Working with People Who Stutter

A Lifespan Approach

Ellen M. Bennett

Speech Therapy Group
El Paso, Texas

PEARSON

Merrill
Prentice Hall

Upper Saddle River, New Jersey
Columbus, Ohio

Library of Congress Cataloging-in-Publication Data

Bennett, Ellen M.
   Working with people who stutter: a lifespan approach / Ellen M. Bennett.
      p. cm.
   Includes bibliographical references and index.
   ISBN 0-13-045432-X
   1. Stuttering. I. Title.

RC424.B455 2006
616.85'5406—dc22   2004027555

Vice President and Executive Publisher: Jeffery W. Johnston
Acquisitions Editor: Allyson P. Sharp
Editorial Assistant: Kathleen S. Burk
Production Editor: Sheryl Glicker Langner
Production Coordination: Thistle Hill Publishing Services, LLC
Design Coordinator: Diane C. Lorenzo
Cover Designer: Ali Mohrman
Production Manager: Laura Messerly
Director of Marketing: Ann Castel Davis
Marketing Manager: Amy Purdy
Marketing Coordinator: Brian Mounts

This book was set in Garamond Book by Carlisle Communications, Ltd. It was printed and bound by R.R. Donnelley & Sons Company. The cover was printed by The Lehigh Press, Inc.

Photo Credits: Ellen M. Bennett, pp. 2, 56, 154, 251, 314, 319, 350, 352, 377, 392, 424, 484; Anne Vega/Merrill, pp. 22, 264; Pearson Learning Photo Studio, p. 96; Scott Cunningham/Merrill, pp. 196, 222.

Pearson Education Ltd.
Pearson Education Singapore Pte. Ltd.
Pearson Education Canada, Ltd.
Pearson Education—Japan

Pearson Education Australia Pty. Limited
Pearson Education North Asia Ltd.
Pearson Educatión de Mexico, S.A. de C.V.
Pearson Education Malaysia Pte. Ltd.

10 9 8 7 6 5 4 3 2 1
ISBN: 0-13-045432-X

I've had many blessings in my life. But none more precious than the angels who watch over me.

This book is dedicated to them: my mother, Sandra Bennett, and my sister of the heart, Cheryl Metz.

Preface

My experience fresh out of graduate school was no different from any other therapist. Joining the Los Angeles Unified School District in 1979, I began my career as an itinerant speech pathologist serving three schools. At Palms Elementary, I had the wonderful, yet frustrating experience of working with a third-grade boy who stuttered quite severely. After a few months of therapy, I began to wonder if I could really help this child. I had one third of a course devoted to this disorder and was armed with Dr. Charles Van Riper's *Nature and Treatment* books. Despite how much I read and reread his worldly words, I could not transform them into therapy activities beneficial to this child. The first parent/teacher conference was approaching, and I was unsure of what to tell this student's father. Despite 3 months of therapy, his son was still stuttering severely. I told him that although I was a speech therapist, I was not competent to help his son and I referred him to the local expert on stuttering. This was a turning point for me in my path toward the treatment of stuttering. I did not like the feelings of helplessness with this client, nor did I want to admit I was not trained enough to make a difference. After all, I had a master's degree from a leading California institution. I had excellent grades in college and I passed the NESBA exam. I made good progress with my clients during clinical training, and my other students were progressing accordingly. So why was it that I, like frequent graduates and seasoned clinicians, felt so inept and so unprepared to work with this population?

The answer to this question is three-dimensional: I lacked knowledge about stuttering, experience with people who stutter, and practical applications of theoretical constructs. I had a tidbit of knowledge about stuttering. I could recall facts memorized for exams. Sometimes a little bit of knowledge can be dangerous, leading to false assumptions and misdirections. I thought, with Van Riper by my side, I could do stuttering therapy. But, in reality, I did not understand the disorder and its complexities. During my education, I had not seen a real person who stuttered. My mind focused

on the behaviors described in the textbooks, not truly understanding that these behaviors are just one component of the communication disorder. I had classified stuttering into its little box, just as I had articulation, voice, and language disorders. This
is what it is and this is what you do. Start at step 1, go to step 2, and so forth. I had
oversimplified the disorder and its impact on the person. With these deficits, I certainly was not capable of applying what I thought I had learned to the real world of
speech therapy.

My experience is not an uncommon one, even after 20-odd years. It is for this reason that I began to study, in detail, stuttering and the people afflicted with this disorder. I sought every opportunity to learn more about stuttering. I started by attending
my first ASHA presentation by Dr. Richard Shine, who demonstrated his Systematic Fluency Training Procedures for Young Children. The year was 1980 and my learning has
not stopped since then. I wish to share with the reader what I have garnered from my
learning experiences over the past 25 years.

This book begins with an overview of stuttering, including definitions and various
characteristics of people who stutter. Next is a discussion of the affective, behavioral,
and cognitive components of stuttering, with a special section addressing covert stuttering. Past and present theoretical beliefs are thoroughly reviewed in chapter 3. The
process of assessment and diagnosis is divided into three stages: planning and information gathering, testing and interpretation, and report writing. I have created a report writing checklist that can be useful to clinicians and supervisors. Chapter 5
covers the full spectrum of treatment paradigms to include examples of established
fluency-shaping, stuttering modification, and integrated approaches. Much detail is
presented on treatment strategies, which may be selected when creating individualized treatment plans. Intervention principles and the client/clinician relationship conclude this chapter. Because of the inclusion of the affective and cognitive components
of stuttering in this book, chapter 6 is devoted to the topic of counseling. Presenting
the need for counseling, various approaches, and the elements of counseling provides
the foundation for implementing counseling strategies that facilitate clinician pre-
paredness to address the various emotions of stuttering: shame, anger, and guilt.

The next group of chapters focus on the treatment needs and relevant information for each of the following subgroups of people who stutter: preschool children,
school-age children, adolescents, and adults. A unique model of intervention, which
can be modified to target each of the age groups, is presented in chapter 9. The House
That Jack Built is a conceptual model of an integrated approach to the treatment of
stuttering. Divided into four stages, this model and its multiple therapy activities aid
the clinician in understanding how to conduct fluency therapy. Multiple figures and
tables are provided throughout this section. The book concludes with a chapter on the
low-incidence fluency disorder of cluttering. This complex, difficult-to-treat condition
is especially challenging for the novice clinician. It is intended that my journey with
stuttering is positively conveyed within the pages of this book and that it provides
hope and direction to future clinicians and their clients who stutter.

Ellen M. Bennett

ACKNOWLEDGMENTS

Writing this book began at the lakeside home of Susan Cochrane in 1998. I cannot express enough my gratitude for Susan's support, ideas, and friendship. Her practical, day-to-day interactions with school-age children who stutter paved the way to several of the activities included in this book. As writing progressed, my dearest friend and colleague, Cheryl Metz, read every chapter and studiously edited the manuscript. Her red pencil colored the many rough drafts and helped me become a better writer. Without her support, this book would not have reached completion.

I would also like to thank several people who helped in different ways. Thanks go to Jennifer Orr, who typed all the references. I am grateful for her many hours of work on this daunting task. This manuscript was reviewed on multiple occasions and provided me with insightful, critical feedback that I greatly appreciated. Special thanks to Stephen Hood for his contributions and willingness to share his expertise with me. Thanks also to my colleagues, Deborah Card and Sofia Muñoz, who provided feedback on several chapters before their final printing. Completing this project, at times, seemed like a endless journey. I would like to thank my editor, Allyson Sharp, for her continuous encouragement and feedback. Last, I would like to say thank you to my mother, Sandra Bennett, who endured my mood swings and short temper during the last stages of writing. She has always believed in me and communicated it through her love and support.

I am also grateful for the helpful comments of the following reviewers: Nancy Martino, Xavier University of Louisiana; Rodney M. Gabel, Bowling Green State University; Lisa R. LaSalle, University of Wisconsin, Eau Claire; Stephen B. Hood, University of South Alabama; Robert W. Quesal, Western Illinois University; Michael Blomgren, University of Utah; Diane Paris, Boston University; Moon K. Chang, Alabama State University; Debra W. Bankston, Stephen F. Austin University; and Sandra R. Ciocci, Bridgewater State College.

Working with people who stutter has provided much joy in my life. I wish to thank all my clients who have crossed my doorstep, my colleagues, and my friends who stutter. You have helped me gain a keener insight into stuttering and become a better clinician. Without you, there would be no book.

ACKNOWLEDGMENTS

Discover the Merrill Education Resources for Communication Disorders Website

Technology is a constantly growing and changing aspect of our field that is creating a need for new content and resources. To address this emerging need, Merrill Education has developed an online learning environment for students, teachers, and professors alike to complement our products—the *Merrill Education Resources for Communication Disorders* website. This content-rich website provides additional resources specific to this book's topic and will help you—professors, classroom teachers, and students—augment your teaching, learning, and professional development.

Our goal with this partnership and initiative is to build on and enhance what our products already offer. For this reason, the content for our user-friendly website is organized by topic and provides teachers, professors, and students with a variety of meaningful resources all in one location. With this website, we bring together the best of what Merrill has to offer: text resources, video clips, web links, tutorials, and a wide variety of information on topics of interest to general and special educators alike. Rich content, applications, and competencies further enhance the learning process.

The *Merrill Education Resources for Communication Disorders* website includes:

RESOURCES FOR THE PROFESSOR

- The **Syllabus Manager**™, an online syllabus creation and management tool, enables instructors to create and revise their syllabus with an easy, step-by-step process course of your class from any computer with Internet access. To access this tailored syllabus, students will just need the URL of the website and the password assigned to the syllabus. By clicking on the date, the student can see a list of activities, assignments, and readings due for that particular class.
- In addition to the **Syllabus Manager**™ and its benefits listed above, professors also have access to all of the wonderful resources that students have access to on the site.

RESOURCES FOR THE STUDENT

- Video clips with questions to help you evaluate the content and make crucial theory-to-practice connections.
- Thought-provoking critical analysis questions that students can answer and turn in for evaluation or that can serve as basis for class discussions and lectures.
- Access to a wide variety of resources related to classroom strategies and methods, including lesson planning and classroom management.
- Information on all the most current relevant topics related to communication disorders, including ASHA and Praxis requirements, IEPs, portfolios, and professional development.
- Extensive web resources and overviews on communication disorders.
- A message board with discussion starters where students can respond to class discussion topics, post questions and responses, or ask questions about assignments.
- A search feature to help access specific information quickly.

To take advantage of these and other resources, please visit the *Merrill Education Resources for Communication Disorders* website at

http://www.prenhall.com/bennett

Brief Contents

Contents

CHAPTER 6

Counseling in Stuttering Disorders   196

CHAPTER 9

The House That Jack Built: A Conceptual Model
of Integrated Therapy for the School-Age Child   314

CHAPTER 12

Cluttering: Another Fluency Disorder   484

Final Thoughts   509

Note: Every effort has been made to provide accurate and current Internet information in this book. However, the Internet and information posted on it are constantly changing, so it is inevitable that some of the Internet addresses listed in this textbook will change.

Working with People Who Stutter

Introduction

CHAPTER OUTLINE

LEARNER OBJECTIVES

- Describe fluency along a continuum of effort, rate, and continuity.
- Define and differentiate fluency and stuttering.
- Elaborate on how stuttering manifests itself differently in each person.
- Describe the speech and language characteristics of people who stutter.

- Outline the insights the research on genetics has provided clinicians working with people who stutter.
- Summarize the current research on the neurological differences of people who stutter.

KEY TERMS

affective component
avoidance behaviors
behavioral component
block
circumlocutions
cognitive component
continuity
core stuttering behaviors
disfluencies
dizygotic
effort

escape mechanism
fluency
fMRI
hesitations
monozygotic
nonfluency
PET
postponement behaviors
proband
prolongations

rate
rCBF
"S" cycle
secondary behaviors
sound/syllable repetitions
SPECT
starter device
stuttering
substitutions
withdrawal

Research resounds with evidence of the lack of confidence, comfort, and competence many speech pathologists experience when working with people who stutter (e.g., Copper & Cooper, 1985, 1996; Cooper & Rustin, 1985; St. Louis, 1997a, 1997b; St. Louis & Durrenberger, 1992; St. Louis & Lass, 1980, 1981; Yaruss, 1999a). This is a most unfortunate finding for both the person who stutters and the profession as a whole. Stuttering is a prime example of a breakdown in communication that speech-language pathologists should be trained to address. With the American Speech-Language-Hearing Association's deregulation of course work and clinical requirements, however, some training institutions are not preparing graduates to work with people who stutter.

PURPOSE OF THE BOOK

This book provides a foundation of knowledge that will enable you to envision the therapy process as a can-do work in progress. Instead of approaching the disorder and people who stutter with fear and a lack of confidence, you will embrace this area with enthusiasm and optimism, knowing you can make a difference. Our universities historically have failed to produce clinicians who feel competent in their ability to adequately serve people who stutter (Brisk, Healey, & Hux, 1997; Cooper & Cooper, 1996; Kelly et al., 1997; Sommers & Caruso, 1995; St. Louis & Durrenberger, 1992; St. Louis & Lass, 1981). Researchers have found three factors that impact the client-clinician relationship negatively: (1) fluency is the least-liked disorder with which to work, (2) clinicians have a weak understanding of this disorder, and (3) clinicians received inadequate clinical and academic preparation in fluency disorders. With practical hands-on therapy examples based on current theory, this book will enhance the clinical training experience of both students studying this profession and those practicing clinicians who want to broaden or strengthen their competencies.

STRUCTURE OF THE BOOK

This text is structured to facilitate readability and comprehension. Each chapter begins with an outline, learning objectives, and a list of key terms that appear in bold print in the text. Critical thinking questions at the end of each chapter provide a study guide. Visual aids facilitate understanding and charts and tables enhance the learning process to prepare you for real-world therapy. Throughout the text, the male gender form is used to refer to the person who stutters, and the female gender is used to refer to the clinician (speech-language pathologist [SLP], clinician, or therapist). Several acronyms are used to avoid wordy repetition of terms, such as person who stutters (PWS), adult who stutters (AWS), or child who stutters (CWS).

This book is divided into two sections. Part I covers the nature of stuttering, beginning with the characteristics of the person who stutters in chapter 1. Characteristics of the disorder itself are discussed in chapter 2 from an affective, behavioral, and cognitive perspective. Chapter 3 surveys past and present theoretical beliefs followed by assessment principles and procedures in chapter 4. An orientation toward the treatment philosophy presented in the text is provided in chapter 5. Part I concludes with chapter 6, which describes counseling theories and practical guidelines as applied to working with people who stutter.

Part II presents treatment suggestions across the age span from preschool to adults. Chapter 7 introduces preschool children who stutter and their particular characteristics and treatment needs. Special issues for this group of children include counseling for parents and involvement in therapy, spontaneous recovery, and concomitant disorders. Chapter 8 discusses the school-age child who stutters, addressing the special issues of teasing, increased awareness of communication differences, and the role of the classroom teacher in treatment. Chapter 9 presents a specific intervention model applicable to the older school-age child who stutters. The House That Jack Built is a conceptual model for an integrated approach to the treatment of stuttering disorders created by this author. Chapter 10 explores the unique needs of the adolescent who stutters. Client motivation, increased peer pressure, and teaching effective coping strategies are discussed. The adult population is covered in chapter 11 with special attention given to the lifelong impact of stuttering, employment and discrimination concerns, and involvement in support groups. Chapter 12 addresses the unique disorder of cluttering.

This book addresses the major issues involved when working with people who stutter. It does not provide a comprehensive study of all areas of investigation. Ideally you will become intrigued with both the topic of stuttering and with the person who stutters and engage in further independent study.

PHILOSOPHY

The disorder of stuttering is a multidimensional, dynamic phenomenon involving **affective** (feelings), **behavioral** (core stuttering), and **cognitive** (thoughts) **components** (Figure 1.1). Interactions with the individual or family must consider all three aspects of the disorder. From assessment to treatment, people who stutter demonstrate unique profiles of strengths and weaknesses reflective of the ABCs of stuttering (see chapter 2). Although the cause of stuttering is unknown, this book discusses the predisposing, precipitating, and perpetuating physiological, genetic, environmental,

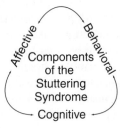

Figure 1.1
Triggers in the form of affective (feelings), behavioral (stuttering), and cognitive (thoughts) components interacting together to create the stuttering syndrome.

and intrapersonal factors that contribute to the emergence and maintenance of fluency breakdowns particular to each client. Let's begin with a discussion of fluency, its components, and what happens when fluency becomes disrupted.

DEFINITIONS

Fluency

Starkweather (1987) described **fluency** as a multidimensional behavior made up of the components of rate, effort, and continuity. **Rate,** the amount of information disseminated at any given period of time, can be calculated as the number of continuous sounds per unit of time, which is a function of articulatory control and coarticulation (Starkweather, 1987, p. 25). Rate of speech is faster for longer utterances and impacts speech comprehension when it is more than 275 words per minute (Foulke, 1971, cited in Starkweather, 1987). Any combination of factors, such as word length, word familiarity, message significance, situational concerns, coarticulation, phoneme sequences, stress, and prosody, may disrupt rate.

Fluent speech is produced in an effortless manner, requiring little thought or muscular exertion. An increase in **effort** may present itself through the perception of tense articulatory contacts, glottal fry, or breathstream irregularities. Bloodstein (1984) contended that as tension increases in the speech mechanism, the individual is likely to fragment or shorten speech elements. Finally, **continuity** is the equivalent of smooth flowing speech void of excessive or inappropriately placed pauses. There is predictability and usefulness for "conventional pauses . . . that a competent speaker makes for emphasis or to signal something linguistically important, while idiosyncratic pauses are an aspect of performance, reflecting hesitations or uncertainty over word choice, style, or syntax" (Starkweather, 1987, p. 20). Conventional pauses, commonly called **hesitations**, serve four functions: (1) as a planned pause to create dramatic effect; (2) as a tactic to allow time to formulate the language components of the message; (3) as a method of planning the neuromotor productions required to execute the message; or (4) as an avoidance mechanism to delay the moment of stuttering. When smooth flowing streams of sounds are produced in an effortless, timely manner, the speaker is judged to be fluent.

Disfluencies

Johnson and his associates (1959) classified fluency disruptions, that is, **disfluencies,** into eight categories: interjections, part word repetitions, word repetitions, phrase repetitions, revisions, incomplete phrases, broken words, and prolonged sounds. These categories are useful when determining how typical or usual a person's speech may be. Table 1.1 provides examples of each category of Johnson's classification system. Campbell and Hill (1987) provided a similar framework to classify breaks in the speech flow. Their More Typical and Less Typical paradigm differentiated between normal nonfluencies and those

Table 1.1
Johnson's classification system of disfluencies.

Category	Examples
1. Interjections	"uh" "er" "well"
2. Part word repetitions consisting of sound or syllable repetitions	"a a a apple" "ca ca ca candy cane"
3. Word repetitions	Mommy, mommy, I want to go home.
4. Phrase repetitions	"I want I want a cookie."
5. Revisions	"I was - I am going."
6. Incomplete phrases	"She was - and after she got there, he came."
7. Broken words	"I was g - (pause) - oing home."
8. Prolonged sounds	"Sh-------e was nice to me."

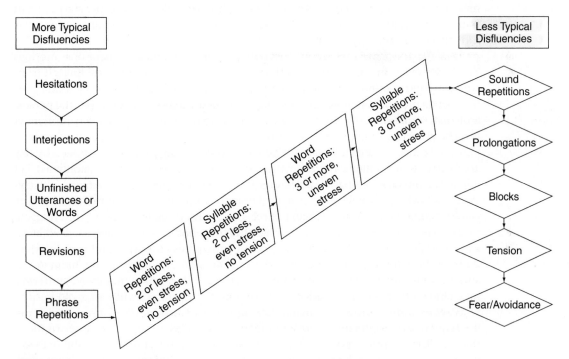

Figure 1.2
A progression of more typical to less typical speech behaviors.
Source: Based on Campbell and Hill (1989).

disfluencies that indicate the child is moving into stuttering by tensing and fragmenting speech efforts (Figure 1.2). Let's look at their classification of disfluencies:

Hesitations → Interjections → Unfinished Utterances or Words → Revisions → Phrase Repetitions → Whole Word Repetitions → Syllable Repetitions → Sound Repetitions → Prolongations → Tense, Silent Blocks → Secondary Behaviors.

Stuttering

Although there are many ways of describing stuttering, Wingate's (1988) definition is, perhaps, all inclusive. It relates four elements to the subjective observation of events present in a person's speech. **Stuttering** is (1) a disruption in fluency of verbal expression that is (2) characterized by involuntary, audible, or silent repetitions or prolongations in the utterance of short speech elements, namely, sounds, syllables, and words of one syllable. (3) These disruptions usually occur frequently or are marked in character, and (4) they are not readily controllable.

From a simplistic point of view, stuttering is judged present when a break occurs in the forward flow of speech (Van Riper, 1971), which, according to Conture (2001), is characterized by certain disfluencies (i.e., whole word, syllable, or sound repetitions, prolongations, and/or silent pauses). These **core stuttering behaviors** may or may not be accompanied by **secondary behaviors,** that is, escape, starter, postponement, and/or avoidance mechanisms; symptoms of negative feelings (affect); or thoughts (cognition) about talking.

Escape mechanisms are learned behaviors used to end a moment of stuttering. The individual is in a moment of stuttering and utilizes a trick to release himself from stuttering and continue with his communication effort. **Starter devices** are used to get the speech mechanism moving (i.e., to start a speech attempt). For example, the person anticipates a moment of stuttering and uses a starter to get the speech mechanism moving. These tricks can take many forms (e.g., interjections, throat clearing, head nods or tilts, eye blinks, or facial grimaces). When used successfully, they are reinforced by the ability to continue talking. However, these lose effectiveness as they are habituated, becoming an unconscious part of the stuttering episode. The person is now faced with trying a new behavior to get speech started or stop stuttering, thus compiling a series of faculty coping mechanisms that do not release him from the moment of stuttering.

Postponement behaviors and **avoidance behaviors** are strategies used in response to anticipated stuttering. The person anticipates stuttering and uses interjections or hesitations (postponement devices, or *stallers*, delaying the moment of stuttering) to buy time in an effort not to stutter. Or the person may avoid stuttering by changing words (**substitutions**), talking in circles purposefully to avoid certain words (**circumlocutions**), or by not talking at all (**withdrawal**). Figure 1.3 presents the sequence of events that represent the full scope of stuttering from predisruption, fluency disruption, and postdisruption perspectives (Hood, 2003). The inability to say what one wants to say leads to a myriad of feelings, including frustration, anger, embarrassment, and shame (Murphy, 1999). During these moments, the person begins to develop self-defeating thoughts surrounding communication, such as "I can't talk" or "I am not a good talker." With continued stuttering, the client enters a vicious cycle of stuttering, feelings, and thoughts that triggers spiraling down the stuttering cycle, producing further feelings of helplessness and copelessness.

The Stuttering Cycle

Stuttering is cyclic and variable. It is considered a heterogeneous disorder with symptoms manifested differentially in each individual. This variability contributes to the

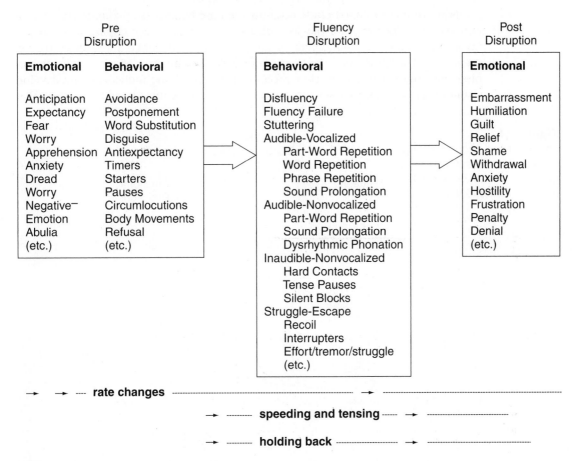

Figure 1.3
Timing of events before, during, and after the moment of stuttering.
Adapted with permission from S. Hood.

complexity of the disorder. After years of working with many people who stutter, the **"S" cycle** was developed as a conceptual framework to help parents/teachers/people who stutter understand the development of this disorder. The stuttering cycle includes two components: first, the stuttering behavior itself, and second, the emotional reaction to the moment of stuttering. As Figure 1.4 illustrates, the person initially produces a moment of stuttering, usually brief and effortless (a small "s"). There occurs a slight, just barely conscious, emotional reaction to the break in speech flow (a small "e"). This minor reaction (affective and/or cognitive) results in an increased level of tension and fragmentation that produces a slightly larger moment of stuttering. As the moment of stuttering grows, so does the emotional reaction. This cycle continues until both the stuttering (a very large "S") and emotionality (a very large "E") are so substantial that effective communication no longer exists.

Stuttering behaviors include not only the core behaviors of sound/syllable repetitions, prolongations, and blocks, but also a series of faulty coping mechanisms (avoidance, escape, postponement, or starter devices) developed in response to communication failure. The emotional reactions may take the form of anger, guilt, embarrassment, and/or frustration. After prolonged stuttering, the individual may develop shame-based reactions to the stuttering and negative cognitive thought processes that

Figure 1.4
The stuttering cycle involving movement between two key variables: stuttering and the emotional reactions to the stuttering.

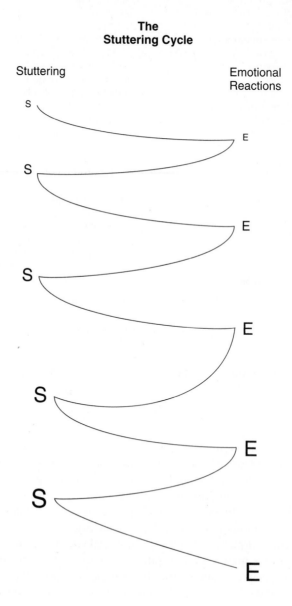

The Stuttering Cycle

Stuttering

Emotional Reactions

hinder the ability to cope effectively. Of course, not all individuals start their "stuttering life" in the depths of the stuttering cycle. However, it is possible to have an individual, within weeks postonset, exhibit core stuttering behaviors accompanied by avoidance reactions and a high level of awareness.

The Fluency Continuum

This text adheres to the philosophy that fluency lies along a continuum based on variations in the rate, effort, and continuity of speech production. Fluency does not occur 100% of the time. Everyone has breaks in the forward flow of speech, referred to as normal **nonfluency.** Nonfluencies typically take the form of hesitations, interjections, revisions, unfinished utterances/words, phrase repetitions, or brief whole-word repetitions. These are effortless free-flowing episodes that do not inhibit the speaker's ability to continue his communicative intent. Increases in tension cause the individual to fragment the speech attempt, producing short, more aberrant breaks, such as **syllable/sound repetitions.** When the individual cannot move forward with speech effort through repetitions, tense sound elongations (**prolongations**) are attempted. However, this may not produce the desired outcome as the person tenses more and is unable to produce any speech. This results in a **block,** representing the opposite end of the spectrum from fluency. A person's speech may include movement up and down this fluency continuum (Barasch, Guitar, McCauley, & Absher, 2000; Bloodstein, 1995) depending on the nature of the communication exchange and the degree of negative emotion attached to talking. Nonfluency and stuttering should not be confused. The behavior called stuttering is just one manifestation of a breakdown in any or all dimensions of fluency (rate, continuity, and effort). The frequency and degree of tension, effort, and rate differentiate between normal nonfluency and stuttering.

Before venturing further into the various characteristics of PWS, it is important to recognize the extensive research and clinical efforts of Nicoline Ambrose, Gene Brutten, Kristin Chmela, Susan Cochrane, Edward Conture, Janice Costello, David Daly, Carl Dell, Hugo and Carolyn Gregory, Barry Guitar, Stephen Hood, Ellen Kelly, William Murphy, Robert Quesal, Peter Ramig, Nan Bernstein Ratner, Richard Shine, C. Woodruff Starkweather, Kenneth St. Louis, Martine Vanryckeghem, Janice Westbrook, Dean Williams, Ehud Yairi, J. Scott Yaruss, and Patricia Zebrowski, all of whom I credit for my increased understanding of both fluency and stuttering.

CHARACTERISTICS OF PEOPLE WHO STUTTER

Prevalence and Incidence

Approximately 5% of the population will have stuttered at some point in their lives, with an overall prevalence rate of 1% of the general population (Bloodstein, 1995; Guitar, 1998). Age inversely influences the incidence rate; that is, a greater number of young children stutter than older adolescents and adults. According to the Stuttering

Foundation of America, over 3 million Americans stutter. When working in the public schools, the speech pathologist may encounter as many as 6% to 8% of a school's population who exhibit symptoms of stuttering. Stuttering is considered a low-incidence disorder; however, it is believed many clinicians underdiagnose the presence of stuttering in hopes the child will recover spontaneously without requiring direct intervention.

Onset

Most clinicians and researchers agree stuttering is a childhood disorder that develops between 2 and 5 years of age (e.g., Bloodstein, 1995; Conture, 2001; Guitar, 1998). Fully developed stuttering can be observed as early as 2 years of age (Starkweather, 1997a, 1997b), a time characterized by a transition from a lexically driven language production system to a grammatical, rule-governed system (Bernstein Ratner, 1997b). Children with persistent stuttering often exhibit later onset times, with a mean onset around 38 months of age (Throneburg, Yairi, & Paden, 1994). As the child enters adolescence, the likelihood of developing stuttering symptoms decreases. It is rare to see sudden onset of stuttering in an adult; however stuttering may emerge after a cerebral vascular accident or head trauma, and it is referred to as *acquired* or *neurogenic stuttering*.

Genetics

Researchers have long been interested in a possible genetic link to explain the presence of stuttering. Stuttering appears to be a male predominate disorder according to long-standing reports of a 3–4:1 ratio of males to females, and it often has a high familial incidence rate (Bloodstein, 1995; Buck, Lees, & Cook, 2002; Felsenfeld, 1996, 1997; Kidd, 1980, 1984; Poulos & Webster, 1991). This gender and familial bias spurred researchers to delve into the genetics of stuttering using three types of research designs: adoption studies, twin studies, and family studies.

Adoption studies investigated the emergence of stuttering behaviors in children not raised by their biological parents. Despite the thesis that adoption studies would provide the strongest support for a genetic basis to the disorder, few studies have been conducted due to the cost and difficulty of finding subjects. Felsenfeld (1997) reported preliminary results of one study suggesting "that having a biological parent with a reported history of speech disorder appeared to be more important for the development of these conditions than being reared by a parent with a positive history" (p. 7). However, until more adoption studies are conducted, the role of genetics in adopted children is not clearly defined.

Twin studies shed a bit more light on the heritability of stuttering. These studies have used behavioral genetics as their foundation, focusing on factors that would explain the presence of individual differences among fraternal (**dizygotic**) and identical (**monozygotic**) twins. Genetic theory predicts that for a trait to be considered inherited, one would expect it to be present more frequently in monozygotic twins who share the same genetic material. Howie (1981) studied 36 twin pairs with at least one member either a recovered or current stutterer. He found that 63% of the monozygotic twins were concordant for stuttering as compared to 19% of the dizygotic pairs. *Concordant* means that both individuals exhibit the behavior under investigation. Bloodstein (1993) concluded that pooled figures from twin studies "demonstrate beyond question that if one member of a pair of identical twins stutters, the other will also be found to stutter in the great majority of cases" (p. 128).

Perhaps the greatest insight into the role genetics plays in stuttering comes from the findings of family studies. Two designs have been employed when investigating stuttering in families: high-density and case-control designs. High-density studies look closely at families with multiple members who stutter. Case-control design studies identify a single member, called the **proband,** who stutters, and they closely investigate the characteristics of this individual's family. Early studies estimated that approximately one third to one half of all stutterers surveyed had a current or recovered stutterer in the family (Felsenfeld, 1997). Additional studies conducted by Kay (1964), Kidd (1984), and Ambrose, Yairi, and Cox (1993) supported and extended our knowledge of the role of genetics in stuttering. Felsenfeld summarized the findings from these three landmark studies:

- Fifteen percent of first-degree relatives report a history of recovered or current stuttering.
- Male relatives are at a greater risk for stuttering than females.
- Female relatives of stutterers are more likely to recover than male relatives, and they recover at an earlier age.
- Sons of female probands are more likely to stutter.
- Females require greater genetic loading in the transmission of stuttering.
- Severity of stuttering does not impact the likelihood that stuttering will develop in family members.

In conclusion, genetic studies indicated a strong, yet unknown, genetic factor related to stuttering. It is known that stuttering runs in families, is more predominant in males as compared to females, and monozygotic twins have a higher concordance rate than dizygotic twins. However, genetics alone cannot explain the presence of this disorder. Other factors, such as environment, may interact with this genetic predisposition, thereby allowing stuttering to emerge in certain individuals (Felsenfeld, 2002; Felsenfeld, Kirk, Zhu, Statham, Neale, & Martin, 2000; Yairi, 2004; Yairi, Ambrose, & Cox, 1996).

Intelligence

The question of intellectual differences between PWS and their nonstuttering peers has been posed numerous times with few definitive answers. Johnson and associates (1959), in the book entitled *The Onset of Stuttering*, reported no significant differences in IQ between the stuttering and nonstuttering children who participated in his studies. In contrast, Okasha, Bishry, Kamel, and Hassen (1974) reported slightly lower IQ scores for CWS, with Andrews et al. (1983) reporting at least a one half standard deviation difference between stuttering and nonstuttering children. Bloodstein (1995, pp. 256–257) provided a summary of the research on this issue, concluding that PWS function at slightly lower intellectual levels, albeit in the average range, than their nonstuttering peers. However, Batik and Bennett (2001) administered the Test of Nonverbal

Intelligence to 8 stuttering and nonstuttering children, and they failed to find group differences. More recently, Yairi (2004) wrote, "there are no other indications of a meaningful intellectual deficit in PWS" (p. 99). It has been the clinical experience of this author that people who stutter function no differently in the area of intellectual functioning. However, more systematic studies are needed to understand better the role of intelligence in stuttering disorders.

Concomitant Disorders

Schwartz and Conture (1988) addressed the need to consider subgroups of stutterers who exhibit certain patterns of skills. It has been well documented that children who stutter differ in their speech and language skills, therefore requiring subgrouping (e.g., Bloodstein, 1995; Bernstein Ratner, 1997b; Conture, 2001; Guitar, 1998; Louko, Edwards, & Conture, 1990; Melnick & Conture, 2000; Nippold, 1990; Ramig & Bennett, 1995, 1997a; Yairi, 2004). The presence of phonological disorders, language differences, and/or word-finding difficulties in children who stutter are three prominent concomitant problems often reported in the literature.

Phonological Disorders

During the 1980s and 1990s, researchers sought to determine how stuttering and phonology were related. Two reasons exist for this area of investigation. First, the literature refers to the high rate of the co-occurrence of stuttering and phonological disorders in children (Caruso, Ritt, & Sommers, 2002; Conture, 2001; Nippold, 1990; Ruscello, St. Louis, & Mason, 1991; St. Louis, 1991; St. Louis & Hinzman, 1988; St. Louis, Murray, & Ashworth, 1991). Conture (2001) reported co-occurrence rates that ranged from 24% to 45% of young children. Van Riper (1973) classified 25% of children who stutter as "track II stutterers," experiencing either articulation or learning disabilities. Secondly, the Covert Repair Hypothesis (Postma & Kolk, 1993) described stuttering as a breakdown in the phonological encoding skills required for fluent speech production. The presence of a faulty or hypersensitive internal speech monitor may be the source for errors characterized as stuttering.

The profiles of stuttering children appear to be highly similar to those of phonologically disordered children. Both disorders occur more frequently in males than in females, they run in families, they are characterized by oral-motor coordination components, and periodically, stuttering emerges after phonological intervention. The similarity in profiles, along with the high rate of coincidence, requires one to question the relationship between the two disorders.

Wolk, Edwards, and Conture (1993) discussed three views regarding the coexistence of stuttering and phonology. First was Bloodstein's (1995) psychosocial perspective, which suggested children with communication disorders develop a sense of failure around speech and begin to struggle with speech. Second is the common predisposition underlying both disorders. Lastly, stuttering and phonological disorders are related to the same phenomenon—a central neurological processing deficit. This last hypothesis has gained support in the literature on stuttering and phonological disorders (Butterworth, 1992; Byrd & Cooper, 1989; Crary, 1993; Kent, 1984; St. Louis, 1991; Webster, 1993; Wijnen & Boers, 1994). Many researchers have investigated the characteristic patterns of stuttering and phonological disorders when they co-occur. The following summarizes these authors' findings and reflections:

- Of the children who stuttered, 24% to 45% also exhibit disordered phonology (Arndt & Healey, 2001; Conture, 2001; Louko et al., 1990).
- Children, at the onset of stuttering, appear to be delayed in phonological skills (Yairi, 2004).
- Stuttering subjects exhibit more atypical processes and greater frequency of cluster reduction than fluent peers (Louko et al., 1990; Wolk, Blomgren, & Smith, 2000).
- Stuttering plus disordered phonology children exhibit longer sound prolongations as compared to stuttering plus normal phonology (Wolk et al., 1993). This has particular relevance when considering the sound prolongation feature may be important in the differential diagnosis of young stutterers (Schwartz & Conture, 1988).
- Poor phonological skills in the early stages of stuttering may differentiate between persistent PWS and recovered PWS (Paden, Ambrose, & Yairi, 2002; Paden & Yairi, 1996).
- Stuttering does not necessarily occur on phonologically difficult sounds, syllable shapes, or multiple syllables (Howell & Au-Yeung, 1995; Throneburg et al., 1994).
- There are inconsistent findings on whether words with phonological errors are more likely to be stuttered on than those spoken error free (Caruso, Ritt, & Sommers, 2002; Melnick & Conture, 2000).
- More severe stuttering does not necessarily mean a greater number of phonological processes will be present in the child's speech (Anderson & Conture, 2000; Louko et al., 1990; Ryan, 1992; Wolk et al., 1993; Yaruss, Lasalle, & Conture, 1998).
- Phonological patterns are not significantly different between children who stutter and their fluent peers (Wolk et al., 1993).
- Children who stutter and have disordered phonology may take longer to recover from stuttering (Conture, 2001; Nippold, 2002; Paden, Ambrose, & Yairi, 2002; Paden, Yairi, & Ambrose, 1999).
- Frequency, duration, and types of stuttering are not significantly different for children who stutter and those who also have phonological disorders (Wolk, Blomgren, & Smith, 2000; Yaruss & Conture, 1996).

The influence or interaction between these two disorders is becoming clearer through longitudinal studies currently in progress. Paden and Yairi's (1996) research indicated that poor phonological skills in the early stages of stuttering differentiate persistent from recovered PWS. Paden, Ambrose, and Yairi (2002) further delineated the interaction between stuttering and phonological disorders. Investigating the development of phonological skills in children who do and do not stutter over a 2-year period, they observed six group trends: (1) the mean percentage of phonological error for the children who were persistent with stuttering was higher than those who recovered from stuttering; (2) one year later, the number of phonological errors no longer differentiated between the two groups of subjects; (3) mastery of the 10 error patterns investigated occured by year 3; (4) by age 5.5, 20.3% of recovered children no longer meet criteria as phonologically impaired as compared to only 13.6% of the persistent children; (5) a larger percentage of girls in the recovered group (35.5%) no longer met the phonological criteria as compared to 18.2% in the persistent group; and (6) children with persistent stuttering demonstrated slower phonological progress. These authors conjectured that stuttering interferes with phonological development, slowing down its rate for a subgroup of children who stutter.

We do not know why phonological disorders frequently appear in the profile of a subgroup of children who stutter. Perhaps there is an underlying, developmental glitch unknown at this time that contributes to the systemic speech breakdown in these children. Answers may be provided with future research, and, until then, the co-occurrence of stuttering and phonological disorders has a certain degree of predictability and must be considered during assessment and treatment decisions.

Language Differences

The presence of language disorders among adults and children who stutter has been debated over the years. Andrews et al. (1983), in their landmark review of the literature, concluded that children who stutter perform poorly on some standardized tests. Nippold (1990), in her review of the literature, failed to find sufficient support for the contention that children who stutter are more likely to have language delays. Watkins, Yairi, and Ambrose (1999), in a longitudinal study of preschool children who stutter, found "on virtually all the measures of expressive language employed herein, the groups of children were similar in skill and near or above developmental levels" (p. 1134).

However, Ryan (1992) found significant language delays in his subject pool; Arndt and Healey (2001), based on a survey of speech-language pathologists, found 72 (15%) of 467 children had both language and fluency problems. So what are the language characteristics of children who stutter (CWS)? The following summarizes the current research in this area:

- CWS score lower on measures of receptive language than children who do not stutter (Bernstein Ratner, 1997b; Meyers & Freeman, 1985a; Ryan, 1992).
- Children with persistent stuttering score lower than those who have recovered on measures of receptive and expressive language (Yairi, Ambrose, Paden, & Throneburg, 1996).
- CWS exhibit greater variability in their language production skills (Watkins & Yairi, 1997).
- CWS exhibit more stuttering when producing grammatically complex and long sentences (Logan & Conture, 1995, 1997; Melnick & Conture, 2000).
- CWS are more likely to exhibit stuttering on utterance where the grammar is not yet established (Bernstein Ratner, 2001).
- CWS exhibit a greater difference in their receptive and expressive skills compared to their nonstuttering peers (Anderson & Conture, 2000).
- CWS exhibit more stuttering when attempting to produce sentences that exceed their typical mean length of utterance, a measure of linguistic proficiency (Zackheim & Conture, 2003).

- CWS exhibit a slower speech reaction time when generating sentences in the absence of priming sentences (Anderson & Conture, 2004).
- CWS benefit more from syntactic priming than their nonstuttering peers (Anderson & Conture, 2004).
- Some children with persistent stuttering exhibit above-average expressive language abilities (Yairi, 2004).

The literature does not provide a clear picture regarding the language skills of children who stutter. This author concurs with Watkins, Yairi, and Ambrose in their belief that children who stutter do not, as a group, exhibit gross language disorders. However, as others have suggested (Anderson & Conture, 2000; Bernstein Ratner, 1997b; Conture, 2001; Nippold, 1990; Ratner, 2004; Schwartz & Conture, 1988; Starkweather, 1991), a subgroup of children may exist who exhibit subtle language deficits co-occurring with stuttering. Perhaps the use of standardized measures of language is not sufficient to detect the subtle language differences suspect in children who stutter (Ratner, 2004; Watkins, Yairi, & Ambrose, 1999; Weber-Fox, 2001). Bernstein Ratner (2000) keenly described the use of standardized tests as "not the best net with which to fish for subtle linguistic abilities" (p. 338). The possibility exists of subtle differences in the processing and generation abilities of people who stutter. The clinician must recognize the possibility that this pattern exists and make appropriate assessment modifications to determine the presence of a concurring language disorder.

Word-Finding Difficulties

Clinicians (Conture, 2001; Gregory, 2003; Rustin, Botterill, & Kelman, 1996; Telser, 1971) report cases in which children who stutter exhibit word-finding difficulties. However, studies investigating the link between word-finding ability and stuttering produce conflicting results (Batik, Bennett, & Yaruss, 2003; Shine, Johnson, DeMarco, Hough, & O'Brien, 1991). Telser (1971) measured response latencies on a rapid autonomic picture naming task for a group of stuttering and nonstuttering children. It was found that 55% of the CWS had longer response latencies than the nonstuttering children, perhaps indicative of a word-finding problem. Shine et al. (1991) revealed findings contradictory to those of Telser. Examining the word-finding ability, as measured by accuracy and response latency on a picture-naming task of 8 stuttering and nonstuttering preschoolers, Shine et al. found no group differences. They concluded that stuttering and word retrieval were possibly two separate problems that happen to coexist in a small subgroup of children who stutter.

Clinical reports on the co-occurrence of word-finding problems and stuttering appear to support Telser's beliefs. Rustin, Botterill, and Kelman (1996) reported a large number of CWS exhibiting word retrieval difficulties. They stated that a delay in retrieval disrupts the forward flow of speech, resulting in the use of disfluencies to fill the pause. Gregory and Hill (1980) noted that CWS who have word retrieval difficulties may respond to the resultant pauses in speech with emotional reactions (i.e., with frustration). They predicted that a subsequent increase in disfluencies would be observed in situations placing higher demands on word retrieval. However, Conture and Caruso (1987) acknowledged the difficulties in distinguishing between the pauses in the speech of CWS as a result of word retrieval problems or to the disorder of stuttering itself. Conture

(2001) expressed the opinion that the Test of Word Finding (TWF) (German, 1989) was, currently, the only objective way to measure word-finding skills in CWS. However, Conture pointed out that it cannot be determined if the TWF can actually "distinguish stutterers' response latencies due to difficulties in word finding from those due to stutterers' hesitating or pausing because of reluctance to say a particular sound, syllable, or word" (p. 75). Batik, Bennett, and Yaruss (2003) used German's TWF to investigate the possible relationship between the two disorders, but they found no difference in the mean score on the TWF for CWS as compared to nonstuttering children. The absence of differences in word retrieval may be attributed to the simplistic skills required to perform this single word-naming task. It may be that CWS exhibit word-finding problems that become apparent only at higher levels of communication, such as discourse, which place greater demands on the speech generation system. Further research is necessary to explore fully the relationship between the prevalence of stuttering and word retrieval disorders.

Brain Differences

Early theories of stuttering attributed the disorder to an insufficient dominance of the left hemisphere for processing speech information (Travis, 1931). Now, technology (Positron Emission Test [**PET**]; Single Photon Emission Computed Tomography [**SPECT**]; and functional Magnetic Resonance Imaging [**fMRI**]) allows researchers to systematically assess the accuracy of Travis's contentions by measuring regional Cerebral Blood Flow (**rCBF**) in cortical and subcortical areas of the brain during speaking tasks (for a review of these research methodologies, see Watson & Freeman, 1997). One of the earliest studies to use this technology was conducted by Wood and his colleagues (1980). Measuring blood flow during perceptual versus speaking tasks, they found inadequate left hemisphere processing during speaking but not during perception. Pool, Devous, Freeman, Watson, and Finitzo (1991) used SPECT technology to investigate rCBF in adults during rest. They found increased right hemisphere activation in the anterior cingulate area for stuttering subjects. During a silent reading task, DeNil, Kroll, Kapur, and Houle (2000) observed simultaneous activation of Broca's area and the anterior cingulate cortex for stuttering subjects, whereas the fluent speakers demonstrated higher activations in the primary motor cortex. Wu et al. (1995) found decreased activation in the Broca's and Wernicke's areas of the left hemisphere during choral speaking tasks. DeNil et al. (2000) observed increased right hemisphere activation during oral reading. This abnormal right hemisphere activation during various speaking tasks has been confirmed by several other studies (Braun et al., 1997; Fox, Ingham, & Ingham, 1996; Ingham, 2001; Ingham, Fox, Ingham, & Zamarripa, 2000; Van Borsel, Achten, Santens, Lahorte, & Voet, 2003).

Researchers continue to find different neural organization patterns in PWS (Foundas, Bollich, Corey, Hurley, & Heilman, 2001; Ingham, 2001; Ingham, Fox, Ingham, Zamarripa, Martin, Jerabek, & Cotton, 1996). One issue of the *Journal of Fluency Disorders* (2003) was devoted to the discussion of brain differences in adults who stutter. See the complete text of these studies for details regarding designs, subjects, and a thorough description of results. The following is a brief introduction to the preliminary findings from the works of Fox; Ludlow and Loucks; Ingham, Ingham, Finn, and Fox; Blomgren, Nagarajan, Lee, Li, and Alvord; DeNil, Kroll, Fafaille, and Houle; and Neumann et al.

- Reduction of left hemisphere dominance during stuttering.
- Abnormal temporal sequencing of speech-associated activation in PWS.
- Abnormalities of myelin structure in the left rolandic operculum of PWS.
- A shift to right hemispheric processing as a result of excessive right inferior premotor activation.
- Reduced activations in auditory association regions.
- Hypoactivation in the left caudate nucleus during fluency and stuttering.
- Greater right caudate nucleus activation with lower supplemental motor area activation in fluent and stuttered conditions.
- Possible gender differences in areas of activation during stuttering.
- Disproportionate right hemisphere activity in persistent stutterers indicative of a shift from left to right anterior insula function during speech.
- Highly variable activation patterns for both stuttering and nonstuttering subjects during lexical access tasks, yet stuttering subjects exhibited bilateral activation during a word description task.
- Activation of the motor cortex and cerebellum during silent reading.
- Overactivation of cerebellar and cortical sensorimotor regions during speech.
- Deactivation in the left precentral and bilateral occipital regions of the brain.

The differences found in these studies do not directly reflect a causative relationship between stuttering and irregular neural organization. Such differences may be the by-product of lifelong stuttering because we know the brain is placid and prone to reorganization. According to Ludlow (2000), "brain activation patterns observed in stuttering adults are perhaps the result of individually adapted systems that evolved during childhood and early adolescence in an effort to produce fluent speech" (p. 2). Büchell and Sommer (2004) also indicated that the reported brain differences in PWS may "not be the cause of stuttering, but rather a compensatory process" (p. 161).

This conclusion is evident in the research on treatment effects using this research methodology (DeNil, 1999; DeNil, Kroll, & Houle, 2001; DeNil, Kroll, Lafaille, & Houle, 2003; Ingham, Kilgo, Ingham, Moglia, Belknap, & Sanchez, 2001; Neumann et al., 2003). Utilizing a pre-post treatment design, studies found increased cerebellar activity directly after treatment, reflective of increased attention to speech production. One year posttreatment, a significant decrease in cerebellar activity was attributed to the development of automaticity in motor and cognitive processes. Specifically, treatment may produce a reorganization of neural processes, such as in DeNil's (1999) study in which an increase in activation in the cortical motor regions in the left hemisphere was noted after an intensive behavior treatment program. Concurrently, treatment changed the activation patterns of the anterior cingulate region, reflective of a change in cognitive and emotional states posttreatment.

DeNil, Kroll, Lafaille, and Houle (2003) investigated changes in neural activation 1 year postparticipation in an intensive behavior treatment program. This study found significant changes in lateralization with a shift toward left hemisphere activation. At the 1-year follow-up mark, subjects exhibited increased bilateral or right hemisphere activation.

Neumann et al. (2003) also investigated changes in neural organization pre-post treatment. During the pretreatment overt reading task, PWS exhibited widespread overactivation in the right hemisphere to include the sensorimotor, frontal motor, parietal, right temporal, right insula, and limbic regions. Posttreatment patterns reflected a change in loci of activation to include greater bilateral activation, especially in the frontal, temporal, and parietal regions of the brain. However, these changes were not stable at the 2-year follow-up period with a return to overactivation in the right hemisphere. More studies are needed before we are able to make any definitive conclusions regarding brain functioning and stuttering. The use of neuroimaging technology in stuttering research is certainly in its infancy.

Ludlow (2000) summarized the impact of this research trend with the following comments: "It is likely that the dysfunction is not one of a simple laterality difference as was suggested many years ago (Travis, 1978). As new technologies emerge which are non-invasive and have improved temporal resolution, studies in children who stutter during the critical period of speech development may provide understanding of how this dysfunctional system emerges" (p. 4). Thus, these authors contend, in general, the primary dysfunction is located in the left hemisphere with hyperactivation of the right hemisphere. Although this dysfunction may not be the cause of stuttering, it may be a result of compensatory processes from lifelong stuttering. The future holds potential for gathering significant information on brain organization and functioning of PWS.

CHAPTER SUMMARY

This book provides a reader-friendly tool for the dissemination of information on fluency and stuttering from the preschool years through adulthood. The concepts of fluency and stuttering must be understood. One way to conceptualize fluency is along a continuum comprising more typical and less typical disfluencies. As the person tenses his speech mechanism, fragmentation of speech efforts occur (i.e., sound, syllable repetitions). The stuttering cycle provides a graphic representation of the dual components involved in the movement and interaction between the stuttering behaviors and the emotional reactions to these behaviors. People who stutter differ in how they react to stuttering, reinforcing the heterogeneous nature of the disorder whose origin remains unknown. It is believed the predisposition to stutter is a genetically transmitted trait that interacts with the individual's environment. It emerges during early childhood and manifests more often in males than in females. A great majority of children who stutter recover from stuttering, with females spontaneously recovering more than males. Severity of stuttering does not appear to be an inherited feature of the disorder. People who stutter function at the same level of intelligence as the general population with subgroups of the population characterized by certain concomitant disorders. Although it is clear that children who stutter are more likely to have phonological disorders, research is not definitive with regard to the presence of language or word-finding difficulties. Modern technological advances have allowed researchers to investigate the presence of brain differences in people who stutter, and the future holds promise for gathering greater insight from continued study in this area.

STUDY QUESTIONS

1. Describe how you would use the S cycle to explain the development of stuttering to a parent of an adolescent who stutters severely.

2. How can the speech pathologist differentiate between normal nonfluency and stuttering?

3. What are the secondary characteristics of stuttering? Explain how they develop.

4. Discuss insights gained about people who stutter from the research presented in this chapter.

5. Think about any myths or preconceived notions you had about people who stutter before reading this chapter. Discuss what you have learned.

6. Describe the speech and language characteristics of people who stutter.

7. What insights has the research on genetics provided clinicians working with people who stutter?

8. Summarize the current research trends into the neurological differences of people who stutter.

The ABCs of Stuttering

2

CHAPTER OUTLINE

Affective Components of Stuttering
    The Psychology of Stuttering
    Emotions
    The Impact on the Self-Concept
    The Grief Process
    Temperament

Behavioral Components of Stuttering
    Physiological Aspects
    Linguistic Aspects
Cognitive Components of Stuttering
    Perceptions of Stuttering
    Attitudes Toward Communication

LEARNER OBJECTIVES

- Identify the characteristics of emotions and describe how emotions develop.
- Define, compare, and contrast the unique features of shame versus guilt.
- Describe how situational shame relates to the stuttering experience.
- Describe the physiological characteristics of respiration, phonation, and articulation in stuttering.
- Predict where stuttering will occur within the linguistic structure of the language.

- Discuss the relationship between length and complexity of utterance and the possible impact on stuttering frequency.
- List the common listener perceptions reported in the literature.
- Discuss the relationship between attitudes and stuttering moments.
- Discuss the interaction among the affective, behavioral, and cognitive components of stuttering.

KEY TERMS

acceptance
anger
audience punishment guilt
bargaining
class shame
clinician-induced guilt
closed category words
cognitive
cognitive distortions
core emotions
covert responses
debilitating guilt
denial
depression
domain-specific self-concept
emotion
evaluative emotions

existential shame
exposed emotions
global self-concept
guilt
healthy shame
incongruence
interpersonal aspects
intrapersonal aspects
listener perceptions
maladaptive responses
mean length of utterance (MLU)
narcissistic shame
objective self-awareness
open category words
overt behaviors
primary emotions

primary guilt
resistance
secondary guilt
self-concept
self-talk
shame
shame spirals
situational shame
therapy-induced guilt
timing guilt
toxic shame
unhealthy shame
voice onset time (VOT)
voice reaction time (VRT)
within-word disfluencies

Fluency specialists view stuttering as a dynamic disorder composed of *Affective*, *Behavioral*, and *Cognitive* elements (or the ABCs of stuttering). To work with people who stutter, the clinician must understand these components and how they may manifest in each individual. What we know about stuttering is limited, yet research and clinical experience have provided insight into certain predictabilities within each element.

AFFECTIVE COMPONENTS OF STUTTERING

PWS may experience an array of emotions related to their communication difficulties (Kendall, 2000). Repeated experience with communication failure and social penalties builds a wall of emotions, each brick representing a negative communicative exchange and the resultant emotional reaction. Of particular relevance are the feelings of anger, guilt, and shame prior to, during, and after moments of stuttering. People who stutter are not psychologically different in any way. However, the psychological impact secondary to stuttering can change the way the individual approaches communication exchanges, thus becoming an essential part of the therapy process.

The Psychology of Stuttering

Stuttering is a complex, intricate disorder involving cognitive processes associated with emotions elicited by communication failures. Previously, Mower (1967) hypothesized that stuttering was a symptom of neurosis. The "conscience has succeeded in getting its message into the individual's main communication channel in such a way that, if the message itself cannot be clearly transmitted, it can at least 'jam' and distort that which the ego or self-system is trying to say" (p. 70). Mower suggested that in the therapy process, the client resolve conflicts between the ego, self-system, and consciousness so stuttering would be alleviated. Goldstein (1958, cited in Sermas & Cox, 1982) hypothesized that stuttering individuals were more anxious, tense, and socially withdrawn when compared to nonstuttering subjects.

Yet research on the personality traits and psychotherapy outcomes of people who stutter have not supported the hypotheses just described (Peters & Hulstijn, 1984; Sermas & Cox, 1982; Sheehan, 1968; Webster, 1977). PWS are not inherently different psychologically from the general population. It is well accepted that no single personality pattern exists for all people who stutter, nor are they different from the general population (Conture, 2001; Guitar, 1998; Sheehan, 1968; Silverman, 1996). Peters and Hulstijn (1984) investigated anxiety in people who stutter, finding no differences between stuttering and nonstuttering people on measures of personality and physiological anxiety. They did observe variances, however, in the subjective anxiety results for people who stutter. Stuttering subjects exhibited increased anxiety related to speech tasks. General conclusions were that stuttering was not elicited by anxiety, thus refuting the hypothesis that stuttering comes from a general factor of anxiety. This is further supported by Sermas and Cox (1982) who investigated the personality correlates of people who stutter. Using the MMPI, TAT, SCL-90-R, and Rorschach test, they found that PWS scored significantly higher on the Interpersonal Sensitivity Scale that "reflects feelings of personal inadequacy, uneasiness, inferiority, and discomfort together with negative expectations during interpersonal interactions" (p. 151). These investigators concluded that "although obsessive personality trends and sensitivity in social situations may be found among stutterers, no particular character structure can be defined" (p. 156).

This line of research has ventured into the area of psychotherapy for stuttering disorders. Webster (1977) evaluated the records of 648 PWS who had received speech therapy and psychotherapy over several years. He noted that 92% of these subjects showed either no improvements or only slight improvements in their fluency characteristics after psychotherapy. If the disorder of stuttering had as its etiology some psychological derivation, then therapy of this nature would have reduced stuttering symptoms. However, "this form of therapy has little effect on the gross fluency characteristics of these individuals" (p. 254). Stuttering produces emotions that impact the client's ability to cope with everyday verbal exchanges. Yet the source of these emotions is not an underlying psychological deviancy.

What is agreed on is the presence of affective and cognitive responses to the behavior of stuttering (Conture, 2001; Cooper, 1993; Manning, 1996; Shapiro, 1999), which may influence the ability of the PWS to manage their speech. The consequences of stuttering influence the client's belief system. Anticipation and avoidance behaviors develop as a result of these consequences, fostering the development of more severe stuttering. In a review of the literature on anxiety and stuttering, Menzies, Onslow, and Packman (1999) concluded that "positive findings in the literature provide clues about the possible relationship between stuttering and anxiety" (p. 8). These authors noted the situational nature of anxiety as a by-product of stuttering, concurring with the findings of other researchers (Bloodstein, 1995; Kraaimaat, Janssen, & Brutten, 1988; Peters & Hultijn, 1984; Sermas & Cox, 1982; Van Riper, 1973). The following sections describe the role of emotions in the development and maintenance of stuttering.

Emotions

> I believe the greatest gift I can conceive of having from anyone is to be seen by them, heard by them, to be understood and touched by them. The greatest gift I can give is to see, hear, understand and to touch another person. When this is done I feel contact has been made. (Satir, 1976, n.p.)

To be seen, heard, understood, and touched by another during everyday interactions is basic to human existence. For some people, however, this simple communicative exchange results in anger, guilt, and shame. An understanding of the emotions attached to the experience of stuttering will help you design treatment plans to address the affective components of this impairment.

Definition of Emotion

A straightforward definition of **emotion** is not easily found in the literature. *Webster's Collegiate Dictionary* (1990) defines emotion as follows:

> (a) the affect aspect of consciousness; (b) a state of feeling; (c) a psychic or physical reaction (as anger or fear) subjectively experienced as strong feeling and physiologically involving changes that prepare the body for immediate vigorous action. (p. 407)

Emotions are motivated and preceded by the individual's physiological reaction to environmental stimuli. It has been suggested that emotions, as determined by individuals' perceptions and interpretations of themselves and their experiences, form the core of the motivational process and serve to direct behavior. Gonzalez, Barrull, Pons, and Marteles (1998) presented a simplified interpretation of emotion characterized by the following features:

- Emotion is constant, ever present.
- Emotion varies as a function of the experience or stimuli present in the environment.
- Emotion is not always available for conscious thought (as in suppression).
- Emotion is situational.
- Emotion is the immediate evaluation of the likelihood of survival.

Gonzalez et al. (1998) contended that emotions serve to notify the individual of the pending outcome from environmental stimuli in terms of survival. If the stimuli elicit a favorable survival rating, the emotion is positive. On the contrary, if the stimulus brings forth an unfavorable prospect of survival, the emotion will be negative. In other words, "emotion is the subjective measurement (or evaluation) of the probability of survival of the organism in a given situation or in front of any perceived stimulus" (p. 4). Gonzalez et al. presented a dual-component representation of emotion involving quantitative and qualitative components. The quantitative component of emotion involves the magnitude in which the emotion is expressed (such as little, enough, a lot, great, some, etc.). The qualitative component is expressed by means of the words used to describe the emotion—love, friendship, fear, insecurity, and so forth (see Figure 2.1).

Emotional Development

Lewis (1992) described the development of emotions as a set of steps that outline how different emotions are transformed and integrated into the self system of an individual:

Step   1.   Emergence of the **primary emotions** to include joy/happiness⇒ surprise⇒interest; distress⇒sadness and/or disgust⇒anger⇒ fear. These basic emotions develop early in the life of the child.

Step   2.   Development of the cognitive capacity for objective self-awareness, which interacts with the environmental socialization process.

Step   3.   Development of self-conscious emotions as the child becomes aware of the self. These are nonevaluative and not correlated with thoughts, actions, or

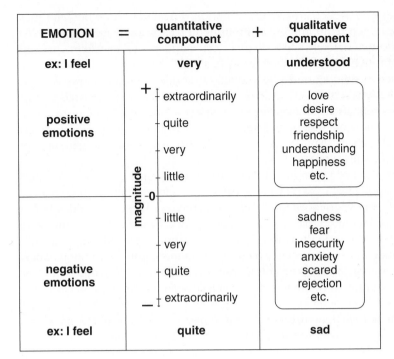

EMOTION =	quantitative component +	qualitative component
ex: I feel	very	understood
positive emotions	+ extraordinarily, quite, very, little	love desire respect friendship understanding happiness etc.
negative emotions	-0, little, very, quite, — extraordinarily	sadness fear insecurity anxiety scared rejection etc.
ex: I feel	quite	sad

(magnitude, along vertical axis)

Figure 2.1
Gonzalez, Barrull, Pons, and Marteles's (1998) dual-component model of emotion. *Source: www.biopsychology.org, reprinted with permission of the authors.*

feelings. **Exposed emotions** include embarrassment, empathy, and envy. Megacognitions, the ability to reflect on memories, set the stage for self-conscious emotions.

Step 4. Appearance of self-conscious **evaluative emotions** as the child begins to own the rules, standards, and goals of the environment. Higher level cognitive processes are involved in developing the evaluative emotions of pride, embarrassment, shame, and guilt.

Learning about social rules and standards in one's community (home, school, and/or town) interacts with the development of **objective self-awareness** to produce exposed and evaluative emotions. From a cognitive attribution point of view, Lewis (1992) proposed, first, that the person's success or failure in meeting the social standards of the community produces a signal to oneself. Second, this signal affects the organism and elicits self-reflection. Self-reflection is made on the basis of self-attributions (internal and/or external, from the environment) that influences the resultant exposed emotion. If the exposed emotion is accepted by the environment, pride and positive self-attributions occur. However, if the exposed emotion receives a negative evaluation, shame may develop. The evaluation of emotions is highly variable and depends on factors of (1) early failures in the self-system, (2) harsh socialization experiences, (3) high levels of reward for success, and (4) high level of punishment for failure (Lewis, 1992). These attributions may lead to the development of anger, guilt, and/or shame.

As individuals experience a particular emotion repeatedly, these become their **core emotions,** which recur and are often difficult to acknowledge (Field, 1995). As emotions build qualitatively, the individual may suppress them. Clients may appear to be out of touch with their feelings or in a state of denial. Denial of feelings implies the person is holding on to his hidden emotions, unable to express them. Suppressed emotions keep the client in a state of low self-esteem. Related to stuttering, the client repeatedly experiences unexpressed negative emotions in response to communication difficulty. After a period of time, these emotions are suppressed and the client may not be able to identify the emotional garbage collected over years of stuttering.

The repeated recall of a memory of an experience is similar to the development of stuttering. The individual experiences repeated difficulty communicating in a certain environment. He experiences the feeling of exhibiting these difficulties before and recalls them as uncomfortable, uncontrollable events. Reacting to these moments of disfluency begins the growth cycle of stuttering: Stuttering producing reactions that in turn produces more stuttering, which results in more intense emotions. These emotional overlays contribute to the communication difficulties of people who stutter as shown through the development of secondary behaviors (e.g., head nods used to get out of a stuttering moment, avoidances, fears, and/or circumlocutions). Negative self-attributions arise to include **interpersonal aspects** ("They won't like me if they know I stutter") and **intrapersonal aspects** ("I can't do this right"). As these secondary behaviors develop and the stuttering patterns become more severe, the individual experiences increased social consequences. Feelings of being different, not liked by others because of this difference, ostracism, teasing, and ridicule all contribute to the development of shame (Karen, 1992).

Field (1995) stated that a healthy, balanced emotional life requires an individual to experience a feeling, recognize, accept, and express it, and then let it go. To help clients with this process, clinicians must understand the emotions of stuttering. PWS report various emotions surrounding their speech experiences (Ginsberg, 2000). Three emotions frequently reported are anger, guilt, and shame (e.g., Murphy, 1999; Sheehan, 1953, 1958, 1969; Van Riper, 1973). These emotions vary in degree and intensity, as supported by Gonzalez's paradigm, based on the individual's perceptions of impending danger from environmental stimuli and his own history with these emotions. Not all PWS have experienced anger, guilt, and/or shame, but for those who have a profile of avoidance behaviors accompanied by secondary features, emotional reactions to stuttering will require attention in therapy.

Anger

Anger may be defined as a strong feeling of displeasure involving a cognitive response or interpretation of a social event. Anger is considered an emotion of choice, a way of communicating (Tavris, 1989), and may even block one's awareness of other painful emotions. According to Tavris, some myths regarding anger are not true. First, anger is a biochemically determined event. Second, anger and aggression are instinctual to humans. And third, it is healthy to ventilate when angry.

Table 2.1
Perceptions and habits that increase or reduce anger reactions.

Anger-Arousing Perceptions	Anger-Reducing Perceptions
• Injustice: "It's not fair"	• "Bad things happen"
• Shattered expectations	• Empathy for the other person
• Blaming: "Your fault"	• "I can't fight every battle"
• "Not treating me right."	• "She couldn't help it"
• Shattered belief in a just word	• Humor and silliness
• "She's condescending to me"	
• "I deserve better than this"	
• "Those people are breaking the rules"	

Anger-Intensifying Habits	Cooling-Off Habits
• Yelling	• Count to 10 (or to . . .)
• Sulking	• Sleep on it
• Plotting revenge	• Exercise (noncompetitive)
• Hitting, other violence	• Nip argument in the bud
• Competitive games	• Meditation, relaxation
• Accusations: "You never . . ."	• Distraction (baking bread, reading, movies)
• Arguing while angry	

Source: Summarized from Anger: The Misunderstood Emotion *by C. Tavris, 1989, p. 289.*

A person chooses to engage in angry behaviors. Individuals interpret their environment in a particular way and believe they have been wronged. The interpretation of unfairness precipitates anger. Replaying the event, either in one's mind or through verbal rehearsals, acts to enhance rather than reduce the feeling of anger. "Expressing hostile feelings is not a sufficient condition for the reduction of anger" (Tavris, 1989, p. 141). Anger can be triggered in two ways: (1) arousal/stress that leads to certain trigger thoughts in which the person responds with anger or (2) trigger thoughts that produce heightened arousal/stress, which results in anger (see Table 2.1).

Three side effects of anger are relevant to therapy. First, anger is associated with both rigidity and resistance and keeps the person from moving forward. When rehearsed, the client's belief system becomes inflexible. The individual may even resist interpreting the precipitating event in any other way. Lerner (1985) stated that "venting anger may serve to maintain, and even rigidify, the old rules and patterns in a relationship, thus ensuring that change does not occur" (p. 4). Second, angry people begin to feel helpless in situations eliciting this emotion. The feelings of helplessness reinforce clients' beliefs that something is wrong with them. McKay, Rogers, and McKay (1989) outlined how thoughts emerge as the client experiences helplessness. First, the client tells himself, "I'm in pain. Something is wrong with me." Next, he says, "Others should fix my pain." The client has successfully shifted responsibility for his behavior onto another, most likely the therapist. He may make comments such as "You're the expert. Tell me what to do" or "There has to be something you can do for me." Shifting responsibility for behavior change is problematic and a negative influence on the therapeutic relationship.

PWS may engage in anger rehearsal behaviors as they tell stories about their stuttering experiences. Clients who have been in therapy for a long time may come to believe they "should" be able to change their speech. Their repeated failure may elicit feelings of anger, first toward the therapist and eventually toward themselves. This irrational belief sets clients up for failure and frustration. Different clients may respond to this frustration with varying degrees of emotions, only one of which is anger. You must listen to clients talk about their lives of stuttering and determine if anger is a factor in treatment prognoses.

Guilt

Guilt is another emotion often present in the communication profile of PWS and their parents. Guilt is attributed to transgressions, reparative in nature, and comes from the conscience. The person focuses on the action of the transgression ("That was mean of me to tell that story") rather than the self ("I am mean"). "Guilt comes from the limits and values our parents and other adult figures taught us which we internalized" (Middleton-Moz, 1990, p. 57). The desire to make restitution for one's actions is strong, the emotion being less intense than shame, and more capable of dissipation (Lewis, 1992). Guilt is the normal reaction to breaking a social rule. Luterman (1991) reported guilt as the single most pervasive feeling that individuals and families of disabled clients experience. Parents may comment, "What did I do to make him stutter" or, "If I had only come here earlier" indicating feelings of guilt that their child stutters because of some action they did or did not take.

Guilt may be present in the belief system of the person who stutters, too (Sheehan, 1997). He may apologize for his inability to communicate and act in ways that avoid creating discomfort for the listener. The focus on listener reaction is indicative of the individual's guilt surrounding stuttering. Individuals feel guilty for what they have or have not done. In the case of therapy, the client may be guilt ridden because of his inability to utilize the techniques he has learned. Comments such as "I should be able to use the pullouts" or "If I could just do what I learned" may indicate the presence of guilt. A certain degree of guilt may be necessary for motivation. However, **debilitating guilt** is nonproductive and keeps the person from making amends and moving forward.

Sheehan identifies six sources of guilt reactions in stuttering. First is **primary guilt,** the feeling that precedes and leads to moments of stuttering. Here the client believes his stuttering behavior is wrong and not something he wants to do. Next is **secondary guilt,** or the feeling of failure after one has stuttered. Sheehan noted, "The constant suggestions of neighbors and strangers to the stutterer to take a deep breath, to think *about* what he has to say, to slow down, to try some trick—all these imply that stuttering is a simple problem with an easy solution if the stutterer will just follow the proffered (*sic*) advice" (p. 70).

Audience punishment guilt originates in the client's perception that his stuttering is offensive or aversive to the listener. The client experiences guilt over feeling angry at himself or the therapist because he does not perceive any benefit from therapy, called **therapy-induced guilt.** This may also be described as "not doing enough" by the client. **Clinician-induced guilt** occurs when the therapist blames the client for failure to make progress in obtaining a certain level of fluency. As Sheehan stated, the clinician uses the concept of acceptance of the stuttering to imply to the client that "after all, remember that you're a stutterer, and you might as well accept that fact" (p. 73). Lastly, **timing guilt** is another factor in treatment. At particular times during therapy, a client may be ready to perform certain tasks while at other times not prepared to perform. The clinician's job is to assess this readiness to perform throughout therapy. Asking clients to perform tasks before they are ready sets them up for failure and results in subsequent feelings of guilt. As these scenarios recur, clients internalize feelings of inadequacy and self-deprivation that embed feelings of guilt into their belief system.

Shame

Shame, in contrast, involves the evaluation of the self rather than one's actions. Feelings of failure, inadequacy, and the desire to cover up, hide, or withdraw are characteristic of shame (Ferguson, Stegge, & Damhuis, 1991; Karen, 1992; Lewis, 1992; Schneider, 1977). Although triggered by the same event as guilt, the distinction lies in the individual's interpretation of the event and subsequent reflection on the failure. Shame can be characterized by both external and internal components. Averting eye contact (not wanting others to see you in your state of exposure), nervously touching the body, shrinking of the body, blushing, and an inability to speak are external manifestations of shame (Lewis, 1992; Schneider, 1977; Zahn-Waxler, cited in Lewis, 1992). Bradshaw (1988) commented that shame is an "excruciating internal experience of unexpected exposure. It is a deep cut felt primarily from the inside. . . . We disown ourselves and this disowning demands a cover-up" (p. 3). Internally, the individual wishes to vanish, shrink, disappear as the result of exposure of their inadequacy. Shame is a social experience of sudden exposure of one's inadequacy resulting in a decrease in self-esteem (Karen, 1992; Lewis, 1992; Nathanson, 1992).

Karen (1992) identified two meanings for shame: one to denote healthy attitudes that define the person's character and one to denote feelings. **Healthy shame** has socializing power that assists in the adherence to social standards set by one's community (Lewis, 1992; Schneider, 1977). Healthy shame is influenced by family, neighborhood, nation, and the era in which one grew up (Nathanson, 1992) and reminds us of our limitations and faults. **Unhealthy shame** is linked to negative evaluations of communication exchanges that leave their mark on a person's self-concept. Individuals interpret the environment's reaction to their stuttering as negative and feel the need to escape. Feeling flawed and helpless, the person begins to internalize this inadequacy as a failure to meet social standards for communication over which he has no control. Continued experiences reinforce the emotions, eventually leading to **toxic shame.**

Karen (1992) classified shame into four different categories. First is **existential shame**, in which the individual suddenly sees himself as perhaps others do. This can involve the sudden awareness of hurting another person, being selfish, or insensitive. This type of shame lacks the negative self-affirmations commonly derived from early childhood shaming experiences. Second is **class shame,** derived from being a different color, socioeconomic status, and/or gender. These group differences serve mainly as a function of social power. **Narcissistic shame** is pathological and suggests a negative self-portrait that one is unable to fight against. The fourth category is **situational shame,** a passing shame experience that arises from the breaking of some social standard and has a temporary effect on one's identity while one feels rejected and humiliated. An example of situational shame would be the passing of gas or body odor. In relation to the person who stutters, situational shame could be the momentary inability to say one's name or answer a question aloud, being teased or mocked by one's peers, and/or failure to gain employment because of one's speaking difficulties. These experiences, repeated often enough, can lead to lasting wounds for the individual.

Schneider (1977) viewed shame somewhat differently: before the act and after the act. Before the act, "shame as discretion," implies external volition under control of the individual. Issues of an ethical nature would fit into this category. Comments like, "You're not going to do that and embarrass me, are you?" would occur in before-the-act shame. "Shame as disgrace" is an after-the-event emotion. Schneider stated that shame as disgrace is a "painful experience of the disintegration of one's world" (p. 22). Being put to shame (shame as disgrace) versus shame as seen in modesty and blushing (shame as discretion) are distinctly different. When one is shamed by another, the self experiences a sudden disruption. This leads the person to become more aware of his or her actions, thus growing into a sense of confusion and disorientation. Disorientation is followed by a reflexive moment of consciousness, an act of self-attention (Schneider, 1977) as the "self views the self with unkind eyes" (Karen, 1992). Figure 2.2 is a drawing representative of this "All eyes on me" belief.

Like Nietzsche (cited in Schneider, 1977), this author firmly believes there should be freedom from shame. No one should be put to shame, although society needs healthy shame to function as a whole (Hultberg, 1988). PWS need to relieve themselves of and/or be prevented from developing toxic shame in the early stages of stuttering. The following quote exemplifies this author's belief regarding shame:

> "Whom do you call bad? Those who always want to put to shame.
> What do you consider most humane? To spare someone shame.
> What is the seal of liberation? No longer being ashamed in front of oneself."
>
> (Nietzsche, cited in Schneider, 1977, p. 7)

The PWS begins to feel shame around communication failures if the topic is not open to discussion in the family or therapy setting. The secrecy and silence instill a sense of isolation that encourages the child to hide his failures. The more he hides and fears failure (stuttering), the bigger the shame grows. He interprets this silence as disgrace and fears that if the family secret is told, he will be abandoned. As shame increases, the individual feels he can never be accepted or loved by others (including himself).

An example of this shame appears in a poem written by Juan, an 8-year-old boy who stutters. *Juan's Secret* (1990) (Table 2.2) exemplifies the impact the conspiracy

Figure 2.2
"All Eyes on Me" portrait drawn by a child who stutters.

of silence around stuttering can have on the development of the self in children. Being communicatively disabled in a society that puts considerable emphasis on communication skills can have a major impact on self-perceptions. Emerick (1988) stated, "because oral communication is so elementary to being human, an impairment in speech, particularly one that has no obvious basis and is intermittent in nature, affects a person in a very human sort of way" (p. 257). Shame-based reactions to stuttering develop as the client experiences multiple failures to meet expectations (Bennett, 1995; Bennett & Chmela, 1998; Murphy, 1999; Quesal, 1997a). These reactions pile up and become a vivid part of the client's stuttering history.

Table 2.2

A story written by a young child who stutters, exemplifying the concept of secrecy in stuttering.

Juan's Secret (1990)

Once upon a time, not long ago, there lived a boy named Juan.

His life was all right, most of the time.
His mom was nice, his dad had a car,
his brother could pop his knuckles,
and his sister usually left him alone.

But Juan had a problem, a secret problem,
that no one seemed to suspect.

Sometimes when he talked, his throat felt tight. It was hard to breathe, and his words got stuck. He wanted to walk right up to his mom and say
"Hey, mom, I have trouble talking."

But he didn't because he thought no one knew his secret problem.
"She must not have noticed, or she would have said something by now", he thought.
"Maybe no one knows—no one but me.
Maybe I'm just imagining it.

"Or maybe this is something you're not supposed to talk about . . . like burping or the stomachache. Maybe she might even punish me," he thought, "if I tell her I have trouble talking."

So Juan kept the secret all to himself.
He tried not to think about it.
But it came back in his dreams at night,
And in the day, it lurked behind him, teasing. "I'm not going to look at it!" Juan thought. "If I don't look at it, maybe it will go away."

Juan imagined that the "thing" was a monster, He thought it must be ugly and grim. "I bet it has teeth like a shark, And eyes like a devil," he thought.
"It must be green, and its fingernails long.
Its belly must be fat from eating boys like me."
So day after day Juan kept looking straight ahead. He never looked back for fear he would see "IT."

Then one day a small little voice inside him
said, "Hey, man! Don't be afraid! You're no kid! You watch scary movies! You don't run from anybody!"

"Just take a peek," the little voice said.
"Maybe its just fake . . . like Freddie Krueger."

So the next time Juan's throat felt tight, he turned quickly and said to the monster,
"Hey, what are you doing?" like you would talk to a thief stealing your bike.

From inside his throat came the monster's reply, "I'm just making your throat tight . . . that's all!" "Well, quit it!" said Juan. "I don't like your teasing!" "But I love it when you're scared," said the monster.
"I can hold your breath. I can squeeze your muscles. There's nothing you can do!"

"We'll see about that!" said Juan, mad as could be!
Then he shifted his braid to FREE CHOICE!

Like Luke Skywalker when he conquered the Empire,
the FORCE by his side, Juan told his throat what to do! The monster's green skin turned a sickly pale blue, his teeth fell out and his fingernails melted.

His cheeks turned all red, and his belly exploded! "No, not FREE CHOICE!" he sputtered as he died.

Juan watched in amazement as the "Thing" disappeared. First one part of it was gone, and then another. Little pieces remained, but he said to himself: "With FREE CHOICE in me, I need never fear.
One day it'll be gone . . . all gone indeed! I'll soon look around, and see nothing but me!"

Shame Spirals

The stuttering cycle, presented in chapter 1, describes the interaction between the moment of stuttering and the reaction to this event. As the client swings back and forth, the stuttering and reaction portions grow. A similar pattern exists for shame development. Potter-Efron and Potter-Effron (1989) described how waves of shame develop into **shame spirals.** Healthy shame occurs in waves, and it is quickly resolved if the individual attends to it. However, when ignored, the shame spirals in a downward direction causing the person to dwell on the negative aspects of the self. Let's look at how these authors describe the progression into a spiral of shame:

> In a typical shame spiral, a person might become aware of a shortcoming. It could be trivial such as forgetting to make a phone call. Perhaps suddenly embarrassed, this person has shameful thoughts and feelings. This is immediate shame. He may withdraw from the situation to regain his composure. So far, this is perfectly normal. . . . But serious problems can develop at this point, particularly if he is shame-based. Current shame can trigger recollections of past shame. That is why it is difficult to feel a "little" shame. Once a person starts to feel shame, it can quickly become excruciating. The spiral can accelerate as a person remembers other times when he felt shame. He becomes flooded with uncomfortable and scary thoughts. . . . This signals the need for a general retreat from situations that could increase the shame. For instance, a person who initially avoided someone who said things that bothered him won't go to the building where the person works. The person who feels shamed becomes more vigilant, needing to guard against exposure of his shame. (p. 35)

This description of shame spirals closely parallels the behaviors that clients exhibit who are shamed by their stuttering. The person accumulates episodes of past shame and recalls these events as hurtful and uncomfortable. Avoidance behaviors are selected to decrease the eminent feelings of shame. Clients may avoid using the telephone even though this behavior is impractical. They may even choose to drive to a store to see if it is open rather than to use the phone. As clients spiral down into shame, their decisions negatively impact their communication efforts, making the disorder more severe. These shame-based reactions to stuttering will eventually impact the client's self-concept (Bennett & Chmela, 1998).

Shame and Resistance

All clinicians encounter resistant clients at some point in their careers. **Resistance** occurs when the client unconsciously avoids the pain of past memories (Bohart & Todd, 1988). Resistance may manifest in particular client behaviors, such as missing appointments, not completing assignments, and/or evading certain topics of discussion. The client may attempt to draw you off the topic of stuttering by talking about trivial concerns not related to speech. It is believed the underlying source of resistance is the shame the client feels about his stuttering. Therapy encourages the client to share negative memories of the shame experienced when stuttering. A natural instinct is to avoid situations in which pain occurs; therefore the client shows up late for the session or fails to come altogether. Be cognizant of the client's level of self-acceptance and proceed cautiously with the resistant client.

Impact on the Self-Concept

The negative self-evaluations of people who stutter impact their **self-concept** as effective communicators. A further look into the definition of self-concept, the development of the self, and how one's experiences shape the self-concept is necessary to understand the individual who stutters. Okun (1997) defined self-concept as "the perception we have of ourselves based on information from significant others and from our experiences" (p. 291). Strein (1995) noted two distinctly different models: **global self-concept** versus **domain-specific self-concept.** The global view is an overarching, broad-based characterization of the person's self-evaluation. This perspective is considered traditional and "probably the more common view among counselors and therapists" (p. 1). In contrast, the domain-specific model proposes a set of self-evaluations based on situational variables. This multifaceted perspective might include various types of self-concept such as academic, social, physical, and communication. Related to stuttering, the PWS may have a positive, global self-concept, yet his self-concept as a communicator is flawed and incongruent with his global self-perceptions.

Such **incongruence** will negatively impact the development of a healthy self-concept. Rogers (1961, 1986) identified certain characteristics of personality: the *self* (a person's conscious sense of who and what they are); the need for *positive regard* from others; and the need for *positive self-regard*, or acceptance from within. When all three aspects of personality are consistent, the individual is in a state of congruence. Incongruence occurs when a gap is perceived between the person's self-concept and his real-life experiences. Incongruence creates anxiety and defensive behaviors such as denial and distortion.

For the PWS, periods of incongruence may be present when trying to hide stuttering, pretending to be a fluent speaker and then being unable to be fluent. The self-concept is wounded when the person realizes stuttering has occurred and negative listener reactions are perceived. This may be especially true for the covert stutterer who makes every effort to hide his stuttering through circumlocutions, avoidances, and various secondary behaviors. With every avoidance or trick, the self-concept becomes at risk for damage. When these avoidance mechanisms no longer work, the client condemns himself for this failure, entering the throes of a shame spiral. Although this damage occurs to the domain-specific self-concept as a communicator, the person still suffers the internal degradation of negative self-thoughts, placing him in a state of low self-esteem. Repeated degradation may create a sense of hopelessness in the client, precipitating grief over the loss of ability to communicate effectively. With a firm grasp of the grieving process you may assist clients during their journey toward the acceptance of stuttering.

The Grief Process

You may find family members or clients who react to the diagnosis of stuttering with grief. The news that their child does indeed stutter may send parents into a state of panic, distraught about the future. It is common for parents to project how stuttering is going to impact their child's life years from now. Understanding the grieving process is essential to helping parents stay in the present and manage their child's speech disorder. Crowe (1997) contended that the grieving process is typically time limited for most losses. However, for those who have communication disorders, the loss may be reinforced daily, making recovery from grief a protracted process. Kubler-Ross (1969) outlined the grieving process in these five stages: (1) denial, (2) anger, (3) bargaining, (4) depression, and (5) acceptance.

Denial

Denial is a normal reaction to unpleasant information. During the denial stage, the parent/client reacts to the diagnosis with disbelief. After all, most parents have been told their child will outgrow stuttering. They are instructed to ignore the stuttering; however, when this does not work, they feel guilty and sad. They may obtain a second opinion from another therapist before the realization sets in that their child is indeed stuttering. You can help parents/clients move through this stage by providing accurate and complete information and being available to answer questions as intervention begins. Many times clinicians begin their therapy routine without allowing time in the lesson plan to address parental/client concerns. As the client-clinician relationship is being established, listen with empathy to parental/client concerns and provide information and direction.

Anger

Anger is the second stage of the grieving process. Clients begin to question themselves and others, seeking answers to the question "Why me?" Parents may express anger toward the individuals who advised them to wait until the child got older or to the doctor who said their child would outgrow it. Adult clients may be angry about previous therapy that has not provided relief from stuttering. You must be prepared to acknowledge these responses as normal, allowing the client to express their feelings in therapy. However, "anger clouds the therapy process, making it difficult for a client to see the purpose and course of therapy" (Crowe, 1997, p. 36). If parents/clients appear to be holding on to their anger, you may need to refer them to a grief counselor.

Bargaining

Bargaining, the negotiation between client and clinician, is the third stage of grief. During this period, clients appear eager and willing to attend therapy and do their work in exchange for a "cure," but they must be told there are no guarantees in the practice of speech-language pathology. It is not an exact science. One cannot state or imply that by doing what the clinician says to do, they will be fixed or cured. Too many external and internal factors can influence treatment outcomes. Clients and parents must be informed of this from the start of therapy. Setting treatment goals together may help the client establish realistic therapy expectations and move beyond the bargaining stage.

Depression

Depression follows bargaining as clients realize no matter what they say or do, the disorder remains an everyday factor in their life. The term *depression*, as used in this model, does not refer to clinical depression. The clients' feelings of sadness and despair over having a communication disorder encompass their depression. These feelings may keep them from making progress in therapy. Inattentiveness and what appears to be a lack of motivation are symptoms of feelings of depression. Allowing clients to express their concerns in therapy will help you judge the extent of the depression and its impact on therapy. Monitor the duration of this affective state and, if the client does not appear to be moving out of depression, refer him to another agency.

Acceptance

Acceptance, the last stage of the Kubler-Ross grief model, comes with the belief that the communication disorder exists and it is up to the client to do something about it. Clients become more engaged in therapy, putting forth a concerted effort to improve their communication skills. Parents follow through more consistently, often being more positive toward their child and therapy as a whole. Crowe (1997) noted that acceptance depends on the severity of the disorder, extent of family support, individual personalities, and the clinician's counseling skills. You can promote and maintain client acceptance by continuing to listen empathetically to their concerns, engage them in the therapy process, and motivate them.

The grieving process, although described in linear terms, is a variable process influenced by client and clinician factors. Client personality, previous emotional history, and the tendency to use certain defense mechanisms may impact the progression through this cycle. Clinician personality, counseling skills, and knowledge of the disorder of stuttering will either enhance or impede client progress. At any point, clients may relapse into a previous stage of grief, requiring support from the therapist. Be careful to remain cognizant of this possibility when interacting with clients and families of people who stutter.

Temperament

Another affective component present in some people who stutter is a reactive **temperament** (Conture, 2001; Conture & Melnick, 1999; Guitar, 1997, 1998, 2003; Lewis & Golberg, 1997; Oyler & Ramig, 1995; J. Riley, 2002). Guitar (1998, 2003), citing the works of Kagan on temperament, wrote that some people who stutter may have greater reactivity to uncomfortable or unfamiliar events. A subgroup of people who stutter report a high degree of sensitivity to changes in daily routines along with perfectionistic tendencies. These individuals exhibit behaviors that indicate they are not comfortable with mistakes (e.g., tearing up a drawing/report when they make a perceived error). The individual's frustration at not being able to speak in a fluent, forward manner is fueled by his temperament.

J. Riley (2002), in an excellent article on counseling for speech-language pathologists, discussed various components of temperament: activity, rhythmicity, approach, adaptability, intensity, mood, persistence and attention, distractibility, and threshold (pp. 14–15). *Activity* refers to the level of physical activity the individual displays across different tasks (i.e., playing quietly versus a preference for running instead of walking). *Rhythmicity* includes a person's adherence to daily routines in terms of regularity or organization (i.e., eating, sleeping, bath time). Another aspect of temperament is the person's response to new situations, called *approach*. Is the individual hesitant or shy in new situations? Can the client adapt to situations over time? The time it takes for the client to adapt or adjust in novel environments refers to his *adaptability. Intensity* describes the amount of energy put into responding to the environment (i.e., does the client fatigue quickly or is he loud versus quiet).

The consistent *mood* of the client is an additional part of temperament. The clinician wants to observe any consistent pattern of pleasant versus irritable, and so on. The ability of the client to sustain attention and complete tasks makes up the next part of temperament: *persistence and attention. Distractibility* describes the person's ability to be redirected when he becomes distracted. Some individuals can easily go back to the original task and complete it. Some become disorganized, needing to be reoriented. The last component of temperament described by Riley is *threshold*, which involves the client's sensory reactions to textures, odors, light, and so on. Riley recommended that clinicians look for patterns of temperamental characteristics and cautions against jumping to rash conclusions based on minimal observations. Understanding the temperament of the person who stutters provides the foundation for treatment success.

For this particular population, therapy may need to be approached in a slightly different manner. Guitar (1997) discussed a treatment plan for an individual in which the initial work focused too directly on the individual's stuttering, thereby creating resistance to the therapy process. Guitar described how he had to modify the treatment based on the client's fear of stuttering and perceived failure. Gather information on temperament, sensitivity, and perfectionistic tendencies of people who stutter prior to determining the direction of treatment.

Conture (2001) suggested that information be obtained relative to the following characteristics: (1) sensitivity to novelty; (2) continued reaction to novelty long after the event has occurred; (3) difficulty separating from parents (for children); (4) decreased verbal output when confronted with change, novel situations, or stress; and (5) strong, persistent fears. You must understand that the temperamental features of people who stutter *do not* cause them to stutter. Rather, a highly "sensitive to mistakes" temperament may interact with other factors to exacerbate or maintain stuttering.

BEHAVIORAL COMPONENTS OF STUTTERING

The specific speech behaviors exhibited prior to, during, and after a moment of stuttering have certain physiological and linguistic characteristics. Before delving into these features, you must understand that the categorization of stuttering according to discrete, behavioral events is not the best representation of such a complex disorder.

An example of such a classification might be Conture's (2001) criteria of three or more **within-word disfluencies** per 100 words used to classify an individual as exhibiting stuttering behaviors. Within-word disfluencies include (1) sound or syllable repetitions; (2) sound prolongations; (3) monosyllabic whole-word repetitions; and (4) within-word pauses, also referred to as blocks. Three important factors must be considered when defining this complex disorder as absolute, discrete events. First, the age of the client will influence your evaluation of the presence of stuttering. Young preschool children often exhibit within-word disfluencies that are not considered stuttering. The frequency of disruption in the flow of speech and effort put into talking impact the listener's evaluation of a young child's fluency. Second, stuttering is a highly variable disorder that fluctuates from situation to situation and day to day. The behaviors exhibited during an evaluation session may not be characteristic of the individual's typical speech production patterns. The third factor is the presence of the client's covert manifestations of stuttering. Most definitions isolate the observable, measurable **overt behaviors** considered stuttering. However, the client may engage in **covert responses** to stuttering that you may not see during initial evaluation sessions. The client using covert responses does not want stuttering to emerge and makes every effort to hide it through word changes, avoidances, and subtle postponement devices. These covert reactions may reduce the observable moments of stuttering, appearing to decrease the frequency of the behavior. So consider the behaviors of stuttering in terms of frequency counts as just one aspect of this highly variable, dynamic disorder (Smith, 1999; Smith & Kelly, 1997).

The behavioral component of stuttering is the most widely researched aspect of the disorder. Most of these findings can be categorized into either physiological or linguistic areas of study. Physiological studies have investigated the role of respiration, phonation, and articulation during the fluent and stuttered speech of people who stutter. Linguistic studies have focused on the *loci*, or location of moments of stuttering within the language structure of the speaker. The following is a brief overview of the relevant conclusions drawn from the literature.

Physiological Aspects

Several theories have proposed stuttering as a temporal sequencing disorder (Kent, 1984; Perkins, 1986; Perkins, Rudas, Johnson, & Bell, 1976). During the 1970s and into the 1980s, many researchers investigated the respiratory, laryngeal, and articulatory systems of people who stutter (e.g., Adams, 1978, 1981; Adams & Ramig, 1980; Caruso, 1991; Colcord & Adams, 1979; Commodore & Cooper, 1978; Cross & Luper, 1979, 1983; Cullinan & Springer, 1980; Freeman, 1979; Gracco, 1991; Hillman & Gilbert, 1977; McKnight &

Cullinan, 1987; Peters, Hulstijn, & Starkweather, 1989; Till, Reich, Dickey, & Sieber, 1983; Watson & Alfonso, 1982; Zimmerman, 1980a, 1980b). The majority of this research was conducted on adults who stuttered using various reaction time paradigms. Measurements of **voice onset time (VOT), voice reaction time (VRT),** respiratory air flow, sequential movements of the upper lip, lower lip, and jaw, as well as tracking of articulatory movement, have been gathered for the sole purpose of determining if neuromotor deficits in the timing of articulatory gestures might explain the presence of stuttering.

Although this and current research has not found the source of stuttering, it certainly has provided several puzzle pieces related to the respiratory, laryngeal, and articulatory functioning during stuttering. However, as Silverman (1996) writes, "no differences in physiological functioning, other than those that occur during the moment of stuttering, have been demonstrated unequivocally to differentiate persons who stutter from their normal-speaking peers" (p. 55). The following sections summarize research findings on the respiratory, phonatory, and articulatory performance of people who stutter.

Respiration

Respiration is an essential component of speech production. When disrupted, speech becomes difficult to produce. Bloodstein (1995) noted that one of the first factors studied in the search for the cause of stuttering was the disordered breathing of PWS. Currently, researchers continue to investigate the respiratory functioning of PWS during fluent and stuttered speech (Baken, McManus, & Cavallo, 1983; Williams & Brutten, 1994). Baken et al. (1983) observed qualitatively different patterns of chest wall posturing in adults who stuttered. Often the breathing patterns observed during stuttering are not the same as when the person is silent (Bloodstein, 1995).

Additionally, Williams and Brutten (1994) investigated the respiratory events prior to speech production in adults who stutter by measuring the air flow shape and latency between respiration and the initiation of laryngeal movements. They found that PWS took longer to reach peak air flow for speech and exhibited concurrent contraction of the abdomen and rib cage mechanisms. Nonstuttering subjects contracted the abdomen and expanded the rib cage upon respiration. The stuttering subjects contracted both structures. They also observed a greater lag time between respiratory initiation and the first indications of laryngeal movements, perhaps reflective of a delay in prephonatory vocal fold closure. In his review of more than 17 early publications, Bloodstein made the following conclusions: (1) during stuttering there are anomalies of a number of different kinds; (2) these anomalies are not present during silence; and (3) many of the disturbances observed in the speech of PWS are also present in nonstutterer's speech (p. 146).

Phonation

Clients often report that "they feel as if their throat is jammed shut" when they stutter. The loci of tension appears to be directed at the laryngeal mechanism, that is, the ability to turn on vocal cord vibration in a timely fashion with respiration and articulatory movement. One child told this author he had a "peach pit stuck in his throat," which is why he talked like he did. Clinicians and researchers have long been interested in the role of phonation in stuttering.

Dworkin, Culatta, Abkarian, and Meleca (2002) summarized the research findings of their study that directly observed the functioning of the larynx during stuttering. They concluded that PWS exhibit (1) "excessive vocal fold supraglottal activity, (2) prolonged contraction levels, (3) long periods of premovement activation, and (4) abnormal reciprocity between abductor and adductor muscle groups" (p. 216). This hyperfunctioning of the vocal mechanism was also reported by Freeman and Ushijima (1978) and Shapiro (1980) and may produce systemic discoordination, as Perkins, Rudas, Johnson, and Bell (1976) proposed. Some researchers have developed specialized treatment programs to specifically address this oral-motor coordination deficit in PWS (Riley & Riley, 1991, 2000). However, the role of phonation in stuttering goes beyond just that of coordination. Investigators began to look at the ability of PWS to turn on the vocal mechanism in a timely manner (Caruso, 1991).

Research on the laryngeal timing of PWS, using voice onset time (VOT) measurements, has produced inconsistent results. Some studies observed significantly slower VOT for stuttering subjects; others did not. What is clear about the voice onset timing characteristic is the presence of greater variability (Jancke, 1994; Janssen, Wieneke, & Vaane, 1983; Wieneke & Janssen, 1991; Williams & Brutten, 1994). This variability appears to be related to stuttering severity, with more severe stutterers exhibiting greater group variability than mild or nonstuttering subjects (Caruso, Abbs, & Gracco, 1988; McClean, Kroll, & Loftus, 1991; Watson & Alfonso, 1987).

For voice reaction time (VRT), the research is more robust in its conclusions: Adults who stutter exhibit slower VRT than nonstutterers (Bakker & Brutten, 1989; Dembowski & Watson, 1991; Prosek, Walden, Montgomery, & Schwartz, 1979; van Lieshout, Hulstijn, & Peters, 1991; Watson & Alfonso, 1982). It is also apparent that this response time differential varies according to the type of stimuli used and the level of linguistic complexity. Van Lieshout et al. (1991) found significant differences in speech reaction times for PWS when naming pictures versus words. Peters and Hulstijn (1987) found greater response time latencies for PWS as linguistic demand increased. In summary, Bloodstein wrote that the "delay that stutterers often manifest in their vocal reaction times is very small, but the regularity with which researchers have obtained this finding is nevertheless impressive" (p. 199). However, clinicians are reminded that the vocal mechanism does not function in isolation (Denny & Smith, 1997). The clinical implications of the findings just cited are not clear at this time. For a thorough review of the studies investigating the role of phonation in stuttering, see the writings of Bloodstein (1995).

Articulation

Zimmerman, in his landmark 1980 studies, noted aberrant motor sequencing of the lip and jaw in the fluent and stuttered utterances of PWS. These observations pointed a finger at the role of coordination of the articulatory mechanism in this disorder. Smith, Denny, and Wood (1991) observed imprecise timing of the articulators occurring around a moment of stuttering. Guitar, Guitar, Neilson, O'Dwyer, and Andrews (1988) observed reversed sequencing of lip muscles for PWS. Discoordination between movements of the upper lip, lower lip, and jaw have been noted in several other studies (Archibald & DeNil, 1999; Caruso, Abbs, & Gracco, 1988; DeNil, 1995; DeNil & Abbs, 1991). However, Smith (1990) did not confirm such timing irregularities.

Archibald and DeNil (1999) proposed that adults who stutter have difficulty managing small movements of the articulators. They investigated the ability of subjects to track minimal movements of the jaw with and without visual feedback. The moderate to severe subjects exhibited significantly slower articulatory movements when relying only on proprioceptive feedback (no visual feedback). Their findings support the presence of an oral kinesthetic defect in a subgroup of adults who stutter.

Another study by McClean, Tasko, and Runyan (2004) investigated the orofacial movements associated with the fluent speech of PWS. Measuring the speed and duration of vocal tract opening and closing, they found variable performance for both stuttering and nonstuttering subjects based on the nature of the task, stuttering severity, and direction of movement. For PWS, they exhibited significant differences in lower lip and jaw closing movements when producing nonsense phrases; however, orofacial speed did not vary between groups. Stuttering severity, either high or low, did impact tongue opening movements. PWS with low stuttering exhibited higher speeds with significantly lower speeds for those subjects with high stuttering. The authors attribute these differences to the possibility of two distinctly different control processes working during sentence production. PWS with more severe stuttering may have utilized learned adaptive strategies to enhance speech fluency during the experimental tasks. They concluded that the elevated speed for those subjects with mild stuttering was a contributing factor to speech disfluency assuming these subjects were not relying on adaptive speech motor processes.

Caruso (1991) reviewed the growing body of evidence on the physiological factors involved in speech production. He concluded that "stutterers may take more time to organize and/or execute their speech movements to reach the same spatial targets that normals achieve in producing perceptually fluent speech. This agrees with the most consistently replicated finding in more than 60 years of research on stuttering; that is, stuttering is a disorder of timing" (p. 103). These timing differences in adults who stutter involve the temporal control of speech and nonspeech movements. However, one question remains to be answered: Do children who stutter exhibit similar physiological differences like adults?

Preliminary findings suggest children exhibit variances in VOT, VRT, and articulatory movements that also appear to be influenced by age and stuttering severity. Conture (1991) summarized the literature on VOT, Voice Initiation Time (VIT), and Voice Termination Time (VTT), only to concur with the equivocal findings of significant differences, most likely attributed to differences within the groups of children under study (i.e., the co-occurrence of phonological disorders). Research on the speech production of children who stutter measures temporal asynchrony between respiration, phonation, and articulation. The research of Conture and his colleagues have not supported the temporal discoordination hypothesis. However, more recent studies (Chang, Ohde, & Conture, 2002; Subramanian, Yairi, & Amir, 2003; Yaruss & Conture,

1993; Zebrowski, Conture, & Cudahy, 1985) continue to investigate the formant transitions and coarticulation abilities of children who stutter compared to their peers. However, the limited number of studies are insufficient to provide any definitive conclusions at this time. Studies on VOT in children failed to find consistent differences on measures of laryngeal timing (Conture, Colton, & Gleason, 1988; Cullinan & Springer, 1980; DeNil & Brutten, 1991; Hall & Yairi, 1992; Howell, Sackin, & Rustin, 1995); others have found significantly longer times for measures of VRT (Cross & Luper, 1983). Bishop, Williams, and Cooper (1991a, 1991b) found slower reaction times (RT) with greater variability in task performance related to levels of complexity. Age appears to be an important variable influencing reaction times for children: RT appears to decrease in length and variability as children become older.

Recent research has utilized a priming technique to assess the speech reaction times (SRT) of children who stutter (Anderson & Conture, 2004; Melnick, Conture, & Ohde, 2003). Melnick et al. studied the ability of preschool children to name pictures rapidly during three conditions: no prime, related prime, and unrelated prime. Results indicated that for all children, both stuttering and nonstuttering, SRTs were shorter when provided with a related prime. However, CWS with delayed articulatory mastery demonstrated longer SRTs. The authors interpreted these findings to infer a "somewhat" less developed articulatory/phonological system for CWS compared to their nonstuttering peers. However, Anderson and Conture (2004) failed to find significant differences in SRTs between these two groups of children. One possible explanation for these different results possibly lies in the response demands used in the two studies. Melnick et al. looked only at the SRT when naming single words, whereas Anderson and Conture's responses required the children to generate a simple declarative sentence involving greater syntactic demands. As the next section demonstrates, linguistic complexity appears to have a negative impact on the ability of PWS to generate fluent speech production.

Linguistic Aspects

The linguistic aspects of stuttering also have a long research history. From the early works of Brown (1938a, 1938b, 1945), studies have investigated the loci and frequency of stuttered events related to the phonetic, lexical, syntactic, and pragmatic components of language. The intent of this body of research is to identify any consistency effect present in both children and adults who stutter. The following summarizes the general conclusions drawn from several reviews of the literature and recent studies in this area (Bloodstein, 1995; Bernstein Ratner, 1997b; Dayalu, Kalinowski, Stuart, Holbert, & Rastatter, 2002; Howell, Au-Yeung, & Sackin, 1999, 2000; Natke, Grosser, Sandrieser, & Kalveram, 2002; Prins, Hubbard, & Krause, 1991).

Phonetic Features

There are four apparent regularities in the phonetic features of words and the moment of stuttering. First, longer words are stuttered on more frequently than shorter words. Secondly, most stuttering occurs on the initial position of words, usually the first syllable of the word (the onset and nucleus position). When the word is multisyllabic, stuttering most commonly occurs on the accented or stressed syllable of the word. The last factor is related to the frequency of sounds in the English language. An inverse relationship exists between the frequency of phoneme occurrence and stuttered events (i.e., stuttering decreases as word initial phoneme frequency increases). The likelihood of stuttering occurring on any given sound appears to be an individual, case-by-case foundation. Studies have failed to find group tendencies to stutter more frequently on certain English phonemes.

Lexical Features

Stuttering has been associated with lexical organization and retrieval processes. Lexical retrieval is a complicated process that occurs at an extremely fast rate. Bernstein Ratner (1997b) reported lexical retrieval rates ranging from 2 to 3 words per second up to 11 plus words per second. Two major lexical factors influence this retrieval process: word frequency and class category. The frequency of words influences stuttering episodes in that stuttering increases with less frequent words for both children and adults. This frequency effect is also impacted by word familiarity. Less frequent words may be less familiar; therefore less familiar words are more likely to be stuttered, too.

The category of words (open versus closed) contributes to the frequency of stuttering. There are major lexical differences between words classified as open and closed. The **open category words** is a large repertoire of vocabulary items that grows throughout the lifespan. It contains nouns, verbs, adjectives, and adverbs. The **closed category words** are a small, limited set of words with very few new members. This category contains primarily function words, such as pronouns, conjunctions, prepositions, inflections, interjections, and auxiliary verbs. Open-class content words vary in their phonetic characteristics, whereas closed words have simpler syllable shape, greater linguistic predictability, and carry less prosodic features, such as stress. Retrieval rate is shorter and more automatic for closed versus open words, each being processed in different centers in the brain (Bernstein Ratner, 1997b; Dayalu et al., 2002).

Adults stutter more on high, information-bearing open category words, whereas children stutter more often on closed category words (Howell et al., 2000). This differential effect between children and adults appears to be related to the development and use of grammatical features in children (Au-Yeung, Howell, & Pilgrim, 1998; Bernstein Ratner, 1997b). Children use function words to initiate their utterances more often than content words, which adults typically use to start their communication efforts.

Syntactic Features

Syntax involves the planning, ordering, and construction of lexical and phonological units to express one's communicative intent (Levelt, 1989). It requires time to plan these syntactic elements. Bernstein Ratner (1997b) noted a 0.75-second prespeech latency time for simple sentences, increasing to 7- to 9-second latencies for complex structures. As the speed requirements increase, breakdowns are inevitable for both the fluent and nonfluent speaker. The location of stuttering within the syntactic organization is strongly connected to stuttering. Bloodstein (1995) reported that over 90% of stuttering occurs on the initial sound or syllable of a word. Stuttering is more likely to occur at the beginning of an utterance or at clausal boundaries. Verb selection appears to be a difficult task for children who stutter but not for adults.

The issue of length and complexity of utterance has speared the interest of many researchers (e.g., Bernstein Ratner, 1995; Bernstein Ratner & Sih, 1987; Costello & Ingham, 1993, 1999; Logan & Conture, 1995; Logan & LaSalle, 1999; Melnick & Conture, 2000; St. Louis & Hinzman, 1988; Zackheim & Conture, 2003). The literature suggests that when considering length alone, stuttered utterances are generally longer than fluent utterances and may be related to the fact that speaking rate increases with length of utterance. Complex utterances are more likely to exhibit Stuttering Like Disfluencies (SLDs), particularly when the length of the utterance exceeds the **mean length of utterance (MLU)** (Zackheim & Conture, 2003). Utterance length and syntactic complexity interact to increase the likelihood of stuttering.

Pragmatic Features

Pragmatics is the study of the social aspects of language and has been conjectured to impact the frequency of stuttering (Bernstein Ratner, 1997b; Kelly & Conture, 1992; Weiss, 1995). Various factors may influence the ability of the child or adult to manage fluent speech production: the number of people in a conversation; type of speech act (requests, demands, comments); social stature of the conversational partners; situational dynamics; and cultural differences. However, systematic studies of the relationship between pragmatics and stuttering are limited and in "their infancy" (Bernstein Ratner, 1997b, p. 111). Weiss (1995) failed to find differences between stuttering and nonstuttering children's number of assertive or responsive utterances. However, children who stutter are more likely to be fluent when responding to parental requests as compared to making their own requests. The conversational tempo, as measured by speaking rate of the conversational partners, does not appear to influence the stuttering child's speaking rate. Having parents slow their speech rate does not ensure a similar rate reduction will happen in the child's speech. Further studies are certainly needed before any pattern of regularity can be differentiated among those who stutter.

COGNITIVE COMPONENTS OF STUTTERING

Cognitive components of stuttering encompass the thoughts generated before, during, and after the stuttering experience. **Cognitive** is defined (*Webster's Collegiate Dictionary*, 1990) as relating to or involving cognition that is "the act or process of knowing including both awareness and judgment" (p. 257). The person conceptualizes his knowledge through the generation of thoughts. According to Ellis (2001), a prime source of cognitive functioning involves human thinking (p. 18), which he clearly links to the process of change. Thoughts are shaped by the individual's own perception and interpretation of events, which may or may not be based on reality. Related to stuttering, thoughts can be categorized into two themes: thoughts about the self and thoughts about the listener.

The individual develops certain thought patterns about his speaking abilities after repeated experiences with stuttering. How the client views himself as a communicator will impact how he approaches speaking situations. Every day, people generate positive and negative self-thoughts based on their social experiences. For the PWS, these repeated thought patterns often turn into self-fulfilling prophecies. If the client thinks often enough, "I can't say my name," he will approach this speaking task with apprehension and predictably have difficulty saying his name. The individual's view of himself and his abilities in a given role determines the type of thought generated.

The next category of thoughts include how the speaker views the audience or listener. According to Meyers (1991), "the development, persistence, and maintenance of stuttering is a bi-directional process involving both the listener and stutterer" (p. 41). Many people who stutter develop a heightened awareness and concern about listener reaction to stuttering. Comments such as "If they know I stutter, I won't get the job"; "They will think I am stupid if I stutter"; or, "I let them finish my sentences because it must be very hard to listen to my stuttering" exemplify the speaker's concern about what the listener is thinking about his stuttering. Some clients develop clever ways of hiding their stuttering in efforts to avoid the punitive effects of listener reactions. One client, an adult who was often interviewed on television, hid his stuttering by developing an extensive vocabulary of synonyms related to his work so he could change any word he thought might be difficult to say. However, the downside to this was a loss in communicative effectiveness because the words chosen did not always convey the exact meaning he wished to communicate. His covert or hidden stuttering eventually brought him into therapy. At the initial visit, he recounted the mental energy he extended each day at work because he was concerned about what his coworkers might think of his stuttering.

Perceptions of Stuttering

Listener perceptions of stuttering and people who stutter provide a foundation for the client's belief system. Stated another way, what the individual thinks about himself and his perceptions of what the listener is thinking influences the occurrence of stuttering. Listener reaction to or perceptions of stuttering have been researched over the years. Several groups of listeners were surveyed to obtain their perspectives and beliefs about people who stutter. They include teachers (Crowe & Walton, 1981; Lass et al., 1992; Yeakle & Cooper, 1986); pediatricians (Yairi & Carrico, 1992); administrators (Lass et al., 1994); special educators (Ruscello, Lass, Schmitt, & Pannbacker, 1994); employers and colleagues (Ayre, Wright, & Grogan, 1998; Christmann, 1998a, 1988b); school-age children (Franck, Jackson, Pimentel, & Greenwood, 2003); students in speech pathology (Diedrich, Jensen, & Williams, 2001); and college professors (Dorsey & Guenther, 2000). Added to these studies were investigations of listeners in general

(Dietrich et al., 2001; Doody, Kalinowski, Armson, & Stuart, 1993; Kalinowski, Stuart, & Armson, 1996; Manning, Burlison, & Thaxton, 1999; Patterson & Pring, 1991; Wenker, Wegener, & Hart, 1996). Overall, research has uncovered the following beliefs of listeners regarding the disorder or person who stutters:

- PWS are characterized as having a more negative personality and are described using terms such as *tense, anxious, nervous, quiet, reticent, introverted*, and *guarded*.
- Educators believe stuttering is caused by psychological and physical problems.
- Teachers feel stutterers are characterized by negative personality traits, such as shyness, nervousness, being quiet, insecurity, and anxiousness.
- However, the majority of teachers agree that stuttering does not negatively impact academic performance.
- Some employers perceive PWS as less capable than fluent coworkers.
- Male stutterers are perceived by the listener as less well adjusted, less intelligent, and less employable.
- Adult stutterers are perceived as afraid, anxious, nervous, passive, and sensitive regardless if they are speaking or not.

The research studies are highly consistent in their findings regarding listener perceptions toward stuttering. As Hulit and Wirtz (1994) wrote, "we have come to a crossroads in researching attitudes toward those who stutter. . . . The results have been remarkably consistent. Researchers report that attitudes are generally negative and consistent with common stereotypes about the personalities and competencies of those who stutter" (pp. 256–257).

Certain variables or factors have been proposed to explain why the general public continues to hold these beliefs, despite published reports failing to find personality differences. Among the variables is the amount of exposure to people who stutter, having a family member who stutters, knowledge about stuttering disorders, method of evaluation (hypothetical PWS or direct observation), educational level of the listener, age and gender of the listener, as well as the listener's own self-confidence as a speaker. Research findings are inconsistent regarding the impact of any of these variables on listener perceptions. What the research does indicate is that listeners believe PWS are different from fluent speakers. However, the origin and nature of such beliefs have yet to be identified.

Attitudes Toward Communication

Writers historically have expressed interest in the belief system of the person who stutters (e.g., Bennett, Ramig, & Reveles, 1993; Bloodstein, 1995; Brutten, 1984; Brutten & Dunham, 1989; Craig, 1990; DeNil & Brutten, 1991; Erickson, 1969; Luper & Mulder, 1964; Manning, 1996; Murphy, 1999; Quesal & Shank, 1978; Ramig & Bennett, 1995, 1997a; Sheehan, 1969; Silverman, 1970; Van Riper, 1973; Vanryckeghem & Brutten, 1996, 1997; Williams, 1985; Woods, 1974). This literature reveals the need to address the client's concern about communicative effectiveness and heightened sensitivity toward stuttering episodes that produce negative attitudes toward interpersonal interactions. To better understand this relationship, the following definition of *attitude* is presented. As Ajzen (1988) contended, "the formation of beliefs may lead reasonably to the development of attitudes that are consistent with those beliefs" (p. 32). He defined an attitude as a "disposition to respond favorably or unfavorably to an object, person, institution, or event" (p. 4). The acquisition of attitudes occurs through the learning process, that is, the learning of responses from one's environment. Accordingly, attitudes have certain dimensions and therefore can be measured, organized, changed, predict behavior, and have meaning to the individual. PWS develop attitudes about their communication competence based on their daily social interactions. The emergence of negative communication attitudes is founded on the client's self-evaluations of these interactions.

A possible source of negativity lies in the individual's cognitive thought processes that occur before, during, and after the moment of stuttering. Negative **self-talk** (thoughts in your mind) contributes to the individual's beliefs about his communication abilities. As the person thinks a task is formidable, so becomes the task and the subsequent reinforcement of the person's self-defeating beliefs. For example, a particular client once reported having difficulty naming his career. With each opportunity to say his occupation, he anticipated stuttering and would ruminate in his mind with thoughts such as "I *never* can say that word" and "Why *can't* I say it?" When he had to tell a new acquaintance his occupation, he inevitably experienced a severe block, which confirmed his belief that saying the word was difficult. What the client did not realize was that at other times he produced the word in the absence of stuttering. He did not attend to these occasions but rather focused on situations that confirmed his negative self-talk.

Viewing this disorder from a social-cognitive perspective, such self-defeating beliefs contribute to the person's feelings of helplessness and withdrawal from communication exchanges. Applied to stuttering, this perspective is based on the construct that a PWS wants to communicate yet fears the outcome and attempts to avoid the negative consequences often experienced when stuttering. This fear is based on the client's belief system, which tells the person that speaking is a difficult, often painful, experience. With repeated experiences, the client develops cognitive distortions (Burns, 1980) that impact any hope of lasting recovery from stuttering.

Cognitive distortions are irrational thoughts created by the individual that hinder the ability to view life from a healthy perspective. Expressions such as *must*, *should have*, *can't*, or *always/never* may indicate the presence of a self-defeating belief system. Burns (1989) called self-defeating beliefs "twisted thinking" and provided a classification system for the most common cognitive distortions. Table 2.3 provides examples of these cognitive distortions as they apply to stuttering. We know an interaction exists between thoughts and emotions. Burns outlined this connection in his list of negative thoughts that bring about certain emotions (Table 2.4).

According to Daly (1996), people engage in cognitive thoughts at a rate of 1,200 words per minute with 75% of these thoughts being negative, counterproductive, and working against the individual. It is believed attitudes are influenced by the amount of time stuttering; therefore the following sections address separately the attitudes of adults versus children who stutter.

Table 2.3
Speech-related examples of distorted thinking.

Ten Forms of Twisted Thinking		
Type of Thinking	Definition	Speech-related Example
All-or-nothing thinking	You see things in black-or-white categories	"I've got to do a perfect job on my oral report."
Overgeneralization	You see a single negative event as a never-ending pattern of defeat by using words such as *always* or *never* when you think about it.	"I never can say my name fluently."
Mental filter	You pick out a single negative detail and dwell on it exclusively, so your vision of all of reality becomes darkened, like the drop of ink that discolors a beaker of water.	"I just couldn't stop thinking about the way I sounded when I couldn't say my name. The rest of the evening I avoided talking."
Discounting the positive	You reject positive experiences by insisting they "don't count."	"I can't believe I stuttered. I was right at the end of my presentation and all of a sudden I couldn't get a word out."
Jumping to conclusions	You interpret things negatively when there are no facts to support your conclusions. Mind reading: Without checking it out, you arbitrarily conclude that someone is reacting negatively to you. Fortune telling: You predict things will turn out badly.	"If I tell them I stutter, they will think I am stupid." (Mind reading) "I'll probably stutter. My mind will go blank and I won't be able to say it." (Fortune telling)
Magnification	You exaggerate the importance of your problems and shortcomings, or you minimize the importance of desirable qualities.	"This stuttering is terrible. I just can't deal with it anymore!"
Emotional reasoning	You assume your negative emotions necessarily reflect the way things really are.	"I feel like an idiot when I stutter."
"Should" statements	You tell yourself that things should be the way you hoped or expected them to be.	"I should be able to talk like everyone else."
Labeling	Labeling is an extreme form of all-or-nothing thinking. You identify your shortcomings with a label.	"I can't believe I stuttered when I asked her out. I am such a loser."
Personalization and blame	You blame yourself for something you weren't entirely responsible for, or you blame other people and overlook ways that your own attitudes and behavior might contribute to a problem.	"I try hard not to stutter because it makes people uncomfortable listening to me."

Source: Based on Burns (1989).

Adults Who Stutter

Adults who stutter have reported negative attitudes toward communication (Andrews & Cutler, 1974; Bloodstein, 1995; Breitenfeldt, 1998; Brutten & Shoemaker, 1967; Cheasman & Everard, 2003; Craig, 1998; Erickson, 1969; Prins, 1997; Starkweather, 1987; Van Riper, 1973; Zebrowski & Kelly, 2002) and often develop a series of avoidance mechanisms and situational, word, and phonemic fears in response to long histories of stuttering. Clients may avoid certain social situations because of the belief they will be embarrassed or shamed by their stuttering. They may even choose

Table 2.4

Negative thoughts that lead to certain emotions.

Negative Thought	Emotion
Loss or rejection	Sadness and depression
Unfulfilled expectations	Frustration
Danger	Anxiety and panic
Being bad	Guilt
Inadequacy compared to others	Inferiority
Unfairness; life isn't fair	Anger
Not being good enough	Shame
No end to one's problems	Hopelessness

Source: Based on Burns (1989).

careers that require minimal verbal interaction in response to their stuttering. Adults anticipate negative speech evaluation from listeners and begin to fear communication exchanges, often exhibiting increased levels of communication apprehension (Kelso, 2003). Repeated feelings of loss of control create a sense of helplessness and perceptions of decreased communicative competence. Boberg and Boberg (1990) reported that some married clients even keep their stuttering hidden from their spouses. It is hypothesized that these subjects believed their partners would view them negatively if stuttering was revealed. The development of covert reactions to stuttering (i.e., hiding one's stuttering) is a manifestation of the individual's negative attitudes regarding the disorder.

The belief in the inevitability of stuttering accompanied by dislike for the disorder may lead to other **maladaptive responses.** PWS develop the ability to scan ahead and reliably predict words on which they will stutter (Martin & Haroldson, 1967; Peins, 1961; Van Riper, 1971; Wingate, 1988), leading to a heightened awareness of words most difficult to say fluently. Using postponement devices (*uhm, ah, oh*), circumlocutions (talking around the topic), or word substitutions, the client cleverly avoids anticipated stuttering. Whether successful or not, this behavior reinforces the individual's attitudes, thus contributing to the severity of the problem. The presence of negative attitudes toward communication is an important variable to consider during treatment. Several studies have reported a high relationship between change in communication attitudes and maintenance of speech change after treatment.

Guitar (1976) investigated the relationship between pretherapy attitudes of adults who stutter and posttherapy treatment outcomes. Using the Eysenck Personality Instrument, Erickson's S-24 Scale, and the Stuttering Self-Rating of Reactions to Speaking Situations, Guitar found that the posttherapy percentage of stuttered syllables was highly correlated to pretreatment measures of attitude, particularly those involving avoidances. Subjects with high pretreatment speech avoidances exhibited significantly higher posttreatment stuttered speech. Guitar contended that the clinician may predict therapy outcomes from pretreatment attitudes. Guitar's conclusions were further supported by other researchers who believed the process of therapeutic change involves not only the development of smooth speech production but also modification in negative speech-related attitudes (Andrews & Craig,

1988; Feinberg, Griffin, & Levey, 2000; Guitar & Bass, 1978; Kraaimaat et al., 1988). The adult's belief system impacts his behavior, which, in turn, influences the ability to cope effectively with stuttering. If beliefs remain unchanged posttherapy, adults will soon revert to their old thought patterns and return to their anticipatory-avoidance cycles.

Children Who Stutter

Do children, who have had less time with the experience of stuttering, develop intricate situational and word avoidances like the adult? Clinical experience and research findings indicate that CWS clearly have negative attitudes toward communication (Bennett et al., 1993; Blood, Blood, Tellies, & Gable, 2001; DeNil & Brutten, 1991; Murphy, 1999; Vanryckeghem, 1995; Vanryckeghem & Brutten, 1996; Vanryckeghem, Hylebos, Brutten, & Peleman, 2001). The most extensive work on children's attitudes toward communication has utilized the Communication Attitude Test (CAT) (DeNil & Brutten, 1991; Vanryckeghem, 1995; Vanryckeghem & Brutten, 1992, 1996, 1997; Vanryckeghem, Hylebos, Brutten, & Peleman, 2001). The following summarizes their findings:

- CWS have significantly higher negative attitudes toward communication compared to nonstuttering peers.
- Negative attitudes have been observed as early as age 6.
- Negative attitudes increase as the child becomes older.
- The extent of negative attitudes may be impacted by stuttering severity.
- Parents may not be reliable judges of their child's communication attitudes.
- Negative attitudes are often accompanied by negative emotions.

However, like the adult, the exact nature of these negative attitudes has not been studied systematically. Is there a certain pattern of items on the CAT that is consistently identified by CWS or are the attitudes independent, based on the individual's experience with stuttering? Another hypothesis might contend that the experience of stuttering creates a commonality in attitudes toward communication among children who stutter. These negative attitudes apparently can take the form of either an interpersonal versus intrapersonal orientation (Bennett, Ramig, & Reveles, 1993). Interpersonal concerns about communication involve speaking interactions with another individual, typically peers for children who stutter. Teasing is an excellent example of an interpersonal exchange that influences the development of negative attitudes. Langevin, Bortnick, Hammer, and Wiebe (1998) found that 81% of their sample of CWS reported incidences of teasing and bullying, most commonly on the school playground or in the classroom. Teasing reflects an imbalance of power with the intent to be hurtful to another. Children who stutter are frequently teased about their speech because it is "an external difference that invites teasing and bullying" (p. 19).

Intrapersonal concerns about communication abilities are thoughts that involve the child's self-reflections, or within-the-self beliefs, not directly related to a particular interpersonal situation. For example, when the child makes the comment that "he doesn't talk right," there is no reference to another individual. Comments such as "I talk better with a friend" or "Reading aloud in class is hard" imply a social interaction of some type. It is believed that intrapersonal attitudes develop out of negative interpersonal exchanges

Table 2.5
Examples of interpersonal and intrapersonal concerns of children who stutter.

Interpersonal Concerns	Intrapersonal Concerns
• Being teased by peers because of stuttering. • Answering questions aloud in class. • Making new friends. • Talking on the phone. • Ordering in restaurants. • Asking strangers questions. • Introducing themselves to the opposite sex. • Speaking in front of groups. • Speaking in group discussions. • Afraid of not being accepted because of stuttering.	• Avoidance of the topic of stuttering as though not talking about it would make it go away. • Words get stuck in my mouth. • Feeling not worthy of another's friendship because of stuttering. • Talking is troublesome and difficult. • Not achieving in life because of stuttering. • Being less intelligent because of stuttering. • Loss of control over stuttering.

repeatedly experienced by the child. For example, the experience of being teased over and over may produce negative thought patterns to develop, and the child begins to believe he is unlikeable because of his stuttering. This belief fosters the additional belief of being different (i.e., being less than his peers in some way). This cycle of negative thoughts or cognitive distortions spreads to other areas of the child's life in which the child now believes he is incapable of making friends, achieving, or even changing his speech. Intrapersonal attitudes are shaped by the child's perception of how he thinks the world should be, and they are not necessarily based on reality. Clinical reports note a pattern of avoidance, fear, and cognitive distortion present in the profiles of children who stutter in both interpersonal and intrapersonal constructs (e.g., Blood et al., 2001; Chmela & Reardon, 2001; Conture, 2001; Guitar, 1997; Murphy, 1999; Ramig & Bennett, 1995, 1997a).

Table 2.5 contains a list of common concerns of children who stutter in each of these dimensions. These concerns, according to Hugh-Jones and Smith (1999), can impact the development of friendships for children who stutter. In their study of the short-term and long-term effect of teasing, the majority of their 276 respondents reported episodes of teasing with 46% indicating some degree of long-term impact. Clinicians, parents, teachers, coworkers, and significant others must address teasing and bullying about stuttering when interacting with people who stutter.

CHAPTER SUMMARY

This chapter addresses the affective, behavioral, and cognitive components of stuttering disorders. Although presented as dichotomous variables, researchers understand the direct interaction or influence of one component on another. For example, any change in the client's feelings may result in the anticipatory thoughts that are reacted to through certain stuttering behaviors. These trigger feelings, actions, or thoughts that can create an imbalance within the individual, placing him at risk for further stuttering. The person who stutters is not psychologically different from the fluent speaker. Because of repeated experiences with communication failure, however, the person who stutters can develop negative emotion. Moving from anger and guilt into shame spirals can produce debilitating effects on the individual's self-concept and perspective as an effective communicator.

Much is known about the behavior of stuttering and the predictability within the phonological, lexical, syntactical, and pragmatic communication dimensions. Both frequency and location effects have been identified for phonetic and word class language features. PWS produce less stuttering on frequent sounds and words, and utterance length and complexity negatively influence the rate of stuttering. The majority of stuttering is observed at the beginning of the utterance, typically on the first sound or syllable of the initial word. Rate of turn taking during conversational speech may impact stuttering, but more research is needed in the area of pragmatics and stuttering. As behaviors of stuttering increase, so do the cognitive aspects of the disorder.

People who stutter generate certain thoughts, or cognitions, regarding their abilities to communicate. With repeated stuttering, a negative belief system may develop, predisposing the individual to further communication failures. As the client "thinks he can't speak correctly," he enters situations ready to fail, and thus he fails. These cognitive distortions become a self-fulfilling prophecy leading to despair and feelings of shame. Concern over listener perceptions and their own attitudes toward communication feed the shame clients feel because of stuttering. The cycle of stuttering continues to fester as the client experiences negative affective and cognitive responses to the behavior of stuttering.

OUTSIDE ASSIGNMENT

Assume the role as a person who stutters for a day. Engage in three community interactions with people you do not know. Your speech should contain moderate-severe core stuttering behaviors with accompanying secondary features. Keep a journal recording your feelings, behaviors, and thoughts before, during, and after each interaction. You may use Appendix A to record your experiences. Reflect on your day as a person who stutters. Describe your experience in terms of the affective, behavioral, and cognitive components of stuttering. Make note of the listener's reaction to your speech. Be prepared to discuss your experience in class.

STUDY QUESTIONS

1. In this highly variable disorder, discuss the predictable patterns that exist.
2. What are emotions and how do they develop?
3. Provide an example of a shame-based reaction to stuttering for an adult client.
4. Why would a person who stutters feel anger because they stutter?

5. Which type of self-concept can be directly applied to the person who stutters?

6. Differentiate between guilt and shame as related to stuttering experiences.

7. Why does the clinician need to understand how emotions may impact clients' ability to manage their speech?

8. Discuss how the PWS's speech mechanism functions differently from the fluent speaker.

9. How might the communication attitudes of the adult differ from the school-age child who stutters?

10. Discuss listener's perceptions toward stuttering and how this might impact a communication exchange with an adult who stutters.

Theoretical Foundations

CHAPTER OUTLINE

Psycholinguistic Foundations and Theory
    Models of Speech Production
    Temporal Programming Disorder
    Stuttering as a Sequencing and Timing
       Disorder
    Phonetic Transition Defect Theory
    Covert Repair Hypothesis (CRH)

Suprasegmental Sentence Plan Alignment
Current Theoretical Beliefs
    Theory of Neuropsycholinguistic
       Functioning in Stuttering
    Demands-Capacity Model
    Dynamic Multifactorial Model

LEARNER OBJECTIVES

- Discuss early theories related to stuttering.
- Give examples of fluency-inducing conditions and explain why these conditions reduce the frequency of stuttering.
- Outline and discuss Levelt's model of speech production as it has been applied to stuttering disorders.
- Explain the theoretical foundations for defining stuttering as a temporal programming disorder.

- Describe how learning theory has been applied to stuttering.
- Apply the demands-capacity model to the early development of stuttering in the preschool child.
- Discuss the factors that influence stuttering according to Smith and Kelly's model.
- Compare and contrast current theoretical models of stuttering.

KEY TERMS

capacity
cerebral dominance
choral reading
coda
consequences
covert repair
delayed auditory feedback
  (DAF)
demands

diagnosogenic theory
dichotic listening
discoordination hypothesis
distraction
fault line
fluency-inducing conditions
  (FIC)
frequency altered feedback
  (FAF)

grammatical encoding
internal speech monitor
lalophobia
lemma
lexeme
masking
negative reinforcement
nodes
nonlinearity

nucleus	primary stuttering	secondary rewards
onset	propositionality	slots-and-fillers model
phonetic plan	punishment	speech errors
phonological encoding	response-contingent paradigms	spreading activation
positive reinforcement	rhyme	surface structure
primary rewards		

Researchers and clinicians have spent years conjecturing about the nature of stuttering, attempting to identify factors that influence the emergence, development, and maintenance of the disorder. Various theories of stuttering include the areas of environment, linguistics, medicine, neurology, physiology, and psychology. This chapter provides an overview of past and present theoretical beliefs about stuttering. Much can be learned from the past and will help guide future researchers, who may one day provide us with answers to the puzzling questions about stuttering.

Theoretical perspectives can be classified into several categories: organic, psychological, semantic, auditory/perceptual, learned behavior, motor breakdown, psycholinguistic, and interactionist. Figure 3.1 is a flowchart illustrating the various theories researchers have proposed over the years. The shapes used differentiate the theorists and theories.

This chapter emphasizes more contemporary theoretical beliefs; see Bloodstein's *Stuttering: The Search for a Cause and Cure* (1993) and Silverman's *Stuttering and Other Fluency Disorders* (1996), for more details concerning past theories of stuttering.

PAST THEORETICAL BELIEFS

Physiological Theory

The physiological theory of stuttering posits that some type of physical defect causes this mysterious phenomenon. From the time of Aristotle, stuttering was believed to have organic origins, suggesting a sluggish tongue was unable to keep up with the thoughts of the person. Combie reinforced Aristotle when he proposed that stuttering was the result of an "ineffectual organ of language" trying to keep pace with the "larger organs of intellect." Moving from this assumed coordination difficulty, Galen conjectured the tongue was too short or thick and swollen to manage the movements necessary for speech. In 1583 Mercurialis applied the ancient principles of medicine, which looked at different levels of moisture and temperature to understand disease. He believed the tongue was lacking moisture; therefore he proposed applying different warming or moistening substances on it. Sir Francis Bacon, in 1627, prescribed wine as a means to "heateth" the tongue. Dieffenbach, in 1841, believed stuttering was due to a spasm of the vocal folds. He prescribed surgery in which a horizontal incision was made at the root of the tongue, excising a triangular wedge across it (Silverman,

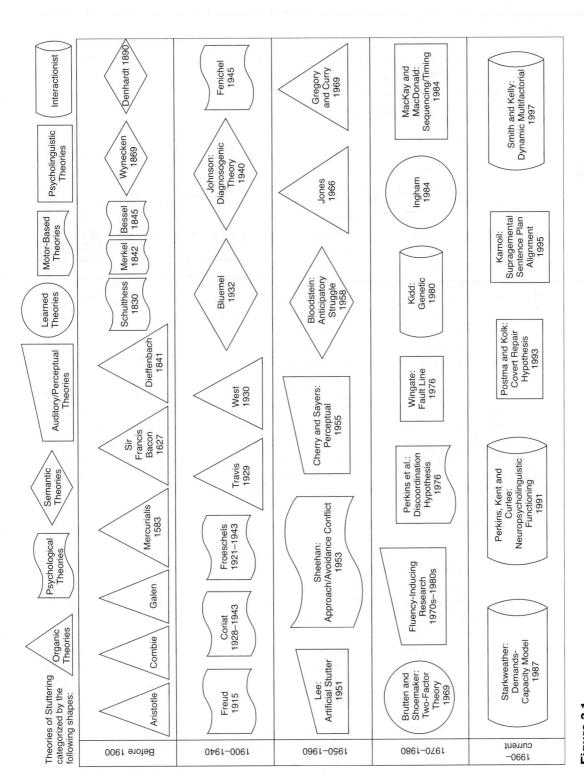

Figure 3.1
Theoretical developments over the years.

59

1996). It is no wonder stuttering was decreased after this procedure; the pain alone would keep anyone from speaking. During the early 19th century, beliefs shifted from a physiological explanation to a psychological emphasis.

Psychological Theory

Stuttering has been described as a psychological disorder in which the individual exhibits an underlying weakness within the psyche. Schulthess, in 1830, called stuttering **lalophobia,** and he defined it as a phobic reaction to the articulation of speech. A lack of confidence in one's ability to communicate was Merkel's explanation for stuttering blocks in 1842. Bessel, in 1845, proposed an approach-avoidance theory to explain stuttering. He suggested the person's struggles during the act of stuttering were by-products of attempts to overcome a real, or imagined, moment of stuttering. This psychological orientation continued through the end of the century. In 1869 Wynecken stated the stutterer was a "speech doubter," and Denhardt, in 1890, blamed stuttering on the person's fixed beliefs in the inherent difficulty of speech production (Bloodstein, 1993, 1995; Silverman, 1996; Wingate, 1976). Moving into the 20th century Freud appeared in the forefront of psychology with his writing on neurosis, and his influence spread to stuttering disorders.

Freud wrote that many neurotic behaviors have their origins in the early stages of psychosexual development. He proposed that stuttering results from conflicts with excremental functions, and he suggested the stuttering block represents a need to satisfy deep and complex psychic needs. Coriat (1928; 1943) expanded on Freud's beliefs. He maintained that stuttering is an attempt to satisfy unresolved oral-erotic needs in that speech is primarily an oral activity, and the individual perceives it as "pleasurable." Fenichel, in 1945, attributed stuttering to a fixation at the anal-sadistic stage of psychological development. He placed greater emphasis on the latent hostility and guilt stutterers had when talking, derived from their desire to speak conflicting with the fear of hurting the listener with their speech.

Organic Theory

The organic theorists suggested, that a cerebral anomaly is present in PWS, an idea that became popular during the late 1920s and early 1930s. The birth of the American Academy of Speech Correction is attributed to an increase in systematic research on stuttering disorders. Robert West, the association's first president, hypothesized that stutterers suffer from a "biochemical imbalance." His idea led to a series of medically oriented research projects. According to Bloodstein (1993), it was West who originally proposed a "general model of organic theories of stuttering that has never been improved upon" (p. 38). A combination of predisposing (genetic) and precipitating (environmental) factors interact to create an "organ deficit whose exact nature has not yet been discovered" (p. 39). West's beliefs led to research in the genetics of stuttering. His observations of the higher incidence rate of stuttering in families provided the foundation for the belief that an inherited trait may be present in the genetic makeup of people who stutter. West, unknown to him at that time, was prophetically accurate with his hypothesis.

Concurrently, Lee Edward Travis, the first person to obtain a PhD in speech disorders in 1924, investigated the role of **cerebral dominance** in stuttering. Travis (1931) based his beliefs on the observations that more PWS were left handed or had their handedness changed as a child. He called such individuals "dextrosinistrols." Knowledge regarding hemispheric lateralization of language function led him to reason that there must be a mechanism for synchronizing information between both hemispheres. He asserted that PWS lacked a "safe margin" of dominance of one hemisphere (the left) over the other (the right) during speech production. Without equivalent, simultaneous activation of the nerves on both sides of the body, discoordination may occur in the form of stuttered speech.

Semantic Theory

Semantic theorists attributed stuttering to a reaction on behalf of the client or parent to the meaning of the word *stuttering*. This shift in thinking occurred with Bluemel's paper (1932) describing **primary stuttering.** Initial word, syllable, and sound repetitions were the main characteristics of primary stuttering. Bluemel believed these characteristics would fade away if the listener (i.e., the parents) did not draw attention to them through their suggestions. Froeschels (1943) described the early symptoms of stuttering as the child's effort to avoid normal disfluency. He called this phenomenon "physiological stuttering."

Wendell Johnson, a student of Lee Edward Travis, also had difficulty differentiating between the speech of nonstuttering and stuttering children. He noted that both groups of children exhibited similar types of breaks in the flow of speech. He interviewed the mothers of children who stutter, and he asked them to describe their child's speech. He reported that the mothers of stuttering children described the effortless repetitions of words, sounds, or syllables, ironically similar to the description from mothers of nonstuttering children. Johnson and his associates (1959) concluded that "stuttering begins not in the child's mouth, but in the parent's ear." They reported that when the parent labels the child's speech as "stuttered," it becomes disordered (thus the term Johnson's **diagnosogenic theory** of the origins of stuttering). Johnson's theory led to a hands-off treatment orientation for the young child, claiming the speech disfluencies were normal and would fade away if ignored by the parents. For decades, many parents were told to disregard their child's speech disfluencies with the hopes these developmental behaviors would mature and subside. This wait-and-see approach to early childhood stuttering has, unfortunately, left many parents waiting for a miraculous fix as their preschoolers move into elementary and middle school, beyond the period of most spontaneous recovery. Despite current information disputing Johnson's diagnosogenic theory, many speech pathologists and physicians continue to adhere to the belief that children will outgrow stuttering, and they delay the onset of evaluation and treatment procedures for the young preschool child.

Approach-Avoidance Model

Through the 1950s Johnson's research focused on adults who stutter and investigated the concept that stuttering is the product of an individual's attempt to avoid stuttering. He drew three conclusions from a series of studies: (1) stuttering decreases when communicative pressure is reduced; (2) stutterers are more fluent when distracted from focusing on their speech; and (3) some of the situations in which people become fluent are situations in which the cues for stuttering are not present (Bloodstein, 1993).

Johnson's ideas intrigued someone else interested in the area of stuttering, Joseph Sheehan (1958). Utilizing information on learned behavior, Sheehan hypothesized that stuttering results from a conflict between the desire to talk (approach gradient) and the desire to refrain from talking (avoidance gradient). As these two drives conflict, different speech scenarios arise. In one scenario, the approach drive exceeds the avoidance drive and the individual is fluent. When the avoidance gradient is stronger than the approach gradient, the individual may withdraw from the communication effort totally. In another scenario, both drives are equal and the individual is unable to move forward with the flow of speech. As the individual experiences this conflict over and over again, guilt develops and contributes to the speech difficulties. Sheehan (1958) noted that secondary guilt is a significant contributory factor in the maintenance of stuttering. "Secondary guilt refers to the feelings the stutterer develops as a result of his inevitable knowledge that his blocks are distressing to others, more so at times than to himself" (p. 135). He believed guilt was an important development that explains the precipitation and maintenance of avoidance behaviors and, therefore, therapy must assist the individual to increase the approach to communication drive while directly confronting avoidance mechanisms, thus breaking the link between guilt and stuttering.

Anticipatory Struggle Hypothesis

In 1958 Bloodstein discussed his anticipatory struggle theory of stuttering, which incorporated many of Johnson's tenets regarding the belief system of PWS. Bloodstein believed the PWS respond to anticipated stuttering with fear and tension. As the feared word approaches production, the PWS tenses the speech musculature with maladaptive preparatory sets, almost ensuring he will stutter. This anticipatory process can be broken down into a sequence of events (Bloodstein, 1995, p. 67):

1. A suggestion, in the form of some outside stimulus, of imminent difficulty in speech.
2. An anticipation of failure.
3. A feeling of need to avoid it.
4. Abnormal motor planning for the voluntary articulation of the speech activity.
5. Mustering of certain preparatory sets for this purpose.
6. The production of tension and fragmentations that interfere with the normal speaking process.

Bloodstein (1984) stated, "Whenever we are overwhelmed by the difficulty of a complex, automatic, serially ordered motor activity, we are likely, first, to initiate the activity with excessive tension, and second, to fragment the activity—that is, to break it up into manageable segments, and especially to repeat the first part of the activity until we gain the conviction to execute it as a whole" (p. 173). The core features of stuttering, that is, repetitions of words, syllables, and sounds, are reflections of the fragmentation process attributed to the excessive tension when approaching speech.

Although Bloodstein (1984) considered his hypothesis representative of the learned theories of stuttering, he acknowledged the role of heredity and environment in this learning process.

Auditory-Perceptual Defect Theory

Deficits in the stutterers' auditory feedback system used to monitor speech is the underlying tenet of the auditory-perceptual defect theory. Around the time Sheehan and Bloodstein were investigating the learned components of stuttering, Lee (1951) made a remarkable discovery. An engineer, he realized that when auditory feedback is delayed through the use of headphones and an audiotape recorder, the normal speaker becomes highly disfluent. This "artificial stutter" intrigued researchers, who proposed that the nature of stuttering is perhaps due to a deficit in the auditory perceptual feedback loop. The research findings of Cherry and Sayers (1956) boosted the theory of stuttering as a perceptual defect. They found that when PWS were exposed to loud white noise in both ears, they began to speak fluently. They hypothesized that stuttering is due to an unstable feedback loop used by speakers to monitor their speech. It was not until the late 1960s and 1970s that many researchers investigated Lee's "artificial stutter" and Cherry and Sayer's masking effect.

Organic Theory—Revisited

The 1960s brought about a renewed interest in the theory of cerebral dominance through several major research findings. In 1966 Jones, a neurosurgeon, used the Wada test on four of his patients who had experienced some type of brain lesion. The Wada test consists of an injection of sodium amytal into one of the carotid arteries. "If the person temporarily loses the ability to speak when sodium amytal is injected into a carotid artery, it is assumed that a center for mediating speech and language is located in the hemisphere of the cerebral cortex to which the artery supplies blood" (Silverman, 1996, p. 59). Jones found language activity on both sides of the brain in all four subjects. Hence the search for brain differences in PWS began once again.

Another finding by Curry and Gregory (1969) reinforced the organic bases theory of stuttering. Utilizing a **dichotic listening** task, the individual performed a series of listening tasks presented through headphones. It was conjectured that most people would respond more rapidly to the speech stimuli processed through the right ear because the auditory signal leads directly to the left hemisphere. It is commonly known that the left hemisphere is dominant for speech and language. This was considered a right ear advantage (REA). Those who responded more accurately to the stimuli presented on the left side had a left ear advantage (LEA). Curry and Gregory found that 11 of the 20 PWS in their study exhibited a LEA, otherwise inferring right hemisphere dominance for language. Their findings spurred considerable research during the 1980s; yet findings have been equivocal. If there is a difference in the location and/or functioning of the language centers of the brain in people who stutter, only the research of the future, using advanced technology (PET, rCBF, SPECT, and fMRI), will provide any definitive answers.

Genetic Basis Theory

Researchers have long supported the genetic basis of stuttering as an explanation for the high incidence rate of stuttering in families. In fact, research on the genetics of stuttering may lead to greater insights into the nature of the disorder. Bloodstein (1995), Felsenfeld (1996, 1997, 1998, 2002), and Kidd (1984) provided a clear overview of epidemiology and the genetics of stuttering. The genetic basis of stuttering has been researched through three types of methods: twin studies, adopted studies, and family studies.

Kay's (1964) Newcastle Study, Kidd's (1980) Yale Family Study, and Ambrose et al.'s 1993 study utilized the case-control family study methodology in which a proband (PWS) is identified and immediate and extended family members are investigated. The following summarizes what they learned from these genetic studies:

- One-third to one-half of PWS report a positive history of familial stuttering.
- Male relatives (father, brother, son) of a PWS are at greater risk for stuttering than female relatives.
- The male offspring of a female PWS is at greater risk for stuttering.
- Gender ratios consistently report a 3:1 ratio of males to females.
- Female relatives are more likely to recover, and they do so at an earlier age.
- Although the presence of stuttering appears to be familial, stuttering severity is not.
- For female stutterers, greater genetic loading is required for stuttering to be expressed.

Kidd (1984) added that the predisposition to stutter interacts with environmental factors. Genetics alone is insufficient to predict high concordance rates. He noted that results of twin studies "clearly demonstrate that nongenetic factors can be important in the development of stuttering" (p. 154). Certain children may be prone to stuttering when environmental demands negatively influence the capacity of the speech production to produce fluency. These demands may vary for each individual child. Researchers do not have enough information regarding the nature of stuttering to make definitive claims regarding the genetic etiology of stuttering.

Learned Theory

Learned theorists propose that stuttering can be categorized as behaviors that are systematically reinforced through conditioning from one's environment. Out of the works of B. F. Skinner and Ivan Pavlov, researchers sought to find the effect, if any, of behavioral principles of classical and instrumental conditioning on stuttering behaviors (Ingham, 1984). Brutten and Shoemaker (1967, 1969) proposed a two-factor model of the development of stuttering in which repetitions and prolongations (factor 1) are the result of classically conditioned negative emotion to the disintegration of speech fluency. Avoidance and escape responses (factor 2) are instrumentally conditioned responses to the anxiety associated with these fluency failures. Learning theorists state that upon presentation of a particular stimulus, the client exhibits a response that is followed by a consequence. The client's evaluation of the consequence determines the likelihood of the response recurring or diminishing. **Consequences** can be classified as reinforcement or punishment. There are two types of reinforcement: positive or negative. **Positive reinforcement** may take the form of **primary rewards** (food) or **secondary rewards** (social praise, performance-specific feedback, or token) that increase the likelihood the desired behavior will recur. **Negative reinforcement** is the removal of a negative stimulus upon the occurrence of a desired behavior that serves to increase a desirable behavior (Ingham, 1984). **Punishment** decreases the frequency of a particular behavior, either when the individual tries to escape or avoid an unpleasant consequence (noise, time-out) or when a positive stimulus is removed upon the occurrence of an undesirable behavior.

The effect of fluency using **response-contingent paradigms** was reported by several researchers (Andrews, Howie, Dozsa, & Guitar, 1982; Hanson, 1978; Hegde & Brutten, 1977; James, 1981, 1983; Martin & Haroldson, 1979, 1982). Hegde and Brutten (1977) investigated the effects of positive and negative reinforcement on stuttering frequency in three adults. Upon receipt of a dime for periods of fluency, all three subjects increased fluency. The effect of punishment was more inconsistent. Some disfluencies decreased when punished; other disfluencies increased. Hegde and Brutten identified prolongations and repeated syllables as two types of stuttering behaviors that were least influenced by the punishment paradigm. Interjections were the easiest to extinguish.

Martin and Haroldson (1979) found significant reductions of stuttering frequency in conditions where subjects were told "wrong" or received a time-out at the moment of stuttering. Accompanying this reduction of stuttering was a decrease in the duration of moments of stuttering. Subjects who experienced decreases in stuttering in the time-out also exhibited similar effects in the delayed auditory feedback (DAF) and metronome conditions. The largest amount of stuttering reduction was in the time-out condition. Other researchers were interested in the effects of punishment strategies on the frequency of stuttering. James (1981) compared the percentage of stuttering of 36 subjects in four conditions: (1) contingent time-out from speaking, (2) contingent tone but no time-out, (3) noncontingent tone, and (4) noncontingent time-out. James was interested in determining whether punishing stimuli needed to be contingent to produce reductions in stuttering frequency and whether a particular stimuli would be more effective than another. The outcome of this study was that only the contingent time-out group experienced a significant reduction in frequency of stuttering. James interpreted these results as an indication of factors other than distraction or attention to stuttering as influencing stuttering frequency. The tone condition without a time-out was not sufficient enough to decrease stuttering frequency, indicating the necessity of the time-out factor in the reduction of stuttering. James noted that there were individual differences in the subjects participating in the study.

Individual differences appear obvious in the research of subjects' ability to self-administer time-out procedures contingent on moments of stuttering (Hanson, 1978; James, 1983; Martin & Haroldson, 1982). Hanson (1978), using a single-subject research design, investigated the effects of a contingent flash of white light when stuttering occurred. During the attention condition, subjects depressed a hand switch indicating a moment of stuttering. In the contingent condition, the experimenter depressed the switch that activated a light on a moment of stuttering exhibited by the subject. The subjects also clicked when they perceived a moment of stuttering. Results indicated varied performances between the two subjects. For one subject, stuttering decreased in all conditions, although the subject underestimated the amount of stuttering during the conditions. The other participant exhibited fewer stuttering moments in both attention conditions, yet overestimated the amount of stuttering during the contingent condition. Hanson stated that the contingent stimulus effectively reduced stuttering rates, but it did not reduce the number of stuttering moments. Hanson indicated that these findings did not support the "attention" hypothesis because of the inconsistent self-identification of moments of stuttering by the subjects.

Martin and Haroldson (1982) also found response-contingent stimuli to be effective in reducing stuttering frequency. Their study involved 30 adult stutterers divided into three groups: (1) experimenter-administered stimuli, (2) self-administered stimuli, and (3) noncontingent stimuli. For all three conditions, the mean percentage of stuttered words did not differ significantly between the self-administered versus the experimenter-administered time-outs. Time-outs produced reductions in stuttered words; however, the study showed that this extinguished rapidly. Martin and Haroldson reported less extinction and generalization for the self-administered group with weak agreement on the loci of stuttering between the subjects and the experimenters.

A third study further demonstrated an inability of subjects to administer self-initiated time-out effectively despite decreases in stuttering frequency (James, 1983). James looked at the effects of self-initiated, fixed versus flexible time-out durations on stuttering frequency under three conditions: (1) experimenter-administered time-out with a fixed duration, (2) experimenter-administered time-out with the duration determined by the subject, and (3) subject-initiated time-out with a fixed duration. Results of his study indicated that although subjects were less accurate in administering time-outs, stuttering decreased in all three conditions. James noted that although the subjects' abilities to identify moments of stuttering and to administer a time-out procedure was imprecise, punishment still reduced stuttering frequency. Perhaps the subjects' perception of when to administer the time-out was sufficient to change their routine speaking process. This added factor of attention to personal speech patterns might suffice to produce stuttering reductions.

The research findings imply that response-contingent paradigms positively affect the amount of stuttering exhibited by subjects. However, several researchers have raised the question of maintenance and/or generalization of these effects (Hegde & Brutten, 1977; James, 1983; Martin & Haroldson, 1979, 1982). Martin and Haroldson (1982) found that subjects able to self-monitor exhibited greater generalization of their increased fluency during a "telephone" generalization task. Further analysis of the factors that assist in the transfer process may shed light on how response-contingent paradigms influence the speech behaviors of people who stutter. Whether these factors are termed "distraction," "attention getting," or "punishment," the positive effects are well documented. There is still much to learn about why response-contingent paradigms produce significant reductions in stuttering frequency.

Fluency-Inducing Conditions

The 1970s and 1980s can be described as a time of searching to understand why people become fluent in certain situations, that is, **fluency-inducing conditions (FIC)**. The positive effects of novel conditions on the frequency of stuttering have long been recognized in the profession (e.g., Kalinowski & Saltuklaroglu, 2003; Kalinowski & Stuart, 1996; Ramig & Adams, 1980, 1981; Stager & Ludlow, 1991, 1993, 1998; Starkweather, 1987; Van Borsel, Reunes, & Van den Bergh, 2003; Van Riper, 1971; Wingate, 1969, 1976, 1981). Decreased stuttering frequency is associated with the novel conditions of singing, pacing, masking, rhythm conditions (speaking to the beat of a metronome), delayed auditory feedback, and choral reading. Understanding the powerful impact of these conditions on the speech of PWS will help develop a foundation for understanding the strategies used in stuttering therapy.

Singing

Singing is one of the most commonly identified fluency-inducing conditions (Wingate, 1976, 1988). Most people who stutter report the absence of stuttering when singing (Bloodstein, 1993). This phenomenon is well researched, and other findings support this common observation (Andrews et al., 1982; Colcord & Adams, 1979; Healey, Mallard, & Adams, 1976; Johnson & Rosen, 1937; Stager & Ludlow, 1993; Van Riper, 1971; Wingate, 1981). Several explanations for the increased fluency while singing have been proposed. Possibly the speaker is distracted from his own speech by focusing on the tune. Perhaps the fluency is a result of decreased demand for language formulation required during this task or the imposed rhythm implicit in the meter. Wingate, in 1976, identified three major distinctions between speaking and singing. First, singing involves the predominant feature of phonation with increased duration of voiced phonemes. Wingate referred to this pattern as the "line" or "legato" condition. Second, singing requires more speaking time through extended vowel duration and the subsequent decreased speaking rate. Third, singing requires more volume. The increased need for breath support when singing assists to regulate this function.

Subsequent to Wingate's statements, several researchers sought to test the factors associated with decreased stuttering when singing. Among them were Healey et al. (1976). Their study looked at the role of language familiarity and speech production while singing and reading. Using familiar versus unfamiliar lyrics, Healey et al. (1976) found subjects exhibited longer utterance duration and the greatest reduction in stuttering frequency when singing familiar versus unfamiliar lyrics. The authors concluded that repeated motor practice aids in the reduction of stuttering frequency (Healey et al., 1976). Andrews et al. (1982) concluded that for the singing condition, stuttering frequency was reduced by 90%, mean phonation duration increased, and articulation rate decreased. The slowed fluent speech rate was a by-product of either the reduction in articulatory rate or the increased pausing that occurred. Similar to Healey et al. (1976), Andrews et al. (1982) concurred that part of the decrease in stuttering frequency was due to the reduced demands for language formulation that occurred when singing.

Colcord and Adams (1979) investigated the role of vocal sound pressure levels (SPL) when singing. Following Wingate's comments of increased volume when singing, these authors investigated the effects of increased SPL during reading and singing on both normal and disfluent speakers. The control group, fluent speakers, exhibited a significant increase in voicing duration, peak vocal SPL, and average vocal SPL when singing. The experimental group, the disfluent speakers, experienced increased voicing durations but no significant change in vocal SPL levels. Authors were unsure why the fluent speakers increased their SPL levels when singing. Overall results confirmed Wingate's extension of voicing when singing hypothesis. However, Colcord and Adams did not find changes in vocal SPL were a component of the manner of vocalization that occurred in this condition.

Rhythm/Pacing

Decreased stuttering when speaking to a prescribed rhythm is one of the "universal facts about stuttering" (Martin & Haroldson, 1979; Van Riper, 1971; Wingate, 1976). Johnson and Rosen (1937) investigated the effects of 12 fluency-inducing conditions, one of which was rhythm, on the frequency of stuttering. All but speaking rapidly enhanced fluency with the rhythm conditions having the greatest impact. Johnson and Rosen explained these effects in terms of the "distraction" hypothesis. For example, the individual's attention is focused on the timing aspect of rhythm and not the actual speech production. Wingate (1976) further discussed three lines of thinking that, at this time, were applied to the rhythm effect. First was the fact that rhythm encouraged the stutterer to slow down his speech. Second, rhythm acted as a form of masking where the speaker was forced to concentrate on the beat of the message. Third, rhythm provided regularity in speaking.

Research performed since then has shed light on other factors that contribute to rhythm's fluency-enhancing properties. Wingate (1988) strongly believed the rhythm effect is a product of emphasized phonation, focused attention on syllable nuclei, and stress patterns that are produced in an intentional manner. Van Riper (1971) also recognized that the rhythm effect is more than just distraction. He found that subjects decreased stuttering frequency when reading aloud to the beat of a metronome while writing concurrently. Even with a very conscious form of distraction (i.e., writing) subjects did not experience the same degree of improved fluency as in the rhythmic metronome-only condition. Van Riper commented that the "rhythm facilitates the timing of motoric patterns which are prone to asynchrony" (1971, p. 407).

Hutchinson and Norris (1977) systematically investigated the effects of three different auditory stimuli on stuttering frequency and behaviors during oral reading and conversational speech. Their results indicated that metronome pacing had the greatest reduction in stuttering in both conditions. Next, Hutchinson and Navarre (1977) looked at the aerodynamic patterns of stuttered speech segments during metronome and nonmetronome conditions. Subjects read a passage designed to have a balance of four classes of sounds: voiceless stops, voiced stops, voiceless fricatives, and voiced fricatives. Lower peak intraoral air pressure, longer pressure durations, and decreased airflow rates were characteristic of the stuttering subjects in the pacing condition. They concluded that "paced speech creates conditions more conducive to CNS coordination of vocal tract events" (p. 202).

Along these lines of thought, Hayden, Adams, and Jordahl (1982) investigated the relationship of voice initiation times (VIT) of PWS speaking under conditions of novel stimulation. In one study, Hayden et al. (1982) found that the VITs under the condition of pacing were significantly less for the stuttering group. The authors noted that the shorter VIT during the pacing condition could be attributed to the effect of rhythm. Increasing predictability for phonatory onsets, the pacing condition allowed subjects to make the necessary prephonatory adjustments prior to the onsets. In the second study by these authors, speech initiation times (SIT) were significantly slower for the stuttering subjects with sound pressure levels (SPL) significantly less in the pacing condition. Again, these results provided partial support for investigating laryngeal involvement in the disorder of stuttering.

Masking

Speaking in the presence of **masking** noise has long been recognized as a powerful fluency-inducing environment (Andrews et al., 1982; Hayden et al., 1982; Hutchinson & Norris, 1977; Lechner, 1979; Martin & Haroldson, 1979; Stager & Ludlow, 1993; Wingate, 1976). The fluency produced under the noise condition was originally thought to be a by-product of the distraction the speakers encountered. Not being able to hear his own speech, the stutterer could not self-evaluate, thereby becoming less anxious (Wingate, 1976). However, research in this area has provided additional insight about the fluent speech of people who stutter under the masking condition.

Wingate (1976, 1988) succinctly reviewed some of the early research in this area. Accordingly, Wingate stated that Shane, Cherry and Sayers, and Maraist and Hutton were among the first to report the effects of masking on stuttering frequency. They reported that stuttering frequency decreases under continuous masking. However, masking during silent periods also produces decreased stuttering. This finding had a significant impact on the credibility of the auditory dysfunction hypothesis in that auditory feedback was not an active factor during silent periods. How then could masking noise, which changes the auditory feedback loop system, effectuate change when the individual is not speaking?

Murray, as cited in Van Riper (1971), found that continuous masking was more effective than random stimuli, and contingent masking had no significant effect on stuttering frequency. The volume of masking noise had an inverse relationship with stuttering frequency: the louder the noise, the greater the reduction in stuttering frequency (Cherry & Sayers, 1956). A common report in the literature on masking is the presence of the Lombard effect during masking conditions (Hayden et al., 1982; Starkweather, 1987; Wingate, 1976). Wingate (1976) described this phenomenon as the occurrence of increased vocal intensity under conditions of masking noise. With increased loudness, Wingate hypothesized an accompanied change in the manner of vocalization. Additionally, researchers investigated the laryngeal component to the fluency of stutterers under masking settings.

Lechner (1979) investigated the fundamental frequency of stutterers and non-stutterers when speaking with masking. Utilizing a reading task, Lechner found with masking, subjects exhibited an increased mean and median fundamental frequency. However, stutterers did not differ in their total speaking time in the masking and normal feedback conditions. Martin and Haroldson (1979) also found no significant reduction in the duration of stuttering moments under the noise condition.

Hayden et al. (1982) measured voice initiation times under the conditions of pacing and masking. For the ten adult stutterers included in this study, there existed a non-significant "trend" toward decreased VITs with masking. The lack of improved VIT during the masking condition was attributed to the Lombard effect, which includes an increase in vocal intensity. Along with this increase, Hayden et al. believed other aerodynamic and physiological adaptations occurred that may have accounted for the VIT behaviors of the stutterers. Slower speech initiation time (SIT) during masking was observed in the second study by Hayden, Jordahl, and Adams (1982). Including a control group, they found another nonsignificant "trend" toward slower SIT for the stuttering versus nonstuttering subjects across all conditions. Both groups increased their vocal intensity, again, to a nonsignificant degree. The authors concluded that the fluency-inducing effects of masking cannot be attributed to initiation of phonation alone. Increases in vowel durations and vocal intensity might account for the masking effect (Hayden et al., 1982).

Andrews et al. (1982) looked at 5 speech pattern characteristics of stutterers' speech under 15 fluency-inducing conditions. For masking, they found that stuttering frequency decreased minimally, but they could not find any consistent change in any of the speech patterns measured. Again, these authors attributed these changes to the Lombard effect and the impaired auditory feedback occurring in this condition.

Later Stager and Ludlow (1993) investigated speech production changes of fluent speakers under masking. They found that vowel duration, vocal intensity, peak pressure, peak flow, and pressure velocity all increased significantly. They identified increased vowel duration as the consistent change in speech production across the four novel conditions of masking, choral reading, delayed auditory feedback (DAF), and rhythm. Perhaps a better understanding of how masking changes the speech of fluent speakers might shed light on the impact of this condition on the speech of people who stutter. Overall, researchers have not clearly identified the factors that may be responsible for the fluency-inducing effects of masking. The theories of faulty auditory perception, change in the manner of vocalization, and/or motor discoordination may all explain the masking effect.

Delayed Auditory Feedback

Information gained from research on **delayed auditory feedback (DAF)** supports the concept of an auditory dysfunction in stuttering. DAF occurs when the speaker's auditory signal is delayed by milliseconds via an electronic device. Several studies have investigated the effects of delayed auditory feedback on the speech of fluent speakers. Wingate (1976) and Van Riper (1971) provided comprehensive reviews of some of these earlier studies. Lee (1951) and Black (1951) noted disturbances in speech production similar to stuttering in the speech of fluent speakers when speaking in DAF conditions. Lee termed these speech disturbances "artificial stuttering." Wingate (1976) stated that the "artificial stuttering" created by DAF was distinctly different from stuttering. He noted that disfluencies in the DAF condition occur after speech has been initiated.

Starkweather (1987) reported repetitions in DAF speech that occurred at the end of units. True stuttering occurs prior to initiation and/or as speech is attempted, and at this point, auditory feedback is not operative (Wingate, 1976, p. 230). The absence of secondary, expectancy, and/or ancillary behaviors further acts to differentiate these two speech patterns. Wingate also noted that sound repetitions did not appear in DAF speech, a behavior consistently characterized as stuttering.

Neelley's (1961) perceptual study differentiated between the DAF speech patterns of fluent and nonfluent speakers. Having listeners judge DAF and non-DAF speech segments of fluent and stuttering subjects, listeners told the difference between the stutterers' DAF speech and the fluent speakers' speech. The DAF speech from both groups was judged to be comparably "disturbed" (Wingate, 1976, p. 230). Lastly, stutterers were able to identify differences in their stuttering patterns in DAF and non-DAF conditions.

Again, Wingate (1976) hypothesized that other speech pattern characteristics of DAF speech might explain this fluency-producing effect. Stager and Ludlow (1993) looked at the speech production changes of fluent speakers under various novel conditions. When reading in the DAF environment, nonstuttering subjects exhibited significantly longer vowel durations and decreased speech rate. Andrews et al. (1982) also found increased mean phonation duration and slowed fluent speech rate of stuttering subjects when speaking under DAF conditions.

Decreased articulatory rates were associated with a decrease in stuttering frequency in the DAF condition. Although no significant differences in the percentage of vocalized time between stuttering and nonstuttering groups were noted, stutterers took significantly longer to read a sentence. For both groups, DAF was associated with longer total time. Martin and Haroldson (1979) investigated the effects of experimental treatments on stuttering. They found that for stuttering subjects, 85% experienced a decrease in percentage of stuttering under DAF conditions. Mean stuttering duration also decreased with DAF treatment. The ameliorative effect of delayed auditory feedback is well documented.

More recently, another condition has been investigated that produces immediate fluency: **frequency-altered feedback (FAF)** (Armson & Stuart, 1998; Hargrave, Kalinowski, Stuart, Armson, & Jones, 1994; Ingham, Moglia, Frank, Costello-Ingham, & Cordes, 1997; Kalinowski, Stuart, & Armson, 1996; Kalinowski, Stuart, Wamsley, & Rastatter, 1999; Stuart, Kalinowski, Armson, Stenstrom, & Jones, 1996). Frequency-altered feedback produces similar fluency effects to delayed auditory feedback. Alterations in frequency in the upward or downward direction result in a decrease in stuttering frequency, although it does not eliminate it entirely. As researchers continue to utilize this new methodology, it is presumed the fluency by-product will, once again, be attributed to changes in the manner and mode of vocalization used when speaking in this novel condition.

Choral Reading/Unison Speech

The fluency-evoking effects of **choral reading** (concurrent reading) are attributed to several factors: (1) distraction, (2) masking, (3) decreased communicative responsibility, (4) limited self-evaluation, (5) rhythm, (6) unusual stimulation, and/or (7) a change in manner of vocalization (Barber, 1939, as cited in Wingate, 1976; Johnson & Rosen, 1937; Van Riper, 1971; Wingate, 1969). Johnson and Rosen investigated the effects of choral reading on the fluency of people who stutter. Imposed rhythm and distraction were attributed to the consequent fluency effects. Later, Barber found that choral reading of similar materials produced significant improvement in speech fluency. Again, these effects were attributed to the lack of self-evaluation of speech performance. Bloodstein (1950) found a high degree of speech improvement when reading similar versus dissimilar material. Bloodstein stated that these effects were due to decreased anxiety and the "strong and unusual stimulation" of the choral reading condition.

Pattie and Knight (1944, as cited in Wingate, 1976) looked at the impact of speaker proximity and choral reading. In one condition, the two speakers were in the same room, reading a similar and different sample. In the other condition, the speaker was not present. Again, reading similar samples produced greater fluency regardless of the presence or absence of the other speaker. Pacesetting and rhythm, according to the authors, were important factors in the increased fluency of the subjects. More recent research continues to reinforce these earlier findings of the ameliorative effects of choral reading.

Ingham and Packman (1979) investigated the perceptual differences of the speech of PWS as compared to fluent speakers when speaking in chorus and nonchorus conditions. The study found that the chorus condition resulted in the greatest reduction in percentage of words stuttered, which was associated with an increase of words per minute. Ingham and Packman concluded that some people who stutter may respond to choral reading settings by decreasing speaking rate, and yet, not all individuals will respond in such a manner. Adams and Ramig (1980) did not corroborate Ingham and Packman's findings in their study of the vocal characteristics of normal speakers and stutterers in chorus with a tape recorder. Measuring vowel durations, sound pressure levels, and continuity of phonation during choral reading, they found that the mean vowel duration for the stuttering group was 30 milliseconds longer than the model in the nonchorus condition. During choral reading, vowel duration decreased, approximating that of the model. The normal group did not exhibit any significant differences in vowel durations in either condition. Continuity of phonation and sound pressure level were not influenced by choral speaking for either group. As reported by other researchers (Andrews et al., 1982), stutterers exhibited a significant reduction in stuttering frequency from the nonchorus to chorus condition in this study.

Contrary to Wingate's belief that vowel durations increased during choral speaking, Adams and Ramig suggested that the structure of their experimental condition might have an effect on subjects' vowel durations. In that participants spoke in chorus with a prerecorded sample, the model's vowel durations were held constant throughout the experiment. Subjects, in order to synchronize their speech with the model's, had to adjust their durations to match those of the recording. Any modification of vowel durations in their speech would result in different speech rates. Wingate (1981) studied the spectrographic characteristics of speech patterns during novel conditions. Results of this investigation confirmed Adams and Ramig's findings that vowel duration and amplitude changes are not significant factors involved in the fluency-inducing effects of choral conditions. Wingate attributed the reduced stuttering in choral reading to emphasis on phonation and modulation of stress contrasts.

Stager and Ludlow (1993) evaluated the speech production changes under fluency-evoking conditions of fluent speakers. Assessing various physiological behaviors, Stager and Ludlow found that the subjects demonstrated significant decreases in peak pressure, peak flow, and pressure velocity in the choral reading condition. They concluded that the nonstuttering subjects modified some aspect of speech production in the fluency-inducing condition, but they were not consistent in which variable they modified across conditions. The only consistent modification observed was increased vowel duration.

Previous explanations of stuttering as a by-product of an auditory dysfunction are not reinforced by the research findings just described. The task of choral reading and/or speaking is more complex, and it involves rapid auditory processing (Starkweather, 1987). Perhaps the factors of language generation and timing play a role in producing increased fluency when speaking in chorus. Perhaps the extended vowel durations noted by Stager and Ludlow (1993) can be attributed to this effect. Or maybe the change in stress contrasts is the relevant factor. The research does not provide consistent answers to the many questions raised regarding the fluency-evoking effects of choral reading/unison speech.

Understanding Novel Conditions

Explanations for why these conditions have such fluency effects have been proposed. The following discussion describes the hypothesized beliefs regarding the nature of the fluent speech production under novel conditions.

Distraction Hypothesis. Johnson and Rosen (1937) reported the effects of rhythm on stuttering. They found that speaking rapidly did not enhance fluency with the rhythm conditions producing the greatest reduction in stuttering frequency. Johnson and Rosen attributed these results to the **distraction** the subjects experienced under these conditions (Wingate, 1976). Unable to concentrate on their own speech to self-evaluate, anticipate, or analyze it, subjects experienced less anxiety, and they became more fluent. Distraction can take many different forms: assuming a role, using an accent, slurring sounds, and so on (Bloodstein, 1993). The distraction hypothesis has been used to explain the effects of many of the fluency-enhancing conditions. Bloodstein (1993) cleverly called it the "masquerade effect." When the mask is removed, the effect of the novelty wears off, or it vanishes.

Auditory Dysfunction/Feedback Disturbance Hypothesis. The belief that stuttering is caused by faulty auditory processing was common during the early part of the 20th century. In 1913 Bluemel coined the term *transient auditory amnesia* when referring to auditory involvement in stuttering (Wingate, 1976). Investigations that reported the effects of masking and delayed auditory feedback were used as evidence of the auditory dysfunction in people who stutter (Starkweather, 1987; Wingate, 1976). During the 1930s several researchers began to investigate the incidence of stuttering in the deaf and hard-of-hearing population as a test of Bluemel's hypothesis. Other researchers found that stuttering did occur in these populations; however, the incidence was far below that of the normal hearing population (Wingate, 1976). When noting the speech characteristics of this population, that is, slow speech rate, extended vowel duration, imprecise consonant articulation, and less varied pitch and intensity levels (Wingate, 1976), one may surmise these features can be attributed to the lower incidence rate rather than the hypothesized auditory dysfunction Bluemel attributed as the cause of stuttering.

Reduced Propositionality/Decreased Communicative Responsibility Hypothesis. The fluency-inducing effects of singing, shadowing, and choral speaking have been attributed to decreased language formulation, or **propositionality,** and communicative responsibility (Andrews et al., 1982; Perkins et al., 1976; Starkweather, 1987). The individual experiences decreased stuttering because the speech production decisions of rate and rhythm have already been made by the other speaker. The factors of language generation and linguistic stress, known to play a role in stuttering (Wingate, 1984a), are predetermined by the nature of the tasks themselves. These fluency-inducing conditions do not contain the added aspect of exchange between communication partners, which increase the timing and speech demands on the PWS, making the likelihood of a speech breakdown more likely.

Vocalization Hypothesis. Wingate (1981) played a major role in identifying and understanding the characteristics of fluency produced under novel conditions. After years of research, Wingate hypothesized that the fluency produced by stutterers when speaking under novel conditions is not a product of distraction or faulty auditory perception. The fluency by-product of these conditions is due to a change in the manner and mode of vocalization (i.e., the way in which the person actually speaks). "Emphasis on phonation" through extended vowel duration, decreased rate, and modulation of stress contrasts is primary to Wingate's phonetic transition defect hypothesis (Freeman, 1979; Wingate, 1981, 1984a, 1984b).

Discoordination/Effective Planning Time Hypothesis. Perkins et al. (1976) proposed that phonatory coordination with respiration and articulation is the basis of stuttering. Although not causing stuttering, Perkins (1986) believed these dissynchronies are stuttering. He proposed that as the amount of "effective planning time for phonetic voice-onset coordinations" increases, stuttering decreases (p. 87). If strategies like slowed speech rate were used to facilitate transitions from sound to sound, there would be more time for the remaining coordinations. This enhancement of the motor coordinations for speech would facilitate fluency (Andrews et al., 1982; Perkins, 1986). Perkins (1986) and Adams (1981) felt the role of the larynx in moments of stuttering is crucial and needs to be incorporated into treatment plans for people who stutter.

Commonalities and Conclusions

What are the similarities and commonalities of the fluency of PWS when they speak in novel conditions? Wingate proposed this question in 1976. Upon reviewing the relevant research, these features clearly stand out. Certain conditions produce fluent speech, which is characterized by increased vowel duration, decreased rate, increased pause duration, and slower articulatory rate. Other conditions elicit speech that features decreased vowel duration with no change in rate of speech. Fundamental frequency increases in variability, sound pressure levels increase, and voice onset times are delayed in other settings. What becomes apparent is that the effect of fluency-inducing conditions relates to one or more aspect of vocalization. Without a doubt, Wingate's vocalization hypothesis has gained much support from the research in this area.

Singing, rhythm, masking, DAF, and choral reading are just a few of the environments in which PWS become fluent. This fluency differs from that of fluent speakers, however, and perceptual studies bear this out. The characteristics used to categorize the fluent speech segments of stuttering versus nonstuttering speakers involved slowed speech rate and abnormal cadence (Adams, 1981). Perhaps these perceptual features reflect a change in the manner of vocalization that occurs when speaking during fluency-inducing conditions. Adams and Runyan (1981) addressed the fluency versus stuttering dichotomy succinctly:

> [S]tuttering and fluency are viewed as events along a continuum, so that as speech flows forward there is a drift, sometimes gradual, sometimes rapid, toward stuttering. The closer a speaker comes to that overt stuttering event, the more abnormal the speech produced, and the more perceptibly different the speech fluency. Similarly, after stuttering has occurred, there is a relatively gradual return toward normal fluency. During this post stuttering transition, subtle anomalies are still present in the speech signal, and fluency remains distinguishably different from normal. (Crichter, 1979).

Perkins's discoordination/effective planning time hypothesis is also strongly supported by the research on fluency-inducing conditions. Andrews et al. (1982), after reviewing the literature on stuttering, wrote that fluency-inducing conditions have their effect because they simplify the complex task of speech motor control. This simplification may come from many aspects. Perhaps the decreased demand for language formulation provides time for voice initiation or the synchronization effect of rhythm is responsible for the fluency by-product. Whether the effects are due to the increased time to make prephonatory adjustment (Hayden et al., 1982) or longer total speaking time (Lechner, 1979), when the environment is conducive to central nervous system coordination, fluency is produced (Perkins et al., 1976). Perkins (1986) identified several ways to facilitate the coordination of phonetic voice onsets: (1) use rhythm; (2) decrease the number of onsets through shortening phrase length; and (3) prolong syllables. The effects of singing, rhythm, DAF, choral reading, and masking in one way or another increase the planning time for speech.

Emphasis on phonation is a key component in Wingate's vocalization hypothesis. The research on fluency-inducing conditions spurred many investigations on the laryngeal involvement in stuttering. Note that other physiological and aerodynamic factors are involved in the occurrence of stuttering. Freeman (1979) reviewed the research on the role of phonation in stuttering and noted several studies that indicated differences in voice initiation, voice termination, voice onset, fundamental frequency variability, and intraoral air pressure values of speech segments of fluent and disfluent speakers. Fiberoptic examination of the larynx during fluent and stuttered productions is another research direction. Adams (1981) mentioned the inappropriate laryngeal behaviors concurrent with part-word repetitions. Adams also emphasized the role of the vocal folds in moments of stuttering.

Prosody, the expression of linguistic expression, has been identified as a major component in the disorder of stuttering (Packman, Onslow, & Menzies, 2000; Prins, Hubbard, & Krause, 1991; Starkweather, 1987; Wingate, 1981, 1984b). Wingate (1981) found that primary stress patterns are directly related to the moment of stuttering. He concluded that extended duration is not the central element in fluency-inducing conditions. The fluency effects were more related to both emphasis on phonation, as implemented by increased duration, and the modulation of stress contrasts during prosodic expression (Wingate, 1981, p. 115).

These results were partially contradicted by Weiner (1984), who did not find any significant difference in the proportion of stressed versus unstressed stuttered syllables. Wingate (1984a) identified three major stress dimensions: pitch, loudness, and duration. Stressed syllables are produced with higher fundamental frequencies and slightly more intense voice (Starkweather, 1987). As vocal intensity increases, vocal tension also increases. Tense vocal cords may throw off the balance between the vocal folds and subglottal air pressure creating abnormal glottal tension adjustments (Starkweather, 1987). Starkweather further noted that if the person pushes hard to get air out, as when struggling with a moment of stuttering, the optimal vocal fold tension is not achieved and may result in the locking of the vocal folds. Wingate (1984b) concluded that the laryngeal voice source is a major dimension of prosodic formation.

In a study conducted by Prins, Hubbard, and Krause (1991), Wingate's conclusions regarding stress and stuttering were verified. Using a reading task, they set out to determine if there is a significant coincidence between stuttering events and syllabic stress. Their results indicated that stuttering occurs on stressed syllables twice as often as unstressed syllables. Additionally, there was a significant tendency for stuttered events to occur more often on polysyllabic words. These findings, like Wingate's, clarified the role of prosody in stuttering.

PSYCHOLINGUISTIC FOUNDATIONS AND THEORY

Several psycholinguistic theories were proposed during the mid-1980s and early 1990s stating that stuttering could be attributed to deficits in higher level linguistic processing above the level of motor production (Karnoil, 1995; MacKay & MacDonald, 1984; Perkins, Kent, & Curlee, 1991; Postma & Kolk, 1993; Wingate, 1984b). These theories are based on various models of speech production with their interrelated linguistic and cognitive concepts. Having the knowledge of such models is essential to understanding normal speech production and how disruptions in this normal process are represented as speech disorders (i.e., stuttering, phonological disorders, and word retrieval difficulties). Levelt (1989), Shattuck-Hufnagel (1979), and Dell (1986) have outlined various principles of speech production that were applied to stuttering disorders (Kolk & Postma, 1997; MacKay & McDonald, 1984; Wingate, 1988). The following sections present a brief overview of these models. Refer to the original references for a more detailed description.

Models of Speech Production

Levelt's Model

The speaker is a highly complex information processor who transforms intentions, thoughts, and feelings into fluently articulated speech (Levelt, 1989). Using a model that combines serial and parallel processing, Levelt (1983, 1989, 1992) described a speech production system that includes a conceptualizer, formulator, articulator, speech monitor, and speech comprehension system (Figure 3.2).

The Conceptualizer generates the preverbal message, which consists of conceptual information used to realize the speaker's intentions. To encode a message, the speaker must have two kinds of knowledge: procedural and declarative. Procedural knowledge is equivalent to an "if X then Y" condition/action pair. This information is stored in the working memory, attended to by the speaker. Declarative knowledge is

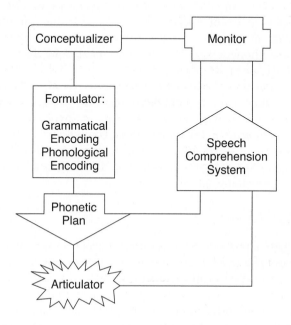

Figure 3.2
Levelt's model of speech production.
Source: Adapted from Speaking: From Intention to Articulation, *by Willem Levelt, 1989. Cambridge, MA: MIT Press. Copyright 1989 by MIT Press. Reprinted with permission.*

propositional, and it consists of knowledge about the present situation and life experiences stored in long-term memory, also part of conceptualization. This mechanism is a highly controlled process available to monitoring (Blackmer & Mitton, 1991; Laver, 1980; Levelt, 1989). The output of the Conceptualizer, the preverbal message, functions as the input to the Formulator. The Formulator involves the processes of grammatical and phonological encoding to produce the phonetic plan. Next, the Articulator receives information from the formulator in the form of the phonetic plan and unfolds and executes the plan as a series of neuromuscular instructions that produce overt speech.

The process of formulation is highly detailed, and it requires more discussion to understand thoroughly its role in speech production. The formulator accepts fragments of the message from the conceptualizer, and it translates them into a linguistic surface structure. The process of translating the concept-to-be-verbalized into a linguistic surface structure involves both grammatical and phonological encoding. **Grammatical encoding** involves the retrieval of **lemmas** (words) from the mental lexicon and the generation of syntactic building procedures reflected in the preverbal message. This process converts the preverbal message into the phrase structure including lemmas and their grammatical relations. Lemmas assist in locating word-form information. The **surface structure** has information relevant to rhythm, mood, focus, and sentence prosody. Surface structure is the mediating representation between grammatical encoding and phonological encoding.

Phonological encoding creates the phonetic plan for the concept-to-be-verbalized, consisting of a string of **lexemes** (phonemes) corresponding to the lemma. The major source of information accessed during phonological encoding is lexical form (i.e., the information about an item's internal composition—phonology and morphology). Phonological encoding can be divided into three major processing levels: morphological/metrical spellout (using lemmas to retrieve a word's morphemes and metrical structure); segmental spellout (using morphemes to access the word's syllables and segments); and phonetic spellout (using segments and clusters to address stored phonetic syllable plans) (Levelt, 1989, p. 319).

The syllable is the basic unit of articulatory execution (Sussman, 1984). It consists of phones, which are characterized by complex, temporally overlapping articulatory gestures. Each syllable plan is marked for syllabic structure involving onset, nucleus, and coda. The dynamic properties of the phone depend on where it appears in the syllable and on the environment surrounding it. Two theories regarding the process of phonological encoding are relevant to understanding the loci of the moment of stuttering: slots-n-fillers and spreading activation.

Slots-and-Fillers Model

Shattuck-Hufnagel (1979) described a two-step control structure to explain the phonological encoding process. This control structure involves a *selection step* followed by a *check-off step*. Shattuck-Hufnagel's **slots-and-fillers** model is based on two hypotheses: (1) processing of sublexical information in speech production planning makes use of representational units that correspond to single phonemic segments; and (2) this planning process includes a mechanism for the serial ordering of individual phonemic segments, referred to as the sublexical serial ordering mechanism. The basic premise behind the function of this mechanism is that segments and their slots are represented independently (Shattuck-Hufnagel, 1992). An association process connects segments to their slots, and this mechanism operates during a preexecution planning process (Shattuck-Hufnagel, 1979). This association process occurs in a left-to-right manner, over the length of some processing chunk of the utterance, perhaps the phrase. A scan-copier mechanism is proposed that scans from a set of retrieved units the correct unit and copies it into the slot. "The essence of this model is that the organizing frame provides the instructions for scanning a particular class of segments in the buffer that contains the segments of the lexical candidates for the utterance" (Shattuck-Hufnagel, 1992, p. 245). This scanning is done sequentially, proceeding slot by slot and unit by unit from the beginning of the utterance to its end. As soon as a given unit is inserted into a slot, it is checked off by the monitor and marked "used."

In the slot-filler model of speech production, word forms are created out of segments, segment sequences, and zero segments. Syllables have three slots each, corresponding to the syllabic constituents of **onset, nucleus,** and **coda.** Each slot accepts a single segment, segment sequences, or a zero segment as insert. Zero segments take the onset or coda positions of syllables that begin or end in vowels. Shattuck-Hufnagel (1992) suggested that slots and inserts might also be marked as stressed or unstressed syllables. The following comments extend the belief that an interaction may exist "between stress and word position . . . that, within this scan set, lexical stress is one of the factors determining similarity between candidate segments. Thus when two onset segments share lexical stress, there is higher probability of mis-selection between them" (p. 247).

The process of integrating the planning frame with the lexical candidates incorporates a risk of information loss or misordering of segments. Shattuck-Hufnagel (1992) noted that continued research on both spontaneous and elicited speech errors provides "a clearer picture of both the major components and the details of the phonological planning process" (p. 250). In contrast to the slots and fillers model just described is Dell's (1986) spreading activation theory of phonological encoding.

Spreading Activation Model

Dell's (1986) theory of phonological encoding uses the connectionist language of parallel distributed processing. Using **spreading activation** principles, an algorithm is implemented in a network of connected **nodes,** establishing states of activation that spread throughout the network. A concept is nothing more than an activated collection of nodes, called a distributed representation (Dell, 1986). Important to this theory is the concept of parallel activation of structural frames that control the order in which activated nodes are boosted (Dell & Juliano, 1991). This model is organized into four strata, or levels, of nodes: semantic, syntactic, morphological, and phonological. These nodes are processing units. Nodes are stored in long-term memory, and when activated, they spread activation to connected nodes at other levels via links. The syntactical stratum involves activation of lemmas and diacritical features. Morphological-level nodes determine the stem and affixes or address of the frame. Syllable constituents and phoneme nodes are activated at the phonological stratum. This spelling out is done by activation or priming, processed in the serial order of left to right. Only one node is considered the "current node" for that level and it has the highest level of activation, resulting in selection. Node activation occurs in a bidirectional flow (i.e., nodes at different levels provide feedback to one another). After a node is selected, activation levels go to zero. This is similar to Shattuck-Hufnagel's check-off procedure. All nodes show an exponential decay of activation if not selected.

Dell's model attempts to represent the interactive nature of lexical processing through bottom-up and top-down feedback links. When a node is selected, and its activation decays, feedback is sent through the system. If an incorrect segment is tagged for selection, the feedback loop will become dyssynchronous, and the system will be alerted to this imbalance (Dell & Reich, 1980). "The construction of a representation at each level goes on simultaneously with that of the other levels. . . . The processing at each level is yoked to the one above it, but the higher one can get ahead" (Dell, 1986, p. 287). Speech errors result from activation of inappropriate nodes and the construction of multiple representations (Baars, 1980). Martin, Weisberg, and Saffran (1989) supported Dell's interactive theory of lexical retrieval. They stated, "lexical retrieval of a target word is determined by a fluctuating balance between activation processes (feed-forward and feedback) and context (linguistic and nonlinguistic). Thus, as conditions under which a name is retrieved vary, so do the activation levels of the target lexical node and its competitors" (p. 483).

Speed-Accuracy Trade-Off Model

Another factor in retrieval accuracy is rate of speech. MacKay (1982) discussed two main components of fluency: speed and accuracy. He observed that as the rate of speech increased, so did the probability of speech errors entering the speech output. This "speed-accuracy trade-off" was the premise of his 1982 article, and it led him to add an additional component, flexibility, to the definition of fluency. As the speech production system becomes more flexible, increased fluency results. Practice is a common variable in developing flexibility and influencing the speed-accuracy trade-off phenomenon. Flexibility in speech production is reflected through the strength of the connections between nodes. The strength of these connections is influenced by the amount of activation and usage, or practice, each node receives. MacKay (1982) used research findings on high-frequency words and their retrieval rates as evidence of connection strength and practice (Levelt & Wheeldon, 1994; Regan, 1978). As a word is practiced, stronger connections develop. This strength is equivalent to the amount of activation needed for selection. Newly practiced, or high-frequency words, have a lower activation threshold, whereas less frequent words require a greater amount of activation for selection and insertion into the speech plan.

A rise in speech rate may increase the presence of speech errors at all levels of speech production (conceptualizer, formulator, and articulator) (Dell, 1986; Levelt, 1989). Gracco (1991) viewed changes in speaking rate as reflecting a change in the output of the "central rhythm generator." An increase in speaking rate produces a subsequent increase in the generator's output, which may produce characteristic changes in segments and their sequencing. MacKay (1982) explained this paradox through his node-structure approach to speech production.

When an individual begins to process the preverbal message, nodes become activated in a parallel fashion. This activation process involves a time element. If speech rate is fast, the activation and selection process may be compromised. Dell (1986) noted that activation, selection, and decay rates are constant and independent of speaking rate. If speech rate exceeds this constant, a competing node may be selected prematurely, creating an error in the plan. As speed decreases, there is ample time for the correct node to reach the set activation threshold and to be selected for insertion into the speech plan (Dell & Reich, 1980). This activation-selection process occurs at both the grammatical- and the phonological-encoding levels of speech production.

Flexibility in speech production is reflected through the strength of the connections between nodes. The strength of these connections is influenced by the amount of activation and usage, or practice, each node receives. MacKay (1982) used the research findings on high-frequency words, and their retrieval rates, as evidence of connection strength and practice (Levelt & Wheeldon, 1994; Regan, 1978). As a word is practiced, stronger connections develop. This strength is equivalent to the amount of activation needed for selection. Newly practiced, or high-frequency words, have a lower activation threshold, whereas less frequent words require a greater amount of activation for selection and insertion into the speech plan.

Issues of rate, or speed-accuracy trade-off principles, are familiar to the topic of stuttering (e.g., Bloodstein, 1995; Conture, 2001; Guitar, 1998; Van Riper, 1971). Rate control strategies (Brutten & Shoemaker, 1967; Perkins & Curlee, 1969; Shine, 1980; Van Riper, 1971) have been well recognized as fluency-inducing techniques. Perhaps these speech manipulations involve a time element that allows the correct node to reach activation and to become selected, thus reducing error rates. Rate of speech may also enhance the monitoring function in speech production (Kolk, 1991). Provided with more time, the internal monitor becomes more efficient at detecting or implementing stringent criteria for error detection. Possibly, covert repair rates increase with a subsequent decrease in overt speech repairs.

Speech Monitoring Model

Levelt (1989) discussed the role of an **internal speech monitor** in this process. Internal speech consists of phonetic representations that can be analyzed by the speech comprehension system. Speakers can detect errors in the internal speech product before execution (Blackmer & Mitton, 1991; Fromkin, 1973, 1993; Kolk, 1991; MacKay, 1982). Monitoring occurs in the speech comprehension system, involving the interpretation of one's own speech sounds as meaningful words or sentences. Levelt (1989) presented his "main interruption rule," which stated that error detection is equivalent to a moment of interruption in the flow of speech. During the interval, which may have a latency of 200 milliseconds (Blackmer & Mitton, 1991), replanning and implementation of the repair occurs. Postma and Kolk (1992a, 1992b) found that PWS could monitor their speech without auditory feedback, as in delayed auditory feedback and masking conditions, thus supporting Levelt's internal monitor condition. Additionally, Neilson and Neilson

(1991) noted that monitoring of internal speech is not a continuous process, but rather it is intermittent due to the neural demands that monitoring places on system functioning. This intermittent monitoring was supported previously by the findings of Nooteboom (1980) and Laver (1980), who indicated that speakers may not correct all overt **speech errors.** Laver (1980) noted that failure to correct a slip was not to be equated with failure to detect the slip. Laver further clarified that the degree the error impacts communication may be a factor in whether or not the error is corrected.

Levelt (1989) utilized a flow-through monitoring system to determine appropriateness of the communicative intent, lexical accuracy of the message, and phonological form correctness. Monitoring occurs at the level of conceptualization in Levelt's model. Errors in grammatical or phonological encoding will be processed through the system without delaying further processing. Through feedback loops, the monitor detects the presence of some errors and implements corrective actions resulting in a higher incidence of overt speech errors. Levelt's flow-through monitor may be contrasted with Laver's (1980) hold-up monitor.

A hold-up monitor delays processing of the phonetic plan, prevents overt errors, and produces a greater incidence of hesitations (Blackmer & Mitton, 1991). Laver's (1980) monitoring model incorporates multiple monitors so replanning occurs at the locus of the error. This localization results in rapid detection-to-repair rates. Levelt's single-monitor system predicts slower detection-to-repair rates because of the use of feedback loops that must pass through the conceptualizer. Actions that involve the conceptual process are believed to entail more time than actions at the lower levels of speech production (Blackmer & Mitton, 1991). Currently, research evidence supports both the flow-through and hold-up models of monitoring (Blackmer & Mitton, 1991; Dell, Juliano, & Govindjee, 1993).

Speech Errors and Repairs Model

The characteristics of speech errors assist researchers in hypothesizing about how speech production is accomplished. Levelt's (1989) and Laver's (1980) research, along with others, provides support for the idea that monitoring occurs prior to production. The monitoring system checks for the accuracy and completeness of the plan. Levelt (1989) explained that the presence of filled pauses, like "uh" and "um," may be indicative of incomplete planning. The repetition of prior material, sound/syllable repetitions, may reflect plan revisions of an inappropriate nature. Blackmer and Mitton (1991) conjectured that the repair times may vary according to the classification (complete planning versus plan revision) of the speech error. They classified errors as either production based or conceptually based in origin.

Results of Blackmer and Mitton's (1991) study indicated that speakers make rapid repairs once every 4.8 seconds, and the repair times frequently are very brief. Surprisingly, they noted that some repairs had cut-off-to-repair times equal to 0 milliseconds and were, at times, accompanied with the prolongation of the segment prior to the repair. They interpreted this finding as supporting the buffer system in speech production. With buffering, the inner speech monitor has time to scan the plan before utterance initiation. However, "during rapid unbuffered speech, the articulator must frequently start a phonological phrase before material has arrived to complete it. If material arrives in time, speech will be flawless; but if material arrives too late, the articulator will run out of material and come to a halt" (Blackmer & Mitton, 1991, p. 191). Although the cut-off-to-repair times are thought to be generated by the articulator, their source may be at the level of lexical access or phonological encoding. Blackmer and Mitton found that production-based repairs were shorter than conceptually driven repairs, perhaps indicating a greater ease in repair as compared to conceptually based problems. The absence of buffering was attributed to these slower repair times.

> In slower repairs, problems may have been detected too late to allow the entering of the repair into the ongoing stream of plans. . . . In slower repairs, fluency has been broken down, speaking has come to a halt, the articulatory buffer is empty, and the speaker must not only plan the repair but also re-establish the intricate coordination of the components of speaking. (Blackmer & Mitton, 1991, p. 193)

The halting process may be similar to the blocking behaviors observed in stuttering. Perhaps when a PWS exhibits a block, complete cessation of speech, the buffering component of speech production is not functioning, whereas when rapid sound/syllable repetitions are produced, the buffer is engaged. Repetitions are characteristic, or equivalent to, rapid cut-off-to-repair rates and use of the buffer system, whereas blocks are characteristic of slower cut-off-to-repair rates and no buffering component. Extending these assumptions further, perhaps sound/syllable repetitions are production-based problems and blocks are conceptually based problems.

Temporal Programming Disorder

Kent (1984) presented his temporal programming disorder theory of stuttering utilizing the research findings from studies on cerebral dominance, genetics, and fluency-inducing conditions. The basic premise behind this theory is that PWS lack the capacity to generate temporal programs necessary for speech. This temporal uncertainty is somewhat similar to the Perkins et al. (1976) **discoordination hypothesis** in that stuttering will decrease for any condition that facilitates initiation of phonation in coordination with articulation, thereby increasing the temporal predictability of speech. Kent (1983, 1984) hypothesized that linguistic uncertainty and temporal uncertainty interact to precipitate stuttering. MacKay (1969) also concluded that linguistic uncertainty is an influential factor in the disorder of stuttering. Such linguistic and temporal dimensions are identified above the level of motor programming in most models of speech production. Kent did not specify which processing domains influence a temporal breakdown. He noted that findings from speech error research support the dissociation of prosodic from segmental information (Fromkin, 1973) and that speech is planned and monitored before overt production (Blackmer & Mitton, 1991; MacKay, 1969). These notions may lead us to point to cognitive functions of lexical access and phonological encoding for insight into temporal uncertainty in stuttering.

Stuttering as a Sequencing and Timing Disorder

MacKay and MacDonald (1984) tied speech asynchronies to a sequencing and timing disruption in PWS at higher levels of speech production. MacKay and MacDonald asserted that it is important to understand the process of normal speech production in order to comprehend disruptions to the process. Although these authors acknowledged the role of motor coordination in stuttering, they stated that other factors, such as lexical access and phonological encoding, may influence the loci of speech breakdowns in the hierarchy of speech production. "The hypothesis that stuttering reflects a malfunction within the muscle movement system, of course, does not imply that higher level processes cannot contribute to the frequency of stuttering" (p. 276).

Utilizing a connectionist model of speech production, they discussed interactions among content, sequence, and timing nodes. "Content nodes," the basic component to speech motor control, are organized into three independent systems: muscle movement system, phonological system, and sentential system. Each node shares three dynamic properties: priming, activation, and linkage strength. Priming involves "excitatory input that active nodes pass onto other nodes connected to them" (p. 266). Priming effects are additive in nature. Activation is equivalent to the highest level of excitatory input for a node. The long-term characteristic of the connections between nodes defines linkage strength, affecting the rate of priming of other system nodes. Practice effects influence the degree of strength for such links.

Sequence nodes are a "nonspecific activating mechanism" (p. 266) whose purpose is activating nodes in the proper serial order. Sequence nodes will activate the node with the greatest priming. MacKay and MacDonald called this the "most-primed-wins principle" (p. 266). Timing nodes represent components of an internal clock determining when sequence nodes are triggered. These provide an underlying basis for node organization. Overall, there are timing nodes, sequence nodes, and content nodes for each level of processing: sentential, phonological, and muscle movement.

Accordingly, errors occur when the intended-to-be-activated node has less priming than another node. This inappropriate priming results in reverberating effects from top-down and bottom-up connections. A delay or a disruption in the feedback loop system may lead to stuttering. MacKay and MacDonald explained the incidence of repetitions within this activation framework. Nodes, once activated, exhibit the tendency to be reactivated. The nodes for people who stutter may be characterized by an abnormal priming and recovery (or decay) cycle.

Another possibility is that priming summates too slowly, and nodes rebound sharply, so activation may begin again. This sharp rebound produces the sound repetitions characteristic of core stuttering behavior. MacKay and MacDonald explained that this repetitive cycle does not last forever because nodes fatigue, and they do not meet the highest primed qualification for selection. Another possible explanation is that as the sound is repeated, the system is provided more time for the correct node to reach the necessary activation level needed for selection. This model of speech production, as applied to stuttering, was one of the first of its kind known to this author. Later, the principles of spreading activation, priming, and speech error analysis were applied specifically to the dynamic disorder of stuttering (Bosshardt, 1993; Postma & Kolk, 1990, 1993; Postma, Kolk, & Povel, 1991; Wijnen & Boers, 1994).

Phonetic Transition Defect Theory

Wingate (1988), in his book the *Structure of Stuttering*, described his beliefs regarding the nature of stuttering and its psycholinguistic foundations. He defined stuttering as a disorder in oral language expression or a defect that extends above the level of motor execution. The difficulties of PWS are linked to linguistic stress and the inherent complexities in the elaboration of stress features. Utilizing Shattuck-Hufnagel's (1979) slot-filler model of phonological encoding, Wingate stated that stuttering involves a deficit in the sequencing from sound to sound, which he terms the *phonetic transition deficit*. The initial phone is available for production, but the timing is disrupted with delayed activation of the syllabic nuclei (the vowel) prohibiting generation of the rest of the word. This breakdown occurs at what Wingate called the **fault line,** which represents the boundary between two syllable constituents: **onset** (initial consonant) and **rhyme** (vowel + final consonant).

Crystal (1991) defined *onset* as a term used to "refer to the opening segment of a linguistic unit," usually the syllable (p. 242). *Rhyme* refers to a single constituent structure comprising the nucleus (vowel) and coda (final consonant). Onset and rhyme play important roles in theoretical models of speech production (Levitt, Healy, & Fendrich, 1991). The fault line, according to Wingate (1988), is especially vulnerable to a breakdown. The expression of this breakdown is at the motor execution stage; however, Wingate wrote that the fault line extends from higher levels of neural organization to the level of motor production. In conclusion, Wingate (1988) related stuttering to an impairment involving a lack of synchronicity in lexical retrieval, assembly, and phonological representations that may lead to a breakdown in prosody and timing. Such timing disruptions may result in the core stuttering behaviors of repetitions and prolongations.

Covert Repair Hypothesis (CRH)

Postma and Kolk (1993) presented a model of speech production that attempted to explain stuttering in relation to self-repairs made during the production process (Figure 3.3). Utilizing Levelt's (1989) model of speech production, Postma and Kolk postulated that stuttering originates from a deficit in phonological encoding of an utterance in which generating the **phonetic plan** is especially vulnerable to errors. This deficit may have its source in the monitoring component of the production process. Each system has an internal monitor that detects errors before overt articulation (Baars, Motley, & MacKay, 1975; Blackmer & Mitton, 1991; Levelt, 1989; MacKay, 1982; Van Wijk & Kempen, 1987). If the correction is successful, speech flow will not be disrupted. **Covert repair** (before speech is produced) interrupts the forward flow of speech by either halting or stalling execution of the upcoming plan. The halting or stalling are overtly expressed as sound/syllable repetitions, prolongations, or audible blocks.

Figure 3.3
Postma and Kolk's adaptation of Levelt's model of speech production.
Source: From "The Covert Repair Hypothesis: Prearticulatory Repair Process in Normal and Stuttered Disfluencies," by A. Postma & H. Kolk, 1993, Journal of Speech and Hearing Research, 36, pp. 472–487. Copyright 1993 by the American Speech-Language-Hearing Association. Reprinted with permission.

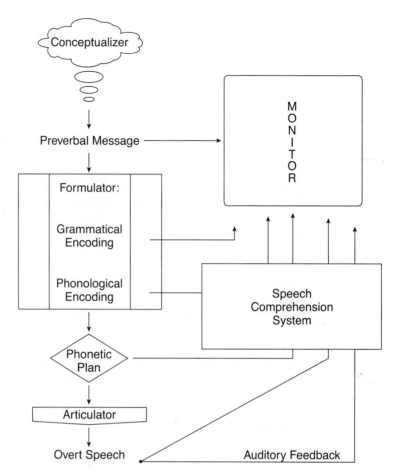

Postma and Kolk (1993) contended that with PWS, the internal monitor is "flawed," thereby detecting errors that are not errors, termed *superfluous corrections*. The internal monitor may utilize deviant criteria for detecting speech errors. Postma and Kolk (1993) stated that this defective monitor may account for the high frequency of repairs or moments of stuttering. PWS attempt to repair these "perceived" errors. This is a process that consumes resources, and it makes the complete plan temporarily unavailable for implementation. Postma and Kolk noted that the internal monitor has a look-ahead function. He or she is able to spot errors, or the potential for errors, in the current plan or while they are stored in the articulatory buffer. Buffering phonetic plans gives the internal monitor time to check for errors. According to Levelt (1989), the buffer may hold up to a few phonological phrases at a time. Spreading activation and speech rates influence the ability of the internal monitor to inspect the plan before motor execution (MacKay, 1982). Kolk (1991) noted that to improve fluency, PWS need to slow their speech rate, thereby allowing time for the correct elements to be activated and selected. This slower speech rate thus enhances the functioning of the internal monitor.

Postma and Kolk (1993) utilized Levelt's classification of speech errors, and they outlined stuttered moments from this perspective. The breakdown in the flow of speech can occur through speech errors or speech disfluencies. These events may be viewed as lying on a continuum of fluency with both disruptions coming from the same mechanism (Postma, 1991). Taking the three types of core stuttering behaviors (repetitions, prolongations, and audible blocks), they explained the origin of these behaviors in speech production terms.

repetitions

A repetition occurs when an individual has begun overt articulation and either detects an error in the plan or the rest of the plan is not available for processing. The individual then selects a repair strategy based on the locus of the interruption, well recognized as frequently being at the syllable level (Postma, 1991; Sussman, 1984; Wingate, 1988). Postma (1991) noted that "phonemic errors can usually be handled by backtracking to the beginning of the interrupted syllable" (p. 16). Syllables can be divided into the constituent parts of onset and rhyme. As previously noted, stuttering occurs most often at this juncture. Postma extends Wingate's fault line, the demarcation between onset and rhyme, to include the boundary between the nucleus and coda components of rhyme. The person institutes a retrace or restart strategy, repeating the portion of the phonetic plan already established, awaiting arrival of the remaining constituent parts.

prolongation *blocks*

The prolongation is exhibited when only the initial sound becomes available for articulation and the system is waiting for activation, revision, or for a selection of tasks to be completed. A block, which prohibits any sound production, results when the activation of the articulatory plan is completely halted. This total cessation of speech may have as its source both a failure in lemma access or phonological encoding. These postponement and restart strategies buy time for the speech production system to perform the elaborate series of intricate processes necessary for fluency.

Postma and Kolk (1993) categorized restart and postponement strategies based on the source of the internal error. Phrase repetitions have as their source an error in the semantic or syntactic levels of speech production, which involve implementing the restart process at the level of the phrase. Word repetitions are considered lexical access errors. They result in restarting on the previously produced word. Phonemic errors are associated with smaller units of reiteration. Blocks, prolongations, and subsyllabic repetitions involve initiating a restart strategy at the beginning of the syllable. Postponement strategies are utilized on both semantic and phonemic errors. Again, the locus of the interruption functions as an indicator of the type of repair being implemented. Silent pauses greater then 200 milliseconds are indicative of errors of a semantic or lexical nature where the individual is holding up execution awaiting reformulation. Prolonging a noninitial sound serves to provide time for arrival of the rest of the phonetic plan. Broken words, another form of blocking behavior, serve a similar function to the noninitial prolongation.

There appear to be several similarities between speech errors and core stuttering behaviors (Postma & Kolk, 1990). Both increase significantly with increased speaking rates (Dell, 1986; Postma & Kolk, 1992b; Postma & Kolk, 1993; Starkweather, 1987). Word initial and syllable initial position constraints apply to both speech errors and stuttering, along with the impact of stress (Hubbard & Prins, 1994; MacKay & MacDonald, 1984;

Postma & Kolk, 1993; Prins, 1991; Prins et al., 1991; Wingate, 1988). Use of editing terms observed during speech errors appears similar to the use of fillers or interjections in stuttering (Postma & Kolk, 1992b). Linguistic complexity influences speech production and stuttering rates (Bernstein Ratner & Sih, 1987; MacKay, 1969; Watson & Alfonso, 1982). Even cognitive stress interferes with the adult's ability to produce fluent speech (Caruso, Max, McClowry, & Chodzko-Zajko, 1998). Stuttering, speech errors, and their covert repairs respect both clause boundaries and the onset-nucleus and nucleus-coda demarcation (Bloodstein, 1995; Jayaram, 1984; Wall, Starkweather, & Cairns, 1981; Wingate, 1988).

Suprasegmental Sentence Plan Alignment

Karniol (1995) presented a theory of the development of stuttering in children that emphasizes the role of suprasegmentals in speech production. Karniol proposed that there exists a need to realign the suprasegmental features of speech when errors occur. The core stuttering behaviors of repetitions and prolongations represent the actions of the alignment process between the planned and revised suprasegmental features. This alignment is necessary so there is consistency in the suprasegmental characteristics between these two plans.

Karniol's model is based on the following factors: (1) words are produced differently in a sentence frame than in isolation; (2) the way a word is produced depends on the sentence in which it is embedded; (3) suprasegmental features are determined prior to utterance initiation; (4) people change their speech plans "online"; (5) lexical search time is required during online changes; and (6) prolongations and sound/syllable repetitions represent points of interference among the planned and revised suprasegmental features. Online changes, according to this model, will occur before plans are completed, and they are accomplished through frame shifts and frame elaborations. A frame shift occurs when the initial plan is changed and a different syntactic frame is implemented. Frame elaborations retain some part of the original utterance and retracing occurs when additional elements are inserted into the plan. In summary, Karniol's model "posits that disfluencies of all types are a result of the fact that speech is an intricate process that combines both preplanned elements and active, online revisions" (p. 111). When conflict exists between these two events, stuttering may occur.

CURRENT THEORETICAL MODELS

The late 1980s through the 1990s can be categorized as the interactionist period during which theoretical philosophy began to meld components of one theory with another through the publication of several models to explain stuttering behaviors. With the exception of Postma and Kolk's covert repair hypothesis (1993), a common thread across these models is that dynamic individual influences working together with nature, that is, genetics, explain the manifestation of stuttering (Perkins et al., 1991; Smith & Kelly, 1997; Starkweather, 1987).

Theory of Neuropsycholinguistic Functioning in Stuttering

Perkins et al. (1991) proposed a theory of neuropsycholinguistic function in stuttering (Figure 3.4). Components of this theory are time pressure, awareness of cause of disruption, and loss of control. Speech disruption and time pressure are considered necessary and sufficient to account for stuttered and nonstuttered disfluencies. Perception of loss of control further distinguishes stuttering from normal nonfluencies. Pressure to continue with a disfluency, the cause being unknown to the speaker, is reflected as stuttering. Disfluency of known origin is viewed as a normal nonfluency and is less likely to interrupt the flow of speech.

Perkins et al. also use Shattuck-Hufnagel's (1979) slots-and-fillers model of speech production in their theory. Speech sounds are used to fill the slots and are drawn from a store of segments (nodes) that are scanned for those with the highest level of activation. These are then selected for insertion into the phonetic plan. Perkins et al. used the analogy of an assembly line to demonstrate this principle. Mistiming "of arrival of

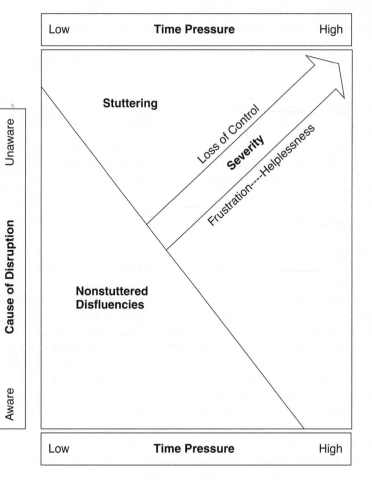

Figure 3.4
Perkins, Kent, and Curlee's theory of neuropsycholinguistic functioning in stuttering. *Source: From "A Theory Of Neuropsycholinguistic Functions in Stuttering," by W.H. Perkins, R. Kent, & R. Curlee, 1991, Journal of Speech and Hearing Research, 34, pp. 734–752. Copyright 1991 by the American Speech-Language-Hearing Association. Reprinted with permission.*

either slots (syllable frames) or phonetic fillers (segmental content) for those slots would disrupt fluent flow of speech" (p. 737). Disfluencies occur when the paralinguistic-prosodic and the language-segmental systems are "dyssynchronous." Perkins and his colleagues hold two major assumptions regarding neural speech processes and stuttering: (1) competition for neural resources affects efficiency of performance, and (2) speech is a complex performance composed of multiple components processed in different brain systems (p. 739). In communication, the two systems interact together: the paralinguistic and linguistic systems. Levelt (1989) noted that paralinguistic and linguistic information is generated at the level of grammatical encoding. Any disorganization or mistiming at this level may influence the assembling of segmental information and subsequent phonological encoding necessary for fluent speech production.

The Perkins et al. theory is very comprehensive in its hypotheses and underlying assumptions. The basic premise of this theory is that disfluency (normal and stuttered) results when dyssynchrony exists between the paralinguistic and linguistic systems. Speakers then react to this dyssynchrony in two ways: (1) pressing to continue with disruptions of unknown cause or (2) pressing to continue with a disruption of known origin. What makes the disruptions known or unknown is the degree of awareness of the delay in processing syllable frames with their corresponding content. According to this theory,

> If dyssynchrony is caused by delayed segmental input, the disfluency is of symbol-system origin; the cause is relatively available to awareness. If the cause is delayed syllable-frame input, probable origin of the disfluency is delayed signal-system processing, a cause that is relatively unavailable to awareness. When speakers press to continue dyssynchrony-disrupted utterances of unknown cause, the disfluencies will be stuttered. (p. 742)

Stuttered disruptions are marked by the feeling of loss of control. The preceding is only a brief summary of its components related to speech production. For more details, see the authors' comprehensive description of this model of stuttering.

Demands-Capacity Model

Starkweather (1987) proposed a model for understanding the development of stuttering in children. It is well recognized that stuttering is a childhood disorder (Yairi, 1997a, 1997b). The onset usually occurs between the ages of 2 to 5 years with rare occurrences during preadolescence (Andrews & Harris, 1964). During this preschool period, the child experiences rapid growth in language skills accompanied by the development of capacities to manage such growth. Starkweather contended that a balance between environmental or self-imposed **demands** and the child's **capacities** to manage them must be present for fluent speech production: "When a child's capacity for fluency exceeds the demands, the child will talk fluently, but when the child lacks the capacity to meet demands for fluency, stuttering, or something like it, will occur" (p. 75).

Fluent speech requires certain capacities. Among these capacities are the increasing control over the movements of the vocal mechanism, language skills, social/pragmatic knowledge of when and how to communicate, and cognitive development (Starkweather, 1997). Demands placed on the child's fluency encompass these same categories. Motor control demands might include perceived time pressure, coordination of the rapid articulatory adjustments required for speech, and the anticipatory reactions that trigger stuttering. Language production demands may fluctuate according to whether the child is currently experiencing the common "language spurt" for this age. Examples of language demands include vocabulary, increased syntactic requirements, phonological knowledge of speech errors, and pragmatic awareness of the environment's reaction to breaks in the forward flow of speech. Social/emotional demands may take the form of "being put on the spot for big-boy speech," as in telling grandparents about a school event or having to perform before an audience. Any speaking situation, in which there exist high demands for cognition, requires the child to recall events, organize, and communicate them according to adult standards. The interaction of these four demands and the child's capacity to handle them reflects the major components of the demands-capacity model (DCM).

Several issues have been raised regarding the validity of Starkweather's demands/capacity model (Bernstein Ratner, 2000; Curlee, 2000; Kelly, 2000; Siegel, 2000; Yaruss, 2000). These concerns center around several themes: terminology, implied relationships, observable capacities, and circular reasoning. Siegel (2000) contended that a major weakness of this model lies in the use of the word *capacity* and the way it is used in the model. Siegel stated that the model more precisely measures the child's "performance" when encountering various environmental demands. Performance can be observed and thereby is measurable, whereas capacities are difficult to assess because many are not directly observable. According to the model, clinicians are asked to develop treatment plans based on the child's capabilities without being able to determine them directly. Siegel stated that, in actuality, clinicians are looking at the child's performance under various demands: "Performance provides a window to the underlying capacities" (2000, p. 325). Siegel would prefer to reframe the name of the model to reflect these contentions, calling it the demands-performance model.

A second issue with the DCM lies in its implied relationships between changes in demands reflecting positive changes in the level of fluency exhibited in the child. Curlee (2000) admitted a degree of usefulness in the DCM, yet questions the clinical application of the model. According to Curlee, the demands frequently targeted in treatment have been found to have inconsistent effects on the fluency of children. The demands outlined by Starkweather are often external of the child, exhibited by the environment. However, Curlee suggested that the model is best applied to the internal constraints present within the child. He provided an example of internal demands when discussing Riley and Riley's (1979) component model for assessing and treating children who stutter. This model directly measures the child's abilities in the domains of attending, auditory processing, sentence formulation, and oral motor skills. Despite his concerns regarding the focus on environment instead of internal factors within the child, Curlee did acknowledge use of the DCM principles when guiding parents. Curlee wrote that he uses this model in his efforts to "reduce any concerns or guilt and some of the 'mystery' of stuttering for parents and to suggest things to do that may help them feel that they are helping the child" (p. 334).

Bernstein Ratner (2000) was, perhaps, more critical of the DCM for its focus on changing parental behaviors that have not been empirically supported in the literature. The DCM encourages clinicians to focus on the more observable behaviors of the environment, that is, the parents. However, Bernstein Ratner wrote that the DCM is "wrong in its attention to parents' behaviors with its ensuring potential for guilt and remorse" (p. 342). What is correct in the model is the assumption that the system breaks down when it cannot handle a particular task. Factors that influence this breakdown are more probably related to less known within-the-child variables of language capacity and instability in the speech motor production system.

Yaruss's (2000) commentary on the DCM reinforced both Curlee's and Bernstein Ratner's statements. Yaruss agreed that certain capacities, such as lexical access, syntactic formulation, anxiety, or coarticulation, are difficult to assess. However, like Curlee, he presented an example of using measures of DDK to assess the capacity of the child's speech motor system to rapidly move the articulators in a sequential manner. Yaruss firmly stated the importance of investigating the motoric, linguistic, cognitive, and socioemotional foundations in the development of stuttering, as proposed by the DCM. Although the reasoning may be circular, knowledge of the child's performance leads to assumptions regarding inferred capacities. As Kelly (2000) precisely summarized, performance is indeed "the surface manifestation of the interaction between underlying capabilities (or capacities) and contextual influences" (p. 360). Such knowledge is essential to the management of childhood stuttering. Although there has been recent debate regarding the validity of Starkweather's model, researchers and clinicians have found a certain degree of usefulness in the model's principles when working with young children who stutter and their parents.

Dynamic Multifactorial Model

Smith (1999) and Smith and Kelly (1997) presented a model of stuttering that provides a comprehensive framework for understanding the complexities of this disorder. They stated that previous models attempted to isolate a phenomenon that is forever changing. Three problems with such models were identified: (1) they attempt to account for stuttering as an event; (2) they are linear, positing a singular problem from which all stuttering evolves; and (3) they are narrowly focused on "putative linguistic processes," thus failing to capture the complex nature of the disorder (Smith & Kelly, 1997, p. 205). In their efforts to develop a dynamic, multifactorial framework for use in both clinical and research areas, Smith and Kelly succinctly outlined a model that is a "best-fit" with this author's view of stuttering (i.e., stuttering needs to be viewed as a "nonlinear, emergent phenomena"). Using a continuum of stability and instability, the clinician can account for changes in the system in any number of areas, such as cognitive, linguistic, emotional, and/or motor levels (Figure 3.5). Each individual person who stutters has his or her own continuum of stability-instability reflective of a profile of strengths and weaknesses. What are the multiple factors that contribute to the development of stuttering?

Smith and Kelly's model distinguished between the explanation sought for stuttering and various levels of analysis that contribute to the explanation. On one hand, the environment interacts with the factors of genetics, emotion, cognition, language, and speech motor production. These factors contribute to the emergence of the disorder, they change over time, and they vary in the degree of representation. On the other hand, observations are made of the person who stutters. These include sociocultural, acoustic, kinematic, psychological/behavioral, perceptual/linguistic, electromyographic, measures

Figure 3.5
Stability continuum with various factors that may shift and become unbalanced producing stuttering symptoms.
Source: Based on Smith and Kelly (1997).

of CNS function, and/or autonomic measures. These observations are used to explain what happens before, during, and after the actual moment of stuttering.

Another feature of this model is the concept of **nonlinearity.** "A signature characteristic of dynamic systems is nonlinearity. Thus, a very small change in one parameter may produce very large changes, even qualitative shifts, in the output behavior of the system" (Smith & Kelly, 1997, p. 208). So, any change, for example, in the individual's environment may produce changes in the ability to manage stuttering moments. For any given person at any given time, a sudden shift in one factor may disrupt the balance and lead to the diagnosis of stuttering. "The paths of different individuals into (and out of) the stuttering diagnostic space may be quite distinctive" (Smith & Kelly, 1997, p. 209). They also noted that a given individual may have all the characteristic factors that would predict the emergence of stuttering yet not receive the diagnosis.

Three characteristics of dynamic systems are relevant to this theory: (1) these factors change over time, (2) they vary in degree of representation, and (3) a small change in one may produce a large change in another, manifested as a sudden increase in behaviors diagnosed as stuttering. Smith (1999) wrote that stuttering takes place within individuals that function as self-organizing systems. These systems that have "many interacting components can suddenly produce patterns in space and time, and can display nonlinear behavior, that is shifting from one pattern of output to another very rapidly" (p. 39). Overlapping factors that balance on a continuum will interact together to determine a relative outcome that varies widely with time. This multifactorial dynamic theory of stuttering helps clinicians understand this heterogeneous disorder.

CHAPTER SUMMARY

After numerous investigations, we have bits and pieces of knowledge about this complex disorder. Propositions have been made regarding the psychological, physiological, interpersonal, linguistic, cognitive, and neurological makeup of people who stutter. Genetic studies have, perhaps, provided the most conclusive findings (i.e., stuttering is familial, more males than females stutter, and a genetic predisposition appears to interact with the environment to produce the stuttering syndrome). We know that PWS can become fluent under an assortment of fluency-inducing conditions (e.g., singing, DAF, FAF, masking, rhythm, and choral speech). We have learned much about the fluent speech characteristics under these conditions: vowels are longer, there is an emphasis on phonation, loudness increases, and there is a slower speech rate. These changes in the manner and mode of vocalization work together to produce speech fluency.

Most theorists agree that the breakdown in speech production (i.e., stuttering) occurs above the level of articulation. Stuttering has been viewed as a breakdown in language processing, most predominantly involving the development of the phonological structure of the utterance. The inability of adults to formulate language in a timely fashion, as well as the comorbidity of phonological disorders and stuttering in young children who stutter, are indicators of this deficit in language generation. Even levels above phonological encoding have been indicated in several of the recent theories. Organizing the syntactic structure of the utterance with the appropriate stress features may also be problematic for people who stutter.

Some theorists view the development of stuttering during the preschool years as an interaction between nature and nurture. The young child has certain capacities for fluent speech production. When various demands rise beyond the child's capacity to manage them, this process is impaired. For older children and adults, the feelings of loss of control play a major role in the continuation with speech that is not fluent. The emotional reaction to the inability to move forward with speech fuels the person's feelings of loss of control and increases the person's perceived time pressure to continue speech production.

As the most current theories propose, stuttering is more than just the behavior exhibited by the individual. It is a dynamic disorder with multiple factors (e.g., language, sociocultural, neuromotor, genetics, psychological/behavioral, etc.) interacting together to influence the client's ability to communicate effectively. The dynamic representation of stuttering manifests differentially in each individual. Chapter 4 discusses ways in which the speech-language pathologist may assess these differences involving the ABCs of stuttering.

STUDY QUESTIONS

1. Of the early theories related to stuttering, which one intrigues you the most and why?

2. How has Johnson's diagnosogenic theory impacted the advice given to parents of preschool children who stutter?

3. Using the stuttering cycle presented in chapter 1, how may you relate Bloodstein's approach/avoidance behaviors to the cycle of stuttering and emotional reactions?

4. What genetic factors appear related to the incidence of stuttering?

5. Discuss how stuttering has been considered a learned speech motor behavior.

6. A frequently asked question of speech pathologists is "Why do people sing without stuttering?" How would you respond to this question?

7. Summarize the findings of fluency-inducing conditions. Can you project the clinical significance of these findings?

8. Think of the word *cat*. Can you outline the tasks required to produce this word?

9. Discuss the timing components of stuttering as described by MacKay, MacDonald, and Kent.

10. Compare and contrast the overt and covert speech errors in the speech of people who stutter.

11. How might you use the demands/capacity model to explain the emergence of stuttering in a 2½-year-old child?

12. Explain the variability of stuttering according to Smith and Kelly's model.

Assessment and Diagnosis

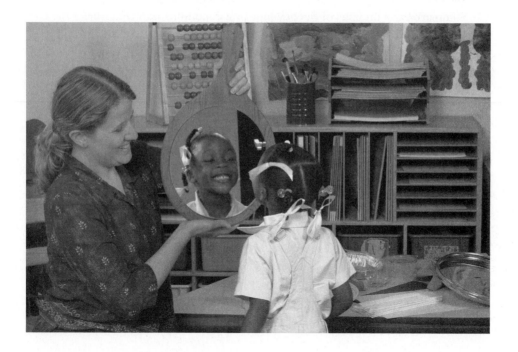

CHAPTER OUTLINE

LEARNER OBJECTIVES

- Design a treatment plan incorporating the concepts of triangulation and interviewing skills to obtain the most beneficial information available.

- Understand the need to establish a solid client-clinician relationship as a basis for assessment procedures.

- Differentiate between quantitative versus qualitative fluency measures.

- Determine client's fluency profile of strengths and weaknesses.

- Identify ways of assessing client's attitudes toward communication.

- Utilize formal and non-standardized procedures when conducting an evaluation.

- Incorporate various sources of information when determining stuttering severity.

- Outline components of a diagnostic report on children and adults who stutter.

- Interpret test findings to make appropriate diagnoses and treatment recommendations.

- Understand the distinctions between impairment, disability, and handicap.

KEY TERMS

automaticity
avoidance behaviors
circumlocution
clustering
communicative competence
diagnostic profile
differential diagnosis
disability
escape behaviors

funneling
handicap
impairment
iterations
loci of tension
metric
minimal encouragers
pattern analysis
prognostic indicators

redirection
reflective comment
rephrasing
secondary symptoms
stalling devices
starters
stimulability
triangulation

The assessment of fluency is a detailed, thought-engaging process. The goal of assessment is to understand thoroughly the client's speech behaviors, thoughts, and feelings, that is, their fluency profile (Figure 4.1). You will want to learn as much as possible about the person's communicative patterns so you can develop an appropriate treatment plan.

Healey, Susca, and Trautman (2002, 2004) conceptualized the diagnostic process as involving five individual areas of investigation: (1) *Cognitive*, (2) *Affective*, (3) *Linguistic*, (4) *Motor*, and (5) *Social* (CALMS). Figure 4.2 provides a visual representation of their CALMS Model of Stuttering. The extent of information gathered in each of these five domains depends on the age of the client. For example, older school-age children or teenagers should have little difficulty talking about how they feel about stuttering, yet preschool children may not have the vocabulary to put their feelings into words. The linguistic component of stuttering may have

Figure 4.1
Determining the diagnostic profile of an individual who stutters includes the dimensions of affect (A), behavior (B), and cognition (C).

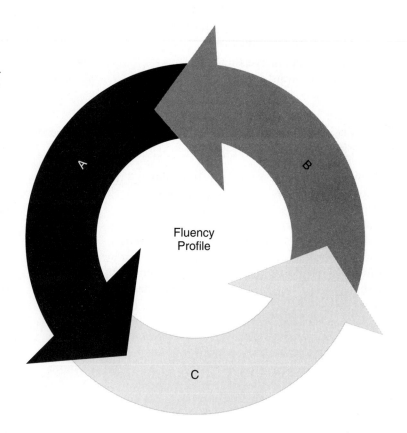

greater impact on the disorder for the preschooler when language is beginning to expand into rule-governed constructions. The social component of the CALMS model may have more prominence for teenagers or adults whose stuttering has inhibited their social interactions and/or vocational goals.

The information in this chapter will assist you in determining the client's relative strengths and weaknesses in the CALMS components through a three-stage assessment process: planning and information gathering, testing and interpretation, and report writing (Table 4.1).

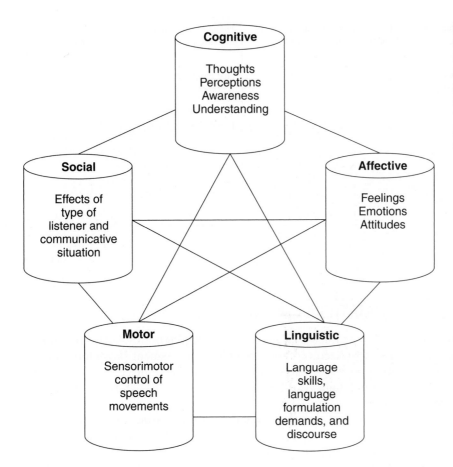

Figure 4.2
CALMS Model of Stuttering.
Source: E. Charles Healey, Michael Susca, and Lisa Scott Trautman, 2002. Reprinted with permission of the authors.

Table 4.1
Three-stage assessment guidelines.

Stage 1				
Planning			Information Gathering	
Ideal Assessment	Points to Remember	Case History	Client/Clinician Relationship	Interviewing
Review instruments	Be thorough	Review form	Use funneling	Prepare for opening interactions
Determine if age appropriate	Audiotape and videotape	Determine missing details	Be open and honest	Be spontaneous yet flexible
Select type of samples to obtain	Plan methods to assess stimulability and consistency	Outline questions to ask client/parent	Exhibit good listening skills	Monitor nonverbal and verbal behaviors
Select interactions to obtain	Manipulate linguistic complexity	Identify concomitant areas	Respond with empathy	Vary question types
Organize nonstandardized procedures	Plan fluency disruptions and topics for discussion	Check equipment/ gather materials	Communicate the possibility of change	Be prepared for emotional reactions (e.g., tears or anger)

PLANNING AND INFORMATION GATHERING

Planning is required for any fluency diagnostic and includes both standardized (norm reference) and nonstandardized (criterion reference) assessment procedures. In developing a diagnostic plan, you must decide the flow and methods to use for each individual case. Costello and Ingham (1984) discussed several characteristics of an ideal fluency evaluation methodology.

First, a diagnostic method should distinguish a stutterer from a nonstutterer. The Stuttering Prediction Instrument (SPI) (Riley, 1981); Protocol for Differentiating the Incipient Stutterer (Pindzola, 1987); and Systematic Disfluency Analysis (SDA) (Campbell & Hill, 1987) meet this criterion. Second, the ideal assessment method should be

Stage 2				Stage 3
Testing		Interpretation		Report Writing
Quantity	Quality	Impact	Prognostic Indicators	Section 1: Opening paragraph
Frequency counts	Loci of tension	Impairment	Identify positive indicators: • > 12 months postonset • female • absence of secondary symptoms • high variability, periodic • lack of awareness • few SLDs • good stimulability	Section 2: Background information
Iterations	Attitudes toward communication	Disability		Section 3: Evaluation results
Linguistic complexity	Secondary symptoms	Handicap	Identify negative indicators: • familial history of stuttering • male • < 14 months postonset • sudden rise in SER • concomitant disorders • struggle and avoidances • clustering • < 3 iterations • unable to produce rote, automatic tasks fluently • increase in SLDs • signs of awareness • other confounding factors	Section 4: Diagnostic impressions
Pattern analysis	Consistency	Strengths		Section 5: Recommendations
Speech rate	Stimulability	Weaknesses		Section 6: Signatures
Stuttering Severity				

appropriate for use with children and adults. The Stuttering Severity Instrument: 3 (Riley, 1994) (SSI), SDA, and Personalized Fluency Control Therapy Assessment (PFCT) (Cooper & Cooper, 1985) meet this standard. Third, the chosen method should provide for a wide range of samples, such as picture naming, monologue, dialogue, and reading. Instruments that adhere to this guideline include the SSI, the SDA, and Shine's (1980) assessment procedures. The fourth recommended methodology includes assessment of the variability in speaking abilities. Cooper and Cooper's PFCT protocol, Shine's assessment, the SDA, and, to some extent, the SSI, investigate the issue of variability. Finally, the ideal evaluation methodology would provide a composite picture of the client's manner of speaking. The SDA, PFCT protocol, and Shine's procedures are examples of this recommendation.

Like all clinical procedures, as a experienced speech-language pathologist you might select desired components from any of the assessment procedures just cited because they are all excellent tools. You may augment any one procedure with additional tasks or tests to learn more about the individual. Inclusion of criterion-referenced tasks supplement the diagnostic process. Selecting pictures and reading material, developing situational hierarchy checklists, or determining the types of interactional samples to obtain are client-dependent variables. However, certain key points are important to remember during diagnostic planning.

Key Points to Remember

The determination of the client's relative strengths and weaknesses is the foundation of the assessment process. Stuttering is a highly variable, heterogeneous disorder, so it is crucial to use the concept of triangulation to plan thoroughly for the diagnostic interaction (Figure 4.3).

Triangulation means viewing the client from multiple perspectives—in this case, three. Observations must be planned and purposeful (Conture, 1997) to capture the client's fluency fluctuations. Perspectives might include time of day, communica-

Figure 4.3
The diagnostic process involves purposeful observations of the client from different perspectives. The term *triangulation* refers to the identification of three different settings, time of day, or communication partners in which the therapist wishes to observe the client.

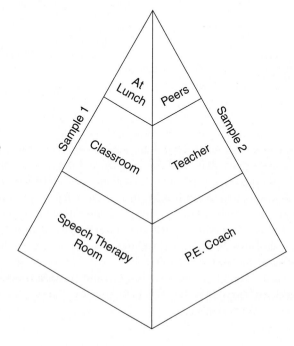

tion partners, environmental setting, or any combination of identified factors. Whatever triangulation perspectives you select, here are six important points to remember when planning a fluency diagnostic:

1. There are no shortcuts when it comes to assessing fluency; whatever you do, be consistent and thorough.
2. Always audiotape and/or videotape your interactions with the client and family.
3. Assess the variability of fluency across different settings and speaking tasks.
4. Assess stuttering in structured tasks that control for linguistic complexity, such as dialogue, monologue, reading, and so on.
5. Assess fluency in tasks involving various degrees of time pressure (e.g., interruptions, rapid questioning, distractions).
6. Assess fluency while varying the topic of discussion (e.g., home, work/school, speech therapy, friends, peer pressure, social events, etc.).

Depending on the purpose of the evaluation, the time available for detailed transcriptions, and the nature of the client's difficulties, certain procedures will meet your minimum needs and some will provide an extensive profile of the client's strengths and weaknesses. The first source of information that will guide your planning decisions is the case history form, available in most diagnostic textbooks. Appendices B and C are samples of child and adult case history forms. Whatever form you choose to use, these pieces of information are necessary components: general client information; referral source and reason for testing; background histories to include family structure, pregnancy, birth, medical, motor, speech, academics, work environment, and demands; specific inquiries regarding the history of stuttering and/or therapy; and the client/parent's desired outcomes if treatment is required.

You will use the information you obtain from the case history form and/or phone contact to determine the necessary components that need testing. An overriding principle to keep in mind when reviewing the case history is that the child is a whole person, so the assessment process must address all components of communication. Voice, language, articulation, oral motor skills, hearing, academic performance, and intellectual functioning are all parts of a fluency diagnostic. Base the amount of time you spend assessing each component on the child's individual strengths and weaknesses. Regardless of the selected evaluation tools, the actual diagnostic should represent a well-organized plan that can be modified at any time.

Once the plan is designed, you begin the information-gathering phase of the assessment. Establishing a positive client/clinician relationship will impact the amount and type of information you can obtain when interviewing the client and his family members. When the client/parents arrive for an evaluation, they may be apprehensive. This may be their first experience addressing the fluency problem or seeking help from a professional. Like visiting a doctor to get the results of blood tests, the patient is scared of the unknown, not unlike our client or parent awaiting news regarding the diagnosis and prognosis. To be successful at obtaining information under these less than optimal conditions, you must establish a positive client/clinician relationship and understand the interview process.

Client/Clinician Relationship

The relationship between client and clinician is the foundation of stuttering assessment and intervention and must be characterized by trusting, honest, and respectful interactions. Gregory (1986) presents three reasons why it is important to make efforts to understand the client, especially during the initial contact. First, most clients appreciate the interest. Second, what is done in our early interactions establishes some of the basic conditions of therapy. Ultimately, the process of talking initiates a client-driven self-evaluation and reorganization of thinking, thus opening the way to receive new information and direction from the clinician. Getting to know the client as a person first helps take some of the direct attention off the disorder of stuttering, leading into dialogue about the disorder.

You might try **funneling** to get to know your client (Figure 4.4), which involves initiating a general conversation to establish an environment conducive to the open exchange of ideas. Inquire about the client's interests and hobbies to demonstrate an interest in the whole person. Slowly ask questions regarding general speech experiences and gradually move into the topic of stuttering. Identify the client's definition of stuttering, what he thinks causes stuttering, and how stuttering may have shaped his life. With the establishment of trust and genuineness, it is safe to inquire about the client's experiences in speech therapy. If appropriate, ask him to model the strategies he learned and rate the relative effectiveness of these techniques in the management of the disorder.

Here is a sample dialogue of a clinician using funneling:

Clinician:	"It's nice to meet you, John. Tell me about yourself."
John:	"Well, I'm 16 years old and I work part time at the Old E1 Paso Factory. I go to Andress High School and do okay in school."
Clinician:	"What's okay?"
John:	"Well, my grades are okay. I get ABC grades."
Clinician:	"ABCs are okay."
John:	"I really like my P.E. class. I'm on the golf team so I get A's in there."
Clinician:	"So you enjoy playing golf. My son plays golf too. It's a good sport."
John:	"Yeah. I go play with my dad. We go on Sundays sometimes."
Clinician:	"What other things do you like to do, with or without your dad?"
John:	"I like to hang out with my friends and play Nintendo. That's about all."
Clinician:	"It seems to me that playing golf or Nintendo don't require a lot of talking. Tell me about situations in which you have to talk."
John:	"Gee. I, uh, I'm not much of a talker. I have always been a really quiet guy."
Clinician:	(Nods her head)
John:	"Yeah, I've never been like, into talking. You know, with stuttering, you just can't do it so easily."
Clinician:	"Let's make a list of different situations that require you to talk. (The clinician pulls out a piece of paper and writes the client's responses.)
Clinician:	"I don't see using the phone on your list. Let me ask you a question. Do you talk much on the phone with your friends?"
John:	"No. I don't use the phone much. People hang up on me sometimes and I get real mad."

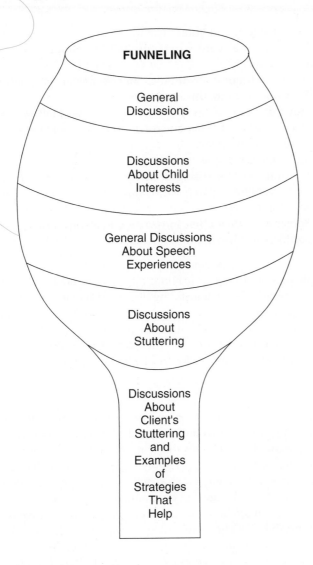

Figure 4.4
Funneling schemata used when planning a diagnostic session.

Clinician:	"Hmm. So talking on the phone is not much fun?"
John:	"No. Not really."
Clinician:	"Tell me about situations in which you enjoy talking."
John:	"I don't mind talking when I'm around my close friends, but to strangers it's harder. I really don't like asking questions of people I don't know."
Clinician:	"Why is that?"
John:	"Cause I stutter."
Clinician:	"What do you mean stutter?"
John:	"Like I can't get my words out. Like it's hard to talk."
Clinician:	"You can't get your words out and it's hard to talk."

John:	"Yeah, I stutter and I don't like it."
Clinician:	"You used the word *stuttering.* Tell me about this word. What is stuttering?"
John:	"It's when I repeat a word over and over again. Like bababababall."
Clinician:	"Why do you think this happens?"
John:	"Hey, I don't know. My mom says it's because I talk too fast."
Clinician:	"You talk too fast. What do you do to keep from talking too fast?"
John:	"I use my slow speech."
Clinician:	"Show me what slow speech sounds like."
John:	"It sounds like this." (Using an exaggerated prolonged vowel approach.)
Clinician:	"And this helps get your words out?"
John:	"Sometimes, yeah."
Clinician:	"Sometimes. What else can you do when you stutter?"
John:	"Nothing, just use my slow speech."

When first interacting with a person who stutters, it is best to start the discussion away from the topic of stuttering. You may not know how much emotionality exists around the subject. Opening the diagnostic by directly "touching the stuttering monster" might threaten the client and start the session on a sour note. Funneling provides the opportunity to get to know the client, gradually creating a safe environment for open discourse. Funneling depends on the efficiency of your interviewing skills and your creation of a positive environment for the assessment process.

Interviewing

Interviewing the client and/or parents is another component of the information-gathering and planning process involving several clinician competencies. Shipley (1997) identified clinician characteristics that contribute to effective interviews and classified them into five broad groups: (1) spontaneity and flexibility; (2) openness, honesty, and trustworthiness; (3) concentration, self-awareness, and emotional stability; (4) belief in people's ability to change and commitment to people; and (5) good communication skills and academic/clinical competence in speech-language pathology.

Spontaneity is the ability of clinicians to respond appropriately and quickly when needed. *Flexibility,* as a sign of clinician security and knowledge, is an underlying skill that allows a change of interview direction when needed. There is no one way to interview all clients. Modify your interview plan according to the interviewee and the flow of the discussion. *Openness* and *honesty* are essential to the development of trust and respect. "Clinicians must be able to hear, understand, and accept the values and feelings of other people. . . . They also must be careful not to inappropriately impose their values on others" (Shipley, 1997, p. 12). You must be honest in your responses to questions posed to you. Clients know when you are being forthright with your answers. A trusting relationship must be established through honesty.

Emotional stability and *self-awareness* are critical to effective interviewing. The saying "clinician know thyself" applies to how well you know your own strengths and weaknesses, biases, and beliefs. Certainly clinicians who have tried to change some aspect of themselves will have a better understanding of the effort and commitment needed to change behavior. Part of self-awareness is confidence, which enables you to concentrate during the interview and pay attention to the details provided. Effort during the interview cannot be compromised by you losing focus or being concerned about what you are "doing" or "saying." The ability to follow the client's discourse and reflect this understanding in appropriate ways is a required skill. Learn to recognize nonverbal signals of discomfort, confusion, and stress and respond to such signs in a professional way. The clinician who is secure and emotionally mature will be able to maintain concentration throughout the interview.

You must believe people can change and you can assist the client in the change process. Commitment to people is the driving force of those entering the field of speech-language pathology. Without an interest and commitment to people with disabilities, the likelihood of success in this field is minimal. The clinician who is dedicated to people communicates this commitment both nonverbally and verbally to clients and becomes a more effective interviewer and therapist. Clinical knowledge, competence, and wisdom sum up the characteristics of the effective clinician. As Gregory (1986) noted, we are products of our training. As we interact more with clients and parents, we learn, evaluate, modify, and generate new ideas so we can say, "We are clinicians in the process of change." As a new clinician, you may not have all these characteristics, but they will develop with experience and continuing education. Development and mastery of effective interview skills should be your goal.

Opening Interactions

The purpose of the initial interview is to obtain information. The interaction of those involved in the interview will influence the outcome—getting answers to questions. The client case history will provide you with ample information. However, direct questioning of the client and/or parent is often required. New clinicians often ask the parent questions already clearly answered on the case history form. This redundancy can irritate the interviewee.

A strategy you can use when interviewing clients for the first time involves completing the Information Composite Sheet (Table 4.2). Answer the questions on this sheet based on the case history or phone contacts. Then highlight the remaining questions that need answering or clarification. During the actual interview, refer to this worksheet to gather information from the client and keep you from being redundant and appearing unprepared or unorganized. Along with the Information Composite Sheet, particular verbal and nonverbal behaviors, when used appropriately, enhance the effectiveness of the interview. Use of minimal encouragers, body posture, silence, redirection, and open/closed questions are just a few of these behaviors.

Minimal encouragers are brief comments that signal the interviewee to continue talking (Shipley, 1997). These comments might include "uh huh," "yes," "hmm," "tell me more," or "I see." Practice using minimal encouragers before you enter a real-life interview. Overuse of this strategy may appear obvious to the interviewee, whereas not providing feedback to the client may be misinterpreted as a lack of interest. Head nods are a nonverbal form of encouragement and communicate to the client that you are listening to his response. Your body posture provides information to the client.

Table 4.2
Information composite sheet useful for gathering information during a fluency diagnostic.

Client's Name: _____ Informants: _____ Date: _____

Using the case history form and information gathered during the initial phone contact, fill in the answers to the following questions. Then highlight those that need answering or clarification.

In your own words, tell me why you are here today.	
What aspect of your child's speech concerns you the most?	
Describe your child's stuttering.	
Demonstrate this stuttering for me.	
Are there any relatives who have had speech and language problems, stuttering in particular?	
When did it start?	
Who first noticed the problem?	
Under what circumstances?	
Were you worried about it in the beginning?	
What did you do about it?	
How did you help your child with his speech?	
Have you used the word *stuttering*?	
Has the stuttering changed since it began?	
Is your child's speech the same in all situations?	
Does your child have trouble saying particular words or sounds?	
Is your child aware of it? If so, how do you know?	
Does your child show frustration, anger, embarrassment, or fear?	
Does your child appear to struggle or become tense when trying to say a word?	
Does your child try to correct the stuttering?	
Does your child avoid any situations to keep from talking?	
How do others react when your child stutters?	
How do you react?	
What helped the most?	

Table 4.2
Continued

Who recommended this help?	
How does your child react to this help?	
How much does your child talk?	
Who does your child talk to the most?	
Have other people mentioned your child's stuttering to you?	
Has your child had any therapy for his speech?	
If so, what did they work on?	
Were you involved in therapy?	
How much progress was made?	
How is your child performing in school?	
Describe your pregnancy and delivery.	
Describe your child's motor development.	
Describe your child's current cognitive development.	
Describe your family's daily routine or schedule.	
Is your child right or left handed?	
Has anyone tried to change handedness?	
Describe his [or her] friends and playmates.	
What are your child's favorite toys or play activities?	
What aspirations and expectations do you have for your child?	

When we lean forward, we demonstrate an interest in what the client is relaying. Leaning backward communicates an unfavorable disinterest with the current interaction. You may not be aware of your body posture and unfortunately communicate a degree of negativity to the client.

Use of silent periods is another technique that encourages the client to continue talking. However, in some cultures, silence can be unbearable. Speech-language pathologists have great difficulty handling periods of quiet. We like to talk and sometimes talk too much. Silence may emerge during the interview when you ask a poorly framed question or you wish the client to talk more. If you do not fill this void, the client will. Using the KMS acronym ("keep mouth shut") might help you monitor your level of talking. As speech-language pathologists we must learn to tolerate silence, particularly during an interview.

You may also be faced with the parent who does not stop talking, thus needing **redirection.** Here it is sometimes appropriate to redirect the client/parent by clearing your throat, rephrasing, or offering a reflective comment that helps you gain control over the direction of the interview. Clearing your throat is a subtle way of communicating you have something you wish to contribute.

Rephrasing, a strategy we also encourage parents to use with their children, involves restating the communicative intent of the interviewee. Rephrasing is very helpful because it shows the client/parent you are attending to their message and allows you then to redirect the flow of questions. For example, after the parent has stated, "Don really is hard to understand when he is stuttering," you might rephrase this statement as "It's hard to listen to the stuttering. Tell me more about his speech during this time."

The third strategy for dealing with parents who talk too much is reflection. Making a **reflective comment** involves summarizing the client's feelings, thoughts, or behaviors. "It seems you have tried to talk to Don about his stuttering, but you feel it was not as successful as you wanted. Let's talk about what else Don does when he stutters" is an example of a reflection of the parent's message followed by the next area of inquiry that helps move along the interview.

The interview process can get bogged down by the type of questions asked. Questions can be classified into two types: open and closed questions. Both types have their purpose, yet you need to use them appropriately. Open questions are broad in nature and do not lead the client in any particular direction. For example, "Tell me more about your speech" or "Expand on your last statement" are open questions that may lead into additional areas of inquiry. Closed questions seek specific answers and do not require elaboration. For example, "What is the most difficult speech situation for you?" or "How many ear infections did your child have before he was 3?" are questions that require a set response from the client or parent. Closed questions can appear to lead the client to respond in a particular way. Questions like "Do you get angry when he does that?" implies you believe the client should be angry at the situation and are not helpful. Formulate a list of open and closed question formats beforehand to use during the diagnostic interview.

The counseling literature is robust with suggestions on how to conduct an interview. The following principles will help you become a more effective and efficient interviewer (Okun, 1997):

1. Decide beforehand the goal of the interview.
2. Allocate a sufficient amount of time for the interview.
3. Establish a pleasant and relaxed atmosphere. Plan to initiate the parent/client interview at the beginning of the diagnostic session. Don't put it off toward the end because it is an anxious one for the interviewee and participants may become fatigued, feel time constraints, or become overwhelmed with the testing process.
4. Let the client/parent talk freely. The more talking you do, the less the client is talking.
5. Avoid dwelling on unimportant matters or wandering off the topic.
6. Don't work too slowly. Have an agenda and ask only the questions that need to be answered to understand the client better.
7. Ask one question at a time. Compound or complex questions may lead to confusion requiring rephrasing and more time.

8. Avoid lecturing the parent. Now is not the time to disseminate information in lengthy monologues.

9. Clarify discrepancies in client responses. A polite way to do this is to shift the responsibility for the misunderstanding on yourself: "I'm sorry. But earlier you said you didn't have difficulty with———. But just now you said "———." Could you clarify?"

10. Let the interviewees tell their story. Allow time for them to release their feelings, fears, and hopes for the future. Listening to their stories will give you a better understanding of the client and improve chances for a successful interview and later therapeutic outcome.

Your place in the interview situation is to gain insight into the client's communication difficulties. Using the strategies just described can enhance the outcome of the information-gathering process. Additionally, Okun (1997) outlines behaviors used by counselors during interviews that impact the effectiveness of the interview process. Table 4.3 provides a visual summary of the facilitating and nonfacilitating verbal and nonverbal behaviors you might remember to use during these interactions.

Table 4.3
Key facilitating and nonfacilitative behaviors of speech clinicians.

Type	Facilitative	Nonfacilitative
Verbal	• Uses understandable words • Reflects back and clarifies statements • Appropriately interprets • Summarizes for client • Responds to primary message • Uses verbal reinforcers • Calls client by first name • Answers questions about self • Uses humor to reduce tension • Is nonjudgmental and respectful	• Interrupting • Advice giving • Preaching • Placating • Blaming • Cajoling • Extensive probing and questioning • Directing, demanding • Patronizing attitude • Straying from topic • Intellectualizing • Overanalyzing • Talking about self too much • Minimizing or disbelieving
Nonverbal	• Tone of voice similar to client • Maintains good eye contact • Occasional head nodding • Facial animation • Occasional smiling • Occasional hand gesturing • Close physical proximity to client • Occasional touching • Relaxed, open posture • Confident vocal tone	• Looking away from client • Sitting far away or turned away from client • Sneering • Frowning • Scowling • Tight mouth • Shaking pointed finger • Distracting gestures • Yawning • Closing eyes • Unpleasant tone of voice • Rate of speech too slow or too fast • Acting rushed

Source: Based on Okun (1999).

Closing Interactions

After the evaluation is completed, summarize the findings for the client and/or family. Several principles can be applied to this dissemination process and make it a supportive experience for all. "Keep It Super Simple," or KISS, is a mnemonic device you can repeat to yourself when addressing the client. Shipley (1997) gave the following suggestions to use when conveying information:

1. Try to sandwich positive and negative points (alternating between good and bad news).
2. Keep language use simple and appropriate (monitor professional vernacular).
3. Avoid relying on test names and protocols (and I would add scores and abbreviations).
4. Continuously watch for signs of misunderstanding or resistance.
5. Accept emotional responses professionally, supportively, and matter-of-factly.
6. If you need to make more than three to five important points, consider alternative methods for conveying the information (such as charts, student profile sheet indicating strengths, weaknesses, and areas to target).

The Student Profile Worksheet (Table 4.4) is a useful way to disseminate information and allow time for the client or parent to internalize the information. Often, we provide too much information at one time and the client/parent is not able to keep up with the details. They look confused or continue to go back to a point presented earlier. When this happens, we often have not allowed time for the information to sink in or provided an opportunity for questions and clarifications. The Student Profile Worksheet is divided into three sections: strengths, areas of concern, and target areas. Present a strength exhibited by the client and write it in the appropriate column. Following this, write the client's concern or weakness in the second column. The process of writing allows the client or parent time to process the information. This is not a completed document you bring to the closing session. It is a work-in-progress type of activity. Continue to add a strength, then a concern, until you have presented the *major* findings of the diagnostic. The next step involves reviewing the information and determining what areas you will target initially in therapy. Goal determination should be a joint effort among clinician, client, and/or parent.

Understanding how clients or parents may react to the diagnostic findings is important to a smooth closure of the assessment meeting. Clients may respond positively or negatively to the information you present at the closing of the diagnostic. Denial, anger, frustration, hope, determination, and sadness are just some reactions to the diagnosis of stuttering. The person's prior experiences and present beliefs may determine their reactions, all of which are highly individual. Shipley (1997) extended Donaghy's ten basic principles of human nature that influence how an individual may respond during the information exchange process. The following summary of these points will help you understand the reactions observed when providing information to clients:

1. No two people are alike.
2. People are conditioned by their environment and past experiences.
3. People behave both verbally and nonverbally on the basis of their needs.
4. Needs may be conscious or unconscious.

Table 4.4
Worksheet used to disseminate information to clients, teachers, and/or parents.

Student Profile Worksheet

Student's Name: _____ Date: _____

Strengths	Areas of Concern	Target Areas

5. Needs have both logical and emotional elements.
6. A person's needs can distort his or her perceptions and recollections.
7. People need the recognition, acceptance, and approval of others.
8. People have a need to organize and structure the world.
9. People have a need to influence the world.
10. Constructive and lasting changes usually come from satisfying successful experiences.

Every client/parent enters the diagnostic environment with their own set of expectations and anxieties. Understanding human nature may prepare you for any response formation. Two scenarios may develop, creating an uncomfortable setting and impact the interview process: when the parent cries and when the parent/client becomes angry. Crying is an emotional reaction to the topic being discussed and should be handled in a positive way. Most therapists recommend giving a facial tissue to the client at the first signs of crying. However, when we offer a tissue before being asked, we may communicate a level of discomfort with crying, as if saying, "Please take this tissue and stop crying." Wait for the client to ask for a tissue or have a box easily accessible. It is important to convey that crying is okay and, in many ways, helps the therapeutic process.

Angry parents convey their emotions in a different manner. Briefly, anger may be a sign of discomfort and frustration. Parents, upon hearing their child is indeed stuttering, may feel disappointment and frustration because they believed their child would "outgrow it." This is what the pediatrician told them, and the shock that this has not happened or they have "wasted time" fuels their frustration and flares into anger. Displacement, the transfer of hostile feelings onto another individual, may occur. You may be the target of the parents' anger because you are the messenger of the news.

Do not, first and foremost, personalize the anger. The parent or client is not upset at you but with the information you are relaying. Acknowledge the level of discomfort the client is experiencing through the use of empathetic statements, such as "You feel upset at this news because you wanted so much to prevent it." Give them their wishes in words, such as "I wish your son were not stuttering." Provide positive strokes for the parent by acknowledging their efforts to help their child both in the past and the future, such as "I am so happy to have you here and to know you want to help your son with his speech." If these strategies do not quell clients' anger, remove yourself from the situation and give them time to collect their thoughts. Using the excuse of needing a bathroom break or getting a drink of water is a polite way to leave the immediate situation. Anger is a natural response to unfavorable information. Although not often faced with the angry client/parent, you must be prepared to handle these situations.

TESTING AND INTERPRETATION

Following the planning and information-gathering phrase of assessment is stage 2, testing and interpretation. Based on the information obtained from parental interviews and the case history, you design a testing plan that may include a series of standardized and nonstandardized assessment tools/procedures. The procedures/instruments presented next are widely represented in the literature. Credit is given to the following for their insightful assessment ideas that have been incorporated into the proposed assessment ideas presented in this book: Campbell and Hill (1987), Conture (2001), Cooper and Cooper (1985), Gregory and Hill (1999), Guitar (1998), Healey, Susca, and Trautman (2002), Pindzola (1987), Riley (1994), Schwartz and Conture (1988), and Shine (1980). Ramig and Bennett (1997a) compiled a checklist of assessment instruments for stuttering that evaluated 9 assessment tools according to 29 components (Table 4.5). This checklist provides a comprehensive overview of available instruments on the market. Regardless of what procedures you use in assessing

Table 4.5

Analysis of 29 assessment tools that may be used during the information-gathering phase of the evaluation process.

	Systematic Fluency Assessment	Stuttering Prediction Instrument	Stuttering Severity Instrument	Cooper Personalized Fluency Control Therapy	Assessment of Fluency in School Children	Systematic Disfluency Analysis	Stuttering Intervention Program Protocol	The Fluency Development System	Assessment Program for Dysfluent Children
Age Prescribed For:	3–9	2–9	Children-Adults	Children-Adults	Any	Any	3–9	2–9	Any
Administration/Analysis Time	2.5	?	?	?	3+	4+		?	2–2.5
Manual Provided	▲	▲	▲	▲	▲	▲	▲	▲	▲
Case History Obtained	▲	▲		▲	▲	▲	▲		▲
Audio Recording Required	▲	▲	▲	▲	▲	▲	▲	▲	▲
Video Recording Required						▲		▲	
Verbatim Transcription Required	▲				▲	▲		▲	
Number of Samples Obtained	2+	1+	2+	3+	3+	3+		2+	
Monologue Sample Analyzed	▲	▲	▲	▲	▲	▲			
Dialogue Sample Analyzed	▲	▲		▲	▲	▲			
Parent-Child Interaction		□				▲		▲	
Reading Sample Obtained	▲		▲	▲	▲	▲			▲
Rate of Speech Calculation						□		▲	
Duration Measures		▲	▲	▲		▲		▲	
Percentage of Stuttered Words	▲	▲	▲	▲	▲			▲	▲
Percentage of Stuttered Syllables	▲			▲		▲		▲	

(continued)

Table 4.5

Continued

	Systematic Fluency Assessment	Stuttering Prediction Instrument	Stuttering Severity Instrument	Cooper Personalized Fluency Control Therapy	Assessment of Fluency in School Children	Systematic Disfluency Analysis	Stuttering Intervention Program Protocol	The Fluency Development System	Assessment Program for Dysfluent Children
Stuttered Words Per Minute	▲								
Stuttered Syllables Per Minute	▲								
Physiological Factors	▲				▲				
Secondary Behaviors	▲	▲	▲	▲	▲	▲			
Attitudes	□	□		▲	▲	○			
Personality Factors									▲
Severity Ratings	○	▲	▲	▲		▲		▲	
Language Factors	▲				▲	▲	▲	▲	▲
Parent Interview	▲	▲		▲	▲	▲	▲	▲	▲
Teacher Interview						○			
Client Self-Evaluation						○			▲
Therapy-IEP Information Included	▲			▲	▲	▲	▲	▲	▲
Normative Data Available	?	▲	▲	?	?	?	?	?	?

Nine assessment instruments are described according to 29 components which may be considered when choosing an assessment tool. Represents components incorporated in the assessment instrument. ▲ Indicated that the feature is obtained for other tools and included in the particular instrument. ○ Denotes items which are indirectly assessed. □ Means item is not indicated in the manual? This is meant as a guide during the assessment process. Each instrument may be utilized differently depending upon clinician style and training. The reader is referred to the manuals of these instruments for more details.

Source: From Curlee, Siegel, Nature and Treatment of Stuttering: New Directions, *2/e. Published by Allyn and Bacon, Boston, MA. Copyright © 1997 by Pearson Education. Reprinted by permission of the publisher.*

the individual who stutters, you can classify the information obtained into either quantitative or qualitative features of the client's communication profile.

Assessment outcomes for stuttering include both quantitative and qualitative measures (Figure 4.5). Quantitative measures might include frequency counts, number of iterations, influence of linguistic complexity on stuttering frequency, pattern analysis, and speech rate measurements.

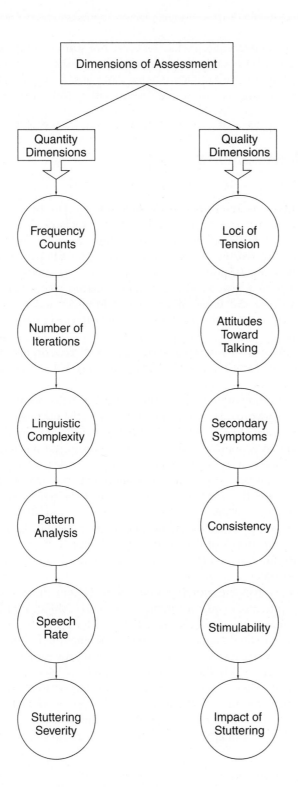

Figure 4.5
Dimensions of a fluency assessment involving quantitative and qualitative measurements.

However, percentages and percentile ranks, alone, are not sufficient for the diagnosis of stuttering. Qualitative measures include identification of the loci of tension, attitudes toward talking, presence of secondary behaviors, consistency, stimulability, and situational hierarchies. Measures of stuttering severity fall in both categories, depending on how it is measured.

Quantitative Measurements

Frequency Counts

Basic frequency counts of stuttered speech are the foundation of the most traditional assessment guidelines (e.g., Conture, 1997; Johnson & associates, 1959; Riley, 1994; Shine, 1980; Van Riper, 1971; Yaruss, 1997). However, four measurements issues identified by Yaruss (1997) are worthy of discussion: what type of behavior to measure, what metric to use, how much should be sampled, and how to handle clustered moments of stuttering. The first issue is what type of disfluency to count or what Yairi (1997a) called "identifying the target phenomena." Johnson and associates were among the first to establish a list of speech disruption behaviors (1959). Their classification system included these speech behaviors: phrase repetitions, interjections, revision-incomplete phrases, word repetitions, part-word repetitions, disrhythmic phonation (broken words and prolonged sounds), and tense pauses (audible tension between words).

Conture (2001) uses the within-word disfluency as his main index. When a child exhibits 3 or more within-word disfluencies per 100 words, the diagnosis of stuttering is considered. As previously discussed, Yairi (1997a) introduced the SER (sound/syllable repetitions) and SLD (sound/syllable repetitions, prolongations, and blocks) as prominent features of disfluent speech. A child exhibiting more than 3 SERs per 100 words or more than 3 SLDs per 100 words is considered at risk for stuttering. Campbell and Hill's SDA calculates the percentage of more typical, less typical, and total number of disfluencies per 200 syllable samples. As alluded to in the discussion on the fluency continuum, frequency counts of all disfluent behavior can be beneficial in understanding the fluency patterns of the child. A disturbance in fluency is any interruption in the forward flow of speech. If we believe this to be so, we should obtain measurements of all breaks.

Another concern involves the **metric,** or unit of measurement, used for analysis. Some therapists use stuttered words per minute (SW/min) (Shine, 1980) as the expression of stuttering frequency. However, using time as a basis may be misleading, especially when the client exhibits long, tense blocks. The client could have a relative low-frequency count only because much of the time during the sample was spent in silence. Another issue arises in whether to use words versus syllables as the base metric. For the younger child, speech typically consists of monosyllabic words so using words as the index is theoretically sound. However, as children begin to develop a multisyllabic vocabulary, use of words instead of syllables may result in an underestimation of the frequency of stuttering. Not only does stuttering begin more often on the initial syllable of an utterance, but it can occur in the middle of multisyllabic words (Wingate, 1976, 1988). The syllable is considered the basic unit of speech (Levelt, 1989); therefore "a syllable-based metric more accurately reflects the amount of speech affected by disfluency" (Yairi, 1997a, p. 52).

In obtaining frequency counts, how should multiple disfluencies on one word, called **clustering,** be counted? Yairi (1997a) stated counting clusters as one incident might misrepresent the individual's difficulties. Understanding the source of clusters might shed some light on this problem. Clustering occurs when the child initiates one type of disfluency that fails to release him to continue his communication effort, so he tries another behavior. "I wa wa w———a want an apple" is an example of clustering that includes a syllable repetition followed by a sound prolongation and another syllable repetition before the person completes his intended message. Do we count this as one disfluency on the word *want* or do we count each type as a separate unit of disfluency?

The SDA (Campbell & Hill, 1987) includes clusters in their own category, thus weighting them differently. Clustering may be representative of reactive behavior to the temporary loss of control over speech. Researchers have investigated clustering behaviors in preschool children and determined that this behavior was indicative of more advanced stuttering (Hubbard & Yairi, 1988; LaSalle & Conture, 1993, 1995). This author concurs with these findings and believes the presence of clustering may be a negative prognostic indicator for spontaneous recovery. Separating them from single units of disfluency is very important in understanding the client's particular patterns of stuttering (Hubbard & Yairi, 1988).

Next, the size of the sample obtained is important to consider. Campbell and Hill (1987) obtained 200 syllable samples of differing interactions, for example, parent-child interaction, reading, monologue or storytelling, and dialogue with the clinician. The number and type of samples obtained, of course, depends on each child and his or her particular situation. Conture and his colleagues obtained samples of 100 words, whereas Meyers and Woodford (1992) recommend samples of 350 words. Even larger samples of 500 syllables are obtained by Yairi (1997a). The types of samples obtained and their representativeness of the client's difficulties should be considered when deciding the number and length of samples. Several short, yet typical, samples may be better than a longer sample that is atypical of everyday communication. Guitar (1998) suggested using the samples exhibiting the most severe stuttering. Such decisions will vary depending on the individual being assessed.

Iterations

The number of repeated speech units is termed **iteration** and has diagnostic significance (Ambrose & Yairi, 1995). Yairi and Lewis (1984) found that nonstuttering preschoolers typically had one extra unit compared to the children who stutter two or more units. They concluded that three iterations were above average for both stuttering and nonstuttering preschoolers. When transcribing the client's speech sample, take care to note the number of iterations accurately. Sometimes you may have to listen to a particular segment numerous times before achieving an accurate count of the iterations. Because of the prognostic value of the number of iterations, the client's diagnostic profile must include information on iteration length.

Linguistic Complexity

The influence of linguistic complexity on stuttering is well documented in the literature (Bernstein Ratner & Sih, 1987; Gaines, Runyan, & Meyers, 1991; Logan & Conture, 1995; Starkweather, 1987) and therefore must be evaluated. According to Starkweather (1987), if the demands for language generation are low, the child is able to speak fluently. Language tasks that are low in demands are typically overlearned behaviors characterized by high **automaticity,** that is, the client does not have to think about the task. As the demands increase, fluent speech production becomes more difficult requiring a greater degree of conscious effort. Theoretically, if we think about the establishment of associational pathways in the mental lexicon through Dell's theory of spreading activation, the more experience the person has with certain vocabulary, the stronger their phonological-lexical representation becomes. Strong representations require less activation to be selected for use during language formulation. Weaker representations or damaged representations require greater activation, that is, greater demands.

Shine's (1980) assessment procedures provide a nice organization for assessing the interaction of the demands for linguistic performance and the capacity to manage their motor equivalents. Beginning with rote naming tasks, the client is asked to name numbers, recite the ABCs, days of the week, and months of the year. When a client is unable to produce these automatic speech efforts fluently, it may be a sign that stuttering is ingrained in his speech production system. Even the initiation of voicing for vowels results in a laryngeal spasm or block the client does not know how to manage effectively. When this happens, progress in therapy is usually slower and requires extensive drill in retraining the areas of basic speech production, such as place, manner, and voice characteristics of sounds.

The next level of linguistic complexity involves imitation of speech. Repeating single words, short phrases, and longer sentences are examples of changes in complexity and degree of automaticity. Imitation is a fluency-inducing condition much like choral speaking. The replication of another's utterance is low on the demands scale, resulting in high fluency. Again, it is a negative prognostic indicator when the client is unable to obtain fluency when imitating speech. Picture naming requires greater involvement of the grammatical encoder within the mental lexicon; thus it is considered a task higher in language demand. Naming a series of 36 pictures on a page gives you an opportunity to observe the language formulation process in action. The client may observe several behaviors that are indicative of awareness of stuttering or the likelihood of stuttering on a word. Irregular pausing or posturing before a word, use of interjections, and eye movements may signal awareness that a moment of stuttering is approaching or even attempts to postpone or circumvent them.

Next, the client is required to generate a story while looking at a series of pictures. Sequence story pictures provide a general language framework for the child to use, a simpler task compared to spontaneous story retelling. Ask the client to tell what is happening in each picture. This allows you to observe the client's organizational and syntax skills while noting the level of fluency. You may observe an increase in revisions because the client has a greater number of opportunities to avoid certain words or sounds thought to be problematic. Interjections may increase as the client buys time to formulate or circumlocute feared words.

Reading is another task that provides insight into the client's speech patterns. An important factor to consider when selecting the reading material is the level of reading proficiency needed to perform the task. The reading level should always be one to two grade levels below the client's current reading abilities. This task is not evaluating reading ability and it may be difficult to determine if the client is having problems "reading" the word or "saying" the word if the material is at a challenging reading level.

Three distinct patterns emerge from the reading task. First is the client who has no difficulty reading the story fluently. This may be due to the provision of language and phonological structures, punctuation used to manage pauses, and/or the lack of bidirectional communication.

The second profile is the client who exhibits severe stuttering throughout the reading sample. The client, when reading, is not able to use the many learned avoidance behaviors he is accustomed to using to produce fluency. When reading, you can't change the word and there is no getting around the feared words or sounds. You might observe more interjections used as postponement devices until the client can produce the target word. Sometimes, clients will drop words from the reading passage just so they don't have to produce them.

The third profile is typical of most children who have not developed anticipatory behavior. They stutter on words and generally read the sample with some degree of fluency. Moments of stuttering occur on the beginning word of the utterance or sentence with smooth movement until the next breath is taken. Rhythm is not dramatically disturbed as it is with the second profile. You must develop fine-tuned observational skills in order to differentiate among these three patterns that emerge when reading.

As we move up the linguistic hierarchy, we reach the level of monologue, dialogue, and multiple-interaction scenarios. Monologue speech requires the client to engage in a one-way discussion, for example, about events in his favorite movie. The client can choose his own linguistic structures for production, having a greater opportunity to change words. The clinician may see two patterns emerge during monologue speech. First, the client who stuttered severely during the reading sample may exhibit less stuttering here. The freedom to select words and to organize sentences allows the individual to avoid anticipated difficulties. Second, the client who read the passage fluently may exhibit greater stuttering due to the increased language demands involved in the monologue. The sole burden for language formulation is placed on the client during this task. Next, the client is asked specific questions that require personal information. Saying his name, describing his home and family structure, and talking about his speech have an added element of emotionality that may or may not disrupt fluency. From here, you and the client engage in a dialogue, a back-and forth exchange of ideas. You can assess the impact of frequent questions, interruptions, simu-talk (talking at the same time), fast articulatory rate, and frequent pauses on the fluency of the client. Stuttering manifests itself differently in each person. How clients respond to certain stimuli, language tasks, and environmental pressure becomes part of their fluency profile that you will use when planning treatment.

Pattern Analysis

Insight into the client's stuttering profile can be obtained through **pattern analysis** of moments of disfluency. It is not sufficient to know just how much clients are stuttering; we must also know what they are doing when they stutter. The cases of Jim and Lisa illustrate how percentage of stuttering alone can be misleading and not very helpful (Table 4.6).

Jim and Lisa were evaluated using the SDA procedures. Both exhibited approximately the same amount of disfluency for a monologue sample. Jim had a total of 21% disfluency consisting of 5% more typical disfluencies and 16% less typical disfluencies. Lisa had 21% total disfluency broken into 2% more typical and 19% less typical disfluencies. Jim's more typical behaviors included mainly whole-word repetitions. His less typical or stuttering behavior was the consistent use of short, brief blocks involving labial tension on the /p/ sound. He had an equal distribution of prolongations and sound repetitions during this sample. No secondary signs of struggle were present. He did a lot of talking with frequent yet brief breaks in the forward flow of speech.

Lisa's profile, however, is somewhat different. She had very few more typical behaviors and less typical disfluencies characterized by long, tense blocks involving facial grimaces, hand gestures used as escape mechanisms, pitch rises, head nods with turning, and interjections used as postponement devices. Lisa said very little in this sample and had long breaks in the forward flow of speech that severely distracted from her communication efforts (Table 4.7).

Pattern analysis provides you with two important aspects of the client's stuttering: what types of stuttering are predominant in his speech and how the client combines these behaviors when reacting. In these cases, knowledge of Jim's patterns helped plan his individual education plan (IEP), which was very different from Lisa's plan. Jim's profile indicated he had developed anticipatory responses to the /p/ sound resulting in posturing prior to saying words starting with /p/. He had no difficulty releasing himself from the moment of stuttering and had only a few instances of clustering.

Table 4.6
Systematic Disfluency Analysis frequency counts: When numbers don't tell us enough.

	Jim		Lisa	
	Number	Percentage	Number	Percentage
More Typical Disfluencies	22	5%	3	2%
Less Typical Disfluencies	63	16%	26	19%
Total Disfluencies	85	21%	29	21%

Although he did not like his speech, he had not developed faulty coping mechanisms as secondary behaviors. His plan was to confront his belief that saying the /p/ sound was difficult, reduce his anticipatory behaviors, and involve him in tension reduction tasks. He chose to utilize the *bounce* strategy (brief, tension-free sound or syllable repetition) for managing his stuttering.

Lisa was very different in her patterns and reaction to stuttering. She had extreme difficulty releasing from the moment of stuttering and responded with secondary devices that were ineffectual. Instances of stuttering did not cluster around particular sounds or words. Lisa tried to hide her discomfort with stuttering. Lisa's plan started with basic voicing practice to help release her from the moment of stuttering with an easy initiation of phonation. Once she was able to get her voice moving, she could complete her utterance. She chose to use the prolongation or "slide" as a way to manage her speech. Lisa required much desensitization to the topic of stuttering and to stuttering itself. She was encouraged and rewarded for open discussions about the disorder of stuttering or insertion of easy, voluntary stutters.

Table 4.7

The distribution of more typical and less typical disfluencies for two clients with the same total percentage of stuttering.

	Jim		Lisa	
More Typical Disfluencies				
Hesitations	1		0	
Interjections	2		0	
Revisions	3		0	
Unfinished Utterances/Words	0		0	
Phrase Repetitions	3		0	
Word Repetitions	13		3	
Clustered Components 2–3	0		0	
Clustered Components 4+	0		0	
Less Typical Disfluencies				
Word Repetitions	0		2	
Syllable Repetitions	2		4	
Sound Repetitions	6		4	
Prolongations	7		4	
Blocks	39		9	
Clustered Components 2–3	9		3	
Clustered Components 4+	0		0	
Number of Syllables	405		135	
More Typical Disfluencies	22	5%	3	2%
Less Typical Disfluencies	63	16%	26	19%
Total Disfluencies	85	21%	29	21%

Both cases help demonstrate the need for differential diagnosis that leads to differential treatment (Gregory & Hill, 1999). **Differential diagnosis** consists of frequency counts, as well as knowledge about patterns or types of disfluencies across differing samples specific to each individual client. Differential treatment is designed according to the individual needs of the client. Once you understand the client's communication profile, you are better able to develop profile-dependent treatment plans, as well as track any change in patterns over time. Patterns of disfluency change over the course of treatment and must be documented in the client's records.

Change is a gradual process (Goldberg, 1997) and comes in small steps. It is unlikely that a child who exhibits severe stuttering will go from one extreme (stuttering) on the fluency continuum to the other (fluency). For example, the child who exhibits blocks and tense prolongations with secondary behaviors will gradually change the amount of tension in the speech mechanism allowing repetitions to emerge. The client is not holding speech back, and sound and syllable repetitions are now available for shaping into easy whole-word repetitions. The freedom to use easy onsets promotes continuity in tension-free speech efforts, that is, the production of fluency. Remember, fluency is not void of disfluencies. Everyone's speech includes the more typical disfluencies of whole-word and phrase repetitions, hesitations, and interjections. The therapy process involves the gradual movement along the fluency continuum from less typical to more typical disfluencies.

Knowing the distribution between more typical and less typical disfluencies can aid in documenting such change. The following is an example of a fourth-grade student who started therapy in January and received therapy for 2 years prior to being dismissed from speech therapy at the end of sixth grade. Alex's profile involved the use of many interjections and revisions, which he used as stallers to buy time to arrange his thoughts. However, these techniques did not always work and he would eventually produce a sound repetition or short-tense block. Word-finding difficulties were ruled out as a source of the interjections and revisions because language skills were within normal limits on standardized tests of language and narrative discourse. Table 4.8 demonstrates Alex's fluency change over the course of treatment.

Table 4.8
Fluency patterns on the Systematic Disfluency Analysis over a 2-year period of time for a fourth-grade boy receiving services in the public schools.

	Jan.	Oct.		April		Feb.
# MT	63	14	37	11	10	7
# LT	44	2	2	1	5	5
% MT	12.6%	11.02%	15.6%	4%	3.96%	2.66%
% LT	8.0%	1.5%	.8%	.36%	1.98%	1.9%
Total %	21.7%	12.5%	16.45%	4.37%	5.95%	4.56%
# syllables	498	127	237	274	252	263

The next case is an example of a change in total percentage of disfluency accompanied by an obvious change in the client's patterns of talking (Table 4.9). Joseph, a 5-year-old kindergartener, was initially tested in June when he entered therapy for the first time. He was 2 years postonset and his parents expressed much concern because his speech was not getting better as the pediatrician had predicted. He was retested in January after 6 months of integrated therapy. The table indicates not only the drop in overall frequency of stuttering but a change in his patterns of disfluency. Joseph went from predominantly sound repetitions and blocking behaviors to tension-free brief prolongations. It is important to note that the stuttering modification strategy of voluntary stuttering was taught because Joseph had already established negative attitudes and avoidance behaviors. This child would bang his head on the floor and cry "Why can't I talk!" The increase in short, easy prolongations can be attributed to his slide strategy that had not yet been normalized. He continues to exhibit two-item clustering with a large number of interjections. While working with Joseph, it became apparent he used interjections as a postponement device. Although his frequency counts were dramatically reduced, he continues to be at risk for continued stuttering due to his avoidance behaviors and presence of less typical disfluencies.

Table 4.9
Changes in both frequency of stuttering and patterns exhibited by a 5-year-old boy.

	Pretreatment Dialogue with Clinician	After 6 months of Treatment Dialogue with Clinician
More Typical Disfluencies		
Word Repetitions	4	0
Unfinished Word	2	0
Interjection	4	7
Revision	0	1
Two Item Cluster	1	0
Less Typical Disfluencies		
Syllable Repetitions	4	2
Sound Repetitions	13	1
Prolongations	4	9
Blocks	14	2
Two-Item Cluster	8	6
Three-Item Cluster	5	1
Four+-Item Cluster	1	0
Total Syllables	212	340
Total # MT	12	8
Total # LT	49	21
Total Number	61	29
% MT	5.7%	2.3%
%LT	23.1%	6.2%
Total % Disfluency	28.8%	8.5%

Speech Rate

Determining speaking rate is an important part of a fluency diagnostic. Speech is produced at a rate of 15 phonemes per second or two to three words per second (Levelt, 1989). The clinician wants to discover how the client manages this remarkable feat. Some clients may slow their speech rate as a response to their stuttering; others may increase their speech rate in fear that once they stop, they will stutter again upon initiation of speech. Vanrychkeghem, Glessing, Brutten, and McAlindon (1999) conducted a study that investigated the interaction between rate of speech and stuttering severity. They found that adults who stuttered the most exhibited increased stuttering when reading in the slow, normal, and fast rate conditions. However, those adults who stuttered were not impacted by speech rate. Be aware of the differential effects of rate of speech on stuttering frequency. There are two commonly used methods for evaluating speech rate: criterion versus norm-referenced procedures. Criterion referencing relies on your perceptual judgment regarding the rate of speech produced by the client. Speech intelligibility and rhythm influence such judgments. For some clients, producing speech at a fast rate results in a compromise in articulation. The client whose rhythm is irregular may actually produce less speech, perhaps as a result of his avoidance behaviors or time spent in tense blocks. If you conclude that either profile is apparent for the client, calculate actual figures and compare them against normative data.

Determining speech rate can be influenced by the age of the client. As speech motor control develops, the individual is better able to coordinate the approximately 100 muscles necessary for speech production (Levelt, 1989). Guitar (1998) presented speech rate norms for children in Vermont and speculated that there would be little difference for children in other states. Andrews and Ingham (1971) provide us with figures for adults. Table 4.10 summarizes these guidelines for making judgments regarding speech rate for children, adolescent, and adult populations. Interpretation of rate measures will differ based on the profile of each client. A low syllable per minute figure may indicate the presence of long, tense blocks that consume much time. The actual articulatory rate may be average; however, due to time spent in a block, the calculated speech rate appears significantly slow, especially when compared to the norms. Proceed cautiously and ensure proper interpretation of normative data on individual performance measures as well as subjective judgments.

Table 4.10
Speech rate guidelines for children, adolescents, and adults.

Age (year)	Range in Syllables per Minute
6	140–175
8	150–180
10	165–215
12	165–220
Adolescent and Adult	162–230

Source: Based on Andrews and Ingham (1971) and Guitar (1998).

Qualitative Measurements

Loci of Tension

Identifying the **loci of tension** for each client is important in learning their patterns of stuttering and essential to the planning process of treatment. For example, if laryngeal blocking is a prominent feature of speech production, you will have to allocate time for voicing drills on vowel sounds with a focus on proprioceptive feedback. Bloodstein (1995) strongly advocates for the role of tension in the fragmentation of speech efforts. It is your responsibility to observe and/or ask the client where he "feels" the most tension during a moment of stuttering. Some clients may have extreme tension in the laryngeal area prohibiting the easy initiation of speech. Others may exhibit labial tension that results in frequent blocking on bilabial sounds.

Attitudes Toward Communication

The attitudes of people who stutter have long been of interest to researchers (e.g., Andrews & Cutler, 1974; Bennett, Ramig, & Reveles, 1993; Brutten & Dunham, 1989; Cooper & Cooper, 1985; DeNil & Brutten, 1991; Erickson, 1969; Guitar & Bass, 1978; Manning, 1996; Van Riper, 1971; Vanryckeghem & Brutten, 1992, 1996, 1997; Watson, 1987, 1988; Yovetich, Leschied, & Flicht, 2000). They contend that this population exhibits negative communication attitudes and perceptions of social inadequacy when compared to nonstuttering individuals (DeNil & Brutten, 1991; Erickson, 1969; Silverman, 1970; Woods, 1974). There are several inventories you can administer to assess attitudes toward talking. Those mentioned here are merely a sampling.

Attitudes develop out of the learning process and establish the person's belief system. Therefore, a fluency diagnostic must include an evaluation of the attitudes toward stuttering of not only the individual who stutters, but also of the significant others in his environment (e.g., parents, teachers, spouses, siblings, etc.). Ideally, it would be comprehensive to assess all individuals within the client's communication community. The lack of feasibility of such efforts, however, often results in focusing on attitudes of the child, parent, and/or adult.

Children Who Stutter. An abundance of literature and research on children's attitudes toward stuttering is also available (e.g., Brutten, 1984; Brutten & Dunham, 1989; Conture, 2001; Craig & Hancock, 1998; Culatta, Bader, McCaslin, & Thomason, 1985; DeNil & Brutten, 1991; Devour, Nandur, & Manning, 1984; Hancock & Craig, 1998; Peters & Guitar, 1991; Silverman, 1970; Vanryckeghem & Brutten, 1992, 1996, 1997; Vanryckeghem, Hylebos, Brutten & Peleman, 2001; Woods, 1974). This research suggests that the child's continued experience with stuttering produces increased emotional reactions and awareness. Teasing from peers and parental suggestions to "stop and think before you talk" reinforces the concept of being different. The feelings of loss of control (Perkins, Kent, & Curlee, 1991) interact with the child's thoughts about being different to create more stuttering. Knowledge of the child's attitudes toward communication is an important part of his fluency profile.

The Communication Attitude Test (CAT) (Brutten, 1984) assesses the young child's perceptions of talking on a 35-item, true-false measure (Table 4.11). Research found

Table 4.11

Communication Attitude Test©, an instrument designed to assess children's speech-associated attitude.

Name: _____ Age: _____ Sex: _____ Date: _____

Read each sentence carefully so you can say if the sentence is true or false FOR YOU. The sentences are about your talking. If YOU feel that the sentence is right, circle true. If YOU think the sentence about your talking is not right, circle false. Remember, circle false if YOU think the sentence is wrong and true if YOU think it is right. Please make sure that all 35 sentences are circled either true or false. Remember, there are no right or wrong answers to these sentences.

1. I don't talk right.	<u>True</u>	False
2. I don't mind asking the teacher a question in class.	True	<u>False</u>
3. Sometimes words will stick in my mouth when I talk.	<u>True</u>	False
4. People worry about the way I talk.	<u>True</u>	False
5. It is harder for me to give a report in class than it is for most of the other kids.	<u>True</u>	False
6. My classmates don't think I talk funny.	True	<u>False</u>
7. I like the way I talk.	True	<u>False</u>
8. People sometimes finish my words for me.	<u>True</u>	False
9. My parents like the way I talk.	True	<u>False</u>
10. I find it easy to talk to most everyone.	True	<u>False</u>
11. I talk well most of the time.	True	<u>False</u>
12. It is hard for me to talk to people.	<u>True</u>	False
13. I don't talk like other children.	<u>True</u>	False
14. I don't worry about the way I talk.	True	<u>False</u>
15. I don't find it easy to talk.	<u>True</u>	False
16. My words come out easily.	True	<u>False</u>
17. It is hard for me to talk to strangers.	<u>True</u>	False
18. The other kids wish they could talk like me.	True	<u>False</u>
19. Some kids make fun of the way I talk.	<u>True</u>	False
20. Talking is easy for me.	True	<u>False</u>
21. Telling someone my name is hard for me.	<u>True</u>	False
22. Words are hard for me to say.	<u>True</u>	False
23. I talk well with most everyone.	True	<u>False</u>
24. Sometimes I have trouble talking.	<u>True</u>	False
25. I would rather talk than write.	True	<u>False</u>
26. I like to talk.	True	<u>False</u>
27. I am not a good talker.	<u>True</u>	False
28. I wish I could talk like other children.	<u>True</u>	False
29. I am afraid the words won't come out when I talk.	<u>True</u>	False
30. My friends don't talk as well as I do.	True	<u>False</u>
31. I don't worry about talking on the phone.	True	<u>False</u>
32. I talk better with a friend.	<u>True</u>	False
33. People don't seem to like the way I talk.	<u>True</u>	False
34. I let others talk for me.	<u>True</u>	False
35. Reading out loud in class is easy for me.	True	<u>False</u>

(Items underlined receive a score of 1. Vanryckeghem and Brutten (1997) found the mean score for children who stutter was 17.44 and nonstuttering children was 7.05.)

Source: From "Speech-Associated Attitudes of Stuttering and Nonstuttering Children," by L. F. DeNil & G. J. Brutten, 1991, Journal of Speech and Hearing Research, 34, *pp. 60–66. Copyright 1991 by the American Speech-Language-Hearing Association. Reprinted with permission.*

Table 4.12
Concerns of children who stutter.

Interpersonal Concerns	Intrapersonal Concerns
• Being teased by peers because of stuttering. • Answering questions aloud in class. • Making new friends. • Talking on the phone. • Ordering in restaurants. • Asking strangers questions. • Introducing themselves to the opposite sex. • Speaking in front of groups. • Speaking in group discussions. • Afraid of not being accepted because of stuttering.	• Avoidance of the topic of stuttering as though not talking about it would make it go away. • Words get stuck in my mouth. • Feeling not worthy of another's friendship because of stuttering. • Talking is troublesome and difficult. • Not achieving in life because of stuttering. • Being less intelligent because of stuttering. • Loss of control over stuttering.

that the stuttering subjects received a mean score of 17.44, whereas nonstuttering subjects scored a 7.05. The CAT significantly identifies those children with negative speech-associated attitudes that appear to be related to the age of the child; that is, negative speech-associated attitudes increase as children continue to stutter (Vanryckeghem & Brutten, 1997).

Additionally, the CAT provides insight into the intrapersonal and interpersonal beliefs surrounding communication. Bennett, Ramig, and Reveles (1993) separated the items on the CAT into two groups: interpersonal and intrapersonal. Interpersonal involves the bidirectionality of communication, what others think about one's speech. Intrapersonal communication attitudes involve beliefs about themselves and the ability to talk (Table 4.12). Bennett et al. found that for younger children, attitudes focused on the interpersonal aspect of communication. Younger children are more concerned about peers, teacher, and parent perceptions. As age increases, children's attitudes became more internalized, centering on the self. Comments such as "I don't talk right" or "I don't like the way I talk" are examples of intrapersonal, within-the-person, attitudes. The more internalized the attitudes become, the greater the impact stuttering may have on children. They begin to doubt their abilities, focusing on the weaknesses they exhibit, and possibly, distorting reality through negative thought processing. The "I don't talk right" statement may become reshaped to "I can't talk right" or even "I will never talk right." Knowledge of children's attitudes toward speech adds another dimension to their profile-dependent treatment plan.

Parental Attitudes. The child is not alone when communicating but is part of a dynamic family system of which parents are an essential component (Rustin, Botterill, & Kelman, 1996). Parents often bring a myriad of behaviors into the treatment process. There is a corpus of research on selected verbal and nonverbal behaviors of parents of children who stutter. Turn-taking behaviors (Kelly, 1994); rate of speech (Kelly, 1993, 1994; Kelly & Conture, 1992; Meyers & Freeman, 1985b; Stephenson-Opsal & Bernstein

Ratner, 1988); interruptions (Kelly & Conture, 1992; Meyers & Freeman, 1985a); and eye contact (LaSalle & Conture, 1991) are just a sample of parental behaviors that have been researched and reported in the literature.

Added to this literature base is the topic of parental perceptions of their child's communicative competence and attitudes toward stuttering (Bernstein Ratner & Silverman, 2000; Rustin & Purser, 1991; Vanryckeghem, 1995). Bernstein Ratner and Silverman (2000) researched the congruence between parental perceptions of communicative competence and actual test performance of young children who stutter. They found that parents of children who stutter were accurate informants regarding their child's linguistic performance. However, in a study looking at the congruence between parents' and children's attitudes toward stuttering, parents of children who stutter were found to be "poor predictors" of their child's attitudes toward stuttering, often reporting more negative attitudes than self-reported (Vanryckeghem, 1995). This lack of parent-child agreement brings forth the issue of how much the parents' belief system influences their scoring on assessment questionnaires. Parents may not share "a common reality with that of their child" (p. 200). If so, more information needs to be gathered on parental perceptions.

A neglected part of this research is information on the feelings of parents toward the disorder of stuttering. Parents of children who stutter (CWS) may experience feelings of isolation, guilt, and denial (Meyers, 1991; Riley & Riley, 1984; Rustin et al., 1996; Zebrowski & Schum, 1993). Such feelings are highly variable and must be assessed prior to the educational portion of early intervention, that is, the provision of advice on what to do or not do when your child stutters (Starkweather, Gottwald, & Halfond, 1990). However, what are the parents' perceptions or attitudes toward the label of stuttering? Cooper and Cooper (1985) developed The Parent Attitudes Toward Stuttering Checklist (PAT) (Table 4.13), a 25-item "agree" or "do not agree" inventory for which a total score is obtained for each category. A higher score in the "do not agree" category is indicative of more favorable attitudes toward stuttering. This tool provides insight into a wide realm of concepts related to the development, management, and maintenance of stuttering. An important procedural guideline is to give each parent his or her own PAT to complete. Gender differences exist: Men and women think and act very differently. Rustin et al. (1996), based on their extensive experience with families, noted that parents differ in their overall attitudes toward their child's communication difficulties. We want to know the beliefs of mothers and fathers as individuals. So always have duplicate forms available for completion at the time of the diagnostic evaluation.

Adults Who Stutter. Much has been written and researched regarding the attitudes of adults who stutter (e.g., Andrews & Craig, 1988; Andrews & Cutler, 1974, Bennett & Chmela, 1998; Erickson, 1969; Guitar, 1976, 1998; Leith, Mahr, & Miller, 1993; Manning, 1996; Murphy, 1999; Van Riper, 1971, 1973). There is a general consensus between researchers and clinicians that a negative attitude toward communication develops as a result of years of stuttering. Negative attitudes do not cause stuttering, but they may maintain or exacerbate it. As the person continues to stutter, he may anticipate stuttering with tense posturing. The anxiety builds as he waits to see if he will fulfill the prophecy, that is, will I stutter or not. When reinforced, the belief that

Table 4.13

Assessment instrument that is part of the Personalized Fluency Control Therapy—Revised.

Parent Attitudes Toward Stuttering

Name: _____ Date: _____ Child's Name: _____

Instructions: Put a check in the *Agree* or the *Do Not Agree* column after each statement. Make your decision as to how you feel about the statement as quickly as you can. Even if you cannot decide which answer is right for you, check the answer that seems closer to your feelings.

	Agree	Do Not Agree
1. Most of the time I feel I just do not know what to do about my child's stuttering.		
2. I guess I frequently believe that if I ignore the stuttering, it will probably go away.		
3. I do have doubts if speech therapy is necessary for my child.		
4. In thinking about my child's stuttering, I sometimes have the feeling that I might have caused it.		
5. Stuttering is probably a mental or an emotional problem.		
6. Stutterers seem to have certain personality traits.		
7. I guess it is best not to talk about my child's stuttering with my child.		
8. I would agree that parents should help the stuttering child avoid speaking situations in which the child has trouble.		
9. I doubt if my child will ever be able to talk without stuttering being a big problem.		
10. Teachers should not make my child answer questions in class if they think my child will stutter on the answer.		
11. Sometimes I have the feeling that my child could stop stuttering if a little effort was put to it.		
12. I had best encourage my child to plan to do things where there is little demand on speech.		
13. I worry a great deal about my child's stuttering.		
14. Sometimes I find myself wondering if other children will pick up stuttering from playing with my child.		
15. If my child would stop worrying about the stuttering, it would probably go away.		
16. It seems to me that sometimes my child uses the stuttering as a way of getting attention.		
17. I should not expect my child to do as well in school because of the stuttering.		
18. My child's stuttering has been getting progressively worse over the last year or so.		
19. In comparison with others I have known who stutter, my child's stuttering is bad.		
20. I think that I should punish my child in some way each time I hear the stuttering.		
21. Frankly, I am embarrassed in public when I hear my child stutter.		
22. I am afraid that if I talk with my child about his or her feelings about stuttering, it may make it worse.		
23. There is little doubt in my mind that my child is emotionally "different" from other children because of the stuttering.		
24. I have found that telling my child to stop and start over again when he or she stutters has been helpful.		
25. I doubt if the way I feel or act has any effect on my child's stuttering.		
Total		

Source: From Cooper Personalized Fluency Control Therapy (PFCT-3) for Adolescents and Adults, *by E. B. Cooper and C. S. Cooper, 1985, Allen, TX: DLM. Copyright 1985 by DLM. Reprinted with permission.*

talking is difficult is entrenched in the preparations for talking. The development of avoidance behaviors, which are not always effective, frustrate the client who then tenses more and continues to proceed down the stuttering cycle. Unfortunately, such beliefs impact progress in therapy. Treatment efficacy has been linked to the modification of attitudinal concerns as well as speech production.

Guitar (1976) investigated the relationship between pretherapy attitudes of adults who stutter and posttherapy treatment outcomes. Using the Eysenck Personality Instrument, Erickson's S-24 Scale, and the Stuttering Self-Rating of Reactions to Speaking Situations, Guitar found posttherapy percentage of stuttered syllables highly correlated to pretreatment measures of attitude, particularly those involving avoidances. Subjects who exhibited high pretreatment speech avoidances exhibited significantly higher posttreatment stuttered speech. Pretreatment communication attitudes were found to be independent of pretreatment stuttering frequency, perhaps indicating that attitudes make up an entirely different dimension of the disorder of stuttering. For example, a high frequency of stuttering does not necessarily coincide with high levels of negative attitudes toward talking. However, Guitar (1976) concluded that one may predict therapy outcomes from the level of pretreatment attitudes.

Guitar's conclusions are further supported by the findings of Andrews and Cutler (1974), Guitar and Bass (1978), Kraaimaat, Janssen, and Brutten (1988), Sheehan (1969), and Webster (1977). The process of therapeutic change involves not only the development of smooth speech production, but also change in the negative speech-related characteristics. Change in the person's self-concept as a speaker is imperative to therapeutic success (Andrews & Cutler, 1974). Guitar and Bass (1978) firmly believe that modification of one's fluency skills does not automatically ensure changes in communication attitudes. The research studies all conclude that one should not ignore the cognitive aspects of the disorder of stuttering.

Numerous instruments are available to assess attitudes toward stuttering. Erickson (1969) developed the Scale of Communication Attitudes (S-24), which Andrews and Cutler (1974) later modified. The S-24 is a 24-item true-false measure designed to compare attitudes of stuttering and nonstuttering adults (Table 4.14). Another viable instrument is the Stutterer's Self-Rating of Reactions to Speech Situations (Darley & Spriestersbach, 1978) (Table 4.15). This is a 40-item checklist broken into avoidance, reaction, stuttering, and frequency components of the disorder. Woolf (1967) developed the Perceptions of Stuttering Inventory (PSI), a 60-item tool that studies the struggle, avoidance, and expectancy aspects of stuttering. Any of these instruments may become part of the diagnostic profile for the adult client.

Secondary Symptoms

Guitar (1998) defines **secondary symptoms** as behaviors learned in response to continued stuttering. There are two types of secondary symptoms: escape and avoidance behaviors. **Escape behaviors** occur when the speaker is stuttering and attempts to terminate the stutter and finish the word (p. 12). Eye blinks, head nods, hand gestures, or body movements are samples of escape mechanisms. **Avoidance behaviors** occur in response to the person's efforts to prevent stuttering. As the individual foresees a moment of stuttering, he may attempt to stall or postpone it until he is assured he will

Table 4.14

Modified Erickson's Scale of Communication Attitudes (S-24).

Name: _____ Date Completed: _____

Directions: Read each item and decide if the statement is true or false for you. Circle either true or false for each statement:

1. I usually feel that I am making a favorable impression when I talk.	True	False
2. I find it easy to talk with almost everyone.	True	False
3. I find it very easy to look at my audience while speaking to a group.	True	False
4. A person who is my teacher or boss is hard to talk to.	True	False
5. Even the idea of giving a talk in public makes me afraid.	True	False
6. Some words are harder than others for me to say.	True	False
7. I forget all about myself shortly after I begin to give a speech.	True	False
8. I am a good mixer.	True	False
9. People sometimes seem uncomfortable when I am talking to them.	True	False
10. I dislike introducing one person to another.	True	False
11. I often ask questions in group discussions.	True	False
12. I find it easy to keep control of my voice when speaking.	True	False
13. I do not mind speaking before a group.	True	False
14. I do not talk well enough to do the kind of work I'd really like to do.	True	False
15. My speaking voice is rather pleasant and easy to listen to.	True	False
16. I am sometimes embarrassed by the way I talk.	True	False
17. I face most speaking situations with complete confidence.	True	False
18. There are few people I can talk with easily.	True	False
19. I talk better than I write.	True	False
20. I often feel nervous while talking.	True	False
21. I find it hard to make talk when I meet new people.	True	False
22. I feel pretty confident about my speaking ability.	True	False
23. I wish I could say things as clearly as others do.	True	False
24. Even though I knew the right answer, I often failed to give it because I was afraid to speak out.	True	False

Scoring Procedures: Adults who stutter received a mean score of 19.22 with a range from 9–24 on the S-24. Nonstuttering adults received a mean score of 9.14 with a range of 1–21. To receive a total score, each statement earns 1 point if the response matches the following:

1. False	7. False	13. False	19. False
2. False	8. False	14. True	20. True
3. False	9. True	15. False	21. True
4. True	10. True	16. True	22. False
5. True	11. False	17. False	23. True
6. True	12. False	18. True	24. True

Source: From "Stuttering Therapy: The Relation between Changes in Symptom Level and Attitudes," by G. Andrews & J. Cutler, 1974, Journal of Speech and Hearing Disorders, 39, pp. 312–319. Copyright 1974 by the American Speech-Language-Hearing Association. Reprinted with permission.

be able to complete it fluently. **Stalling devices** might include interjections, such as "ah" or "um," **circumlocutions** (talking around the intended word), or excessively long pauses before a word. Guitar (1998) describes the use of **starters** as avoidance reactions to the moment of stuttering. Starters function as a means to jump-start the speech production system. The client may insert a starter before the initial word of an utterance, such as "uh I want to go now."

Table 4.15

Self-Rating of Reactions to Speech Situations used with adults who stutter.

Name: _____ Age _____ Sex _____
Examiner _____ Date _____

After each item put a number from 1–5 in each of the four columns. Start with the right-hand column headed Frequency. Study the five possible answers to be made in responding to each item, and write the number of the answer that best fits the situation for you in each case. Thus, if you habitually take your meals at home and seldom eat in a restaurant, certainly not as often as once a week, write number 5 in the Frequency column opposite item No. 1. "Ordering in a restaurant." In like manner respond to each of the other 39 items by writing the most appropriate number in the Frequency column.

   Now, write the number of the response that best indicates how much you stutter in each situation. For example, if in ordering meals in a restaurant you stutter mildly (for you), write the number 2 in the Stuttering column. Following the same procedure, write your responses in the Reaction column, and finally write your responses in the Avoidance column.

Numbers for each of the columns are to be interpreted as follows:

A. Avoidance
1. I never try to avoid this situation and have no desire to avoid it.
2. I don't try to avoid this situation, but sometimes I would like to.
3. More often than not I do not try to avoid this situation, but sometimes I do try to avoid it.
4. More often than not I do try to avoid this situation.
5. I avoid this situation every time I possibly can.

B. Reaction
1. I definitely enjoy speaking in this situation.
2. I would rather speak in this situation than not.
3. It's hard to say whether I'd rather speak in this situation or not.
4. I would rather not speak in this situation.
5. I very much dislike speaking in this situation.

C. Stuttering
1. I don't stutter at all (or only rarely) in this situation.
2. I stutter mildly (for me) in this situation.
3. I stutter with average severity (for me) in this situation.
4. I stutter more than average (for me) in this situation.
5. I stutter severely (for me) in this situation.

D. Frequency
1. This is a situation I meet very often, two or three times a day, or even more on the average.
2. I meet this situation at least once a day with rare exceptions (except Sunday perhaps).
3. I meet this situation from three to five times a week on the average.
4. I meet this situation once a week, with few exceptions, and occasionally I meet it twice a week.
5. I rarely meet this situation—certainly not as often as once a week.

Table 4.15
Continued

	Avoidance	Reaction	Stuttering	Frequency
1. Ordering in a restaurant				
2. Introducing myself (face to face)				
3. Telephoning to ask price, train fare, etc.				
4. Buying plane, train or bus ticket				
5. Short class recitations (10 words or less)				
6. Telephoning for a taxi				
7. Introducing one person to another				
8. Buying something from store clerk				
9. Conversation with a good friend				
10. Talking with an instructor after class or in his/her office				
11. Long distance call to someone I know				
12. Conversation with father				
13. Asking a girl for date (or talking to a man who asks me for a date)				
14. Making short speech (1–2 minutes)				
15. Giving my name over telephone				
16. Conversation with my mother				
17. Asking a secretary if I can see the employer				
18. Going to house and asking for someone				
19. Making speech to unfamiliar audience				
20. Participating in committee meeting				
21. Asking instructor question in class				
22. Saying hello to friend going by				
23. Asking for a job				
24. Telling a person a message from someone else				
25. Telling a funny story with one stranger in a crowd				
26. Parlor game requiring speech				
27. Reading aloud to friends				
28. Participating in a bull session				
29. Dinner conversation with strangers				
30. Talking with my barber/hairdresser				
31. Telephoning to make appointment or to arrange to meet someone				
32. Answering roll call in class				
33. Asking at a desk for book or card to be filled out, etc.				
34. Talking with someone I don't know well while waiting for bus, class, etc.				
35. Talking with other players during game				
36. Taking leave of a host or hostess				
37. Conversation with friend while walking				
38. Buying stamps at post office				
39. Giving directions to stranger				
40. Taking leave of a girl/boy after date				
Totals				
Average (divide total by # of answers)				

Your observations of the type and quantity of escape and avoidance behaviors used by the client become part of the client's diagnostic profile. These behaviors are symptomatic of the client's level of discomfort with stuttering. Occasionally, the client may report verbally that he doesn't "mind" the stuttering, but you observe the presence of secondary tactics. It is important to understand that secondary behaviors are initially voluntary behaviors, but because of learning principles they become habituated and function at an unconscious level. What was originally a successful strategy to escape or avoid stuttering now is no longer effective. The client, indeed, may not be aware of their presence. A discrepancy between client report and your observations is just one example of the negativity the client feels toward stuttering.

Consistency

Stuttering is highly variable in its frequency and can change at any moment in time. The assessment profile obtained must include information on the client's consistent and/or inconsistent patterns. Samples obtained across differing setting, people present, topics of discussion, and so on, will contribute to determining what may be fluency inducing for each particular client. Chapter 3 outlined the different fluency-enhancing conditions that can be evaluated. In addition to these circumstances, you may also evaluate the client's adaptation response. The adaptation effect occurs when the person who stutters performs an oral reading task repeatedly (Johnson & Knott, 1937) resulting in a reduction in all types of disfluency. This reduction is temporary and does not necessarily transfer to other reading materials or settings. Because the amount of adaptation varies for both adults and children, it must be examined during the course of the diagnostic session(s). Results of adaptation probes will guide the clinician during the beginning stages of therapy. If the client responds favorably to adaptation, use of this strategy may build the client's self-confidence or faith that he can change his speech, thus empowering him to change.

Stimulability

A determination regarding the degree of **stimulability** for managing stuttering is another valuable part of a fluency diagnostic. You may structure a series of tasks, also called trial therapy, to gauge how successfully the client may implement both fluency shaping and stuttering modification strategies. The purpose here is to determine if the client has any prior knowledge/proficiency with therapy techniques or vocabulary and to assess the ability to learn such strategies when provided with instructions and models. The following is an example of clinician/client dialogue during baseline measurements:

Clinician:	"Have you ever heard of a pullout?"
Client:	"No. It doesn't sound familiar."
Clinician:	"Have you heard the expression *easy onset*?"
Client:	"Yes."
Clinician:	"Tell me the definition and show me an easy onset."
Client:	(Client performs task but speech is not noticeably different.)
Clinician:	"Say the word *apple* just like I do." (Clinician models an easy initiation of phonation.)

Client:	(Attempts to reproduce but efforts turn into a real stutter.)
Clinician:	"Try starting your voice real slow on the 'a' in apple. Like this 'a'–pple."
Client:	(Client's productions are successful.)
Clinician:	"Good. Now I want you to use that easy onset when you say the next 20 words."

Certain procedural guidelines are recommended for use when obtaining pre-treatment baseline measures:

- Materials selected for use when obtaining baseline measurements should not be used during actual treatment.
- Collect a sufficient number of trials to determine proficiency, for example, 20 for each level of complexity.
- Use a testing paradigm in which you schedule a series of tasks that start at a difficult level and gradually become easier for the client. For example, you might have different sets of stimuli (20 items) for the sentence level, phrase level, two-word combinations, single words, or syllable productions. Ask the client to generate a sentence for each picture.
- Make no comment about the client's speech efforts. Let him know ahead of time that you will not be providing any feedback during this probing time and you cannot answer any of his questions.

Situational Hierarchy

Over the course of stuttering, clients may develop certain situations in which they anticipate having difficulty with communication. Perhaps one day the client stutters when asking a store clerk for directions. This occurs again and the client establishes a link between stuttering and asking strangers questions. This link is reinforced with repeated experiences and the client establishes the concept that it is difficult to ask strangers questions. This is an example of how feared situations develop in PWS; however, how a client reacts to a particular experience is highly individual. Part of a fluency diagnostic is to determine what situations/words/sounds the client anticipates stuttering so therapy can address these irrational beliefs. You may use both standardized and criterion-referenced checklists to determine such a hierarchy. For children, a worksheet such as Easy-Hard Checklist (Table 4.16) can be completed to provide this information.

The second part of stage 2 is interpreting the information obtained from the testing procedures. Here you use clinical judgment and research information to determine if a problem exists, the severity of the problem, and the overall impact of the problem on the client's ability to communicate effectively. In determining if a problem exists, answer the following questions based on the information gathered during the diagnostic session(s):

1. Does the client's manner of speaking draw adverse attention from the listener?
2. Are parents, teachers, spouses, and/or peers concerned about the speaker's communication?
3. Is the speaker concerned about the ability to get his ideas across or contribute to classroom or work-related discussions?

Table 4.16

This checklist provides a means for obtaining information on a child's situational hierarchy of easy to difficult situations or speech tasks.

Name: _____ Date: _____

	Real Easy	Not So Easy	Hard	Real Hard	Target Areas
Talking to my parents					
Talking to my friends					
Talking about stuttering					
Feeling relaxed when talking					
Introducing myself to people					
Talking to a stranger					
Ordering in restaurants					
Talking on the telephone					
Talking in front of a group					
Reading in front of a group					
Talking to teachers					
Talking without being afraid of sounds					
Talking without changing words					
Raising my hand to answer questions in a group					
Talking without being embarrassed					
Looking at people when I talk					
Feeling good about myself when I talk					

Source: Modified version of an original worksheet by J. Westbrook, unpublished document. Reprinted with permission.

4. Do the speaker's communication abilities inhibit his interactions in educational or occupational environments?

5. Does the speaker believe stuttering has handicapped him in some way?

Stuttering Severity

If a problem exists, you must determine the extent or severity of the problem. Two tools are specifically designed to measure stuttering severity: Riley's (1994) Stuttering Severity Instrument for Children and Adults (SSI-3) and the Iowa Scale of Severity of Stuttering (Sherman, 1952). The SSI-3 (Table 4.17) consists of three scales: frequency, duration, and physical concomitants. Frequency counts of "repetitions or prolongations of

Table 4.17

Stuttering Severity Instrument-3.

Name: _____ Date: _____

Frequency (Use Readers Table or Nonreaders Table, but not both)

Readers Table				Nonreaders Table	
1. Speaking Task		2. Reading Task		3. Speaking Task	
Percentage	Task Score	Percentage	Task Score	Percentage	Task Score
1	2	1	2	1	4
2	3			2	6
3	4	2	4	3	8
4–5	5	3–4	5	4–5	10
6–7	6	5–7	6	6–7	12
8–11	7	8–12	7	8–11	14
12–22	8	13–20	8	12–21	16
22 & up	9	21 & up	9	22 & up	18

Frequency Score (use 1 & 2 or 3) _____

Duration

Average length of three longest stuttering events timed to the nearest 1/10th second		Scaled Score
Fleeting	(.5 sec or less)	2
Half-second	(.5–.9 sec)	4
1 full second	(1.0–1.9 secs)	6
2 seconds	(2.0–2.9 secs)	8
3 seconds	(3.0–4.9 secs)	10
5 seconds	(5.0–9.9 secs)	12
10 seconds	(10–29.9 secs)	14
30 seconds	(30.0–59.9 secs)	16
1 minute	(60 secs or more)	18

Duration Score (2–18) _____

Physical Concomitants

Evaluating Scale   0 = none   1 = not noticeable unless looking for it
2 = barely noticeable to casual observer   3 = distracting
4 = very distracting   5 = severe and painful-looking

Distracting Sounds	Noisy breathing, whistling, sniffing, blowing, clicking sounds 0　1　2　3　4　5
Facial Grimaces	Jaw jerking, tongue protruding, lip pressing, jaw muscles tense 0　1　2　3　4　5
Head Movements	Back, forward, turning away, poor eye contact, constant looking around 0　1　2　3　4　5
Movement of the Extremities	Arm and hand movement, hands about face, torso movement, leg movements, foot-tapping or swinging 0　1　2　3　4　5

Physical Concomitants Score _____

(continued)

Table 4.17

Continued

Total Overall Score		
Frequency _____ + Duration _____ + Physical Concomitants _____ = _____, Percentile _____, Severity _____		

Percentile and Severity Equivalents of SSI-3 Total Overall Score for Preschool Children (N–72)

Total Overall Score	Percentile	Severity
0–8	1–4	Very Mild
9–10	5–11	
11–12	12–23	Mild
13–16	24–40	
17–23	41–60	Moderate
24–26	61–77	
27–28	78–88	Severe
29–31	89–95	
32 and up	96–99	Very Severe

Percentile and Severity Equivalents of SSI-3 Total Overall Score for School-Age Children (N–139)

Total Overall Score	Percentile	Severity
6–8	1–4	Very Mild
9–10	5–11	
11–15	12–23	Mild
16–20	24–40	
21–23	41–60	Moderate
24–27	61–77	
28–31	78–88	Severe
32–35	89–95	
36 and up	96–99	Very Severe

Percentile and Severity Equivalents of SSI-3 Total Overall Score for Adults (N–60)

Total Overall Score	Percentile	Severity
10–12	1–4	Very Mild
13–17	5–11	
18–20	12–23	Mild
21–24	24–40	
25–27	41–60	Moderate
28–31	61–77	
32–34	78–88	Severe
35–36	89–95	
36–46	96–99	Very Severe

Source: From Stuttering Severity Instrument for Children and Adults *(3rd ed.), by G. D. Riley, 1994, Austin, TX: Pro-Ed. Copyright 1994 by Pro-Ed. Adapted with permission.*

sounds or syllables including silent prolongations" (p. 4) are obtained for both readers and nonreaders. The three longest stuttering events are chosen to obtain an average duration measure. The physical concomitants subscale includes rating of the following categories: distracting sounds, facial grimaces, head movements, and movements of the extremities. A total overall score is then obtained and compared against age-appropriate norms. The Iowa Scale of Severity of Stuttering (Table 4.18) is a categorical measure in which various observers rate the speaker's level of severity. The scale ranges from 0 (no stuttering) to 7 (very severe) with a brief explanation for each numerical value.

Keep in mind that stuttering severity is an essential component of the diagnostic portfolio, yet it can be influenced by your perceptions (i.e., nonstandardized, subjective evaluations). Your judgment alone is insufficient for determining severity ratings. In some work settings, the speech-language pathologist does not remain at one site for any length of time (e.g., the public schools). In the era of documentation and treatment efficacy, it is your role and duty to assess each individual properly and

Table 4.18
The Iowa Scale of Stuttering Severity.

Speaker: _____ Age: _____ Sex: _____ Date: _____
Rater: _____ Identification: _____

Instructions: Indicate your identification by some such term as "speaker's clinician," "clinical observer," "clinical student," or "friend," "mother," "classmate," et cetera. Rate the severity of the speaker's stuttering on a scale from 0 to 7, as follows:

0   No stuttering
1   Very mild—stuttering on less than 1 percent of words; very little relevant tension; disfluencies generally less than one second in duration; patterns of disfluency simple; no apparent associated movements of body, arms, legs, or head.
2   Mild—stuttering on 1 to 2 percent of words; tension scarcely perceptible; very few, if any, disfluencies last as long as a full second; patterns of disfluency simple; no conspicuous associated movements of body, arms, legs, or head.
3   Mild to moderate—stuttering on 2 to 5 percent of words; tension noticeable but not very distracting; most disfluencies do not last longer than a full second; patterns of disfluency mostly simple; no distracting associated movements.
4   Moderate—stuttering on about 5 to 8 percent of words; tension occasionally distracting; disfluencies average about one second in duration; disfluency patterns characterized by an occasional complicating sound or facial grimace; an occasional distracting associated movement.
5   Moderate to severe—stuttering on about 8 to 12 percent of words; consistently noticeable tension; disfluencies average about 2 seconds in duration; a few distracting sounds and facial grimaces; a few distracting associated movements.
6   Severe—stuttering on about 12 to 25 percent of words; conspicuous tension; disfluencies average 3 to 4 seconds in duration; conspicuous distracting sounds and facial grimaces; conspicuous distracting associated movements.
7   Very severe—stuttering on more than 25 percent of words; very conspicuous tension; disfluencies average more than 4 seconds in duration; very conspicuous distracting sounds and facial gestures; very conspicuous distracting associated movements.

Source: From Johnson, Darley, Spriestersback, Diagnostic Methods in Speech Pathology, *2/e. Published by Allyn and Bacon, Boston, MA. Copyright © 1978 by Pearson Education. Reprinted by permission of the publisher.*

have a complete record of their assessment history. Using a published instrument rather than just personal perceptual judgement allows the next therapist to understand the basis for placement and be able to measure changes in severity over time.

Overall Impact on Communicative Competence

Once a problem is identified and the severity classified, you must determine the extent to which the individual's manner of speaking impacts his **communication competence,** that is, his ability to interpret and impart information in an age-appropriate, timely, and socially acceptable manner. The presence of a disorder does not necessarily imply a handicap or disability is present. Prins (1997) discussed the World Health Organization's classification system of human behaviors involving "impairment," "disability," and "handicap" as related to stuttering. Let's review Prins's definitions for these terms:

- **Impairment:** loss or deficit that may underline the evidence of a disability, for example, the neurological system is inadequate to handle the motor demands placed on it during certain situations.
- **Disability:** observable breakdown in performance, that is, the emergence of core stuttering behaviors in the speech of the individual.
- **Handicap:** effect of the disability on attitudes and beliefs of the individual. For people who stutter, the extent of the handicap may have little to do with the degree of disability. "Clients who stutter infrequently and with little overt evidence may represent the extremes of handicap. However irrational, they may blame stuttering for virtually all their self-perceived shortcomings. In such cases the disability, however slight, is a fundamental impediment of self-image, social inadequacy, and vocational attainment" (p. 336).

Determining the extent to which stuttering handicaps the individual will be based on the age and/or daily environment of the client. The school-based therapist must determine if the presence of a fluency disorder impacts the child's educational functioning. A narrow interpretation of the "educational impact statement" has been and is currently used to exclude a child who stutters, who is not having academic difficulties, from receiving services in the public schools. However, academic success goes beyond just grade evaluations. In any school curriculum, there are essential elements of instruction requiring oral communication proficiency as well as the development of the self-concept as a contributing member of society. These components of instruction can be applied to the "functional implications" requirements to be met for inclusion in speech therapy within the school setting.

The adult who stutters may experience workplace discrimination and self-perceived beliefs regarding the ability to perform in certain occupations. Clients may express a long-standing desire to become a "police officer," but because of their belief they would not be able to talk on demand, they did not pursue this career. Clients' attitudes and beliefs interact with their speech behaviors to impact their overall functioning, thereby creating a handicap.

Interpretation of test results also involves the determination of whether the client is likely to recover from stuttering without intervention. Making this prognosis is especially relevant for the young preschool child who is showing signs of stuttering. The literature states that anywhere from 40% to 80% of children who stutter recover spontaneously on their own. The work of Conture, Guitar, and Yairi and many other colleagues provide much insight to help make a prognostic statement. Table 4.19 lists positive and negative **prognostic indicators** that have been reported in the literature.

You may also use Riley's Stuttering Prediction Instrument (SPI) (1984) when testing the young child who stutters. The SPI includes seven sections: history, reactions, part-word repetitions, prolongations, frequency, and norm tables for children who stutter and those who have recovered from stuttering. Performance on sections II through V produce scores that are added together to get a total score. Section VI contains a table of the distribution of SPI scores for 85 children who stutter between the ages 3 and 8 years. Section VII contains a table of the distribution of SPI scores for 17 children whose disfluencies had not become chronic. The total score is converted to a stanine and percentile rank, which is equivalent to severity ratings ranging between subclinical to very severe for both populations of children. Table 4.20 provides basic fluency counts you may use to differentiate between normal nonfluency and beginning stuttering.

Table 4.19
Positive and negative prognostic indicators for spontaneous recovery from stuttering without treatment.

Positive Indicators	Negative Indicators
• Less than 12 months postonset	• Family history of persistent stuttering
• No familial history of stuttering; or a history of recovered stuttering	• Male
	• Greater than 14 months postonset
• Female	• Increased number of SLDs
• Absence of secondary symptoms	• Sudden rise in SERs
• High variability	• Concomitant disorders
• 1–2 iterations in repetitions	• Signs of awareness
• Lack of awareness	• Struggle and avoidances
• Few SLDs	• Clustering of disfluencies
• Good stimulability	• Greater than 3 iterations
• Good language and articulation skills	• Unable to produce rote, automatic tasks fluently
	• Other confounding factors

Table 4.20
Quantitative differences in the speech characteristics of nonstuttering and stuttering preschoolers.

Characteristic	Nonstuttering	Stuttering
Total Disfluency Rates	6–8/100 words	15/100 words; 17/100 syllables
Number of SERs	2/100 words	9/100 syllables
Number of SLDs	3/100 words	11/100 syllables
Number of Iterations	1 repetition/word	2+ repetitions/word
Number of Clusters	not present usually	6 times as many
Number of Head/Neck Movements	present at times	2 times as many

REPORT WRITING

Stage 3 of the diagnostic process involves the dissemination of findings through written documentation (i.e., the diagnostic report). Diagnostic reports differ depending on the work setting of the clinician. Some reports provide the bare necessities; others are detail-oriented, extensive client profiles. The following recommended diagnostic report format consists of five sections and is a general guide for organizing and synthesizing information into a written document. Sample diagnostic reports are located in Appendices D and E. When writing the diagnostic report, you (and your supervisor) can utilize Bennett's Report Writing Checklist (Table 4.21) to determine if all components are included in the report. Simply check each section at a time, indicating with a check mark whether the information is or is not provided. Report writing takes practice, and even the best clinician can use a helpful guide at times.

Fluency Evaluation

Opening Paragraph: Who, When, Where, and Why

The opening of the evaluation includes information on who came to the session, when (date of evaluation), where the diagnostic was held, and why the client was there. Be sure to identify the referral source, if there is one. Referrals come from many different sources (e.g., teachers, parents, employers, spouses, etc.). Knowing this information sets the tone for the following sections.

Summary of Background Information

Information in this section depends on whether the client is an adult or child. Present a chronological sequence of events starting with birth through the present.

- Open this summary with a statement regarding the child's family structure. For example, "Greg, a 7-year 8-month-old boy, is the youngest of three children in the Jones family. He lives with both parents and siblings Eric (12 years) and Susie (10 years). English is spoken in the home and was the language used throughout the evaluation."
- The next section includes information on the prenatal, natal, and postnatal histories reported by the mother or on the case history form. If a significant event occurred during any period, make sure you include it in this summary. At times, a simple statement, such as "Prenatal, natal, and birth histories were unremarkable," is all that is required.
- Medical history is next. Here you present the client's general health picture. Report any information on childhood diseases, accidents, or injuries. Any history of recurrent otitis media is especially important to note. If the client has a positive history of ear infections, obtain and report the frequency and treatment received for this condition. Knowledge about the type of medication received is especially important because a high or repeated dose of antibiotics can impact hearing acuity and speech development. If pressure equalization tubes (PET)

Table 4.21
Bennett's Report Writing Checklist, a useful guide for writing diagnostic reports.

Task Description	Yes	No
Section 1: Opening Paragraph		
Who came with the client?		
When was the evaluation?		
Where was the evaluation?		
Why did the client/parent request the evaluation?		
Was there a referral source?		
Section 2: Background Information		
Is the client's name, age, and family structure identified?		
Is the language spoken by the client or in the home identified?		
Is the language of the evaluation identified?		
Is information on prenatal, birth history, and postnatal events identified?		
Is there a description of client's general medical history?		
Is there any mention of recurrent otitis media and its treatment?		
Are developmental milestones in the area of motor development reported?		
Are speech milestones reported?		
Is there a detailed description of the client's current speech skills related to reason for the evaluation?		
Is there mention of any prior evaluations or speech therapy? If so, where, when, and what were the outcomes?		
Is there mention of the academic history of the client?		
Is there a description of what the client/parent hopes to achieve from the diagnostic session?		
Is there mention of the client/parent goals if therapy is warranted?		
Section 3: Test Results		
Hearing:		
Was a screen performed or a formal test given?		
If so, is there mention of frequencies tests and at what level?		
Is there mention if the client passed or failed the exam?		

(continued)

Table 4.21
Continued

Task Description	Yes	No
Oral Motor Examination:		
Was a screen utilized or a formal examination completed?		
Is there mention of the structure and function of the oral mechanism?		
If oral motor planning difficulties were seen, are DDK rates reported?		
Intellectual Performance:		
Is there any comment regarding intelligence?		
Was a standardized IQ test administered?		
If so, what test was given and by whom?		
What are the scores obtained on this test?		
Voice:		
Was a screen utilized or a formal examination completed?		
Is there mention of the client's vocal quality, pitch, and intonation?		
Articulation:		
What instrument was administered?		
Is there a description of the client's error patterns?		
Is there a description of the client's error consistency?		
Is there a description of the client's stimulability?		
Is there a comment regarding the client's intelligibility?		
Language:		
Were receptive and expressive language skills screened?		
Is there mention of the test names?		
If the client failed the screen, is there mention of additional testing?		
If so, what were the test names and derived scores?		
Was a language sample analyzed?		
If so, what were the results of the analysis?		
Is there mention of consistencies between standardized tests and nonstandardized observations?		
Is there mention of specific client strengths and weaknesses?		
Is there mention of the client's interactional/pragmatic skills?		
Fluency:		
Is there mention of the number, type, and size of samples obtained?		
Is there mention of the instrument used to analyze the samples?		

Table 4.21
Continued

Task Description	Yes	No
Are any of the following counts reported? • Stuttered words/minute • Percentage of stuttered words • Percentage of stuttered syllables • Number of iterations • Speech rate		
Is there mention of the impact of increases in linguistic complexity?		
Is there a description of the speaking patterns of the client?		
Is stuttering severity reported?		
Is the loci of tension reported?		
Were the client's attitudes toward talking assessed?		
Is there mention of the client's comments regarding his speech?		
Is there mention of situational fears and avoidance behavior?		
Is there mention of the consistency of the client's speaking patterns?		
Is there mention of the client's stimulability factors?		
Section 4: Diagnostic Summary		
Is there mention of the parameters in which the client has difficulties?		
Is there mention of the severity of the client's difficulties?		
Is there mention of the parameters in which the client is within normal limits?		
Is there mention of the impact these difficulties have on client's communication skills?		
Is there mention of any confounding variables?		
Is there a prognosis for improvement statement?		
Section 5: Recommendations		
Is there mention of who received the recommendations?		
Is there mention of whether therapy is indicated?		
If so, is there mention of the frequency, duration, and service delivery model?		
Is there mention of the direction of treatment?		
Is there mention of the role of parent/significant other in therapy?		
Is there mention of required re-evaluations?		
Is there mention of any needed referrals?		
Is there a signature of the evaluator with degree, title, and license number indicated?		

were inserted, obtain information on when, how long they were in place, and whether they remediated the frequency of ear infections.

- Report development milestones in the areas of both motor and speech. Many standard case history forms have extensive motor developmental milestones but are weak on speech milestones. You may want to supplement this information with a more detailed investigation of speech development.
- The history of speech difficulties experienced by the client comes next. Note when the difficulties were first noticed, by whom, and under what circumstances. Other relevant information may include a steady progression in stuttering, the parents' perceptions of why their child is stuttering, and what they do to help. Is the client aware of his difficulties? Report any comments the child has made regarding his speech. Indicate if there is a familial history of speech/language disorders.
- Previous therapy for stuttering comes next. Report answers to the following questions: Has the client received any assistance for his speech, and if so, what did it involve and how long was the therapy? What does the parent/client think was most helpful and what was the least helpful? Any other comments about the client's stuttering should be reported here, preferably using the words spoken or written by the individual.
- Academic information, such as school, teacher, grades, strengths and weaknesses, and enrollment in special education is important to the child's diagnostic profile. During the parent interview and evaluation process, you will have ascertained the overall success or failure experienced by the child in the school environment. When reporting this information, make sure you note if the parent is providing the information or if you actually talked with the teacher.
- Reflection on what the client/parent hope to achieve from speech therapy services concludes the background information section of the diagnostic report.

Test Results

A general comment about the client's demeanor and behavior during the diagnostic starts this section. Note three types of behaviors: level of cooperation, interaction, and knowledge. For example, "Steve entered the diagnostic session without any hesitation. He cooperated fully with examiner requests and completed all tasks required of him, despite being shy and quiet."

- *Hearing.* A comment is usually made regarding performance on the hearing screening or tympanometric finding with an overall impression of hearing acuity by the examiner.
- *Intellectual Performance.* Indicators can be obtained through several sources: school reports or standardized testing. I prefer to administer a nonverbal IQ test to rule out the possibility of intellectual functioning as a confounding variable to treatment outcomes.
- *Oral Peripheral Examination.* Make a brief comment regarding the structure and function of the oral mechanism, noting any significant observations that may help clarify the client's speech behavior. It has been suggested that the oral motor system in PWS may be inferior to that of nonstuttering peers. In fact, Riley and Riley

(1986) reported approximately 69% of children who stutter in their study exhibited deficits in oral motor coordination. If oral motor difficulties are suspect, obtain and report diadokokinetic rates or administer a formal measure, such as Riley's (1986) Oral Motor Planning assessment procedure.

- *Voice.* A subjective evaluation of the client's pitch, intonation, and quality of speech meets the minimum requirements of an informal screen. An ENT referral is indicated when vocal quality appears raspy or hoarse, indicative of possible vocal pathology, such as vocal nodules. Occasionally, vocal pathology may be present due to the excessive tension in the laryngeal area when stuttering. The PWS who experiences severe laryngeal blocks with an explosive release may develop vocal nodules or polyps.

- *Articulation.* An examination of the client's articulatory abilities is essential, especially when testing children who stutter. Conture (2001) reported that 25% to 45% of children who stutter also had deficits in articulation. Disordered phonology coexists with stuttering in 40% of children according to Louko, Edwards, and Conture (1990). These research studies and many clinical observations confirm phonology as the most prevalent of all concomitant problems. A thorough look at the client's articulation strengths and weaknesses is crucial to the development of the treatment plan.

- *Language.* Language skills are an important factor influencing the client's communication abilities; therefore, an informal screen of receptive and expressive language ability is minimally necessary. Nippold (1990), in a review of the literature, failed to find support for a high co-occurrence rate of language delays and stuttering. Although a subgroup of children may exhibit both language and fluency problems, there is not a high probability this will be the case in the majority of children who stutter. However, you must ascertain if the client has age-appropriate language skills and assess accordingly.

- *Fluency.* The organization of information on the client's speech fluency may follow a particular flow, beginning with the basic frequency counts and patterns obtained from the transcribed language analysis. A discussion of the client's patterns of speech breakdowns, that is, more typical and less typical disfluencies, supports the numerical data already provided. This discussion may include information on clustering, number of iterations, rate of speech, secondary behaviors, and loci of tension. Comments about attitudes toward communication, avoidance behaviors, and situational hierarchies come next. Report severity ratings as well as the outcome of trial-therapy efforts and any measures of consistency gathered. To conclude the fluency section, make a subjective statement regarding the impact of stuttering on the client's overall communicative effectiveness.

Diagnostic Summary

The diagnostic summary is a short paragraph of the relevant findings of the evaluation. Begin the summary with an indication of the presence of a difference, delay, or disorder in what parameter(s) and to what degree of severity. A comment on the parameters that were within normal limits should follow. Bring any confounding variables,

Table 4.22
An example of a diagnostic statement written for insurance reimbursement.

Patient Name: Brian S.
Reason for treatment: Stuttering Disorder (307.00)
Date of Initial Diagnosis: September 17, 1999

   I. ***Functional Abilities/Strengths:*** Voice, hearing, language, and articulation skills were judged to be strengths for Brian.

   II. ***Functional Limitations/Diagnosed Difficulties:*** Brian exhibits a moderate fluency disorder (**307.00**) that interferes with his ability to communicate effectively with family, school, and community members. His speech is characterized by sound/syllable repetitions accompanied with excessive tension that disrupts the continuity of speech. He currently has difficulty initiating phonation, which he reacts to with visual signs of struggle (i.e., facial grimaces). He is beginning to show awareness of his communication difficulties through comments such as "I can't talk right" and "My words stick."

   III. ***Comments/Clinical Summary:*** It is recommended that Brian enroll in individual speech therapy (**92507**) to improve his speech fluency. Prognosis is judged good due to Brian's age, strong language skills, and his parents' desire to help their son.

   IV. ***Short-Term Goals:*** Time Frame 3–6 months
      1. Brian will use easy onsets, light articulatory contacts, and phrasing techniques to establish fluency in words, phrases, and sentences.
      2. Brian will name the parts of the body used to make speech and identify what he does with these speech helpers when he stutters.
      3. Brian will openly discuss stuttering and insert easy repetitions and prolongations into his speech in therapy, home, and school settings.
      4. Parents will follow through on home assignments.

   V. ***Long-Terms Goals:*** Time Frame 6–12 months
      1. Brian will use his fluency strategies in home, school, and community settings.
      2. Brian will improve his speech-monitoring skills when interacting with others.
      3. Brian will decrease his reactive behaviors to speech breakdowns.
      4. Parents will be active participants in the treatment process to ensure transfer to other environments.

Rehabilitation Progress: GOOD

   VI. ***Treatment Plan/Modalities:***
      Frequency: 2x/week Duration: 45 min. Anticipated Discharge: 12 months

Betty Jones, Ph.D., CCC-SLP	Date
Speech Language Pathologist	
Texas License #44491	

factors that may impact therapeutic success, to the attention of the reader. A statement regarding prognosis for improvement with and without therapy concludes the diagnostic summary.

Recommendations

Several components should be in the recommendation section of a diagnostic report:

- Who received the recommendations?
- Is speech therapy indicated?

- Where is the therapy to be provided?
- If so, what is the recommended frequency of sessions, length of each session, and type of service delivery model (i.e., individual or group therapy)
- What is the recommended direction of treatment (e.g., fluency shaping, stuttering modification, or an integrated approach)?
- Expectations for parental involvement and follow-through with assignments should be written into the recommendations.
- Any referrals to outside agencies if deemed necessary.
- If you feel the information obtained on the child's communication patterns was not sufficient, include a recommendation for further testing.
- Close the recommendation section with signature lines indicating who conducted the evaluation along with credentials and license number.

Certain employment settings may require the clinician to develop a diagnostic statement for submission to insurance companies. This should be a concise one-page document, providing the necessary information the insurance company requires for reimbursement of therapy services. The diagnostic statement might include, but is certainly not limited to, the following components: functional abilities/strengths, functional limitations/diagnosed difficulties (including ICD 9 codes), comments/clinical summary, short-term goals with projected time frame, long-term goals with projected time frame, rehabilitation progress/prognosis, frequency and duration of services, and anticipated discharge. Table 4.22 provides an example of a diagnostic statement for a child who stutters.

CHAPTER SUMMARY

When determining the fluency profile for a person who stutters, you engage in a three-stage process: planning and information gathering, testing and interpretation, and report writing. Establishing a positive client/clinician relationship through effective interview skills enables you to understand clients and their particular affective, behavioral, and cognitive responses to stuttering. You then assess the quantitative and qualitative features of the disorder to determine the severity of the problem and its overall impact on the person's communicative competence. Your last responsibility is to summarize this information in a professional document representative of the client's strengths and weaknesses, that is, the fluency profile. This profile sets the stage for the development of client-dependent treatment plans in which you and the client enter into a therapeutic relationship with certain goals established.

STUDY QUESTIONS

1. What are the characteristics of an ideal fluency assessment?
2. Triangulation is based on what theory of stuttering?

3. Why is the client/clinician relationship critical to understanding the client?

4. Name the three stages of the assessment process.

5. Define funneling and describe its use during an interview.

6. Generate five closed questions. Can you rephrase these to make them open questions?

7. How might you organize the diagnostic findings for the parent/client?

8. What is the role of pattern analysis in the assessment process?

9. Why do frequency counts fail to capture the essence of stuttering?

10. Pair up with a classmate. Take turns practicing SOLER during a 5-minute listening exercise. Discuss the experience.

11. Why is it important to treat each parent as an individual when measuring attitudes toward stuttering?

12. Differentiate between escape and avoidance behaviors.

13. Describe a scenario in which an impairment and disability exist, yet a handicap is absent.

14. Differentiate between quantitative and qualitative features of a person's fluency profile.

5

Intervention Paradigms and Procedures

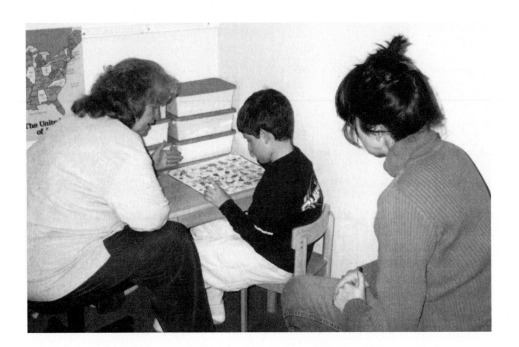

Normal Speaking Process Interference Education
Hard versus Easy Contacts
Negative Practice
Three-Way Contrast Drills
Speech Assertiveness and Openness
Voluntary Stuttering
Cancellations
Pullouts and Freezing
Hierarchy Analysis

Reducing Avoidance Behaviors
Facilitating Awareness and Monitoring
Developing Positive Speech Attitudes
Guiding Principles of Intervention
Success-Driven Model
Teaching Paradigm
Speech Analogies
Treatment Philosophy
Client/Clinician Relationship
Adolescent/Adult Considerations
Child-Based Activities

LEARNER OBJECTIVES

- Differentiate among fluency-shaping, stuttering modification, and integrated approaches to the treatment of stuttering disorders.

- Identify factors that influence the development of the client's treatment plan.

- Define the various components that may be selected for a client's treatment plan.

- Provide a rationale for inclusion of certain treatment strategies in a client's treatment plan.

- Describe the differences between teaching versus testing instructional paradigms.

- Understand the role of analogies in the therapy process.

- Describe how automaticity of speech strategies may influence the client's progress in therapy.

- Understand the importance of establishing a strong client/clinician relationship during the initial stages of therapy.

KEY TERMS

automaticity
autonomy
cancellations
change process
choice making
client/clinician relationship
desensitization
easy contacts
empowerment
fixed-ratio of reinforcement

fluency initiating gestures
fluency-shaping therapy
freezing
habit
integrated therapy
intermittent modeling
modeling
negative practice
phrasing

pseudostuttering
pullouts
reinforcement
speech assertiveness
stuttering modification therapy
success-driven model
triads
volition
voluntary stuttering

The dynamics of working with people who stutter are fascinating, yet challenging. Awareness of difficulties communicating may lead the individual deep into the stuttering syndrome with affective, cognitive, and behavioral factors becoming strongly entrenched in the person's communication style (Cooper, 1993; DeNil & Brutten, 1991; Leith, 1984). For the majority of people who continue to stutter, therapy must move from an indirect focus on fluency orientation to a more integrative approach specifically addressing the behaviors, feelings, and thoughts experienced when stuttering. But first, let's review the different types of intervention approaches found in the literature that may be used with people who stutter. Gregory (1979) and Guitar (1998) provided an excellent review of three types of treatment approaches for stuttering disorders: fluency-shaping, stuttering modification, and integrated therapy.

TREATMENT PARADIGMS

Fluency-Shaping Therapy

Based on learning principles and the effects of delayed auditory feedback, **fluency-shaping therapy** came to the forefront of stuttering intervention during the 1960s (Bloodstein, 1995; Curlee & Perkins, 1969). The primary goal is to achieve either controlled fluency, spontaneous fluency, or normal fluency. Characteristics of fluency-shaping programs include (1) establishment of fluent speech, (2) use of behavioral principles, (3) quantitative measurements, (4) a highly structured therapy routine, (5) emphasis on data collection, and (6) systematic, planned transfer (Figure 5.1). Programmed therapies, such as Costello Ingham's Extended Length of Utterance (ELU) (1980, 1983, 1999) and Ryan's Gradual Increase in Length and Complexity of Utterance (GILCU) (1971, 1974, 1986), are examples of two widely used fluency-shaping paradigms.

Janice Costello Ingham

Costello Ingham (1983, 1999) discussed a fluency-shaping program incorporating the use of behavior principles in the establishment of spontaneous, natural-sounding stutter-free speech. The Extended Length of Utterance (ELU) behavioral treatment program is appropriate for young children between the ages of 3 ½ to 6 or 7. Although involving a set of specific steps, this program can be individualized for each client using "an overarching set of principles" (p. 75), that is, speaking tasks, measurements, and response-contingent feedback. Speaking tasks, such as monologue, reading, and conversational speech, are controlled for length and complexity through the ELU program (see Table 5.1). The first step is to have the individual talk as much as possible. Most of the therapy is conducted at the conversational level, unless the client requires a more structured monologue. Spontaneously fluent utterances are reinforced with positive feedback and tokens, whereas stuttered speech receives immediate negative feedback. A major feature of this program is its use of ongoing measurement through

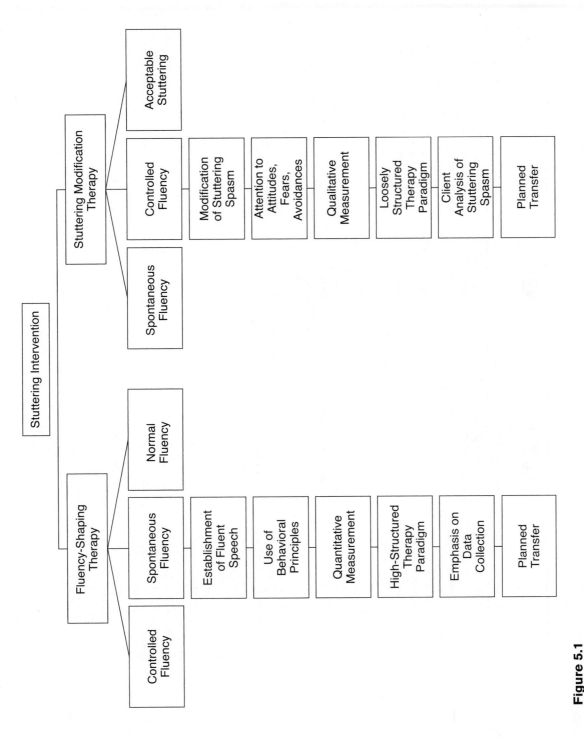

Figure 5.1

Presentation of the characteristics of fluency-shaping and stuttering modification therapy for stuttering.

Source: From "Working with 7–12 Year Old Children Who Stutter: Ideas for Intervention in the Public Schools," by P. R. Ramig & E. Bennett, 1995, Language Speech and Hearing Services in Schools, 26, p. 140. Copyright 1995 by the American Speech-Language-Hearing Association. Reprinted with permission.

Table 5.1

Outline of a therapy paradigm designed to establish fluency in children.

		Extended Length of Utterance Program			
Step	Discriminative Stimuli	Response (+ & −)	±Consequences and Schedules	Criteria	Measurement
1	Minimum of 50 cards containing pictures labeled by monosyllabic words within vocabulary range of client—presented without model—one card at a time. Example: car, leaf. Instructions: "Say each word."	+ : Stutter-free 1-syllable word. − : Stuttered syllable	+ : Positive social reinforcer ("Good!" "Right!" "Excellent!" "Perfect speech!" etc.), 1:1 Positive token reinforcer, 1:1 (Tokens exchanged for backup reinforcers throughout the program as follows: 10:1, 20:1, 35:1. The exchange rate may be altered backward as longer responses are required or when declining levels of correct responding indicate the need for increased motivation) − : "Stop," said by clinician during or immediately following a moment of stuttering; client must stop speaking briefly; 1:1.	Pass: 10 consecutive stutter-free responses Fail: 7 consecutive stuttered trials or 100 trials without meeting pass criterion.	(+) Each stutter-free response (−) Each stuttered response At completion of step, calculate % correct responses and number of trials required to meet criterion.
2	Minimum of 50 cards containing (a) pictures labeled by 1-syllable words presented in pairs, plus (b) a minimum of 50 cards containing pictures labeled by 2-syllable words, plus (c) a minimum of 50 cards containing pictures to evoke two-syllable syntactic utterances. Example, (a) car-house, (b) mother, (c) my cat. Instructions: "Tell me what's in these pictures."	+ : Stutter-free 2-syllable utterance − : Any stuttered syllable	+ : Same as above − : Same as above	Same as above	Same as above
3	Same kinds of stimuli as a, b, c above except selected to evoke 3-syllable word strings, single words, and syntactic word combinations.	+ : Stutter-free 3-syllable utterance − : Any stuttered syllable	+ : Same as above − : Same as above	Same as above	Same as above

4	Same kinds of stimuli as a, b, c above except selected to evoke 4-syllable utterances.	+ : Stutter-free 4-syllable utterance – : Any stuttered syllable	Same as above	Same as above	Same as above
5	Same kinds of stimuli as c above except selected to evoke 5-syllable utterances (NOTE: Do not include 5-syllable words).	+ : Stutter-free 5-syllable utterance – : Any stuttered syllable	Same as above	Same as above	Same as above
6	Same kinds of stimuli as c above except selected to evoke 6-syllable utterances	+ : Stutter-free 6-syllable utterance – : Any stuttered syllable	Same as above	Same as above	Same as above
Practice	Minimum of 50 pictures containing lots of activity, toys and play, topic cards. Instructions: "Tell me about this (present one stimulus) and keep talking until I say 'OK.' I want you to talk for 3 sec. I'll show you." Describe one picture in relatively slow, simple, connected speech and stop at the end of 3 sec, in the middle of a sentence, if necessary, and click the stopwatch at the same time. Show the child that the stopwatch is at 3 sec. Demonstrate on two or three different stimuli. Then say, "Now it's your turn. Keep talking until I stop the watch and say 'OK.'" For some clients it may be necessary to practice using "story retell" tasks wherein the clinician speaks about the picture for 3 sec and then the child repeats the task in his or her own words for 3 sec.	+ : Continuous talking in connected speech for a duration of 3 sec (stuttering allowed) – : Pauses, problems thinking of things to say, etc. Be sure client learns to stop as soon as the watch stops, even if utterances is not completed. Be sure client does not increase speaking rate in an attempt to complete utterance before the time is up.	+ : Positive social reinforcer, 1:1 – : Re-explain and/or change stimulus materials. Helpful to let child watch the clock.	Pass: 3 consecutive correct responses Fail: Continue task as practice until child meets pass criterion.	Start timing with stopwatch when client begins talking. Do not initiate child's response by saying "Go!" and thereby imply that a fast speaking rate of hurried speech is appropriate. Just say "Start when you're ready" and start the clock when the child begins speaking.

(continued)

159

Table 5.1
Continued

Step	Discriminative Stimuli	Response (+ & −)	±Consequences and Schedules	Criteria	Measurement
7	Same picture, topic cards, and toy stimuli as above, presented in random order. Instructions: "Tell me about this one and keep talking until I say 'OK,' just like you've been doing." If necessary, give "story re-tell" models until the child is able to generate utterances independently.	+ : Stutter-free 3-sec monologue connected speech utterance (monologue = uninterrupted by the clinician) − : Any moment of stuttering	+ : Positive social reinforcer, 1:1 Positive token reinforcer, 1:1 − : "Stop," said by clinician during or immediately following moment of stuttering; client must briefly stop speaking; 1:1 (Be sure you do not say "stop" at the end of stutter-free utterances when the required speaking time has been reached. Say "Good," etc.)	Pass: Ten consecutive stutter-free monologue responses Fail: Seven consecutive stuttered trials or 75 trials without passing the step	(+) Each stutter-free response (−) Each stuttered response At the completion of the step, calculate percent of correct trials required to meet criterion
8	Same stimuli and instructions as above	+ : Stutter-free 5 sec monologue connected speech utterance − : Any moment of stuttering	+ : Same as above − : Same as above	Same as above	Same as above
9	Same stimuli and instructions as above	+ : Stutter-free 10-sec monologue connected speech utterance − : Any moment of stuttering	+ : Same as above − : Same as above	Same as above	(+) Each stutter-free response (−) Each stuttered response For every third or fourth trial, count number of syllables spoken in 10 sec and multiply × 6 for approximate SPM speaking rate. At completion of the step calculate percent of correct trials, number of trials required to meet criterion, and average SPM (based on all trials for which rate data were taken).

160

10	Same stimuli and instructions as above	+: Stutter-free 20 sec monologue connected speech utterance −: Any moment of stuttering −: Any utterance >160 SPM	+: Same as above −: Same as above −: Reminder to speak a bit more slowly, 1:1.	Same as above	Same as above (for rate data, multiply 20-sec syllable count × 3 for approximate SPM for each trial).
11	Same stimuli and instructions as above	+: Stutter-free 30-sec monologue connected speech utterance −: Any moment of stuttering	+: Same as above: "Refreshing" the stimuli used as positive reinforcers may also be appropriate here, or at any time in the treatment when the child's attention/focus appears to wane −: Same as above. Also, for some children it may be appropriate to increase the in-fluence of feedback for stuttering by adding the removal of one token for each stuttered response (response cost). This can be added here, or whenever it seems apparent that additional focus/effort is required on the child's part.	Same as above	Same as above (for rate data, multiply 30-sec syllable count × 2 for approximate SPM for each trial).
12	Same stimuli and instructions as above	−: Any utterance > 160 SPM +: Stutter-free 1-min monologue connected speech utterance −: Any moment of stuttering Any utterance >160 SPM	−: Reminder to speak a bit more slowly, 1:1. −: Reminder to speak a bit more slowly, 1:1 +: Same as above −: Same as above −: Same as above	Same as above	Same as above (for rate data, count syllables for 15 sec of each 1-min response and multiply × 4 for approximate SPM).

(continued)

Table 5.1
Continued

Step	Discriminative Stimuli	Response (+ & −)	±Consequences and Schedules	Criteria	Measurement
13	Same stimuli and instructions as above	+ : Stutter-free 2-min monologue connected speech utterance. − : Any moment of stuttering − : Any utterance >160 SPM	+ : Same as above − : Same as above − : Same as above	Pass: 10 consecutive stutter-free monologue responses Fail: 7 consecutive stutter trials or 50 trials without passing the step	Same as above (for rate data count syllables for four different 15-sec intervals during the 2-min response and add for approximate SPM)
14	Same stimuli and instructions as above	+ : Stutter-free 3-min monologue connected speech utterance. − : Any moment of stuttering − : Any utterance > 160 SPM	+ : Same as above − : Same as above − : Same as above	Pass: 5 consecutive stutter-free monologue responses Fail: Same as above	Same as above
15	Same stimuli and instructions as above	+ : Stutter-free 4-min monologue connected speech utterance. − : Any moment of stuttering − : No rate requirement	+ : Same as above − : Same as above − : (No feedback regarding rate unless stuttering occurs associated with high SPM)	Same as above	Same as above
16	Same stimuli and instructions as above	+ : Stutter-free 5-min monologue connected speech utterance. − : Any moment of stuttering	+ : Same as above − : Same as above	Pass: 4 consecutive stutter-free monologue responses Fail: 20 trials without passing the step	Same as above

162

Step	Description	Contingency	Reinforcement	Pass/Fail Criteria	Measurement
17	Topics introduced by clinician and by child for conversation. Include clinician questions, interruptions, overlapping utterances, topic changes, etc.; i.e., mirroring natural conversational interactions (but keep clinician utterances short)	+ : 2 min of stutter-free conversation (Note: 2 min based on cumulative child speaking time) − : Any moment of stuttering	+ : Same as above − : Same as above	Pass: 10 consecutive stutter-free conversations Fail: 7 consecutive stuttered trials or 50 trials without passing the step	Same as above, plus use stopwatch to cumulate child speaking time (i.e., 2 min of child talking time, rather than a 2-min conversation, including clinician talking time)
18	Same as above	+ : 3 min of stutter-free conversation (Note: 3 min based on cumulative child speaking time) − : Any moment of stuttering	+ : Positive social reinforcer, 1:1 Positive token reinforcer, 2:1 − : Report number of stutters to child at end of trial. Do not stop child at the moment of stutter	Same as above	Same as above
19	Same as above	+ : 4 min of stutter-free conversation (Note: 4 min based on cumulative child speaking time) − : Any moment of stuttering	+ : Positive social reinforcer, 1:1 Positive token reinforcer, 2:1 − : Report number of stutters to child at end of trial. Do not stop child at the moment of a stutter	Pass: 7 consecutive stutter-free conversations Fail: 30 trials without passing the step	Same as above
20	Same as above	+ : 5 min of stutter-free conversation (Note: 5 min based on cumulative child speaking time) − : Any moment of stuttering	+ : Positive social reinforcer, 1:1 − : Report number of stutters to child at end of trial. Do not stop child at the moment of a stutter	Pass: 6 consecutive stutter-free conversations Fail: 25 trials without passing the step	Same as above
21	If child continues to stutter, develop transfer program in natural environment				

Source: From J. C. Ingham, "Behavioral Treatment of Young Children Who Stutter: An Extended Length of Utterance Method." In R. F. Curlee (Ed.), *Stuttering and Related Disorders of Fluency (2nd ed.).* New York: Thieme Medical Publishers, 1999, pp. 101–109. *Reprinted by permission.*

online data collection procedures. Parents and siblings are trained to implement therapy in the home environment to obtain fluency generalization.

Bruce Ryan

Ryan (1971, 1974, 1986) introduced a programmed instruction, operant conditioning system for the establishment of fluent speech called Gradual Increase in Length and Complexity of Utterance (GILCU). This approach outlines sequential steps in which fluency is obtained at one level before progressing to another. Ryan used positive reinforcement with token rewards, as well as punishment for stuttered speech. His "good" or "stop, speak fluently" performance feedback continues through the two major components of his program: gradual increase in length and complexity of utterance (GILCU) and delayed auditory feedback (DAF). GILCU is a 54-step procedure using reading, monologue, and conversation (Table 5.2). The DAF is a 26-step process in which the child uses slow, prolonged fluent speech with the DAF device set at a 250-millisecond (msec) delay. This delay is gradually faded out in 50-msec intervals. Ryan recommended implementation of the GILCU portion first, followed by the DAF component if necessary. After this establishment phase, the child enters into the 17- to 32-step transfer portion of the program. Transfer activities include careful manipulation of physical settings, audience, telephone use, home, school, and other environments. Once the client is successful, he moves into the 5-step, 22-month maintenance phase. Success in this program depends on the coordinated efforts of the entire treatment team: child/client, parent(s)/significant other, and clinician (Ryan & Van Kirk Ryan, 1995). Research studies have determined that the GILCU treatment paradigm produces significant positive results, short term and long term, with school-age children who stutter (Ryan & Van Kirk Ryan, 1995, 2002).

Teaching fluency-shaping skills can be implemented in intensive or nonintensive routines. ELU and GILCU present specific therapy principles most commonly used with children in nonintensive therapy settings, such as in the public schools where therapy is scheduled two to three times a week for a brief period of time. However, for the adult who stutters, intensive fluency-shaping programs provide a different opportunity to obtain fluency in a relatively short period of time. Chapter 11 discusses several intensive fluency-shaping programs appropriate for use with adults.

Stuttering Modification Therapy

Stuttering modification therapy has as its goals the end product of spontaneous fluency, controlled fluency, and/or acceptable stuttering (Guitar, 1998). Characteristics of this type of therapy might include (1) modification of the stuttering spasm, (2) attention to attitudes, fears, and avoidances, (3) qualitative measurements, (4) loosely structured client-centered treatment sessions, (5) client analysis of the stuttering spasm, and (6) planned transfer (Ramig & Bennett, 1995). Van Riper, Williams, and Dell all have written about their modification therapies. Others adhere to the same modification philosophy, but only these three remarkable pioneers in the area of stuttering modification therapy for adults and children are discussed here.

Table 5.2
Fluency-shaping establishment program used with children and adults.

GILCU Establishment Program		
Activity		**Criterion/Consequences**
Criterion test in reading, monologue, and conversation	5 min each speaking model	
Reading aloud in clinic setting: 1. Single words 2. Two words 3. Three words 4. Four words 5. Five words 6. Six words 7. One sentence 8. Two sentences 9. Three sentences 10. Four sentences 11. 30 sec 12. One min 13. One min and 30 sec 14. Two min 15. Two min and 30 sec 16. Three min 17. Four min 18. Five min Reading in home environment:	5 min reading daily	0 SW/min Correct: "Good" Incorrect: "Stop. Read fluently."
Monologue in clinic setting: repeat steps above	Say the following words fluently	0 SW/min Correct: "Good" Incorrect: "Stop. Say it/read it fluently."
Reading and monologue in home environment	2-min reading, 5-min monologue daily	
Conversation in the clinic setting: repeat steps above		0 SW/min Correct: "Good" Incorrect: "Stop. Say it/read it fluently."
Reading, monologue, and conversation in home environment	2-min reading, 2-min monologue, and 5-min conversation daily	
Criterion Test in reading, monologue, and conversation	5 min in each speaking mode	Two or fewer stutters per mode

Source: From B. P. Ryan, "Treatment of Stuttering in School Children." In W. H. Perkins (Ed.), Stuttering Disorders. New York: Thieme Medical Publishers, 1984, pp. 95–106. Reprinted by permission.

Charles Van Riper

Charles Van Riper has long been considered the father of stuttering modification therapy. In his landmark text, *The Treatment of Stuttering,* Van Riper (1973) outlined the goals and procedures utilized in stuttering modification therapy for the adult who stutters. Using a problem-solving approach to therapy, Van Riper seeks to desensitize the individual to moments of stuttering through counterconditioning principles. The PWS responds to the anticipation or experience of stuttering in a more adaptive manner, thereby neutralizing the self-reinforcement of stuttering. In summary, the goal of Van Riper's modification therapy is to learn to stutter in an easy way without negative affective or cognitive reactions. By decreasing the fear of stuttering and eliminating the maladaptive responses learned by the person, fluency emerges. To achieve this goal, Van Riper uses four stages of therapy: identification, desensitization, modification, and stabilization.

In the *identification* phase, the client collects information about his core stuttering behaviors, how he reacts behaviorally in response to stuttering, and what feelings accompany the moment of stuttering. Figure 5.2 demonstrates this identification process. Specifically, Van Riper has the client identify these elements:

1. Target behaviors
2. Avoidance behaviors
3. Postponement devices
4. Timing behaviors
5. Verbal cues
6. Situational cues
7. Core behaviors
8. Loci of tension
9. Repetitive recoil behavior
10. Poststuttering reactions
11. Feelings of frustration
12. Feelings of shame
13. Feelings of hostility

Figure 5.2
Identification in action:
A worksheet produced
by a teenager attempt-
ing to identify the affective, behavioral, and
cognitive components
of stuttering.

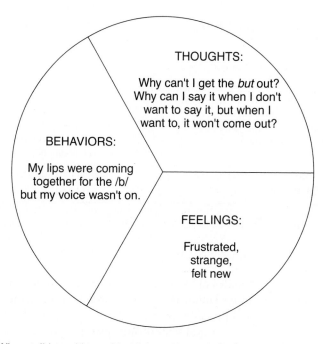

THOUGHTS:

Why can't I get the *but* out?
Why can I say it when I don't
want to say it, but when I
want to, it won't come out?

BEHAVIORS:

My lips were coming
together for the /b/
but my voice wasn't on.

FEELINGS:

Frustrated,
strange,
felt new

"When talking with my friend, I couldn't say the word *but* and *I* . . ."

The **desensitization** phase of therapy has as its goal the disassociation of the avoidance or escape responses from their stimuli. "Our purpose in desensitization therapy is to reduce the strength of the attendant emotional upheaval enough to enable the stutterer to learn new ways of coping with the expectancy and experience of broken words" (p. 267). Desensitization involves the reduction of fears and negative emotions surrounding speech through confrontation activities, holding on to the moment of stuttering, and pseudostuttering to counteract concerns about listener reactions. Steps taken during desensitization therapy include the following tasks:

1. Recognize negative emotionality.
2. Construct hierarchies.
3. Confront the disorder.
4. Desensitize to listener reaction.
5. Practice counterconditioning.
6. Use assertive responses.
7. Implement relaxation techniques.
8. Incorporate pseudostuttering.
9. Provide reassurance and hope.

Modification strategies, perhaps the best contribution of Van Riper (Bloodstein, 1995), include cancellations, pullouts, and preparatory sets (these are elaborated on later in this chapter). The hallmark of this stage of therapy is change (p. 302) in which the client is asked to experiment with new ways of feeling, speaking, and thinking. The goal of the modification phase of therapy is variability, which can be accomplished through the following tasks:

1. Exploring of self
2. Varying habitual patterns
3. Role-playing scenarios
4. Varying the stuttering behaviors
5. Varying the escape behaviors
6. Teaching a fluent form of stuttering
7. Using proprioception monitoring
8. Implementing cancellations
9. Utilizing pullouts
10. Rehearsing and using preparatory sets

Stabilization involves maintaining therapy gains and establishing the client as his own therapist. Van Riper contended that, although therapy has established a new set of responses to the anticipation of stuttering, it is impossible to prepare the client for all impending responses to old cues to which the stutterer may respond with avoidance and struggle (p. 350). During the stabilization period, the client sets aside periods of time for his self-therapy. Journaling is used to share the client's maintenance with the clinician during less frequent individual sessions. Therapy tasks might include the following:

1. Reconfigure fluency.
2. Use continuous oral reading to practice phrasing.

3. Increase speech rate.
4. Reflect on and share success stories.
5. Automatize sets and strategies through mass practice exercises.
6. Prepare for contingencies.
7. Employ pseudostuttering to practice cancellations and pullouts.

To learn more about Van Riper's therapy, look at his original work. The Stuttering Foundation of America rents a series of videotapes of Van Riper conducting therapy with an adult client, demonstrating each phase of his approach.

Dean Williams

Another approach to treatment was developed by Dean Williams, considered the master of all clinicians. At the time of early research, in 1971, the majority of research and literature was geared either toward the adult or preschool child who stuttered. Williams's therapy involved a positive approach to learning for the school-age child through a series of tasks: (1) examining the child's basic assumptions about stuttering and what he thinks causes it; (2) providing considerable information about talking; (3) helping him understand and accept his feelings; (4) helping him become more aware of the purpose of talking (i.e., that of verbal communication); (5) helping him experiment with and explore the versatility of his behavior that is called talking, and (6) demonstrating and then reinforcing what he can do to talk easily and spontaneously (p. 1076). Williams (1985) later commented that his therapy approach emphasized facilitating the client during the discovery process of therapy. He suggested the clinician not "tell" the child what she is doing, but facilitate the child's discovery through a "set of structured experiences." Conture (2001) summarizes Williams's procedures in a list of five components used to change the child's beliefs about speech and stuttering:

1. What's wrong? The clinician begins by exploring what the child thinks is wrong.
2. What are you doing to help? The clinician helps the child discover, through describing activities, what he "does" during a moment of stuttering.
3. What's going on? The clinician assists the child in determining if what he is doing really helps.
4. When we learn, we make mistakes. Emphasis in on the fact that making mistakes is part of the learning process.
5. Changing behavior depends on what the child does. The clinician helps the child understand that change occurs through action, through *doing*.

Carl Dell

In Dell's (1979, 1993, 2000) treatment paradigm, the first procedure involves removing the mystery of stuttering through pseudostuttering, desensitization, and increased fluency. Second is nurturing independence for the child who stutters. It is Dell's goal to have the child become his own clinician, assuming responsibility for therapy gains. He uses the concept of "choice making" to establish this self-direction in therapy. "Children need to develop their own strategies that will help them persevere" (p. 61). Children must believe they have earned their fluency through active decisions made regarding how they choose to talk. This helps the child develop self-analysis skills needed for relapse periods.

However, before children can make such choices, they must learn to identify their moments of stuttering. Dell believed children must learn about stuttering in general and their particular loci of tension as part of the therapeutic process. Once the child can identify where he stutters, he must be allowed the opportunity to "experience this tension in an accepting environment so that he . . . can become desensitized" (p. 63). Emphasizing the tactile-kinesthetic feedback during tension reduction activities assists in developing the crucial skill of self-monitoring.

Modifying stuttering behaviors is a focal point in Dell's treatment. Teaching children to vary their stuttering behaviors is essential for progress. If children are to make choices regarding how they talk, they must be able to produce various types of speech patterns. In his 1979 publication about the school-age stutterer, Dell wrote about three ways of talking: hard, easy, and regular. Having the child who stutters identify, produce, and experiment with these three speaking styles provides an opportunity to build the concept of talking differently and gain the courage to proceed with varying speech. Dell also used in-block corrections or pullouts to demonstrate how to handle "real" moments of stuttering. Finally, **voluntary stuttering,** inserting a short, tension-free repetition or prolongation, empowers the child to be more open with his stuttering.

In summary, Dell's intervention ascribed to three main features: (1) stuttering is intermittent and unpredictable, (2) treatment should remove the mystery of stuttering, and (3) choice making should be incorporated into therapy to establish the concept of flexibility and responsibility. Specifically, Dell's treatment procedures apply to both the mild or severe child who stutters.

Integrated Therapy

The melding of fluency-shaping and stuttering modification approaches is best exemplified by Peters and Guitar's (1991) **integrated therapy** for the intermediate stutterer. Peters and Guitar believed that as the client continues to stutter, environmental and developmental factors interact to produce an increase in core stuttering behaviors, causing the client to react emotionally with tension and fragmentation. Avoidances begin to surface as frustration and embarrassment continue. The goals of this approach are controlled fluency and acceptable stuttering characterized by mild or very mild stuttering. Characteristics of integrated therapy might include (1) the establishment of spontaneous fluency in the clinical setting through fluency-enhancing gestures, (2) modification of moments of stuttering, (3) attention to feelings and attitudes, (4) flexibility in the extent of structured interaction between student and therapist, (5) data collection varying with the degree of structure, and (6) planned transfer activities.

Ted Peters and Barry Guitar

Peters and Guitar (1991), in *Stuttering: An Integrated Approach to Its Nature and Treatment*, presented a comprehensive overview of integrated approaches for the advanced (adult), intermediate (adolescent), and beginning (child) stutterer. Their approach to therapy utilizes a well-controlled balance between fluency-shaping and stuttering modification therapies to meet the individual goals of each subgroup of clients. For the beginning stutterer, Peters and Guitar implement a predominantly fluency-shaping regime that incorporates parents in the therapy process. As the client gets older, greater emphasis is placed on the attitudes and feelings that emerge with continual stuttering. An emphasis on modifying the moment of stuttering begins with the older adolescent and adult who stutters. Goals, rationales, and procedures, with useful informational pamphlets, are available.

Eugene and Crystal Cooper

Personalized fluency control therapy (PFCT) was first introduced by Gene and Crystal Cooper in 1976 and revised in 1985. This approach involves four distinct stages: identifying and structuring, examination and confrontation, cognitive and behavior orientation, and fluency control. PFCT emphasizes the client/clinician relationship while addressing the affective, behavioral, and cognitive components of stuttering disorders. Cooper (1984) stressed the importance of training in self-reinforcement, believing this skill is essential to long-term maintenance. **Fluency initiating gestures** (FIGs) are introduced as one way of achieving the program goal: "the feeling of fluency control" (p. 11). The following are definitions of these fluency strategies:

> *Slow speech:* a reduction in the rate of speech typically involving the equalized prolongation of syllables.
>
> *Easy onset:* the initiation of phonation with as little laryngeal area tension as possible.
>
> *Deep breath:* a consciously controlled inhalation prior to the initiation of phonation and typically used in conjunction with the easy-onset FIG.
>
> *Loudness control:* a conscious and sustained increase or decrease in the volume of the client's speech.
>
> *Smooth speech (easy contact):* a reduction in phonatory adjustments; also light articulatory contacts with plosive and affricate sounds, typically being modified to resemble fricative sounds.
>
> *Syllable stress:* a deliberate variation of volume and pitch. (p. 20)

Richard Culatta and Stanley Goldberg

Culatta and Goldberg (1995) developed an integrated approach called PROLAM-GM. Six intervention strategies combined with generalization and maintenance principles comprise this program. Intervention options include *p*hysiological adjustments (P); *r*ate manipulation (R); *o*perant control (O); *l*ength and complexity of utterance manipulations (L); frequently *a*ttitude change (A); and *m*onitoring (M). The generalization (G) phase of therapy is highly structured, incorporating learning principles. Maintenance (M) is carried out through a series of daily routines, regular clinic contacts, refresher programs, and self-help group meetings. Relapse is discussed during maintenance because of the high likelihood of regression to previous old habits.

Hugo Gregory and Diane Hill

Gregory and Hill (1999) proposed a differential treatment approach for the confirmed person who stutters. This paradigm involves the modification of speech and change in attitudes with the amelioration of other contributing factors, such as language or phonological disorders. Gregory and Hill described the use of less specific and more specific speech modification strategies. They begin with the less-specific approach for the development of fluency and only use more-specific strategies to handle residual stuttering. An example of a less-specific strategy would be their ERA-SM: easy, relaxed approach with smooth movements on the initial CV or VC segment of the utterance. Easy transition into the word or phrase is accomplished through slow, smooth initial movements with the rest of the utterance maintaining normal rate and prosody. In this less-specific approach, they do not analyze the moment of stuttering. Pausing, relaxation, and resisting time pressure are additional strategies used in this phase of therapy.

Moving into a more-specific approach occurs when the client continues to exhibit moments of stuttering. Here the clinician models different types of stuttered speech with the client imitating this behavior. Practice in tension reduction during the moment of stuttering would occur so the client has the experience of catching, reducing tension, and moving out of the stuttering with easy, relaxed speech. If necessary, voluntary stuttering may be used to desensitize the client to stuttering episodes.

Attitudinal change is another aspect of Gregory and Hill's approach. The clinician is encouraged to teach the client how to describe stuttering moments using specific statements, such as "Your lips are squeezing together." They found analogies to be useful when assisting the client in understanding what is happening with the speech production system when stuttering. An important feature of attitudinal change involves the clinician's ability to listen to the client and allow for the expression of feelings. Gregory and Hill contended that the clinician must be prepared to help the individual learn how to label and handle the feelings he experiences when stuttering.

Peter Ramig and Ellen Bennett

Ramig and Bennett (1995, 1997a) presented an integrated approach to therapy based on the concept of a continuum of fluency-shaping and stuttering modification methods. This orientation to therapy is appropriate for all age groups because it is based on the philosophy that each treatment plan is individualized according to client needs. It allows for maximal flexibility to accommodate daily fluctuations in the client's affective, behavioral, and cognitive profile.

Ramig and Bennett (1995) recommended a fluency-shaping orientation to address the fluency concerns of the young preschool child who stutters. When necessary, the clinician may choose to implement a more direct modification through the use of play-based therapy activities. To shape the fluency of the young child who stutters, they recommend these seven principles:

Principle 1:   Explain in simple, understandable terms what you want the child to do. Example: "We are going to look at some pictures of zoo animals. When I hold up the card, I want you to tell me the name."

Principle 2:   Be consistent in the terms you use to reinforce the target behavior. If you are calling his new way of talking "easy talking" (or "easy speech," "super smooth speech," "nice-n-easy"), everyone in his environment (parents and teachers) should be familiar with the terminology and use the same wording. It may be appropriate for the child to choose the words he wants to use to describe this "new way of talking."

Principle 3:   Consistently model the target behavior you wish the child to adopt. Example: Use a slower rate while producing soft contacts on the initial sound or syllable of each word in saying, "The truck is big."

Principle 4:   Model slower, relaxed speech throughout your interaction with the child, both in and out of the therapy room. Your speech model should be consistent regardless of where the interaction takes place (e.g., in the halls, coming off the bus, or in the cafeteria).

Principle 5:   Model slower, relaxed body movements as you interact with the child before, during, and after the session. Example: When walking to the speech room with a kindergarten and/or first-grade student, model "walking like a turtle" (Meyers & Woodford, 1992) to facilitate the use of slow, easy speech once in the speech setting. Do the same thing on the way back to class, after the session. This warm-up and wind-down time is especially important.

Principle 6:   While working on specific fluency-enhancing strategies, such as a slow stretch on the initial sound, syllable, or complete word, use a concomitant slow, relaxed forward movement of the hand or arm as you model the target behavior. Example: You can move your arm in front of you from left to right in the shape of a rainbow as you slowly say "tiger." The child produces this movement with you as he says the word. You may, for example, wish to label this activity as "rainbow speech" or "rainbow talking." This facilitates fluency through providing a slower model of speaking and moving for the child. Whenever possible, use concrete, conceptually based activities during the therapy interaction. Moving a small toy car, doll, or ball across the surface of the table while you model the desired behavior facilitates comprehension of a slower, easier speech production (Gregory & Hill, 1980).

Principle 7:   Reinforce with praise to the degree appropriate for the individual child. Fostering the child's feelings of self-worth is important and reinforcement is one of many ways this can be accomplished. (p. 141)

For the older school-age child, Ramig and Bennett discussed a direct approach to modifying speech through the analogy of the "House That Jack Built" (Bennett-Mancha, 1992). (See chapter 9.) This conceptual model involves four interactive phases of therapy: laying the foundation of knowledge, installing the plumbing, building rooms and walls, and building the roof of fluency. A strong aspect of this integrated approach is the attention drawn toward the attitudes and feelings of the child who stutters.

For the adult who stutters, therapy must combine aspects of fluency-shaping and stuttering modification therapies appropriate to the profile of the adult. Lifelong debilitating affects of stuttering leave their mark on the affective, behavioral, and cognitive characteristics of the individual. Therapy activities will depend on client characteristics, with greater client-driven decision-making/problem-solving therapy activities rather than clinician-directed therapy.

PROFILE-DEPENDENT TREATMENT PLANS

Therapy for the person who stutters should follow an integrated framework, regardless of the client's age. The flexibility inherent in this approach allows the speech pathologist to tailor the treatment of each individual client, a principle mandated by federal law (P.L. 94–142). Fluency-shaping and stuttering modification therapies fall along a continuum with fluency on one end and easy stuttering on the other. Each client who stutters has individual needs. They should not be slotted into predetermined therapy programs. An integrated treatment approach allows the speech pathologist to develop a specific program for the client based upon his own personal profile while modifying it according to special circumstances.

As Williams (1971) espoused, the therapy process is one of planning, carrying out, and assessing each and every day. You must be prepared to disregard the original lesson plan if the client's immediate needs do not reflect your original plan. For example, one day, you may plan a predominantly fluency-shaping therapy session for a group of fifth-grade boys who stutter. As they enter the room, one child appears visibly upset. It would be inappropriate for you to pretend not to notice his mood. The lesson must be modified to probe the client's concerns, having the group problem-solve or discuss the client's difficulty. Suppose it was discovered this boy had been teased at lunch and was sent to the principal's office for reacting negatively to the situation. This would be an opportune time to address attitudes and feelings rather than focusing on the planned fluency-enhancing activities.

Profile-dependent treatment plans are based on the concept of "tailored/customized intervention" (Ramig & Bennett, 1997a). The first step in this process is to determine the particular profile of strengths and weaknesses through a comprehension assessment, as described in chapter 4. Next, you look at the quantitative as well as qualitative aspect of the client's stuttering to select the specific components that may facilitate speech change. Certain therapeutic strategies are useful when changing specific stuttering behaviors. For example, if the client exhibits short, tense silent blocks, establishing light articulatory contacts directly targets this behavior. If the client uses long prolongations, instruction on the use of breath-stream management would be appropriate. Table 5.3, from Ramig and Bennett (1997a), presents intervention components that address observed speech behaviors. This author supports such a component model as a means of creating profile-dependent plans. The following sections reviews 18 specific treatment techniques.

Table 5.3

Recommended intervention components that target observed speech behaviors.

Tailoring Therapy: Intervention Components and Observed Speech Behaviors

Speech Behavior	Increase Length and Complexity	Regulate and Control Breathstream	Establish Light Articulatory Contacts	Control Speaking Rate	Facilitate Oral-Motor Planning	Discuss Normal Speaking Process	Discuss Interference Process	Hard versus Easy Contrasts	Negative Practice	3-Way Contrast Drills-Triads	Hierarchy Analysis	Speech Assertiveness and Openness	Voluntary Stuttering	Cancellations	Pullouts and Freezing	Reduce Avoidance Behaviors	Facilitate Awareness and Monitoring	Instill Positive Speech Attitudes	Transfer Skills	Establish Maintenance Plan	Involve Others in Intervention
Short, Tense Silent Blocks		*	*			*	*	*	*	*			*	*	*	*	*		*		
Excessively Long Prolongations		*				*	*	*	*					*	*	*	*		*		
Rapid, Tonic Repetitions			*	*		*	*	*	*	*			*	*	*		*		*		
Hard Glottal Attack		*	*				*	*	*	*				*	*				*		
Excessive Fillers and Interjections			*			*	*	*	*	*		*	*	*		*	*		*		
Distortion of Speech Signal																	*	*	*		
Quick, Shallow Inhalation		*		*	*	*	*		*							*	*		*		
Talking on Exhausted Breathstream		*	*	*	*	*	*	*	*					*			*		*		
Jaw Clenching			*		*	*	*	*	*	*			*				*		*		
Limited Articulatory Movement			*		*	*	*	*	*	*		*		*		*	*	*	*		
Negative Comments * about Speech												*				*	*	*	*		*

174

Struggle Behaviors

Situational Avoidances and Fear

Specific Sound or Word

Highly Variable Stuttering

Anticipatory Posturing

Excessive Hesitancies in Speech

Choppy Quality to Speech

Difficulty Comprehending Message

Limited Oral Expression

Expected Language Involvement

Tailored Treatment can be achieved by identifying observed speech behaviors and the appropriate intervention component as indicated by the *. This list is not exhaustive and should be viewed as a possible list of components that might be included in therapy. These components have been described elsewhere by Ramig, Stewart, Orgrodnick, and Bennett, 1994.

Source: From Curlee and Siegel's Nature and Treatment of Stuttering: New Directions (2nd ed.). Published by Allyn and Bacon, Boston, MA. Copyright © 1997 by Pearson Education. Reprinted by permission of the publisher.

Increasing Length and Complexity

Research is unequivocal regarding the impact of increased sentence length and complexity on instances of stuttering (Bernstein Ratner & Sih, 1987; Logan & Conture, 1995; Ryan, 1984; Yaruss, 1999b). Longer sentences require more complex motor planning sequences, thus increasing the likelihood that stuttering will occur (Starkweather, 1987; Yaruss, 1999b). If the child's profile indicates he frequently stutters on longer utterances, therapy might start at the word level, gradually manipulating responses to increase in length and/or complexity. You may choose to establish fluency following the GILCU or ELU programs previously discussed.

Regulating and Controlling the Breathstream

Speech production begins with respiration. For some children who stutter, the process of inhalation, exhalation, and phonation is disrupted (e.g., when a child speaks on inhalation or holds his breath for too long and then spits out his words). Teaching the child how to regulate and control breath stream is critical for coordinating respiration with phonation. Riley and Riley (1983) noted that the building of the speech support process, as airflow management, is an elementary goal in any fluency program. You may use the visual aid of a slide to demonstrate the inhalation requirements of speaking. As the child climbs up the steps of the ladder to the top of the slide, he inhales air into the lungs. As the child slides down, he exhales and begins vocal fold vibration. Having the child trace with his finger the steps of the ladder while slowly moving down the slide provides concrete, tactile feedback to facilitate comprehension of this concept. You can have the child contrast fast versus slow inhalation-exhalation patterns to feel the difference in his body.

Establishing Light Articulatory Contacts

Bloodstein (1958, 1997) hypothesized that with continued stuttering, the individual reacts through increased tension and fragmentation. This tension may surface in the characteristic of tense articulatory contacts. If present in the child's profile, you may choose to introduce "soft contacts" as Peters and Guitar (1991) described them: "By this we mean that the movements of the articulators (tongue, lips, and jaw) should be slow, prolonged, and relaxed. These articulatory movements should not be fast and tense" (p. 231). During personal communication with Lois Nelson (1990), she discussed the importance of emphasizing the proprioceptive feedback loop in therapy. We instruct children to "feel the words in their mouth," drawing attention to the main speech helpers and their movement during speech. This skill is a precursor to many of the speech modification tools children may use to manage their stuttering. It is essential that children have experience and proficiency with this technique.

Controlling Speaking Rate

Wall and Myers (1995) speculated that slowing speech rate may allow the individual to make the adjustments necessary for fluent speech production. Some people who stutter increase their speech rate as a reaction to stuttering, as if to get as much out before they have to stop. However, this coping mechanism is not conducive to either fluency or effective communication. You may decide to model different rate control strategies, such as prolonged vowel production, easy relaxed transitions, continuous phonation, or delayed auditory feedback. One strategy helpful to children is called **phrasing.** You can demonstrate phrasing through the analogy of "chunks." Get three candy wrappers from the chocolate candy bar called Chunky. Tell the child that for each candy he may take two to three bites (words). Explain that eating the whole candy bar at once would be too much in his mouth. Model for them how each bite is like a chunk, getting just enough to enjoy the candy. Then talk about enjoying speech by saying a chunk at a time while tapping with your finger on each candy wrapper as you say each phrase. This is a concrete way to help the client understand the concept of managing the number of words per utterance or phrase.

Facilitating Oral-Motor Planning

Riley and Riley (1979, 1984, 1991, 2000) have long established that the majority of children who stutter have oral-motor planning deficits. The ability to sequence syllables into words and words into phrases can be a cumbersome task characterized by reduced articulatory excursions and jaw clenching. Teaching the child to overarticulate sounds is one way to enhance fluency. For some children who stutter, systematic oral motor drills may be warranted. Therapy focusing on accurate and smooth productions of syllable sets with the gradual increase in production rate is just one treatment option. Riley and Riley's Oral Motor Programming Program is a useful tool (see their program for specific details).

Normal Speaking Process Education

Many clinicians believe children need to have a core vocabulary to use when describing their speech, that is, the language of talking (Conture, 2001; Dell, 1993; Ramig & Bennett, 1995; Williams, 1971, 1985). This author believes that, for some children, building an understanding of how people talk in general provides a nonthreatening environment in which the student-clinician relationship can be established. Discussing the processes of respiration, phonation, and articulation provides the basic foundation necessary to investigate how sounds are produced and incorporated into words and larger language units. After learning about the normal speaking process, clients are ready to learn about ways anyone can disrupt this process.

Normal Speaking Process Interference Education

Clinicians often ask children what they do when they stutter, failing to realize the client may not have the language to explain this event, thus getting the response "I get stuck." Through the series of activities presented in chapter 9, you can help children discover and describe how they interfere with the normal speaking process through core stuttering behaviors (i.e., within-word repetitions, prolongations, and blocks).

Using concrete representations as visual aids can help clients confront their stuttering. Having the child draw his own picture symbol of stuttering establishes ownership and self-responsibility. You may take the child's pictures and put them on a worksheet for him to tally each time he exhibits a particular type of stuttering. Such identification is essential to future progress.

Hard versus Easy Contacts

The ability to produce **easy contacts,** as stated earlier, is an essential component of several therapy techniques. Providing opportunities to experiment with both types of speech allows the client to feel the difference between the two. The feeling of tension then becomes a signal of possible stuttering to which the client can modify with easy contacts. Have the client practice hard and easy contacts with all the speech helpers using fun gamelike activities. For example, you may direct clients to produce a word that begins with the /m/ sound (a bilabial sound) with hard and then easy contacts. Encourage them to describe how the two productions fell. This exercise continues until the clients have produced each sound of the English language in a hard and easy way.

Negative Practice

Practicing what he fears can assist the person who stutters in learning how to modify his speech. Gregory (2003) describes a two-step procedure in which the client first says a word in a tense, hard way. Then he repeats the word with half the tension. Again, focus is on the feeling aspect of this drill. There are several benefits to **negative practice** for the person who stutters: he (1) confronts stuttering, (2) learns to stay in the moment without attempting to escape, (3) has an opportunity to calm himself during purposeful stuttering, and (4) feels a sense of empowerment in that he has taken charge of the stuttering and changed it bit by bit. When approached with enthusiasm, clients begin to feel comfortable playing around with their speech.

Three-Way Contrast Drills

A modification of the negative practice technique is the three-way contrast drills (also called **triads**) presented by Ramig and Bennett (1997a). This drill consists of a three-step procedure: producing the word the "hard way," producing the word with an easy repetition, then producing the word with an easy prolongation (Figures 5.3 and 5.4). These three efforts are said without any interruption so that the client can concentrate on feeling the difference between productions. "This affords a gradual reduction in tension, improves desensitization, and allows the child to experiment with different forms of easy stuttering" (Ramig & Bennett, 1997a, p. 303), referred to in this text as *bounces* and *slides*.

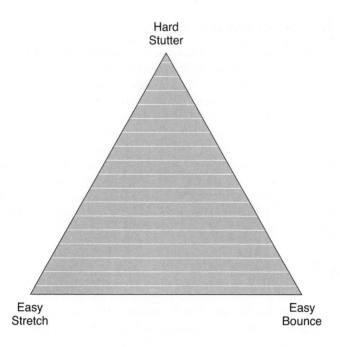

Hard
Stutter

Easy
Stretch

Easy
Bounce

Figure 5.3
Manipulating
stuttering: Three-way
contrast drills.

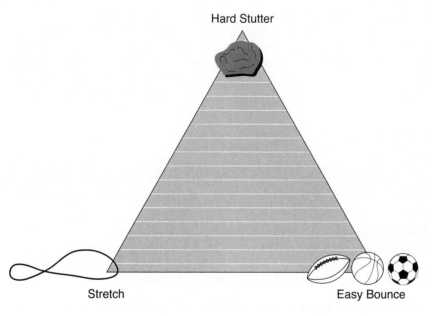

Hard Stutter

Stretch

Easy Bounce

Figure 5.4
A visual representa-
tion of triad drills
appropriate for
children who stutter.

Speech Assertiveness and Openness

As clients experience repeated frustration with talking, they may develop shame-based reactions to their stuttering (Bennett, 1995). These reactions can fall within two domains: intrapersonal or interpersonal. *Intrapersonal* reactions might range from concealment of stuttering, avoidance of social situations, and/or refusing to talk. These reactions will eventually dominate the client's desire to communicate. If such behavior continues, treatment progress will be negatively impacted (Bennett, 1995). Getting stuttering out in the open and educating others about this disorder are samples of **speech assertiveness** activities. Responding to teasing and ridicule falls within the *interpersonal* reaction category. Understanding why people tease, being assertive when teased, and responding appropriately to labels and false characterizations helps build the child's self-confidence. Chapter 9 provides numerous activities and suggestions for creating speech assertiveness in children who stutter.

Voluntary Stuttering

The concept of voluntary stuttering, also called **pseudostuttering,** has a long history in the treatment of stuttering disorders. Bryngelson, Dell, Murphy, Sheehan, Van Riper, and Williams are just a few of the experts who have advocated this stuttering modification strategy. During a presentation given by Carl Dell in the mid-1990s at Southwest Texas State University, he modeled his form of voluntary stuttering, brief sound/syllable repetitions. He related voluntary stutters to that of a vaccination. Although a bit painful initially, the long-term effects are worthwhile. By inserting stuttering into his speech, the client receives a boost of fluency. The fear of stuttering is reduced because this action is purposeful. Stuttering is out in the open and there is no sudden exposure of inadequacy, that is, shame. Starting on nonfeared words in simple linguistic constructions, the client experiments with bounces and slides. Some clients may prefer bounces; others, slides. One strategy may feel better and be easier to use than another. Let each client decide on his own which one to practice. The client must discover what works best for him rather than be told by the clinician.

Cancellations

Cancellations are a modification tool used to analyze the moment of stuttering. Van Riper (1973) initially proposed that the cancellation be used as a means of nullifying the reinforcement from the moment of stuttering through a time-out from communication. These are the steps for performing a cancellation:

1. The client finishes the word he has just stuttered on.
2. The client pauses, calms himself, and reflects on the stuttering moment.
3. The client rehearses, first overtly and then covertly, a new, easier form of stuttering.
4. The client repeats the stuttered word using an easy stutter.

Cancellations create an awareness of the behavior exhibited during stuttering. However, it is a difficult technique and may not be appropriate for the younger school-age child. To perform a cancellation, the client must be aware of the stuttering and be able to stop directly after the word. Often several words will slip out upon release of the moment of stuttering, which becomes the reinforcing power behind stuttering. Being able to stop and reflect on one's speech requires a certain degree of metalinguistic knowledge. This technique is recommended for use with older children or adults who demonstrate the ability to analyze their language abstractly.

Pullouts and Freezing

Van Riper (1973) stated that the "modifications of behavior through cancellations tend to move forward in time to manifest themselves during the period of stuttering itself" (p. 328). Clients are now required to catch the moment of stuttering before the word is completed. They **freeze** midstream, reduce tension levels, and gradually move out of the moment of stuttering and complete their communication. Although proposed for use with adults, **pullouts** have been incorporated into the treatment plans of school-age children who stutter (Conture, 2001; Guitar, 1998; Murphy, 1999; Ramig & Bennett, 1997a; Williams, 1984). Teach this technique first in drill-type activities until the client develops a sense of mastery and automaticity, gradually moving into tasks that require more extemporaneous speech efforts.

Hierarchy Analysis

Some clients come into therapy with a long list of self-perceived feared words and situations. It is your job to help the child and adult problem-solve and rank-order these situations from easiest to hardest. We recommend you and your client select the situation with no fear or minimal fear to start increasing the approach drive to talking. We want to focus on the strengths of the client to ensure success, working from a success-driven model so we do not set him up for failure. As the child achieves success with the task, he should receive much praise and reinforcement. Keep in mind that what the client is being asked to do is very difficult and threatening. We want each client to succeed; therefore, we structure the situational task down to the last detail. Think about the basic *wh* questions to guide this activity: who, what, where, when, how, and why. For example,

> Eric will use a voluntary stutter:
> Who = a friend, Jack
> Where = in the cafeteria
> When = standing in the lunch line
> What = "I'm hungry."
> How = bounce on the /h/ sound at the beginning of *hungry*.

You and your client role-play and practice with the group in the therapy room, gradually moving into the cafeteria. This prepares him for the task as best as possible and increases the likelihood of completion. In our experience, speech therapists work exceptionally well creating these speech hierarchies.

Reducing Avoidance Behaviors

As one of his ground rules for therapy, Fraser (1978) suggests eliminating all avoidances. This goal is easier said than done. To stop avoidance behavior, you must analyze the client's reaction patterns and teach him to become aware of these avoidances. After awareness comes change. Together with your guidance, the client outlines a plan to eliminate these avoidances. A word of warning: When removing a behavior, the client will often replace it with another inappropriate one. Make sure these avoidances have developed out of a fear of stuttering. If the client continues to fear stuttering, he will just replace one behavior with another faulty coping mechanism. Therefore, the client must reduce the fear of stuttering through voluntary stuttering, openness and speech assertiveness, and knowledge. Another strategy the client can employ is positive self-talk. Comments such as "I can do this" or "This is difficult and I will try my best" fit into the category of positive affirmations. Other ways to reduce behavior through positive self-talk and knowledge are presented in chapter 9.

Facilitating Awareness and Monitoring

Speech pathologists often express their concern about creating awareness of stuttering through direct intervention. For the preschool child who has not been stuttering for a prolonged period of time, we do not want to draw awareness to the laborious task of talking. However, for some children whose profile is filled with negative awareness, anticipation, and avoidance, facilitating a positive awareness of stuttering is important to progress.

Goldberg (1997) maintained it is difficult to change behaviors you are not aware exist. The client must be able to identify and label a behavior before he can make the conscious choice to change it. Experience tells us that many school-age children who stutter, and certainly adolescents and adults, are aware they are different in some way. Some can tell you exactly about their stuttering problem right from the start. Others need guidance in learning about their disorder and how it manifests itself in their speech. Helping clients understand what they do, feel, and think when they stutter serves to demystify the disorder and facilitates the change process.

One way to increase awareness is to allow the client to evaluate his own productions. Of course, when you teach clients how to use a technique, much performance feedback is provided. You tell them how easy they started, how smooth their speech was, or how to improve its connectedness. We constantly tell them "Good, nice easy start," "Good slide out," or "Good change" and seldom allow the client to evaluate his own performance. Then later you must allow the client to judge his own productions. This self-evaluation leads to increased awareness and monitoring and is a part of each therapy session.

Developing Positive Speech Attitudes

Having fun in therapy is necessary but not sufficient to change the negative communication attitudes of people who stutter. DeNil and Brutten (1991) found children who stutter exhibited greater negative attitudes toward communication when compared

Table 5.4
Support groups and resources.

American Speech-Language-Hearing Association	Stuttering Foundation of America
10801 Rockville Pike	P.O. Box 11749
Rockville, MD 20852	Memphis, TN 38111
(800) 638–8255	(800) 992–9392
www.asha.org	www.stutteringhelp.org
Board-recognized fluency specialists:	**Friends**
www.stutteringspecialists.org	1220 Rosita Road
National Stuttering Association	Pacifica, CA 94044
119 W. 40th Street, 14th Floor	(866) 866–8335
New York, NY 10018	www.friendswhostutter.org
(800) We Stutter	**Stuttering Home Page**
www.WeStutter.org	www.stutteringhomepage.com

with their peers. These attitudes may take either interpersonal or intrapersonal directions. Bennett, Ramig, and Reveles (1993) found young children who stutter exhibit mainly interpersonal concerns about talking. As they get older these concerns become more internalized and take on an intrapersonal perspective. The older child who has been stuttering for a long period of time has most likely suffered social consequences that he has internalized as criticisms. He may begin to exhibit a low self-concept about the ability to change his speaking patterns. This negativity can persist into adulthood and impact treatment outcomes (Guitar & Bass, 1978).

Learning about stuttering, talking about famous people who stutter, and interacting with other people who stutter can reduce the sense of isolation and increase objective perspectives. Just having the experience of repeated success in modifying one's speech helps increase positive thinking. Support groups for adolescents and adults are essential to accepting the trials and tribulations one may experience in the journey to change one's stuttering (Ginsberg, 2000). Table 5.4 provides a list of support groups and resources to share with clients. The integrated model of intervention provides multiple opportunities to increase the client's positive perspectives toward becoming an effective communicator.

GUIDING PRINCIPLES OF INTERVENTION

Ramig and Bennett (1995, 1997a) present several tenets for working with school-age children who stutter that can be expanded to describe guiding principles of intervention for all people who stutter. The following principles represent the minimal expectations for all speech-language pathologists choosing to work with individuals who exhibit stuttering disorders:

1. Have at least a basic understanding of the phenomena of stuttering and be able to explain stuttering in concrete terms.
2. Allow, encourage, and reinforce any expression of feelings regarding talking.

3. Develop highly flexible treatment plans designed to meet the changing needs of the client.
4. Utilize positive reinforcement over punitive techniques, maintaining a positive environment for the person who stutters.
5. Be consistent in the terms you use when describing target behaviors.
6. Consistently model slower, relaxed speech and body movements throughout your interactions with the client.
7. Develop automaticity of skills through mass practice.
8. Follow a success-driven paradigm for therapy.

Success-Driven Model

It is recommended that you adhere to the principles just listed at all stages of intervention and work from a **success-driven model.** Attempt to make all interactions with clients as successful as possible. Continually ask yourself, "What skills does the client need to be successful at this task?" "What are the precursor skills necessary to perform this task?" To accomplish this goal, we use a teaching paradigm accompanied by speech analogies.

Teaching Paradigm

You must teach the skills necessary for successful speech management, not just present a stimulus, get a response, and provide a consequence. This is a testing paradigm that serves to assess not teach the skills necessary to succeed. For example, during a therapy session, you present a picture to the client to use a pullout modification strategy. The client is unable to perform successfully and explodes out of the stuttering block. You model the strategy again. With this feedback, another attempt is made.

This scenario is not indicative of a success-driven approach. Teaching from a success-oriented perspective, you would dissect the task just described into small sequential steps and then decide at what level the client can successfully begin. In order to utilize pullouts, the client must be able to know he is stuttering; catch his moments of stuttering before finishing it; freeze in the middle of stuttering; modify tension in the speech mechanism; and initiate phonation in an easy, smooth way in order to continue with his communication effort. If you divide complicated tasks into simpler steps, you will be better able to help the client by moving up and down the hierarchy of skills, thus decreasing frustration.

Speech Analogies

Conture (2001) suggested the use of analogies to assist children in understanding the therapy process and allow them to take a more active role in changing their speech. Use of analogies breaks down complex tasks into terms and concepts the child can understand, thus taking the mystery out of talking and stuttering. The normal talking process may be conceptualized as the process of making a pizza. Using a garden hose, Conture (2001) demonstrated the role of pressure in the eventual production of speech blocks. The House That Jack Built is a conceptual model of intervention that facilitates the learning process through the use of various analogies. Comparing the process professional athletes endure when developing and refining their skills can help the adolescent understand the importance of daily assignments to therapy progress. If the adult client owns a house, you and your client can problem-solve all the home maintenance tasks that must be completed on a routine basis. Certain tasks are required to be done once or twice a year; others must be attended to daily. As the adult client discusses the many chores involved in maintaining a house, you can make the association to the many chores involved in maintaining his speech gains.

Treatment Philosophy

The integrated approach to treatment described in this text includes three important principles. Automaticity, choice making, and understanding the change process are underestimated factors that impact therapy progress. You must understand the role of automaticity in skill development, empower the student through choice making, and manage the arduous process of establishing long-lasting speech change.

The Role of Automaticity

Stuttering and secondary accessory behaviors develop as maladaptive responses to a break in the forward flow of speech. This reaction becomes reinforced and habitual. **Habit** is an acquired pattern of behavior that has become involuntary as a result of frequent repetition (Jeffers, 1988). Thus replacing old habits with new habits requires much drill. Gregory (1991) commented that clients need structure and considerable repetition in order to change speech patterns. Prins (1997) reinforced this belief when he wrote, "If it is to be effective, the responses that replace old stuttering reactions must become automatic, done without special attention or effort" (p. 349). To establish **automaticity**. focus on increased response rate, manipulating certain variables during therapy, and reinforcing self-monitoring with automatic skill development.

Response Rate

The number sufficient to say a habit has been changed must be determined on an individual basis. Certain stages of therapy involve tasks requiring the client to demonstrate the ability to modify his speech. Modifying it once is not enough. Therapy is attempting to "reprogram" the client's speech "computer." Goldberg (1997) put it nicely when he wrote, "Nothing becomes automatic without consistent practice" (p. 52).

Think of what a client does when correcting a frontal lisp. The client is required to demonstrate proficiency and automaticity at the isolation step before moving into syllables. First, production is slow and purposeful with maximum direction from the therapist. As the client learns the new motor pattern, he produces syllables faster with less cognitive effort. Then he proceeds to the word level and slowly practices the new patterns in familiar grammatical forms. As the new way replaces the old way of saying the sound, rate of production increases again. This sequence of slow, purposeful productions gradually moving into faster, automatic efforts applies to clients working on speech modification strategies.

Therapy Variables

Clinicians often express concern regarding the ability of their clients to transfer newly learned behaviors outside the therapy room. Comments such as "He has the skills but just doesn't use them" reflect this therapy dilemma. Transfer of learned behaviors is a systematic process, one that you and your client must purposefully plan. Campbell and Hill (1989) outlined several therapy variables that, when manipulated, can facilitate transfer and maintenance. These variables, once put together, comprise the puzzle of therapy. As a puzzle piece (say listener reaction) is manipulated, you check for its impact on speech production before changing the next factor. If the client sustains his skills, you focus on another factor, say language formulation. This process continues until the client has sustained the skills in different therapy activities in which all variables have been manipulated to some degree. The client's puzzle, for this setting, is now complete. Change the setting, and you start over again, manipulating variables until the client has demonstrated mastery with all factors introduced. Let's look further into some of these variables.

1. *Topic/Materials.* You often select the stimuli used during each session. Sometimes you and the client develop word lists based on common interests to use when practicing strategies. As proficiency is mastered with one set of stimuli, introduce new words or topics to challenge the client. Many times clients practice everyday vocabulary words and overlearn them; they fail to transfer their skills to less common words.

2. *Physical Activity.* Manipulating physical activity changes the demands placed on the client as a particular point in time. For example, you may choose to ask the client to stand while saying single words. Then, the client walks around the room while performing the same speech task. As performance is maintained, the client may also try to juggle while saying his words, walk backward, play hopscotch, and so on.

3. *Location.* Therapy should take place in different locations. Initially, therapy starts in the clinician's room where the client becomes very comfortable with where he sits and the surroundings. At each step of the therapy process, the client should practice his skills in different environments. For example, the adult client has mastered the use of light articulatory contacts on single words and everyday phrases within the therapy room. The next step would be to change the location in which he practices this material, such as in the hallway, in the waiting room, at the local restaurant, outside the office building, or in the cafeteria.

4. *Listener Reactions/Distractions.* Clients must build up a tolerance for negative listener reactions and/or distractions. You probably often sit attentively, listening to the client. However, as the therapy process continues, model behaviors that may distract the client. Looking away while the client talks, tapping a pencil on the table, and coughing or sighing during a moment of stuttering are examples of behaviors clients

need to learn to tolerate. Auditory distractions are also useful when attempting to de-sensitize the client. Introduce a recording of noise from common environments and activities (such as restaurants, shopping malls, the movie theater, dinner table, or children playing) to help your client practice his speech strategies in real-life situations.

5. *Modeling.* In the early stages of therapy, modeling is critical. You must be able to model the behaviors you want your clients to learn. **Modeling** begins in a direct manner with you providing a sample at a one-to-one ratio (Clinician says, "ball" and the client immediately repeats "ball."). As proficiency develops, incorporate **intermittent modeling:** You say a word, interject a comment, and then the client produces the word (Clinician says, "Ball. Now it's your turn." The client says "ball."). However, as therapy progresses, reduce the extent of your modeling. If a new topic or a change in location is planned, you may need to change the modeling schedule based on client performance.

6. *Reinforcement.* Clinicians often reinforce client efforts to change through either verbal and/or token reinforcement. **Reinforcement** typically proceeds from a fixed ratio (1-to-1 reinforcement to 2-to-1, to 5-to-1) to a variable schedule of reinforcement (1-to-1, 5-to-1, 3-to-1, 10-to-1). Modify the reinforcement schedule systematically based on the client's current level of success. Some programs may use time as a basis for reinforcement. However, for the person who stutters severely, this type of reinforcement schedule can be highly punitive. Exercise caution when considering the use of time-based reinforcement schedules.

7. *Language Formulation.* Changing the level of language formulation may put a greater demand on the speech production skills of the client who stutters. You can plan therapy systematically to include gradual changes in linguistic complexity and utterance length to facilitate client progress. As a change is made in language formulation, you and your client must closely monitor the level of stuttering. If large jumps are made in this area, the client may not be able to implement his strategies, thus becoming frustrated.

8. *Persons Present.* Most therapy sessions include the client and the clinician, with perhaps other children if therapy is within the school setting. Introducing a new person into the therapy session may be a sufficient enough change to challenge the client's ability to use his strategies. Periodically, it is a good idea to ask someone new to participate in therapy to help the client adapt to such changes.

Self-Monitoring

The ultimate goal of therapy is for the client to become his own clinician. To reach this goal, clients must have the opportunity to self-monitor their speech efforts under the guidance of the speech pathologist. Often, you are the sole person evaluating the client's attempts to change his speech. Clients may become dependent on you to evaluate their speech progress. Then, when asked to perform in environments where you are absent, the client is unable to evaluate his performance accurately or thoroughly. During the early stages of therapy, ask the client to self-evaluate his speech. For example, both of you can rate, on separate pieces of paper, the client's ability to catch stuttering moments. Then compare these ratings and discuss any discrepancy. The client engages in another therapy task, ranks his speech performance, and compares it to your ranking. This helps the client develop a realistic evaluation system and provides multiple opportunities to self-monitor his speech. At each stage of therapy (establishment, transfer, and maintenance), incorporate self-monitoring into client tasks. Chmela and Reardon (2001) provide several worksheets that are useful for children who stutter to self-evaluate their speech. These 7-point Likert scales can easily be modified for use with the adolescent and adult who stutters.

Choice Making

Another component of our treatment model that empowers the client to become an active participant in therapy is **choice making.** Throughout the activities presented in the upcoming chapters, you will notice the clients are allowed to make even the simplest decisions, such as picking the color of their speech folder, what stickers they want to earn, or whether to use crayons or markers. Offering a choice means you must be prepared to accept the client's decision. This communicates to clients that they are important and can make choices on their own, thus developing a sense of empowerment (Kaufman; 1980; Kaufman & Rafael, 1990) and autonomy (Faber & Mazlish, 1980).

Empowerment emerges when provided with a choice. Kaufman and Rafael (1990) equated choice making with power. Individuals can be responsible for their behaviors and feelings by making choices about their behavior and feelings. You can share with your clients this famous quote: "You may not have the choice of whether you stutter or not. But you do have the choice of how you are going to stutter." Enabling clients to make decisions regarding their treatment direction develops self-responsibility. Accepting responsibility for speech change is necessary for long-term stabilization of newly learned behaviors (Leith, 1984). You must utilize different strategies to empower students to be active participants in therapy.

Autonomy is independence that leads to increased self-confidence and internal locus of control. Autonomy dissipates feelings of helplessness, worthlessness, and frustration (Faber & Mazlish, 1980). If the client asks, "Do you want me to use my stretches?" you might respond, "Do you want to use stretches? What feels most comfortable to you?" Communicating respect for the client's insight reinforces self-responsibility. This encouragement also develops self-monitoring skills, a basic necessity of treatment progress (Leith, 1984). Faber and Mazlish (1980) list six skills therapists may use to encourage autonomy: (1) let clients make choices; (2) show respect for a client's struggle; (3) don't ask too many questions; (4) don't rush to answer questions; (5) encourage the client to use sources outside the home; and (6) don't take away hope (p. 139). Through the act of **volition** (the act of freely choosing a course of action or behavior), the client asserts personal responsibility for his behaviors (Goldberg, 1997).

Understanding the Change Process

The **change process** is challenging. By reflecting on behaviors you have tried to change in yourself, you will be reminded that probably the journey was not an easy one and was filled with frustration, relapse, and self-doubt. Understanding the difficulties and problems inherent when attempting to change affective, behavioral, and cognitive mind-set is essential to understanding the therapy process in its entirety.

Goldberg (1997) has an outstanding chapter on the change process in his text *Clinical Skills for Speech-Language Pathologists.* Change occurs when clients accept responsibility for both their current and future behaviors, are motivated to change, and possess knowledge of the change process. The basis for change lies in the client's knowledge of how to use specific strategies, practice routines, and retrieve strategies in nonclinical settings. Goldberg suggests behaviors that change gradually last longer, particularly if rewarded and reinforced. Praise the client for small accomplishments, small steps toward their goal. Teach the client to become his own change agent by explaining how change occurs and the pitfalls of change before he engages in the process.

CLIENT/CLINICIAN RELATIONSHIP

The initial therapeutic meetings of client and therapist are critical to establishing a solid relationship based on trust and acceptance. This **client/clinician relationship** has often been expressed as the most critical variable in the treatment process (Crowe, 1997; Gregory, 1991; Manning, 1996). The first few days of rapport building sets the groundwork for successful stuttering therapy (Guitar, 1998; Manning, 1996). You must demonstrate a sincere interest in the client as a person of value and worth before you attempt to modify speech behaviors.

Adolescent/Adult Considerations

Some adolescents and adults enter the therapeutic process with accumulated emotional garbage from years of stuttering. Take the time to understand the client's unique feelings and belief system. Listening to the client's story or his history of stuttering is an effective way of building a strong client/clinician relationship (Bloom & Cooperman, 1999). Knowing the client's story should precede any dissemination of information. When you attempt to provide answers for the older person who stutters, disempowerment occurs and possibly reinforces the sense of helplessness present in this age group. Shipley (1997) said effective client/clinician communication is based on sensitivity, respect, empathy, objectivity, listening skills, and motivation. These conditions, particularly relevant for adolescents and adults who stutter, is discussed further in later chapters.

Child-Based Activities

The activities here demonstrate the process of establishing a bond between therapist and student based on honesty, trust, openness, and a sincere interest in one another as unique individuals. These activities were developed for use with children who stutter receiving services in the school setting. Not all activities are adaptable for use with adolescent or adults, whose particular needs are addressed in subsequent chapters.

ACTIVITY 1:   THIS IS ME. WHO ARE YOU?

Objective:	The client will identify and state the reason he is coming to therapy.
Procedures:	The therapist, upon meeting with the student for the first time, explains who she is and states her position at the school. The walk from the child's classroom to the therapy room includes a casual conversation of introductions to all children in the group, school, and what the children enjoy doing. She explains to the children that she receives a list of children eligible for services and their names are on the list. Here is a possible scenario:
Clinician:	"Well, hello Jimmy. My name is Miss Jones. I am the speech pathologist here. It's time for you to come to speech. I'd like you to meet Jessie, Armond, and Fran. They are students who also come to speech with you."
Jimmy:	"Hi, I'm Jimmy."
Students:	"Hi Jimmy."
Clinician:	"You have been in the third grade now for a week. How do you like your teacher?"
Jimmy:	"Great, she seems really nice so far."
Clinician:	"What do you like about your classroom?"
Jimmy:	"I like our nature center. We have snakes, a turtle, and an aquarium of fish."
Clinician:	"Wow, that sounds great!"
Clinician:	"I told you as we walked here from your classroom, my name is Miss Jones. I am your speech therapist. On the first day of school, the principal gave me a list of students who are lucky enough to get to come to speech and your names were on the list. This is where I need your help. There are only names on this list. This list does not tell me why you are coming to speech. Do you know, Jimmy?"
Jimmy:	"I'm not sure."
Clinician:	"Some children I work with need help saying sounds. When they want to say /r/, they might say /w/, for instance. Do you have trouble saying sounds?"
Jimmy:	"No, not really any one sound. It's more like I get stuck on my sounds, like they won't come out of my throat."
Clinician:	"Oh, yes. I have worked with a lot of children who talk about that happening. There is a name for that. Do you know it?"
Jimmy:	"Yes, my old speech pathologist called it stuttering."

Clinician:	"That's right. That's the name—stuttering. That's what we call it when sounds or words get stuck in our throat or mouth. So is that why your name is on my list?"
Jimmy:	"Yes."
Clinician:	"It's important we know and remember the name. Stuttering. Let's say it together."
Both:	"Stuttering."

ACTIVITY 2: RULES AND EXPECTATIONS FOR OUR ROOM

| Objective: | To create a set of rules and expectations for therapy. |
| Procedures: | Upon entering the therapy room and being seated, ask the students if they know something about rules—rules in their class, home, library, and so on. Then as a group, create rules for the speech room. With a large piece of construction paper and black marker, ask the students to brainstorm rules and expectations they believe may be necessary and fair. Write down, accept, and validate all ideas. When an exhaustive list has been completed, the group discusses and decides on what rules to keep. A sample conversation follows: |

Student:	"I know a rule! Listen to the teacher."
Clinician:	"Yes! Listening is very important."
Student:	"How about no running around."
Clinician:	"Write that one down."
Student:	"Take turns talking."
	(Students continue adding to the list.)
Clinician:	"It looks like we have a thorough list of all kinds of rules. Let's decide together on the five we want to keep."

ACTIVITY 3: CREATING THE SPEECH FOLDER

| Objective: | To create a personalized student portfolio. |
| Procedures: | Gather the following materials together: varied colored pocket folders, markers, colored pencils, crayons, glitter, and other various decorations. Children enter the speech room and take their seats. Tell the students that because of the "great information and fun creations" they will be getting and making during speech time, they will need a folder to store them. Multiple choices are offered the students as they create their personalized folder. Comments during this time are nonjudgmental, reaffirming |

individuality. Observations and verbalizations from the children are wel-
comed, however not expected or necessary. If they occur, positive reflections on the *content* of the message are made, although nothing is
said about *production* of the message. Dialogue may sound like this:

Clinician: "Oh John, I see you have chosen blue. And Tosha, you picked green. We all have different likes. We are all different in different ways."
John: "I like spaceships. Do you have any stickers with rockets?"
Clinician: "I don't think so, but you could draw one on your folder."
Tosha: "I see star stickers. I want them!"
Clinician: "Help yourself to any stickers you like."

ACTIVITY 4: GETTING TO KNOW YOU!

Objective: To instill feelings of acceptance and importance in the student.

Procedures: Gather the following materials together: standard outline of child, various colored construction paper, colored pencils, markers, crayons, glue,
and magazines. Tell the students to (1) cut out the outline of the child
and glue it on the construction paper of his choice; (2) draw on hands,
face, and so on, to decorate the person; (3) look through magazines and
cut out pictures and/or words that tell about who they are and what is
important to them; and (4) glue the pictures next to the outline of the
person. Model what you expect the children to do, commenting positively on the choices each child makes. Make no comments about
speech production. Conversation proceeds:

Clinician: "Oh, I found a picture of shrimp. Shrimp is my favorite food. I am cut-
ting this out."
Clifford: "I found a race car. I am cutting it out and gluing it here."
Clinician: "I found the word *nice.* I think I am nice so I am going to cut it out."
Clifford: "I found another race car going really fast. My mom says I go really fast
sometimes. I'm gonna cut it out."

ACTIVITY 5: STAND FOR

Objective: Child will identify and share areas of interest.

Procedures: You will need a list of statements that include common childhood interests. This game involves students standing up to identify their likes and
dislikes. If a child agrees with the statement made by the therapist, he

stands up. The children remain standing until a statement is made in which they disagree. Throughout the game, children will be standing and sitting as the statements change. As the game continues, comments are made about how different we are with regard to our likes and dislikes, that none of them are wrong, only different. To introduce the game, you might say, "When I make a statement you agree with, stand up." The dialogue might sound like this:

Clinician: "You like to ride bikes."
              (Everyone stands.)
Clinician: "Your favorite soda is Coke."
              (One sits down.)
Clinician: "You enjoy cleaning your room."
              (All but one sits down.)

ACTIVITY 6: GETTING TO KNOW ME BINGO

Objective: To reinforce that differences are okay.

Procedures: Gather together the following materials: Bingo boards, beans, chips, or some other sort of marker for the game; list of interests, activities, foods, actors, athletes, and so on, that interest the children. The first person to have a diagonal, horizontal, or vertical line wins. This child names the things that were covered and dialogue ensues. During the game, conversation may proceed like this:

Clinician: "Who *likes to watch football?*"
    Joey: "Oh, that's me, that's me! I got it!"
    John: "Not me, too long. I hate that game."
Clinician: "I see you two have different feelings about football. That's fine!"
    John: "But Mrs. Smith [therapist], you can't tell me you like football. It's boring, don't you think?"
Clinician: "I have watched football in the past. I have my own opinions and you have yours. Neither is right nor wrong, only different."

During these rapport-establishing activities, a child may make reference to his or another's speech. This is an opportunity for you to begin addressing differences in everyone's speech while discovering the child's attitudes and beliefs. Document the terminology the child uses when describing his speech in order to associate further learning with his current frame of reference. For example, dialogue during this activity might sound like this:

Clinician: "Now I want you to find and cut out pictures or words from the magazine that describes you."

John:	"I found the word *afraid*. I feel that way when I have to answer questions in class."
Clinician:	"You are afraid to answer questions in class. Glue it on your paper."
John:	"Sometimes I am trying to answer and the word won't come out."
Clinician:	"The word won't come out."
John:	"I know the answer and I am trying to say it, but it's like it feels real tight. Almost like I am going to choke, right here" (places hand around throat).
Clinician:	"Wow, like you're going to choke. Wow, show me again where it feels tight." (Again, student places hand around the throat. Clinician places her hand around her own throat, simulating what the child is doing.) "Has anyone else ever felt tight in the throat?" (Several group members nod yes.)
Joe:	"Not tight in my throat. My sounds get caught right on my tongue. They stay there and they are stuck."
Clinician:	"Joe feels stuck on his tongue sometimes and John in his throat. The first day we met, we talked about the name of the word that means getting stuck, caught, or feeling tight. Do you remember it?"
Students:	"Stuttering."
Clinician:	"Excellent! You remembered! From the games we have been playing and our discussions, it seems like we are different in many ways, including how we bump, or using the real word, how we stutter. Let's review some ways we are different."
John:	"We like different things to eat."
Clinician:	"Thank you, John."
Joe:	"We all have different bedtimes."
Clinician:	"That's true."
Jenna:	"We stutter differently."
Clinician:	"Yes, we even stutter differently."

The dialogue just described emphasizes the belief that beginning therapy should focus on the client, not the stuttering (Guitar, 1997). Establishing rapport is extremely important and does not occur in one session. Allocate time to this process and do not underestimate the need for a trusting, open, and reciprocal environment.

CHAPTER SUMMARY

Determining treatment plans for an individual who stutters involves multiple decisions made by the clinician and client. First, what is the best treatment paradigm to use in therapy? Is a fluency-shaping, stuttering modification, or a combination of both approaches the best way to address client needs? Next, the particular therapy strategies must be selected for instruction. The chapter reviewed 18 instructional strategies based on the client's speech profile.

Guiding principles of intervention serve to assist the therapist when planning actual instructional tasks for the client. Using a teaching versus a testing paradigm facilitates learning and enhances motivation. Speech analogies are an excellent instructional strategy to present abstract concepts in simplistic terms. Your philosophy of treatment should center around several basic constructs: automaticity, high response rates, manipulating therapy variables, and increased self-monitoring. Additionally, therapy becomes more client centered when choice making is allowed. Choice making provides the client with decisions regarding the direction of therapy, thus empowering him to change. With this power, the client begins to take more responsibility for his actions, thus developing autonomy and self-confidence. These feelings, along with knowledge of the change process, strengthens the client/clinician relationship, a critical factor in therapeutic success. Establishing a bond of trust and caring between client and clinician will vary depending on the age of the client. Considerations may be made for the adolescent and adult that may not be present for the younger child who stutters.

STUDY QUESTIONS

1. Describe the events of a therapy session when the therapist adhered to the philosophy of an integrated approach.

2. Describe the characteristics of the client who might benefit from a stuttering modification orientation to therapy.

3. Why is it important to establish automatic use of therapy strategies?

4. Generate an analogy you would use to help clients understand some aspect of treatment.

5. Develop a treatment plan for an 18-year-old male client with the following characteristics: high scores on the PSI, facial grimaces and lip posturing, loss of eye contact, and limited social opportunities to talk.

6. How would you implement the concepts of autonomy and empowerment in a therapy session for an adult versus a child who stutters?

7. What treatment variables would you incorporate into the therapy plan for a preschool child who stutters with little awareness of her disfluencies?

8. What factors would you consider when deciding the appropriate approach to therapy you would use with someone who stutters?

6

Counseling in Stuttering Disorders

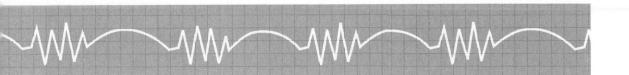

Expressing Empathy
Brainstorming
Self-Talk
Goal Setting

Shame Resolution
   Shame-Attacking Therapy
   Breaking Down the Wall of Silence
   Shame in Children
Anger: A Special Situation

LEARNER OBJECTIVES

- Describe the characteristic features of client-centered therapy.

- Implement SOLER during personal interactions within the classroom.

- Define empathy and describe ways of expressing one's understanding to clients.

- Differentiate between Rogers's client-centered therapy and Ellis's rational-emotive behavior therapy.

- Describe how the clinician may use Ellis's A-B-C technique with the person who stutters.

- Explain how shame can be resolved through the client/clinician relationship.

- Describe ways of managing anger in therapy.

- Explain the need for ongoing self-study in the area of counseling.

KEY TERMS

active listening
alternative perceptions
brainstorming
cognitive constructs
cognitive distortions
cognitive rehearsal
cognitive techniques
CPC Cycle
core message
disparity
disputing process

emotional overlays
empathy
genuineness
irrational beliefs
mantras
mastery
minimal encouragers
misperceptions
musturbatory
pleasure

principle of autonomy
principle of humanity
principle of humility
questioning
role play
self-efficacy
self-talk
shadow side of listening
SOLER
unconditional positive regard

The clinician is in a position to assist clients in reducing anger, guilt, and shame associated with stuttering. Many of the traditional stuttering modification activities have secondary effects on these emotions. However, specific counseling tasks may be needed to target reduction of the emotional reaction to stuttering. These techniques will require an understanding of basic counseling principles, knowledge of various counseling approaches, and facility with certain counseling strategies. A special note is required: Not all clients who stutter experience anger, guilt, and shame. Only the clinician may engage in counseling activities if your client's profile indicates a need (Luterman, 1991; Murphy, 1999; Quesal, 1997a; Rustin, Cook, & Spence, 1995; Schum, 1986; Shipley, 1997; Zebrowski & Schum, 1993).

NEED FOR COUNSELING

Addressing the affective and cognitive aspects of stuttering requires clinicians to have knowledge and skills in counseling (Bloom & Cooperman, 1999; Cooper, 1997; Luterman, 1991; Manning, 1996; Riley, 2002; Shapiro, 1999). People who stutter report feelings of loss of control, fear, and hopelessness at certain periods in their lives. The clinician/client relationship can help clients working through these feelings to improve their communication confidence. Cooper (1997) stated counseling is appropriate when certain conditions exist that interfere with therapy progress: misperceptions, emotional overlay, and a disparity between the way the stutterer thinks and feels about himself and his stuttering. The following discussion delves into a triad of conditions that requires the use of counseling skills.

Some people who stutter may exhibit **misperceptions** regarding their stuttering and the impact it has on their communicative effectiveness. They may be unable to identify what their lips, tongue, and jaw are doing during a moment of stuttering. They may not realize the extent to which their speech interferes with communication or how their speech mannerisms are distracting to the listener. Or they may perceive their stuttering is so severe that they are not worthy of the listener's attention. They may believe listeners perceive every bobble in their speech as negative. Cooper stated that extreme misperceptions may create emotional feelings attached to stuttering, impacting the client's ability to work on his speech. Clients' self-perception of the need to work on speech may impact therapy progress.

Emotional overlays, extreme reactions to the stuttering condition, may create a sense of hopelessness. With these feelings, the client may not even enter therapy voluntarily and if he does, may not believe it is going to help him. You may find you are putting more energy into the therapy process than the client. Missed therapy sessions and incomplete home assignments are two examples of noncompliant behavior due to emotional overlays. Cooper proposed that clients must feel their speech is important enough to warrant putting in the energy for therapy.

Another situation calling for counseling skills occurs when the client exhibits a **disparity** between his feelings and thoughts around stuttering. The client may tell you one thing, yet his behavior reflects the opposite. For example, clients may say they are bothered by their speech and want very much to work on getting better. Yet they forget to do their first outside assignment. "A stutterer may be intellectually aware of the need to modify his speech but may not be emotionally committed to doing so" (Cooper, 1997, p. 21). Therapy activities incorporating counseling skills will help clients better understand the interaction among their feelings, thoughts, and behaviors. Once you identify the need to implement counseling skills, however, you must be knowledgeable about various counseling approaches.

COUNSELING APPROACHES

There are many approaches to counseling in the literature, for example, Gestalt, person-centered therapy, psychoanalytic, humanistic, existential, cognitive, and behavioral. For the purposes of this text, only those approaches that have been applied directly to people who stutter are discussed. Two of the most commonly used with people who stutter are the client-centered and cognitive-behavioral approaches (Bloom & Cooperman, 1999; Conture, 2001; Guitar, 1998; Manning, 1996; Rustin, Cook, & Spence, 1995; Shapiro, 1999; Silverman, 1996; Van Riper, 1973).

Client-Centered Therapy

Carl Rogers (1961), in his book *On Becoming a Person*, outlined the basic premise of client-centered therapy: to respect and facilitate the self-generated growth of the individual. To achieve this goal, you must believe (1) there are many possible realities to any given experience, that is, no right or wrong ways to view a situation, and (2) if you show trust and respect for clients, they will move in a positive direction toward self-actualization. To accept clients as they are means to listen nonjudgmentally. Acceptance does not mean agreement. You may acknowledge the client's views on his speech, yet not support certain behaviors in which the client engages because of his perceptions of reality. Again, Rogers contends that the clinician must accept and respect the multiple realities for the client. To demonstrate acceptance and respect, Bohart and Todd (1988) present seven rules of conduct. The clinician does not:

1. Give advice on how clients are to solve their problems.
2. Give general advice on how clients should live.
3. Judge clients.
4. Label clients.
5. Develop treatment plans for clients.
6. Direct clients to talk about certain topics.
7. Interpret the meaning of clients' experiences.

The client-centered approach to counseling is a process-oriented way of interacting with clients, which means it focuses on the behavior the client is doing, facilitated through a strong client/clinician relationship. Rogers emphasizes the role of the therapist in the client's process toward self-actualization. He believed certain personal qualities of clinicians impact the therapeutic process: unconditional positive regard, empathy, and genuineness.

Unconditional positive regard encompasses certain features of the therapist: (1) care for the client that builds trust, (2) care must be nonpossessive or noncontrolling, and (3) respect for the autonomy of the client with the belief that he is capable of making change. The client is valued as a person regardless of the negative or positive behaviors exhibited. The clinician sets aside all judgment and allows the client to express himself in a warm and safe environment, which, according to Rogers, is essential to the client/clinician relationship. "The safety of being liked and prized as a person seems a highly important element in a helping relationship" (p. 34).

Empathy is the ability to view events from the client's perspective. Do not allow your own experiences to color your perceptions of the client's situation. True empathy is an attempt to feel what the client has experienced from his point of view. Your understanding of the thoughts and feelings expressed by the client is essential to therapeutic growth. Expressing empathy is a skill that requires practice. One strategy used to convey empathy is the *reflection of feeling* technique. Reflecting the client's feelings conveys the clinician's comprehension to the client. The clinician may convey a reflection of feeling as well as a reflection of meaning, as demonstrated in the following example:

Client: "I really tried not to change my words with my date. It's just so hard to let go and not worry about what she may think of me when I stutter."

Reflection of Feeling: "You sound confused and fearful."

Reflection of Meaning: "You're saying that showing your stuttering might change how shefeels about you."

Being empathetic creates trust between the client and clinician. With trust, clients will be more willing to be open about important issues in their lives. As clients share their experiences, the empathetic clinician can model how to reflect on these experiences, subsequently allowing the client to emulate this reflection strategy. When using the reflective technique, the clinician is training the client to listen to and capture the meaning of his experiences (Bohart & Todd, 1988, p. 140).

Genuineness is used to convey a sense of honesty, congruence, and authenticity on your part. Clinicians are said to be genuine when what they do and say accurately reflects how they think and feel about matters of importance. Rogers wrote the following about what being "real" means: "I need to be aware of my own feelings, in so far as possible, rather than presenting an outward facade of one attitude, while actually holding another attitude at a deeper or unconscious level. Being genuine also involves the willingness to be and to express, in my words and my behavior, the various feelings and attitudes which exist in me" (p. 33). The clinician may demonstrate genuineness through periodic self-disclosure, introducing a personal problem to the client. Two cautions regarding clinician use of self-disclosure, however: First, the problem disclosed should be relevant to the client's issues currently being addressed. Second, disclosure should be used as a means of facilitating client progress and not as a venting exercise

for the clinician. Self-disclosure can create empathy, which, according to Rogers, is therapeutic itself. Developing and refining your skills in demonstrating empathy will certainly enhance your therapeutic relationship with people who stutter.

In summary, Rogers's client-centered counseling focuses on the demonstration of
respect for the client through empathetic listening behaviors. The clinician is non-
judgmental of the client, attempting to view his experiences through the client's eyes.
Clinicians, congruent or genuine in their own lives, use reflection of feeling and meaning, as well as self-disclosure, to strengthen the client/clinician relationship.

Cognitive-Behavioral Therapy

Cognitive-behavioral therapy is oriented to the thoughts clients have regarding their
reality. The cognitive perspective contends that one's thoughts mediate or shape the
individual and can be modified through counseling. Four different cognitive-behavioral
approaches are summarized next: personal construct therapy, social learning theory,
Aaron Beck's cognitive therapy, and Albert Ellis's rational-emotive behavior therapy.

Personal Construct Theory

The psychologist George Kelly developed a theory of personality in the mid-1950s. He
conjectured that personality consists of sets of **cognitive constructs** based on the individual's anticipation of recurring events. "What these statements mean is that a person makes sense of the world by developing cognitive categories which he can then
use to try to predict, that is, anticipate, events" (Bohart & Todd, 1988, p. 222). These cognitive categories usually take the form of opposites, or dichotomous values, such as
"good" versus "bad" or "happy" versus "sad." Constructs can be considered rigid or
loose, open or closed to possible change. A person can have constructs that are not in
agreement with one another, causing cognitive confusion. Personal construct counseling helps people use their cognitive constructs to make sense of their world and
motivates them to reshape constructs for greater congruency.

Personal construct theory has been applied to the disorder of stuttering most no-
tably by Lena Rustin, Frances Cook, Willie Botterill, and David Shapiro. Kelly's self-
characterization and repertory grid are two techniques they use to gain insight into
the client's views of himself, his stuttering, and significant others. Clients write a character sketch about themselves as a means of gathering information on the client's constructs and issues of concern. Rustin, Cook, and Spence (1995) provide directions for
this task: "Write a character sketch of yourself as if you were a close friend of yours,
someone who knows you very well, probably better than anyone really does, a sympathetic friend" (p. 175). You can learn more about the client's personal constructs
through analyzing their characterization, particularly the first and last sentences. Botterill and Cook (1987) contend these statements "are often amongst the most reveal-
ing about the person" (p. 153).

Another task used to gather information about the client's personal constructs is
the repertory grid technique. The repertory grid is a series of constructs, relevant to
the client, rated along a continuum of 9 points, such as joyful one end (1 point) and

angry at the other (9 points). These constructs are outlined by the client and clinician, identifying grid elements pertinent to the client's history. Grid elements may include friends, family members, people admired by the client, or teachers. Next, the grid is constructed with elements along the top axis and constructs down the vertical axis. The client then rates how he views each construct for each element on the grid. The resultant matrix often provides information about particular constructs that may shape the client's treatment plan.

They also described a three-stage process, called the **CPC Cycle,** for developing an awareness of possible alternatives to one's behavior: (1) circumspection, (2) pre-emption, and (3) control. During circumspection, the client engages in a problem-solving exercise about a particular problem. The client and clinician brainstorm all possible alternatives to the problem, allowing even the absurd to be considered. Botterill and Cook (1987) instruct clients to "present the first thing that comes into your head no matter how crazy it may seem" (p. 163). Once a list has been constructed, they enter the preemption stage, considering the consequences of each solution. The control stage involves testing each solution for actual success. "The level of success or failure the chosen strategy achieves is less important here than the elaboration of the construct system which produced it. Either outcome is likely to lead to further elaboration and development of the individual's construct system which will in turn lead to the development of further more adaptive strategies" (p. 163).

Shapiro (1999) writes of the application of personal construct theory to school-age children, adolescents, and adults who stutter. Seven of Kelly's 11 corollaries with illustrations are discussed and related to people who stutter. The following summarizes Shapiro's applications:

1. "*Construction corollary: A person anticipates events by construing their replications.*" This means we anticipate our future on the basis of our past. A 55-year-old client cannot envision what it might be like to talk fluently because stuttering is all he has ever known. People who stutter anticipate the words and situations when they will stutter. Clients' motivation in treatment will continue only if they have experienced, and thereby can anticipate, success. A clinician's attitude toward stuttering therapy and the likelihood of a client's success will be affected by the relative success of treatment with previous clients.
2. "*Dichotomy corollary: A person's construction system is composed of a finite number of dichotomous constructs.*" In other words, people view the world in terms of opposites. The common conceptualization of people as "stutterers" or "fluent speakers" embodies a dichotomous construct that obscures the reality that fluency is a continuous variable and people who stutter (and their clinicians) are a heterogeneous population.
3. "*Choice corollary: A person chooses for himself that alternative in a dichotomized construct through which he anticipates the greater possibility for extension and definition of his system.*" This means all people have and make choices, either implicitly or explicitly. Both stuttered and fluent speech are the consequences of what someone does, feels, and thinks. Once provided ownership of stuttered and fluent speech as realistic options, the person who stutters may choose, with guidance, accordingly.

4. "*Experience corollary: A person's construction system varies as he successively construes the replication of events.*" Building on the construction corollary means both our anticipation of events and our view of the world evolve on the basis of past and particularly repeated experiences. This is how stuttering gains habit strength. "I have always stuttered. I stutter. Therefore, I will stutter." However, you can use this same corollary to break the habit strength of stuttering by creating an opportunity for the client to build a foundation of successful fluency experiences on which he begins to anticipate future fluency success. In other words, by creating opportunities for success (a primary objective in effective treatment), success begets success.

5. "*Individuality corollary: Persons differ from each other in their constructions of events.*" This means people are likely to hold vastly different interpretations of the very same observed event. Because all people who stutter are different in how they construe and predict the world, treatment must be tailored to fit each individual. Also, this corollary may explain why clinicians hold different treatment recommendations for the same client.

6. "*Commonality corollary: To the extent that one person employs a construction of experience which is similar to that employed by another, his psychological processes are similar to those of the other person.*" This argues for the client and clinician to create and use opportunities to shift perspective so as to consider other points of view—that is, for the client to see through the eyes of (experience the construct system of) fluent speakers, and the clinician to see through the eyes of the client.

7. "*Sociality corollary: To the extent that one person construes the construction process of another he may play a role in a social process involving the other person.*" This is an extension of the commonality corollary. People often do share common perceptions of the same experience. Examples might include the camaraderie noted at conventions held by self-help and support groups for people who stutter or the sense of inclusion experienced by members sharing a cultural identity. Clients, at least temporarily, can come to see as others do by shifting perspective. To the extent we can share the perspective of another person, we begin to understand and participate within his or her reality. (pp. 121–122)

Shapiro strongly advocates clinicians to be aware of the client's view of himself as a communicator in a social world. With this knowledge, you can facilitate client change in the future. However, clients must also be actively involved in the change process. They must identify, reassess, and revise their own person constructs conducive to long-term maintenance of fluency. This is a useful reference for those who wish to explore this theory related to people who stutter.

Social Learning Theory

Social learning theory incorporates several key issues that are relevant to working with people who stutter. This theory contends that learning emerges as a person associates an event with certain stimuli because of its predictive value. Bandura (1977, 1986) proposed that behavior is associated with anticipated consequences, regardless of whether these consequences occur. The client develops a sense of **self-efficacy,** which is one's perception of a certain level of competence to perform a behavior. Self-efficacy is situation specific, that is, a client can feel competent to answer the phone at home but does not feel competent to do so at work. A client who has low self-efficacy will avoid situations, develop defense mechanisms in response to their perceptions of incompetence, and give up when he perceives the behavior is too difficult. A person who stutters may have low self-efficacy as a communicator and avoid speaking situations or develop secondary behaviors (or defense mechanisms). He may lack the persistence to stay in therapy when challenged by performance-based therapy tasks. Bandura believed the client benefits most from both observing and performing behaviors that increase self-efficacy (Bandura, 1986). You must be prepared to demonstrate what you want the client to do, modeling high self-efficacy. *Seeing* and *doing* are two constructs that are highly relevant to speech therapy for stuttering.

Cognitive Therapy

Cognitive therapy, as proposed by Aaron Beck, is a structured, systematic approach to the resolution of dysfunctional cognitions. Originally designed for implementation with the depressed individual, Beck's therapy has been applied to other disorders, including stuttering. Beck described a three-dimensional characterization of the client entering cognitive therapy: (1) holds a negative view of himself, (2) holds a negative view of his personal future, and (3) holds a negative view of his current experiences (Bohart & Todd, 1988). The goal of cognitive therapy is to identify dysfunctional cognitions, see how they trigger depressive feelings and behaviors, and learn how to modify them. Beck was interested in *how* the client thinks, not *what* he thinks. He asks clients to develop hypotheses to test real-life experiences as a means of gathering evidence to contradict the client's perceptions and cognitive beliefs.

Bohart and Todd (1988) described the behavioral and cognitive techniques Beck uses to address the dysfunctional cognition of the client. Behavioral intervention includes a series of tasks in which the client engages to develop a sense of mastery. Clients are instructed to keep an hourly daily log of all activities. This provides information for the client to use when performing the mastery-pleasure rating task. **Mastery** is the sense of accomplishment one receives from doing a task; **pleasure** is how the client feels about the task. Here the client rates each activity along a continuum, much like a 7-point Likert scale. Next, the client and clinician use these ratings to outline a series of graduated task assignments. These scheduled tasks are arranged in a hierarchy from easy to more difficult to accomplished.

Additional techniques include cognitive rehearsal and role play. **Cognitive rehearsal** takes place when, first, the client and clinician break down a task into individual steps. Then the client rehearses the activity out loud. This verbal practice helps the client prepare for the actual task in advance and allows for feedback and discussion from the clinician. **Role play** is another common technique used in counseling. In a pretend interaction, clients assume the role of significant other, or in the case of the person who stutters, they assume the role of listener. They verbalize how they would respond to various scenarios, and the clinician takes the client's role, modeling effective coping strategies. Role playing is used to assist the client in developing a more flexible way of viewing events in his life.

Cognitive techniques include creating an awareness of the connection between the client's thoughts and feelings. Again, daily logs are used in which the client records his automatic thoughts in certain situations, as well as the feelings evoked by these thoughts. As this skill is mastered, the clinician asks the client to write down **alternative perceptions** of the situation. Another technique employed by cognitive therapists is **questioning:** The therapist asks questions to help the client test and explore his hypothesis about reality. Three types of questions are used: (1) What's the evidence? (2) What's another way of looking at the situation? and (3) So what if it happens? It is the clinician's job to question the client's statements about his perceptions regarding life's experiences.

Rational-Emotive Behavior Therapy

Rational-emotive behavior therapy (REBT) (Ellis, 2001; Ellis & Harper, 1975) is a form of cognitive therapy that focuses on the client's rational and irrational belief system. For Ellis, how the client interprets an event creates an emotional or behavioral reaction. The emphasis is not on what the client thinks but what the event *means* to the person. The individual interprets the event using extreme terms, such as *should, must,* or *have to,* indicating the client's **irrational beliefs.** Although these beliefs cannot be verified empirically or scientifically, the person remains attached to them. The person who stutters may make statements such as "I must be fluent to make a good impression" or "I should be able to say my name but I can't." Ellis calls this type of behavior **musturbatory** because the client turns preferences into needs.

Ellis presented a formula to demonstrate the sequence of events related to the development of irrational beliefs. The A-B-C formula reads as follows: *A* (objective event) → *B* (person's interpretation of the event) → *C* (emotional/behavioral reaction to the event). During early childhood, children experience an event, interpret it to mean something is wrong with them, and then act in ways to compensate for feelings of inadequacy. When this cycle repeats itself, the irrational belief becomes entrenched in the individual's belief system, shaping his behavior. Ellis (2001) identified three major irrational beliefs or absolutes held by humans: (1) "I must achieve outstandingly well in one or more respects or I am an inadequate person!" (2) "Other people must treat me fairly and well or they are bad people!" and (3) "Conditions must be favorable or else my life is rotten and I can't stand it!" (p. 61).

REBT is often short term, using direct confrontation of the client's beliefs about his life. Ellis utilizes techniques derived from various approaches, including operant conditioning, desensitization, assertion training, role playing, interpersonal skills training, modeling imagery, shame-attacking exercises, and bibliotherapy (reading materials). The clinician engages the client in the **disputing process** involving the logical challenge of beliefs. This process includes four stages: identify self-limiting beliefs; attempt to validate these beliefs; realize they cannot be validated; and replace them with more rational views. The ultimate goal is for the client to learn how to think scientifically. To reach this goal, beliefs need to be challenged repeatedly with active experiential exercises to test out beliefs. Ellis provides the client with homework assignments of disputing beliefs in which the client records his experiences in the daily log.

The basic principles of REBT have been implemented in the work of other psychologists who have described specific therapy tasks effective at disputing irrational beliefs. Burns, in *Feeling Good: The New Mood Therapy* (1980) and *The Feeling Good Handbook* (1989), outlines several cognitive therapy tasks to help clients cope better with their problems. Many of Burns's (1989) ideas apply to working with people who stutter (see these original resources for additional information). The following are key aspects of Burns's cognitive therapy:

1. People can change the way they think, feel, and behave.
2. Thoughts lead to certain emotions.
3. Positive thoughts produce greater self-esteem.
4. Negative thoughts decrease self-esteem.
5. Thoughts influence how we behave.

Burns emphasized the role of one's thought processes in the development of **cognitive distortions** or irrational beliefs. Negative thoughts create an array of emotions, depending on the nature of the individual's thoughts. More important, negative thoughts are a normal part of life. (In chapter 2, Table 2.4 provided examples of the connection between the type of negative thought and the emotion elicited by it.) When one suffers a loss, such as a death in the family, sadness and depression are expected. However, when protracted, these negative thoughts may lead to distorted or twisted thinking or distorted thoughts. Burns used many of Beck's and Ellis's techniques to help the client change thought patterns, such as the daily log. Using a three-column format, Burns has the client write down his automatic thoughts and estimate his belief in each one on a scale of 0 to 100. Next, he identifies the distortion present in each thought. Then the client substitutes a more realistic thought and estimates his belief in each one. When done repeatedly, the client's self-perceptions begin to change and become less self-damaging.

The approaches to counseling just described will help you utilize principles of unconditional positive regard, genuineness, and empathy to enhance your interpersonal skills. Identifying the client's personal constructs and knowledge of self-efficacy development will increase his likelihood of achieving speech goals. You may also incorporate activities to help clients confront their cognitive distortions and develop positive beliefs surrounding communication.

ELEMENTS OF COUNSELING

Few graduate programs in speech-language pathology include courses in counseling clients with communication disorders. This is unfortunate because you will often be placed in positions in which knowledge and skills in counseling would positively impact the therapy process. The following elements of counseling should provide some basic guidelines for those of you learning to counsel clients. As Meier and Davis (2001) noted in the preface of their book *The Elements of Counseling*, "one cannot become a counselor simply by memorizing" a set of guidelines and rules. Practice in role plays with knowledge of a theory of counseling are essential for all counselors. For the speech-language pathologist, professional development activities are essential to develop or strengthen the skills introduced in this chapter. Of Meier and Davis's 43 counseling guidelines, 11 have been selected here for their usefulness and applicability to speech therapy.

Counseling Guidelines

- **Speak briefly.** Communicate in one or two sentences and use minimal encouragers. It is the client's job to do the talking in counseling.
- **When you don't know what to say, say nothing.** It is okay to have silence in the therapy session. Avoid the temptation to fill the gap during periods of silence.
- **Notice resistance.** Pay attention to clients who abruptly change the topic or forget important assignments. Resistance may be an indicator of the client's lack of readiness for change.
- **When in doubt, focus on feelings.** As the client relates his story, ask him how he feels about his speech. Some clients may have difficulty recognizing their feelings or be unable to describe them. Learn to recognize feelings in your clients and help them express these feelings through statements such as "I feel anger because people cut me off when I stutter."
- **Avoid advice.** Do not give advice in the early stages of the client/clinician relationship. The rush to give advice puts you in the position of the person "having all the answers" and the client having none.
- **Avoid premature problem solving.** Help clients define the problem fully before developing a plan of action. Early problem solving, as in giving advice, places you in the position of power. If the plan fails, the client will most likely blame you.
- **Avoid relying on questions.** Direct questions may be threatening to the client and can make him defensive. Use open questions that allow the client to elaborate on his thoughts.
- **Listen closely to what clients say.** Specific words used by the client may provide information on how he views his speech. Use of the word *problem* instead of *stuttering* may indicate an underlying discomfort with this label and its hidden meaning. Words like *always*, *should*, and *must* tell you about the client's perceptions of his world and will need to be challenged later in therapy.
- **Do not assume change is simple.** Clients and beginning clinicians often view change from an unidimensional perspective: Do this and all will be better. However, clients do not live in a vacuum. Numerous factors may interact to keep the client from making significant changes in his speech. Clinicians and clients must identify these factors together and address them during therapy.
- **Do not assume you know clients' feelings, thoughts, and behaviors.** Avoid making comments like "I know how you feel" because you may incorrectly label the client's feeling. This is particularly relevant if you are a fluent speaker and it is inconceivable you would know how it feels to stutter.
- **Do not assume you know how clients react to their feelings, thoughts, and behaviors.** The way you respond to certain experiences may not represent how the client would respond. Be careful about overgeneralizing your reaction to that of the client.

Principles of Counseling

Certain principles of counseling may help you, as a beginning clinician, counsel people who stutter. Klevans (1988) published a list of major considerations relevant to the client/clinician relationship:

1. Techniques should be geared optimally to the achievement of reasonable specific therapeutic objectives identified early in the course of treatment.
2. The therapeutic process should be designed to meet the unique needs of the individual client and thus should be applied flexibly, sensitively, and in ways that are maximally meaningful to the client.
3. Steps should be taken to foster a good therapeutic relationship (working alliance) from the beginning of therapy, thus enhancing the client's active participation and creating a sense of collaboration and partnership.
4. Clinicians should resist the temptation to persuade the client to accept a particular "solution," to impose their values, or to diminish the client's striving for freedom and autonomy.
5. Rather than viewing therapy predominantly as a set of "technical operations" applied in a vacuum, clinicians need to be sensitive to the importance of the human elements in all therapeutic encounters.
6. All good therapeutic experiences lead to increments in the client's self-acceptance and self-respect; consequently, continual care should be taken to promote such experiences and to guard against interventions that might have opposite effects. (p. 205)

Positive Self-Concept

Developing a positive self-concept as an effective communicator is a very important goal of therapy. For some individuals, stuttering overshadows communication efforts, damping the self-concept or the "child's sense of their own personal worth and social identity" (Meyers & Woodford, 1992). By ages 8 through 10, a child's self-image is stabilized and reflects the experiences the child has encountered and judged to be successful or unsuccessful. A component of the child's self-concept might be the perception of an inability to communicate effectively. You must make efforts to shift these perceptions in a positive direction to ensure long-term maintenance of fluency gains. Berg (1990) presented nine ways to improve one's self-concept: (1) accept compliments, (2) make realistic comparisons, (3) don't overreact to failure, (4) minimize criticism, (5) recognize strengths, (6) expect what is reasonable, (7) expect success, (8) praise yourself, and (9) take credit for your achievements.

People who stutter may have difficulty recognizing their fluency strengths, often focusing on fluency failures. The stuttering dominates their thoughts, preventing them from viewing the communication effort in its entirety. They may be highly critical of their speech and have set unrealistic expectations for themselves. Many clients set themselves up for failure through anticipatory sets that are realized over and over.

Shifting to "anticipatory sets for fluency success" is a major goal for these clients. Murphy and Quesal (2002) provided a list of ways speech pathologists can help clients develop self-esteem; these include (1) keep an *I Did It List* (each day write a list of five things you did that day that made you feel proud); (2) expect to make mistakes; (3) don't compare yourself to others; (4) don't set unrealistic goals (changing your stuttering takes time); and (5) do good things for yourself (do at least one thing a day that is good for your brain and body). You must identify which clients are in need of such exercises and plan therapy tasks that will move them toward a more positive self-concept.

COUNSELING STRATEGIES

Counseling the person who stutters requires both knowledge and skills. You must learn how to listen actively and display both verbal and nonverbal behaviors conducive to an unconditional environment. During the therapy process, you may use active listening, minimal encouragers, expressions of empathy, brainstorming, self-talk, and goal setting to encourage clients to move in positive directions. These are only a brief sample of counseling strategies you may use when working with stuttering. Again, these strategies are only as effective as you make them. Practice is essential.

SOLER

When counseling the person who stutters, you need to develop certain listening skills. Egan (1998) sums these up in the acronym **SOLER**: *S*, face the client squarely indicating a posture of involvement; *O*, adopt an open posture where hands and legs are not crossed, but open in the direction of the client; *L*, lean forward slightly indicating to the listener you are attending; *E*, don't stare, but maintain steady eye contact with the client so he knows you are listening; *R*, remain relaxed; reduce fidgety behaviors and distracting facial expressions. Although SOLER appears a straightforward way to listen to clients, it does take practice. Resisting the urge to provide advice or even talk can be challenging for the novice listener. In the classroom activity you can practice implementing SOLER and openly discuss your performance with other students.

Classroom Activity

Divide the class into partners. Each student should take turns being the client and/or the counselor. Engage in a discussion and practice SOLER for 3 to 5 minutes. Reverse roles and continue with the interaction. As a class, discuss these interactions, directing your comments to each component of SOLER. Each student should try to use this strategy with people outside the class and be prepared to discuss their experiences at the next class period.

Active Listening

Effective counseling relies on your ability to listen to the client's story and understand his point of view. **Active listening** requires concentration and attention to both verbal and nonverbal components of the client's message. According to Egan (1998), listening involves (1) listening to and understanding the client's verbal messages; (2) observing and reading the client's nonverbal behavior—posture, facial expression, movement, tone of voice, and the like; (3) listening to the context—that is, to the whole person in the context of the social settings of his life; and (4) listening to sour notes—that is, things the client says that may have to be challenged (pp. 65–66).

Listening to and understanding the client's verbal message is the first step. In the beginning of therapy, clients often tell their stories of stuttering to the clinician that contain a mixture of information ranging from the client's experiences, behaviors, and affect (Egan, 1998). Clients may relate what happened to them during a particular interaction. For example, the client may say, "That lady just cut me off when I started to stutter. She didn't let me finish." The experience of the client involves a listener who interrupted him. The focus is on the other person and what he or she is doing. Clients may also include information on their behavior, what they did or did not do in the situation. For example, the client just described may continue his story by saying, "I just kept my mouth shut because I knew she wouldn't let me talk." The client's behavior would be described as "not saying anything more." Some clients may include information on their feelings during the interaction, such as "I got so angry when she cut me off." In summary, the client's **core message** could be summed up in the following statement reflected back to the client: "So when the lady cut you off, you became angry and stopped talking." When reflecting the client's message, use the words the client uses as a way to demonstrate listening.

The client's nonverbal cues will also provide useful information. Egan reported that effective helpers should attend to six particular behaviors: bodily behavior (posture, body movements, and gestures); facial expressions (smiles, frowns, raised eyebrows); voice-related behaviors (tone of voice, pitch, voice level, pauses, inflection); observable autonomic physiological responses (breathing, blushing, paleness); physical characteristics (fitness, height, weight, complexion); and general appearance (grooming and dress). The client's nonverbal behaviors confirm or refute what is being discussed or demonstrate client confusion and disorientation. Look for congruence between how clients are acting compared to what they are saying.

Listen to clients' behavior in the context of their life (i.e., past, present, and future interactions). Clients live in a social environment that influences their daily behaviors. As you attend to the client's behaviors when relating events around stuttering experiences, the context of the message will influence how you interpret the nonverbal behaviors. Do not isolate certain nonverbal behaviors, or as Egan stated, "Do not become overly fixated on details of behavior" (p. 72). Look for consistency of behaviors and reflect back to the client your observations, asking for insight into their meaning.

Finally, be sure to acknowledge "sour notes" expressed in the client's message that may need to be challenged later in therapy. These may include beliefs about stuttering or beliefs about the client's stuttering behaviors that negatively influence the likelihood of success. The *should, musts,* and *can'ts* are irrational beliefs that block progress. The client may make a comment, such as "I can't say my name," when in reality he just introduced himself by name. The client may express the notion of perfectionism when stating, "I should be able to be fluent. I have had enough therapy." But wait to confront the client on his beliefs until you have established a strong, trusting relationship. In the meantime, record the client's exact words in the session notes and use them as future topics for discussion.

Listening is more complex than you might imagine. It takes practice and mastery to be an effective listener. Egan introduces the **shadow side of listening** to emphasize this complexity. The downside of listening might entail inadequate listening, evaluative listening, filtered listening, labels as filters, fact-centered rather than person-centered listening, rehearsing, sympathetic listening, and interrupting. Table 6.1 provides definitions and examples of behaviors that might interfere with the listening process.

Table 6.1
Shadow side of listening with relevant examples related to stuttering.

Type of Listening	Definition	Speech Example
Inadequate listening	Becoming distracted by our own thoughts or problems.	Thinking about your reactions during a previous interaction with a salesclerk who was rude.
Evaluative listening	Judging the person as you listen to them. You begin thinking in terms of good-bad, acceptable-unacceptable. Thinking the client is a victim of wrongdoing and offering immediate advice on what he should do in the future.	The client believes he was denied a job opportunity because of his stuttering. You react with the following statement: "They can't do that. You should sue them."
Filtered listening	Cultural, sociological, and personal filters, learned early in life, may bias our listening. Prejudice distorts our listening.	When the clinician thinks, "This is a typical response for a man. He just wants to be in charge of everything."
Labels as filters	Using diagnostic categories to describe the client.	"I see my stutterer next." "The stutterer is waiting to see you."
Fact-centered rather than person-centered listening	Asking multiple questions as if getting all the facts will solve the problem.	"What did the person say to you? What did you say back? What was the expression on his face? What did you do after that?"
Rehearsing	Focusing on how you will respond to the client. When thinking about the best words to use, you have stopped listening.	"I need to use the right word. What word did he use when referring to his speech?"
Sympathetic listening	Taking one side of the story as the complete story.	The clinician begins to see only the client's views of events without considering other possibilities.
Interrupting	When you interrupt, you stop listening.	Cutting off the client when he is telling his story when the clinician feels there is something important that needs to be addressed or when the clinician wants to change the topic.

Source: Based on Egan (1998).

Minimal Encouragers

During the process of listening, you may use **minimal encouragers** as signals to the client to continue talking (Shipley, 1997). These are brief comments that reflect your attention, such as "Mmm," "Uh-huh," "I see," "Keep going," or "That's helpful." These vocalizations have been shown to be highly effective at increasing client verbalizations and enhancing the client/clinician relationship. However, the client may interpret the overuse of minimal encouragers as nonlistening. Sometimes, saying nothing is better than repeating the same vocalization over and over. Use encouraging comments when you want clients to know you are interested in what they have to say and that it is okay to continue talking.

Expressing Empathy

The expression of empathy by the clinician has been repeatedly identified as a major factor influencing the client/clinician relationship (Burns, 1989; Egan, 1998; Okun, 1997; Scheuerle, 1992; Shipley, 1997). As discussed earlier, empathy is the ability to perceive and communicate accurately what another person is feeling. Egan (1998) presents a formula for expressing empathy: "You feel . . . (here name the correct emotion expressed by the client) because (or when) . . . (here indicate the correct experiences and behaviors that give rise to the feelings)" (p. 84). After listening to the client's core message, you can incorporate the components of the message into this formula. Again, it takes much practice to refine one's skill at being empathetic. Appendix F provides several examples related to working with people who stutter that you can use to practice expressing empathy. Ultimately, you will move past this formula and be able to express empathy by using a single word ("Great"), phrase ("You're on cloud nine"), experiential statement ("You feel you conquered the task"), or behavioral statement ("You feel like shouting at the top of your lungs").

For some clients, the expression or feelings may be too direct and you may need to concentrate first on the experiences and behaviors. Egan emphasizes selectively focusing on one aspect of the client's core message at a time. You will not be able to respond to all the client's messages during a session. Instead, listen to the heart of the client's story, to the context surrounding the client's message. At times, you will be wrong in your empathy statement and need to recover. When this happens, the client will let you know of your error. It is okay to acknowledge wrong perceptions because this demonstrates that you, too, can make mistakes. Egan contends it is important the clinician "not pretend to understand." If you are not following what the client is saying, acknowledge it with a comment such as "I think I've lost you." Here are Egan's suggestions for using empathy:

1. Remember that empathy is, ideally, a way of being and not just a professional role or communication skills.
2. Attend carefully, both physically and psychologically, and listen to the client's point of view.
3. Try to set your judgments and biases aside for the moment and walk in the shoes of the client.

4. As the client speaks, listen especially for core messages.
5. Listen to both verbal and nonverbal messages and their context.
6. Respond fairly frequently, but briefly, to the client's core messages.
7. Be flexible and tentative enough that the client does not feel pinned down.
8. Use empathy to keep the client focused on important issues.
9. Move gradually toward the exploration of sensitive topics and feelings.
10. After responding with empathy, attend carefully to the cues that either confirm or deny the accuracy of your response.
11. Determine whether your empathic responses are helping the client remain focused while developing and clarifying important issues.
12. Note signs of client stress or resistance; try to judge whether these arise because you are inaccurate or because you are too accurate.
13. Keep in mind that the communication skill of empathy, however important, is a tool to help clients see themselves and their problem situations more clearly with a view to managing them more effectively. (p. 99)

Brainstorming

Often in the therapy process, you will engage the client in problem-solving troublesome situations. Together, you will brainstorm possible solutions to a problem. Egan describes rules for **brainstorming**, a series of questions used to further client understanding: (1) suspend judgment, (2) produce as many ideas as possible, (3) use one idea as a takeoff point for others, (4) get rid of normal constraints to thinking, and (5) produce even more ideas for clarifying ideas on the list. Table 6.2 contains a list of questions you may use to probe clients understanding of the benefit of certain choices they have listed while brainstorming. These questions also help clients think about the future rather than the past.

Self-Talk

Use of positive self-talk has been widely reported in the literature on stuttering (e.g., Blood, 1995; Bloom & Cooperman, 1999; Chmela & Reardon, 2001; Conture, 2001; Daly, 1988; Manning, 1996; Ramig & Bennett, 1995; Van Riper, 1973). The purpose of positive

Table 6.2
Questions clinicians may use when probing clients during brainstorming sessions.

1. What would the situation look like if you were managing your speech?
2. What changes in this situation make sense?
3. What would you be doing differently with your speech?
4. What patterns of behavior would be in place that are not in place now?
5. What current patterns of behavior would be eliminated?
6. What would you have that you do not already have?
7. What accomplishments would be in place that are not in place?
8. What would this opportunity look like if you developed it?

self-talk is to reprogram the client's internal filter, or auditory feedback loop, that may produce negative, self-defeating comments. Daily **mantras** are positive affirmations a client says to himself that puts him in charge of the situation. These may include comments such as "I have a lot to share with people" or "There is no need to be completely fluent." The client writes down power-inducing comments on an index card. He then rehearses these with meaning, initially overtly and then covertly in his mind. A schedule is made for practicing these mantras on a routine basis. Before entering a stressful situation, the client retrieves this card and selects a mantra to rehearse.

Just thinking positively may not alter the client's belief system, however. In fact, if the client does not believe in the mantra, all the practice in the world will not make it effective. Incorporate cognitive therapy principles to help the client identify trigger thoughts that plunge him into the throes of negative emotion. A useful tool is an activity called "Friendly Thinkin'" and "Stinkin' Thinkin'," used for school-age children who stutter. Divide a piece of paper in half. On one side write "Friendly Thinking" and on the other write "Stinking Thinking." The following dialogue provides an example of how to open the discussion:

Clinician:	"Every day we talk to ourselves in our head. How many of you have done this?"
Alex:	"Sure, I do. Sometimes, when I am walking to school, I will be saying things to myself. But not out loud."
Clinician:	"Right. We are talking in our heads. Sometimes, we may say things that are helpful, kind thoughts. Who can think of something kind you would say about yourself?"
Roberta:	"I look good today."
Alex:	"I am smart."
Clinician:	"That's right, Alex. You sure are smart, and Roberta, you look good today. When you say things like that you are being kind to yourself. However, sometimes, you may have a bad day and say things that are hurtful or unkind. Who can think of a hurtful comment?"
Alex:	"I am clumsy. Sometimes I think I am so fat that nobody likes me 'cause I am so fat."
Clinician:	"Saying you are clumsy and fat is hurtful to you. You are calling yourself a name. That's not being kind to yourself. What else might someone say to themselves?"
Roberta:	"You are stupid because you stutter."
Clinician:	"Wow. That's stinking thinking. That hurts. How can you change that thought so you don't hurt yourself?"
Alex:	"We could say I stutter, but that doesn't make me stupid."
Clinician:	"That's friendly thinking. You are being kind to yourself. What else might you say to be kind?"

Burnell (1990), in the *Power of Positive Doing*, presented a cycle of self-talk that people need to understand in order to change. "To shift your mental processes, you must first understand how your mind works" (p. 109). Burnell's thought cycle goes like this: How I think determines → What I think determines → My attitude determines →

What I do determines → My environment reinforces → How I think → and the cycle repeats itself. Identifying trigger thoughts is very important to changing this cycle. Clients need to discover what type of self-talk they use before and after moments of stuttering.

Changing before-the-act thoughts is the first step in modifying self-talk. Clients must be able to detect the presence of self-talk, identify if it is helpful or hurtful, and determine the source or reason for the self-talk. For example, the adult who stutters enters a store and approaches a salesclerk. He begins to feel anxious about this communication exchange and starts saying to himself, "She's going to laugh when I stutter." He catches this thought process and identifies the negativity present in the statement. He then reflects on his underlying discomfort with his stuttering and determines this to be the source of his negative thoughts. At this point, he has the opportunity to change his thoughts to make them more positive. He might comment to himself, "So what if I stutter."

Changing after-the-act thoughts, called *coping in retrospect* (McKay, Rogers, & McKay, 1989), is a strategy used after an episode to manage the tendency to perseverate on one's speech performance. This retrospection occurs regardless of whether the speaker is fluent or not. For example, after a moment of stuttering, some clients may rehearse this moment over and over, building anxiety and concern about their speech. Or, after a fluent moment, the speaker focuses too intently on the fluency in hopes of replicating it. However, this leads to anticipatory behaviors, setting the client up for the possibility of fluency failure. This rehashing can be eliminated by using mantras, allowing the client to move forward. Together you and your client can problem-solve various statements that the client practices everyday. No one response will be appropriate for all situations, so generate several for selection. Coping statements for fluent speech might be "I handled that one pretty well" or "I am taking charge of my speech." Coping statements in retrospect after one stutters might be "I can laugh about it," "I'm getting better at this," "Shake it off," or "There goes another stutter." The key point to remember is that the client copes with the aftermath of the event and moves on.

Goal Setting

For the older adolescent and adult who stutters, discussing specific speech-related goals is critical during the early stages of therapy. As you establish a relationship with your client, make mental notes of his readiness to develop an action plan. The clinician who tells the client what he needs to do to change his speech does not allow the client to make informed choices, which may sabotage the therapy process. The ultimate goal of therapy is the creation of clients as their own therapists. To achieve this goal, the client plays an active role in the decision-making process of therapy. Egan (1998) believed goal setting provides the tools for empowerment. When the client actively sets goals for himself, he (1) focuses his attention and action, (2) is mobilized with energy and effort, (3) becomes motivated to search for strategies to accomplish his goals, and (4) will persist with goals stated in specific terms. Once the client has developed a set of specific goals to achieve, this opens the door for dialogue on how to achieve such goals. You are in a unique position to offer suggestions to the client because he has asked for assistance. Using a toolbox of strategies, the client learns what each technique involves, its purpose and rationale, and the specific procedures for implementation. The client, then, selects the appropriate tool to use to address the particular speech problems encountered. The ultimate choice is left up to the client, yet you provide much guidance.

SHAME RESOLUTION

Potter-Efron and Potter-Efron (1989) describe a two-stage process to reduce shame in adults: understanding phase and action phase. The understanding phase includes five steps: (1) Be patient—shame heals slowly, (2) become fully aware of your shame, (3) notice your defenses against shame, (4) investigate the five sources of your shame, and (5) accept your shame as part of the human condition (p. 121). In step 1, clients come to realize it will take time to heal the wounds from stuttering. There are no quick fixes to the buildup of shame-based reactions to stuttering. Next, clients must face their shame, which is an uncomfortable feeling for most. Learning about the disorder of stuttering, learning about what the client does when stuttering occurs, and dissecting the thought processes will help clients face their shame. Next, clients will discover the faulty coping mechanisms, or defenses, they use because of stuttering. These might include denial ("I don't really stutter all that much"); withdrawal (avoiding speaking situations); anger/rage (thinking people are deliberately humiliating you because of your stuttering); and/or perfectionism (holding off shame by trying to be fluent).

Shame-Attacking Therapy

Clients now must identify the source of their shame. Potter-Efron and Potter-Efron (1989) list five sources of shame: our genetic and biological composition, our families of origin, society's expectations and demands, current relationships, and ourselves. The person who stutters might have a family history of persistent stuttering, possibly influencing his ability to manage stuttering. The way in which the client's family handled stuttering may have led to feelings of rejection and inadequacy creating shame. Or shame may have its source in the social circles of the client. Perhaps there is a high demand and expectation for "fitting in" and "being perfect" that the client attempts to meet. When the client perceives himself a failure because of his stuttering, he experiences shame. Lastly, the client, himself, may induce shame through negative thoughts, such as "I am just not good enough for them."

Entering the action phase of shame resolution involves five steps: (1) Get some help—you don't have to do this alone; (2) challenge the shame; (3) set positive goals based on humanity, humility, autonomy, and competence; (4) take mental and physical action to move toward those goals; and (5) review your progress regularly (p. 121). "People who are shamed keep vast areas of their lives a secret because they believe that others would scorn them if others knew who they really were" (p. 133). This secrecy is often seen in the covert stutterer who is desperately trying to hide stuttering through circumlocutions and other avoidance behaviors. Having the client share his stuttering with significant others helps reduce the feelings of shame. Even as simple as having the child tell his parents about the parts of the body used for talking helps set the stage for later discussions about stuttering.

Next the client must challenge the shame. To do this, clients must have identified their source(s) of shame because each source must be challenged differently. In response to comments such as "Why me?" the client can challenge the shame with a response like "There goes my genes." Cultural shame may be challenged by rehearsing comments such as "These people talk so quickly, but I don't have to keep up with them." Adults who stutter, in addressing familial shame around stuttering, may choose to talk with their parents about what they have learned about stuttering and break down the conspiracy of silence from the past. The teenager who stutters might confront his feelings of shame by talking with his girlfriend about his therapy and discussing how she might be able to help him in the future. Lastly, the client must also challenge the shame he, himself, induces. Comments such as "I am tired of hating my stuttering. I am okay even with my stuttering" will reduce the feelings of inadequacy brought on by repeated negative self-evaluations.

You can help clients set goals based on four basic principles. First is the **principle of humanity,** in which everyone belongs to the human race and no one is excluded because of their shame. The person who stutters must learn to interact with others and feel a sense of belonging. Joining self-help groups, such as those sponsored by the National Stuttering Association, demonstrates movement in a positive direction. The **principle of humility** states that all people are equal and accepted. A person who stutters needs to feel he is no better or worse than another. Everyone has strengths and weaknesses that emerge at different times. These differences do not make the person inferior or superior. The **principle of autonomy** contends that each individual has the right to live his life in any way he likes. This means the person does not have to be bound to please others. Stutterers may be overly concerned with listener reactions to their stuttering and try to ease their pain by avoiding certain words or carefully planning their words to avoid stuttering. This need to please results in behaviors that negatively influence the client's ability to confront and change his speech. Lastly, every person has the ability to contribute to society, the premise of the *principle of competence.* We do not have to be perfect in our ability to communicate. It is okay to be just good enough. For the person who stutters, developing communicative competence rather than fluency counters the shame derived from the need to be perfect.

The next step in resolving shame is to develop a plan of action geared to reduce past and present feelings of shame. Develop a hierarchy of tasks that promote openness and acceptance of stuttering. Gradually, one task at a time, engage in the activity and reflect positively on how you are changing that source of shame. You must understand this action plan involves a long-term process in which the client will need much encouragement and a safe environment to discuss successes and failures. Ultimately, all clients need to routinely review their progress in shame reduction. Shame habits are hard to break and will resurface periodically. Potter-Efron and Potter-Efron (1989) present four questions clients might ask themselves when reviewing their progress (reworded to relate to the person who stutters):

1. What have I done in the last few days to help me feel good about my communication? Have I shared my stuttering challenges with someone?
2. Have I acted as if I am a fluent speaker? Have I pretended to be a fluent speaker to make an impression?
3. Am I treating myself as a victim of my stuttering? What can I do to gain control of my thoughts and actions?
4. How am I acting competently or incompetently? Can I now settle for "good enough," or does my speech have to be "perfect"?

Breaking Down the Wall of Silence

Getting the individual to "own" (Lewis, 1992) the stuttering is important in the shame resolution process. Acknowledging and confronting the stuttering in an open, accepting environment is crucial to therapeutic success. Talking openly about stuttering is a way to dissipate the shame surrounding the disorder. Boberg and Boberg (1990) investigated the extent of this openness with 15 spouses of stuttering clients. Interestingly, these 15 wives reported they did not discuss stuttering with their husbands or children. Many had developed codependent roles, answering the phone or ordering in a restaurant, as a means of hiding the stuttering from others. If silence is determined to be a factor in the maintenance of stuttering, you can generate a list of tasks with the client to reduce the shame due to silence. These tasks might include voluntary stuttering, sharing reading materials with significant others, posting literature on stuttering for public review, or even hanging a poster in one's office displaying pictures of famous people who stutter. Together as a team, you and the client can establish a series of tasks to break down systematically the wall of silence around stuttering.

Therapy that allows words to describe the stuttering behaviors and demystifies the disorder can be effective for people who stutter (Ramig & Bennett, 1995, 1997a; Williams, 1985). Shame subsides when the individual can explain a chance behavior in terms of a logical consequence of personal habits (Hultberg, 1988). Discussing how stuttering develops may assist the client in understanding the reaction process and how negative cognitive and/or behavioral reactions can exacerbate speech behaviors. Shane (1980) noted one way to deal with cognitive shame is to explore, acquire, and master the skills to become competent, thereby overcoming cognitive shame. This learning process is essential to recognizing and accepting shame around the disorder of stuttering. Nothing is so shameful as coming face to face with one's inadequacies. "Putting shame into words with a trusted companion enables one to step outside it. It no longer seems to penetrate one's entire being and allows some self-forgiveness to emerge" (Karen, 1992, p. 68). You are the client's trusted companion, consistently providing support, listening, and understanding.

Shame in Children

The counseling component of therapy for people who stutter will vary from client to client, based on the person's socialization experiences and how his communication difficulties were and/or are received by significant others. Lewis (1992) commented on the role of parents in the development of shame. The child comes to view himself through the eyes of his parent(s); therefore, the establishment of a supportive and tolerant attitude toward one's failure (Sidoli, 1988) would be essential to any intervention plan. The elimination of "deficiency messages" (e.g., "You are not good," "Slow down a little," or "You're not trying hard enough") is crucial to growing up without shame (Potter-Efron & Potter-Efron, 1989). Establishing an environment of openness around the topic of stuttering is extremely important modeling for the child that feelings are neither good nor bad and need to be accepted (Luterman, 1991). The Stuttering Foundation of America publishes several books directed at educating parents about the proper handling of dysfluent speech in children. Creating an environment in which the child is accepted for who he is despite the presence of stuttering is essential to recovery in the child who stutters.

ANGER: A SPECIAL SITUATION

For a small group of people who stutter, anger may be a predominant theme in their stories of stuttering. Tavris (1989) suggested that the resolution of anger involves the mind and body. "People who want to 'let go' of anger have to rearrange their thinking as well as lower their pulse rates" (p. 288). She presents various strategies for targeting the perceptions that elicit anger. Table 2.1 in chapter 2, listed client perceptions and habits that increase or reduce anger reactions. An important first step in reducing anger is to acknowledge and accept responsibility for it. The client must understand no one can make him angry, only the client who is holding on to his beliefs. A useful task is to have the client keep a journal of episodes in which he becomes angry. He should record "what triggers the anger," the frequency of anger, the intensity of anger, the duration of anger, and the mode of expression (what did he do). The client is now able to analyze his journal entries and discover patterns of reactions and interpretations. With this knowledge, he is now in a position to change his reaction cycle.

Clients can generate a list of positive self-thoughts that will help them cope with their anger. Bilodeau (1992) stated that a person must take responsibility for his anger. The statement "I feel (angry) when I think (how you see the event)" helps clients identify their feelings triggered by certain thoughts. The client first identifies a situation to target from his anger log. He writes the anger formula on the top of a piece of paper and completes the anger statement. For example, the person who stutters may feel anger when coworkers do not allow him to finish his sentences. He writes this situation on the top of the paper. Then he completes the formula statement "I feel angry when I think my coworkers don't want to listen to my stuttering." The following dialogue exemplifies the problem-solving process between client and clinician:

Client:	"I feel angry when I think my coworkers don't want to listen to my stuttering."
Clinician:	"So you think they aren't interested in what you want to say?"
Client:	"Right."
Clinician:	"How do you know they aren't interested?"
Client:	"They wouldn't be cutting me off if they wanted to hear what I had to say."
Clinician:	"Can there be another explanation for their behavior?"
Client:	"I don't know."
Clinician:	"Sometimes people will fill in another's words because they think they are helping that person."
Client:	"That never crossed my mind."
Clinician:	"Have you ever discussed this with your coworkers?"

Try having the client practice other positive self-affirmations when he begins to experience anger. Tavris (1989) talked about cool thoughts, problem-solving thoughts, ultimate control and escape routes, and self-rewarding thoughts that help reduce anger. Cool thoughts include comments such as "Take a deep breath and chill out" or "Getting pissed off won't help your speech." Problem-solving thoughts might be "It's OK to feel annoyed" or "OK, develop a plan. What's the first thing I want to do?" The ultimate control and escape routes involve planned time-outs and self-reinforcing statements such as "I'm in control of myself" and "Move away and get your act together." Self-rewarding thoughts might be "I'm hanging in there" or "I feel great because I'm coping with my stuttering rather than avoiding it."

The use of humor also reduces the impact of anger and allows the client to add perspective to his speech experience. Manning (1996) writes about using humor in the therapy process. "Humor reflects a person's ability to step away and distance himself from his situation in order to gain a degree of insight" (p. 18). Being able to laugh at oneself is the ultimate form of reappraisal (Tavris, 1989). Humor allows the client to change his thoughts of "injustice" to one of "absurdity," or, as Manning states, experience a conceptual shift. Developing a more objective view of a problem helps the client distance himself from the anger-provoking situation. The client continues with activities to help him identify thoughts surrounding interactions that elicit anger. The clinician who listens attentively to the client's concerns can guide him in the direction of healthier habits for coping with anger surrounding the topic of stuttering. If the client's anger is more pervasive, a referral to the appropriate personnel would be indicated.

CHAPTER SUMMARY

When the therapist is able to "provide the client a glimpse of alternative modes of behavior, which are healthier than his present coping mechanisms" (Shane, 1980, p. 351), success in the therapeutic process is more likely to occur. Counseling that includes modeling a variety of coping strategies may enhance the success of the client. In reference to stuttering, teaching the client who stutters several ways of managing his affective and cognitive reactions to stuttering may be essential to success and long-term maintenance. To achieve these goals, you need to implement counseling skills when working with the client who stutters. Being an active listener, using minimal encouragers, and listening with empathy establishes a good client/clinician relationship conducive to change. Once this is established, the client will be more willing to engage in brainstorming, self-talk, and goal-setting therapy tasks. Counseling activities that engage the active change of negative cognitive constructs, provide choices for clients, and openly address the topic of stuttering may have long-term benefits for the person who stutters.

STUDY QUESTIONS

1. When is it appropriate to confront a client about his irrational beliefs around stuttering?
2. Describe how you would establish a trusting relationship with an adult who stutters.
3. Contrast client-centered therapy with rational-emotive behavior therapy.
4. How does shame develop in the person who stutters?
5. What strategies might you use to help the client manage feelings of anger?
6. When interviewing a person who stutters, describe the counseling strategies you might use.
7. Describe the characteristics of a school-age child in need of counseling to resolve issues around stuttering.

7

Preschool Children Who Stutter

CHAPTER OUTLINE

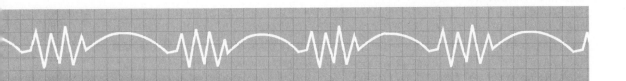

Behavioral Guidelines
Issues of Spontaneous Recovery
Prevention versus Intervention
Treatment Goal and Design

Indirect Strategies for the Preschool Child
Direct Strategies for the Preschool Child
Current Models of Therapy
Treating Concomitant Disorders

LEARNER OBJECTIVES

- Label the common characteristics of early childhood stuttering.

- Identify at-risk factors and prognostic indicators related to the onset and continuation of stuttering.

- Describe the speech, language, and attitudinal characteristics of parents of children who stutter.

- Recognize the importance of early identification.

- Differentiate between indirect and direct treatment directions.

- Exhibit the ability to choose the appropriate treatment paradigm for the preschool child who stutters based on the individual's fluency profile.

- Understand the possible role of concomitant disorders on treatment planning and progress.

KEY TERMS

blended approach
cognitive-behavioral orientation
concurrent intervention
direct strategies
discrete approach
heterogeneity

indirect strategies
prevention
proactive prevention
reactive prevention
response-contingent paradigm

response time latency (RTL)
restimulation
sequential intervention
spontaneous recovery
turn taking

Working with the preschool child who stutters presents four unique challenges. The first involves differentiating between normal nonfluency and signs of beginning stuttering. If the child is exhibiting signs of early childhood stuttering, the second challenge arises: Will this child recover from stuttering without intervention? Next, if treatment is indicated, what type of intervention approach is best? Lastly, how do we approach intervention for the child who also has some type of concomitant speech or language problem?

THE ABCs OF STUTTERING

Affective Components

Negative feelings about talking emerge gradually with repeated communication failures. The majority of preschool children have minimal negative feelings about their moments of stuttering, yet some do exhibit strong emotions. It is not uncommon to see a young child express anger and frustration, making comments such as "Why can't I talk" or "My words won't come out." Although many of these preschool children do not have the metalinguistic ability to talk specifically about their stuttering, parents may report that their child is not completing sentences and beginning to show signs of struggle and/or avoidance (Ambrose & Yairi, 1994). Yairi (2004) indicated that awareness of speech difficulties progresses rapidly between ages 4 and 5. Do not assume preschool children will not have significant affective factors contributing to their speech difficulties. Even the possibility of awareness of speech differences by their peers may be present at an early age.

Ezrati-Vinacour, Platsky, and Yairi (2001) investigated nonstuttering preschool and first-grade children's awareness of stuttering-like disfluencies and found surprising results. They reported that at age 3, children show beginning signs of awareness of speech differences that become fully developed around age 5. "It is interesting to note that there was an almost unanimous agreement at age 4 that disfluent speech was not good and that a fluent speaker was a preferred friend rather than one who stutters" (p. 377). Careful monitoring of reactions of preschoolers, both fluent and stuttering, by parents and clinicians is essential because of the progressive nature of this disorder and the impact of negative emotions on the behavioral components of stuttering.

Behavioral Components

A common vocabulary is essential as a point of reference when discussing fluency breakdowns in the preschool population. Yairi (1997a) and his colleagues, in numerous publications, describe two speech classifications that have the power to differentiate between the nonstuttering and stuttering preschooler. One index is the Short-Element Repetition (SER) containing syllable and word repetitions. The SER index is representative of the normal nonfluencies of early childhood speech with a decline in SERs, a feature of normal speech development. Another index is the Stuttering-Like Disfluency (SLD). SLDs, which occur in the speech of all preschool children, are made up of syllable and monosyllabic word repetitions, dysrhythmic phonation, and tense pauses. We must become familiar with the characteristics of preschool nonstuttering children in order to identify the preschooler who stutters.

Yairi (1997a) published an extensive review of the literature on the speech characteristics of stuttering and nonstuttering preschool children. This section summarizes Yairi's key findings along with an update on current literature since 1997. Speech characteristics of preschoolers are described from quantitative and qualitative perspectives. Ambrose and Yairi (1999) noted significant quantitative and qualitative differences between stuttering and normal disfluency. You must be prepared to differentiate between the two in order to make appropriate treatment recommendations.

Quantitative Characteristics

Table 7.1 displays several significant findings regarding the quantitative differences between nonstuttering and stuttering preschoolers. Nonstuttering preschoolers may have 6 to 8 disfluencies per 100 words, whereas stuttering children have a total rate of disfluency almost twice as high as nonstuttering children (15 disfluencies per 100 words). The disfluency patterns of the stuttering preschooler reflect three to five times as many SERs and SLDs with twice as many *iterations* (the number of times a word, sound, or syllable is repeated). Nonstuttering preschool children rarely exhibit *clusters*, more than one type of disfluency during a moment of stuttering. Yet frequent and longer clusters are a predominant component of the stuttering preschoolers' speech. Additionally, Schwartz and Conture (1988) found that the sound prolongation feature may be important in the differential diagnosis of young stutterers.

What we know about normal fluency development includes the following:

- Disfluency peaks near the latter part of year 2 followed by a downward slope.
- Age 3 is typical of large variations in the frequency of disfluency.
- Number of part-word repetitions declines with maturation.
- SLDs are a minor part of the disfluency patterns for nonstuttering preschool children.

Table 7.1

Quantitative differences in the speech characteristics of nonstuttering and stuttering preschoolers.

Characteristic	Nonstuttering	Stuttering
Total Disfluency Rates	6–8 /100 words	15/100 words; 17/100 syllables
Number of SERs	2/100 words	9/100 syllables
Number of SLDs	3/100 words	11/100 syllables
Number of Iterations	1 repetition/word	2+ repetitions/word
Number of Clusters	Not present usually	6 times as many
Number of Head/Neck Movements	Present at times	2 times as many

Qualitative Characteristics

The speech of nonstuttering preschoolers can be described as qualitatively different from the speech of stuttering preschoolers. Nonfluencies are tension free, rhythmic, brief, and rarely accompanied by secondary behaviors. The child usually does not show signs of awareness of breaks in fluency and will continue to attempt to talk regardless of the manner of talking exhibited. In contrast, the speech of the young stuttering child is perceptually tense and dysrhythmic with rapid changes in tempo. Preschoolers who stutter may also exhibit twice as many head and neck movements as signs of awareness of communication difficulties. Another qualitative feature in the speech of preschool stutterers is the presence of secondary features (e.g., head, eye, and body movements). Yairi (2004) reported that for children with persistent stuttering, the presence of secondary behaviors increased after a few months of onset. Those preschool children who recovered from stuttering demonstrated a decrease in secondary behaviors over the course of 6 months after onset.

Cognitive Components

Determining the cognitive components influencing the preschool child's fluency is difficult to assess because of the developmental level of these children. It is uncommon to observe children express negative thoughts or make statements that would provide insight into their belief system. You must work with the parents to determine what processes might be interfering with the preschooler's speech. Another aspect to investigate is the parents' belief system regarding stuttering, therapy, and their child. Using instruments such as the Parent Attitudes Toward Stuttering Checklist, presented in chapter 4, is one means of gaining insight into what parents believe and how they might react toward their child's stuttering.

SPECIAL ISSUES

The preschool population presents several unique challenges. The SLP must become familiar with factors related to the development and maintenance of stuttering. Identification of the specified speech characteristics assists in evaluating the likelihood of spontaneous recovery from stuttering. Knowledge of these topics helps to guide the parents of the preschooler who stutters.

Predisposing, Precipitating, and Perpetuating Factors

Several factors make a child at risk for continued disfluency or stuttering. These can be classified into predisposing, precipitating, or perpetuating factors (Shapiro, 1999). *Predisposing* factors incline the person to stutter, whereas *precipitating* factors make stuttering surface. *Perpetuating* factors contribute to the continuation or maintenance of stuttering. A predisposition for fluency breaks may be present in the child who has

(1) a familial history of stuttering, perhaps indicative of the genetic transmission of ineffi-
cient neural pathways for speech and language tasks (Guitar, 1998). Another factor may
be an underlying neurological difference in people who stutter. Guitar postulated that
accompanying this genetic factor is a predisposition toward a sensitive temperament
attributed to a possible overreactive lymbic system. Predisposing factors are nonalter-
ing by nature.

Precipitating factors might include (2) rapid speech and language development occurring during the preschool years in which the child is unable to manage adequately
the increased demands placed on his speech and language mechanism. Environmental stressors, such as a hurried home schedule or verbal competition among siblings
for communication time, may contribute to the emergence of stuttering during this
period. A third precipitating factor may also be the social adjustment children encounter upon entering preschool (Shapiro, 1999). A fourth factor of concomitant
speech and language disorders may imply the presence of a more vulnerable, weaker
language production system for children who stutter. And lastly, Guitar (1998) believed
the child's increased sensitivity to stress makes him vulnerable to fluency breaks. Precipitating factors can be modified to varying degrees.

Perpetuating factors are more concrete, thus amenable to change by the child and
his environment. These might include an (3) overly critical home atmosphere, highly mature linguistic models, and speech criticism from the child's home and school settings
(Shapiro, 1999). Also, continued experience with stuttering results in the development
of learned behaviors (avoidance, escape, and postponement) that further draw negative attention toward the child's speech. With continued use, a strong habitual pattern
develops that is often difficult to change without assistance.

In summary, understanding the role of the factors just described is crucial to the
differentiation of normal nonfluency and the signs of incipient stuttering. The literature indicates that stuttering does run in families. It appears more frequently in males
than females, with females recovering from stuttering more often than males. Disfluencies appear in the speech of most preschool children; however, for some children,
they develop a powerful habit strength of faulty coping behaviors that exacerbate
their communication difficulties. Children who stutter may be more highly sensitive
to environmental stressors, thereby reacting to any comment regarding their communicative performance. The genetic predisposition to stutter interacting with environmental precipitating and perpetuating features may be sufficient for the emergence of
stuttering.

Characteristics of the Preschool Child Who Stutters

The development of fluency waxes and wanes during the early period of speech development. Between the years of 2 and 4, most children experience a burst in language skills characteristic of movement from a semantically driven system to a
syntactically governed, rule-based system (Bernstein Ratner, 1997b). This transition
creates a temporary imbalance between the child's speech motor production abilities and the cognitive demands placed on the speech system. Stuttering appears to
be triggered by the child's inability to generate syntactic representations in a timely

fashion. Speech becomes fragmented, resulting in fluency breaks. Bluemel (1932) initially described these fluency breaks as easy repetitions devoid of physical or emotional tension. Johnson et al. (1942) defined early stuttering as the experience of conflict resulting from a desire to speak, operating in opposition to a desire to avoid expected stuttering. He later, in 1959, noted that the single most important feature that differentiates normal from abnormal disfluency is listener evaluation. Both Bluemel and Johnson viewed early childhood disfluency as a normal phenomenon experienced by all children. However, as we learned in chapter 1, recent studies contradict this assumption.

Yairi (1997a) suggested that certain speech behaviors differentiate the preschool child who stutters from his nonstuttering peers (refer to Table 7.1). To summarize, the preschool child who stutters is most likely to have word and syllable repetitions (SERs), as well as monosyllable whole-word repetitions, syllable repetitions, prolongations, and tense pauses (SLDs) to a greater extent than the nonstuttering preschooler. Accompanying these moments of stuttering is twice as many head and neck movements, indicative of awareness of speech difficulties. A rise in SERs is a valid cause for professional concern. As CWS continue having difficulty, they are more likely to exhibit clustered disfluencies. Conture and Kelly (1991) found that children who stutter were more likely to exhibit eyeball movement to the side and eyelid blinking. The research of Armson, Jenson, Gallant, Kalinowski, and Fee (1997) added another identifying feature in early childhood stuttering: the degree of audible struggle. They observed that listeners consistently ranked young children's speech containing various degrees of audible struggle as stuttered speech.

Most CWS show an early profile of normal fluency with the emergence of stuttering around 30 to 36 months of age. Approximately 10% or more disfluency is considered significant enough for concern, particularly when 3 or more within-word disfluencies appear per 100 words (Conture, 2001; Guitar, 1998; Yairi, 1997a). Signs of awareness will be present in 20% of CWS at the onset of stuttering. There is three times the likelihood of having a familial history of stuttering, with more males than females stuttering. Girls begin stuttering earlier than boys because they reach the stage of rule-governed speech production sooner than most boys.

Curlee (1999) clearly stated that the incipient stutterer can be reliably identified. He suggested that the clinician attempt to answer four questions to guide the decision-making process: (1) What kinds of speech disruptions are eliciting parental concern? (2) Have the child's speech disruptions changed since the parents first became concerned? (3) How long have the parents been concerned about the child's fluency? and (4) How valid do the parents' concerns about stuttering appear to be?

Risk Factors

The patterns of early childhood stuttering are highly variable in their representation from child to child. There are certain risk factors you can look for when attempting to determine who will recover from stuttering and who will not. These at-risk indicators may include the presence of tense articulatory contacts and articulatory posturing; visual signs of tension and struggle; a rise in pitch during moments of stuttering; lengthy prolongations and blocks; presence of the schwa; and a disruption in phonation between parts of the repetition (Conture, 2001; Starkweather, 1987). The greater number of risk factors present in the profile of the child, the greater the likelihood of continued stuttering. However, it must be said that, because of the **heterogeneity** of the disorder, one might assess a child who has all the potential risk factors present but does not progress into the cycle of stuttering. Through continued research and study, ideally answers will help clarify this misty picture. Until then, we must use prognostic indicators to make the most-informed decision possible.

Prognostic Indicators

Positive Indicators

One important positive prognostic indicator involves the amount of time that has lapsed since the onset of symptoms (Pellowski & Conture, 2002). When time postonset is less than 12 months, it is more likely the child will recover from symptoms providing the following characteristics are present in the child's profile: the child has no familial history of stuttering, has a history of recovered stuttering, and/or is female. Certain speech characteristics may also help predict those who may not be encumbered by stuttering. The absence of secondary symptoms, only one to two iterations in their repetitions, and few SLDs are positive indicators. The child who responds positively to trial therapy, exhibits good stimulability, and has good language and articulation skills can utilize these strengths to work through the early stages of stuttering and move into fluency.

Negative Indicators

Some children lack the traits just listed and are at a higher risk for continued stuttering. Specifically, the child who is male, has a family history of persistent stuttering, and has been stuttering for longer than 14 months is less likely to recover on his own. Signs of awareness through struggle and avoidance behaviors, the presence of concomitant disorders, a rise in SERs and SLDs, and the presence of clustering also contribute to a negative prognosis. It has been this author's experience that when the child is unable to produce rote automatic tasks (such as counting, saying the ABCs, singing, imitation tasks) fluently, prognosis for improvement without intervention is unfavorable. Rote automatic tasks place few demands, cognitive or motor related, on the child who should be able to perform such tasks with ease. When this does not happen, perhaps stuttering is an ingrained component of the child's speech production system that will require direct intervention to change.

Spontaneous Recovery: What Does It Mean?

A large percentage of preschool children who show signs of stuttering will recover spontaneously on their own. Attempts have been made to explain this phenomenon through research findings and clinical observations (Ingham & Cordes, 1998;

Throneburg & Yairi, 2001; Watkins & Yairi, 1997; Yairi, 1997a, 1999). The issues surrounding spontaneous recovery are threefold:

1. What percentage of children actually recover from stuttering without intervention?
2. What are the characteristics of those children who recover spontaneously?
3. When should we intervene with the preschool child who stutters?

The actual percentage of children who recover spontaneously from stuttering ranges from 32% to 80% (Bloodstein, 1995; Conture, 2001; Silverman, 1996). One possible explanation for such a wide range concerns the methods used to obtain these figures. Client retrospective, self-report, parent report, clinical observations, and longitudinal studies are a few methods reported in the literature. The problem with self-report and retrospective report methods involves the accuracy of information obtained. Variability in the definition of stuttering, clarity of recall of exact behaviors exhibited during this period, and the nature of one's experience with stuttering may influence the person's memory trace. If the individual had unfortunate teasing, shame, and frustration, he may recall this time frame with vivid recollection. Others may have only vague feelings of having a speech difference. In one well-designed longitudinal study of 84 preschool children who stutter, Yairi and Ambrose (1999) reported a conservative estimate of 74% recovery rate with 26% persistency rate.

Age is closely related to the issue of spontaneous recovery (Yairi, 1999). Andrews (1984) reported half the risk of ever stuttering is passed by age 4, three quarters by age 6, and virtually all by age 12. What are the characteristics of these children who are spared a "life bound up in words" (Jezer, 1997)? Those children who spontaneously recover usually do so within 14 months postonset. Silverman (1996) noted that recovery can occur at any age, with the younger more likely to recover than the older person. Females recover more than males; children exhibiting mild to moderate stuttering are more likely to recover than those with more severe profiles (Bloodstein, 1995). Amster (1995) noted that children who are perfectionistic may be more likely to react negatively to moments of stuttering. This may perpetuate their movement into the stuttering cycle described earlier. Ramig (1993a) questioned the high rates of spontaneous recovery and cautioned clinicians.

This leads into the last question: When do we intervene with the preschool child who stutters? Johnson and his associates imprinted in the minds of both the professional and layperson the "wait and see" approach to early childhood stuttering. The "ignore it and it will go away" 1950s mentality is not acceptable, especially for the 20% to 68% who do not recover spontaneously. We must provide support when indicated, whether it is in the form of indirect intervention, parent counseling, or hands-on clinician-directed treatment. Bernstein Ratner (2001) reframed the old "wait and see" phrase to "wait and watch," inferring the importance of closely monitoring the young child who may be at risk for continued stuttering. Other fluency specialists recommend immediate intervention with the preschool child who stutters because of the progressive nature of the disorder (Ramig & Bennett, 1995; Yaruss, 2002; Yaruss & Reardon, 2003). Of course, the extent of this intervention will vary according to the level of parental concern and the child's ABC profile. It is the role of the speech-language pathologist to assess thoroughly and identify at-risk factors for continued stuttering.

Parents of Children Who Stutter

Parents often bring with them a myriad of behaviors into the treatment process. Since the era of the diagnosogenic theory, it has been assumed parental speech characteristics in some way negatively impact stuttering. Bernstein Ratner (1993) precisely stated, "the clinical presumption here is clear, that the manner in which parents converse with children has tangible effects on their communicative behaviors" (p. 243). However, the research has failed to shed light on any definitive patterns of interactions between parental speech behaviors and the fluency level of their child.

Speech and Language Characteristics

Certain speech characteristics of parents of children who stutter have been researched over the years: *rate of speech* (Bernstein Ratner, 1992; Guitar & Marchinkoski, 2001; Guitar, Schaefer, Donahue-Kilburg, & Bond, 1992; Kelly, 1993, 1994; Kelly & Conture, 1992; Kloth, Janssen, Kraaimaat, & Brutten, 1995; Meyers & Freeman, 1985b; Stephanson-Opsal & Bernstein Ratner, 1988); *interruptions* (Guitar et al., 1992; Kelly, 1993; Kelly & Conture, 1992; Meyers & Freeman, 1985a; Mordechai, 1979; Yaruss & Conture, 1995); *turn-taking behaviors* (Kelly, 1993; Mordechai, 1979; Bernstein Ratner, 1992, 1993); *question usage* (Langlois, Hanrahan, & Inouye, 1986; Weiss, 1993; Weiss & Zebrowski, 1992; Wilkenfeld & Curlee, 1997); and *eye contact* (LaSalle & Conture, 1991). In the following section a summary of the findings, based on the literature just cited, is provided for each characteristic.

Speech Rate. Findings on parental speech rate appear to indicate that parents of children who stutter do not, as a group, talk any faster than parents of nonstuttering children. When they do speak faster, little evidence suggests this impacts the child's speech rate negatively. However, there is evidence that a reduction in maternal speech rate produces an increase in speech fluency (Starkweather & Gottwald, 1993). Guitar et al. (1992) found a high correlation (0.70) between the mother's speech rate and the fluency level of her stuttering child. While the mother's speech rate decreases, the child does not respond similarly, although he becomes more fluent. Why this happens is not totally clear. Earlier research (Bernstein Ratner, 1992; Kelly & Conture, 1992; Stephanson-Opsal & Bernstein Ratner, 1988; Yaruss & Conture, 1995) failed to find a significant interaction between parental and child speech rates. However, more recent research findings (Guitar & Marchinkoski, 2001) appear to conflict with previous studies. Differences in research conclusions may be attributed to the varying methods used in each study. Guitar and Marchinkoski (2001) conjectured that looking at individual mother/child dyads versus group comparison designs was a better way of researching these dynamic interactions. They found that for five out of six mother/child dyads, speech rates for the child who stutters decreased as the mother spoke slowly.

Further research using single subject mother/child dyads will, perhaps, shed light on the interaction among parental speech rate, children's speech rate, and level of fluency. Collectively, the findings on any possible interaction between parental speech rate and episodes of stuttering are ambiguous at best. Miles and Bernstein Ratner (2001) summarized the research in this area and concluded that "Although numerous comparison and intervention studies have examined this aspect of parental verbal interaction, they have neither demonstrated unequivocally that rapid parental speech rates exacerbate stuttering in children nor generated conclusive evidence rate differences among mothers of children who stutter and mothers of fluently speaking children" (p. 1117).

Interruptions. Interruptions may be a common characteristic of mothers in general (Meyers & Freeman, 1985a). However, research findings are inconsistent when talking about the frequency of interruptions for parents of children who stutter. Mordechai (1979) found that mothers of children who stutter interrupted more frequently than mothers of nonstuttering children. Guitar et al. (1992) found that fathers interrupted more frequently than mothers. Kelly and Conture (1992) failed to find differences between these two parent groups. Yet there is agreement that when stuttering severity increases in frequency and duration, the likelihood of interruptive behaviors also increases (Kelly, 1993; Yairi, 1997a).

Turn Taking. The exchange between listener and speaker, that is, **turn taking,** has been indicated as a possible exacerbating factor in the maintenance of stuttering in young children (Bernstein Ratner, 1992; Conture, 2001; Guitar, 1998; Kelly & Conture, 1992; Shapiro, 1999; Starkweather, 1987). If communication is conceptualized as a give-and-take sharing of ideas between speaker and listener, both partners need to be respectful of each other's right to talk. **Response time latency (RTL)** is one measure of the time between turns. Kelly and Conture (1992) measured the RTLs of mothers and their children who stutter. They found that mothers exhibited longer RTLs compared to their stuttering children. Newman and Smit (1989) found that adult RTLs positively impacted the RTL of children. As the RTL increased in length for the adult, a similar increase was observed in the speech of the child. Winslow and Guitar (1994) reported a significant decrease in stuttering-like disfluencies during structured turn-taking tasks that manipulated RTL. They concluded that structured turn taking may have reduced the perceived threat of interruption by the listener.

However, this bidirectional influence in speaker's RTL (Kelly, 1993; Meyers, 1991) may be highly variable across children who stutter and needs to be assessed during the diagnostic process. Do not assume this bidirectionality will be present in a particular child's profile. Bernstein Ratner (1992) made an excellent observation when she wrote that some children may be intolerant of longer RTLs, resulting in an increase in interruptions. "It is not at all unusual to observe children who stutter to frequently interrupt people while they are talking, talk for others, talk out of turn or exhibit difficulty waiting their turn to talk" (Conture, 2001, p. 171). Although the literature is unclear about the exact relationship between turn taking and interruptions, the possibility of a negative influence on the speech fluency of the child may be present.

Question Usage. Research on the frequency and impact of parental questioning behaviors has yielded inconsistent findings. Langlois et al. (1986) determined that mothers of children who stutter asked more questions than mothers of nonstutterers. However, other studies failed to find a higher proportion of requesting behaviors among this group of parents (Weiss, 1993; Weiss & Zebrowski, 1991, 1992) or that questioning behaviors elicited stuttering (Wilkenfeld & Curlee, 1997). Kelly (1993) concluded that little consistent evidence supports the belief that parents of children who stutter exert communication time pressure through frequent use of questions. In fact, Weiss and Zebrowski (1992) found children were more likely to be fluent when responding to questions in contrast to making assertions. These authors hypothesized that responding to requests (i.e., questions) required little communication responsibility, utilizing a demands-capacity model to explain their findings. Their overall conclusion stated "as fewer demands for topic management were left in the hands of the children, fluency was easier to manage" (p. 220).

Miles and Bernstein Ratner (2001) expressed concerns over the application of the demands-capacity model to intervention suggestions for parents of preschool stuttering children. Their study found no significant differences in the linguistic behaviors of mothers of stuttering children versus mothers of nonstutterers. The absence of linguistic demands conflicts with the common advice given to parents to simplify their speech when talking with their child. This advice could have detrimental effects on the linguistic development of the young child entering a period of rapid language development. These authors support their opinion with literature indicating language development is enhanced when parents speak at a slightly higher level than their children (p. 1125).

Eye Contact. A singular study investigated the extent of eye contact between mothers and their children who stutter (LaSalle & Conture, 1991). This study is particularly relevant to the topic of preschool stuttering because parents are often counseled to "look at their child when he/she is talking" (Ainsworth & Fraser, 1988; Yaruss & Reardon, 2003). LaSalle and Conture (1991) found mothers of children who stuttered established eye contact more often during moments of stuttering compared to mothers of nonstuttering children. They hypothesized that the establishment of eye contact served as a means to demonstrate to their child that they were listening to the child's communication effort, as well as to monitor such efforts. Just the opposite behavior was exhibited by mothers of nonstuttering children, who decreased eye contact when their child was disfluent. A special note is made regarding the use of eye contact between speaker and listener. Certain cultural influences may interplay with loss of eye contact, so each parent/child dyad must be evaluated in terms of the cultural appropriateness of maintaining eye contact.

In summary, we do not fully understand the relationship between parental speech behaviors and stuttering in the young preschool child. Conflicting findings may reflect the complexity of this heterogeneous disorder, presenting a challenge to both researchers and clinicians. It appears that as parents decrease speech rate and lengthen their response time latency, their child becomes more fluent. This fluency is not a result of a concurrent decrease in the child's speaking rate. Nor is it a reflection of a change in linguistic complexity of the parent's speech model or frequent use of questions. The inconsistency in the research findings puts us in a bind regarding instructions we typically give to parents during intervention.

Attitudes Toward Stuttering

Added to this research are studies investigating parental perceptions of their child's communicative competence and parental attitudes toward stuttering (Crowe & Cooper, 1977; Bernstein Ratner & Silverman, 2000; Rustin & Purser, 1991; Vanryckeghem, 1995). Bernstein Ratner and Silverman (2000) researched the congruence between parental perceptions of communicative competence and actual test performance of young children who stutter. They found that parents of children who stutter were accurate informants regarding their child's linguistic performance. Zebrowski (1993) concluded mothers of children who stutter are accurate in their judgments of what was considered typical stuttering episodes. However, in a study looking at the congruence between parents' and children's attitudes toward stuttering, parents of children who stutter were found to be "poor predictors" of their child's attitudes toward stuttering, often reporting more negative attitudes than self-reported (Vanryckeghem, 1995). This lack of parent-child agreement brings up the issue of how much the parent's belief system influences their scoring on assessment questionnaires. Parents may not share "a common reality with that of their child" (p. 200).

Parents may feel varying degrees of guilt surrounding their child's stuttering (Conture, 2001; Murphy, 1999; Yaruss & Reardon, 2003; Zebrowski & Schum, 1993). This guilt may stem from the belief system held by the parents. Parents are accurate when estimating their child's linguistic performance and judgments of what is stuttering, yet inaccurate in their estimates of attitudes toward stuttering. These judgments are derived from the parents' beliefs about stuttering; therefore, you must assess such parental attitudes. Cooper and Cooper (1985) included in their assessment program a checklist for parents to complete that provides some insight into this area (Table 4.13).

This instrument was used in a preliminary study of parental attitudes by Bennett and Orr (2001). In their sample of 16 subjects, they identified one item as consistently marked as "agree" by parents: "Most of the time I feel I just do not know what to do about my child's stuttering." Despite feeling at a loss about what to do when their child stutters, 56% of the parents identified that telling their child to "stop and start over" was helpful advice. Supporting this finding is Glasner and Rosenthal's (1972) research, indicating that 65% of their parents gave similar advice to their children who stuttered. Shine (1980) reported that parents encourage their children to stop and start over and view this advice as supportive.

Parental belief system may be threatened by common suggestions provided to parents from speech-language pathologists. Starkweather, Gottwald, and Halfond (1990) commented that parents are often put in a bind by the advice they receive to ignore stuttering. Such advice may place parents in a state of chaos, producing guilt and possibly increasing the "emotional strain already placed on the family" (Meyers, 1991, p. 56). Instead of encouraging and reinforcing parental feelings of competence, such advice may confuse parents by asking them to stop doing what they believe will help their child. Parents often have a strong desire to do something concrete (Luper & Mulder, 1964). Before we begin to advise parents on what to do or not do, we need to gather information on their belief system so we support and empower the parent.

TREATMENT DIRECTIONS

Early intervention is highly effective at ameliorating life-impacting effects of stuttering. Five areas are worthy of discussion when considering either indirect or direct treatment for the preschool child: case selection criteria, behavioral guidelines, issues of spontaneous recovery, prevention versus intervention, and treatment goal and design. With the following information, the clinician and parents can make well-rounded decisions on behalf of the child who stutters.

Case Selection Criteria

Four possible scenarios may arise when determining who should or should not receive early intervention (Curlee, 1999). The first group consists of children who exhibit few signs of beginning stuttering, and it is unlikely they will develop such problems. The next group includes children who are evidencing inconsistent signs of beginning stuttering and need further observation or assessment. The third group of children show consistent signs of beginning stuttering and an appropriate plan should be developed and implemented. Those children who are already showing signs of chronic stuttering and remission is unlikely in the absence of professional intervention form the fourth group. Not all children fit nicely into these four categories. Williams (1984) strongly believed the goal of intervention for the preschool child who stutters is the prevention of the development of negative emotions toward communication. Three variables may influence your decision to intervene: (1) assessment of type, frequency, and extent of disfluencies; (2) exploration of the nature of the parents' interactions and reactions to their child and to the way he talks; and (3) observations of the reactions of the child and others to the way he is talking (Williams, 1984).

Behavioral Guidelines

Conture (2001) prescribed certain behavioral guidelines that may be used when determining if direct intervention is warranted. Six factors may influence your decision to intervene or not. First, when prolongations make up 30% or more of the child's stuttering behaviors, therapy may be warranted. The presence of clustered moments of stuttering is a definite warning sign. Looking at all the disfluencies present in the child's speech, concern should arise when 70% of all disfluencies are stuttering-like disfluencies. Loss of eye contact with the listener, at least 50% of the time, is another risk factor. The presence of negative comments about talking and delays in speech and language development completes Conture's list.

To paraphrase Van Riper (1973, p. 450), we should not wait to intervene with these young children, and we must put forth a concerted effort to prevent the development of habitual stuttering behaviors. If there is uncertainty about the possibility of recovery, it is recommended you err on the cautious, conservative side (Curlee, 1999; Harrison & Onslow, 1999; Williams, 1984). Let the parents decide whether or not they want intervention. Parents are a reliable source of insight regarding their child's communication difficulties. Zebrowski (1993) found that parents of children who stutter correctly identified broken words and prolongations as stuttered speech more often than parents of nonstuttering children. If they have sought your assistance, they are most likely concerned about the problem and will require your assistance, one way or another, in helping their child.

Issues of Spontaneous Recovery

When to intervene with the preschool stuttering child has been a long-standing controversial issue within the profession, partially because of research findings on the high rates of **spontaneous recovery** for this population. If so many young children will recover without treatment, how do we decide who needs treatment and who does not? Curlee and Yairi (1997) discussed several beliefs clinicians hold regarding the necessity of early intervention. Those clinicians who subscribe to immediate intervention soon after onset support their beliefs with the following statements:

1. The real rate of remission without treatment is substantially lower.
2. Fewer than half of these early remissions occur without the child having received some form of intervention, and most of those who do stop without direct or indirect treatment are assisted by self-directed parental intervention or that of other caregivers.
3. Once a child has begun to stutter, withholding treatment for any period of time places a child at a higher risk for chronic stuttering problems.
4. Clinical treatment of young preschoolers who stutter is highly effective.
5. Early treatment does no harm. (p. 9)

However, not all clinicians adhere to these beliefs, preferring to wait a certain amount of time postonset to determine if children will spontaneously recover on their own. Curlee and Yairi (1997) provided five beliefs of clinicians who prefer to wait a period of time before initiating treatment:

1. Most children stop stuttering on their own within the first year to two of onset without treatment.
2. Additional remissions continue to occur at decreasing rates for a number of years in the absence of professional intervention.

3. Remission and persistent stuttering are related to a child's family history of these outcomes.

4. The effects of self-directed efforts by parents and caregivers to reduce or eliminate stuttering are unknown.

5. No evidence indicates that waiting a year or more to intervene with young preschoolers will make treatment goals more difficult to achieve, increase the amount of treatment needed to achieve those goals, or result in less satisfactory treatment outcomes. (p. 9)

As we will see, clinicians apply various guidelines regarding when to intervene with the young child who stutters. Starkweather and Gottwald (1993) recommended initiating treatment as soon as parents become concerned. Harrison and Onslow (1999) utilized a conservative time frame of 6 months postonset when determining if therapy is warranted; Yaruss and Reardon (2003) recommended an even more conservative timeline of 2 to 3 months postonset of symptoms. Curlee and Yairi (1997) broaden the timeline to 15 to 18 months postonset. And for some children exhibiting highly variable signs of stuttering, they extended this boundary to 2 years postonset.

Ingham and Cordes (1998) disagreed with Curlee and Yairi's stance on withholding treatment for the young preschool child who stutters. After careful review of data from several studies, they concluded that "treatment should be offered to young children who stutter, and that delaying treatment, even for as little as 15 months post onset, may diminish the chances that children will recover" (p. 11). Starkweather and Gottwald (1993) also concluded that a delay in the onset of treatment may lengthen its actual duration. With discrepancies in the current literature on spontaneous recovery and the necessity of treatment for preschool children, more research must be conducted in order to better understand the developmental nature of stuttering and remission.

For today, however, "the more important implication of these findings, actually, is that parents should be given information about the benefits that may occur if they do try to intervene in their child's stuttering" (Ingham & Cordes, 1998, p. 11). There is no evidence that employing intervention will cause stuttering to increase or persist over time, nor can we assure parents their child will recover without treatment (Ingham & Cordes, 1998; Packman & Onslow, 1998; Williams, 1984; Yaruss & Reardon, 2003). The clinician is often faced with certain realities of everyday work with families of children who stutter. Zebrowski (1997) made the following comments, which are reinforced in the writings of this book:

> The reality is that we cannot refuse to engage in some sort of professional relationship with these children on the grounds that we don't have a sufficient amount of scientific data to predict treatment outcome or efficacy with a high degree of accuracy or reliability. Young children who are exhibiting the signs of beginning stuttering will (and should) continue to be referred to us for help and it is our responsibility to offer some form of assistance to these children and their families. (p. 21)

It is clear that we do not know if treatment outcomes from early intervention programs are reflective of the treatment provided or to spontaneous remission (Curlee & Yairi, 1997; Ingham & Cordes, 1998; Packman & Onslow, 1998; Bernstein Ratner, 1997a;

Zebrowski, 1997) "The management of young children who stutter depends not on a formula but on the decision-making and problem-solving skills that are part of the armory of every well-trained clinician" (Packman & Onslow, 1998, p. 9). During this decision-making process, there will be a certain level of false positives, enrolling children in treatment who might otherwise have recovered from stuttering without treatment (Onslow, 1992). Bernstein Ratner (1997a) made an interesting analogy with the field of medicine that is useful when discussing the controversy over spontaneous recovery:

> Overtreatment does not worry the medical profession, in many cases. We routinely vaccinate all children, even if few would contract a particular disease. In many cases, we have decided that the benefits to a relatively small group of children outweigh the marginal cost to the population of children in general. We need such a risk/benefit analysis for stuttering treatment." (p. 32)

In fact, we may never know with any degree of certainty if a particular child will recover from stuttering without some form of professional assistance. For those of us who have seen the debilitating effects of lifelong stuttering on the individual, the odds may be worth the cost of treating those who might recover on their own. Onslow (1992) used the term *logically justifiable* when clinicians decide to assist families of children who stutter. Clinicians must always consider the characteristics of each individual family, reflect back on the research data on spontaneous recovery, and, together with the family, make the most informed decision possible. If intervention is deemed necessary or desired by the team, what treatment model to choose is the next challenge.

Prevention versus Intervention

Starkweather et al. (1990) differentiated among three types of **prevention**: primary, secondary, and tertiary. Primary prevention refers to activities directed toward the general population that lead toward the prevention of a disease or disorder. Secondary prevention targets a specific population that may be at risk for a disease or disorder. And tertiary prevention focuses on a population already identified as having the disease or disorder. I use the terms *proactive* versus *reactive* prevention. **Proactive prevention** incorporates aspects of the primary and secondary definitions, whereas reactive prevention is similar to tertiary, after-the-fact intervention. Treatment decisions for early childhood disfluency may involve a proactive and reactive stance due to the possibility of spontaneous recovery issues. It is unknown whether any one child will recover from stuttering without intervention. It is known that early intervention with the young incipient stutterer is effective (Conture, 2001; Curlee, 1999; Guitar, 1998; Meyers, 1991; Shine, 1980; Starkweather et al., 1990). Taking a proactive stance through screening and intervention for this population may decrease the number of people who have life-impacting effects from stuttering (Onslow, 1992).

Reactive intervention, beginning after the disorder has established itself in the communication style of the individual, can be effective but may not be as effective as early intervention. For some children, stuttering will remain a factor and have an impact on their development long after they enter the early elementary school years. For this reason, it is recommended that therapy for the preschool child who is suspected of stuttering begin early in the stages of the disorder with indirect parent counseling orientation, leading into a more direct approach to treatment when necessary.

Treatment Goal and Design

The basic clinical goal for early childhood stuttering is to do what is necessary to prevent the development of negative emotions and aberrant motor reactions to speech disruptions (Williams, 1984). Factors affecting this clinical goal are (1) the severity of stuttering, in that the more disfluent the child, the more likely he is going to have negative emotions; (2) high standards imposed by parents; (3) emotional reactions to environmental pressures; and (4) variables in the communication process that produce stress. The clinical management of the preschool child who stutters must identify which of these four factors are potential confounding variables to successful treatment and design an individualized plan to change such variables.

An individualized treatment plan may take the form of indirect versus direct management strategies (Figure 7.1). **Indirect strategies** attempt to change the child's behavior by targeting the home environment. It is important for the parent to understand that "the environment does not cause a child to stutter; however, certain aspects of the environment may make it more likely that a child will exhibit increased stuttering in some situations" (Yaruss & Reardon, 2003). The indirect model relies on general parenting instruction intended to modify parent-child interactions, as well as monitoring of the child's speech. Initially, treatment sessions are infrequent, once or twice per month, and may increase in intensity if behavioral change is not observed.

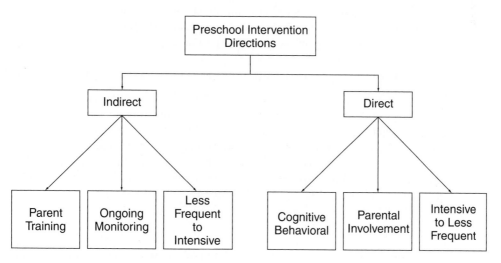

Figure 7.1
Visual representation of the components of indirect and direct treatment approaches for the preschool child who stutters.

Direct strategies follow a **cognitive-behavioral orientation,** relying on response-contingent conditioning programs, fluency training, and/or stuttering modification procedures to decrease stuttering. Parents are involved in the therapy process in ways similar to indirect therapy. However, they also receive direct training in speech modification techniques to facilitate transfer and maintenance of speech fluency in their child. Direct intervention typically begins more intensely, twice or three times per week with a gradual reduction of direct contact as the child learns to speak fluently.

Indirect Strategies for the Preschool Child

Indirect strategies are typically utilized for children who have not begun to show signs of tension or struggle associated with stuttering. They seldom notice or make comments regarding their speech. Time postonset of stuttering is short and their speech behaviors are highly variable. Parents exhibit a mild degree of concern yet wish to prevent the further development of stuttering in their child. There are certain principles to follow when implementing the following indirect treatment procedures. (A special note regarding the term *indirect*: This may be misleading to the beginning clinician. Therapy is certainly directly addressing environmental changes necessary to create a fluency-enhancing setting for the preschool child. However, indirect attention is made toward the child himself. Do not confuse indirect with a hands-off approach toward treatment.)

Basic Principles of Intervention

- Get to know the parents before disseminating information or advice.
- Know the child and his specific profile of stuttering.
- Provide a consistent model throughout all interactions.
- Focus on the parent and environmental factors rather than the child.
- Empower parents to be active change agents through involvement.
- Listen to the core messages of the parent and reflect hope and encouragement back to them.
- Remember that changes occur in small steps, and convey this to the parents.

The goal of indirect therapy is the creation of fluency that will remain stable over time. You may choose from the following treatment procedures to achieve this goal: parent counseling; ongoing monitoring of the child's speech in order to document improvement and determine if changes in procedures or strategies are warranted; the modification of situations, activities, and/or behaviors within the home environment that disrupt the child's speech; and parent training. Select these procedures for implementation based on family and child needs.

Parent Counseling

Begin the counseling process by providing parents with information regarding early childhood stuttering. Yaruss and Reardon (2003) convey to parents that (1) most children stop stuttering, (2) help is available for families and children who stutter, (3) stuttering does not have to ruin the child's life, and (4) parents are not alone in the quest to help their child. Additionally, it is beneficial for parents to understand the continuum

Dear Parent(s),

Take the time to observe other people talking.
Watching the news is a good source for this activity.
Listen for any "break in the forward flow of speech,"
that is, hesitations, interjections (uhms), phrase
repetitions (I can I can go), word repetitions (my my),
syllable repetitions (I wa wa want), sound repetitions
(I w w w want), stretching of sounds (w--------want),
or complete stoppage of sound. Each time you hear
a disfluency, put a tally mark on the TV. Bring it to your
next session.

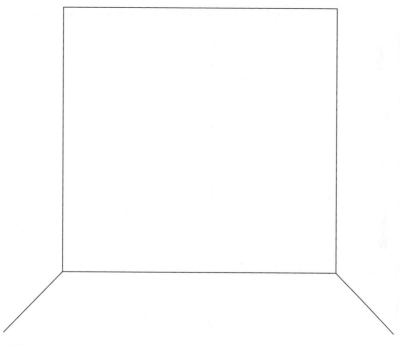

Figure 7.2
Watch People Talk is a chart for tallying disfluencies when listening to other people talk.

of fluency and be able to identify all types of disfluencies. The clinician may ask parents
to listen to speakers and make note of their observations. For example, provided with
a chart (Figure 7.2), parents are instructed to watch the news and listen for and mark
disfluencies in the speech of the people being interviewed.

 This form is returned at the next visit and leads the discussion into what happens
when the individual begins to react to these breaks in speech production. Explanation
of the stuttering cycle (Figure 1.4 in chapter 1) facilitates the parents' understanding
of the ABCs of stuttering. Now you can direct the parents' attention toward their
child's speech. Have parents chart their child's activities and behaviors that disrupt
fluency. Table 7.2 is an example of a form parents can use to note specific behaviors

Table 7.2
A charting worksheet useful for parents during the early stages of therapy.

Home Charting Worksheet

Date	Where was your child?	What was your child doing?	Describe your child's speech.	Was your child aware?	How did you help your child?

of both the listener and speaker during disfluent episodes. You and the parents begin to explore the multidynamic nature of stuttering together through discussions that often elicit further inquiries from the parents.

Parents often ask why their child stutters. Be sure to answer this question in a way that does not make the parents feel responsible. Describing the disorder as a puzzle may help them cope with the fact that we do not know, with certainty, the cause of stuttering. We have several facts or puzzle pieces that fit together and make sense, yet we are missing many pieces. Stressing the multifactorial, dynamic feature is essential to understanding how stuttering manifests in each individual. Most likely, a genetic predisposition to stutter is influenced, in varying degrees, by environmental factors. At this point in the discussion, you must look at the particular profile of the client to determine exacerbating, confounding variables. Parents may be highly sensitive to this information, so provide material in small segments, always identifying positive as well as negative behaviors. Just as you did when discussing diagnostic findings with the parent, present this information in a three-column format of environmental strengths, exacerbating conditions, and then together as a team, you and the parents can decide which behaviors you will target initially.

Starkweather (1997b) presented a three-way process children use when modifying their speech: awareness, acceptance, and change. We have applied this process to parents as a means of facilitating environmental change. First, parents must be aware of behaviors exhibited by themselves, their child, and other family members that contribute to the development and/or maintenance of stuttering. This information will be used to make decisions regarding the direction of therapy. Next, parents must accept the stuttering and openly address it with their child and the clinician. Parents are encouraged to acknowledge their child's stuttering through comments such as "that was a bumpy word" or "that was a hard one to say." Logan and Caruso (1997) presented four categories of statements parents may use to promote objective talk around stuttering (Table 7.3).

Table 7.3
Descriptions and examples of four categories of statements that parents can model to facilitate their child's ability to talk objectively about speech disfluency.

Type of Model	Description	Examples
Talking Objectively About Speech Disfluency		
Labeling	Parents model simple, factual statements that describe their child's behavior.	"That word sounded bumpy." "You feel angry." "That took a little while to say."
Informing	Parents model simple explanations about the nature of child's behavior or feelings.	"People make mistakes when they are learning." "Sometimes we become frustrated when we find something is hard to do."
Assuring	Parents model accepting/reassuring statements.	"It's okay with Mom and Dad if you repeat words." "Sometimes Mom and Dad repeat words, too."
Reframing	Parents model alternate ways for their child to interpret events.	"This is a good chance for you to learn how to deal with kids who tease you."

Source: From K. J. Logan & A. J. Caruso, "Parents as Partners in the Treatment of Childhood Stuttering." Seminars in Speech and Language 1997; 18(3): 319. Reprinted by permission.

Another form of acceptance is to have parents insert tension-free, whole-word/syllable repetitions into their speech (Starkweather, 1997b). The parents now have the opportunity to reflect on their disfluency with a comment like "Yes, I did trip on that word a little, didn't I? It isn't always possible to say things just the way you want" (p. 275). With your guidance, parents are in a position to model appropriate behaviors and interactions to promote acceptance in their child. The premise is that one cannot change behaviors they are unaware of nor accept the need to change.

Parental readiness for change is the third step. Using the information gathered so far in therapy, you and the parents begin to identify behaviors that need to be modified. The literature is robust with suggestions on what parents should and should not do when interacting with their child who stutters. Again, before you tell a parent to modify a behavior, make sure it is relevant to the particular fluency profile of the child. Generating a standard list of suggestions and routinely giving these out may not be the best method. Not all suggestions apply to all parents. It is hopeful parents will discover which factors are pertinent to their child, rather than you didactically telling them. However, for the beginning clinician, this list is a beneficial guide when counseling parents:

- Listen to *what* your child is saying not *how* he or she is talking.
- Openly acknowledge your child's communication difficulties.
- Openly acknowledge your child's feelings surrounding these difficulties.
- It is *okay* to use the word *stuttering*.
- It is *okay* to stutter.

Ongoing Monitoring

Ongoing monitoring of the child's speech is an essential component to any early childhood intervention program. However, parents need to learn how to monitor their child's fluency as well as stuttering behaviors. Use of a daily log can assist parents with this process of learning about situations that help or hinder their child's fluency abilities. This log might include a list of set activities, circumstances, and persons with whom the child typically interacts, making it easier for the parent to recall when stuttering peaks. Reliance on verbal reports from parents is subject to inconsistency and decreased reliability. Written documentation also helps in tracking the child's speech performance over the course of therapy. Other information on such a form might include talking while excited, competing for listeners' attention, speaking under time pressure, reciting or performance speech, and/or competing with siblings for floor space.

You may also require weekly recordings of a 5-minute parent-child or child-sibling interaction that are periodically analyzed to validate parental reports on progress or lack of progress. This is particularly important for those who are at risk for continued stuttering. If stuttering worsens during this monitoring period, encourage parents to bring their child back for further follow-up. If the child's speech is improving or maintaining, follow-up may be delayed, but parents should continue systematic monitoring. Onslow (1992) described a cost-efficient method for managing cases that have been placed on an at-risk register. Brief parent interviews or mail questionnaires are conducted regularly to determine if the child should remain on the at-risk register. He asks parents a series of eight questions requiring yes or no responses. The child remains at

Table 7.4

Monitoring questionnaire used to determine if modifications to the preschool child's treatment plan are needed.

Questions	Yes	No	Comments
At any time in the past months, have you noticed any of the following associated with your child's speech:			
1. Many repetitions of the first part of a word, or a number of words (for example "d-d-d-daddy" or "I want-want-want-want to play" or "Can I, can I, can I, can I go to the store?").			
2. Periods of silence, or "blocks," when attempting to speak.			
3. Prolongations of sounds when attempting to speak (for example, "that's a caaaaat").			
4. Blinking, facial twitching, or grimacing when attempting to speak.			
At any time in the past months, has your child said anything or have you noticed anything that made you think your child has:			
5. Had any kind of involuntary disruption of efforts to speak.			
6. Lost control of the ability to speak (for example, "Mommy, I can't say it.").			
At any time in the past months:			
7. Have you thought that your child may be stuttering?			
8. Has any other person or persons told you that your child may be stuttering?			

Source: Based on Onslow (1992).

this level if the parent responds no to all questions (Table 7.4). If a yes is present, the child's status is upgraded and an appointment is made with the parents to consider any required modifications. Monitoring and indirect treatment procedures should continue until remission occurs or there is no improvement. Onslow recommended a schedule of observations be conducted at least every 2 to 3 months for young children, decreasing in frequency as the child gets older.

Modification of Home Environment

Adams (1993), in a summary of 35 studies investigating the home environment of children who stutter, concluded that these children do not grow up in a home environment that is blatantly unhealthy. There does not appear to be any distinguishing pattern of behaviors between parents of stuttering versus nonstuttering children. However, during the monitoring period, certain environmental interactions may be identified as fluency disrupting, thus requiring direct attention. One common practice in the literature is the establishment of a routine "talk time" exercise (Botterill, Kelman,

& Rustin, 1991; Mallard, 1991). Parents agree to set aside a predetermined amount of time (3, 4, or 5 minutes initially) four, five, or six times per week. They play with their child in a room alone with no distractions, such as the television or radio playing in the background. The parent is to follow the child's lead, allowing him to choose a toy or game for interaction. It is emphasized that parents listen to *what* the child is saying not *how* he is talking. Mallard suggested these interactions be videotaped, if possible, to review with the clinician at a later date. Each parent evaluates their listening performance with notations in a talk time log. Also be cognizant of the different types of interactions of mothers and fathers of children who stutter. Kelly (1994, 1995) stressed the importance of involving both parents in the treatment process.

Parental follow-through with talk time activities helps provide insight into the parents' commitment to the therapy process. For some families, commitment to therapy places no strain on the daily routine of the home. However, for other families, this may not be the case. Remember, in today's society, parents have many concerns to handle throughout the day. Work schedules, family dynamics, demands from siblings, and so on, may place a strain on the family, influencing their ability to follow through on assignments. If parents are not able to complete this relatively easy listening task, it may be even more difficult for them to commit the time required to change certain interactions that disrupt fluency. Not all families will be good candidates for family-directed intervention. Accept this reality, treat all families with unconditional regard, and adapt treatment plans accordingly.

Parent Training

You might provide parents with several suggestions or strategies to create a communicative exchange conducive to fluency (Bennett-Mancha, 1990; Conture & Melnick, 1999; Kelly & Conture, 1991). Kelly (1993) concluded, from a review of the literature on parent-child factors that facilitate fluency or exacerbate stuttering, that the research does not provide conclusive support for the common suggestions provided parents. However, as Ingham and Cordes (1998) noted, "problems exist when we assume that averaged findings from a large group are applicable to any one particular subject" (p. 16). Therefore, such suggestions should be applied on a case-by-case basis because any one of these behaviors may or may not play a central role in the maintenance of stuttering. The following is a list of possible suggestions that may help parents aid in increasing their child's fluency.

1. Use positively reinforcing communications.
2. Promote acceptance, acknowledgment, and openness around stuttering.
3. Speak less hurriedly.
4. Pause more frequently ("think in phrases").
5. Allow your child to finish his thoughts.
6. Rephrase the child's responses using fluency-enhancing behaviors, also called **restimulation.**
7. Maintain eye contact.
8. Recognize the communicative strengths of your child.

Being able to implement these suggestions is not an easy task. Parents must have systematic training opportunities to practice the strategies and receive reinforcement from you. Never just tell parents to "slow down" their speech without showing them how to do it. Logan, Roberts, Prieto, and Morey (2002) published findings from a study that investigated adults' ability to implement four rate reduction strategies as a means of decreasing conversational pace. Techniques included articulatory rate (AR), increased utterance pauses (IUP), turn switching pauses (TSP), and self-devised method (SDM). Articulatory rate reduction was accomplished by elongating phonemes within each syllable to 1 to 2 seconds in duration. Increased utterance pauses required adults to increase the frequency and duration of pauses within and between utterances. The turn switching pauses involved increasing the duration between conversational turns by 1 to 2 seconds. The last strategy asked adults to produce speech that was 25% slower than their customary speech rate without any direction on how to accomplish this goal. Results of this study have particular relevance for training parents of children who stutter.

First, all adults were able to employ these techniques after a relatively short period of training (i.e., several training sessions). When provided with specific instructions on how to decrease their speech rate, adults had a greater mean rate of reduction than when left on their own (SDM) to determine how to do this. Second, the adults in this study did not naturally change other aspects of speech production that were not trained. Therefore, we cannot assume parents will automatically change untrained parameters of speech in the same manner as those they have previously trained. You must provide direct training, albeit not requiring much time, on each suggestion you are asking parents to implement during parent-child interactions.

Direct Strategies for the Preschool Child

Direct strategies are utilized for children who have begun to show signs of tension or struggle associated with stuttering and/or have not benefited from indirect therapy. Parents often report that the child has made negative comments about talking and will even stop talking when he encounters a moment of stuttering. There are certain principles to follow when implementing the following direct treatment procedures.

Basic Principles of Intervention

1. Keep demands low for the beginning of therapy.
2. Keep tasks within the child's current level of language ability.
3. Incorporate fluency tasks centered around common vocabulary.
4. Scaffold fluency tasks into gradual increases in linguistic demand.
5. Be consistent in the structure of your therapy sessions.

Let's look at each principle in more detail. It is important that the child experience success in the early stages of therapy; therefore, do not impose high demands for either language or motor production. Shine (1980) incorporated this principle when he selected simple monosyllabic words that the client can fluently produce for practice using an "easy speaking voice." Keep therapeutic tasks within the child's language level

Table 7.5
Five levels of requests varying in linguistic demand.

Level	Explanation
Level I	Requests obligate single-word responses that repeat one of the words in the examiner's question/request. For example, "Is it red or blue?" This includes all yes/no questions, with the exception of clarification requests.
Level II	Requests typically obligate single-word responses: the name of a common object present in the examining situation but not given in the question. For example, "What is that?" This level also would include requests that require more than a single-word response when the question elicits "the red car" or "the green truck" and requests for clarification.
Level III	Requests elicit responses consisting of prepositional phrases or complete sentences but the referents are not present and are not named in the request. For example, "Where did you put it?"
Level IV	Requests often elicit a series of attributes not named in the request, and the syntactic form of the request is not constrained by the nature of the request. For example, "Tell me everything you know about skiing."
Level V	Requests are open ended and elicit the greatest variety of responses both in form and content. For example, "Make up a story about pumpkins."

Source: A. L. Weiss, "The Pragmatic Context of Children's Disfluency." Seminars in Speech and Language 1993; 14(3): 220. Reprinted by permission.

as a way to decrease the demands the child must manage. Determine what the child's interests are and use this vocabulary during structured tasks. Client-centered therapy provides the benefit of engaging the child in topics and activities he is interested in while promoting fluency.

Next, there is a consensus in the literature that the length of an utterance is associated with the occurrence of stuttering (Logan & Conture, 1995; Wilkenfeld & Curlee, 1997). A unique way of scaffolding fluency tasks so they gradually increase linguistic load is by using the Stocker Probe paradigm, presented here as modified by Weiss (1993) (Table 7.5).

Five levels of demand comprise this organization, all of which may be manipulated within the course of each session. Moving from a multiple-choice task (Is this red or blue?), the child is then asked to label in response to "What is it?" Level III requires more language processing, requiring the child to use phrases or sentences. A verbal elaboration task ("Tell me everything you can about a car") is followed by a Level-V demand to generate a series of events in the form of a story. You can move up and down the linguistic hierarchy in response to the child's current performance. Refine your observational skills so you can identify upcoming fluency breakdowns and redirect the child or change the linguistic task before stuttering happens.

The last principle of intervention suggests you maintain consistency in the structure of each therapy session, particularly during the initial stages of therapy. Such structure helps children predict what they will do, thus reducing the stress of sudden changes in routine. As the child gains some degree of fluency control, you can gradually reduce the structure of the session and increase the unpredictability. If the child is unable to maintain his fluency, return to a more structured scheme. Van Riper (1973) described a similar procedure in which the clinician begins to insert various fluency

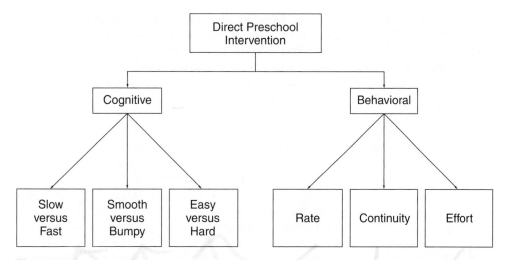

Figure 7.3
Depiction of the cognitive and behavioral equivalents of direct treatment for the preschool child who stutters.

disruptions into the therapy session to build the client's tolerance level. If the clinician observes a reaction on behalf of the child, the disruption is removed allowing the child to return to his fluency baseline. Over time, Van Riper hypothesized that this would desensitize the child and increase the tolerance of unexpected demands.

Treatment Procedures

Direct treatment procedures for the preschool child who stutters can be classified as cognitive-behavioral in orientation (Figure 7.3). Behaviorally, the concept of fluency can be divided into the components of rate, continuity, and effort (Starkweather, 1987). However, young children may have difficulty understanding these concepts due to their limited metalinguistic development (Bernstein Ratner, 1993). Putting these fluency components into a cognitive perspective helps make these terms concrete and comprehensible to this young population. The cognitive translation of rate might be taught through activities emphasizing "slow versus fast"; continuity principles can be demonstrated through "smooth and bumpy" tasks. The last component of effort is easily translated into "hard versus soft" exercises. The following section targets how to convey the behavioral aspect of fluency through cognitive activities.

Slow versus Fast. Preschool children can comprehend the concepts of slow and fast. They can sort items that move slow or fast, imitate corresponding physical actions, and cut out pictures of people going fast and slow. Meyers and Woodford (1992) presented a story format to communicate this concept. Utilizing a race horse and a tortoise, an analogy is made when the race horse goes too fast and stumbles over his feet, yet the tortoise, who takes its time, wins the race. Although too lengthy for some young children, this coloring storybook is useful for most preschool children.

Another way of contrasting slow and fast is to have the children color pictures in a slow way, making comments about the quality of the output. Then have the group color quickly, which may provide the opportunity to make a comment such as "When we go fast, sometimes we make mistakes, like tearing the paper or coloring on the table." Make sure you comment that "mistakes are okay" but you prefer the slow way of coloring. You can do the same contrast activity with modeling clay. The child tries to make a snake but rolls too fast and breaks the clay, whereas going slow and taking your time, you can make a well-formed snake. Again, gradually move this contrast toward the child's speech efforts, that is, "into the mouth." While coloring fast, model excessively fast speech and acknowledge when you stumble on your words. Then model excessively slow speech and ask the children if they like that type of speech. Create games for the children to play that provide opportunities for them to sense the difference between fast and slow speech.

Congruence between your physical movements and speech model is a necessity. You may confuse the child by using fast hand or body movements, such as when dealing cards or erasing the blackboard. Take every opportunity to utilize slow physical movements throughout the therapy sessions. Slowly manipulate stimuli within the activity, slowly pick up the toys when finished, and slowly walk the child back to his classroom or waiting room area.

Smooth versus Bumpy. The concept of smooth versus bumpy speech sets the framework for later use of easy, voluntary stuttering (i.e., bounces). Here, the children can go on a scavenger hunt, finding objects that feel smooth or bumpy, putting them in their corresponding paper sacks. You can model slow, smooth speech as you place items in the smooth bag. In contrast, bumpy speech is produced for items that feel rough or bumpy. For example, you can say, "I f-f-found a piece of sandpaper." Gradually shape this model into easy, rhythmic repetitions void of extensive tension. You can further extend this activity by having the child taste smooth versus bumpy foods (e.g., smooth versus crunchy peanut butter, grapes versus raisins, or plain yogurt versus yogurt with granola).

Reinforce any efforts by the child to produce these different types of speech. Comments such as "That was an easy bumpy" or "You really said that smoothly" demonstrate to the child the concept of acceptance. Game board activities can be created in which the child moves along the board practicing smooth versus bumpy speech (see Figure 7.4). Along with clinician and parent modeling, the child learns how to modify his speech in a positive way.

Easy versus Hard. Fluent speech production is often described as "easy" for the young child. You can label this new way of talking using a variety of terms: easy speech; slow, easy speech; and/or superslow speech. To make this term more concrete, have the child sort objects that are soft versus hard. Using tactile cues helps the child grasp the feeling component of easy sounds. Another activity is to have the child squeeze your finger with a lot of effort. Comment on how hard he was trying. Then have the child just barely touch your finger, again, reflecting back to the child

Figure 7.4
Stretchy and bouncy bags and folders made by children who stutter.

on the ease of his efforts. Gradually move this activity toward the child's speech, explaining how sounds can be made in an easy versus hard way. Cooper and Cooper (1985) have a game board, "Hard as Nails, Easy as Pie," in which the child has the opportunity to practice both types of speech. Not only do these activities desensitize the child to fluency breaks, they also teach him to have control over the way he talks.

The last note on direct intervention for the preschool child is regarding the words you provide when describing stuttering or fluent speech. Let the child label his new speech with whatever terms he wishes. Some children may react to the term *turtle talk* or *slow speech*, saying they "don't want to talk like a turtle" or "turtles don't talk." When children create their own label, it can be empowering, showing them they have a say in the therapy process. A downside of this choice is that you have to remember the label picked by each child in therapy. Use of a self-stick note with the child's label located on the child's folder will help eliminate embarrassing situations in which you use the wrong term.

Current Models of Therapy

There are several published therapy models you may choose to implement with the preschool child who stutters. The following brief overview of these programs is presented in alphabetical order to avoid inferring preference for one program over another. When you are in the process of developing a treatment plan for a child, include aspects of any one of these programs based on the individual needs of the child and family.

Extended Length of Utterance

Costello (1980, 1983, [Costello Ingham] 1993, 1999) described a fluency-shaping program designed for the young child who stutters. The program incorporates operant conditioning principles with a strong emphasis on structured manipulation of linguistic complexity that can be used in either group or individual therapy. The Extended Length of Utterance system establishes fluency through reinforcement schedules and a well-outlined sequence of therapy objectives. This program is very useful for the beginning clinician who may be trying to establish a certain level of clinical proficiency. Clear guidelines and instructions are available. One weakness of the program is its limited consideration of transfer and maintenance issues of fluency therapy. For some children who stutter, getting them fluent is a relatively easy task; keeping them fluent is the challenge.

Fluency Development Program

The Fluency Development Program for Young Children (TFDS) (Meyers & Woodford, 1992) is a cognitive-behavioral therapy program intended to establish fluent speech in young children. Child-centered activities are described in the manual, which promotes the teaching of certain fluency rules designed to promote understanding of (1) slow versus fast speech, (2) smooth versus bumpy speech, and (3) turn-taking concepts. Children are also taught how to handle time pressure and difficult speaking situations. This program can be implemented in either group or individual settings. The manual includes 13 behavioristic exercises and ideas for clinicians to use when counseling parents.

Gradual Increase in Length and Complexity of Utterance

Ryan (1974, 1984, 1986) described a behavior-oriented therapy program using reinforcement schedules and step-by-step instructions with children who stutter. The program includes four management components: (1) programmed instruction, (2) delayed auditory feedback, (3) punishment, and (4) gradual increase in length and complexity of utterance (GILCU). Fluent speech production is targeted through a traditional sequence of therapy, that is, establishment, transfer, and maintenance. Ryan recommended the GILCU portion of the program be utilized with the young, less severe child. Like ELU, Ryan's program is a useful tool for the beginning clinician just learning about therapy for children who stutter.

Hugo Gregory and Diane Hill

Gregory and Hill (1980, 1993, 1999) described a prevention and management program for preschool stuttering (Table 7.6). The implementation of the prevention versus management program is based on differential assessment and diagnostic findings. They define prevention as referring to the action that may prevent stuttering from increasing and become a major communicative barrier. Three major treatment strategies comprise this approach in which the goal is to establish and maintain fluent speech production through parent counseling and direct client interactions.

Table 7.6

Prevention and management of stuttering strategies and procedures.

Treatment Strategy	Procedures
I. Preventive parent counseling: child typically disfluent	Parent feedback Discussion of interactive styles Increase understanding of communicative stress Increase understanding of speech and language development Provide information through reading
II. Prescriptive parent counseling: Brief child therapy: child borderline atypically disfluent without complicating speech or language factors	Parent feedback Charting disfluent episodes Modeling positive communicative styles conductive to increased fluency Reassessment of child and parent-child interaction
III. Comprehensive therapy program: child borderline atypically (definite stuttering behaviors); disfluent with/without complicating speech or language or behavioral factors	Facilitating child's fluency Increasing tolerance to fluency-disrupting influences Developing competence in skills with the potential to interfere with fluency

Source: Based on Gregory and Hill (1993).

Treatment strategy I involves preventive parent counseling for the child who is typically disfluent. It consists of five components: (1) provide parent feedback, (2) discuss parent-child interactive styles, (3) increase understanding of communicative stress, (4) increase understanding of speech and language development, and (5) provide information through reading. Treatment strategy II entails prescriptive parent counseling through brief therapy with the child who exhibits borderline atypical disfluent speech without complicating speech or language factors. Four tasks make up this strategy: (1) provide parent feedback, (2) chart disfluent episodes, (3) model positive communicative styles conducive to increased fluency, and (4) reassess child and parent child interaction. Treatment strategy III is a comprehensive therapy program for the child with borderline atypical disfluency with complicating speech or language factors or atypically disfluent (demonstrating more definite stuttering behaviors) with or without complicating speech, language, or behavioral factors. Three activities are systematically structured for achievement of fluency: (1) facilitate fluency, (2) increase tolerance to fluency-disrupting influences, and (3) develop competence in skills that have the potential to interfere with fluency.

The Lidcombe Program

The Lidcombe program (Harrison & Onslow, 1999; Jones, Onslow, Harrison, & Packman, 2000; Onslow, 1996; Onslow & Packman, 1999) is a parent-administered fluency-shaping intervention program for early childhood stuttering. The program outlines goals for the parent, child, and clinician incorporating clinician-directed parent training with parent-directed home activities (Harrison & Onslow, 1999). The goal for the child is to use stutter-free speech in all speaking situations and to maintain this fluency for at least 12 months postintervention. Parents are taught how to conduct the treatment and measure their child's fluency until the stuttering is eliminated. The clinician assists the parents in learning about and implementing the program.

Treatment procedures are clearly outlined in the program, which include weekly 1-hour visits to the clinic with daily home activities. A substantial amount of time must be set aside each day for speech work. The program recommends two 10- to 15-minute parent-child interactions in which the child is praised for stutter-free speech. Note that "stuttered speech is corrected at times, but much less frequently than clinician and parent praise for stutter-free speech" (p. 74). There are specific examples of corrective feedback strategies for the parent/clinician to utilize in the program. The program acknowledges the role of client sensitivity to correction, allowing for an emphasis on the positive aspects of the child's communication with infrequent punishment for stuttering. The basic rules for these daily sessions are (1) the child should enjoy the therapy activities, (2) any activity the child reacts to in a negative way is terminated immediately, and (3) all components of the program are applied with a degree of flexibility to meet individual needs of the child and family (Harrison & Onslow, 1999, p. 70). Weekly clinic visits and daily home practice continues until the child meets the criteria for dismissal, less than 1% stuttered speech in the clinic and 1.5% SMST (stutters per minute speaking time) outside the clinic. According to Jones et al. (2000), this process takes approximately 11 clinic sessions with some variability depending on the extent of the child's initial level of stuttering. The child then enters the maintenance phase of treatment characterized by a reduction of home activities by the parents with half-hour clinic visits gradually decreasing in frequency over the next 12 months.

Peter Ramig

Ramig (1993b) described an early childhood intervention design stressing the parent-clinician relationship. His three-stage therapy process incorporates both indirect parent counseling and direct client management, a combination approach found to be effective for the young child (Ramig & Wallace, 1987). Stage 1 stresses parent education. Here, the parents are encouraged to describe what they classify as stuttering. The clinician explains the unknown etiology of stuttering, reviewing myths and the realities of the disorder. During this stage the parents express their feelings about stuttering in an open, accepting environment.

Stage 2 involves facilitating parent awareness of communication and interpersonal styles that are conducive to fluency. Parents practice using a slower speech rate, like Mr. Rogers' Speaking Model. This may be facilitated by having the parents listen to speech played on a variable speech tape recorder. The clinician models fluency-enhancing behaviors and discusses with the parents various interactions that disrupt fluency (e.g., interruptions).

Parents begin to participate as observers and participants during stage 3. They observe interactions between clinician and child, attending to the clinician's speech rate, turn-taking pauses, and relaxed communication demeanor throughout the session. Gradually, parents participate in the session implementing the strategies they learned about during stages 1 and 2. Parents are to assume more responsibility for demonstrating fluency-enhancing behaviors during times when their child is fluent and disfluent. As a major component of this approach, Ramig asks parents to "facilitate fluency in the home environment in a positive and supportive manner" (p. 233).

C. Woodruff Starkweather, Sheryl Gottwald, and Murray Halfond

Starkweather et al. (1990) outlined their direct therapy approach for early childhood stuttering, which includes three dimensions: parent education, attitude change, and behavioral change. Parental education focuses on the exchange of information about stuttering and its manifestation in the child; alignment of parental expectations with reality; and eliminating the conspiracy of silence surrounding the topic of stuttering. This program is administered across several sessions, dispersing information gradually, in bits and pieces. One particular component of parental education addresses the resistance of parents when confronting the disorder. Starkweather et al. (1990) advised parents to acknowledge their child's stuttering with comments such as "You had a hard time saying that word" and to insert voluntary stuttering into their own speech as a model for demonstrating how to cope with stuttering. Length of treatment is considered relevant to discussions because parents often want to know how long the family will be involved in therapy. Starkweather et al. (1990) have identified several predictors of the need for prolonged treatment in this population: the presence of stuttering in a parent, negative parental emotion to the child's moments of disfluency, and the amount of time lapsed since the onset of stuttering. This last statement has been refuted by research by Onslow and his colleagues (1996, 1999, 2003), who contend that length of treatment may not be related to time postonset of stuttering. Further research will help clarify this especially important issue.

Attitude change is the second component of Starkweather et al.'s early intervention program. Teaching parents how to handle their guilt and anger through desensitization, exploration, and identification tasks is a major attitude aspect of this program. They believe it is important to point out to the parents the large amount of fluency the child has in his speech. Parents will often focus on the stuttered speech far more than the fluent portion. It is your goal to assist the parents in redirecting their attention toward the fluency in their child's speech. Praise the parent for the behaviors they exhibit that contribute to this fluency. Equally important, though, is the goal of identifying breaks in the forward flow of speech, whether these are more typical or less typical of preschool children. Understanding the fluency continuum helps parents categorize disfluencies and improve the accuracy of parental reports. This type of discussion naturally leads into the topic of stuttering and the need to be open and talk about it. Be available to answer questions regarding the nature and treatment of stuttering that models a nonemotional, factual demeanor. You can provide multiple examples of how parents may respond when their child is stuttering, such as "That was a tricky word to say" or "Sometimes words are hard to say."

When conducting parent counseling sessions, Starkweather et al. emphasizes that "parents learn better through self-discovery rather than instruction" (p. 70). The tasks geared to change the parents' attitude toward stuttering should be conducted with this principle in mind. Another aspect of their counseling process is addressing particular issues parents may have about their child's stuttering. Issues regarding the past,

Table 7.7

Past, present, and future issues expressed by parents of preschool children who stutter.

Past	Present	Future
Child's history in relation to possible etiology	Anxiety over effectiveness of stuttering prevention program	Worry about prognosis for fluent speech
Guilt in relation to etiology and informal treatment	Curiosity and doubt about value of specific therapeutic techniques	Anxiety about regression
Anger toward self, child, family, and professionals	Curiosity about the relationship of stuttering to other issues (e. g., toilet training, discipline) and relationships (family or peers)	Anxiety about potential school problems
Disappointment about previous professional therapeutic interventions		Worry about continuation with a new clinician
		Worry about termination of therapy
		Desire for support and network system

Source: Based on Starkweather et al. (1990).

present, and future may negatively impact the effectiveness of the intervention if not discussed openly with the parents. Table 7.7 outlines some of the possible concerns exhibited by parents.

The third component of Starkweather's et al. (1990) program targets changing the behaviors called stuttering through indirect and direct methods. These behaviors may be targeted toward either the child or the parent and include the following: speech rate reduction, increasing pause time between conversational turns, slower motor/body movements, decreasing frequency of interruptions, increasing use of commenting versus questioning, and daily "special talking time." Starkweather's talk time activity is similar to Botterill et al. (1991) in that it includes a 15-minute period in which the parent devotes time talking, reading stories, and playing quiet games with the child without any form of distraction. Again, the goal of this activity is to build the child's level of confidence as a worthy communicator.

Stuttering Intervention Program

The Stuttering Intervention Program (SIP) (Pindzola, 1987) is a fluency management system for children 3 to 8 years of age. The program includes assessment procedures, parent counseling ideas, guidelines for writing individualized education plans (IEPs), and teacher information. The primary focus of the speech modification portion is manipulating linguistic complexity to facilitate the use of soft, smooth, and slow speech. Three main concepts encompass this program's theoretical foundation. The first component involves the reinforcement of fluency and punishment for stuttering. The clinician is instructed to say "stop" when stuttering is present. Token reinforcers are given to the child for fluent speech.

The second concept underlying SIP is the enhancement of fluency through rhythmic syllable productions. The child is taught to stretch the beginning of an utterance using a soft voice with smooth, slow movement. Various cognitive analogies, such as a boat sailing on the water, are used to assist the preschooler in understanding clinician requests. The third concept of the SIP emphasizes linguistic manipulation through word level practice, short utterance practice, and longer utterances in conversational speech. The instructional components of this part of the program ("how to do this") are vaguely outlined in the manual. The program does include many helpful informational worksheets for parents and teachers. A unique aspect of this program is the IEP provided in the appendixes.

Systematic Fluency Training

The major goal of the Systematic Fluency Training Program for Young Children (Shine, 1980, 1984) is to establish a simple **response-contingent paradigm** along various levels of linguistic complexity that require a gradual increase in speech motor demands. Upon selecting a core set of vocabulary items that the child can produce fluently, the clinician begins direct training on using an easy speaking voice during structured activities. Shine's activities include a picture identification task, a story book activity, picture matching games, and a surprise box. Each session is structured so there is time for each activity. As fluency is established, more time may be allocated to tasks involving more complex language production. Parents and significant others (such as siblings or peers) are gradually included in therapy sessions to facilitate transfer and maintenance of the child's newly learned fluency. The manual provides a detailed outline of therapeutic steps to follow to achieve speech fluency in conversation.

Treating Concomitant Disorders

Phonological Disorders

Stuttering and phonology: What is the connection? The literature has attempted to answer this question with relative but not complete success. Much insight has been garnered from the research efforts of various investigators (Ambrose, Cox, & Yairi, 1997; Andrews & Harris, 1964; Louko, 1995; Louko et al., 1990; Paden, Ambrose, & Yairi, 2002; Paden & Yairi, 1996; Paden, Yairi, & Ambrose, 1999; Wolk, Edwards, & Conture, 1993; Yairi & Ambrose, 1999; Yairi et al., 1996; Yaruss et al., 1998). Paden, et al. (2002) provide a thorough review of this literature, which is summarized here:

1. The onset of stuttering is frequently reported between 2 and 4 years of age, a time when children undergo rapid phonological development.
2. Incidence rates for the co-occurrence of stuttering and phonology ranges from 30% to 40%.
3. Children who stutter use more phonological processes compared to their peers, particularly consonant cluster reduction.
4. Children who stutter use similar phonological processes to those nonstuttering children.
5. Children who persist with stuttering have a higher mean phonological error score.

6. A large percentage of children who persist with stuttering have a moderate level of phonological inadequacy.
7. Children with persistent stuttering appear to have delayed phonological development.

Their overall conclusion was that children who persist with stuttering often exhibit poorer phonology than seen in children who eventually recover from stuttering. In a longitudinal study of subjects who have participated in the Stuttering Research Project of the University of Illinois, Yairi and his colleagues reported several findings that continue to add to the literature: (1) phonological development of children who stutter appears to differ from most children only in that it occurs at a slower rate; (2) a large percentage (35%) of children in the recovered group were females compared to 18.2% in the persistent group; and (3) the greatest amount of phonological improvement occurred within the first year after identification. The relationship between the onset of stuttering and phonological development is opaque, not yet known in its entirety (Nippold, 2002). However, we know these disorders appear together frequently and, therefore, must be addressed when developing treatment plans.

Sequential versus Concurrent Intervention. The first step is to determine the type of intervention model you will implement for this subgroup of children. There are two types of orientation to treatment: sequential versus concurrent. **Sequential intervention** treats one problem before the other. Several circumstances might warrant this treatment direction. The child who exhibits a severe phonological disorder may need initial phonological intervention to remediate processes that are impacting speech intelligibility. The child may be experiencing frustration at his inability to be understood, which takes precedence over milder disfluencies. In contrast, a child who exhibits an inability to initiate phonation and is struggling with his speech may need immediate fluency-shaping intervention. These decisions will be made on a case-by-case basis.

Concurrent intervention is another treatment paradigm currently recommended for use with the preschool child who stutters and exhibits disordered phonology. Concurrent intervention attempts "to place fluency skills practice within the context of lowest phonological and linguistic demand" (Bernstein Ratner, 1995, p. 182). Louko, Conture, and Edwards (1993, 1999) described a concurrent treatment program using the modified cycles approach in which several processes are targeted over a certain period of time. They integrate fluency-shaping tasks into phonological intervention plans with specific instructions to avoid overt correction of the child's speech. The modified cycles approach involves the following speech tasks: (1) no direct phonetic placement, (2) modeling, (3) auditory discrimination, (4) increasing linguistic complexity, (5) minimal pairs, (6) facilitating contexts, (7) modified paired stimuli, and (8) overtraining.

Blended versus Discrete. Bernstein Ratner (1995) described two additional organizations to intervention for children with concomitant disorders. A unique

blended approach to treatment in which work toward specific goals is staggered based on current level of client proficiency is contrasted with a discrete approach. The following is her outline of a blended therapy session:

> A period of initial therapy time is devoted to improving performance in a particular area of phonological or linguistic performance. After the child has reached a comfortable level of performance (in a structured environment) within the targeted areas, work on fluency can begin, using the recently mastered forms as the basis for practice. Thereafter, guidelines for fluent speech production are framed overtly during "review" activities, rather than during practice on newer targets." (p. 183)

The **discrete approach** to treatment is similar to the cycles approach of Hodson and Paden (Bernstein Ratner, 1995). Here, blocks of time (or cycles) are set aside for work on fluency; other time periods address either phonological or linguistic concerns. This framework allows for maximum individualization of treatment plans based on client needs. Because of the high degree of fluctuation with fluency disorders, the clinician can quickly modify plans to accommodate such variations. The ultimate goal for children who stutter with coexisting phonological disorders is the development of age-appropriate phonology within the context of increasing children's speech fluency, altering the emphasis from phonology to fluency as needed.

Principles of Intervention. Bennett and Louko (1994) presented 12 principles of intervention to guide the clinician when treating children who stutter who also exhibit disordered phonology. This subgroup of children often presents itself with a set of unique strengths and weaknesses that needs to be assessed prior to the initiation of therapy. With a clear profile of skills, you can then consider the following principles and plan accordingly.

Principle 1. For younger children, use an indirect approach to therapy. The rationale behind this principle is twofold: (1) direct intervention may result in increased tension in the speech mechanism, and (2) direct intervention for phonological errors may be followed by increased fluency concerns.

Principle 2. Utilize a slow, unhurried speech model throughout all interactions. This allows the child time to plan, enhances coordination efforts, and models relatively slow physically nontense speech. Although such models may enhance fluency, there are certain pitfalls. These include unnatural-sounding speech accompanied with over-articulation and a singsong intonation pattern. Make every effort to naturalize your speech to make it more acceptable to the child and/or parent.

Principle 3. Reinforce any attempt by the child to speak in a slow, easy manner. Children often need encouragement to use slower speech production that will assist in decreasing their articulatory rate. When making reinforcing statements, be sure not to draw attention to the child's articulatory accuracy.

Principle 4. Avoid all implicit or explicit correction of speech sound errors or disfluencies. Attention to the motor component of speech production may increase the level of tension within the system, thus increasing the likelihood of stuttering. As stated previously, an increase in tension often leads to the fragmentation of speech efforts (Bloodstein, 1984).

Principle 5. Blend activities from one area into activities for the other. Blending activities may be one way to meet the multiple needs of a particular child. A blended approach involves the concurrent work on fluency objectives within the context of phonology activities. Conture et al.'s (1993) pilot study supported the use of a blended approach to therapy.

Principle 6. Gradually increase linguistic complexity. As previously discussed, changes in linguistic complexity may be associated with increases in stuttering; therefore, it is important that you monitor subtle shifts in length and complexity. Bernstein Ratner (1995) noted that fluency activities should avoid the production of linguistically complex utterances outside the child's expressive repertoire.

Principle 7. Model appropriate turn-taking pauses when interacting with the child. The focus on communication effectiveness is an overlapping goal for the child who stutters; thus it is equally important for the child who exhibits phonological disorders. By increasing the time between communication exchanges, the child may utilize this planning time to increase fluency.

Principle 8. Employ overtraining strategies and activities to assist in the transfer of skills. The child who exhibits both stuttering and disordered phonology may have a weak speech production system. To accommodate this possibility, ensure the child has multiple opportunities to practice skills. The development of automaticity, the use of a skill without mental effort, will enhance the transfer and maintenance of learned skills.

Principle 9. Model correct articulatory productions. Basic to all therapy, model the skills you want the child to demonstrate. Auditory bombardment and modified auditory bombardment tasks are examples of tasks in which you can repeatedly model the correct production of articulation targets.

Principle 10. Develop the concept of being an effective communicator. This principle places the focus on the child's content, which shifts the burden off fluency or articulatory proficiency. The attention is now on "what" the child is saying, not "how." By focusing on conversational interactions, the pressure of verbal competition is reduced. Reward the child for any contribution made to the group. Reinforce "rules for talking," such as (1) wait your turn, (2) do not talk while others are talking, and (3) look at the person to whom you are talking.

Principle 11. Use a group intervention approach. Group intervention has advantages for changing both speech and other related behaviors. The emphasis on group dynamics and peer interactions is especially relevant for this subgroup of children because it deemphasizes the individual child's speech difficulties. Group intervention also provides for a multitude of differing adult and peer interactions not possible during individual sessions.

Principle 12. Involve the parents. Parents need to learn how to make appropriate fluency-facilitating changes in the home environment. Involvement of parents in therapy also provides an opportunity for them to observe you modeling behaviors they can incorporate at home. Without these observations, parents may inadvertently correct their child's speech production efforts in a way that exacerbates the child's ability to develop fluency.

Language Disorders

Little has been written on working with preschool children who stutter also exhibiting language and/or word retrieval disorders. In fact, there is inconsistent evidence supporting the contention that these disorders co-occur with greater frequency than would normally be expected (Arndt & Healey, 2001; Batik et al., 2003; Bernstein Ratner, 1997b; Nippold, 1990; Ryan, 1992; Schwartz & Conture, 1988; Shine et al., 1991; Watkins et al., 1999). Researchers, disagreeing on the co-occurrence rates of language and stuttering disorders, have provided little guidance regarding intervention strategies appropriate to the subgroup of children who may exhibit both disorders.

Intervention Direction. However, decisions made regarding the appropriate approach to treatment would be similar to those discussed in the preceding section. You may choose to implement treatment goals in a sequential versus concurrent order based on the client's most immediate needs. Another choice would be to select either the blended or discrete approach as described by Bernstein Ratner (1995). A major factor in determining the best treatment approach is the client's ability to establish and maintain fluency when language demands are increased. For preschool children, changes in linguistic complexity produce a rise in disfluency. Their therapy must be highly structured to ensure a gradual shift in both complexity and length of utterance. Other preschoolers may not react to increased language demands with increased stuttering. Incorporating language concepts into systematic fluency therapy can produce significant improvements in both disorders. The following principles are recommended when planning therapy for this subgroup of children.

Principle 1. Reinforce any attempt by the child to speak in a slow, easy manner. Children often need encouragement to use slower speech production that will provide the planning time necessary to generate accurate language constructions. When making reinforcing statements, be sure not to draw attention to the child's language accuracy.

Principle 2. Utilize a slow, unhurried speech model throughout all interactions. Your modeling of a slow-paced speech pattern allows time for planning responses and enhancing communication efforts. As noted in the previous section, there are certain pitfalls to such a model. These include unnatural-sounding speech accompanied with overarticulation and a singsong intonation pattern. Make every effort to naturalize your speech to make it more acceptable to the child and/or parent.

Principle 3. Gradually increase linguistic complexity. Changes in linguistic complexity may be associated with increased stuttering. Therapy activities that incorporate subtle shifts in length and complexity are best suited for this population. However, you should monitor the impact these changes might have on the manifestation of stuttering and adjust the language level when appropriate.

Principle 4.   Model appropriate turn-taking pauses when interacting with the child. The focus on communication effectiveness is an essential goal for this subgroup of children who stutter. Structure therapy so the client is maximally successful. Increasing the time between communication exchanges aids the child in planning time, which often increases fluency.

Principle 5.   Employ overtraining strategies and activities to assist in the transfer of skills. The child who exhibits both stuttering and disordered language may require multiple opportunities to master the complex language generation system. Ensure the child has multiple opportunities to practice skills through a wide variety of child-centered, language-focused activities. Again, the development of automaticity is essential to the transfer and maintenance of learned skills.

Principle 6.   Involve the parents. As with all therapy involving preschool children, parents are an essential component of intervention. Discuss with them the impact language can have on fluency so their interactions at home are positive for fluency. Have the parents monitor their child's fluency patterns relative to the type of language interactions of the home (e.g., competing for talking time, interruptions, excitement, and rapid succession of questions). Helping parents understand their child's stuttering and language strengths and weaknesses empowers them to change the dynamics of communication exchanges occurring in the home environment.

CHAPTER SUMMARY

Preschool children who stutter have the fortunate likelihood of spontaneous remission from stuttering if their fluency profile is dominated by positive prognostic indicators. A certain percentage of these children, those whose history is filled with negative indicators, may persist with stuttering, however. For both groups of children, parental speech and language behaviors play an important role in the development of a positive self-concept as an effective communicator. The parents' attitude toward stuttering may shape parent-child interaction. It is important to assess these attitudes prior to dispensing suggestions.

Determining treatment directions for the child who persists with stuttering involves consideration of numerous factors. Several case selection criteria and behavioral guidelines were presented in this chapter. The issue of the type of treatment, the treatment goal, and design of therapy must be outlined in the child's plan. Two types of strategies (indirect vs. direct) may be selected for implementation with the preschool child who stutters. The difference between these approaches involves the extent to which the parent or clinician is directly involved in the management of the child's speech. Parent counseling, ongoing monitoring, and modification of the home environment through parent training are the major components of indirect treatment. Direct strategies incorporate more frequent therapy sessions in which the clinician models fluency-shaping behaviors for both the child and parent to emulate. Several current models of direct therapy are available to use with the preschool child who stutters.

This chapter concluded with a discussion of the treatment for children with concomitant disorders, specifically phonological and language disorders. A large percentage of young children who stutter also exhibit speech sound errors that must be addressed in therapy. There is little in the literature regarding the best approach to use with this subgroup of children who stutter. More research will shed light on the relative effectiveness of concurrent, sequential, discrete, and/or blended therapy designs. Until more information is available, 12 principles of intervention were presented for consideration when developing and implementing therapy plans for the preschool child who stutters and exhibits phonological disorders. The incidence rate of language disorders in children who stutter has yet to be determined. Researchers disagree regarding this particular subgroup of children with even less written about how to treat language-impaired stuttering preschool children. Six principles of intervention were presented as guidelines when developing treatment plans for these children.

STUDY QUESTIONS

1. What are the ABC characteristics of the preschool CWS?
2. List negative and positive prognostic indicators for spontaneous recovery.
3. What are the at-risk factors for continued stuttering?
4. Describe the speech and language characteristics of parents of CWS.
5. What might explain the common co-occurrence of phonological disorders and stuttering in the preschool population?
6. Compare and contrast treatment paradigms for the preschool CWS.
7. Pretend you are counseling parents of a 2.5-year-old boy who is showing signs of beginning stuttering. What questions might you ask the parent, and how would you respond to their concern about directing attention toward their child's speech by coming to speech therapy?

School-Age Children Who Stutter

CHAPTER OUTLINE

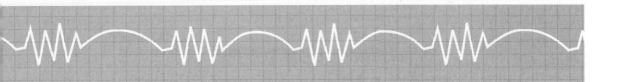

LEARNER OBJECTIVES

- Identify changes in the ABC profile of the school-age child who stutters.

- Explain the impact of federal legislation on services provided in the school setting.

- Differentiate between the various types of service delivery models available in the school setting.

- Identify academic areas in which a student's stuttering may impact his present level of performance.

- Describe and generate meaningful and attainable IEP goals and benchmarks for school-age CWS.

- Discuss the issue of treatment outcomes for public school therapy.

- Discuss how fluency specialists may provide assistance for school systems.

- Understand the main issues to consider when planning a teacher inservice for stuttering disorders.

- List three types of innovative therapy designs for CWS.

- Become familiar with treatment programs and materials used with school-age CWS.

KEY TERMS

administrative-centered
  interactions
case-centered interactions
classroom-based model
client-centered tasks
cognitive set
collaborative consultation
consultee-centered tasks
encouraging praise
ERA—SM
evaluative praise
FAPE

functionality
glide
IDEA '97
IEP
intensive cycle
intermittent schedule
learning effects
less specific-more specific
  approach
LRE
nontreatment variables

objective attitude
outcome
primary rules
Public Law 94–142
pullout model
REEF
secondary rules
social effects
summer camps
treatment relationship
universal rules

School-age children who stutter present a unique set of characteristics in the ABC domains of stuttering. The majority of these children have received some form of intervention, probably utilizing a fluency-shaping orientation. Varying levels of fluency have been established, although not maintained over time. Children may exhibit increased awareness to moments of stuttering accompanied with frustration and negative peer reactions. The following section addresses the ABC characteristics of this age group of children who stutter moving into the elementary school years between 7 and 12 years of age.

THE ABCs OF STUTTERING

Affective Components

Children who continue to stutter despite intervention may develop feelings of frustration, guilt, and confusion, as well as the beginning of shame and anger. As noted in chapter 2, emotions attached to stuttering episodes vary according to the individual's self-evaluation of the feelings experienced before, during, and after episodes of stuttering. With increased awareness of differences in communication skills, some CWS may develop feelings of failure, which contribute to their inability to manage stuttering. The development of conscious self-awareness occurs during this time frame, contributing to increased awareness of negative listener reactions. The desire to hide stuttering increases (i.e., the emergence of shame around stuttering) as these children experience repeated communication failures during peer interactions (Dell, 2000). The need to feel accepted by peers and to develop an association with peer groups becomes an essential issue for older elementary children who may feel left out because of stuttering.

Behavioral Components

When children continue to stutter into the school years, the behavioral characteristics of stuttering begin to interact differentially with the affective component of the disorder. In Figure 8.1, a four-quadrant grid demonstrates this interaction between behavioral variability and the individual's reactions to speech breakdowns. CWS can be

Figure 8.1
A graphic display of the interaction between speech behavior variability and the reaction of communication difficulties.

Quadrant 3: Low Variability, High Reaction	Quadrant 2: Low Variability, Low Reaction
Quadrant 4: High Variability, High Reaction	Quadrant 1: High Variability, Low Reaction

classified into four general groups: (1) high variability with low reaction, (2) low variability with low reaction, (3) low variability with high reaction, and (4) high variability with high reactions. Quadrant 1 suggests there is a subgroup of CWS whose speech behaviors are highly variable, similar to preschool CWS with minimal affective reactions (High Variability, Low Reaction).

With time and continued stuttering, some CWS will develop highly predictable and consistent speech behaviors, yet little emotional reaction is present (Quadrant 2: Low Variability, Low Reaction). However, with time, children begin to exhibit less variability in their stuttering patterns with the emergence of negative coping mechanisms in response to uncontrollable stuttering (Quadrant 3: Low Variability, High Reaction). The increased tension in the speech mechanism leads to greater fragmentation of speech efforts as observed through an increase in sound repetitions, prolongations, and tense blocks. As the frequency of stuttering increases, these children move deeper into the stuttering cycle as emotional reactions increase and frustration with communication becomes evident. You may observe an increased use of escape and postponement devices making speech more noticeable to the listener. Quadrant 4 represents a subgroup of children who exhibit highly variable speech behaviors accompanied with a high degree of reaction to stuttering (High Variability, High Reaction). With time, some children mask their stuttering through subtle, covert revisions and word substitutions, making their stuttering behaviors appear to be highly variable. They become masters at hiding their stuttering from the listener at the high price of not being able to say exactly what they want to say at any given point in time.

As children continue to stutter into the upper elementary school years, the interaction between the stuttering behavior and the emotional reactions shift. As the clinician, it is your job to evaluate these components in order to plan appropriately for each individual child. Progression from one quadrant to another may be indicative of a mismatch between the child's IEP, his current level of communication, and communication demands. Because of the social, educational, and verbal expectations common to the elementary school years, children may progress from one quadrant to another based on their ability to manage or cope effectively with stuttering.

Cognitive Components

Continued stuttering may also impact how the child views himself as an effective communicator. Rustin and Cook (1995) contended the school-age child who stutters is "likely to be developing a self-image associated with stuttering, experiencing communication failure, and developing productive and nonproductive strategies for overcoming the problem" (p. 132). The self-image encompasses how the child assigns meaning to events and problem-solves discrepancies between the desired view versus his actual view of himself. Clinicians who have focused on intervention models for school-age children would agree with the statement that the school-age child develops negative cognitions regarding talking and begins to anticipate, fear, and avoid stuttering (Chmela & Reardon, 2001; Healey & Scott, 1995; Murphy, 1999; Ramig & Bennett, 1995, 1997a). These behaviors reinforce the belief system that tells the individual talking is difficult and an unpleasant event to be avoided at all costs.

You may observe CWS reporting they are unable to perform certain school-related tasks. This mind-set of "I can't do it because I stutter" represents a cognitive distortion that begins to limit their curriculum involvement. Fear of answering questions in class, presenting oral reports, or even asking the teacher for help consumes the thought processes, festering the child's "can't do" self-fulfilling prophecy. You must be prepared to identify, monitor, and intervene when such cognitive distortions interfere with progress in therapy.

SPECIAL ISSUES

Several special issues are relevant to working with the elementary child who stutters and is receiving services in the public schools. These include issues around the possibility of spontaneous recovery, which service delivery model to implement, understanding IDEA '97 rules and regulations, obtaining treatment outcomes, developing innovative programs or options, working with teachers, and accessing the fluency specialist as a consultant for the school district.

Spontaneous Recovery

It is commonly acknowledged that a large percentage of children who stutter recover spontaneously by age 7. As these children become older, this percentage decreases significantly. By age 12, the likelihood of recovery is still present but very minimal in degree. You may hear of isolated instances of spontaneous recovery from stuttering in older children and adolescents, yet these stories are rare. Knowing this fact, you must be prepared to address this issue with parents and children. Parents frequently are told that if they just wait and ignore it, the stuttering will go away. Some children grab hold of this idea, hoping they won't have to work on their speech because it is going to go away one day. Approach this topic with both a dose of reality and encouragement. Describe the positive and negative prognostic indicators in the particular profile with the parents and child, emphasizing the literature to support your statements. But don't take away hope. Discuss what can be done to facilitate recovery and assure them stuttering does not have to have a debilitating, handicapping impact on the child. Present the goals of therapy in terms of developing effective communication skills and not just reducing the frequency of stuttering moments.

Service Delivery Models

Types of Models

School clinicians have several options when determining the types of service delivery models appropriate for children who stutter. Neidecker and Blosser (1993) discussed models for speech therapy within the school setting, which can be classified into two groups: the continuum-based model versus the dichotomous traditional model. They affirmed that school-based therapists are "no longer implementing their programs in isolation from the rest of the educational system" and must "design intervention programs which will increase children's potential for benefitting from the educational process" (p. 177). To achieve this goal, they present a continuum of service delivery models that increases the options available to the therapist for meeting individual student needs.

Continuum-Based Model. Four major concepts of service delivery are supported by a continuum-type model: (1) The importance of recognizing the impact of communication impairments on learning success; (2) the need to create an optimal environment for providing speech-language services; (3) the importance of collaboration and sharing of expertise to develop effective program goals, objectives, and intervention strategies for children; and (4) the need to integrate speech-language goals, objectives, and techniques into the student's learning experience (Neidecker & Blosser, 1993, p. 181).

As a speech therapist working in the school system, you are encouraged to use a variety of service delivery models depending on the needs of the student. Among your choices are inservice training, intervention assistance team collaboration, pullout intervention, community-based intervention, and classroom-based intervention. Incorporating inservice training and pullout intervention along with classroom collaboration might meet the needs of some children who stutter. For others, a different combination of models may provide the most benefit from the educational setting. Neidecker and Blosser's intervention assistance team reviews cases being considered for referral for special services. The therapist working in close coordination with the team can facilitate the referral process for children suspected of stuttering so time is not lost before intervention begins. Numerous combinations of services are available to children who stutter under the continuum-based concept of service delivery.

Dichotomous-Traditional Model. Traditional service delivery models typically are categorized into three groups: pullout, classroom based, and collaborative consultation. According to Eger (1999), the **pullout model** involves services provided individually or in small groups in a room other than the student's classroom. Historically, the pullout model has been the primary model used by school-based clinicians. According to Neidecker and Blosser (1993, p. 187), the advantages to pullout therapy are as follows:

1. Students receive individual direct therapy.
2. Some students may be more willing to give oral responses and engage in group language interaction.
3. Pullout intervention also accommodates articulation, fluency, and voice disorders, especially in the early stages of intervention.
4. Distraction is less of a factor.

In the **classroom-based model,** you provide direct services to students within the class. You may work directly in the self-contained classroom, teaming with the classroom teacher to provide language activities related to the IEP objectives of the children in the class. Or you may identify a particular regular education classroom that contains several students on your caseload. Here you engage in a weekly lesson within the class setting to address the student's specific language needs. During these activities, all children in the classroom participate in the activity. According to Neidecker and Blosser (1993), the teacher should observe these lessons and attempt to reinforce the language concepts covered in the lesson throughout the week. Classroom-based intervention is not meant to be a free period for the teacher, but a time to learn how to identify and reinforce the language deficits of the speech-impaired students in her class. Consider the advantages to this model:

1. Greater numbers of students may be served by one therapist.
2. Nonlanguage-impaired students also benefit from the lessons.
3. Service is provided in a more natural environment than is possible in a separate speech therapy room.
4. Examples of language interactions, language modeling, and cuing may enhance the teacher's and the paraprofessional's interaction with students.
5. Language skills are incorporated into the academic curriculum.
6. Enhanced opportunity exists for generalization and carryover of language skills into everyday life.
7. This model is compatible with others.
8. Flexibility of scheduling for the speech-language pathologist is increased. (Neidecker & Blosser, 1993, p. 189)

Collaborative consultation occurs when the team works together to "facilitate a student's communication and learning in educational environments" (Eger, 1999, p. 1). The team may consist of the SLP, classroom teacher, other teachers, parent, paraprofessional, and/or peers. In this model, you observe students within a classroom and assess their overall language competence. You then discuss specific strategies or techniques that may enrich the language development of students within the class. You must always remember routinely to follow up with the consultation to assess its ongoing progress and to address any teacher concerns that may arise over time. Neidecker and Blosser (1993) wrote that collaborative efforts are most beneficial:

1. The model allows for a greater number of students to be served by one SLP.
2. All students benefit from the information shared with the teacher.
3. The SLP learns about the curriculum, the teacher's style, and classroom routines.
4. Greater emphasis on language skills can be incorporated into the curriculum.

Service Delivery Trends. What is the trend in the use of the service delivery models just described? To service all children on their caseloads, 78% of school SLPs utilize a traditional pullout model compared to 13% implementing a classroom-based model with 5% utilizing a collaborative consultation (Montgomery, 1994). With today's economy, heavy caseloads, and personnel shortages, collaborative/classroom models have been suggested as viable alternatives to the traditional pullout model. Additionally, therapists are selecting classroom-based service delivery models for the following reasons:

1. The classroom is the most natural context for the use of language.
2. Carryover and generalization are the most difficult parts of therapy.
3. We have a changing population of children in our schools today: greater needs, more cultural diversity, and more children at risk for academic failure.
4. When SLPs work in the school setting, their employers are educators, not other SLPs or health care administrators. Educators measure the success of speech and language programs by the SLPs' ability to enhance the academic success of identified students. (Montgomery, 1994, pp. 226–227)

However, you must consider the positive and negative consequences to each of these models relevant to each child who stutters on your caseload. Recent emphasis on student achievement of grade-level curriculum benchmarks may put the traditional pullout model of treatment at risk for extinction. Parents, clinicians, and teachers are beginning to question the usefulness of the pullout model and the possible negative impact such a model might have on the child's academic achievement. However, little is written regarding service delivery models specifically for children who stutter. Cooper and Cooper (1991) have developed a Collaborative Oral Language Fluency Program that incorporates classroom activities geared to "demystify fluency disorders and their treatment for teachers and classmates of dysfluent children" (Cooper & Cooper, 1991, p. 28). This program can be useful for public school speech-language pathologists to augment the child's pullout therapy, yet it is not sufficient in its scope to replace traditional models of intervention.

The initial teaching of fluency or modification skills is best done through the traditional pullout model (Dell, 2000; Ramig & Bennett, 1995). Dell (2000) stated that "pullout therapy is an effective service delivery model for stuttering therapy. Children who stutter need quiet time with us to heal the wound of their private shame" (p. 170). Once skills have been mastered sufficiently to transfer into the classroom setting, collaborative and consultative instruction is appropriate. The decision to move from one model to another should be made case by case. Meeting the individual needs of children who stutter is still the primary goal. Yet providing speech therapy services within the school setting presents a unique set of challenges as well as unique opportunities (Yaruss, 2002). The school environment provides multiple social interactions to engage children who stutter in various speaking tasks. From hallway talks to delivering messages to the principal's office, pullout service delivery models used in conjunction with classroom collaboration may form a best-fit model for school-age children who stutter.

Scheduling Practices. Another challenge for the school therapist involves the arduous task of scheduling students for speech therapy. Two scheduling procedures are utilized in most school settings: intermittent and intensive cycle. In the **intermittent schedule,** you establish a yearly schedule based on the number of children on your caseload and the IEP-recommended contact hours. This schedule remains relatively consistent throughout the school year except for admissions or dismissals from the program. Depending on the number of schools you service, the intermittent schedule (i.e., Monday–Thursday, Tuesday–Friday, Wednesday for testing) allows each child to be seen two times weekly throughout the school year.

In direct contrast to this model is the **intensive cycle** scheduling procedure. Students are seen four times a week for a period of 6 weeks and are "on vacation" from therapy for a period of time before participating in the next intensive cycle. Cycle scheduling does not preclude the use of intensive services as individual needs develop throughout the year. Neidecker and Blosser (1993) identified several advantages and disadvantages to this scheduling practice (Table 8.1).

For some school therapists, a combination of both types of scheduling practices may be the most appropriate. A therapist with one campus may schedule a certain block of time for intensive cycle scheduling and allocate the remaining time slots to intermittent scheduling needs. The need for flexibility when scheduling students for speech therapy cannot be understated. Not all children who stutter fit the 30 minutes, twice-a-week mold. Using flexible scheduling provides another opportunity to reach those students and families who need to be jointly involved in the therapy process. You might arrange your schedule along a 12 to 6 p.m. time frame to accommodate after-school therapy. Berkowitz, Cook, and Haughey (1994) described a nontraditional scheduling design used with school-age children who stutter. They arranged for groups of children to attend therapy after school, as well as conducting monthly parent meetings. Another alternative would involve a Tuesday through Saturday work week allowing you to provide intensive Saturday sessions that might include the family unit (Ramig & Bennett, 1995).

The needs of children who stutter are often forced to fit into an inflexible system. However, you can utilize both intermittent and intensive cycle scheduling procedures in a flexible manner to create a program based on student/family needs. This is a realistic option if the school system allows for creative problem solving between administrators and speech pathologists. School districts must evaluate how services are provided to this population and devise creative means of addressing the unique needs of children

Table 8.1
List of advantages and disadvantages to intensive block scheduling practice.

Advantages	Disadvantages
• Greater number of children serviced • Larger percentage of children are dismissed from therapy as having obtained maximum improvement • Length of therapy reduced for children with articulation disorders • Possibility exists for greater carryover of improvement • Development of closer relationships among parent/teacher/therapist/school personnel • Sustained interest in therapy exhibited by students • Requires less time to review lesson plans	• Certain problems may need more frequent contacts on a regular basis • Administration problems may arise when students are leaving the classroom on a daily basis • Monopolization of a shared room for therapy may cause scheduling difficulties

Source: Based on Neideker and Blosser (1993).

who stutter. Perhaps a better understanding of the rules and regulations set under IDEA '97 will emphasize each district's responsibility to all children with disabilities.

Understanding IDEA '97

Another issue facing clinicians working in the schools is understanding and adhering to the rules and regulations set forth by the federal government. Under the mandates of **IDEA '97** (The Individuals With Disabilities Education Act) and the original intent of **Public Law 94–142,** public schools must provide **FAPE,** a *free, appropriate public education* to all children with disabilities. Under the dimension of appropriate stems the concept of an **IEP** (*individualized educational plan*) to assist the child in benefiting from educational opportunities. The term *public* refers to the integration of all individuals with disabilities into the mainstream of education through the **LRE** (*least restrictive environment*). LRE requirements state that the child with a disability must be educated, to the maximum extent possible, in the regular education environment.

Guidelines

The law stipulates certain guidelines for establishing educational need and developing an IEP that school districts must follow to ensure compliance with IDEA '97. These guidelines mandate the following:

1. Testing must be conducted in the dominant language of the child.
2. Assessment must be conducted in a timely manner, by appropriate personnel trained and knowledgeable in the area of testing and the content domain being evaluated.
3. No single instrument can be used to determine eligibility.
4. The child's current level of educational performance must be specified in the IEP with a description of how the child's disability affects his involvement and progress through the curriculum.
5. The amount of time the child is removed from the regular education setting must be stated in the IEP and supported with an explanation of the reasons why LRE must be altered.
6. Classroom modifications must be specified in the IEP with regard to participation in statewide assessments.
7. The IEP must state all special education and/or related services provided the disabled child.
8. The amount of time the child will not participate with nondisabled children must be explained within the IEP.
9. The IEP team must develop measurable annual goals with benchmarks or short-term objectives as a means of measuring the child's progress within the general curriculum.
10. The IEP must discuss transition services, beginning at age 14, for these children addressing a future course of study (e.g., vocational training or interagency coordination of services after the student is no longer eligible for public school services).

Several of these guidelines have particular relevance to working with school-age children who stutter. Determining educational need, writing educationally relevant goals and objectives, identifying the characteristics of meaningful and attainable goals, writing benchmarks and classroom modifications, obtaining treatment outcomes after considering variables that impact outcomes, and understanding the IEP review process require more elaboration.

Determining Educational Need

You must document the extent to which the child is not accessing the general curriculum because of stuttering. Using the school district's benchmarks for each grade level, you can determine which items require verbal interaction and relate this to the current level of performance in the domain of oral communication as described by Susca (2002): "the ability to participate in group projects, give oral reports, or simply ask or respond to questions in class. A student may not reveal his stutter as observable speech events but does reveal the communication disorder through minimal participation in educational matters" (p. 169).

For example, the Texas Education Agency has established certain benchmarks for each grade level. The second-grade TEKS (Texas Essential Knowledge and Skills) has several components highly relevant to the educational performance of children who stutter. In the area of language arts, five major strands could be used to document educational need: (1) The student listens attentively and engages actively in a variety of oral language experiences; (2) the student listens and speaks to gain knowledge of his own culture, the culture of others, and the common elements of cultures; (3) the student speaks appropriately to different audiences for different purposes and occasions; (4) the student communicates clearly by putting thoughts and feelings into spoken words; and (5) the student reads with fluency and understanding in texts at appropriate difficult levels. You should be able to document deficits in one or more of these essential elements based on the student profile established during the evaluation and information-gathering phase of assessment.

There are two specific effects communication disorders may have on educational performance: social effects and learning effects. In the area of fluency, **social effects** fall within the domain of teasing and ridicule by peers because of stuttering. The student may begin to withdraw from speaking situations out of fear of condemnation and embarrassment. **Learning effects** occur because the student withdraws from group learning activities and other socialization tasks, which decreases the opportunity to learn from peers or review previously instructed materials with other students. Some states have included *vocational effects* into the process when determining if an educational need is present. Most applicable to the high school student, stuttering can negatively impact the student's ability to perform well in job interviews, as well as negatively impacting career choices made by the individual who stutters.

In summary, you must be able to document the adverse effects the student's fluency disorder has on his ability to (1) be involved and advance in the general educational program; (2) be educated and participate with other students with or without disabilities; and (3) participate in extracurricular and other nonacademic activities.

Specific examples of how a fluency disorder may adversely effect educational performance include (1) below-grade-level performance in academics; (2) difficulty with language-based activities; (3) difficulty communicating information orally; (4) listener difficulty in understanding the student's verbalizations; (5) difficulty initiating, maintaining, or terminating verbal interactions; (6) teasing by peers; (7) social situation avoidance; (8) negative emotional reactions such as fear, anxiety, and embarrassment; and (9) difficulty participating verbally in classroom, vocational, or extracurricular activities. (www.iep4u.com, 2003)

Table 8.2 provides an example of an Educational Relevant Chart that you may use when determining education impact.

Table 8.2
Educational relevance format useful with school-age children who stutter.

Name: _____ Date of Evaluation: _____

does/does not demonstrate a fluency disorder that negatively impacts the ability to benefit from the educational process.

Academic Impact	Social Impact	Vocational Impact
Academic areas affected by fluency disorder: _____ Reading _____ Math _____ Language arts _____ Other: _____ Impact documented by: _____ Academics below grade level _____ Difficulty with oral reading assignments _____ Difficulty answering questions in class _____ Difficulty with oral reports _____ Difficulty conveying information orally _____ Other: _____ _____ _____	Social areas affected by fluency disorder: _____ Fluency disorder interferes with ability to be understood by adults and/or peers _____ Student has difficulty engaging others in verbal interactions _____ Peers tease student about fluency disorder _____ Student demonstrates embarrassment and/or frustration regarding fluency disorder _____ Student avoids speaking situations _____ Other: _____ _____ _____	Vocational areas affected by fluency disorder: _____ Inability to be understood by coworkers _____ Limits verbal response to coworkers' engagement _____ Unable to answer questions in a concise manner _____ Inability to answer phone and respond to customer inquiries in a timely manner _____ Secondary behaviors distract from communication _____ Other: _____ _____ _____
Comments: _____ _____ _____	Comments: _____ _____ _____	Comments: _____ _____ _____
_____ No academic impact reported	_____ No social impact reported	_____ No vocational impact reported

Developing Educationally Relevant Goals

Your next job is to work with parents, teachers, and/or the student to develop a set of educationally relevant goals. Traditionally, clinicians have chosen to develop three different types of IEP goals: those that emphasize the establishment of fluency, those that emphasize the management of stuttering, and those that focus on overall improved communication. More recently, Yaruss and Reardon (2002) presented several reasons why you should write goals that focus on communicative competence. First, stuttering involves more than just the observable behavior attended to by the listener. Feelings of shame, embarrassment, fear, and avoidance often accompany the behavior of stuttering, therefore requiring attention during therapy. Second, the negative consequences of stuttering are more likely to impact the child's learning potential, thus requiring educationally relevant goals. Third, as the child gets older, the likelihood of spontaneous recovery is dramatically reduced, which necessitates preparing the child to become a successful communicator. Additionally, a subgroup of children who stutter appear unable to utilize fluency strategies successfully to achieve "normal fluency." For these children, the IEP must be individualized so each child can learn to "say what they want to say, when they want to say it" (p. 197). However, even goals that focus on communication competence must be linked to the curriculum.

What might an educationally relevant goal look like? The following examples provided by Eger (1999) have been modified for the disorder of stuttering:

1. By October 2004, Jason will complete 80% of the oral report assignments with decreased speech anxiety while inserting voluntary stuttering into his speech. Speech anxiety will be measured using a self-rating 7-point Likert scale.
2. Alexis will communicate with peers and teachers within the class setting while monitoring the use of light articulatory contacts and phrasing techniques.
3. Nick will use pullouts to modify his speech when identifying the 5 w's of a story read aloud in class.
4. Cassandra will not use avoidance mechanisms when orally paraphrasing a previously read story.
5. Jackie will use rate control strategies when reviewing homework assignments with her parents at home.
6. By midyear, Frank will be able to use slow, smooth speech when reading aloud a passage from his literature book with 80% accuracy as measured by teacher evaluation.
7. Becky will utilize a 2-second response delay to manage time pressure when answering the teacher's questions in the classroom.
8. By midyear, Maria will present a science project on how the respiratory track system (specifically related to how lungs function for speech) to a small group of selected students from her classroom.

Characteristics of Meaningful and Attainable Goals

Much has been written regarding the long-standing focus of the profession on the practice of writing goals and objectives (e.g., Goldberg, 1997; Roth & Worthington, 2001). More recently, there are three emerging trends that differ from traditional patterns of goal writing practice. These involve the identification of outcomes, functionality, and the treatment relationship (identifying interested parties beyond the patient). An **outcome** is defined as the product of intervention (Johnson, 1996). Outcomes can be obtained in two basic ways: *goal-setting strategy on a case-by-case basis* versus an *outcomes-oriented paradigm* (Johnson, 1996). The goal-setting strategy involves the selection of a goal followed by treatment and a measure of the child's progress toward that goal. Frattali (1996) contended that outcome data are gathered by clinicians as a product of every clinical session. An example of a goal using the case-by-case strategy might be "Child will be able to use easy onsets at the beginning of phrases." The outcomes-oriented paradigm focuses on desired outcomes "identified by persons other than the direct service provider," that is, school district, referral agency, or third party payers (Johnson, 1996, p. 3), for example, "Classroom teacher will observe increased class participation by Johnny over the next semester."

Functionality is the second trend of the current outcome movement. Johnson (1996) noted the new outcomes attempt "to be very deliberate in focusing on high levels of communication that extend beyond the treatment session into the patient's living or vocational environment, and impact other areas of performance" (p. 3). An example of a functional outcome measure might be "Johnny will order his food in the cafeteria three times a week." The last trend emphasizes extending the **treatment relationship** beyond the client and clinician. School districts have a particular interest in how the child's speech disorder impacts educational abilities and performance. An example of the treatment relationship might be: "Sarah will organize and participate in a classroom presentation on stuttering disorders for peers and teachers."

Sisskin (2002) described the characteristics of speech therapy goals for children who stutter receiving services in the school setting. Goals should lead to functional outcomes that last, are individualized, and are educationally relevant. Functional outcome goals contain adequate breadth, focus on communication, incorporate maintenance tasks, and reduce the risk of relapse. Individualized goals are need based rather than approach based and reflect symptom variability common to stuttering. Educationally relevant goals should promote the student's involvement in the general curriculum, thus reflecting any adverse impact of stuttering on the student's verbal performance during academic, nonacademic, and extracurricular settings. These goals must also support curriculum-based intervention strategies, such as classroom collaboration and consultation efforts to assist the student in managing his speech within everyday school activities.

Related to the ABCs of stuttering, Sisskin (2002) wrote that school IEPs must address all three components of the disorder: "A child who consistently makes the choice to ask a question in class despite the risk of stuttering (a cognitive goal) will begin to tolerate disfluency, resulting in a milder emotional reaction to his own behavior (an affective goal), resulting in less tension and struggle (a behavioral goal)" (p. 174). Citing the most recent guidelines for practice in stuttering put forth by the Special Interest Division on Fluency and Fluency Disorders, Sisskin identified several areas for which functional outcome IEPs could be developed (Table 8.3).

Along with this instructional emphasis, you must also develop goals that assist the student in developing communicative competence and confidence. Working on conversational skills, pragmatic interactions, and establishing the ability to say "what they

Table 8.3
Content area goals adhering to ASHA's guidelines for practice in stuttering.

1. Reduce the frequency of stuttering behaviors.
2. Reduce severity, duration, or abnormality of stuttering behaviors.
3. Reduce defensive (escape/avoidance) behaviors.
4. Remove process that maintain stuttering behaviors.
5. Make decisions about speaking situations.
6. Increase social activity and speaking behavior.
7. Improve self-esteem.
8. Reduce negative reactions to stuttering.
9. Deal with coexisting problems.
10. Provide information/counseling to others.

Source: Based on Sisskin's (2002) identified school-related goals for clinical practice in stuttering.

want, whenever they want without negative feelings and attitudes" is essential to the child's long-term progress (p. 175). Finally, design goals to encourage client motivation. Goals that reflect the child's immediate needs and interests will enhance the likelihood of transfer and maintenance. When the child is involved in selecting target behaviors relevant to his everyday speaking world, motivation to practice skills may increase as well as the client's feelings of self-responsibility.

Sisskin discussed several strategies that help gather information needed to write attainable and relevant goals: wish lists, hierarchies, assignment organizers, and goal-setting worksheets. A *wish list* is generated by the IEP team to include behaviors that individuals "wish" would change. The parent, teacher, speech pathologist, and child identify things they wish would change to improve the child's communication existence. Figure 8.2 illustrates the end product of this problem-solving process for a third-grade child who stutters. *Hierarchies* involve the listing of situations or speaking tasks according to their level of difficulty as perceived by the child. Hierarchies can be very simple or highly specific outlining the who, what, where, and what of each situation in which the child stutters. The child then selects a task at the easy end of the list and gradually moves up the hierarchy toward the more difficult or feared tasks. Sisskin provided an excellent example of a benchmark for the fluency goal of reduced severity and duration of stuttering behaviors using hierarchies: "Will produce pull-outs in conversation (what?) During group therapy (where?) With the clinician and a peer (who?) while under time pressure (when?)" (p. 176).

Assignment organizers can be created to help students plan for and implement daily speech work in different settings. According to Sisskin (2002), students may forget to do their speech homework if they are not involved in creating the assignment. "When children complete their own assignment forms, the product is more likely to reflect their interests and developmental level," thus increasing the likelihood of compliance and follow-through. For example, a child who is intrigued with the Harry Potter stories and movies might want to draw different shields as symbols of strategies to use in certain environments. These visual reminders can be placed strategically around the home and class, creating a covert system of reminding the student to engage in speech

Child	Parent	Teacher
I wish . . .	I wish . . .	I wish . . .
People wouldn't say words for me.	I knew what to say when he struggles so hard.	He would stand up for himself.
I wasn't the only kid who stuttered.	I didn't worry about him so much.	I knew some ways to stop the teasing.
I never had to read in class.	He gets over this before middle school.	I knew whether to talk to him about it or not.

Figure 8.2
Wish lists generated at the IEP meeting for a third-grade CWS.

change. Only the student knows what these shields mean. Using these visual aids may reduce the number of verbal reprimands to "use your strategies" from parents or teachers, which draw negative attention to the student's speaking difficulties.

Goal-setting worksheets can help the older elementary student understand the therapy process and become an active participant in this process. "Goal setting worksheets help children acknowledge their accomplishments and focus on the future" (p. 177). You help the student identify his successes and where he needs to be in the future. According to Sisskin (2002), some children do not identify their successes, often perceiving a lack of progress in therapy. You can teach the student to identify success by teaching positive self-talk. "I did a good job at saying my name," "I caught my stutter and changed it. I'm taking charge of my speech" are examples of verbal self-reinforcing comments students can learn to help identify success in therapy. Then you can demonstrate how to write these successes on the worksheet and problem-solve the next task in therapy with the student. These worksheets provide insight into the process of change for you as well as the student. Table 8.4 is a modified version of Sisskin's goal-setting worksheet.

Benchmarks. Once goals are established for the student, you must generate *benchmarks*, or short-term objectives. Goals should encompass the full spectrum of Bloom's Taxonomy from knowledge to evaluation (see Table 8.5). Each objective should contain the following information: anticipated date of completion, observable behaviors, conditions, criteria, and level of mastery. Table 8.6 contains examples of the benchmark components often used by the school-based therapist.

The profession has a long history of writing goals and objectives that are observable and measurable. However, under IDEA '97, these goals must be directly related to

Table 8.4
Modified version of Sisskin's Template for Collaborative Therapy Planning.

Goal	Successes	Next Steps
My knowledge about stuttering		
My feelings about being a person who stutters		
My fear of talking in front of people		
Reducing struggle when I talk		
Reducing my own negative reactions to my stuttering		
Changing the way I stutter		
Reducing my word and situation avoidance		
Improving my participation in conversation		

Source: From V. Sisskin, "Therapy Planning for School-Age Children Who Stutter." Seminars in Speech and Language *2002; 23(3): 178. Adapted by permission.*

Table 8.5
Terms for goal writing using Bloom's Taxonomy.

Knowledge	Comprehension	Application	Analysis	Synthesis	Evaluation
count	associate	add	analyze	utilize	propose
define	compute	apply	arrange	categorize	rearrange
describe	convert	change	breakdown	combine	appraise
draw	defend	classify	combine	compile	assess
identify	discuss	complete	design	compose	compare
labels	distinguish	compute	detect	create	conclude
list	estimate	demonstrate	develop	derive	contrast
match	explain	discover	diagram	design	criticize
name	extend	divide	differentiate	devise	critique
point	extrapolate	examine	discriminate	explain	determine
quote	generalize	graph	illustrate	generate	grade
read	give examples	interpret	outline	prescribe	interpret
recall	infer	manipulate	point out	integrate	judge
recite	paraphrase	modify	relate	modify	justify
recognize	predict	operate	select	order	measure
record	rewrite	prepare	separate	organize	rank
repeat	summarize	produce	subdivide	plan	support

Table 8.6
Examples of terminology used when generating Benchmarks for IEP goals.

Anticipated Date of Completion	Observable Behaviors	Conditions	Criteria	Mastery
Project a date when the teacher is anticipating the student will have completed the stated objective and be ready to move to the next objective. • Within the first semester of school • By the end of the semester • Prior to the science fair	State a specific action or act that can be observed and measured by another person. • verbally label • verbally express • choose/select • read sight words • answer questions • tell a story • sequence events	State where, when, and under what circumstances the observable behavior will occur. • request assistance • list • group/classify • describe • share results or report findings • make a prediction • when given questions orally • when communicating with others • during transition periods • during social conversations • when using the school library • when reading a story aloud • when given 10 questions • during collaboration in math class	State the extent of achievement or standard of performance required of the student. • within 5 minutes • three out of 4 trials • four times weekly for 40% of trials • two times daily for 5 consecutive sessions	State the level of achievement required of the student before proceeding to the next objective. Mastery should be at 70% or higher level of success. • seven out of 10 trials • five consecutive trial days • five consecutive weeks • eight out of 10 trial days

the student's present level of performance. Olson and Bohlman (2002) provided an example of a goal and its benchmarks designed for CWS:

Goal 1: Johnny will increase his verbal participation in school by 50% as reported by his teachers and staff. Benchmarks/Objective would include:

1. Johnny will answer five questions a week.
2. Johnny will state his opinion once per week.
3. Johnny will volunteer to read in class at least once a week.
4. Johnny will verbally share his journal entry with the class once a week.
5. Johnny will learn two verbal methods for dealing with teasing.
6. Johnny will make a telephone call to his mother at work from school twice a week.
7. Johnny will learn six facts about stuttering and verbally share two facts with his classmates when his speech-language pathologist gives a classroom presentation about stuttering.
8. By the end of the IEP year, Johnny will demonstrate improved acceptance of his stuttering as indicated by the results of a communication attitude scale. (p. 161)

Classroom Modifications. If there is an educational need for speech services, IDEA '97 stipulates that classroom modifications must be considered to enhance academic performance. Classroom modifications are defined as adjustments to the regular educational procedures and interactions related to instructional, testing, and evaluation methodologies. During the IEP process, the team determines what modifications, if any, the student may require to maximize his academic success. Most districts have preprinted lists of typical modifications such as "allowing student more time during tests," "shortened assignments," or "preferential seating close to the chalkboard." These common adjustments may not be appropriate for the CWS, necessitating individualization of modifications. Consider the fluency profile of each student when determining how best to adjust the regular education setting. The following is a sample list of possible modifications for CWS:

- Allow more time to respond orally.
- Eliminate any peer teasing episodes.
- Allow students to present oral reports in a small group format or individually with the teacher.
- Call on a student only when his hand is raised or he appears willing to participate orally.
- Use a multiple-choice format when asking questions to evaluate comprehension of written material.
- Do not grade students on verbal performance abilities.

Treatment Outcomes. The public school clinician is faced with issues of accountability around the services provided in the public school system. The expectation of accountability in special education was brought forth through IDEA '97 and will ultimately impact how school-based therapists measure progress. Power-deFur and Orelove (1997) recommended school-based SLPs be prepared to answer the following six questions:

1. If young children with language impairments receive speech-language pathology services, will they learn how to read faster or better?
2. What will the effect of services be on academic achievement?
3. What will be the effect of speech-language pathology services on special education eligibility?
4. What will be the effect of speech-language pathology services on social interactions and self-esteem?
5. What part of speech-language pathology services can be effectively provided by others, for example, kindergarten teachers or teachers of students with learning disabilities?
6. How much intervention is necessary to ameliorate a communication impairment in this child?

The American Speech-Language-Hearing Association (ASHA) has established national treatment outcomes for adults and children with communication disorders. You can use these outcome indicators when determining current level of performance at each stage of the IEP process (admission, review, or dismissal). The following are the identified functional communication measures for fluency, rate, or rhythm (ASHA, 1996):

Level 0: CNT/DNT: An aspect of communication or swallowing that could not be tested due to the level of functioning or should have been tested but was not due to time or other factors.

Level 1: Profound impairment: nonfunctional in all environments. Listener cannot comprehend message.

Level 2: Severe impairment: 10% to 20% fluent in some automatic words in restricted contexts. Secondary characteristics always present. No self-monitoring.

Level 3: Moderate to severe impairment: 30% to 40% fluent for words and phrases in restricted contexts. Secondary characteristics always present. Occasional self-monitoring.

Level 4: Moderate impairment: 50% fluent in phrases and sentences in familiar contexts. Secondary characteristics frequently present. Occasional self-monitoring.

Level 5: Mild to moderate impairment: 60% to 70% fluent in sentences/conversation in familiar contexts. Secondary characteristics occasionally present. Occasional self-monitoring.

Level 6: Mild impairment: 80% to 90% fluent in conversation in broad contexts. Secondary characteristics occasionally present. Frequent self-monitoring.

Level 7: Normal fluency, rate, or rhythm.

Variables Impacting Outcomes

Within-the-Child Variables.   Related to the school-age child who stutters, Zebrowski and Conture (1998) discussed several **nontreatment variables** (also referred to as within-the-child variables) that may influence treatment outcomes. These variables include familial history of stuttering, concomitant phonological problems, child's attitudes toward stuttering, child's sensitivity to stuttering, and the child's temperament. Several of these variables can be addressed in therapy and modified accordingly. However, shaping the child's temperament and sensitivity levels may be beyond the scope of the school SLP. The role of genetics in the development of temperament is strong and largely influenced during the early years of development. It remains unknown at this time how temperament impacts the maintenance of stuttering; yet it is certainly a factor that must be acknowledged and addressed when possible (Bloodstein, 1995; Conture, 2001; Oyler & Ramig, 1995).

Systemic Challenges.   Systemic variables or challenges may impact the outcome of treatment in the school setting. These would include large caseloads, dependence on group treatment, lack of parental involvement in therapy, and routine change in SLP campus assignment. Large caseloads have long been a concern of school-based therapists. Despite the ASHA-recommended caseload size of 40, many therapists handle a range of 80 to 100 students. Linked to this variable is the need for group treatment to manage large caseloads. Therapists are forced to schedule 4 to 6 students per group in order to make direct contact with each child as indicated on the IEP. If a therapy session is

30 minutes long with 6 students, approximately 5 minutes might be allocated for each child. Of course, most veteran therapists are competent at integrating multiple IEP goals into one structured lesson. However, not every therapist has this skill. The likelihood of successful therapy increases when groups are structured according to the identified parameter of speech or language disorders (e.g., voice, fluency, language, articulation, or pragmatics). You must advocate for this type of scheduling procedure instead of abdicating to a set time established by administrators.

A good analogy to use with principals and teachers is to structure your day using the block schedule commonly used by regular education teachers. Set a time to see children with articulation only, fluency only, articulation plus language, and so on, and then ask the teacher to select a time for the student to attend therapy. Remember that regular education teachers are not asked or required to teach multiple subjects (e.g., science, social studies, and handwriting) within the same time frame. Nor should the school-based speech pathologist, particularly given the brief period of time allocated to assist students in meeting their IEP objectives. If therapy is watered down, the student will not make sufficient gains in a timely manner, upsetting the parent(s), clinician, and the student. Additionally, you put yourself at risk for conducting therapy that goes against ASHA-preferred practice statements as well as violating the intentions of IDEA '97.

Lack of Parental Involvement.   The third variable that impacts treatment outcomes is the lack of parental involvement in school-based therapy. The majority of parents would like to participate in treatment; however, parental work schedules often prohibit their inclusion in the therapy process. Although you must learn to work within the constraints of the system, there are several activities you may initiate to gain better involvement of parents in their child's therapy.

Allocate 15 minutes a week to make phone calls to parents to address their child's therapy and implementation of strategies within the home setting. Make a contact list with the child's name, parent's name, phone numbers, and a space for comments. Document each phone contact you have with the parent, identifying what was discussed, feedback comments from the parent, and any confounding variables that might impede progress identified by the parent. List modifications that will be made to the child's therapy plan based on the information gathered during the phone conference.

Additionally, schedule monthly support group meetings for parents of children who stutter. Bennett-Mancha (1990) held a series of monthly meetings for parents in the Ysleta school district. Although some of the parents were not from Bennett's own campus, they attended to learn more about the disorder of stuttering and how to help their child at home. Therapists also attended to facilitate these meetings and to learn how to address parental concerns in the area of stuttering. These 1.5 to 2-hour meetings were held at an elementary school.

Another parent training opportunity involves conducting a mini-talk at the monthly PTA (or PTO) meetings. General discussion about stuttering, its development, and ways of responding when interacting with a child who stutters are just some of the topics that might be covered during these meetings. Watching brief video clips of children who stutter talking about their speech disorder aids in making a lasting connection between you and the parents at your campus.

Frequent Campus Reassignment. It is common to hear about school-based clinicians being moved from one campus to another at the end of the school year. Administrators may have their reasons for such reassignment, but one wonders if anyone considered the disruption in services for the speech-impaired children when they have a new therapist each year or two. Time to get to know students, teachers, and campus personnel may take away time from goal-directed therapy. Children who stutter may become frustrated by the turnover rate and begin to withdraw from interactions that they need to establish trust. They may not be as open or share their shame around stuttering for fear of losing this relationship later. School therapists must educate system personnel responsible for placement decisions regarding the impact of frequent reassignment on children who stutter.

The Review Process

The student's IEP remains in effect for one calendar year. After a year of service (or earlier if deemed necessary), the team must meet to review progress made toward the IEP goals as well as to modify the program if needed. You should be prepared to address the gains the student has made and any roadblocks encountered during the previous year's therapy. Information regarding student skills can be obtained through both non-standardized and standardized assessment tasks. You must be able to describe the changes observed in the child's overall communicative competence and confidence across various settings. You may choose to observe the child directly in the classroom setting or ask the teacher to complete the student profile form (Table 8.7). Parent input is also essential to the overall evaluation of treatment. Asking parents to come for a pre-IEP conference to discuss their child's progress or making a phone contact with the parent can facilitate the IEP review process. Table 8.8 provides an example of the student profile form for parents that can be sent home for completion or used to gather information during the phone conference.

You may consider administering the Stuttering Severity Index:3 or obtain new data from the Systematic Disfluency Analysis procedure to determine the specific behavioral changes that have occurred during the year. Readministration of any attitudinal instruments will also shed light on the cognitive and affective changes to the child's stuttering profile. Session notes should record attitudinal changes the child has made throughout the year, as well as any periods of relapse. Noted benchmarks the child has achieved can be shared with the team. Most of this information involves the teacher, parents, or clinician's perspective of the child's progress or lack of it. Ask the child about his work in speech therapy, having him evaluate subjectively his progress, the program, and what changes he would like to see implemented.

The law requires documentation of progress toward achievement of the IEP goals. It is your responsibility to establish a system of accountability so children who stutter benefit from therapy and do not continue year after year with the same IEP goals they are unable to or have not mastered. These measures of accountability should not rely on the readministration of standardized tests alone. Decisions made at these review meetings include the following categories: (1) continued appropriateness of current

Table 8.7
Student profile form to be completed by student's classroom teacher.

Student Profile (Teacher Form)

Child's Name: _____	Date of Birth: _____
School: _____	Phone: _____
Grade Level: _____	Date Completed: _____

---

1. This student is interested in:
2. Things this student is ready to learn:
3. This student is best at:
4. This student needs the most help with:
5. Help this student had received in the past:
6. Problems with this student's current educational program:
7. Problems with this student's current speech therapy program:
8. Possible alternatives and/or additions to this student's current program:
9. Services this student needs:
10. Special concerns I have about this student:
11. Suggestions I have about working with this student:
12. Strengths this student has in the area of:
    -Academics:
    -Speech:
    -Motor:
    -Social/behavior:
    -Vocational/prevocational:
    -Self-help skills:
    -Self-advocacy skills:
13. Concerns I have for this student in the following areas:
    -Academics:
    -Speech:
    -Motor:
    -Social/behavior:
    -Vocational/prevocational:
    -Self-help skills:
    -Self-advocacy skills:
14. When this student leaves high school as a young adult, I expect:

---

goals; (2) modification of goals to ensure greater success and achievement; (3) modification of therapy plans to better aid the student in goal achievement; (4) identifying academic benchmarks student may need assistance within the upcoming school year; and (5) identification of goals achieved but need to be maintained over the next documentation period.

Eger (1999) presented several strategies for monitoring progress that are useful and practical for the school clinician. First, link the original objectives to the benchmarks for the child's grade level. Then generate a checklist of these objectives to track throughout the year. When making observations, utilize your own set of learning descriptors (comment codes) that can be written next to the benchmark currently under attention. Second, develop objectives based on instructional areas to

Table 8.8
Student profile form to be completed by the student's parent.

Student Profile (Parent Form)	
Child's Name: _____	Date of Birth: _____
School: _____	Phone: _____
Grade Level: _____	Date Completed: _____

1. My child is interested in:
2. Things my child is ready to learn:
3. My child is best at:
4. My child needs the most help with:
5. Help my child had received in the past:
6. Problems with my child's current educational program:
7. Problems with my child's current speech therapy program:
8. Possible alternatives and/or additions to my child's current program:
9. Services my child needs:
10. Special concerns I have about my child:
11. Suggestions I have about working with my child:
12. Strengths my child has in the area of:
    -Academics:
    -Speech:
    -Motor:
    -Social/behavior:
    -Vocational/prevocational:
    -Self-help skills:
    -Self-advocacy skills:
13. Concerns I have for my child in the following areas:
    -Academics:
    -Speech:
    -Motor:
    -Social/behavior:
    -Vocational/prevocational:
    -Self-help skills:
    -Self-advocacy skills:
14. When my child leaves high school as a young adult, I expect:

ensure the child is using his new speech skills in all subject domains. Third, develop checklists of skills that help meet the student's IEP goals. Share these with parents and teachers, letting them know mastery of these skills will be the bases of the child's benefit from speech therapy. Use of a proficiency rating scale is beneficial for ongoing monitoring of student progress toward IEP objectives. Code the child's performance on a Likert scale indicating the degree of independent mastery exhibited in the session or when performing outside speech assignments. Ranging from 0 (not observed) to 5 (consistent implementation), you can easily and quickly rate the child's performance level and track progress over time. This system of coding can be used by everyone who interacts with the child both in the school and home setting (Table 8.9).

Table 8.9
Session notes and coding system useful for documenting progress in therapy.

Session Progress Notes

Student's Name: _____ Month/Year: _____

Goals: 1) _____
       2) _____
       3) _____
       4) _____
       5) _____

Date	Goal (#)	Proficiency Rating	Comments

(Five-point scale: 1 = poor; 2 = weak and inconsistent; 3 = developing; 4 = established skill; 5 = mastery)

Innovative Programs

A need exists for innovative, alternative services for children who stutter to override the obstacles inherent in providing therapy through the school system. The school clinician may consider several options to the traditional school-based model of therapy (Bennett et al., 1993; Berkowitz et al., 1994; Westbrook et al., 1992). Semi-intensive camps, mini Saturday camps, and involvement in support groups may augment regular school services provided for CWS.

Semi-Intensive Camps

Many communities are combining with school districts, universities, and funding agencies to respond to the need for alternative services through the establishment of summer camps (Bennett, 2002; Lougeay & Anderson, 2002; Westbrook et al., 1992). **Summer camps** are typically short-term, semi-intensive opportunities for children to receive additional support during a period when speech therapy is not available. Lasting 1 to 3 weeks, camps use a naturalistic environment with structured activities for children to benefit from peer support, family involvement, and total unconditional acceptance. The Stuttering Foundation of America maintains a list of summer camp programs offered around the country and is an excellent resource for therapists and parents.

For example, Ysleta Independent School District (El Paso, Texas) has held an annual fluency camp since 1991. During its first year, the camp involved 19 children who stutter, 5 licensed speech pathologists who volunteered their time, and 10 graduate students from the local university. The campers were divided into five groups of age-similar peers and assigned one SLP and two graduate clinicians. Hours of operation were 9 a.m. to 3 p.m., Monday through Friday. Children engaged in large- and small-group interactions following a predetermined curriculum. The teaching goals involved learning about the normal speaking process, learning about stuttering, learning it is okay to stutter, and learning to take risks, as well as being more open about stuttering. Parents attended a support group, an informational exchange session, in the evening. The camp concluded with a closing ceremony in which each group of campers presented a skit to share what they had learned at camp with their families and community members. This general organization and framework has been repeated each year since 1991 with an ongoing increase of participants and financial support from the district.

Saturday Mini Camps

Bennett, in 1992, conducted four Saturday mini-camps as a follow-up to the semi-intensive Summer Fluency Camp sponsored by her school district. The goals of these sessions were to reinforce previously learned material, identify current concerns of the students, and develop a tentative plan to be followed through by the student's campus therapist. These mini-camps were more individualized than the summer camp and involved a smaller number of students. Again, district therapists volunteered their time to participate in these mini-camps.

Support Groups

The role of support groups for the adult who stutters has been clearly identified as an integral component to their treatment (Ginsberg, 2000; Ramig & Bennett, 1997a; Reardon & Reeves, 2002; Shields & Kuster, 2003). Several groups began to organize similar meetings for children who stutter, ultimately leading to two large support organizations for children who stutter: Friends: The Association of Young People Who Stutter and Young People of NSA's Stutter Buddies. Each group publishes a quarterly newsletter consisting of articles written by children who stutter with occasional suggestions from therapists and parents. Each organization has its own Web site so children can write one another to share their experiences and support each other (www.friendswhostutter.org and www.WeStutter.org). The task of supporting another in need is very therapeutic and should be encouraged and incorporated into therapy plans. Putting words onto paper helps distance oneself from the pain or, stated another way, sharing one's pain reduces the pain itself. This letter was written for a Stutter Buddies issue by a 10-year-old boy who has been stuttering since he was 4:

> My name is MR. I am 10 years old and live in El Paso, Texas. I attend Mesita Elementary school as a 5th grader. About two years ago, I started speech therapy with Dr. Ellen Bennett. With the help of my family and friends, I overcame a fear of stuttering and on Oct. 26, I auditioned for the Milli Lewis International Talent Agency.
>
> As I walked onto the stage with butterflies in my stomach and saw the judges, I wanted to turn back. But then, I looked at my parents and was reassured. As I said my lines for a Jell-O commercial, I started to stutter a little bit. But I said my lines and everything was fine. By doing this audition, I overcame the hugest fear of all. I was selected to go to Dallas, Texas, in January to compete again for the commercial.

Working with Teachers

Teachers play a vital role in the therapy process for children who stutter. From early morning to late afternoon, teachers interact with their students in numerous and various ways. They are in a unique position to facilitate, monitor, and enrich the communicative environment for children who stutter. However, to do so, they must have knowledge about the disorder, the population with this disorder, and the treatments needed to achieve student goals. Historically, teachers have believed that stuttering is caused by psychological and physical problems (Lass et al., 1992; Ruscello, Lass, Schmitt, & Pannbacker, 1994). Additionally, teachers believe children who stutter are characterized by negative personality traits, such as shyness, nervousness, insecurity, and anxiousness. Such "adherence to negative perceptions regarding children who stutter influences the dynamics of the educational environment, placing the child at a disadvantage and possibly limiting the student's potential" (Bennett, 2003, pp. 53–54). Yeakle and Cooper (1986) found teachers who held more acceptable views of stuttering were those who had direct experience with children who stutter. To shape teacher perceptions positively, you can provide opportunities to expose teachers to stuttering and its variable manifestations through inservice training experiences.

Teacher Inservice

Williams and Dugan (2002) stated three reasons for regular teacher conferences: (1) Teachers will have questions as therapy progresses, (2) small amounts of information at each conference will ensure they are not overwhelmed, and (3) it is important teachers understand the objectives of stuttering modification therapy. Teachers are a valuable resource for both the speech therapist and student. No longer do our students sit in one classroom all day, engaging with only one teacher. Many schools are structured to include team teaching; thus teachers have daily encounters with many more students than those in the homeroom.

Strategies. Bennett (2003) presented several strategies to use when planning a teacher inservice. First, inservice programs should be concise and to the point, following the KISS motto: "Keep It Super Simple." Monitor professional jargon used in training sessions and take care to define specific terms relevant to the topic (e.g., *fluency, disfluency, stuttering, block, easy onsets, prolongations*, etc.). Provide sufficient notice of the inservice through flyers displayed at the teachers' sign-in and lounge areas. Bennett recommended using children who stutter as a means for delivering messages or reminders regarding the inservice date. Direct interaction with students sends a positive message regarding the importance of teacher involvement. It also aids in the transfer of speech skills outside the therapy setting.

During the inservice meeting, follow the *3-E rule of thumb*: engage, encourage, and empathize. *Engage* teachers in meaningful dialogue regarding children who stutter. Be creative when planning activities for training sessions. Having teachers pseudostutter, producing the major types of core stuttering behaviors, is one way of educating teachers on the speech characteristics to look for in their students. As teachers pretend to stutter, you can address the level of discomfort that most certainly will be evident. Talking about emotional reactions to stuttering may be new to some teachers, so allocate time to answer any questions that may arise.

Next, *encourage* teachers by praising their efforts to modify classroom expectations to meet the needs of children who stutter. Many excellent teachers in our schools have had positive interactions and influence on children who stutter. However, there are teachers who may think they are helping the student when, from the student's perceptions, their suggestions hinder the student's feelings of communicative competence. Teachers often tell students, "Slow down," "Take your time," or "Think about what you want to say." In reality, our students know what they want to say. They are just having difficulty saying what they want to communicate. It comes as a surprise when you help teachers view stuttering from the student's perspective.

You can express *empathy* regarding the heavy burden teachers face attempting to educate large classrooms filled with too many students and not enough supplies. Empathy is the expression of understanding of the teachers' experiences, behaviors, and feelings in any given situation. Take this opportunity to express your genuine concern and respect for them as educators. Let the teachers know you understand how hard they work each day for the benefit of every student. Let them know you need their committed help in your efforts to provide the best therapy for every child who stutters. Stress the need for teamwork to achieve the goals of every student.

Organization. Start the meeting by distributing an agenda indicating the content to be covered, as well as any time allowed for a question-and-answer period. Selecting the content of your inservice will depend on the predetermined purpose, based on campus needs. Inservice training can have three distinct goals: (1) dissemination of information, (2) experiences shared by children who stutter, or (3) discussions regarding classroom modifications. The following is just a sample of the type of information teachers would benefit from learning: identification of early warning signs of beginning stuttering, recognizing the covert and overt manifestations of stuttering, and understanding the nature of treatment goals (Bennett, 2003).

Follow-up inservice sessions may involve direct observation of children who stutter sharing their experiences with stuttering, how they feel about their disorder, and what they want teachers to do to help them in the classroom. Additionally, students can model their fluency or stuttering management strategies for the teachers so they can provide better feedback regarding student oral performance in the classroom. Having the students explain the ABCs of stuttering is an excellent way to educate teachers and empower students at the same time.

Content. You may also choose to conduct an inservice meeting to address the classroom modifications set in each student's IEP documents. At the beginning of each year, teachers receive a copy of each student's modification page so they may plan how to adjust their classroom to better meet the needs of their students with disabilities. Although you may choose to meet individually with each teacher, a schoolwide inservice would benefit all teachers who interact with such children throughout the school day.

Bennett (2003) provided several general suggestions for teachers to use when interacting with the child who stutters: (1) allow time for the child to respond, (2) avoid completing sentences or filling in words, (3) stop all interruptions, (4) maintain eye contact during interactions, (5) avoid giving advice, (6) eliminate all teasing or ridicule by peers, and (7) pay attention to *what* the student says, not *how* he is talking. Model for teachers how to respond when a student experiences a severe stuttering block with comments such as "That looked like a hard word to say" or "You are so brave to show me your stuttering." Teachers must understand the difficulties inherent in answering questions in class for some of the students. It is recommended that each teacher discuss privately with the child who stutters and the therapist how to handle oral reports, answering questions, and general verbal communication times in the classroom. The compassionate, understanding classroom teacher can facilitate the child's progress by learning how to cope with stuttering, understanding the nature and treatment of stuttering, and feeling free to ask questions of the school therapist. Conducting teacher inservice programs provides an opportunity for you to establish this type of open relationship with teachers.

Educational Materials

Several useful brochures are available from the Stuttering Foundation of America and the National Stuttering Association that provide basic information on stuttering disorders. Tips of how to respond when talking with a person who stutters, how to handle the child who stutters within the classroom environment, and coping with the emotions often accompanying stuttering are just a sample of what is available. The Stuttering Foundation of America has several excellent videotapes of clinicians modeling therapy strategies, talking with parents about stuttering, and experts answering commonly asked questions. You can use these videos as a resource to augment your inservice program. Other teaching tools might include the Teacher Rating Scale (Table 8.10) and Teacher Interview: Fluency (Table 8.11). As a handout, you can review these forms, ask teachers to keep a copy of it at their desks, and consult it when considering referring a child for a speech evaluation.

Special Events

Certain dates throughout the school year are designated times to promote speech services and increase public awareness of communication disorders. You can use these opportunities to disseminate information or encourage open interactions with teachers. May is designated as "May Is Better Speech and Hearing Month" by ASHA and a time most therapists use to increase knowledge levels of parents and teachers. However, two other dates have particular relevance to children who stutter: International Stuttering Awareness Day (ISAD) and National Stuttering Awareness Week. ISAD is scheduled on October 22 each year and involves a worldwide Internet conference in which participants can address specific questions to each author and engage in dialogue over different topics. Access to the conference agenda and papers remains open to input for a month prior to October 22. The day of the conference, each author commits to being available to respond to inquiries that may come from around the globe. It is an exciting learning experience for all who participate.

National Stuttering Awareness Week, the second week in May, is devoted to nationwide informational dissemination on stuttering disorders. The Stuttering Foundation of America coordinates events that might include newspaper and magazine articles, television interviews, as well as designating a spokesperson to head its advertising campaign. This person is usually a well-known person who has not allowed stuttering to hold them back from their achievements. James Earl Jones, John Stossel, Bill Walton, Ken Venturi, Annie Glenn, Bob Love, and Nick Brendon are just a few of those selected for this prestigious honor.

Table 8.10
Teacher rating scale: Fluency evaluation.

Student: _____ DOB: _____ ID#: _____

Teacher: _____ CA: _____ Grade: _____

Please rate the student on his/her smoothness of speech:	Severe	Moderate	Mild	Average	Above Average	
Classroom Participation: Initiates conversations, answers questions, volunteers to respond verbally.	1	2	3	4	5	N/A
Intelligibility: Is readily understood and does not need to repeat verbal responses frequently.	1	2	3	4	5	N/A
Carryover to Oral Reading: • Reads with fluency and speed appropriate for grade level.	1	2	3	4	5	N/A
• Fluency in oral reading improves with repeated practice of the same passage.	1	2	3	4	5	N/A
Reaction of Peers to Speech: Peers are accepting of the speech difficulties.	1	2	3	4	5	N/A
Reaction of Adults to Speech: Teachers and other adults interact with and/or call on the student despite speech characteristics.	1	2	3	4	5	N/A
Socialization: Do you feel the student's communication skills interfere with social interactions and peer relationships?	1	2	3	4	5	N/A
Nonverbal Behaviors During Speech: • Makes appropriate eye contact during speaking	1	2	3	4	5	N/A
• Utilizes normal body posture	1	2	3	4	5	N/A
• Utilizes normal gestures	1	2	3	4	5	N/A
• Resorts to gestures instead of speaking	1	2	3	4	5	N/A
Feelings and Attitudes: Has the student expressed negative feelings or attitudes about speaking?	1	2	3	4	5	N/A
Fluency: • Does the student repeat sounds or words when speaking?	1	2	3	4	5	N/A
• Does the student appear to get stuck when speaking and can't seem to get the words out?	1	2	3	4	5	N/A
• Does the student draw out certain sounds in words when speaking?	1	2	3	4	5	N/A

Comments:
_____
_____
_____

Teacher Signature: _____ Date: _____

Source: Based on the Las Cruces Public Schools Special Education Department, Speech-Language Pathology Program (2001).

Table 8.11
Teacher interview form useful for gathering information on children who stutter.

Teacher Interview

Student: _____ DOB: _____
SLP: _____ Grade: _____
Teacher: _____ Date: _____

Place a check in the appropriate column to rate the student's communication performance.

As compared to peers in the same setting:	Always 1	2	Sometimes 3	4	Never 5
1. Does the student verbalize appropriately?					
2. Does the student verbalize effortlessly?					
3. When verbalizing, are the student's facial and body movements distracting from communication?					
4. Does this student *readily* participate in class discussions or activities that require speaking in front of group?					
5. Do you accept the student's speech as adequate?					
6. Do peers accept the student's speech as adequate?					
7. Do you understand the student's verbal intent without difficulty?					
8. Does this student *readily* participate in conversation with peers?					
9. Does the student's speech allow for participation/progress in the general curriculum?					

Do you have any other observations related to the communication skills of this student?

_____
_____
_____

Teacher Signature _____ Date _____

Fluency Specialists in the Schools: Models of Consultation

The use of fluency specialists as internal and external consultants to the public school therapist has been addressed in the literature (Oyler & Chmela, 2003; Ramig & Bennett, 1995; Westbrook, 1991). ASHA Special Interest Division #4, Fluency and Fluency Disorders, in 1997, recognized the need for specialty training in the area of fluency disorders (Oyler & Chmela, 2003). The elimination of required practicum experience in the area of fluency disorders coupled with the continued feelings of inadequacy by SLPs prompted consumers and professionals to band together and advocate for the recognition of fluency specialists. The first cadre of fluency specialists were recognized by the Specialty Board on Fluency Disorders in July 2000. Although this national recognition was novel, the recognition of specialists has a previous history in the school system. Dallas and Ysleta (in El Paso, Texas) school districts have used the services of in-house specialists for the past decade. These specialists act as mentors to their fellow therapists in the areas of assessment, intervention, and general problem solving. Whether the specialist works from within the system or is an external resource for the school-based therapist, he or she can help improve the services provided children who stutter.

Oyler and Chmela (2003) identified five ways specialists can aid the school clinician. First, the specialist can problem-solve difficult problems present in a particular child. Second, the specialist can provide supplemental therapy and collaborate with the school therapist on methods of intervention. Third, the skills of the school clinician can be advanced through interactions with a fluency specialist, ultimately proving beneficial to numerous children who stutter. Fourth, planning inservices with the intent of engaging parents and teachers in the therapy process may fall within the domain of the fluency specialist. Lastly, the specialist can advocate for the school clinician in the areas of caseload management, educating administrators on the nature and treatment of stuttering, and ways districts can better comply with the rules and regulations set forth in IDEA '97.

Mental Health Model

The ASHA Special Interest Division on Fluency and Fluency Disorders established a task force to address the particular needs of the school-based therapist providing services for children who stutter. The task force presented a report on the role of fluency specialists as consultants in the school setting, recommending the use of Chaplan's mental health model of consultation (Chmela, Bennett, Campbell, Oyler, Scott-Trautman, & Tardelli, 2002). This model is based on psychodynamic theories of human interaction and includes two types of consultation: case-centered and administrative-centered interactions (Dougherty, 1990).

Case-centered interactions may take the form of client versus consultee tasks. **Client-centered tasks** involve the development of a specific plan to address the needs of a particular student. The specialist may assess the student's and consultee's skills, write a report and discuss with the consultee, and follow up to see if the consultee implements suggestions. **Consultee-centered tasks** work toward improving the consultee's ability to implement fluency services. The consultant establishes a relationship with the consultee; assesses problem areas of knowledge, skill, confidence, and objectivity; and provides intervention for the consultee.

Administrative-centered interactions involve two focus directions: the program versus the consultee. *Program-centered* administrative consultation might include establishing a relationship with the administration and exploring the needs of the system. The specialist gathers facts to understand the needs of the system and develops a set of recommendations shared with the administration. An example of a program-centered task would be the development of training modules for parents of children who stutter. *Consultee-centered* administration consultation helps the administration solve problems in personnel management or policy implementation. The process of consultee-centered administrative collaboration includes five steps: (1) understanding relationships within the system, (2) exploring the needs with the administration, (3) determining who the consultee is and discussing with them the role of the consultant, (4) studying the system, and (5) making recommendations to the administration. Implementation of the consultant's recommendations is the responsibility of the administration.

Schein's Model

Another model that is useful when conceptualizing how to use specialists in the school system is Schein's model of consultation (Dougherty, 1990). His model is conceptualized into three domains: the expert model, the doctor/patient model, and the process model. Figure 8.3 presents a graphic organization of Schein's model as applied to communication disorders. The *expert model* involves the hiring of an individual with knowledge or skill to resolve a previously identified problem within the system.

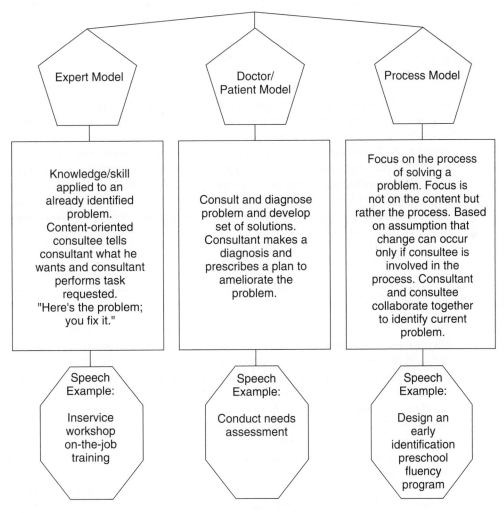

Figure 8.3
A graphic representation of Schein's model of consultation applied to communication disorders.

Table 8.12
Recommended guidelines for success consultation.

1. Requires an experienced specialist in the area of fluency disorders.
2. Requires the specialist to understand how the school system operates.
3. Requires the consultee/school to clearly define issues and needs.
4. Requires the consultant to understand the needs of the consultee/school.
5. Requires that each party involved assumes full responsibility for their role in the consultation process.
6. Requires the consultant positively relate to the consultee, student, parents, teachers, administrators, and others.
7. Requires the consultant to provide recommendations in an appropriate manner.
8. Requires the consultant to identify breakdowns in communication/cooperation between parties when they occur and problem-solve them accordingly.
9. Requires the specialist have the ability to problem-solve in order to most successfully meet the needs identified during the consultation process.
10. Requires the specialist to create a set of recommendations that match the need or ultimate reason for the consultation.

Source: ASHA Task Force on Fluency Services in the Schools (Chmela et al., 2002).

In the *doctor-patient model*, the system hires the consultant to diagnose and prescribe a set of resolutions to the current problem. The *process model* engages the consultant and client in interactions designed to understand how problems are solved within the system versus identifying the content of the problems. Regardless of which model of consultation is implemented by the specialist, successful consultation is contingent on meeting 10 specific requirements (Chmela et al., 2002). Table 8.12 presents these basic guidelines. With increased consumer awareness and the desire to meet the individualized educational needs of this population, the use of fluency specialists might be the wave of the future.

TREATMENT DIRECTIONS

There are many suggestions in the literature for working with preschool or adult clients; however, information on the school-age child who stutters is sparse. During the early 1990s, the Stuttering Foundation of America began to offer annual conferences to address the special needs of the clinician working with children who stutter in the school setting. These workshops and subsequent publications have provided a valuable resource. Although not published programs that can be purchased, the ideas of several of the workshop speakers are presented here. Additionally, several published programs are reviewed. Therapy for school-age children who stutter may incorporate fluency-shaping or stuttering modification principles depending on the needs of each child. Chapter 5 discussed the approaches of several other well-known clinicians. Those, as well as the following methods, are recommended for use with this population.

Treatment methods appropriate for school-age children who stutter fall within the spectrum of approaches described in chapter 5, that is, fluency-shaping, stuttering modification, and integrated approaches to fluency therapy. The following established programs contain many useful ideas when planning therapy for this population.

Fluency-Shaping Intervention

Fluency-shaping intervention focuses on training the child systematically to speak in a new way utilizing behavioral principles of modification. Linguistic length and complexity are controlled, as well as predetermined criterion and consequences for fluent and stuttered speech. Programs such as Costello's ELU and Ryan's GILCU are two examples of fluency-shaping paradigms. The following approaches specifically address the school-age population.

Richard Shine

Systematic Fluency Training for Young Children (Shine, 1980) is a highly structured, easy-to-follow program. It was developed for children ages 3 to 9 and includes both assessment and intervention strategies. Shine emphasizes the use of significant others in the daily implementation of his program (e.g., parents, siblings, or grandparents). Shine's program follows a fluency-shaping model that includes four major activities: (1) picture identification, (2) storybook, (3) picture matching, and (4) surprise box. A token system of reinforcement is used to establish a whispered voice, which is modified into an easy speaking voice and gradually shaped into fluent speech. His manual includes specific steps for the therapist to follow with set criterion levels and specific instructions for advancing to the next highest level of linguistic complexity. This program is an excellent resource for the beginning clinician working for the first time with young children who stutter.

Charles and Sara Elizabeth Runyan

Runyan and Runyan (1986, 1993, 1999) described a Fluency Rules Program (FRP) for implementation with young school-age children who stutter. The goal is to establish naturally fluent speech production through adherence to seven speech rules (universal, primary, and secondary). **Universal rules** are "Speak Slowly (Turtle Speech)" and "Say a Word Only Once." **Primary rules** are "Use Speech Breathing" and "Start Mr. Voice Box Running Smoothly." The three **secondary rules** include "Touch the Speech Helper Together Lightly," "Keep the Speech Helpers Moving," and "Use Only the Speech Helpers to Talk." FRP recommends the following sequence of instructional activities: (1) Observe the child's speaking patterns and determine which rules are broken, targeting them during therapy; (2) teach the language concepts necessary for understanding therapy instructions; (3) develop the child's self-monitoring skills; (4) practice fluent speech production using the fluency rules; and (5) carry over procedures into the

home and class environments. This program provides several useful therapy suggestions to help you implement the program within the school setting. Again, this is an excellent organizational framework for the inexperienced clinician to reference when
planning therapy for stuttering disorders.

Lena Rustin and Frances Cook

Rustin and Cook (1995) discussed an intensive treatment course for the child between
7 and 14 years of age. This treatment program, conducted at the Michael Palin Centre
for Stammering Children in London, includes all those involved in the child's communicative environment because the child is still dependent on his family and teachers
as a resource for development. Following a complete parent and child assessment,
group treatment is initiated based on the "assumption that intervention with individuals who influence the communicative environment of the child who stutters is the
critical component in the treatment of children who stutter" (p. 132). Note that these
authors require parent(s) to attend every therapy session with their child, which may
not be possible in certain work settings, such as the public schools in the United
States. The goals for this treatment program are to (1) increase an understanding of the
nature of stuttering for both the children and their parents, (2) identify the positive
changes that can be made by both the children and their parents, (3) practice changes
in patterns of communication within a secure framework, and (4) offer effective
follow-up schedules following the intensive course.

To achieve these goals, the 2-week course involves a child and parent training
program. The child program focuses on developing fluency in social settings using
social and relaxation skills training as well as fluency control techniques. Social
skills training might address issues from maintaining eye contact to making friends
and developing negotiating skills. Rustin and Cook utilize role-playing and problem-
solving strategies to facilitate skill development. Relaxation training may be initiated if deemed necessary to meet a particular child's needs. They contrast the
body movements of Tin Soldiers versus Rag Dolls and use music to teach children
how to use relaxation "as a coping mechanism when stuttering is particularly
marked" (p. 133).

Teaching fluency control techniques is the second principle component of Rustin
and Cook's intensive program. They utilize a variety of fluency-shaping strategies along
with cognitive problem solving as the child discovers what goes wrong with his
speech and what he can choose to do to change the stuttering. Rate control strategies,
easy onsets, continuous airflow, and blending sounds together are just a sample of the
techniques children are taught to manage their speech.

The parent program is organized around a series of structured group sessions that
involve discussions of certain topics and parent exercises. Parents exchange ideas as
well as learn about their child's treatment program and strategies used in therapy. They
engage in games and exercises similar to their children's therapy so they may better
understand what is required to change speech. Some sessions address particular family dynamics that may interfere with the development and maintenance of fluency. The
goal is to shift responsibility for treatment from the clinician to the family through the

acquisition of "new skills in negotiating conflicts that will persist beyond the timescale of the intensive courses" (p. 133). Follow-up sessions occur 6 weeks, 3 months, 6 months, and 1 year after the intensive course.

Stuttering Modification Intervention

Stuttering modification intervention for the school-age child is designed to draw the student's attention to the moment of stuttering and to teach strategies to modify stuttering. Child-centered activities following Van Riper's identification, desensitization, modification, and stabilization phases of therapy are carefully designed to enhance the development of fluency. The following authors have described their work with schoolchildren, which adds to the ideas of Williams (presented in chapter 5).

Hal Luper and Robert Mulder

Luper and Mulder (1964) were among the first specifically to address the particular needs of the child who stutters receiving services in the public schools. They divide therapy for childhood stuttering into four phases: (1) modification of the incipient stutterer, (2) modification of transitional stuttering, (3) direct therapy with the confirmed stutterer, and (4) modification of advanced stuttering. Phase 1 of therapy focuses on the preschool child (discussed in chapter 7). The phase 2 child usually is between the ages of 6 and 7 with signs of chronic stuttering. For this school-age child, therapy involves increasing the child's communicative confidence as well as learning about and modifying any maladaptive behaviors emerging in the child's speech. The child is instructed on how to produce a "free flow of words" using choral speaking, rhythm, or adaptation principles (p. 88).

Desensitization to stuttering and tension modification strategies are incorporated into therapy activities with open discussions around the topic of stuttering. Additionally, Luper and Mulder provide a program of general speech improvement that offers many successful opportunities for children to talk. The clinician must work with the teacher to encourage the child who stutters to participate in all verbal aspects of the classroom. Allowing the child to withdraw from speaking tasks is not an option.

The phase 3 child receives a more direct approach to therapy due to the development of avoidances, fears, and his confirmed belief that "his way of talking is a problem" (p. 111). Luper and Mulder outline four objectives for this stage of modification therapy: (1) help the child understand the nature of therapy, (2) help him develop realistic personal goals for helping himself, (3) help him become less sensitive about stuttering, and (4) develop a healthy clinician/child relationship.

These authors believe the child must develop an objective attitude in which he admits to himself and others that he stutters. He does not have to like the stuttering, but he must be honest with himself and others by engaging in various "advertising" activities. Therapy includes learning about the disorder or stuttering and what the child "does" when he stutters in a matter-of-fact manner. Next, he must learn to modify his maladaptive behaviors used in anticipation of stuttering. The child must learn what he does when anticipating a moment of stuttering, catch himself during this

Table 8.13
Establishing an objective attitude toward stuttering.

---

1. The individual should feel responsibility for his own behavior and for carrying out the changes that need to be made.
2. He should be willing, temporarily, to place greater emphasis upon how he talks and upon how he feels about speaking than on what he says.
3. He should be willing to allow others to know he stutters and should resist the temptation to hide or minimize his stuttering.
4. He should be willing to experiment with different methods for alleviating the severity of his problems.
5. He should desire to learn as much about the problem of stuttering as he can and his own speech problem in particular.
6. He should become willing to enter difficult speaking situations even though he expects to stutter.

Source: Luper and Mulder's (1964, pp. 150–151) desired attitudinal changes required to establish an objective attitude toward stuttering.

anticipatory process, and change his reactive behaviors. Luper and Mulder utilize the Van Riperian strategies of cancellations and pullouts to assist the child in modifying their moments of stuttering. Last, an important part of the therapy process is having the child observe how others react to stuttering and understand how these perceptions may impact his speech. To achieve this end goal, a strong client/clinician relationship is essential.

Phase 4 therapy involves the modification of advanced stuttering characterized by a strong approach-avoidance cycle of postponement, starting, avoidance, and release devices that no longer work for the older school-age child. The strong emotional reactions to stuttering, with particular emphasis on the social consequences, dominate the mind of the child at this point in his life. Luper and Mulder's approach with this group of children is heavily influenced by Van Riper's treatment philosophy incorporating previously discussed modification strategies. They utilize Van Riper's term **objective attitude** and define it as "the intelligent, unemotional acceptance of an objectional difference as a problem capable of solution" (p. 150).

Table 8.13 provides six attitudinal changes necessary to develop an objective attitude toward stuttering. A major requirement of this stage of therapy involves the active involvement of the child in accepting responsibility for his speech change. Having the child engage in outside assignments is one way to assess self-responsibility. However, these assignments must follow the criteria set forth by Luper and Mulder: Assignments must be meaningful, specific, reportable, and verifiable.

Carl Dell

Dell (1979), in the Stuttering Foundation of America publication *Treating the School-Age Stutterer: A Guide for Clinicians*, provides helpful therapy suggestions and ideas for working with the mild to confirmed child who stutters. School-age children may exhibit behaviors encompassing the entire spectrum of the stuttering syndrome. Dell believes that even the young student may feel embarrassment and shame around stuttering and such feelings must be addressed in the therapy process. For the borderline stutterer, Dell uses an indirect fluency-shaping approach with periodic modeling of milder forms of stuttering. A goal for this child "is to show them how fluent they are most of the time" (p. 34). He suggests increasing the child's awareness of his fluency and the opportunities to use his fluency during tasks that vary in linguistic and cognitive demand. Although primarily addressing fluency with this group, Dell educates the child on both the normal speaking process and stuttering as a means to demystify the disorder.

For the mild child who stutters, Dell begins to shift the emphasis away from fluency and toward a positive awareness of stuttering. The primary goal is to prevent the child from reacting to stuttering with fear and avoidance. The therapy process involves a gradual movement toward directing the child's stuttering as the occasion arises. To begin the confrontation process, the clinician inserts her own pseudostuttering and talks about these episodes with the child. Discussions are conducted in a relaxed, accepting manner, modeling an objective attitude for the child. Next, Dell has the child insert voluntary stuttering into his speech during game activities, all the while monitoring the child's emotional reactions to the stuttering. As the child becomes more desensitized to his stuttering, Dell begins to explore the struggle and tension that remain in the child's speech. Locating where he stutters, playing around with the tension levels of these moments, and instilling the concept of choice making into therapy helps the child reduce the severity of his stuttering.

However, for some children with severe stuttering, this general, yet direct approach to therapy is not sufficient. For the confirmed child who stutters, Dell contends that some children need direct practice with manipulating the moment of stuttering. He described a therapy activity in which the child practices saying a word three ways: (1) the hard way, (2) the fluent way, and (3) the easy stuttered way. This hard-easy-regular activity is a unique way of teaching the child flexibility in the way he talks and conveys the concept of making choices in the way one talks (for details, see chapter 9). Next, the child practices identifying "real" moments of stuttering and changing them to a milder form through easy voluntary stuttering. Gradually, the child is expected to catch his stutter, reduce the tension in the speech mechanism, and bounce out of the stutter using easy repetitions. Dell's description of his modification approach is an excellent resource for clinicians because it provides sample dialogues of client/clinician interactions.

More recently, Dell (2000) describes a nine-session school-based intervention plan. Although including much of the same information just described, Dell's more recent writing elaborates on the principles underlying therapy and provides additional therapy ideas to help implement student goals. The art of therapy involves the establishment of a strong, trusting student/clinician relationship. This relationship, according to Dell, is essential for creating an environment conducive to change. Dell's bottom-line survival thoughts regarding school-based fluency therapy include the following reflections:

1. I have outlined a course of treatment that is effective with children who stutter. It's a course of treatment that is based on the belief that human beings, no matter how young, deserve to understand the nature of the behavior they are trying to change.

Don't expect that if you do everything I have recommended that all students will become magically fluent. This is not a cut-and-dried speech problem and, therefore, it does not have a "one-size-fits-all" solution!

2. Children who stutter must be mystified and confused by their perplexing disorder. Help students understand what parameters in speech are violated when they stutter and what they can do about violations. Once a child understands the intellectual and physiological nature of their stuttering, it is perhaps possible that, together with your help, the student may be able to learn how to become more fluent.

3. Reduce emotions that revolve around stuttering. Sharpen and follow your clinical gut, which will tell you what to do and how far to go with a student in therapy.

4. Keep laughter and real conversation a part of all your work with students. It is *authentic, effective*, and *healing*. (2000, p. 198)

Integrated Intervention

A blending of fluency-shaping and stuttering modification therapy is often used with school-age children who stutter. Similar to Peters and Guitar (1991), the following authors present their designs that range in both structure and form. You will find many useful ideas in their writings.

Edward Conture

Conture (2001) described a creative approach to working with school-age children using multiple analogies useful to enhancing parental and client understanding. Children receiving services are grouped according to the level of parental concern and the child's awareness of communication difficulties. Group 1 are children having no objective-subjective communication problem yet parents are reasonably quite concerned. Despite the child exhibiting age-appropriate fluency during clinician observations, parents contend their child is stuttering at home. Conture noted that parents often have the opportunity to observe their child in speaking situations in which the child's fluency differs from that observed by the speech pathologist. This necessitates assessing the child's fluency in dynamic, interactive communicative situations and considering parental insight as reliable judgments of their child's fluency difficulties.

Group 2 children exhibit stuttering but parents are minimally or completely unconcerned. The clinician engages in various parent counseling tasks to modify any exacerbating environmental factors and monitor the child's speech progression. Group 3 children have some stuttering but parents are also concerned. For these children, therapy involves experimenting with hard and easy speech and identifying the effects of these types of speech on others and gradually in their own speech. Parents are involved in the therapy process and required to follow through with home oral reading and speaking assignments. For the last group of children (group 4), who exhibit a great deal of objective-subjective communication problems and whose parents are quite concerned, the clinician may have to decide when a more direct approach is necessary. Conture outlined six behavioral guidelines useful when making such decisions (Table 8.14). Taking a direct approach means teaching both parents and children about

Table 8.14
Behavioral guidelines used to determine the need for a more direct approach to treatment for the school-age child who stutters.

1. Sound prolongations comprise 30% or more of all stuttering.
2. There is more than occasional presence of stuttering/stuttering clusters in the child's speech.
3. Stuttering comprises 70% or more of his total speech disfluencies.
4. Less than 50% of the time, the child makes eye contact with his listener.
5. The child makes frequent reference to his speech and problems with it (e.g., "Mommy, why can't I talk right?").
6. Delays and/or deviant speech and language development are present.

Source: Based on Conture (2001).

talking and stuttering using a variety of analogies (see Table 8.15). Following the lead of Dean Williams, Conture stressed helping children "see, hear, and feel" stuttering, making it possible to change it.

Hugo Gregory and June Hearle Campbell

Campbell (2003) applied the therapeutic principles of the **less specific-more specific approach** of Gregory (2003) to the school-age population. A less-specific approach to treatment is defined as a speak-more-fluently model, whereas the more-specific approach follows a stutter-more-fluently orientation. Campbell (2003) stated her tendency to start with a less-specific approach with the younger school-age child (age 7) and incorporate more specific strategies only as needed. The less-specific model does not analyze the moment of stuttering because it is believed the child lacks sufficient cognitive development to benefit from such an exercise and may even increase the child's awareness of his difficulties. The main fluency-shaping strategy taught to the child is called **ERA—SM:** easy relaxed approach—smooth movements. The child is instructed to produce the initial consonant-vowel combination "with a more relaxed, smooth movement that is slightly slower than usual" (p. 225) with the remainder of the word produced with normal rate and prosody. Next, the child practices these transitions at the phrase level, gradually moving into sentences and discourse. Emphasis is on easy initiation and smooth transitions at the beginning of each phrase with frequent pausing during dialogue. Choral reading is used to establish speech fluency and as a means to teach this new way of talking to the child.

The more-specific component of this model incorporates several modification tasks. Voluntary disfluency, negative practice, cancellations, pullouts, and resisting time pressure may be selected for practice if the child's profile indicates continued residual stuttering despite implementation of ERA—SM. Campbell addresses this residual fear and dislike for stuttering through incorporating the child in the planning of therapy, thus encouraging the active participation and positiveness toward therapy. Therapy principles of systematic planning, multiple repetitions or drill, consistent clinician modeling, and reinforcement of modified speech attempts work together to create this integrated approach to therapy.

Table 8.15

Examples of some analogies used to help school-age children understand stuttering and the speaking process.

Garden Hose Analogy (parts of the speech mechanism)	The lips are equated with the nozzle of the hose in that both can be constricted to stop or modify airflow (lips) or water stream (nozzle). The vocal tract is analogized with the flexible, bendable, garden hose in that both can be manipulated in such a way (the garden hose can be kinked or bent, and the vocal tract can have the tongue partially or completed occluded airway) as to impede or modify the airflow or water stream. Finally, the larynx or vocal folds (housed in voice box) are equated with the faucet in that both can be constricted or adjusted to stop or modify airflow or water stream. This analogy helps the young child identify the nature and function of each part of the vocal mechanism and the means by which his or her strategies to (*sic*) interfere with speech take place. (p. 193)
Tight Fist Analogy (using time to change tension)	Here, the clinician uses *time* to help the client *gradually* release/change physical tension during speech. This analogy can be used with or without accompanying speech postures, for example, a fixed articulatory contact on /b/. By tensing the fist, and then gradually releasing it, the client can be helped to understand how time can be used to gradually reduce physical tension. (p. 204)
Blown-Up Balloon Analogy (tight closure at laryngeal or vocal fold area)	Since it is difficult for most clients to visualize and understand vocal fold structure and function, some "real-world" analogies are needed. Here a blown-up balloon is squeezed and the aerodynamic "back pressures" are felt by the fingers holding the balloon neck. Likewise, tight vocal fold closure can create aerodynamic back pressure felt at, below, or within the larynx, trachea, and chest. Some of the "tension" that stutterers frequently mention in their neck and chest is undoubtedly due to these aerodynamic back pressures resulting from laryngeal and, at times, supraglottal construction. (p. 199)
Hot Stove Burner Analogy (bodily/physical reactions to unexpected circumstances)	A person exploring a stovetop with his hand unexpectedly touches a lit burner. The person reacts by *physically pulling* the hand *away* and perhaps by gasping, suddenly inhaling, and tensing muscles up in the hand, arm, and elsewhere in the body. Likewise, a person who stutters may react to sudden, unexpected inability to say a sound, syllable, or word by *physically pulling back* the tongue, jaw, head, neck, or shoulders while simultaneously gasping or inhaling. (p. 192)
Jumping Into a Swimming Pool (reaction to unexpected circumstances)	On a hot day in early summer a swimmer might forget that the water is still quite chilly and be surprised (if not shocked) when hitting the cold water. Sudden gasping, inhalations, and/or muscle tensing might all be exhibited by the surprised swimmer, much like the sudden gasping, inhalation, or muscle tensing exhibited by a stutterer when attempting to produce a sound, syllable or word he or she suddenly and/or unexpectedly finds difficult to produce. (p. 191)
Lilipad/Frog Analogy (forward flow of speech)	For a frog to hop across a pond or stream of lily pads, it would have to smoothly, easily, and sequentially hop from one pad to another. However, if it landed on one and repeatedly hopped up and down (repetition) or landed on one in a physically tense, fixed manner (stoppage), it would disrupt forward movement across the pond. Likewise, speech requires physically easy, smooth, sequential behavior to make forward movement from beginning to the end of a sound, syllable, or words. (p. 201)

Source: Based on Conture (2001).

E. Charles Healey and Lisa A. Scott-Trautman

Healey and Scott (1995) outlined a three-phase treatment design for elementary children who stutter. They presented various strategies used to facilitate speech change in children from kindergarten to sixth grade. Basic to their treatment orientation are the following eight principles:

1. You need to be flexible in the design and implementation of a treatment program. This suggests you have a broad knowledge of the different approaches to treatment. Not all stutterers fit into one approach or benefit from one program. Fit the program to the child rather than the child to the program.

2. A good working relationship needs to be established between you and the child. This implies you must take the time to know the child and his interests. Strong relationships are built on trust and respect that evolve over time. The sharing of feelings, attitudes, and experiences will assist in building a strong client/clinician relationship.

3. Also take time to gain a better understanding about how the child cognitively perceives or represents events and experiences in his world. The cognitive component of stuttering therapy (i.e., conceptual knowledge and understanding of "slow talking" and "gentle onset of voicing") is critical to success.

4. Long-term change in speaking more fluently emerges once a feeling of control over the speech process has been developed, positive reactions to the stuttering have occurred, fear associated with speech or stuttering has been reduced, and appropriate changes in the way one talks have been chosen. Moreover, "successful therapy" does not mean the child will exhibit 1% or less disfluency in all speaking situations. Rather, treatment has been effective if the child communicates easily whenever and to whomever he or she chooses (Conture & Guitar, 1993).

5. It is logical to assume a plan for therapy will evolve from data collection during the evaluation. However, if the evaluation is conducted to assess solely whether the child qualifies for services, the data available for planning treatment may be incomplete. When this is the case, an assessment and in-depth analysis of certain aspects of the fluency problem may need to be explored in the initial stages of therapy.

6. Therapy is planned according to the constraints on your caseload size, scheduling of therapy, and the amount of parent involvement. Recognize that the best therapy plan may have limited effectiveness if too many constraints are placed on the delivery of services or there is a lack of support from the parents.

7. Once scheduling and service delivery concerns have been minimized, changes in fluency cannot occur unless there is direct management of the problem. This principle requires you to have the knowledge to make decisions about treatment based on data generated from an assessment of factors that contribute to the stuttering behavior. Those factors should be reevaluated periodically during the course of treatment so changes in the program can be made in a timely manner.

8. It is necessary and reasonable to expect the elementary-age child can assume most of the responsibility of changing and managing the stuttering. Each child should learn and display self-corrective behaviors rather than relying on you for all monitoring. In other words, each child in treatment should be an active participant in therapy. (Adapted from Healey & Scott, 1995, p. 152)

The goal of phase I of their treatment program is the understanding of the child who stutters and the nature of the stuttering problem. To learn about the child, you might engage the child in discussions around favorite movies, video games, or sports. Next, determine the degree of the child's awareness of the fluency disorder. To achieve this objective, you might administer the Communication Attitude Test (Brutten, 1984) or engage the child in positive identification activities to determine the language the child uses when talking about talking. Matter-of-fact discussions and modeling of speech behaviors associated with moments of stuttering helps establish the necessary level of awareness for further speech change.

Phase II of treatment involves the implementation of specific fluency-enhancing and stuttering modification procedures. Healey and Scott reported on a variety of strategies to develop fluency, among which are manipulations in linguistic complexity, speech rate reductions, airflow control, gentle onsets of phonation, and light articulatory contacts. With older school-age children who stutter, stuttering modification strategies may be incorporated in treatment plans. Learning to stutter easily, implementation of cancellations, and voluntary stuttering are three techniques outlined in this particular program.

Phase III of treatment encompasses the transfer and maintenance of skills learned in therapy to environments other than the speech therapy room (e.g., classroom, home, and social community). Incorporation of peers into therapy and using the many different speaking situations of the school environment are samples of the ways children are prepared to transfer their newly learned fluency skills. Healey and Scott also incorporate various fluency disruptions into therapy to prepare the student for real-life speaking. These disruptions may include speaking under time pressure, speaking with a teacher, answering questions, or making a phone call. These speaking tasks are carefully planned prior to implementation to provide maximal success for the child. The use of semantic maps facilitates the problem-solving process between you and the student when planning transfer and maintenance activities.

William Leith

Leith (1984) described an integrated approach to working with children who stutter in the school environment. His treatment approach treats both the stuttering and stutterer through behavior and cognitive methods. With strong foundations in operant conditioning principles, Leith teaches four strategies to help the child eliminate stuttering: (1) slower rate of speech, (2) attending to oral cues or enunciation, (3) easy onset of vocalization, and (4) smooth flow of speech. Together these four aspects of speech are referred to as **REEF**. Additionally, the **glide** is taught to help the child terminate blocks. Leith defines the glide as "the purposeful voluntary movement of the articulators from the initial sound of the word to the intermediate vowel. . . . We are asking the stutterer to think of the rest of the word and to move his articulators into the position of the next vowel" (p. 46). This slow shift from one sound to another reinforces a smooth transition and the forward flow of speech. For older children, Leith may use the DAF device to provide an opportunity for the child to experience a slowed speech rate with exaggerated enunciation.

A second major component of Leith's approach to school-age stuttering involves the cognitive aspects of the disorder. The child's **cognitive set,** defined as the child's view of himself, his stuttering, and the beliefs, attitudes, and feelings experienced when stuttering, are a series of learned behaviors in response to stuttering. Specific factors may influence the development of the cognitive set, such as listener reactions, failure in self-improvement of speech, failure in therapy, and grief. Leith proposed that as the child experiences continued failure and negative reactions to stuttering, he begins to doubt himself and the therapeutic process. To influence this set positively, communicate the hope of change and motivate the child in this direction throughout therapy.

Peter Ramig and Ellen Bennett

Ramig and Bennett (1995, 1997a) presented several ideas for working with 7- to 12-year-old children who stutter. They recommend an integrated approach to therapy to include both the shaping of fluency and modification of stuttering, as well as addressing the negative attitudes toward communication common to this age group. Along with Ham (1990), Ramig and Bennett view therapy along a fluency continuum with speaking manner on one end and fear reduction and symptom control on the other. The tasks actually conducted in therapy depend on the profile of the child at that particular point in time. The rationale for such flexibility is based on the heterogeneity of the disorder and its variable manifestation based on the individual's daily speaking experiences. Within this integrated framework, therapy focuses on utilizing concrete tasks to assist the child in understanding the speaking process and how he interferes with this process through stuttering. During this process of discovery, you might address episodes of teasing and how to respond when teased, as well as negative thinking present in the child's cognitive schemata. They classify thoughts into two groups: 'stinkin' thinkin' (thoughts that hurt) and 'friendly thinkin' (thoughts that help). "Working together to reword these thoughts and providing guided practice in catching, identifying, and changing the child's thoughts is imperative to the successful use of positive self-talk strategies" (Ramig & Bennett, 1995, p. 144).

Within the school setting, Ramig and Bennett address the need to group children who stutter together, particularly during the early stages of therapy. As speech fluency is established or modification strategies become more automatic, incorporation into other groups is appropriate. However, they do recognize the difficulty present when attempting to schedule large caseloads into the therapist's weekly agenda. As a possible alternative, they discuss the possibility of flexible scheduling, the use of fluency specialists, and implementation of mini-camps as means of providing support for school-age children who stutter.

THERAPY MATERIALS AND RESOURCES

Clinicians have access to a wide range of therapy materials that are useful when planning therapy for children with communication disorders. However, the majority of these materials are geared toward the domains of articulation and language.

Little exists in the area of fluency disorders. The following materials specifically address this population and may prove helpful when planning individualized therapy activities.

Easy Does It–1 and 2

Easy Does It—1 (Heinze & Johnson, 1985) is a fluency-shaping program for the preschool through second-grade child. This program provides general activities from which systematic therapy can be developed. It consists of five phases: (1) experiencing fluency, (2) establishing fluency, (3) desensitizing to fluency disrupters, (4) transferring fluency, and (5) maintaining fluency. Home activities are included at each phase of therapy. Easy Does It—2 (Heinze & Johnson, 1987) approaches therapy in an eclectic way combining both stuttering modification and fluency-shaping principles for the age group of 7 through 13. Preparing for fluency, distinguishing fluency from stuttering, establishing fluency, desensitizing to fluency disrupters, transferring fluency, and maintaining fluency comprise the six phases of this program. Attitudes toward speech and teaching the student responsibility for his improvement are inherent in the philosophy of this second program.

Fluency at Your Fingertips

Fluency at Your Fingertips (Ridge & Ray, 1991) is a manual of resource lists clinicians may use when selecting stimuli for therapy sessions with the older elementary-age child who reads. Arranged according to thematic topics (sports, shopping, going to a restaurant, school interactions, going places, and interactions with family and friends), these lists are organized according to the level of linguistic complexity involved and degree of emotionality embedded in the topic. Although not a programmed approach to therapy, the implied therapy orientation is typical of a fluency-shaping program with direct attention to building a tolerance to fluency disruptions. For the therapist working in the school setting, time management is a critical issue. This manual is a useful resource of stimuli that can be accessed easily and quickly.

Fun with Fluency

Walton and Wallace (1998) have succeeded in compiling a series of therapy ideas for working with younger children who stutter from age 2.5 to 7 years. Their manual describes a direct approach to therapy in an easy-to-read format. Topics included in this manual are (1) scheduling of therapy sessions, (2) differential diagnosis, (3) planning and implementing of direct therapy strategies, (4) monitoring of progress, (5) transfer and long-term maintenance, and (6) counseling of children on dealing with their feelings about stuttering. Walton and Wallace use case studies to illustrate how to create conceptually based activities even the preschool child can understand. There are numerous reproducible resources that may be selected for use with the younger school-age child who stutters.

Working Effectively with Attitudes and Emotions

Chmela and Reardon (2001) developed a useful manual providing numerous practical therapy activities to address the affective and cognitive components of stuttering.
The authors state the goal of therapy should be the achievement of balance between
"feeling good about talking, stuttering, and oneself and being able to understand and
use speech modification techniques in order to become an effective communicator"
(p. iv). They acknowledge the variability present in children who stutter and stress
three factors to consider regarding feelings and beliefs around stuttering: (1) The
amount and type of stuttering may not be directly related to the presence of negative
feelings and beliefs, (2) children and families vary in the way they think or view stuttering, and (3) children vary in their ability to understand and talk about their feelings
and beliefs (pp. 2–3). This workbook provides numerous assessment and therapy tools
designed to guide the clinician when working with the school-age child who stutters.
It is an affordable resource all speech pathologists should include in their library.

One example of the appropriateness of the materials available in this manuscript is the adaptation of Faber and Mazlish's (1980) framework for validating and
praising children in a positive manner. Chmela and Reardon demonstrate with several case examples how to establish an environment allowing children to express
their negative feelings subsequent to stuttering episodes. To validate the child's feelings, the first step is to listen actively and acknowledge the child's comments with
a word, such as with minimal encouragers: "mm," "really," or "oh." Next, reflect the
child's message back to him periodically with a confirmation statement, such as "So
what you are saying is . . . " You may also probe for more information by using the
cloze technique of open-ended sentences ("And you don't like talking because . . . ").
Labeling the feeling with a word may be used if you believe you have enough information to conjecture what the student must have felt in the particular speaking situation, such as "That must feel frustrating." The last step is to validate the emotion
with a comment reflecting the acceptance of emotion, such as "It's okay to feel frustrated." The process of validating the child's feeling around talking and stuttering
does not always flow in a sequential, step-by-step way. Chmela and Reardon acknowledge the need to reflect and probe thoroughly before you are ready to label
and validate the child's emotion.

Another crucial skill you need to develop to assist children with their attitudes
and emotion involves the use of praise. Chmela and Reardon have adapted Faber and
Mazlish's definitions of evaluative and encouraging praise to children who stutter.
Evaluative praise infers some degree of value judgment on your behalf. Terms such
as *great, wonderful, terrific*, and *super* appropriately reflect the performance of the
individual as evaluated by the listener, a technique that speech pathologists often use.
However, overuse of evaluative praise fosters dependence on others. The use of **encouraging praise** helps the child develop self-motivation and establishes the skills
for self-monitoring. Encouraging praise includes an observation about the child's behavior followed by a statement about how that behavior makes you feel. The process
of encouraging praise involves three steps. First, make an observation using phrases
such as "I see you are . . . " or "I was noticing . . . " Next, share how the observation

makes you feel through comments such as "I feel proud when you assert yourself." Lastly, sum it up with a word or phrase: "You are learning speech assertiveness."

Related Sources

Several organizations work on behalf of the consumer to improve the quality of services provided for people who stutter, for example, the National Stuttering Association (NSA) and the Stuttering Foundation of America (SFA). The NSA provides brochures, books, and posters to speech pathologists. This consumer-driven organization has a long history of effort and engagement with the profession to help bridge the gap between the consumer and service provider. It holds an annual conference as well as workshops for people interested in stuttering, including children, parents, adults, and clinicians.

The SFA is a nonprofit organization that produces numerous videotapes and informational materials to help clinicians better understand the therapy process. Their flyers, books, posters, and videotapes are excellent resources for clinicians around the world. Additionally, the SFA sponsors workshops for therapists wishing to learn more about stuttering. Ranging from a 2-day inservice training to a 2-week intensive specialization workshop, the foundation is committed to providing continuing education opportunities for school-based therapists.

CHAPTER SUMMARY

School-age children who stutter often present a variety of the ABCs of stuttering. Some continue to spiral down the stuttering cycle with an increase in emotional reactions to speech breakdowns. Others, despite maintenance of their behavioral patterns of stuttering, continue to exhibit minimal affective or cognitive reactions. With age and lack of success at speech change, these children begin to exhibit consistent stuttering behaviors with high reactions. A subgroup of children who stutter develop covert means of hiding their stuttering, often appearing to have highly variable stuttering behaviors. You must learn to recognize how the disorder is developing in each child as he enters and passes through the elementary school years.

Issues related to this age group pertain to certain federal regulations put into force through the IDEA '97 legislative act. Certain guidelines and procedures must be complied with when providing speech therapy services in the school environment. The goal of IDEA '97 is to legislate proper testing and placement in appropriate educational settings to ensure academic success. You must be able to document how stuttering impacts each student's performance in the regular education curriculum and develop educationally relevant goals and benchmarks. Once these have been developed and students are enrolled in speech therapy, you face the challenge of scheduling and grouping these students. Working within the constraints of the school system, you can consider implementing innovative programs to augment ongoing therapy. Finally, working with teachers through teacher inservice programs can enhance the effectiveness of the services provided to CWS.

The chapter ended with a discussion of several current treatment programs, materials, and resources. Depending on the student's individual ABC profile, you may choose from several fluency-shaping, stuttering modification, or integrated therapy paradigms to help the student achieve his goals and objectives. Several consumer organizations have developed useful, cost-efficient materials that can be incorporated into therapy plans to help both the student and clinician work together for therapy success. Working with school-age children who stutter is an exciting, dynamic process because stuttering manifests itself in so many different ways in this age group. Chapter 9 presents a conceptual model of intervention specifically designed for use with 7- to 12-year-old children who stutter.

STUDY QUESTIONS

1. How does the behavioral component of stuttering change for the school-age child?

2. To what might you attribute the student's increase in affective and cognitive reactions to stuttering during the elementary years?

3. Describe how the phenomenon of spontaneous recovery relates to enrollment issues for the school-age child beginning to stutter.

4. Provide an example of an educationally relevant goal for a sixth grader with severe stuttering.

5. What service delivery options are available for school-age children who stutter?

6. In what ways might the school therapist involve the teacher in the therapy process?

7. Describe a scenario in which a school district contracts with a fluency specialist.

8. Compare and contrast two treatment approaches for the school-age child.

9. What resources are available for the school clinician wishing to learn more about stuttering disorders?

The House That Jack Built
A Conceptual Model of Integrated Therapy for the School-Age Child

CHAPTER OUTLINE

Voluntary Stuttering
Advertising
Implementing Strategies
The ABCs of Feelings

Stage 4: Maintaining the Roof of Fluency
Relapse
Choice Making
Maintenance

LEARNER OBJECTIVES

- Design a treatment plan based on the child's profile of skills.

- Implement an integrated approach to the treatment of stuttering in children.

- Differentiate between the four stages of therapy covered in the "House That Jack Built."

- Select appropriate activities designed to teach children about the normal speaking process.

- Assist children in the process of selecting fluency-shaping and stuttering modification strategies useful for their independent stuttering profiles.

- Have knowledge of various activities designed to support children who stutter express their feelings about stuttering.

- Identify factors that contribute to relapse.

- Create maintenance plans for children who stutter.

KEY TERMS

advertising
bouncing
cancellations
choice making
deep breath
easy onsets
ERA—SM
fluency-initiating gesture
fluency report card

loudness control
maintenance
negative practice
phonatory adjustment
pseudostuttering
preparatory sets
pullouts
relapse
relaxation exercises

slow speech
smooth speech
smooth transitions
stretching
syllable stress
triads
vocal track adjustment
voluntary stuttering

For some school-age children who have developed an awareness of communication difficulties, a direct approach that combines fluency-shaping and stuttering modification procedures may be appropriate. The House That Jack Built (Bennett-Mancha, 1992) addresses the child's attitudes, feelings, and speech behaviors surrounding the disorder of stuttering. Designed with the idea of building a house of fluency, this model can assist both you (the clinician) and the child in understanding the therapy process and its direction. This model is a practical way of approaching fluency intervention in the school setting. It consists of four stages of intervention, very similar to Van Riper's therapy paradigm: laying the foundation of knowledge (identification); installing the plumbing (desensitization); building rooms of speech modification (modification); and maintaining the roof of fluency (stabilization). Each stage is described in this chapter, and activities are provided, with objective and procedure as well as sample dialogue, to demonstrate implementation of specific goals. Using this framework, you are now ready to help the child who stutters build a house of fluency. Let us begin by laying the foundation of knowledge as we would the concrete foundation of a house.

STAGE 1: LAYING THE FOUNDATION OF KNOWLEDGE

The beginning of therapy involves many creative experiences for you and the student. Once rapport has been established, you form a unified team searching for the answer to the puzzle of stuttering. The initial goal of therapy is for the student to learn about the normal speaking process and how his stuttering interferes with this process. Williams (1979) believed it is necessary to "direct the stutterer's attention from what he evaluates is happening to him and toward (a) those things he is doing that interfere with talking and (b) those things he is doing to facilitate it" (p. 254).

Teaching the child to replace the inferential subjective terms he uses when talking with objective descriptions helps him develop the "language of responsibility" needed for lasting change. The student needs a core set of terms he will use throughout therapy to describe talking and stuttering. Do not assume students already have this vocabulary just because they stutter. If the goal is for students to be able to identify, categorize, and change their moments of stuttering, they need the vocabulary to describe specifically what is happening in their mouths, minds, and hearts. The goals for stage 1 of therapy are to (1) establish a set of working terms, (2) demystify the disorder of stuttering, (3) dissolve the conspiracy of silence around stuttering, and (4) get stuttering out in the open.

The activities described here help build a strong foundation for the student's house of fluency as he learns about the normal speaking process and how his stuttering interferes with it. Underlying these activities is this philosophy: "The more you read, the more you know. The more you know, the smarter you grow. The smarter you grow, the stronger your voice when speaking your mind or making your choice. The more you know, the further you go." Knowledge empowers the child to make informed choices.

Normal Speaking Process

Being able to explain how speech is produced, discuss the systems used to produce speech, and how "speech helpers" work together to make different sounds is essential knowledge the child who stutters will use later when he attempts to identify moments of stuttering. Scott-Trautman (1998) described Williams's five normal talking processes and how children disrupt these processes through stuttering. Her presentation of Williams's ideas provides a practical framework when initiating therapy at this stage.

Williams's Normal Talking Model

Here is a list of Williams's five normal talking processes. The statements in parentheses indicate what stutterers do to disrupt these processes and how that might be changed.

1. Air from the lungs causes the vocal folds to vibrate. (Breath holding or stopping air before the voice is turned on.)
2. The vocal folds need to vibrate when airflow is started. (Lack of voicing onset, abrupt onsets, letting air escape without voicing. Practice using easy onset of phonation and continuous phonation patterns.)
3. Proper tensing is necessary for normal speech. (Too much tension causes breakdowns in respiration, phonation, and articulation.)
4. Proper timing between the speech systems is necessary for normal speech. (Attempts to start voice without air or moving the articulators before voicing is started. Practice continuous phonation and slow movements of the articulators from one sound to the next.)
5. Sounds are moved with smooth movements between sounds and words. (Tense postures or difficulty making transitions between sounds causes repetitions and prolongations of articulatory movement. Reduce tension associated with articulatory placement and use light articulatory contacts between sounds.)

Quesal (2002) and Quesal and Yaruss (2000) further modified Williams's therapy approach based on the ideas that (1) children need to determine which actions they do create fluency and focus on the fluency versus the stuttering; (2) when stuttering occurs, they are "doing" some behavior that interferes with fluency; (3) they can modify their behaviors to create fluency; (4) the child must become an expert on how he talks; and (5) the goal of therapy is to "become the most effective speaker one is capable of becoming" (p. 1). The following activities teach children who stutter about the talking process as described by Williams, Quesal, Scott-Trautman, and Yaruss.

ACTIVITY 1: SPEECH PIZZA

Objective: Children will understand part to whole relationships related to speaking.

Procedures: Most children like and can relate to making and eating pizza, and the activity stimulates discussions away from the topic of stuttering. It provides a similar thought process and organization for the upcoming discussion about the normal speaking process and provides a memorable experience that children can reflect on later.

Step 1: In the group, initiate a conversation about pizza and what each student likes. Stress the individual differences and choices students can make. Ask if anyone in the group has ever made a pizza from scratch. If so, have them describe the process. Ask the group if they would like to make a personal pizza all by themselves.

Step 2: Gather the materials you will need to make the pizzas (toaster oven, oven mitts, foil, cooling rack, refrigerated biscuits, pizza sauce, shredded cheese, miscellaneous toppings, napkins, plates, utensils).

Step 3: Pass out a piece of foil for each student equivalent to the size of a folded napkin. Give each student a biscuit and demonstrate how to thin it out and shape it into either a rectangle or circle. Place it on the foil. Next spoon on the pizza sauce, remembering not to get it too close to the edge of the crust. Sprinkle cheese and add individual toppings (chop these into small pieces in order to fit). Put the pizzas on the baking pan from the toaster oven and bake at 350°F for 8 to 10 minutes.

Step 4: While the pizza is cooking, write down the ingredients used in this activity on the chalkboard or a large piece of butcher paper. The students describe the steps they took to make their pizza.

Step 5: Let the pizza cool before eating it.

Step 6: Discuss how making a pizza is similar to making speech. We need ingredients and materials used in a systematic order. Discuss what would happen if you attempted to make a pizza without some of the ingredients or out of sequence.

Homework Assignment: Students draw a picture of their pizza experience at home and share it with their parent(s).

Additional Activities: An extension of the pizza analogy is to have the students make a construction paper pizza and hang it in the therapy room (see Figure 9.1). Also, the company called Treats makes a game with pizza pieces. Children can pick an object to put on their pizza while producing easy onsets or light articulatory contacts.

ACTIVITY 2: SPEECH HELPER MAN

Objective: Children will point to and label the major physiological mechanisms they use when talking.

Procedures: This activity reinforces the concept that people make choices throughout the day.

Step 1: Using white butcher paper, trace each child's upper torso, arms, and head with a pencil.

Step 2: Children outline their bodies; give them the choice of using crayons, colored pencils, or markers.

Figure 9.1
Paper plate pizzas.

Step 3: Children draw and label the identified body parts needed to make speech. Remember to use the correct terminology during this activity. The voice box is really the larynx with the vocal folds inside. Dialogue during this step might sound like this:

Clinician:	"John, what do you use to talk?"
John:	"Oh, my tongue."
Clinician:	"Right, we use our tongue to talk. Pick the color you would like to use to draw your tongue."
Alex:	"I use my lips sometimes."
John:	"We have to use our lips to talk."
Clinician:	"We do need our lips to talk. As we will discover, some sounds really need the lips and others don't. What color do you want to use for the lips?"
Tosha:	"What about the air? Where does that come from?"
Alex:	"From the lungs right about here" (pointing to the middle of his chest).

ACTIVITY 3: RECIPE FOR GOOD SPEECH

Objective: Children will outline the steps taken to produce speech from inspiration to articulation.

Procedure: Refer back to the steps used to make a pizza and generate a similar list for steps used to make speech. We have a recipe for good speech just as we have a recipe for good pizza. Stress the sequential order necessary for speech production and what happens during respiration, phonation, and articulation.

Step 1:   Engage the students in a discussion about the steps they took to make a pizza, stressing how important it was to go in sequence. Tie in this analogy with the speech production process. Dialogue for this activity might sound like this:

Clinician:	"Who can remember the first step in making our pizzas?"
Alex:	"We made the crust."
Clinician:	"Right. Now what might be the first step in making speech?"
Tosha:	"We have to breathe."
Clinician:	"We inhale air that fills up the lungs. Then . . . (waits for the students to contribute).
Tosha:	"We have to let the air out and it goes through our voice box."
Clinician:	"That's right. The air leaves the lungs and travels up the trachea and through the larynx that holds the vocal folds."

Step 2:   Ask students to compare and contrast making speech with making a pizza. The purpose of this step is to have the students play around with the terminology and feel more comfortable using the new vocabulary in a familiar context. You will need small balloons to demonstrate vocal fold vibration.

Clinician:	Talking as if to herself, "Well, I wonder what on our pizza looks like the tongue? Maybe the pepperoni or maybe the bell pepper. What do you think, Alex?"
Alex:	"Definitely the pepperoni."
John:	"I think my tongue looks like the bell pepper because it's long and I don't like pepperoni."
Clinician:	"That's what is wonderful about each of us being different people. We like and want different things. Let's take a look at the real vocal folds and see what on our pizza resembles them." (Using a neuroanatomy text, students view the structures of the larynx and find the reference to the vocal folds.)
Alex:	"You mean those things are in my throat? They look like white string."
Clinician:	"Hm, white string. They are stretchy, like rubber bands. We have two of them that come together to vibrate. Kinda like

> when you play around with a balloon that is blown up and slowly let the air out squeezing the mouth. I think I have some balloons somewhere. Do you want to try this? (Children experiment with the balloons.)
>
> Alex: "Wow, that's cool. I think the cheese looks like vocal folds 'cause you can stretch it thin and it's white."

Homework Assignment: Have the student draw a mini-man at home labeling the speech helpers and share it with someone. There are several published forms that can be copied and inserted into the speech folder for those children who need more structuring with their home assignments.

An additional activity to reinforce the speech helpers might be Pin the Helper on the Man, similar to Pin the Tail on the Donkey. You can introduce humor into this game, making fun of how speech would change if the mouth was on the arm. Such absurdity creates a relaxed environment where mistakes are okay. For the upper elementary student, use of the Internet to access information and video clips detailing the functioning of the larynx can be highly useful. Speech pathology texts can be used as a resource as well as obtaining a model of the larynx from a local college. The Speech Helper Game, published in *Learning About Our Speech Helpers* (Jackson & Robbins, 1990) is another way of reinforcing these concepts. This book provides visual aids you can copy and use to create numerous game activities that reinforce how speech is made.

ACTIVITY 4: BUILDING THE LUNGS

Objective: Children will understand and explain the role of inhalation and exhalation in speech production.

Procedure: Each student builds a model of the lungs using the following materials: clear plastic cup, half a drinking straw, one small rubber band, clay, one large and one small balloon, and scissors. Explain to the group the functions of the air stream, lungs, and diaphragm while you assemble this model (see Figure 9.2).

Step 1: Cut a hole in the bottom of the cup approximately the width of the straw. Turn the cup upside down.

Step 2: Insert the straw into the hole, making sure the portion inside the cup is an inch shorter than the rim. Seal the area around the opening with your clay to create an airtight seal.

Step 3: Take the small balloon and tightly attach it with a rubber band to the straw inside the cup. This creates the lung.

Step 4: Cut off the lip of the big balloon. Stretch the body of the balloon across the rim of the cup (which is now the bottom). This creates the diaphragm.

Figure 9.2
Model of the lungs.

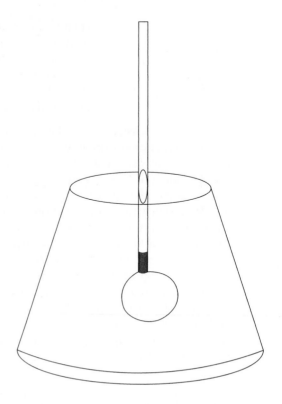

Step 5: Demonstrate that if you pull down on the big balloon (diaphragm), the small balloon (the lungs) expands as air flows through the straw (inhalation). When it is released, the balloon shrinks as air exits the straw (exhalation).

Another activity children enjoy is called the Egg Carton Game, which can be modified in any number of ways for work on all types of speech disorders. This activity provides opportunities for the students to interact with the new vocabulary of the speech helpers, that is, the speech production process.

ACTIVITY 5: EGG CARTON GAME

Objective: Children will use the vocabulary of speech production while playing games.

Procedure: Gather materials needed for this activity: egg carton, strip of construction paper the length and width of the lid of the carton (divided into 12 sections), any object for hiding, and pictures of the speech helpers reduced in size to fit each square on the egg carton strip (see Figure 9.3).

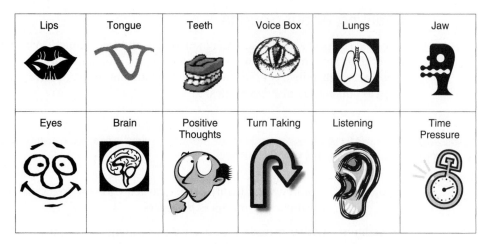

Lips	Tongue	Teeth	Voice Box	Lungs	Jaw
Eyes	Brain	Positive Thoughts	Turn Taking	Listening	Time Pressure

Figure 9.3
The egg carton strip. A fun activity for reviewing the normal speaking process and factors that disrupt this process.

Step 1: Students make the egg carton strip. Take the piece of construction paper and divide it into 12 sections, each centering on one of the portions of the egg carton. The student trims a picture of a speech helper so it fits on a square and pastes it in place. Continue until all 12 squares are filled with different terms or pictures on them. Dialogue during this activity might sound like this:

> Clinician: "Pick a speech helper, John. Where do you want to put it on the strip?"
> John: "Oh, I want the brain. I'll put it here."
> Clinician: "Alex, your turn."
> Alex: "I'll take the lips and glue them next to the brain."
> Clinician: "Yes, we have to have the lips. The lips are used a lot."
> Joe: "I want the air."
> Jessie: "The vocal folds go here."

Step 2: Upon completion of the strip, tape it to the lid of the egg carton. (Laminate these strips so the materials last longer.)

Step 3: Tell the students you will hide an object in one of the egg slots. They will take turns guessing where you put the object. Dialogue might sound like this:

> Joe: "Is the eraser under the brain?"
> Clinician: "No, the eraser is not under the brain. John's turn."
> John: "Is the eraser under the lungs?"
> Clinician: "No, the eraser is not under the lungs. Alex's turn."
> Alex: "Is the eraser under the vocal folds?"
> Clinician: "Yes, the eraser is under the vocal folds. Now you can hide the eraser."

Learning About Sounds

The next series of activities are designed to help children connect information learned about their speech helpers with the sounds of English. In this discovery process, you guide rather than instruct the student. Let the student problem-solve, cuing and modeling as you engage in the activities.

ACTIVITY 6: SOUND GRAB BAG

Objective: Children will identify place of articulation for English sounds using the vocabulary of the speech helpers.

Procedures: Gather materials needed for this activity: paper sack or cloth bag, magnetic letters of the alphabet, pens, and paper. As you put the letters into the bag, identify the sound the letter makes while modeling slow, even-paced speech and body movements. You might say, "The letter *M* goes 'mmmm' (stretching the sound). The letter *P* goes 'puh.'" Remember to model light articulatory contacts.

Step 1: Pick a letter out of the bag. Make the sound and try to determine the main speech helper. "I got a *P* and it makes the sound 'puh.' My lips come together for that sound."

Step 2: Write the letter symbol on the speech helper checklist (Figure 9.4) and check off what students identified as the main speech helper.

Step 3: Upon completion of all the letters, look at the checklist and problem-solve the similarities and differences. "Wow, there are a lot of sounds that we use our tongue for. We have to use the brain and lungs for every sound."

As you play this game, review what sounds the speech helper makes. Pretend you are talking to yourself as you review, and do not ask the students any questions. This is a time to accept what they say unconditionally in whatever manner they say it. You might make comments such as "The lips are used for the *P, B,* and *M* sounds. Okay, I got it."

ACTIVITY 7: STRETCHY/BOUNCY FOLDER

Objective: Children will identify manner of production (stops versus continuants) for English sounds using the terminology of bouncy and stretchy sounds.

Procedure: Gather the materials needed for this activity: manila folder, different-colored ribbons, pinto beans or Cheerios, glue, and markers. Have the child glue strips of ribbon or glue Cheerios on each side of the folder as you discuss how some sounds you can stretch naturally while others you start-stop quickly.

Speech Helper Checklist					
Speech Sound	Lips 	Tongue 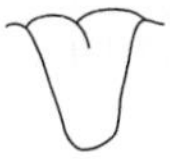	Teeth 	Voice 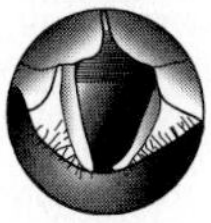	Lungs 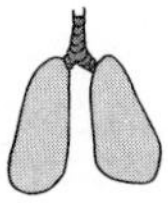

Figure 9.4
A useful checklist to help children identify the appropriate speech helper used when producing sounds.

Step 1: Introduce the concept of stretching and bouncing in general. Students select ribbons. Then cut the ribbon any length. Glue or staple the ribbon to
one side of the board. Dialogue might sound like this:

Clinician: "We're going to make a stretchy/bouncy board."
Rosa: "What's that?"
Clinician: "Some of our sounds are really easy to stretch. We can make
them long, long, long. Or we can make them short. Let's try
stretching the *s* sound. (As you model, hold the ribbon between two fingers, pulling the ribbon through them.) "See
how long we can make that sound? Rosa, what color ribbon
do you want to put on your board?"
Rosa: "I want this pink one."
Clinician: "How long do you want it? About this long or more?"
Rosa: "Right there." (You cut the ribbon.)
Clinician: "Which ribbon do you want next?" (Continue until five to six
ribbons are attached to one side of the folder. Keep in mind
that you want these to vary in length. You can also use a ruler
for a 1-inch stretch, 3-inch stretch, or a foot stretch.)

Step 2: Ask the children what they think goes on the other side. They decide how
many beans they want to put in each row. Remember to vary the number
of beans per row.

Clinician: "What do you think goes on the other side?"
Angel: "The beans. How are we going to do that?"
Clinician: "We will have to glue them in place. Let's make a row of beans
right here. How many do you want, Angel?"
Angel: "I don't know. Six, maybe."
Clinician: "Sounds good to me. Let's put six drops of glue and you put
one bean on each drop. We will have to let this dry before we
move it around."
Rosa: "My turn. I want four."
Clinician: "Good. Where do you want to put your four?" (Continue until
you have five to six rows of beans. As the glue dries, take out
the magnetic letters. Each child picks one and problem-solves
whether it is easy to bounce or stretch. Some sounds can be
categorized either way. However, keep in mind that it is up to
the children to decide what category they think it belongs.
Have them focus on the feeling in their mouths as they attempt
to stretch the sound. There are no right or wrong responses.)

Step 3: Once the board has dried, children practice **stretching** and **bouncing**
with different lengths. For the ribbon, use of tactile cues can facilitate understanding of when to start or stop the sound. As you move your finger
over the ribbon or pull it between your finger, make the sound. When the
ribbon runs out, you stop. For the bounces, children produce the sound

each time they touch one of the beans in the row. For example, if there are six beans in a row, the child would produce the /b/ sound six times: "buh, buh, buh, buh, buh, buh." Dialogue might sound like this:

Clinician:	"Let's practice feeling the difference between stretching and bouncing with our speech. Pick a ribbon and a letter and start stretching as you move it through your finger. Rosa?"
Rosa:	"Like this. /s--------/" (as she pulls the ribbon through her fingers).
Clinician:	"That's right. How did that feel in your mouth?"
Rosa:	"Okay, but I almost ran out of air."
Angel:	"My turn. I want to do a bounce: /m m m m me."
Clinician:	"Wow, you bounced six times on the /m/ sound. How was it? Easy, hard, or just okay?"
Angel:	"Okay, I guess."

Homework Assignment: Children collect objects that feel smooth and bumpy and bring them to speech for the next session. There are no speech production requirements at this time. During the follow-up session, practice sharing objects within the group setting. Have the children practice sliding and bouncing like they did with the ribbon and bean folder. If children are able to demonstrate these easy disfluencies during the session, they may choose to show Mom or Dad the different ways of talking on follow-up home assignments.

ACTIVITY 8: MOTOR ON—MOTOR OFF

Objective:	Children will identify the voicing component of speech production (voiced vs. unvoiced features) for English sounds using the terminology of turning your speech motor on or off.
Procedure:	Gather the materials needed for this activity: yellow, red, and green construction paper, glue, and paper. Each child cuts out a red and green circle, placing it on a strip of yellow paper cut in the shape of a traffic signal. Next, they make another signal and place only the green circle on the yellow paper. Using the analogy of red means "stop" and greens means "go," children sort sounds into the appropriate category based on its voicing feature.
Step 1:	Introduce the concept of traffic lights and the meanings behind red and green lights. Tell the students they will make two traffic lights, one for "on" and one for "off." Dialogue might sound like this:

Clinician:	"How many of you have seen this (holds up a picture of a traffic light) on the streets?"
Roger:	"I see them all the time."
Clinician:	"What does the color red tell you to do?"

Roger:	"Stop. Don't run the red light or you'll get a ticket."
Clinician:	"You are right. Red means to stop, don't move. What does green mean?"
Jessica:	"Go. You can keep on going."
Clinician:	"Right. Green means go and red means stop. When we make sounds, we start and stop our speech in a very special way. Can you think of how we start and stop with our speech?"
Roger:	"We start to talk and stop talking."
Clinician:	"Absolutely. Remember our vocal folds and what happens as air passes over them? Sometimes we make them move or "turn on the motor" and sometimes we "turn off the motor." Who can think of a sound we have to turn our motor on to say?
Jessica:	"What about the /m/ sound?"
Clinician:	"Let's check it out. Put your fingers on your voice box and says the sound /m/. What do you feel?"
Roger:	"I feel something moving."
Jessica:	"Me too."

Continue with this activity as the children discover which sounds are voiced and which are voiceless. Have them place the letters in two piles below the traffic signal with the red or green light. You can elaborate on the role of voicing when stuttering happens and how important it is for the children to become friends with their speech buddies.

ACTIVITY 9: SPEECH PUZZLE

Objective:	Children will provide the place, manner, and voicing characteristics of each sound.
Procedure:	Gather materials needed for this activity: large piece of white construction paper, markers, and paper (Figure 9.5). This activity reviews all three aspects of sound production. Introduce the lesson as putting the pieces together to understand how speech is made.
Step 1:	Set out a large piece of construction paper or butcher paper. Children choose a letter and write it on the paper. Dialogue might sound like this:

Clinician:	"Today we are going to review how speech sounds are made. Who can tell me a speech helper used when talking?"
Alan:	"The tongue and lips."
Clinician:	"Right. We use our lip and tongue to talk. What else do we use?"
Nancy:	"Our vocal folds, too."
Clinician:	"You guys really remember your speech helpers! Now who can remember the different types of sounds we can make?"
Nancy:	"Stretchy and bouncy sounds."
Alan:	"Noisy and quiet sounds."

Speech Features of Sounds			
Sound	Place	Manner	Voice: Motor On—Motor Off
B	lips	stop and go	on
W	lips	stretchy	on

Figure 9.5
Worksheet for helping children identify the features of speech sounds.

Deborah:	"We make sounds in the front of our mouth."
Clinician:	"Very good. Let's make a sound puzzle with all the sounds we use when we talk. Who wants to write the first letter on our puzzle?"

(Continue in a similar fashion until all sounds are represented. Next, cut the paper into puzzle shapes and put them in a paper bag.)

Clinician:	"Let's put our speech back together. When you pick a puzzle piece, I want you to tell me where the sound is made (place), how it is made (manner), and if your motor is on or off (voicing). Who wants to record this information on the chart?"
Nancy:	"I'll write it down. I have good handwriting."
Clinician:	"Thank you for volunteering. You are a good helper. Let's start. Alan, you go first."
Alan:	"I got the /w/. Gee, this sound is made with my lips and it's a stretchy sound. (Putting his fingers on his Adam's apple) My motor is on."
Clinician:	"Super job! Nancy, did you get that on the chart? Who's next?"

Interference Process

After children who stutter understand the normal speaking process, they are prepared to venture into discussions about what happens when normal speaking does not occur, that is, the interference process. Using Williams's talking model, you can demonstrate how stuttering can disrupt each stage of speech production. The goal of the following activities is to assist children in learning how they interfere with the normal speaking process through stuttering. Discussions begin by addressing the role of tension and fragmentation in speech and gradually merge into the arena of stuttering behaviors. These talks should address stuttering in general terms, not specifically related to the speech behaviors of any particular child. It is appropriate to present the S cycle to the group, educating the students on the affective, behavioral, and cognitive components of the disorder. Keep in mind that these activities are "touching the hot potato" and some children may resist, indicating a lack of readiness to address their stuttering. Presentation on the topic of stuttering should be short, brief, and general, providing terms to describe behaviors. As the children demonstrate comfort with this information, you may probe further into each child's own stuttering pattern.

ACTIVITY 10: SPEECH BREAKS

Objective:	Children will define and identify the core stuttering behaviors of sound/syllable repetitions, prolongations, and tense pauses or blocks.
Procedure:	Gather materials needed for this activity: different-colored construction paper cut into 1-inch squares, manila folders, pictures, glue, and symbols

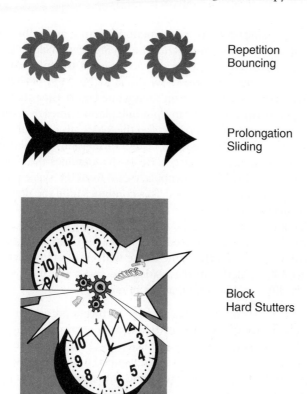

Repetition
Bouncing

Figure 9.6
Core stuttering behaviors.

Prolongation
Sliding

Block
Hard Stutters

of core stuttering behaviors printed on self-adhesive labels (see Figure 9.6). The following steps provide a guide for teaching this goal:

Step 1: Open the discussion with a review of the normal speaking process. Ask students if they know what happens when this process does not work. Use Conture's (2001) analogy of a garden hose to help students understand the relationship between tension and smooth flowing speech. When the garden hose has a kink, pressure builds until the knot is released, resulting in a sudden burst of water from the hose. This is equivalent to a block, one of the core stuttering behaviors. If tension is reduced slightly, water may begin to trickle out of the hose (i.e., a prolongation). Pressure that fluctuates may represent repetitions.

Step 2: Students create a representation of repetitions, prolongations, and blocks. The children share their pictures with the group and hang them on the walls of the therapy room.

Step 3: Introduce your picture representations and explain they will be used in a series of game activities students will make to use in therapy and at home. Model each behavior and then ask students to identify what type of speech break they are making. Continue until all students have a firm grasp at identifying these three behaviors.

Step 4: Pass out the manila folders, construction squares, and adhesive pictures for repetitions, prolongations, and blocks. Students make a game board, gluing the construction squares on the inside of the manila folder in the typical start-to-finish pattern. Allow the students to select whatever colored squares they wish to use on their game board. Glue these in place.

Step 5: Students peel apart the labels and put one picture on each colored square. As the students are putting the labels on the folder, talk about the procedures for playing the game. Each student takes a turn rolling the dice and moving the appropriate number of spaces. He or she identifies the type of speech break to make and selects a vocabulary card from the stack, producing the word in the manner you modeled. This continues until the first player lands on the finish line. You can begin to fade your model as students become more proficient at producing different types of stuttering behaviors.

Step 6: As a home assignment, each student makes a list of 20 words to use when playing this game. Send the game home with written instructions for the parent to follow. At the next session, talk about the child's experience practicing different speech breaks at home.

You can make any number of games using these picture representations. Students particularly like to create their own Bingo boards, checkerboard games, memory match cards, and Uno cards using these stickers. The process of making the game gives you an opportunity to model the behaviors students need to learn. Use specific terms when describing the student's productions during these games. A sample dialogue might sound like this:

Clinician: "Becky, it's your turn to roll the dice."

Becky: "I got a six (counts out the number of spaces). I landed on the arrow."

Clinician: "Pick a card and see what word you will prolong, or stretch."

Becky: "Sunshine. S———unshine."

Clinician: "I heard you stretch the first sound /s/ and then you finished the word. Good looking at me during that prolongation. Oden, it's your turn."

Oden: "I got two (counts out two spaces). Block. I'll block on the word book. . . . Book."

Clinician: "Oden, that was a good block. I saw your lips come together. You were pressing them together really hard and holding your air. Then you exploded and finished the word. Great job."

Describing stuttering in objective terms helps demystify the disorder. You model how to talk about what the child is doing with the speech mechanism to create the stutter. Modeling objectivity teaches children how to reflect on their own speech using concrete terms. You then ask the student to describe his speech breaks and gradually have him describe his own speech behavior during these game activities. An important reminder: Do not spend a lot of time discussing each student's productions. This is an introductory lesson and students may react negatively to the directness of the task. Keep the focus on the game, not necessarily on the speech breaks. As students become more at ease with this exercise, exchange the term *speech break* with *stuttering* while monitoring nonverbal signs of discomfort.

ACTIVITY 11: THINGS TO KNOW ABOUT STUTTERING

Objective: Child will list 10 interesting points about the disorder of stuttering.

Procedure: Gather materials required for this activity: books about stuttering, Internet resources, pencils, and paper. Open the discussion by writing the word *stuttering* on a piece of paper. Ask the students what this word means. Write down all their responses. This often leads into other questions about stuttering. You can show the students how to answer their questions using the resources available to them. Generate a list of information they learned during this lesson. Sample dialogue might sound like this:

Clinician: (As you write the word *stuttering* on the paper) "Who knows what this word means?"

Eddie: "It means you can't talk right."

Clinician: "Let's write that on the paper. Stuttering means you can't talk right. What else does stuttering mean?"

Robert: "It's when the words get stuck in my throat."

Clinician: "Stuttering is when the words get stuck in your throat."

Jose: "Stuttering is saying words hard."

Clinician: "For Jose, stuttering is when words are hard. It's interesting that this word means something different for each one of you. There is no right or wrong answer when defining stuttering. Let's see if we can find more definitions for stuttering in these books I brought to class today."

ACTIVITY 12: FAMOUS PEOPLE WHO STUTTER

Objective: Children will name famous people who stutter. (The goal of this activity is to demonstrate that stuttering does not have to keep children from achieving their dreams.)

Procedure: Gather materials needed for this activity: books written by authors who stutter, flyers from the Stuttering Foundation of America, posters from the National Stuttering Association, newspaper clippings about famous people who stutter, and Internet resources. As children read about stuttering, they may come across a reference to a famous person who stutters. Inquiries into this area are critical for some children who have lost a sense of direction because of their stuttering. You can demonstrate,

Table 9.1
Twenty probes to use for student reflection on issues that arise in therapy.

1. Stuttering is . . .
2. If they know I stutter, . . .
3. Stuttering keeps me from . . .
4. One thing that confuses me about stuttering is . . .
5. A situation that is hard for me to talk in is . . .
6. I was teased about my speech one day when . . .
7. Sometimes my stuttering makes me feel . . .
8. When I stutter in front of a friend, I . . .
9. Sometimes I avoid talking by not doing something such as . . .
10. I am responsible for the way I talk because . . .
11. I wish my parents would . . .
12. Practicing my speech tools is like practicing sports because . . .
13. It may be helpful to share by stuttering with a teacher when . . .
14. I like/don't like coming to speech therapy because . . .
15. It is important for me to use "friendly thinking" because . . .
16. If I could trade my stuttering for another problem I would take . . .
17. The best/worst part of stuttering is . . .
18. I like the way I talk because . . .
19. If I didn't stutter, things would be different and I would . . .
20. I am taking charge of my speech when I . . .

through their stories, how stuttering did not stop these individuals from achieving great things. This opens up the door for discussions on choice making and a discussion of Charles Van Riper's quote on page 344.

ACTIVITY 13: THOUGHT FOR THE WEEK

Objective: Children will reflect, in writing, on key themes involving the topic of stuttering.

Procedure: Gather materials needed for this activity: paper, pens/pencils, and references. This activity provides an opportunity for the student to reflect on some aspect of stuttering that has surfaced in therapy. It might include writing at the top of the paper a statement such as "Stuttering is . . ." and sending it home for the student to complete. Or it might involve an issue directly relevant to the child's history, such as "When I change my words, . . . " or "Having difficulty saying my name means . . . " When the student returns to therapy, this assignment is discussed and placed in the client's portfolio for documentation purposes. Table 9.1 provides a list of possible probes used with the older school-age child who stutters. Figure 9.7 provides an example of a student's response to the probe "What is stuttering?"

Thought of the Week

What is stuttering? . . .

1. It is not my fault.
2. When I repeat sounds or change my words.
3. Something I do when I get stuck.
4. I don't like it!

Figure 9.7
An example of a student's response to the probe "What is stuttering?"

Work done during stage 1 establishes a knowledge base to understand the problem of stuttering. Children need to know how speech is made, what stuttering is, how it is manifested in speech, and how others have dealt with having this disorder. Sharing this information with others, such as parents, teachers, and peers, is essential to breaking down the wall of silence and shame often seen in people who stutter. Students sharing with students empowers them to take charge of their speech and builds their confidence. Building a foundation of knowledge instills a sense of hope for future speech change.

STAGE 2: INSTALLING THE PLUMBING

Stage 2 of therapy involves tasks that assist clients in identifying their moments of stuttering or clogs, as it were. The plumbing is analogous to the speech mechanism, and children attempt to locate the clog in their pipes through purposeful exploration activities. Discussion surrounds topics such as what happens to the house of fluency when you get a clog in the plumbing or a crack in the pipes. If the clog or crack is not repaired, the damage will get worse with time and the repair job will cost more and be more extensive, possibly damaging the foundation. The goals of stage 2 are to (1) continue the desensitization process, (2) begin to identify and categorize moments of stuttering, and (3) establish the concept of "changing one's speech."

The process of achieving these goals include documenting moments of stuttering in a journal or daily log. Establishing a written diary of stuttering helps the child become more aware of stuttering patterns and faulty habits. As children begin to pay attention to their speech, you may initiate activities in which they experiment and manipulate speech through **pseudostuttering**, also called **voluntary stuttering**, that requires children to confront stuttering by doing what they are trying so hard to avoid, thus desensitizing them to the stuttering.

A voluntary stutter consists of a brief sound/syllable repetition or prolongation that is tension free and within the client's control. At times, when children are inserting voluntary stutters into their speech, this voluntary act can turn real or become involuntary. Be sure to recognize this and reward the child's courage when this happens. You can use the analogy of coca-cola, which advertises it is the "real thing." Using an empty Coke can, reward real stutters with a token (pinto bean) to put in the can. When the can is full, the group will have earned a Coke party. Emphasize the bravery of the children in facing their stuttering and taking charge.

As stuttering emerges in their speech, children must practice tension modification tasks in order to develop the precursor skills needed for certain speech modification tools, such as cancellations and pullouts. You can teach children to modify tension in the speech mechanism through negative practice drills. Gregory (2003) describes negative practice as first having clients say the word "just the way you ordinarily would." Next, they repeat the word, reducing tension by 50%. Emphasis is on feeling the difference in the speech mechanism, so clients should be instructed to say both speech efforts without any interceding verbalizations. Say the word with 100% tension; then repeat it with 50%, focusing on the feelings of reduced muscular tension in the lips, tongue, larynx, and jaw.

Another activity that reinforces the variability in speech and the concept that speech can be changed is Dell's (1979) "hard, easy, and regular" contrast practice as described in the Stuttering Foundation of America's booklet *Treating the School Age Stutterer.* The following dialogue from Dell's writings demonstrates the initial introduction of the concept of variability in talking:

Clinician: "Now John, let me talk for a while. We are going to learn about the three ways of saying our words. One way is the regular way. If I was to say a word in the regular way it would sound like this, 'watch' (the clinician points to her watch). Now this is another way I can that word, "wa . . . (the clinician blocks the airflow and struggles a little). Wawawatch'. Whew, that was hard. That is called the hard way of saying a word. This is the third way, 'wwwwatch' (the clinician makes an easy effortless prolongation or repetition). And that was the easy way. Right now you try to say all your words in the regular way but sometimes you get stuck. Saying words in that easy way isn't so bad. Whenever we get stuck on a word instead of saying it in the hard way we are going to learn to do it in that new easy way. Kids that learn to stutter in that easy way don't get stuck so much and later they tell me that more and more of their words start coming out in the regular way. All that's hard to understand right now, but we will practice it." (pp. 64-65)

Try the following activities to achieve the goals just described. Monitor signs of discomfort during these tasks and acknowledge the difficulty inherent in dissecting stuttering. As a general rule of thumb, talk about disfluency should begin in a general fashion, not directly to the child and his particular patterns of stuttering. As observations are made of others' speech, such as on the television and in the school, you can help students classify and describe these episodes objectively. This models for the children how to describe moments of stuttering using descriptive language, for example, "Her lips are squeezed together and she hesitated a minute."

The following steps are a tentative hierarchy of objectives with the intention of teaching children how to catalog their stuttering: (1) Child will label the core stuttering behaviors in the speech of the clinician (repetitions, prolongations, blocks); (2) child will label the loci of core stuttering behavior (using speech helper terms) when stuttering is modeled by the clinician; (3) child will identify type and loci of core stuttering behavior in the speech of other individuals; and (4) child will identify the type of stuttering that occurs in his speech pattern.

ACTIVITY 14: DAILY LOG

Objective: Children will keep a journal of episodes of stuttering.

Procedure: Gather materials for this activity: small spiral notebook, instructions for the construction of journal entries, sample entries, and pens/pencils. Keeping a journal provides an opportunity for the student to think about speech at the end of the day and reflect on both positive and negative experiences. The child can write information on specific situations when stuttering occurred, as well as when the child actively implemented speech modification tools (see Table 9.2). The following is a modification used during the early stages of intervention:

Step 1: Designate a specific time each day to write a small entry in the journal.
Step 2: Select several speech experiences to reflect on in the entry.

Table 9.2
Identification practice worksheet.

Situation	Affective	Behavioral	Cognitive
1/25: Read two sentences in Spanish.	relieved, strong	used easy onsets, relaxed!	That I can do this if I just try!
1/27: Read to my dad.	stressed, frustrated	vocal folds weren't on, very tense	Maybe if I just slow down
1/27: Stuck on *went*.	frustrated, angry, anxious	vocal folds! Lips and mouth formed; head jerked	Why am I in a total block? What's going on?
2/2: Went out to eat, ordered.	felt okay, relieved, embarrassed at first	vocal folds faltered at first, little tense	Glad I didn't hide my stuttering
2/5: Bad stuttering day.	stressed, tired	not in the best of moods, tensed up my vocal folds	Why isn't anything working?

Step 3: Include the following information in your entry: note the date, describe the situation, describe your speech, identify the fluency and stuttering present, and note how you felt about the experience.

Step 4: Bring your journal to speech therapy every session.

ACTIVITY 15: SOMETIMES YOU STUTTER, SOMETIMES YOU DON'T

Objective: Children will understand the variability characteristic of stuttering disorders.

Procedure: Gather materials required for this activity: journal, butcher paper, and pens/pencils. As students write in their journals, point out the variability of situations in which they are fluent or nonfluent. Often both you and the child who stutters will focus too much on the stuttered portion of the child's speech. However, the child typically has more fluency than stuttering. Tape a long piece of butcher paper on the wall and divide it into two columns. On one side, write "Sometimes You Stutter" and on the other write "Sometimes You Don't." Have the children make a list of people, places, and times when they are fluent and not fluent. As a home assignment, students write comments related to their fluency in their journals. Discuss these journal entries at the next session.

ACTIVITY 16: EASY-HARD SITUATIONS

Objective: Children will list speaking situations and rank them according to level of speech difficulty.

Procedure: Gather materials required for this activity: easy-hard inventory (Table 9.3), paper, and pens. As students become more aware of their stuttering, they will be able to identify specific speaking tasks that challenge them. Gathering this information is very important to therapy because you will want to assign practice drills beginning with the least difficult situation. Do not assume you know what is easy or hard for the client. As skills are developed, more difficult situations can be targeted. Periodically, redo this inventory to determine the change in the client's perceptions around these speaking situations.

Step 1: Talk about the specific situations listed in the child's journal in which stuttering was present.

Table 9.3
This checklist provides a means for obtaining information on a child's situational hierarchy of easy-to-difficult situations or speech tasks.

Easy-Hard Checklist					
Name: _____ **Date:** _____					
	Real Easy	Not so Easy	Hard	Real Hard	Target Areas
Talking to my parents					
Talking to my friends					
Talking about stuttering					
Feeling relaxed when talking					
Introducing myself to people					
Talking to a stranger					
Ordering in restaurants					
Talking on the telephone					
Talking in front of a group					
Reading in front of a group					
Talking to teachers					
Talking without being afraid of sounds					
Talking without changing words					
Raising my hand to answer questions in a group					
Talking without being embarrassed					
Looking at people when I talk					
Feeling good about myself when I talk					

Source: Modified version of an original worksheet by J. Westbrook, unpublished document. Reprinted with permission.

Step 2: Together with the child make a list of speaking situations in general (or use Table 9.3). The child ranks each situation according to the perceived level of difficulty: 1 is "real easy" and 5, "most difficult."

Step 3: Rearrange the speaking situations so they now form a hierarchy from easy to difficult. Use this information when planning therapy assignments.

ACTIVITY 17: PRESSURE POINTS

Objective: Children will produce different types of stuttering using each of the speech helpers.

Procedure: Gather materials for this activity: paper bag, speech helper pictures/words cut apart and folded into little pieces, paper, and pencils. This activity will assist children in identifying the loci of stuttering. Each child picks a piece of paper (speech helpers) from the paper sack and says a word, "getting stuck" on that speech helper. Sample dialogue might sound like this:

Clinician: "In this bag I have little pieces of paper with the words of our speech helpers on them. As we pick a paper from the sack, I am going to show you how to "get stuck," or stutter, with that speech helper. Watch Johnny pick from the bag."

Johnny: "I got the lips."

Clinician: "Let's see, what is a word that starts with a lip sound? *Man.* Watch me as I squeeze my lips together. (Clinician blocks on the word . . . man.) "Wow. I was really pushing my lips together hard. I had a block on that word. Let me write down this new word on the paper."

Susie: "My turn. I got the tongue."

Clinician: "Look at the list we made a few weeks ago. What is a sound that uses the tongue?"

Juan: "The /t/ and /k/ sounds are tongue sounds."

Clinician: "Right. What word starts with a /t/ sound?"

Johnny: "*Tongue* does!"

Clinician: "Okay. I am going to repeat the /t/ sound as I say *tongue*. Watch. /t/ /t/ /t/ tongue. I repeated it three times before I finished the word. When you repeat a sound it is called a *repetition* or I call it a *bounce,* like a basketball does (makes the hand gesture as if dribbling a ball). We can also stretch a sound, called a *prolongation*. Who can name a 'stretchy' sound?"

Juan: "What about the /s/ sound? You can make that really long."

Clinician: "Absolutely, I will make that sound long. s---------ong. I stretched the /s/ sound on the word *song*. Stretching is called making a prolongation. So on our paper I have written three types of stuttering—blocks, repetitions, and prolongations. Let's practice doing different types of stuttering with our speech helpers. Who wants to go next?"

ACTIVITY 18: HARD, NOT SO HARD

Objective: Children will adjust tension in the speech mechanism during purposeful speech tasks.

Procedure: Gather materials for this activity: pencil, paper, and picture cards. Draw a line down the center of the paper and write at the top of each column "Hard" and "Not So Hard." This negative practice activity allows students to modify tension in the speech mechanism when stuttering on purpose. Following Gregory's guidelines presented earlier, sample dialogue might sound like this:

Clinician: "Today, we are going to practice cutting our stuttering in half. As you move along the game board, you will say the word you land on with full force, 100% energy. Without saying anything else, repeat the word with half the energy, 50%. Remember to focus on the feeling in your mouth while you modify the tension. When we reduce tension, we increase the likelihood of being fluent. Let's try one. (You roll the dice and move your marker accordingly. You land on a space with the word *team*.) I will say *team* hard and then not quite so hard. T t t t (tense repetitions) team. Tuh tuh team" (less tense repetitions). You then reflect back to the students: "With the first one, I was pushing my tongue up against the bump behind my teeth and I felt a lot of tension in my jaw. On the second one, I still repeated but my jaw and tongue were not as tight. Johnny, it's your turn."

ACTIVITY 19: HARD-EASY-REGULAR SPEECH

Objective: Children will identify and produce hard, easy, and regular speech.

Procedure: Gather materials needed for this activity: 30 picture cards, color dots, three index cards, and markers (see Figure 9.8). Together as a group, students decide how each word will be produced, placing the predetermined colored dot on the back of the picture card. Sample dialogue might sound like this:

Clinician: "We've been talking about different ways of talking. We can talk in the regular way, the hard way, or the easy way. Today, we are going to make a game to practice these three ways speech can be made. First, what color do you want for the 'regular' speech?"

Brian: "How about the green ones?"

Clinician: "Sure, let's put green stickers on the back of 10 cards." (As students select the card, you model saying the word using regular speech. *No* production requirements are made of the students.) "What color do you want for the hard speech?"

Jackie: "Purple, my favorite color."

Clinician: "Purple is good for hard speech. Let's get 10 pictures and put purple dots on the back. Jesse, what color do you want for easy speech?"

Figure 9.8
Ways of talking.

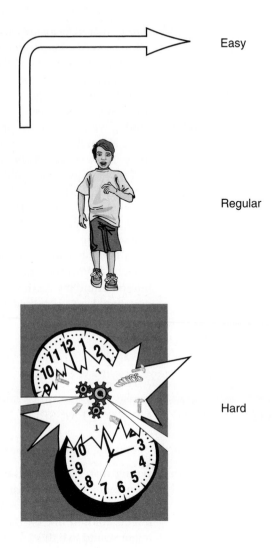

Easy

Regular

Hard

Jesse: "Can I pick yellow?"
Clinician: "Sure. Let's put yellow stickers on the back of the rest of the cards. Jesse, will you write 'easy' on this index card with the yellow marker? Jackie, you write 'hard' with the purple marker. And Brian, you write 'regular' in green."

Once the students create the stimuli, you can begin the therapy activity. To further teach the children, follow a systematic hierarchy to ensure both comprehensive and expressive skills are developed. These might be the objectives for this task: (1) Child will point to the appropriate card when you model either hard, easy, or regular speech;

(2) child imitates easy, hard, or regular speech after the clinician model; (3) child produces easy, hard, or regular speech and you point to the appropriate written word identifying the type of speech produced; and (4) child produces a word and identifies the type of speech used. Sample dialogue sounds like this for each step:

Step 1: Clinician: "Brian, listen to this word and point to the card that says the type of speech I am using. (You say a word in a hard way.) Right, Brian. I say *car* in a hard way so you pointed to purple. Turn the card over and let's see if we were right. (Turns the card over.) Hey, we were right." This continues until all children demonstrate proficiency at identifying your speech.

Step 2: Clinician: "Jackie, pick a card and let's see what color is on the back. (Student picks a card with a green dot.) I will say this word in a regular way and you repeat after me." (You say the word and student repeats it.) "Good job. You said the word *truck* using regular speech just like I did. Jesse, it's your turn. Pick a card . . .)

Step 3: Clinician: "Now I want you to pick a card but don't let me see the color on the back. I am going to try to guess how you say it. Let's see how many I get right. Jesse, pick a card and say the word." (Student picks a card with a yellow dot and says the word in an easy way.) "You said *bus* in an easy way. Yellow. Did I get it right?" (Special note: It is important to tape this activity for times when the student thinks he or she has said a word one way and you disagree. You and the student can listen back to the tape and discuss the bases for your classification.)

Step 4: Clinician: "Now it is your turn to say the words however you want. Let's keep track of the types of speech you use." (Divide a paper into three columns, writing *hard, easy,* and *regular* at the top of each column. Title this paper "Brian's Choices." It is important to stress how students are deciding on their own how they are going to talk. Do not make any suggestions as to which type of speech the students should practice.)

The activities just described are a sampling of desensitization exercises children who stutter can practice to learn more about their stuttering patterns. As they make daily entries in their journals, they identify situations and speech features. In the language of the house of fluency, students identify the type and location of their clogs in preparation for selecting the right type of Drano, or speech modification tool, to implement. With this knowledge, they begin to experiment, or play around, with different types of stuttered speech. Having fun with speech and making choices regarding their speech are two essential principles of stage 2. You may have clients play a Stuttering Trivia game to reinforce information they learned during stage 1 and 2 in therapy (see Figure 9.9).

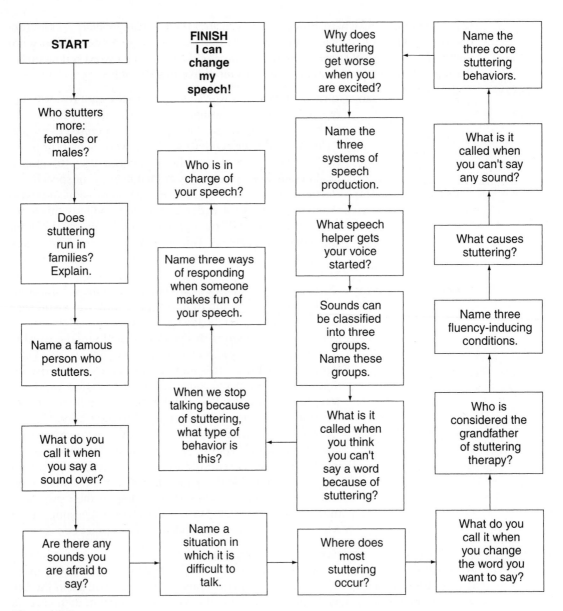

Figure 9.9
Stuttering trivia game.

STAGE 3: BUILDING ROOMS OF SPEECH MODIFICATION

To set the stage for designing the rooms of the house of fluency, introduce Van Riper's famous quote: "We may not always have a choice as to whether or not we will stutter, but we always have a choice as to how we are going to stutter" (unknown reference). Equipped with a toolbox of speech modification strategies, you and the client problem-solve which strategies you will incorporate into future therapy plans (i.e., The House of Fluency). Always remember that each child is different and the same strategies will not always work with everyone. You must individualize the design of the client's house, that is, reinforce the concept of client-dependent treatment plans. No two houses should look the same because no two clients are the same in the affective, behavioral, and cognitive aspects of their stuttering. Figure 9.10 demonstrates the concept of tailoring the house construction to each child's individual needs.

A creative way to conceptualize the house of fluency is to have the students create a shoe box house. Each student selects a shoe box and, using various craft supplies,

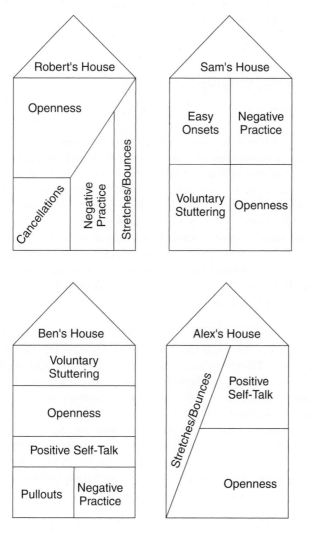

Figure 9.10
Houses of fluency based on individual client profiles.

builds a house out of the box. They label the rooms according to the strategies they have selected for implementation. These houses can be as elaborate (with windows, carpets, curtains, and furniture) or as simple as tongue depressors glued on a poster board in the shape of a house. Each house should look unique.

The goals for stage 3 of therapy are to (1) identify strategies for implementation that meet individual student needs; (2) empower the child through choice making and active involvement in decisions; and (3) practice strategies through drill-like activities to develop automaticity necessary for transfer and maintenance. Achieving these concepts may include the following goals: (1) understand the change process and identify factors that influence the ability to change; (2) learn about teasing and the reaction cycle; (3) learn to recognize and change negative self-talk; (4) utilize voluntary stuttering in everyday situations; (5) develop assertive, nonavoidance habits through advertising; (6) learn, practice, and implement selected strategies; and (7) learn to recognize, accept, and change, when appropriate, the feelings experienced with stuttering. The following topics of discussion will help you achieve the goals for stage 3 of therapy.

Understanding the Change Process

There are five basic tenets of the change process children need to understand. First, children are responsible for their change. No one can make children change the way they speak. It is up to them to assume responsibility for their current speech status. Second, change comes in small steps. Using the analogy of a young toddler learning to walk, the child must first take a few steps and will certainly fall and get back up and try again. Speech change is a gradual process, with small gains that eventually add up to significant change. Third, change is hard, scary, and requires a lot of effort. There are no guarantees the child will receive the desired gains from this effort. Next, change feels strange and different when first learning new skills. Frequently, students comment on "how weird it feels" when trying speech that is so different from their "normal" way of talking. Understand that stuttering feels normal to children who stutter and fluency feels different. Talking about this contrast will help students understand this feeling is typical and will require much practice before fluency feels normal.

Ask the students to write a sentence with their nondominant hand and discuss what they had to do to accomplish this task, that is, increase the focus more on the motor demands, as well as decrease speed and increase purposefulness of hand movements. Help the students discover how imprecise their handwriting appears compared to their usual writing. Point out the amount of attention initially required would decrease as the students continue to write in this manner.

Last, change requires careful thought before starting. Systematically planning tasks, utilizing information gathered prior to this point, ensures greater success in the decision-making process. Spend a large amount of time in problem-solving scenarios and outlining the specific details of the student's behavior before you initiate the actual engagement. If both you and your clients understand the change process and the tenets just presented, achievement of therapy goals will be enhanced.

Teasing and the Reaction Cycle

Children who stutter interact on a daily basis in a social environment that may or may not accept speech differences. As the school-age child gets older, there is greater concern over peer acceptance. There will always be a group of children who take pleasure in tormenting others because of these differences. These bullies who tease others are an unfortunate presence for children who stutter. You can use the Teasing and Bullying Questionnaire for Children Who Stutter—Revised (TBQ-CS) (Langevin, 2002) (Appendix G) to determine if teasing is an issue for a particular client. This instrument elicits information on the presence of teasing, the frequency of teasing episodes, the extent it bothers the person, where teasing occurs, and events that occur during teasing. With insight into the child's perceptions about teasing, you may schedule a specific time to address these concerns. Certainly do not broach the topic of teasing until you establish a strong, trusting client/clinician relationship.

Another alternative is for you to take a proactive versus a reactive stance regarding teasing episodes. Do not wait for your clients to be teased and then address the issue. Be proactive and discuss teasing when there is low emotionality and better reasoning resources available to the students. Routinely plan therapy activities that present possible teasing scenarios for students to problem-solve ways in which they would react or respond. Teasing management involves discussions in the following areas: (1) why people tease, (2) ways we react, (3) consequences of reacting, (4) developing an action plan, and (5) role-playing scenarios.

Why People Tease

Children may not understand why their peers make fun of them. To help them understand, explain that children tease one another usually because they do not feel good about themselves. By teasing someone else, the bully feels better than the other person, which gives him or her a sense of power. The following is a sample dialogue for this discussion:

Clinician:	"Has anyone here ever been teased by someone?"
Judy:	"Yes, I get teased because of my glasses and red hair."
John:	"Ralph always calls me Porky Pig. This gets me so mad."
Clinician:	"Being called a name is hurtful. No one likes to get hurt. Why would Ralph call you that name?"
John:	"Cause he's mean."
Clinician:	"That could be. Usually kids make fun of other kids because they don't like themselves. They don't feel good about themselves. Something bothers them so they want to feel better and, therefore, make fun of you. This makes them feel powerful. Strong. Why would Ralph feel good after teasing you?"

Table 9.4
List of why kids tease and bully.

Kids tease and bully because they:

1. want a reaction
2. want to be cool
3. enjoy it
4. try to get even
5. are jealous of you
6. feel like they're sad
7. like to hear kids cry
8. want to be a big boss
9. want to have power over you
10. want to hide their own things they might get teased about
11. want to prove they're stronger
12. don't feel good about themselves
13. try to look better than the person being teased
14. want to get attention so people will notice them
15. want to control other people . . . and frighten them into doing things

Source: Based on Langevin (2000).

Judy:	"Cause he likes doing it?"
Clinician:	"When he is teasing you, he is not thinking about what is bothering him. Everyone is looking at you not him. Can anyone think of other reasons Ralph would tease John?"

You and your students can continue to list possible reasons for teasing. Remember to put down all the ideas in a nonjudgmental manner. It is important for students to understand that teasing is not about them. It is about the other person as demonstrated in Langevin's (2000) extensive list of reasons why children tease and bully each other (Table 9.4).

Ways We React

Next shift the discussion to a focus on how each child reacts when he or she is teased. Children must learn to take responsibility for their part in the teasing cycle. If children who stutter did not react when teased, it is predicted that children would not tease them about stuttering. When the child reacts to teasing, it is like giving the boxing glove back to the boxer saying, "Hit me again." Sample dialogue might sound like this:

Clinician:	"Remember, there are two parts to the teasing cycle. The first part when the 'teaser' says something mean to you and then there is the 'reaction' part of the cycle. What do you do when someone teases you?"
Judy:	"I start to cry."

Clinician:	"By crying you are reacting to being hurt by that person. When we react to teasing, the bully feels powerful because he has made you feel bad. Doesn't that sound silly? He feels good when you feel bad. Can we change what the bully does?"
John:	"You can tell him to stop."
Clinician:	"Yes, but can you change another person? No. You can only change yourself. You can change the way you react so the bully doesn't feel powerful when he makes fun of you. Let's make a list of all the ways we can respond when being teased."

Consequences of Reacting

The first step in learning not to react is knowing when you are reacting. Once children can identify when they are reacting, they can begin to calm themselves, examine what is happening, and make informed decisions to take care of themselves. After a list of ways to respond has been generated, you and the students can evaluate the consequences of each reaction in relation to advantages, disadvantages, or interesting points (no impact). The following activity demonstrates this problem-solving task.

ACTIVITY 20: PLUSES–MINUSES–INTERESTING POINTS (PMI)

Objective:	Children will evaluate consequences of reacting to teasing.
Procedure:	On a piece of paper, make three columns, writing Pluses, Minuses, and Interesting Points at the top of each column. Students select one of the ways to respond to teasing listed in Activity 19. Write down the positive by-products of responding in this manner. Then write the negative results for this response mode. At times, there may not be any clear positive or negative classification, and these reactions can go under interesting points (see Figure 9.11). Sample dialogue might sound like this:
Clinician:	"Last week, we made a list of all the ways we could react when someone makes fun of our speech. Who can remember one way of reacting?"
Kelly:	"Punch the person."
Raul:	"Walk away."
Zach:	"Tell them to shut up."
Clinician:	"There are many ways we can react when teased. When teased, remember we have to take care of ourselves. So today, let's see what will happen to us when we react in certain ways. Kelly, you said you could punch the person who teased you. How will this help you?"
Kelly:	"I'll hurt him because I'm strong."

Figure 9.11
Problem solving in action.

Clinician:	"So a positive result of punching him is that you will hurt him. Let me write this down under the 'Plus' section on the paper. Now, what would be a minus or negative consequence for punching him?"
Kelly:	"I would get sent to the office and my mom would be called."
Clinician:	"Let me write that down under 'Minus.' Sent to office, mom called." (Continue in the same manner, cataloging consequences for each reaction pattern provided by the students.)

Developing an Action Plan

Langevin (2000), from the Institute for Stuttering Treatment and Research, developed a comprehensive program for the prevention and management of teasing and bullying. Part of coping with teasing is understanding similarities and differences among each other, as well as having an effective strategy to respond when caught in the middle of a teasing event. Entitled "I Can Speak Up," Langevin outlined a five-step procedure to use when responding to teasing. The following activity implements this action plan.

ACTIVITY 21: "I CAN SPEAK UP!"

| Objective: | Children will learn and utilize a positive response strategy when teased. |
| Procedure: | After the group has listed possible responses to teasing and identified possible consequences, present another alternative response pattern |

or plan of action. The introduction to this lesson might sound like this: "Today we are going to learn one more strategy that you can use to handle teasing, bullying, and other kinds of conflicts. Sometimes students want to say something to a person who is bullying but are scared or don't know what to say. It's important to speak up for ourselves, and it's important to do it in a way that is not going to make the situation worse. Speaking up helps us feel better about ourselves, feel more confident, and maintain our power. It lets students who bully know we aren't going to let them get away with what they are doing. Rather than getting even, or suffering in silence, we can speak up for ourselves and say five things": (1) say the person's name: Steven . . . ; (2) tell how you feel: I feel angry . . . ; (3) tell why (describe the behavior): when you call me names; (4) be respectful: Please . . . ; and (5) tell what you want: stop the name calling (pp. 83–84). Students can trace their hand on a piece of paper and write each component on a finger. Writing how they would respond is important because it provides them an opportunity to distance themselves from the injury and reflect on how they felt when teased. Using this five-finger response, students then role-play scenarios in which they have been teased.

Students are also instructed to remember certain key points that will improve the effectiveness of this strategy. These include (1) watch your body language, making sure it is not threatening; (2) stand straight with your hands at your side; (3) don't threaten the other person's space by getting too close; (4) look at the person you are talking to; (5) speak with a clear, polite voice; and (6) if possible, discuss your problem privately (p. 87). *The Teasing and Bullying (TAB) Program* (Langevin, 2000) incorporates several excellent worksheets and additional activities for building self-esteem, developing positive self-talk, and resolving conflicts. The worksheets are easy to follow with examples to guide clinicians. Teasing is an inevitable event for all school-age children, especially if they have a behavior that does not conform to the norm, such as stuttering. Be prepared to address teasing and help children who stutter resolve such conflicts in a positive, self-assertive way.

Role-Play Scenarios

With an action plan in place, students need multiple opportunities to implement this plan when emotions are not high. You can create mock situations in which students assume the role of the person teasing and the person being teased. Utilizing information learned from the previous activities, role-play a teasing scenario and then discuss the perspectives from both sides. Videotaping these sessions is particularly helpful so students can observe and analyze their body language as well as their verbal language to determine overall effectiveness and areas that need continued practice. Two rules must be in place before engaging in teasing role plays. First, students must not make any reference to the other child's family, such as calling the person's mother a name. Second, no foul language can be used during these interactions. The following activities are examples of proactive teasing experiences.

ACTIVITY 22: THE GAUNTLET

Objective: Children will respond appropriately to teasing during role-play activities around the topic of stuttering.

Procedure: Gather all your students in a large, open area. Remember, if you are working in the public schools, children who have articulation and language difficulties also experience teasing and will require the same teasing management strategies. Divide the group into two teams. Line them up facing each other. A volunteer walks down the middle while students on each side tease him. He is to respond with the various strategies outlined previously (the bad look, ignoring, positive verbal comebacks such as "So I stutter," etc.). When he reaches the end of the line, the next person "walks the gauntlet." This continues until all students have participated. Now you can open a discussion about how the students felt and what they were thinking while being teased.

ACTIVITY 23: POP THE BALLOON

Objective: Children will engage in a fun activity to vent feelings they experience when teased about stuttering.

Procedure: Gather materials needed for this activity: balloons, permanent markers, and two chairs. This is a large-group activity similar to The Gauntlet, which involves any child who has been teased in some way. During a discussion about teasing and reacting when teased, ask the students to visualize the face of someone who teased them in the past. Next, they draw that face on a blown-up balloon using the permanent marker (see Figure 9.12). Divide the group into two teams, lining them up at one end of the cafeteria. Place two chairs against the opposite wall. Instruct the students to run to the chair, place their balloon on the chair, and sit on the balloon to pop it. They then run back to their line and the next person takes his turn. The first team to fin-

Figure 9.12
Balloon pops: A
great way to handle
teasing.

ish popping their balloons is the winner. Gather the group together and talk about their experience, emphasizing having fun with teasing strategies.

Positive Self-Talk

Another room in the child's house of fluency could be a room for positive self-talk. The cognitive aspect of stuttering is just as important as the behavioral and affective components. What the child says to himself before, during, and after moments of stuttering will certainly influence the progression of the disorder either positively or negatively. The child who exhibits a pattern of negative, self-defeating thoughts will need to set aside a room in his house to address this behavior.

As noted in chapter 6, the child must first be able to recognize when he is "talking in his head" and make note of these thoughts. Just like cataloging moments of stuttering, the child engages in tasks to gather "thoughts" and write them in his daily log.

You can display a visual representation of positive self-talk in the therapy room to remind clients of the importance of their thoughts (see Figure 9.13). Next, you can help the client analyze these thoughts into either friendly thinkin' or stinkin' thinkin' (see Figure 9.14). Together, you can then take the negative thoughts and classify them according to the type of cognitive distortion being used (Table 9.5).

Figure 9.13
Visual therapy reminders for positive thinking.

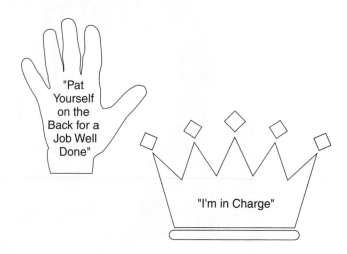

Figure 9.14
A worksheet to use to guide children with identifying the types of thoughts they have about stuttering and communication.

From here, clients can practice reframing their thoughts to be more positive and reflective of reality. The Changing Thoughts Worksheet (Table 9.6) is useful for demonstrating how to change stinkin' thinkin'. You may observe certain recurring terms appear in the child's thought patterns, such as *can't*, *should*, or *would've*. The following activity will help create an awareness of the impact of negative vocabulary.

Table 9.5
Ten common cognitive distortions with examples applied to stuttering.

Type of Thinking	Definition	Speech-Related Example
All-or-nothing thinking	You see things in black-or-white categories	"I've got to do a perfect job on my oral report."
Overgeneralization	You see a single negative event as a never-ending pattern of defeat by using words such as *always* or *never* when you think about it.	"I never can say my name fluently."
Mental filter	You pick out a single negative detail and dwell on it exclusively, so your vision of all of reality becomes darkened, like the drop of ink that discolors a beaker of water.	"I just couldn't stop thinking about the way I sounded when I couldn't say my name. The rest of the evening I avoided talking."
Discounting the positive	You reject positive experiences by insisting they "don't count."	"I can't believe I stuttered. I was right at the end of my presentation and all of a sudden I couldn't get a word out."
Jumping to conclusions	You interpret things negatively when there are no facts to support your conclusions. Mind-reading: Without checking it out, you arbitrarily conclude that someone is reacting negatively to you. Fortune-telling: You predict that things will turn out badly.	"If I tell them I stutter, they will think I am stupid." (Mind-reading) "I'll probably stutter. My mind will go blank and I won't be able to say it." (Fortune-telling)
Magnification	You exaggerate the importance of your problems and shortcomings, or you minimize the importance of desirable qualities.	"This stuttering is terrible. I just can't deal with it anymore!"
Emotional reasoning	You assume that your negative emotions necessarily reflect the way things really are.	"I feel like an idiot when I stutter."
"Should statements"	You tell yourself that things should be the way you hoped or expected them to be.	"I should be able to talk like everyone else."
Labeling	Labeling is an extreme form of all-or-nothing thinking. You identify your shortcomings with a label.	"I can't believe I stuttered when I asked her out. I am such a loser."
Personalization and blame	You blame yourself for something you weren't entirely responsible for, or you blame other people and overlook ways that your own attitudes and behavior might contribute to a problem.	"I try hard not to stutter because it makes people uncomfortable listening to me."

Source: Based on Burns (1989).

Table 9.6
A worksheet designed to help children identify negative thought patterns, the triggers associated with them, and how to change these thoughts in a positive direction.

Changing Thoughts Worksheet		
Column A: Identify what you are saying to yourself when you feel angry or shameful.		
Column B: Write down the kind of trigger thoughts you were using.		
Column C: Rewrite the original statement so that it no longer contains a distorted thought.		

Column A	Column B	Column C

ACTIVITY 24:   POINTS TO PONDER

Objective: Children will explain how certain words impose limitations on their ability to change.

Procedure: Gather materials needed for this activity: construction paper, tape, markers, or butcher paper. When reviewing the student's journal or when the student uses self-limiting terms, write it on the paper under the title "Points to Ponder." Use these comments to reflect on periodically. Keep this list on the therapy wall and add to it throughout the year (Table 9.7). Sample dialogue might sound like this:

Clinician: "Mark, I just heard you say you *can't* keep from changing your words. What type of thinking would this be?"

Table 9.7
Statements used to engage children in discussions about self-limiting thought processes.

Consider this:
    The "CAN'Ts" never will.

Consider this:
    Win the Battle—Lose the War

Consider this:
    What I think of you is none of your business;
    What you think of me is none of my business;
    What I think of me is most important!

Consider this:
    To change I must "know" what to change and take the time to "think" about it.

Consider this:
    Saying it doesn't make it true.

Mark:	"I guess you could say it would be stinkin' thinkin'."
Clinician:	"In what way is this comment not helpful to you?"
Mark:	"The *can't* part, I guess. That's not really what I meant."
Clinician:	"What did you really mean?"
Mark:	"Sometimes I just can't stop it."
Clinician:	"Are you saying that you "*can't*" (stressed) stop? Let's look at our list. What did we learn about the can't? The *can'ts* never will. Is there another way of saying what you mean?"
Mark:	"Well, I can stop but it's hard."
Clinician:	"Right, trying to 'stop avoiding' is hard work. But can you do it? Yes. You are working on it right now and you are learning how to stop. See how you changed a stinkin' thought into one that gives you hope and possibilities?"

Voluntary Stuttering

Voluntary stuttering was previously discussed as a form of assertive nonavoidance. Children advertise the fact they stutter by inserting easy repetitions and short prolongations into their speech. These are purposeful, noticeable moments of stuttering produced without struggle or tension (see Figures 9.15 and 9.16). The rationale for using voluntary stuttering is to desensitize the person who stutters to reactions, self-generated or through the listener. Much like a vaccination, voluntary stuttering builds up resistance to and tolerance for the moment of stuttering, thus decreasing the emotional reaction often accompanying stuttering. A by-product of voluntary stuttering is an increase in fluency. As the child has success with voluntary stuttering, fluency increases and stuttering decreases. Because the child is not avoiding stuttering, a sense of self-control increases along with the confidence to confront any real stuttering that may surface.

Bounces are divided into two segments: **A to B** and **B to C.** The goal of **A to B** is openness and acceptance of stuttering. This segment is produced with exaggerated oral motor movements that are obvious to the listener. The goal of segment **B to C** is connected speech production with continuous flow of information.

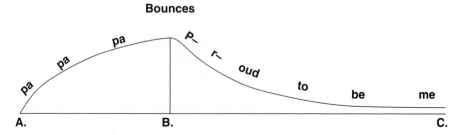

Bounces

The goal of the bounce is to confront stuttering and become desensitized to it. Bounces are syllable repetitions that are produced with an exaggerated beginning, easy initiation of phonation, and no pause between segments. Once the bounce is over, you smoothly transition into the remainder of the word or utterance.

Figure 9.15
Bounces as a form of voluntary stuttering.

When deciding to build a room of voluntary stuttering, guide the child and plan tasks systematically that follow a hierarchy from easy to more difficult situations and people. The child should start with situations/people he perceives as "easy" to advertise stuttering and gradually work toward more difficult situations. Developing proficiency in using easy stuttering is an essential element to successful completion of advertising tasks. Both you and the child should engage in mass practice exercises and role-play scenarios, approximating the selected outside setting prior to actually entering the situation and attempting to advertise the stuttering. Carefully organizing and preparing for these outside assignments increases the probability of success.

Utilizing a *wh* question format can direct the child to consider various aspects that may influence his success when advertising. Determining the who, what, where, when, and how of each exercise provides a structure and a certain degree of predictability for the child who stutters. The following dialogue represents this question framework strategy:

Clinician: "Let's take a look at our house and see where we have been concentrating our work. Ted, it's been a while since you spent time in your advertising room."

Ted: "You're right. I can just tell someone I stutter."

Slides are divided into two segments: **A to B** and **B to C.** The goal of **A to B** is openness and acceptance of stuttering. This segment is produced with exaggerated oral motor movements that are obvious to the listener. The goal of segment **B to C** is connected speech production with continuous flow of information.

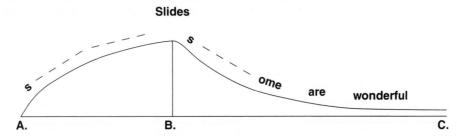

The slide consists of an easy prolongation of the first sound of the word or utterance with a smooth transition into the next word. The goal is to desensitize people who stutter through the insertion of voluntary stutters into their everyday speech.

Figure 9.16
Slides as a form of voluntary stuttering.

Clinician:	"Let's outline the specifics so we know exactly what is going to happen. Think about who, what, where, when, and how questions. First, who do you want to advertise your stuttering?"
Ted:	"Let me think. Uhm. How about my teacher?"
Clinician:	"So you select your teacher. When do you want to advertise?"
Ted:	"Right before going to lunch when we are putting our supplies away."
Clinician:	"Before lunch with your teacher. Now, where will you approach the teacher?"
Ted:	"At her desk. She always waits there for everyone to settle down."
Clinician:	"Before lunch with your teacher at her desk. What do you want to say to her?"
Ted:	"Something about lunch, like what are we having for lunch?"
Clinician:	"Let's write down on this index card the exact words you will say."
Ted:	"Mrs. Smith, do you know what we are having for lunch today?"
Clinician:	"Now, how are you going to say this?"
Ted:	"I'll bounce on *Mrs.* and use a stretch on *lunch*. I'll make the stretch a long one, too."
Clinician:	"Let's summarize. You will go up to your teacher at her desk, just before lunchtime, and show your stuttering twice when you say "M m mrs. Smith. Do you know what we are having for l———unch today? Why don't we practice this? I'll be Mrs. Smith."

Tale of the Three Little Stutterers
and THE BIG BAD BLOCK

Once upon a time, three little stutterers went out into the world to seek their fortune. Now, the first thing each of them had to do was to build a house to keep them safe from the BIG BAD BLOCK.

The first little stutterer met a man carrying a bundle of head jerks, eye blinks, and some umms, ahhs, and you knows. The little stutterer was just settling down nicely, when the BIG BAD BLOCK knocked at his door and said, "Little Stutterer, little stutterer let me in!"

So the little stutterer said, "N-n-n-not b-b-b-by the, you know, hair on m-m-m-my ah, cha-cha-cha-chinny child chin." So the BIG BAD BLOCK huffed and puffed and he blew the house away and that was the end of the first little stutterer.

The second little stutterer built himself a house out of situation avoidances, word, fears, and posing as a fluent speaker. He was watching the telephone ring, when the BIG BAD BLOCK knocked at his door and said, "Little stutterer, little stutterer let me in!"

The second little stutterer said, "Well, no you can't, not even by, you know, the whiskers on my face." So the BIG BAD BLOCK huffed and puffed, and he blew the house away. And that was the end of the second little stutterer.

Now the third little stutterer had met the Great and Powerful SSMP, so he built his house out of advertising, pullouts, prolongations, cancellations, and of course, light contacts.

He had just gotten the higher brain power in place, when the BIG BAD BLOCK knocked at his door and said, "Little stutterer, little stutterer let me in!"

But the third little stutterer advertised, and then said, "Nnnnot bbby the hair on my Chhhinny chin chin."

This made the BIG BAD BLOCK very, very angry, but the third little stutterer just laughed and told a stuttering joke. That really blew the BIG BAD BLOCK's mind. So he huffed and he puffed, and he puffed and huffed, but he could not blow the house away. The house stayed right there, with the third little stutterer safe inside it.

"I shall fix him!" said the BIG BAD BLOCK. "I will sneak down the chimney!" But the third little stutterer had a big pot of negative practice simmering on the fire.

The BIG BAD BLOCK fell right in, and the third little stutterer had the BIG BAD BLOCK for dinner that night.

Figure 9.17
A story written by Dorvan Breitenfeldt (2003) to help young children grasp the concept of being in charge of their stuttering.
Reprinted with permission from D. Breitenfeldt.

Advertising

Advertising, another form of assertive nonavoidance, is defined as the process of actively telling others, either verbally or nonverbally, that you are a person who stutters. The rationale for advertising is to lower speaking anxiety, decrease stuttering, and dis-

Table 9.8
Ten ways in which a child who stutters can advertise stuttering.

1. Wear a T-shirt that makes reference to stuttering.
2. Introduce yourself with the statement "I'm John and I just want to let you know I stutter."
3. Make a comment about working on your speech (e.g., "Today, I have to go to speech class to work on my stuttering").
4. Ask a friend if they know that a famous person stutters.
5. Hand out pamphlets on prevention of stuttering disorders.
6. Write an oral report or conduct a science project about stuttering.
7. Leave materials on top of your desk that make reference to stuttering.
8. Wear the pin from the National Stuttering Association that says, "If you stutter, you're not alone."
9. Hang in your room one of several posters about stuttering from the Stuttering Foundation of America and the National Stuttering Association.
10. Write an article for the school newsletter about stuttering.

solve the conspiracy of silence found with this disorder. By telling people they stutter, children may not suffer the shame that comes from the sudden exposure of stuttering because it is already known. This communicates to the listener a level of self-acceptance. In addition to voluntary stuttering, there are many ways to advertise stuttering. Children can problem-solve ways to advertise both in the school setting and at home. Breitenfeldt (2003a) wrote the *Tale of the Three Little Stutterers and The Big Bad Block*, which is excellent at helping younger children grasp the concept of advertising and voluntary stuttering (Figure 9.17).

Some types of announcements may not require speech production (e.g., wearing a T-shirt with the title NATIONAL STUTTERING ASSOCIATION). Table 9.8 lists several methods of advertising as a form of risk taking. Children should be prepared for possible reactions from others. During therapy, role-play all possible consequences that may occur when you openly confront your stuttering with others. Again, be sure to begin discussions in a general manner, away from the topic of stuttering. The following is an adaptation of Karsten's (1995) activity to initiate conversations around the topic of advertising.

ACTIVITY 25: ADVERTISING ME

Objective: Students will identify the role of advertisements in today's society and generate an advertisement about themselves that identifies personal strengths and attributes.

Procedure: Gather materials needed for this activity: newspaper advertisements, catchy slogans, eye-catching pictures, markers/pens/pencils, paper, glue, scissors, art paper, and magazines. Students look through the magazines, find advertisements that appeal to them, and discuss their reasons for selecting the particular ad. Karsten (1995) suggested children attend to the important aspects of the ads (e.g., the print styles, colors, pictures, and words). Have the group list possible personal attributes that might be included in an ad about a person. Next, direct this activity toward each child, asking him to make a list of personal attributes about himself. Students can make a collage of words, pictures, or phrases cut from magazines that describe them, somewhat similar to a personal ad. Display these advertisements in the therapy room for later reference.

ACTIVITY 26: I'M THE EXPERT

Objective: Children will share information about stuttering with peers and teachers.

Procedure: Murphy (2002) presented a comprehensive outline for in-class presentations given by children who stutter. The rationale for a class visit is to reduce the anxiety, shame, and guilt accompanying stuttering. Class visits will vary in level of abstraction depending on the age of the child. For younger, kindergarten children, topics such as smooth and bumpy or fast and slow would dominate the presentation. The following are the steps you might take when preparing a class visit:

Step 1. Discuss with the child this exercise and move forward only if the child is in agreement.

Step 2. Meet with the classroom teacher to discuss the purpose of the visit and to assess the atmosphere in the classroom. The teacher will be able to tell you if interference is expected from a particular child.

Step 3: Plan the class visit with the child. Decide what the child wants his peers to learn about stuttering, as well as who will do the talking (child or therapist).

Step 4. Develop visual aids and role-play using scripts several times before moving ahead with the actual presentation. The child can give his presentation to another group of children, another teacher, or even a lower grade class before the actual talk.

Murphy (2002) provided a sample guide for third- and fourth-grade class visits that can be modified according to the developmental level of the class. This outline is excellent in its format and organization and has been taken directly from the handout from Murphy's presentation at the National Stuttering Association's annual conference, "Working with School-Age Children Who Stutter: Modifying Negative Feelings and Attitudes and Increasing Self-Esteem."

1. *Introduction.* The speech pathologist introduces herself as the speech teacher and describes her job.
2. *Class participation.* To normalize the concept of receiving speech therapy, ask the children how many of them have been to speech before and what they worked on.

3. *Other speech problems and rationale for coming to the class.* Briefly indicate there are many types of speech difficulties (e.g., pronouncing sounds, using a good voice, learning new words), but today you and the client are going to focus on a problem called stuttering. Let the class know that you and the client want to teach them some interesting things about stuttering, and to educate them, because we all know how important it is to be educated people. If the SLP also stutters, this is a good time to share this information.

4. *Define stuttering and its causation.* Give a brief definition, age appropriate for the class. When speaking to this age level, ask the students if they know what stuttering is and summarize the discussion with explanations such as "Stuttering is a speech problem where some people's speech system doesn't work very well all the time. It doesn't seem to be as coordinated as it should. It gets tripped up or stuck on sounds. We're not sure what causes this but we think maybe some people are just born this way."

5. *Famous people who stutter.* Ask the class if they know anyone famous who stutters. Point out that many famous and successful people have stuttered and then briefly tell them about some of these people. Use some of the posters depicting famous people produced by the Stuttering Foundation of America or the National Stuttering Association as visual aids.

6. *It is no one's fault.* It's very important to stress that no one is responsible for stuttering. People don't stutter because they are dumb or sick. Moms and Dads did not cause it and it's not a disease you can catch.

7. *Different ways to stutter.* Most clients, no matter what degree of speech management skills, can be involved verbally with the class presentation. The clinician and client can demonstrate different forms of stuttering behavior (repetitions, prolongation, and blocks). Ask for volunteers to imitate the various patterns. It can be fun, if done in a friendly manner, having the client grade the attempts of classmates (e.g., A, A−, etc.). The clinician should indicate this type of imitation is for learning purposes only and should not be done at other times. A class discussion should follow in which the children are asked how they would feel and act if they had to talk this way all of the time.

8. *Tools that facilitate smoother speech.* Using the linguistic level at which the child is most comfortable, the clinician and client together demonstrate the speech management techniques the child is trying to incorporate (e.g., pullouts, stretched speech, etc.). It may also be helpful to ask a few of the other children in the class if they can do some of the fluency-enhancing techniques, such as prolonged speech. Here the class may also begin to appreciate the level of difficulty involved in such management techniques.

9. *We can't have 100% success. Change is hard.* It is important that the teacher and the class recognize that speech management in conversation is difficult and the client will continue to have some hard stuttering. Change will come, but it takes time and practice. Influences that make change difficult can be discussed. Items may vary for each child but usually include the following: being tired, competing messages (many people talking at once), and fear of being teased or ridiculed.

10. *Why people make fun of others and how this affects us.* Ask the class to share what they have been teased about. Most elementary-age children are willing to disclose this information and doing so actually creates a stronger bond among the children. Emphasize that anyone who is willing to share something they have been teased about is very brave. It is also helpful to ask the children how teasing makes them feel and behave. Parallels can then be drawn to teasing someone about stuttering.

11. *How the client wants his classmates and teacher to respond to stuttering.* Talk to the class about how they can react to stuttering in a helpful manner. Many elementary children actually welcome their classmates filling in words on which they are stuttering. Of course others want the listener to be patient and wait until they are able to say the word. This portion of the talk should be individualized to meet the child's specific desires, not those of the clinician.

Implementing Strategies

The rooms of the child's house may include fluency-shaping and stuttering modification strategies. Selection of strategies for implementation is based on each individual child and his particular speech profiles. Help the client tailor his house to best fit his wants and needs. Once the rooms of the house have been designed, therapy involves a series of structured tasks to develop automaticity of skills in a variety of settings, people present, and linguistic levels of complexity, ultimately leading to speech modification during conversational speech. The following represent an array of strategies and activities that demonstrate how to address the affective, behavioral, and cognitive components of stuttering.

Speech Controls

There are several speech controls children can use to increase their level of fluency (e.g., easy onsets, light articulatory contacts, and/or controlling speaking rate). Clients must have a variety of strategies available when managing stuttering. No one strategy will work in all situations. When clients are limited in their speech management tools, they may find themselves unsuccessful at producing fluency. Figure 9.18 provides a visual representation of this concept. ERA—SM and fluency-initiating gestures (FIGS) are additional fluency-shaping strategies used with children who stutter (Cooper, 1984; Cooper & Cooper, 1985; Gregory, 2003). These strategies replace stuttered speech with fluent speech through highly structured regimes that manipulate linguistic complexity. Therapy proceeds from establishment to transfer and then maintenance of newly learned fluency skills. The following is an overview of these fluency strategies that can be applied to the school-age child who stutters.

ERA—SM. Easy relaxed approach—smoother movement, or **ERA—SM,** is a fluency-shaping strategy developed by Gregory (2003) and taught to students and

When we limit our speech choices to one technique, we are heading toward danger. What does this mean?

_____

_____

_____

_____

_____

_____

Figure 9.18
Limited choices: What does this mean?

Figure 9.19
A visual guide for utilizing ERA–SM.

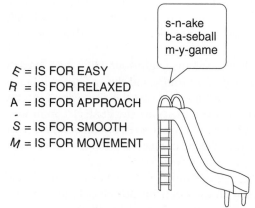

s-n-ake
b-a-seball
m-y-game

E = IS FOR EASY
R = IS FOR RELAXED
A = IS FOR APPROACH
S = IS FOR SMOOTH
M = IS FOR MOVEMENT

professionals at Northwestern University (see Figure 9.19). The philosophy of ERA—SM is based on solid evidence of the difficulty of people who stutter when initiating speech efforts. This strategy directly attacks this difficulty, providing an effective mechanism for the child to use that produces fluent speech.

Here is Campbell's (2003) description of Gregory's speech strategy:

> In practicing words, the initial consonant-vowel (CV) or vowel-consonant (VC) combination is produced with a more relaxed, smooth movement that is slightly slower than usual. The remainder of the word beyond the initial CV or VC is produced at the normal rate and with normal prosody. In phrases, ERA—SM is emphasized on the first CV or VC combination, the remainder of the word and subsequent words in the phrase are blended together. In connect discourse, the child is instructed to focus on monitoring the beginning of each phrase and pausing between phrases." (p. 225)

Along with ERA—SM, the child engages in choral reading and exercises that build his tolerance to time pressure in efforts to establish and transfer newly learned fluency skills. For those children who continue to exhibit signs of negative reactions to stuttering, cancellations, voluntary disfluencies, and negative practice drills are incorporated in their treatment plans. Begin with a less-specific approach in which stuttering is not directly addressed and move toward a more specific modification approach if the needs of the child warrant this change.

Fluency-Initiating Gestures. Cooper and Cooper (1985) used an assortment of fluency strategies in their Personalized Fluency Control Therapy (PFCT) program for children and adults. Strategies are selected based on the child's individual profile of stuttering behaviors. Their strategies are slow speech, easy onset, deep breath, syllable stress, and loudness control, each called a FIG—**fluency-initiating gesture. Slow speech** is defined as the elongation of the starting consonant for varying lengths, measured in seconds. **Loudness control** involves producing syllables in a normal voice, a loud voice, and in a soft voice. **Smooth speech** practice has three component exercises: (1) phonatory adjustment practice, (2) vocal track adjustment practice, and (3) smooth transitions between words. **Phonatory adjustment** refers to the gradual initiation of phonation; **vocal track adjustment** involves the production of stop consonants in a way that does not obstruct the airstream.

Instructions to mainpulate vocal track adjustments might sound like this:"In each set, the first syllable will end with a STOP (*plosive*) sound and the second will begin with a GO (*continuant*) sound. Say the sounds lightly so that the airstream does not stop between syllables . . . " (p. 40). **Smooth transitions** are the gradual, continuous movement from syllable to syllable without stopping the airstream. Instructions might sound like this:"As you go from one word to the next, make a smooth change from one sound to the next. Say the two words as if they were one" (p. 41).

Syllable stress exercises involve the manipulation of stress between the initial and final syllable of words and sentences. With the **deep breath** FIG, children are instructed to take a deep breath before each syllable and exhale as they produce the whole syllable, phrase, and sentence. **Easy onsets** are defined as the process of slowly exhaling and adding voicing to the airflow. Cooper and Cooper's instructions for this exercises are "First, let a little air out of your lungs. Then as the airflow is taking place, start making the first sounds as smoothly and as softly as you can. Finally, gradually and smoothly raise the loudness of the sound" (p. 69). Once children have been introduced to all the strategies, they engage in gamelike activities to practice all six strategies. Cooper and Cooper developed cartoon character representations of these FIGS appropriate for use with younger children (e.g., FIGman, SuperFIG, and SlowFIG). PFCT provides numerous worksheets for practicing each FIG as well as information for parents and teachers.

Relaxation

For a subgroup of older school-age children who stutter, learning **relaxation exercises** can enhance their ability to reduce anxiety and better manage their stuttering moments. Anticipation of stuttering can result in increased muscular tension, and, according to Bloodstein's (1958) anticipatory struggle hypothesis, tension leads to fragmentation. This translates to the individual's inability to connect elements of speech in a smooth, continuous manner. Gregory (2003) provided two rationales for the use of relation exercises with people who stutter:

1. If we can increase our awareness of gradations of tension in the larger, grosser muscles of the body, we can carry that awareness over into monitoring and modifying the tension in the muscles of the speech mechanism—breathing, phonation, and articulation.
2. When we go into a speaking situation in which we feel anxious (we say "tensing up"), if we strive for reduced bodily tension, this will be a competing response that will help us to feel calmer. (p. 192)

Your decision to present this strategy as an optional room in the child's house of fluency will be based on both client and clinician variables. Ham (1999) indicated that the client's motivation, prior experiences with relaxation, and trust in the clinician impacts the effectiveness of this practice. Additionally, your personal characteristics and confidence in conducting relaxation exercises interact with client variables, influencing your decision to select this strategy for implementation. There are several resources you may use if you decide to utilize relaxation in stuttering therapy (Bloodstein, 1995; Conture, 2001; Gregory, 2003; Guitar, 1998; Ham, 1999).

The ability to change muscular tension within the speech mechanism is essential to the implementation of cancellations, pullouts, and preparatory sets. Conture (2001) noted "what IS (*sic*) important, however, is to help the person who stutters learn to physically feel (identify) and change inappropriate amounts and durations of physical movement and tension within the vocal tract WHILE (*sic*) in the midst of normal, although less than pleasant feelings" (p. 197). You can teach relaxation exercises to older children who stutter using Gregory's systematic relaxation procedures described in Table 9.9.

Negative Practice

If the child continues to exhibit excessive tension during stuttering, more work might be required on tension reduction through **negative practice** drills. As previously described, the child says a word with full tension and repeats it with half the tension. Emphasis is on feeling the difference in speech mechanism. Routine drill may be required

Table 9.9
Dialogue for use when instructing clients in relaxation procedures.

During relaxation practice, the clinician should model a slow, relaxed manner of speaking. Each step should be followed by a brief period of silence, about 20 seconds, to allow the client to feel the change in muscular tension. Eliminate all discourse between children during this period. The following is Gregory's (2003, pp. 192–193) dialogue to use in relaxation instruction.

Step 1.	"Beginning with the right leg, extend the foot. Gradually flex the foot and increase the tension all the way up to the hip. When the tension reaches near maximum, let the leg muscles relax and think about the tension flowing out of the leg." Now do the same thing with the left leg.
Step 2.	"Going to the right arm, hold the arm and hand extended in front of you. Gradually flex the hand, slowly making a fist. Increase the tension up the arm and into the shoulder until it reaches near maximum. Then let the arm relax and think about the tension flowing out of the arm, just as you did with the leg."
Step 3.	"We work on the muscles of the chest, abdominal area, and back by deep breathing. When we inhale, we contract muscles that expand the thoracic cavity. Breathe in deeply. Hold the breath for about one second, feel the tension, then exhale. Monitor the release of tension, then breathe quietly for about 10 seconds to feel the relaxation."
Step 4.	"We work on the muscles of the neck by slowly and carefully rolling the head first in one direction and then the other, beginning with the chin against the sternum. Careful movements are very important, as neck muscles can be easily strained."
Step 5.	"Yawning is the last. The first part of the yawn is tensing and the second part is relaxing. Feel the relaxation down in the chest. Think of the body being more relaxed. Think of being more calm."

Source: Based on Gregory (2003).

in some cases. Make sure the words you choose for this practice include ones on which the child anticipates stuttering. During the session, make a list of words on which the child has previously stuttered. Incorporate these vocabulary items into game activities that provide multiple opportunities for the child to practice this skill (i.e., obtain a high response rate in efforts to develop automaticity). As with relaxation, negative practice requires the precursor ability of modifying tension for implementation of modification strategies. Mastery at changing tension levels is essential to therapy success.

Triads

Triads are implemented to assist the person who stutters in gaining a feeling of control and manipulation over stuttering moments. Additionally, triad drills have a powerful desensitizing force as the individual directly confronts his stuttering. Triads are similar to Van Riper's (1973) "stuttering bath" activity in which clients are "flooded" with stuttering in efforts to reduce the amount of emotionality attached to stuttering. During flooding practice, clients may repeat feared words up to 20 to 30 times.

For triads, clients produce the complete triad three to five times until they feel increased control and decreased emotion. There are two phases of triad practice. Phase 1 triads involve the following steps: (1) A hard stutter is produced on a word

> ## My Speech Weeds
> by
> L.W., age 16
>
> ---
>
> I know that many do not usually associate weeds with stuttering, especially me. It's actually a very good, almost accurate, comparison if you give it some thought, as I did. You see, while I was in therapy I was catching quite a few of my larger stutterers. On the other hand, I was letting all of the little ones go. Dr. Bennett pointed this out to me and said how it was all good and well that I was catching the larger stutters, but how I also needed to catch the smaller ones too. Here is where we get back to the weeds.
>
> One day, I went outside to pull all the weeds, and didn't pay much mind to the smaller, so-called, less-important ones. Boy, was I mistaken! The next week (you know, after all the rain), I went outside to once again marvel on what a wonderful job I did. I was horrified to find those so-called little weeds had dropped seeds as they had grown, and now there were literally hundreds of little, evil baby ones. And then I knew that I had to get down to business and pull all the little suckers, no matter what the size. Well, we stutterers knew that there will always be weeds in our flower bed. We just need to learn how to use the proper management, i.e., weed killer.

Figure 9.20
A personal account of an experience with relapse.

followed by a pause; (2) the individual replaces the hard stutter with an easy bounce on the first sound or syllable of the same word followed by a pause; and (3) the word is produced with an exaggerated slide/prolongation on the first sound with a slow, easy transition from sound to sound. By reducing the tension level of each production, the PWS learns how to modify speech. This drill-like task shows the client he has a choice in the way he stutters and provides multiple opportunities for him to change his speech.

As the client makes progress in modifying moments of stuttering, hard stutters are no longer a predominant speech characteristic. However, brief stuttering moments may be present, and the client must learn how to manage them. At times, the client may become comfortable with these small stutters and let them go without any effort to change. There is danger in ignoring these stuttering episodes, however. Use the analogy of pulling weeds in a garden. If you pull only the larger weeds, the smaller ones grow and replace the bigger weeds. This becomes a never-ending, futile exercise as exemplified in an essay written by a 16-year old who stutters (Figure 9.20).

Phase 2 triads can now be initiated to further desensitize the client to smaller moments of stuttering and provide opportunities for modifying them. They involve the following process: (1) Client produces an easy bounce followed by a pause; (2) replaces the easy bounce with an exaggerated slide/prolongation on the first sound with a slow, easy transition from sound to sound; and (3) utilizes an easy onset with light articulatory contacts on the first syllable or sound of the word. Figure 9.21 demonstrates these two types of triad drills.

Figure 9.21
Phases I and II of triad drills.

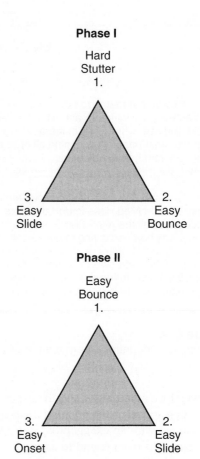

Cancellations

Clients may choose to design a room for cancellations to address the presence of hard moments of stuttering. Van Riper noted that **cancellations** are "designed primarily as a vehicle for learning new responses to the stimuli that trigger the abnormal stuttering responses" (p. 319). For some children who continue to exhibit emotional reactions to stuttering and do not catch their stuttering moments, cancellations need to be practiced intensively and regularly. The cancellation acts to reduce the reinforcing power of stuttering while developing self-corrective patterns. Precursor skills include being able to stop immediately after a moment of stuttering, modification of tension levels, and implementation of easy bounces or slides when repeating the word. This strategy is applicable to older children who stutter because it requires a certain degree of metalinguistic skills to reflect on one's language and speech production. It is not designed for use with younger children who stutter.

Pullouts

Another room in the child's house may include the implementation of **pullouts:** Moving forward in time, the child catches the moment of stuttering and modifies it midstream. Precursor skills for successful use of pullouts include knowing when one is stuttering, being able to stop during a moment of stuttering, modification of tension levels, and easy initiation of phonation with smooth transition from sound to sound as the client continues the speech effort. To teach pullouts, insert hard stuttering into your speech and have the child tell you when to release the stutter. Next, reverse the roles, with you instructing the child to freeze when he stutters and deliberately prolonging the core stuttering behavior until you cue him to say the rest of the word. Next, the child cues himself to pull out of a stuttering block. Guitar (1998) has children clench their fists when they catch a moment of stuttering, hold on to it, and then gradually open their hand as they release the word. This technique helps children understand that they must gradually move out of a stuttering block and not just pop out with the word. Using hand cues can help them pace their pullouts during the initial stages of learning this strategy.

Preparatory Sets

Van Riper (1973) defined **preparatory sets** as the process of teaching the "stutterer to assume a different motor set when he approaches a feared word or sound" (p. 341). Because people who stutter approach feared words or situations with aberrant motor planning and articulatory postures, they must replace these motor sets with new behaviors learned as a product of using triads, cancellations, and pullouts. In response to anticipation of stuttering, "the new slow-motion form of fluent stuttering that had been learned through the cancellation and pull-out modification techniques now appear in the stutterer's speech" (pp. 337–338). Through mass practice using new preparatory sets, the individual moves forward in time to modify possible stuttering before it surfaces in overt speech production. You can direct children to use preparatory sets initially on nonfeared words and gradually attempt them on feared words or sounds. Guitar (1998) provides an excellent visual display of these therapy strategies (Figure 9.22).

The ABCs of Feelings

Children who stutter must recognize, accept, and change, when appropriate, the feelings they experience with stuttering. Chapter 2 introduced several key emotions that may exacerbate the child's ability to manage stuttering (e.g., anger, guilt, and shame). Chapter 6 provided counseling strategies to use when addressing feelings with children who stutter. The following activities will help you introduce discussions about how children feel about their stuttering. We want to initiate these talks in a general way and gradually move into the specific feelings of stuttering. Children may be uncomfortable discussing their feelings during the initial stages of therapy, so carefully consider when it is appropriate to begin. The following activities are adapted from Karsten's (1995) self-esteem workbook for children in grades 5 though 8 and are useful when first addressing the emotions that surround stuttering.

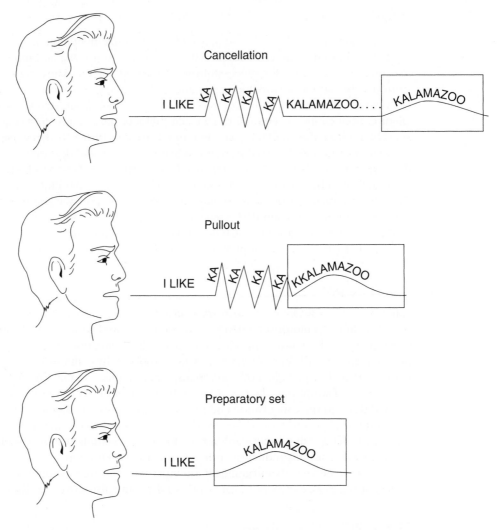

Figure 9.22
Guitar's illustration of Van Riper's stuttering modification techniques.
Source: From Stuttering: An Integrated Approach to its Nature and Treatment, *(p. 219), by B. Guitar, 1998, Hagerstown, MD: Lippincott Williams & Wilkins. Copyright 1998 by Lippincott Williams & Wilkins. Reprinted with permission.*

ACTIVITY 27: WHO AM I?

Objective: Children will record a list of adjectives to describe themselves and write an acrostic name poem using some of those adjectives.

Procedure: Gather materials needed for this activity: pen/pencil, butcher paper, and thesaurus. Engage in a brainstorming exercise having children list many adjectives that could be used to describe a person. The children then select from this list the adjectives they would use to describe themselves. To implement this activity, follow these steps:

1. Using your name, make an acrostic poem to share with the students. For example, the name *Ellen* might be presented as *E* stands for excels, *L* for loving, *L* for likeable, *E* for energetic, and *N* for nice.
2. Brainstorm several positive adjectives for each letter of the alphabet. Students may look up words in the thesaurus if needed. Students take turns writing these words on a piece of butcher paper taped to the wall.
3. Distribute individual sheets of paper. Each student creates a poem to describe who they are.
4. Provide an opportunity for students to share their poems with each other or display them in the therapy room.

ACTIVITY 28: ALL ABOUT ME WITH ZANY WORDS

Objective: Children will create an amusing, fictional tale about themselves and turn it into a story that tells about who they really are and what they think.

Procedure: Gather materials required for this activity: pen/pencils and "Zany Words," "How Absurd," and "A Story of Truth" worksheets (Appendices H, I, and J). Tell the students this activity will help everyone learn a bit more about one another. Follow the steps outlined by Karsten (1995, p. 27) to complete this task:

1. Divide students into pairs. Give each student a copy of the "Zany Words" worksheet and instruct them to record their partner's answers when asked for a word that fits the category described on each line.
2. Give each student a copy of the "How Absurd" worksheet and have them transfer their zany words on the first worksheet into the corresponding blanks on the second worksheet to create a silly story about themselves.
3. Encourage students to read their stories aloud to the group.
4. Give each student a new worksheet, "A Story of Truth," to fill in true words that make sense and tell something about themselves.
5. Invite students to read their real story aloud to the group.
6. Engage the group in a discussion comparing the absurd and real story they created.

ACTIVITY 29: ALPHABET FEELINGS

Objective: Children will generate a list of emotions.

Procedure: Gather materials needed for this activity: pens/pencils, paper, paper bag, magnetic letters, and thesaurus. Open the activity with a discussion of the emotions used when creating their stories in the previous exercise. Challenge students to come up with a list of emotions that begin with each letter of the alphabet. Take turns picking a magnetic letter from the paper bag and write it on the paper. Next to the letter, write various feelings that begin with that letter (e.g., A = angry, agreeable, anxious). Continue until all letters have been selected. Ask the children to give examples of when they felt anxious, angry, or agreeable. This discussion does not have to reflect feelings around stuttering, but feelings in general. Accept all responses with unconditional positive regard.

ACTIVITY 30: COLOR EMOTIONS

Objective: Children will explore emotions by relating them to color.

Procedure: Gather materials needed for this activity: white art paper, construction paper, fabric, markers, and glue. Start this activity with a visualization task: Ask students to close their eyes and picture themselves wrapped in red. Inquire about their feelings and what emotions they associate with the color red. Do this with several different colors. Next, have the group make a list of colors. Using the emotions chart just created, students select an emotion and pair it with a color. Discuss the students' color-emotion pairs and invite them to role-play the scenario in which they feel that color and emotion.

ACTIVITY 31: SPELL-OUTS

Objective: Children will label emotions related to the experience of stuttering.

Procedure: Gather materials needed for this activity: list of feelings produced in the previous activity, pens/pencils, and paper. This activity is an extension of Alphabet Feelings except for its reference to speaking situations and feelings experienced when stuttering. The activity may be organized this way:

Step 1:   Review the emotions list created by the students, acknowledging all feelings as okay. Feelings are not judged as good or bad but just okay.

Step 2:   Direct the students' attention to stuttering and how this disorder may influence how children feel about communication. Write down any feelings expressed by the students on a piece of paper.

Step 3:   Present a word list including terms related to stuttering, such as *control, fluency, therapy, stuttering, change, easy speech*, and so on. Have the students select a word and create an acrostic poem using the letters of that word. Figure 9.23 provides examples of products of this exercise.

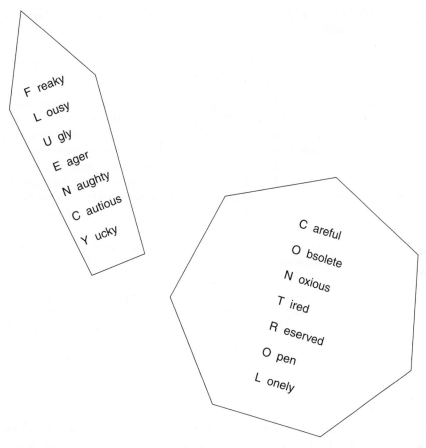

Figure 9.23
Acrostic poems used to help children who stutter express their feelings surrounding stuttering.

As children begin to share their feelings about stuttering, provide an open environment for them to express their emotions. Having a safe place to share shaming experiences leads to the reduction of this emotion, allowing the individual to let go and move forward. Children will share many different emotions and events with you, not all related to stuttering. The trust established between you and the child provides a safety net for him or her to reveal highly detailed personal information. Some children may need someone to talk with about their concerns. The expression of feelings allows them to dissipate. However, you will not always be available to discuss feelings that arise after episodes of stuttering. Students must have strategies in place to help them cope with their feelings. The following activity provides students with a concrete avenue to express their concerns to a trusting rock.

ACTIVITY 32: PET ROCKS

Objective: Children will create a pet rock to share feelings experienced when stuttering.

Procedure: Gather materials together for this activity: glue, craft supplies (feathers, pipe cleaners, eyes, fake hair, felt), scissors, markers, paint, and large rocks. Explain the healing property of talking about feelings, particularly when students are upset because of their communication difficulties. Emphasize the importance of having someone to talk to and make a list of the people they believe they could go to when feeling upset. Discuss how, at times, these people may not be available to listen to the student, so they need to have an alternative plan. Ask them to brainstorm ways they could release their emotions, or "take care of themselves," when a person is not available. This list might include drawing/painting a picture, riding your bike, making something out of Legos, watching cartoons, and/or writing your feelings down on paper. Another option might be to talk to your pet rock. A pet rock never talks back, will be your buddy, and is always there to listen to you, no matter what. Have the children select a rock and decorate it with various craft supplies. The rock becomes a symbol of a trusting companion for the children. Role-play scenarios in which children might use their pet rocks (see Figure 9.24).

ACTIVITY 33: THE STUTTERING MONSTER

Objective: Children will draw a picture of what stuttering looks like to them.

Procedure: Gather materials needed for this task: pencils, markers, paint, paintbrushes, and butcher paper. Read the story "Juan's Secret" (Table 2.2 in chapter 2) to the group and discuss the monster Juan talks about. Ask each child to describe what their "stuttering monster" looks like. The children draw their monsters on butcher paper and talk about their feelings around stuttering as they draw their pictures (see Figure 9.25). Hang the pictures in the therapy room and role-play with the children what they might say to their stuttering monster. As the children make progress in therapy and are coping better with their stuttering, ask them if they want to tear up and throw away their stuttering monster. Make this process a special event, inviting friends, siblings, teachers, or parents to the ceremony.

Building the rooms for the house of fluency represents the major thrust of therapy. Students will spend most of their time in therapy visiting each room in their

Figure 9.24
Three pet rocks created by children who stutter.

Figure 9.25
A picture drawn by a sixth-grade student reflecting his view of the stutter monster.

house, practicing strategies repeatedly, and conquering their fear of stuttering. Work on the affective, behavioral, and cognitive aspects of stuttering provides a well-rounded program that addresses the needs of each individual child. The result of their intensive efforts is an increase in fluency and improved communicative effectiveness. The next challenge involves maintaining this fluency over time.

STAGE 4: MAINTAINING THE ROOF OF FLUENCY

The roof of fluency represents the therapy gains made by the child. Time spent in each room, practicing strategies and engaging in various speech tasks, produces increased fluency. The next stage of therapy entails the process of maintaining and stabilizing this fluency. The roof of the house protects the interior contents from pervading or anticipated dangers. As with all houses, maintenance is required to ensure the stability and integrity of the house's structures. For example, if a leak in a pipe is not attended to, damage may occur to the walls and foundation of the house, requiring major repairs. If children attend to their house of fluency with a regular maintenance plan, these major repairs may be prevented or at least reduced in severity. However, disasters do occur (for example, hurricanes, floods, and windstorms) catching the owner off guard and unprepared. Such relapse is a natural phenomenon that children can cope with better if discussed openly in therapy.

Stage 4 of the House That Jack Built has as its primary goals: (1) comprehension of the concept of relapse and its role in the disorder of stuttering, (2) active involvement of students through choice making, and (3) the establishment of a maintenance plan. Achieving these goals includes activities geared to help the children understand the difficulties inherent in maintaining their newly learned speech skills. Students must be active participants in the therapy process, allowed to make choices regarding their speech management strategies and the development of homework routines, an essential component of this stage of therapy. Lastly, both you and the child must engage in planned therapy activities that enhance automatization of skills learned during the process of building rooms for the house of fluency.

Relapse

Relapse, the loss of previously learned skills, is a common phenomenon in stuttering disorders (Bloodstein, 1995; Conture, 2001; Craig, 1998; Guitar, 1998; Ham, 1999; Manning, 1996; Shapiro, 1999). The age of the client greatly influences the extent of relapse. For the young child who has become fluent, relapse is unlikely. As the child experiences stuttering for longer periods of time, the habit strength of the stuttering grows, making it more resistant to long-term change. Some school-age children who stutter may experience periods of relapse for several reasons. First, the child may have grown dependent on the clinician for feedback regarding his speech skills and have not developed appropriate self-monitoring behaviors. Second, the child may not have established automatic use of his strategies in situations outside the therapy setting. Third, the child may not be compliant in completing outside assignments specified in the maintenance plan. Fourth, greater emphasis was placed on developing fluency and insufficient work was conducted on the affective and cognitive aspects of the disorder. And relapse increases are more likely for the child who does not take responsibility for his stuttering, continuing to describe these failures in terms of the behaviors of others. The following activity may help children understand the importance of assuming responsibility for the choices they make, an essential element of long-term maintenance of fluency (Karsten, 1995).

Table 9.10
Statements that imply the student is assuming responsibility versus dispersing it onto another person.

Responsible Statements	Cop-Out Statements
I noticed that the house needed to be cleaned.	My sister threw my homework away.
I chose to not finish my homework last night.	He made me skip class.
I need to listen in class so I don't miss lunch.	My brother wanted me to play in the street.
I didn't put my homework in the right place.	My friend told me to lie for him.
I know I should not play in the street.	The money was just sitting there so I took it.
I chose to skip class. My friend did not make me.	You never told me that rule.
I can do what is right. I will not lie for a friend.	The teacher didn't give me time to finish.
I know I should not take things that don't belong to me.	The teacher kept me in during lunch.
I should use my time wisely so I complete my work in class.	Mom didn't say I had to clean the house.
I pay attention to the rules and follow them.	My parents were fighting so I didn't do my homework.

ACTIVITY 34: COP-OUTS

Objective: Children will identify excuses and rationalizations (cop-outs) in order to learn the value of taking responsibility for their actions.

Procedure: Gather materials needed for this activity: scissors, glue or tape, art paper, and the worksheets shown in Tables 9.10 and 9.11. Open the discussion by writing the word *responsibility* at the top of a piece of paper. Ask the students what this means to them or how they would define the term. Next, ask students how they would know if someone was taking responsibility for something they had done. Call these *responsible statements*. Write the word *cop-out* at the top of another piece of paper and ask the students what it means to them. Define cop-outs as statements made to shift the responsibility for a particular behavior. An example of a cop-out might be "My mom forgot to tell me to do my speech work." Here the child fails to take responsibility for not doing the homework and shifts the blame onto the mother. Distribute the worksheets on responsible statements and cop-out statements. Have the student cut out the statements from the top portion of the worksheet and match each responsible statement with the corresponding cop-out statement. Next, either use the speech-related statements on the bottom of the worksheet or have students generate their own list of responsible versus cop-out statements. This activity flows nicely into the following task of goal setting.

Table 9.11
Statements related to stuttering indicative of assuming responsibility for one's behavior
versus displacing responsibility.

Responsible Statements	Cop-Out Statements
I chose to watch TV and not to do my homework when my mom went out.	He made me stutter.
I am responsible for my speech folder. I need to keep it in the same place everyday so I can find it.	My teacher wouldn't like me stuttering so hard.
I did not tell my friend that I had homework to do before I could play.	My mom went out last night so I didn't get to practice.
I am choosing to do nothing about my speech.	My mom can't find the speech folder.
I don't like using hard stutters in front of my teacher.	I can't help myself when I stutter.
I get nervous and tense up when I talk with him.	My friend wanted to play and time ran out.

ACTIVITY 35: GOAL SETTING

Objective: Children will list things they like and do not like about their speech and set personal goals from this list.

Procedure: Gather materials needed for this activity: pens/pencils, paper, and the worksheet in Figure 9.26. Introduce this activity with a definition of goals and objectives. Ask students to reflect on a goal they have not yet reached. Problem-solve steps they might take to reach their goal. Gradually direct this discussion toward their speech. Ask students to write down five things they like about their stuttering and five things they do not like. As a group, select one behavior on the list of dislikes and write a goal that would change the behavior. For example, a student writes on the list the following dislike: "I don't like it when I can't pull out of a stutter." Discuss what the child might do to change this dislike. Sample dialogue might sound like this:

Clinician: "So, you don't like it when you can't pull out of a stutter."

Jesse: "It gets me really mad. I go to release and can't move on."

Clinician: "Let's make a list of all the things Jesse might do to change this behavior. Any ideas?"

Larry: "He could practice pullouts everyday."

Rebecca: "He could also visit the negative practice room."

Clinician: "Why would you revisit that room, Rebecca?"

Rebecca: "When Jesse can't release from the block, it's because he is too tight. Well, he's also reacting."

Likes and Dislikes: Goal-Setting Worksheet
THINGS I LIKE ABOUT MY SPEECH
THINGS I DON'T LIKE ABOUT MY SPEECH
WHAT'S MY PLAN?

Figure 9.26
A worksheet to use when helping children who stutter identify various characteristics of speech and set realistic goals to change weaknesses into strengths.

Jesse: "You are right. I am reacting, so of course I tense up and can't reduce the tension."

Clinician: "What else might Jesse do to reduce his reacting behavior?"

Larry: "He could spend time in the room of voluntary stuttering. You do have that in your house, don't you, Jesse?"

Jesse: "No, I didn't put it in. Maybe I need to remodel and make a room for voluntary stuttering."

Clinician: "So how will we write your goal? 'Jesse will insert voluntary stutters into his speech.' How many times a day and in what situations do you think would be most helpful, Jesse?"

The dialogue continues in this manner as a specific plan is designed to address the underlying source of Jesse's inability to use this modification strategy. Continue until each child has identified a speech concern and developed a personal goal to change.

Choice Making

Empowering children to make permanent changes in their speaking patterns requires active participation and **choice making** in therapy. When provided with a choice regarding how to talk, children perceive a sense of power or control over their speech. Remember that one strategy may not always work for the child or be the most appropriate tool for special repairs the child must make. Children must be equipped with a toolbox of strategies to repair their speech. Given the choice, children can select from a variety of tools to implement. However, having this freedom to use different tools also means that children who stutter must develop proficiency in the use of multiple strategies and maintain this proficiency over time. To do this, children must understand the need to practice all strategies routinely, and you can help them in this process.

ACTIVITY 36: WEEKLY RECORD

Objective: Children will practice various strategies on each day of the week.

Procedure: Gather materials needed for this activity: pens/pencils and weekly agenda (Figures 9.27 and 9.28 contain several examples of homework assignment sheets). You and the child decide together on what therapy strategies the child will utilize during the upcoming week. At this point in therapy, the child does not need to create a detailed plan for each speaking situation. The student is instructed to check his list each day in the morning to review what strategies he will implement throughout the day. He can choose to use visual reminders if deemed necessary.

Homework Assignment

Check off each speech task you complete on the day it was assigned. It is important that you do not mark the assignment if you have not completely finished it.

Monday:

_____ 1. Word List

_____ 2. Read aloud 5 pages from "Song of the Brook" using easy bounces.

Tuesday:

_____ 1. Word List

_____ 2. Say your spelling words aloud when you are studying them using stretches.

Wednesday:

_____ 1. When reviewing for your social studies test with your mom, use your easy onsets for at least 15 minutes.

_____ 2. Call Ms. Ellen at 444-8888 and leave a message telling her something about your day. Remember to use your easy speech and not "regular" speech.

Thursday:

_____ 1. Word List

_____ 2. Use easy bounces after school with Mom for 10 minutes.

Friday:

_____ 1. Word List

_____ 2. When you go out for dinner, order your own food and use long prolongations with the waiter. Make sure you maintain eye contact with the waiter.

Saturday:

_____ 1. Word List

_____ 2. When you go the movie theater, use hard stuttering when you ask for your popcorn and soda.

Sunday:

_____ 1. Read three comics aloud to Mom: Stutter hard and pull out of the stutter.

_____ 2. Reflect on the week's worth of speech and write your comments on the back of this paper.

Figure 9.27
An example of a homework assignment for a fourth-grade child who stutters.

During the day, the child makes note of when he modifies his speech or uses his fluency strategies. At the end of the day, he puts a check mark on the calendar indicating the use of each particular strategy. This form is returned at the end of the week or at the next weekly session, and then you both discuss the speech successes and failures.

Home Practice Chart

Name: _____ Return to Speech on _____

Strategy	Mon.	Tues.	Wed.	Thurs.	Fri.	Sat.	Sun.
ERA-SM							
Pullouts							
Bounces							
Relaxation							
Voluntaries							
Openness							

Overall Comments:

_____

_____

_____

Parent Signature: _____

Home Practice Chart

Name: _____ Return to Speech on _____

Date	What strategy I used?	Who was there?	How many times?

Overall Comments:

_____

_____

_____

Parent Signature: _____

Figure 9.28
Two examples of a structured versus unstructured homework assignment for the school-age child who stutters.

Fluency Report Card

The **fluency report card** (originally created by Campbell and Hill, 1989) can be used as a checking mechanism to ensure you are having the child routinely practice all the strategies selected when designing the rooms of the house. This procedure is especially useful for clinicians working in the public schools. Every 6 weeks, report to the parents on the progress each child has or has not made during this period. Use the report card to check off the strategies the child has practiced in this 6-week period and determine (with the child's input) what strategies might be used during the next reporting period. The responsibilities of the public school therapist are many, so time management is a critical skill. This worksheet may help you track this information over the school year as documentation of strategies taught to the child (Figure 9.29). The practice regime for children who stutter must include regular practice of all techniques in order to maintain fluency.

Maintenance

Maintenance refers to the "continuation or persistence of speech and attitudinal change over time" (Gregory, 1982, p. 11). This does not happen automatically and must be planned with systematic procedures to follow (Boberg, 1982). To maintain a certain level of proficiency, the child must know what to do and take the time to think about it. You must ensure the child *knows* the exact steps needed to implement the strategy, when to use it, and why it is used. Next, the child must take the time to *think* about speech in settings outside the therapy room. You can discuss these two components with the children and design symbols to cue them to think about the next speech attempt. For example, the child might color pictures of light bulbs and place them in different areas of his house. When he sees the light bulb, he reflects positively on his speech. The student may also put these light bulbs around his classroom or on the cover of his notebooks as visual reminders to think about speech.

The next step to teaching the skills required for fluency maintenance would be to substitute the light bulbs with symbols representing different techniques. Figure 9.30 provides a sample of different tools the child can select to represent the strategies to implement. For example, the paintbrush might symbolize ERA—SM or exaggerated prolongations used as voluntary stuttering. The screwdriver might represent tension reduction strategies, the hammer symbolizing bounces and the saw, negative practice (cutting the stutter in half). The child selects what tool(s) to use and places its representation in his immediate environment as a visual cue.

Support Our Children

Children who stutter need the support of the clinician throughout the maintenance phase of therapy. Many authors have emphasized the importance of follow-up therapy in the maintenance process (Boberg, 1982, 1986; Conture, 2001; Guitar, 1998; Ham,

Fluency Report Card						
Name: _____ Campus: _____ Year: _____						
Strategy	6 weeks	12 weeks	18 weeks	24 weeks	30 weeks	36 weeks
Negative Practice Drills						
ERA—SM 2–10 minutes						
Can use Rapid ERA—SM						
Cancellations						
Triad Drills						
Resisting Time Pressure						
Pullouts						
Uses Speech Hierarchy						
Voluntary Stuttering						
Openness with Friends						
Aggressive Nonavoidance						
Bounces						
Slides						
Preparatory Sets						
Uses Relaxation						

Figure 9.29
A modified version of Campbell and Hill's original Fluency Report Card.

Figure 9.30
Toolbox of strategies for
managing speech breaks.

1999; Shapiro, 1999). However, what has been written regarding maintenance is directed toward the adult who stutters. Perhaps it is assumed school-age children who stutter are automatically provided with appropriate maintenance plans or they do not need them. The answer to this assumption is unknown. Children receiving services in the school system typically attend therapy twice a week for varying lengths of time. They continue on the same time schedule until released from therapy, purportedly having "achieved their IEP goals." This child then moves into the middle school environment and is lost among active teenagers. The campus therapist will not have this child on her list of students because he was dismissed from therapy. The rigidity of some school systems does not allow for children to be monitored or followed up informally after release from therapy.

Due to these systemic restrictions, it is recommended that clinicians develop unique IEPs that allow for a reduction in contact hours over an extended period of time. Children who stutter need this type of support, and the school-based clinician may have to advocate for such services in order to better serve this population. Ham (1999, pp. 363–364) presented a maintenance schedule for adults who stutter that can be easily applied to the school-age child. You would need to set up a tracking system and engage the cooperation of other district therapists in order to make this type of schedule a reality for the older school-age child and adolescent who stutters.

Maintenance Schedule

Step 1. Reduce the present, twice-weekly schedule to once a week, for about 6 weeks (approximate). Devote nearly every session entirely to preparation for client independence, problem solving, role-play rehearsals, and supervised outside-clinic practice. Prepare client for step 2 in the last session of this step.

Step 2. Reduce session frequency to one meeting every 2 weeks, for about 3 months. During this time period, the client completes a daily log or diary at the end of each day. Focus therapy sessions on discussions of daily records; problem-solve and reinforce efforts as indicated.

Step 3. Drop session frequency to one meeting per month, for about 6 months. During this period, the client completes a summary of his speech successes and failures, which is used as the topic of discussion at the next session. Client is directed to attend to signs of relapse and is instructed to call the clinician for advice and direction or drop back to daily monitoring and evaluation until stability returns.

Step 4. Drop session frequency to one meeting every 3 months for 1 year. Suggest attendance at summer fluency camps or support groups if client appears in need of support or a brief period of focus on his speech.

A Special Precaution

Mistakes will definitely happen during the maintenance of fluency. Do not overreact to these mistakes and take them out of perspective. Support children during this period by helping them problem-solve possible repairs that appear to be needed in the child's house of fluency. Sometimes children need to recarpet their floors, revisiting and reviewing the knowledge they learned about stuttering. Perhaps their speech mechanism begins to clog and they need to spend time analyzing their clogs to determine the appropriate Drano, or speech strategy. Ideally, the client is able to guide himself down the path toward renewed fluency, with the support and encouraging words from the clinician.

CHAPTER SUMMARY

The House That Jack Built is a concrete analogy that helps the school-age child who stutters understand the therapy process. Using an integrated approach to treatment, the clinician and child work together learning about the normal speaking process and how this process is disturbed by stuttering (i.e., the interference process). Obtaining knowledge about talking and stuttering encompass the first building stage. Next, the child installs the plumbing that helps him identify his clog, or identify the type of stuttering present in his speech. The exploration of different types of talking increases the child's ability to describe his stuttering patterns objectively. This skill is necessary if the child is to implement midstream modification strategies.

The third stage of building the house of fluency involves the design and layout of the rooms in the house. With the guidance of the clinician, the child selects the best fit strategies and engages in various activities to master these skills. Knowledge of the strategies, as well as of the change process, teasing and the reaction cycle, and the role of positive self-talk in maintaining fluency, is critical to building the house. Rooms in the house may include strategies addressing any of the affective, behavioral, or cognitive components of the child's particular profile. As fluency develops, the child must maintain his newly learned skills, thus entering the fourth stage of the house, the roof of fluency. Children must understand the possibility of relapse and be prepared with a plan of action. During this maintenance phase of therapy, the responsibility has shifted toward the student through active choice making in weekly and monthly practice routines. Supporting the student during this critical period is essential. Although direct therapy is gradually reduced and phased out, the child who stutters must have a safety net. The clinician can provide this net by routine visits to help children cope with relapse if it occurs.

The analogy of building houses of fluency can guide the clinician when planning fluency therapy for the school-age child who stutters. It provides a concrete organization to therapy for the newly practicing clinician. The house analogy is just one way to engage the child actively in the therapy process, particularly important for older school-age students. It can be implemented with individual or group service delivery models, as well as in different service settings. The House That Jack Built is presented as a conceptual model of intervention that can be modified to meet the individual needs of children who stutter.

STUDY QUESTIONS

1. Outline the four stages of intervention presented in The House That Jack Built.

2. During stage-1 activities directed at learning about sounds, what aspects of speech production are emphasized and why do you think this knowledge is important?

3. Generate five new examples for cop-out statements related to stuttering.

4. Justify the need to advertise stuttering in relation to the school-age child who stutters.

5. What speech modification strategies could be selected for inclusion in a child's house of fluency?

6. When is it appropriate to teach cancellations?

7. How would you teach a child to pull out of a moment of stuttering?

8. Differentiate between the two types of triad drills.

9. Discuss the role of relapse in stuttering.

10. Explain the difference between proactive and reactive teasing management.

11. Discuss the role of automaticity in the establishment of rooms in the child's house of fluency.

12. Describe an original activity designed to assist students in maintaining their fluency.

Adolescents Who Stutter

CHAPTER OUTLINE

Treatment Directions
  Fluency-Shaping Approaches
  Stuttering Modification Approaches

Integrated Approaches
Caveat

LEARNER OBJECTIVES

- Identify the affective, behavioral, and cognitive aspects of stuttering in adolescents.

- Define the period of adolescence in terms of physiological, cognitive, and sociological development.

- Discuss the impact stuttering may have on the adolescent.

- Identify ways clinicians can be innovative when determining service delivery models.

- Determine when it is a good time to temporarily stop therapy for teens.

- Name three theories that help clinicians understand the topic of motivation.

- Name and discuss the 3C's of motivation.

- List ways to make therapy motivating to the teenager who stutters.

- Discuss the similarities and differences among the therapy approaches used with adolescents who stutter.

KEY TERMS

biological motives
cognitive operations
cognitive theory
competency cues
extrinsic motivation

hierarchy of needs theory
intrinsic motivation
optimal challenge
reinforcement theory
self-efficacy

self-esteem
self-fulfilling prophecy
social feedback
social motives
task-intrinsic feedback

Adolescents, in general, can be characterized as having a unique set of psychological, physiological, and social needs. Add stuttering to the equation and this subgroup changes in complexity. This time period of establishing independence and self-direction may be impacted by chronic stuttering (Blood & Blood, 2004; Blood, Blood, Tellis, & Gabel, 2003; Kully & Langevin, 1999; Manning, 2003; Rustin, Cook, & Spence, 1995). The impact of stuttering changes differentially through life as the disorder becomes more or less severe and the person who stutters changes through the process of normal development (Peters & Starkweather, 1989). Such changes may derive from internal and external sources. The hope of spontaneous recovery from stuttering lingers for some adolescents and dims for others. Factors that make one individual recover while others persist with stuttering remain unknown. The psychological development occurring at this time allows the adolescent to reflect on his communication skills and the social consequences of stuttering. Blood and Blood (2004) noted that a subgroup of adolescents who stutter experience social penalties because of the stereotypes associated with the disorder. Added attention to peer reactions and the strong desire to fit in negatively influence the adolescent's beliefs around stuttering.

THE ABCs OF STUTTERING

Affective Components

Adolescence is a time of emotional fluctuations effectively described as a "roller coaster of feelings" (Murphy & Yaruss, 1999). Frustration and anger develop over prior therapy failure, eventually building resentment toward the therapy process. Such emotions can plunge the adolescent's psyche into negative self-doubt and helplessness. The expectation of gaining fluency, along with the knowledge of the relapse phenomena, fuel feelings of despair of ever overcoming stuttering. Shame, coupled with feelings of isolation, becomes more prevalent as the teen attempts to conceal his stuttering from peers. Blood and Blood (2004) reported that the majority of adolescents who stutter perceive themselves as poor communicators and may avoid the common speaking tasks within the school environment (e.g., group discussions, public speaking, interpersonal conversations, and talking with strangers). Such fears can lead to withdrawal and decreased socialization experiences. This frustration weighs heavily on the thoughts of the adolescent, creating low self-esteem and increasing the person's vulnerability to bullying by peers.

Behavioral Components

Very little information is available regarding the speech production abilities of adolescents who stutter (Blood, 1995; Peters & Starkweather, 1989). Conture (2001), in efforts to remedy this deficit, collected behavioral data on a small sample of 15 young adolescents (12–14 years of age) who stuttered. Teens in this sample exhibited a mean rate of 16.5 stuttered words per 100 words spoken with a mean SSI rating of 3.5. Their disfluency type was predominantly part-word repetitions with 10 of the 15 subjects exhibiting a concomitant articulation disorder. Although limited in scope, this research does provide a descriptive picture of the behavioral characteristics of some teenagers who stutter.

Managing stuttering is difficult during this period of life, leading to increased use of tricks and avoidance strategies in an effort to conform to the norm, or status quo, of the teen culture (Blood, 1995; Blood & Blood, 2004; Murphy & Yaruss, 1999). In early adolescence, teens increase the use of escape, postponement, and avoidance devices. However, with the realization of the relative ineffectual nature of such tricks, they eventually drop these secondary behaviors and incorporate covert or subtle ways of managing stuttering. The novice clinician may interpret the decrease in measurable observable moments of stuttering as a sign of progress in therapy, not realizing the development of internalized stuttering is just another means for the teen to hide his imperfections. In reality, these teens are moving further down the spiral of stuttering with increased negative reactions to the disorder.

Cognitive Components

The period of early adolescence is characterized by the alienation of parental influence or contact accompanied with a strong desire to be accepted by one's peer group. Being judged by peers often has a negative impact for adolescents who stutter. The desire to cover up stuttering has its source in the speaker's extreme concern regarding listener perceptions of stuttering (Blood & Blood, 2004; Blood et al., 2003; Manning, 2003).

Intellectually, adolescents are now capable of using metalinguistic skills to figure out ways of hiding episodes of stuttering. They begin to substitute words in which they anticipate stuttering, attempting to hide the overt manifestations of stuttering to avoid negative peer reactions. Perceived peer pressure to conform to group expectations exacerbates the teens' ability to allocate the mental resources needed to modify speech. Teens try every trick to hide this socially unacceptable, penalizing behavior (Manning, 2003). For some teens, social isolation results from their withdrawal because the fear of exposing their flaw far exceeds the desire to engage in peer interactions.

Conture (2001) argued that for some teenagers, the experience of stuttering may "lead to a 'paralysis by analysis' whereby people, places, and things are avoided. Indeed, some teenagers seem to feel that it is better not to act at all than to risk ridicule by their peers for their actions" (p. 219). It is not until the later stages of adolescence (18+ years) that the individual begins to realize the seriousness of the disorder and its handicapping by-products (Peters & Starkweather, 1989). The older adolescent begins to cope more effectively with stuttering and there is a decrease in the use of emotion-based avoidance techniques (Blood et al., 1998).

Working with students who stutter as they move through adolescence involves the management of multiple, interrelated factors. The adolescent's strong desire to appear normal in the eyes of peers may hinder therapy progress, especially if therapy emphasizes openness and direct confrontation of stuttering. You may encounter resistance to therapy as adolescents strive for independence and the desire to be in control of the decision-making process. If you understand this period of adolescence you may be able to turn client resistance into energy for positive speech change.

The following sections define adolescence and discuss the issues facing this population during rapid physical, cognitive, and social development. Next, the topic of motivation is examined in detail with suggestions for coping with and managing the resistant adolescent. Special challenges for the adolescent who stutters are discussed in relation to treatment programs presented in the literature. The chapter concludes with a brief discussion of school modifications to accommodate the special needs of this age group.

Defining Adolescence

Adolescence, a time of trials and tribulation, is a period of physiological, cognitive, and sociological change. The teenager attempts to handle these changes and fit in to the mainstream. The adolescent has a strong desire to not stand out in a negative way from peers, wanting acceptance and participation in activities that bridge the gap between being a child and acting like an adult. Egocentricity is central to all adolescent behavior, focusing on the immediate events of life. Not willing to think about the past and a bit fearful of the future, adolescents remain cemented in the present. Their choices reflect the self-centered perspective characteristic of the period of adolescence, at times hindering their prior family support and connections. Table 10.1 presents an overview of the physiological, cognitive, and sociological factors related to the transition from childhood into adulthood.

Physiological Changes in Adolescence

Adolescence is a period of rapid physical changes due to the release of hormones secreted from various glands. Sabournie and de Bettencourt (1997) summarized the following changes that are observed during puberty: (1) rapid growth in height and weight, (2) development of gonads, (3) growth in reproductive organs, such as enlarged breasts and hips in girls and facial hair and a deepened voice in males, (4) changes in quantity and distribution of muscle and fat, and (5) changes in respiratory and circulatory systems that results in greater physical endurance and strength. Girls experience puberty at an earlier age, usually at 10, with boys beginning their growth spurt at 12.5 years of age (Santrock, 1987). Some adolescents enter puberty early, which is advantageous for boys, who are perceived by peers as more popular and are high achievers. However, early-maturing girls may experience stress because the physical changes are out of sync with their emotional maturity (Myers, 1992), with late-maturing girls showing higher achievement.

Cognitive Development

The adolescents' ability to reason and problem-solve increases during this period of cognitive development. Their ability to think for themselves and consider what others think of them factors into their egocentric reasoning. The world evolves around their unique experiences, which no adult could possibly understand. Adolescents gradually advance into Piaget's stage of cognitive development called *formal operations*. Their ability to use abstract reasoning and logic advances in two stages: emergent formal operational thought and conquest of thought (Rice, 1999). During

Table 10.1

Characteristics of adolescents in the areas of physiological, cognitive, and sociological development.

Task	Stage of Adolescence		
	Early (10–14)	Middle (14–16)	Late (16–20)
Acceptance of the Physiological Changes of Puberty	• Physical changes occur rapidly but with wide person-to-person variability. • Self-consciousness, insecurity, and worry about being different from peers.	• Pubertal changes almost complete for girls; boys are still undergoing physical changes. • Girls more confident; boys more awkward.	• Adult appearance; comfortable with physical changes. • Physical strength continues to increase, especially for males.
Attainment of Independence	• Changes of puberty distinguish early adolescence from children, but do not provide independence. • Ambivalence (childhood dependency unattractive, but unprepared for the independence of adulthood) leads to vacillation between parents and peers for support.	• Ability to work, drive, date, appear more mature; dependency lessens and peer bonds increase. • Conflict with authority, limit testing, experimental and risk-taking behaviors at a maximum.	• Independence a realistic social expectation. • Continuing education, becoming employed, getting married—all possibilities that often lead to ambivalence about independence.
Emergence of a Stable Identity	• Am I OK? Am I normal? • How do I fit into my peer group? • Paradoxical loss of identity in becoming a member of a peer group.	• Who am I? • How am I different from other people? • What makes me special or unique?	• Who am I in relation to other people? • What is my role with respect to education, work, sexuality, community, religion, and family?
Development of Cognitive Patterns	• Concrete operational thought: present more real than future, concrete more real than abstract. • Egocentrism • Personal fable • Imaginary audience	• Emerging formal operations: abstractions, hypothesis, and thinking about future personal interests and emerging identity.	• Formal operations: thinking about the future, things as they should be, options, consequences can be considered.

Source: From Communication Solutions for Older Students, *by Vicki Lord Larson and Nancy McKinley, 2003, Eau Claire, WI: Thinking Publications. Copyright 2003 by Thinking Publications. Reprinted with permission.*

emergent formal operational thought (11 or 12 years of age), adolescents are beginning to find solutions to problems more readily; yet, not until 14 or 15 years of age are they able to explain their solutions based on logical principles and reasoning. Their ability to test hypotheses and deduce conclusions is not fully developed until the later part of adolescence.

Related to therapy, the adolescent may be able to detect flaws in the clinician's explanations regarding her rationale for assignments. You must be competent in your ability to explain why you want the adolescent to perform certain tasks. Providing sound rationale will give you credibility in the eyes of the adolescent, who often is questioning the reasoning skills of adults. The adolescent may challenge you if he believes the rationale is not sufficient to justify the assignment or if he perceives any bit of hypocrisy in the rationale. Cognitive growth becomes more evident as adolescents engage in "deliberate and reflective decision making," which you must accept and support to ensure the sanctity of the client/clinician relationship (Sabournie & de Bettencourt, 1997).

Sociological Development

Adolescents experience great changes in their social development that may exert positive or negative influences on their decision-making abilities. Platt and Olson (1997) identified three major factors that impact adolescents' social development: (1) search for identity, (2) the development of independence and autonomy, and (3) a shift in allegiance from family to peers. In the search for identity, adolescents may experiment with different selves, as if changing masks, until they discover the one that fits best. During this experimentation phase, "most adolescents experience conflict, anxiety, and self-doubt as they try to find out who they are" (Rice, 1999, p. 234). During this period, some adolescents may engage in destructive behaviors, such as smoking, substance abuse, and drinking. The search for their identity continues until the later years of adolescence.

Developing independence and autonomy impacts the adolescents' social development as they ponder their values, morals, future plans, and priorities. Their perceptions of self-control and direction over their behaviors often result in conflicts with authority figures (e.g., parents). Adolescents have their own ideas about how they want to dress, what kind of music to listen to, and the kinds of friends they want to have in spite of their parents' feelings. Steinberg (1989) identified three types of autonomy: emotional, behavioral, and ethical. *Emotional autonomy* is the transition from the adolescent depending on his parents for emotional support to turning to his friends instead. *Behavioral autonomy* involves the adolescent's ability to make his own decisions and follow through on them. *Ethical autonomy* is about knowing what is right from wrong and deciphering between what is important and what is not. As the adolescent ventures into more independent thinking and behaving, the lessening of parental influence can be observed.

The adolescent now becomes highly concerned about peer acceptance and relationships. How the adolescent is viewed by his peers is extremely important during the early stages of adolescence. The adolescent spends much time in egocentric thoughts about the "self" and a preoccupation with how he is viewed by others. Two aspects of egocentrism include the imaginary audience and the personal fable, as described by Elkind (Platt & Olson, 1997). The imaginary audience consists of the adolescent's belief that others are always watching him. For example, feeling that everyone at school is staring at his haircut is egocentric behavior. The personal fable involves the adolescent feeling that he is the only one who is suffering from problems and no other person has ever experienced such feelings.

You must understand the teenager's developmental stage to maximize the success of any therapeutic efforts. The needs of adolescents are unique and must be met for a positive transition into adulthood. These include the need to (1) secure relationships that are meaningful and satisfying, (2) make friends with people of different backgrounds and experiences, (3) be accepted and liked in social groups, (4) shift from homosocial interests to heterosocial ones, (5) learn about social aspects of dating, and (6) learn sex-appropriate behaviors to enhance their masculinity and femininity (Rice, 1999). Blood and Blood (2004) reported that adolescents who stutter are at a higher risk for teasing and bullying than their nonstuttering peers and emphasized the need for adolescents to learn healthy coping strategies to implement when teased. To work effectively with this population, Zebrowski (2002) presented three basic assumptions clinicians must be willing to accept when working with adolescents who stutter: (1) They are the center of their universe, (2) being cool is key, and (3) friends are everything; adults are irrelevant. Acknowledging adolescents' need to feel and act independently, the need to be accepted as they are, and the need to be part of a social group is necessary to establishing and maintaining a trusting relationship with adolescents.

Adolescence and Stuttering

There is general consensus in the literature of a need for more research on all aspects of communication in the adolescent who stutters (Blood & Blood, 2004; Botterill & Cook, 1987; Conture, 2001; Gregory, 2003; Kully & Langevin, 1999; Rustin et al., 1995; Schwartz, 1993). The characteristics of adolescents who stutter vary as widely as those peers who are fluent. You will face at least three possible scenarios involving middle-school students: (1) those students wanting to change their speech and willing to put forth the effort, (2) those who attend therapy because of parental influence, and (3) those who are passive and have no opinion in either direction. Each type of student presents special challenges.

The ideal adolescent client is characterized by a strong desire to change speech. This student initiates the request for therapy, expressing concern over the impact of stuttering on peer interactions. Despite previous therapy attempts and failures, the student remains optimistic about gaining fluency and his ability to manage stuttering. The desire to change speech overcomes the tendency for the adolescent to withdraw from adult interactions. This adolescent who stutters will convey his confidences to the clinician, establishing a strong, trusting client/clinician relationship. Because of the interactions in therapy, the adolescent becomes willing to take risks, challenge his belief systems, and confront the fear of stuttering. However, this is the ideal student who is compliant, assumes responsibility for his speech change, and is motivated to tolerate the long therapy process.

Opposite to this profile is the student who is coerced into attending therapy because of parent, teacher, or clinician concern about stuttering. This adolescent's strong desire to "blend in with the crowd" predominates all his interactions, making speech therapy a signal of one's difference, thus creating sufficient grounds for resistance to therapy (Conture, 2001; Manning, 2003). You may encounter middle-school teens who no longer wish to be removed from class for therapy. Nor do they want to allocate the time required to practice skills in settings other than the speech therapy room. Parents want the adolescent to receive therapy and you are willing to provide the services. However, the student does not want your assistance during this period of his life.

According to Manning (2003), "one realistic option for the adolescent is to decline therapy. . . . If therapy of any type is to be effective, it must be their choice" (p. 13). However, this creates a dilemma producing friction among parents, teachers, and the adolescent. When faced with this particular student and all alternatives have been exhausted, Conture (2001) explicitly stated, "The best course of action when we face the challenge of remediating adolescents is a break from therapy where client and clinician can separate, regroup forces, and wait for a more advantageous time to resume therapy" (p. 256).

A word of caution: A break from therapy does not imply dismissal. Maintain monthly contact with the student, touching base to assess current needs and desires. Always leave the door open for a return to therapy or a booster session when needed. Having a flexible schedule with time included for consultation and monitoring will give you the opportunity to confer routinely with adolescents who stutter. Always keep in mind the role of variability in stuttering. One day the adolescent may not have a need for your services, yet the next week, after a series of speech setbacks, he is ready to make efforts to change. When a break from therapy is initiated, make every effort to be positive about the student's choice to withdraw from therapy. Use the concept of a revolving door policy: the student can come and go as necessary. This communicates to adolescents that it is okay to contact the clinician if events change in their lives. Manning (2003) presented a list of "basic take-home concepts" that would be appropriate to share with this particular group of adolescents (see Table 10.2).

The third profile addresses the student who attends therapy on a semiroutine basis yet passively engages in activities to change. This client enjoys the special attention received from the clinician or even the opportunity to get out of class (if services are in the public school). Outside assignments are rarely returned completed. "I forgot" and "I don't know" become regular responses from the client. Lacking the motivation to assume responsibility for their actions, adolescents like this are, perhaps, the most difficult to engage. Having no desire to work for change but feeling comfortable in therapy is a combination doomed to fail. Working with this group of adolescents requires a thorough understanding of the area of motivation.

Table 10.2
Basic take-home concepts when meeting the adolescent who stutters for the first time.

- You are not alone.
- Stuttering is not your fault.
- You can have a wonderfully successful and happy life even if you stutter.
- Although it may take some time and effort, great success is possible.
- There are several good sources of information that will enable you to become knowledgeable about the nature of stuttering and people who do it.
- There are experienced and wise clinicians who are available when you are ready.
- It is possible to make wonderful and dramatic changes in the way you interpret yourself and your ability to communicate with others.

Source: Based on Manning (2003, p. 14).

SPECIAL ISSUES

Service Delivery Models

The literature on adolescents who stutter provides little guidance regarding the best service delivery model for this population. If the teen is enrolled in therapy, the service delivery model is typically a pullout model with little built-in flexibility. However, because of the teens' increased need to not be different from his peers, the pullout model may not be the most appropriate. Ramig and Bennett (1995) addressed service delivery issues for high school students and provide a unique alternative: speech therapy for credit. Designed as an elective class or a part of the existing (public speaking) course, students (not just those who stutter) sign up for a speech therapy class in which they receive academic credit and grades. Therapists who are at the high school only once a week provide the academic grade for one fifth of the class. If they are providing the course twice a week, the speech portion would be two fifths. There are several advantages to this alternative model:

1. Older teens who are sensitive to being identified as different may accept this as a viable alternative to leaving an already in-session class.
2. Credit toward graduation may help motivate teenagers.
3. Grades are based on the teens' effort and completion of homework assignments, making teens more accountable for their progress.
4. Receiving grades may provide an incentive for teens to take therapy seriously.

Other service delivery alternatives might include before- or after-school therapy, Saturday sessions, or once-a-month weekend (Friday, Saturday, and Sunday) intensive therapy (in place of weekly sessions). Thinking outside the box becomes an essential skill for clinicians working with middle- and high-school teens who stutter. Advocating for innovative service delivery models should be on your agenda and would certainly make the job easier. It is difficult to work with teens who do not want to be singled out as the student with "a problem." These alternatives to routine therapy may keep teens in therapy and support them during this critical developmental period.

Working with Teachers

Middle and high school teachers have a tremendous burden placed on them by the current educational organization. You must remain aware of these constraints when asking for the teacher's assistance with a particular student. "Teachers can become very powerful allies to the SLP in his or her remediation of an older child's or teen's stuttering problem; however, allies, like anything that should grow with time, must be cultivated and develop through continued interaction" (Conture, 2001, p. 278). In the beginning of the year, meet with teachers to discuss the teen's classroom modifications. It is recommended that the teen participate in this meeting because some teens have definite opinions regarding how to address stuttering in the class. Teachers and clinicians must respect the teens' concerns regarding peer awareness of stuttering and absence from class for therapy. Throughout the year, brief notes left in the teacher's box can facilitate communication between you and the teacher (see Figure 10.1). You can arrange for a short meeting every 6 weeks with the teen's teachers to assess academic progress and evaluate speech performance in the classroom. Prior to each student's annual individual educational plan (IEP) meeting, talk with the teacher to identify specific concerns, ideas for new modifications, and need for continued therapy. Working with teachers remains a critical part of the teen's therapy program.

Working with Parents

Parents are an important part of therapy for teens, although teens often want nothing to do with their parents. Schedule routine meetings with the teen's parents to discuss treatment goals, implementation and transfer of goals into the home, and ways in which the parent can facilitate therapy. Teens must play an active role in determining how they want parents to help them with their speech. More important, parents need to learn to cope with stuttering in their teen, just as teens have to learn to cope. Zebrowski (2002) believed teens would like parents to become more open and accepting of stuttering, less concerned about the behaviors of stuttering. She encouraged teens to talk to their parents about therapy goals, what they need from the parents, and acknowledge parental concerns. This becomes an important part of the teen's therapy. "Once the teenager feels ready to talk with parents, we schedule a meeting that includes the teenager, partent(s), and clinician. The teenager basically develops the agenda and runs the meeting. We take a back seat and step in if and when there is a breakdown in communication" (Zebrowski, 2002, p. 99).

For some teens, the agenda may include a discussion about terminating therapy. The question becomes "When is enough *enough*?" The teen who expresses concern about being taken out of class for speech therapy or missing social time because he has to go to therapy is not a good candidate for continued therapy. If the teen doesn't want to be there, neither you nor the parents can force the child to learn what needs to be learned to change stuttering. It is by far a better idea to arrange for periodic checkups, following the dental model, than to continue with the resistant teen. Giving the student a break from therapy is not giving up on the hope of better speech for your child. Conture (2001), in his parting thoughts regarding working with teenagers, wrote, "Most importantly, we have tried to show that it is very helpful to know when to let go; that is, it is professionally correct to terminate therapy when it is obviously going nowhere" (p. 280). However, even if the teen is not in therapy, the parents can receive support from several sources: (1) the therapist, (2) NSA parent newsletters, and/or (3) monthly support group meetings. Parents need our support, too! Parents may express feelings of guilt and abandonment regarding the decision to stop therapy and they need a safe environment to discuss their feelings and problem-solve how they can continue to support their teen who stutters.

During these transitional years, parents can be guided in ways to help their adolescent cope with stuttering. The National Stuttering Association (2001) distributes a Top 10 "To Do" List for Teens designed to empower parents of teens who stutter. Table 10.3 provides a summary of their suggestions for parents.

Notes to Teachers

SPEECH UPDATE

Dear _____: Date: _____

How is _____ doing in your class?

_____

_____

_____

_____

_____

Thanks for the update. Please leave in my box.
Ellen Bennett, Speech Pathologist

SPEECH UPDATE

Dear _____: Date: _____

Are the classroom modifications working to help _____
participate more openly in your class?

_____

_____

_____

_____

_____

Thanks for the update. Please leave in my box.
Ellen Bennett, Speech Pathologist

SPEECH UPDATE

Dear _____: Date: _____

Do you have any new concerns regarding _____ fluency?

_____

_____

_____

_____

_____

Thanks for the update. Please leave in my box.
Ellen Bennett, Speech Pathologist

Figure 10.1
Example of notes clinicians can distribute to obtain information of adolescents who stutter.

Table 10.3
Suggestions for parents of teens who stutter.

Top 10 "To-Do" List for Teens	
Learn about stuttering	Gain knowledge about stuttering
Talk openly with your child	Keep lines of communication open and allow your child to talk about the feelings experienced when stuttering
Empower your child	Empowerment occurs through acceptance and trust
Provide direction and support	Allow your teen to make choices about managing stuttering, even if this choice would not be yours
Choose appropriate therapy	Find a specialist in stuttering therapy and become a part of treatment
Accept your child's stuttering	Accept that stuttering is a part of your teen's life and remember that denial and avoidance of stuttering only fosters its maintenance
Release ownership	Remember that your teen is responsible for his own speech
Be prepared for unexpected changes	Changes in focus and motivation are a part of adolescence and stuttering
Give yourself a break	Remember that change occurs in small steps and learn to appreciate them
Get connected	Connection with others who face the challenge of stuttering in their children will provide hope and encouragement for the future

Source: Handout distributed by the National Stuttering Association, 2001–2002.

Motivating the Adolescent

Motivation can best be defined as an internal desire, want, or need. Motivation comes from the Latin root meaning "to move" (Tavris & Wade, 1987) and can be categorized into two dimensions: biological and social. Eating, sleeping, and seeking shelter are primary or **biological motives** because our bodies seek them out when deprived. **Social motives,** which are learned behaviors, act as "incentives to draw us toward a goal" (p. 350). Human beings are by nature motivated by curiosity, play, exploration, novelty, and understanding. We are motivated to be social, affiliate with others, and to seek love and approval. Mayer (1999) identified seven characteristics of motivated individuals: (1) having a dream, (2) having fun, (3) having a desire, (4) having faith, (5) creating your own luck, (6) accepting failure as a learning experience, and (7) having the determination to persevere. In the therapeutic setting, some clients enter the therapy setting ready and willing to make the sacrifices necessary to make the speech change. However, the majority of adolescents are not engaged in therapy, appearing unmotivated, and present a challenge to clinicians. To better understand the concept of motivation, clinicians need a theoretical foundation.

Theories of Motivation

Theories are useful in helping clinicians understand why people behave in certain patterns. Three theories of motivation (hierarchy of needs, reinforcement theory, and cognitive) are discussed here. The **hierarchy of needs theory** was developed by Maslow to explain human motivation. Maslow believed humans are motivated in certain ways through the desire to have basic biological needs met. This hierarchy of needs ascends from the most basic biological needs to a complex array of psychological/social needs, that is, basic physical needs, safety and security needs, need for love and belonging, esteem needs, and need for self-actualization. Basic physical needs include the necessary elements for survival, that is, oxygen, food, drink, sleep, elimination, and shelter. Once these needs are satisfied, the next level, safety needs, emerges within the individual. Safety encompasses the need to feel protected, through law, order, security, and predictability. The need for love and belonging is the third need to be satisfied through family ties and affection. Esteem needs are divided into two categories: (1) esteem needs fulfilled from within the individual and (2) esteem needs satisfied through evaluation from others, such as praise and acknowledgment from significant others (Wallace, 1993).

With the basic needs achieved, the individual moves toward experiences in which he betters himself through self-actualization. Wallace (1993) describes self-actualization as an individualized process of achieving one's highest potential. The person experiences feelings of discontent and restlessness. These feelings motivate him to strive to better himself. The development of one's innate potential is not an automatic, expectant behavior. The individual must have the courage to engage in risk-taking behaviors with the confidence to overcome obstacles. However, the ability to meet these needs is greatly influenced by society, culture, and the individual's early home environment and experiences. In summary, Maslow's hierarchy of needs theory is just one attempt to explain the behaviors of human beings. Keep in mind that, although presented as a hierarchy, a person may attempt to satisfy needs at multiple levels along the hierarchy (Tavris & Wade, 1987).

Another theory used to explain human motivation is **reinforcement theory.** The adolescent may be motivated through two distinctly different factors: intrinsic versus extrinsic motivators. **Intrinsic motivation** derives from internal rewards, such as pleasure, intellectual challenge, or satisfaction of curiosity (Deci & Ryan, 1992; Harter, 1992; Ryan, Connell, & Grolnick, 1992). The individual engages in an intellectual debate with another and receives internal satisfaction. Outside encouragement to engage in the task is not required because the individual obtains reinforcement in performing the task itself. Intrinsic motivators allow individuals to continue working toward a goal because they want to achieve it.

Extrinsic motivation, in contrast, is based on the need to either respond to societal demands and constraints or behave in certain ways to gain some reward (e.g., money, rewards, stickers, or fear of punishment) (Ryan et al., 1992). The adolescent may continue to perform in therapy to earn the necessary points to receive a reward. Once the external motivators are removed, there is no guarantee the client will continue to work toward the prescribed goal. Only when sufficient success has occurred will the client receive intrinsic feelings of accomplishment necessary to sustain continued therapy efforts without external motivators in place.

Extrinsic factors may initially drive people to be motivated, but intrinsic motivation is what keeps them motivated. A developmental change in motivation orientation (intrinsic → extrinsic) occurs between third grade and the beginning of middle school (Harter, 1992). The education system shifts its emphasis to extrinsic motivation through the focus on the products of learning as evaluated by grades, creating a disinterest in the learning process (representative of a decline in intrinsic motivation). Figure 10.2 illustrates how today's school environment influences student's motivational orientation.

Cognitive theory has as its basic assumption the belief that expectations of success influences motivational levels. If people expect to be successful in accomplishing a goal, they are more likely to work hard at it and reach success. When people feel a goal is unattainable, they are less likely to put the effort toward achieving the goal. This concept is called the **self-fulfilling prophecy** in that if people expect to fail or succeed, they usually meet that expectation (Bandura, 1977, 1986).

Cognitive theory thus places greater emphasis on the individual rather than the environment, contending the individual is an active agent of his behavior (Bandura, 1977, 1986). A major component of this theory is how the individual evaluates the possible outcome of a behavior through **cognitive operations,** that is, goal setting and self-evaluation. The emphasis is placed on the individual's responsibility to change his behavior through goal setting and self-evaluation of performance abilities, that is, **self-efficacy.** Four sources of self-efficacy influence the individual's behaviors, emotions, and thoughts: actual experiences (past successes or failures); vicarious experiences (watching others); verbal persuasion (encouragement); and physiological arousal (physical state).

These sources of self-efficacy interact to build intrinsic motivation and willingness to achieve, thus enhancing one's **self-esteem.** The individual's self-esteem consists of four different attributes: (1) feelings of significance (being valued by others); (2) feelings of competence (capable, adequate, successful); (3) feelings of power (ability to influence and control others); and (4) feelings of virtue (attaining higher moral standards and actively helping others) (Bloom & Cooperman, 1999). For the adolescent who stutters, therapy must utilize all four sources of self-efficacy, building self-esteem, and fostering intrinsic motivation. Intrinsic motivation is a necessary component for any long-term therapy success. In summary, motivation is a function of what researchers describe as the natural need for competence, control, and connectedness (or belonging) (Deci & Ryan, 1992).

The 3 C's of Motivation

The frustration many therapists experience trying to motivate the adolescent who stutters is not uncommon. Teachers have struggled with this problem for years, and researchers have attempted to provide answers. What researchers have learned about motivation and the adolescent can be clearly applied to the therapy setting. You

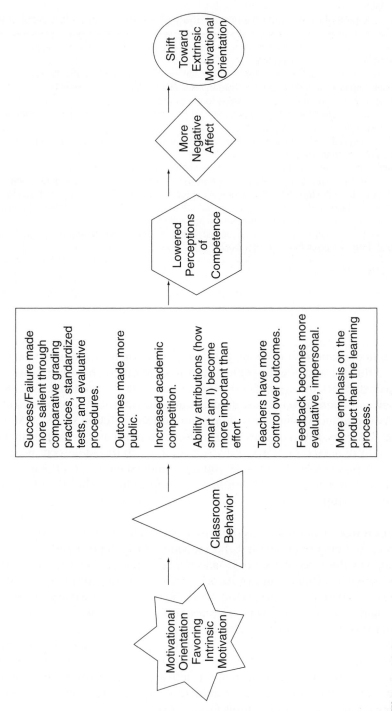

Figure 10.2

Hypothesized model of how changes in the school environment (particularly upon entrance to junior high school) influence competence, affect, and motivation.

Source: From Achinevement and Motivation: A Social-Developmental Perspective, (p. 88), by S. Harter, 1992, New York: Cambridge University Press. Reprinted with the permission of Cambridge University Press.

Table 10.4
Basic principles of motivation covering a variety of variables related to clinical practice.

---

1. Motivation will be high when goals to be achieved are important to the person and there is a good likelihood of reaching them.
2. Motivation will be facilitated if the client can identify with and relate to the clinician.
3. Motivation is enhanced when the clinician links what is deemed important to accomplish something that is of greater concern or value to the client.
4. Motivation is often facilitated if one does enough learning about something to generate at least a moderate level of anxiety about it.
5. Motivation is enhanced if the clinician is concerned more about the ongoing implementation of the process than about the goals alone.
6. Motivation is often increased when there is shared effort and responsibility.
7. Motivated learning is sustained best by a reciprocal flow of information and influence.
8. Motivation is affected by the frequency of contact between the parties, by the tasks that are perceived as being unfinished, by rewards that are acquired on an unpredictable schedule, and by information that is received in appropriate increments.
9. Success bequeaths success! Success with incremental small steps along the way facilitates long-range success toward larger overall goals.

Source: Based on Shipley (1997, p. 24).

should understand events taking place within the therapy room will have a motivational influence on students—either positive or negative. The way information is provided to students, the type of activities you use, your interactional style, the amount of choice or control you give to students, and the opportunities to work alone or in groups will influence the teens' motivation to learn (McCombs, 1991; Meece, 1991; Poplin & Weeres, 1993). Shipley (1997) discussed nine basic principles that often impact motivation (see Table 10.4). If you wish to reach the adolescent who stutters in ways that produce lasting change, you must understand these principles and establish feelings of competence, control, and connectedness (the three C's) in the adolescent who stutters.

Competence. Competence comprises two major factors: (1) the relationship between the target activity and the individual's capabilities and (2) the feedback provided by the activity itself or by another person. First, the activity must involve a certain degree of challenge (not too easy, yet not too difficult). Deci and Ryan (1992) found that students who were intrinsically motivated selected more challenging tasks over simpler, easy ones. You can guide the adolescent in choosing tasks at this level of **optimal challenge,** defined as one step more difficult than the current level of ability. They also found subjects who selected such tasks rated them as more interesting. Secondly, competence is perceived by the individual when feedback is provided through the actual completion of the task or comments made by a significant other (e.g., parent, teacher, peer, clinician). However, a clearer understanding of the nature of this feedback is necessary.

Feedback that fosters intrinsic motivation conveys positive competence in the absence of evaluative comments (Deci & Ryan, 1992). Positive competence feedback is defined as information that affirms competency and supports autonomy on behalf of the client. Competence can be determined in two ways: (1) judgment of performance relative to the individual's experience and personal standards (**task-intrinsic feedback**), or (2) judgment of performance relative to that of others (**social feedback**).

When the teens' attention is drawn toward their ability to perform rather than the learning involved in the task, intrinsic motivation declines. Also, when emphasis is placed "on the products of one's efforts, rather than on the process of learning itself," intrinsic motivation declines. Focusing on the affect experienced during the task ("How did you feel while you were . . . " vs. "How did you do?") increases the teen's perceptions of competence. Harter (1992) indicated that the student's emotional reaction is critical to determining motivational level. You can help teens identify their feelings when performing various tasks and discuss them in relation to the learning process as a whole. Your use of competency cues is another strategy that should enhance the teen's feeling of competence and level of motivation.

Competency cues influence the individual's perceptions of competence in several ways. If external competency cues focus on the individual's attention on the evaluation of his performance, performance anxiety may arise. Therapists who set standards of performance, assign goals, and impose deadlines (without input from the adolescent) foster feelings of less personal control. When external competence cues suggest a task offers a personal challenge to the individual, the task may be experienced by the individual as more meaningful (Harackiewicz, Manderlink, & Sansone, 1992), increasing perceptions of competence.

A sample feedback that focuses on task completion versus performance ability might be "Aren't you proud of yourself? You did it! You didn't let stuttering stop you from making that speech." This provides encouraging feedback that does not impose external evaluative controls. Involving the adolescent in determining goals and expectations is another strategy you can use to encourage positive perceptions of competence. "Motivation is enhanced when clinicians and clients have the same goals" (Shipley, 1997, p. 24). You can help teens select their standards for performance on any given task (e.g., catching two stutters) before they begin the task. This allows the teen to monitor his performance during the course of the task and enhances competence and intrinsic motivation.

Control. Clinicians want the adolescent to be intrinsically motivated; however, many of the routine therapeutic strategies clinicians use to reinforce behaviors in younger clients actually produce negative effects in the adolescent population. Reinforcing compliant behavior with stickers, food, or tokens may produce a decrease in intrinsic motivation for the adolescent, who interprets the clinician's conditions as controlling and self-limiting (Deci & Ryan, 1992). The adolescent interprets the earning of rewards as evaluative behavior on the part of the clinician. Performance feedback ("I like how you reduced your tension on that pullout") is now perceived as an evaluation of them as people, something adolescents are highly sensitive to and to which they may react negatively.

Structure therapy sessions in ways that teach adolescents to focus on the interest, enjoyment, and satisfaction of the task rather than the evaluation of performance ability (Amabile & Hennessey, 1992). When task performance is evaluative ("You did well reading that passage"), adolescents perceive the feedback as controlling and negative. Their interest in the task will decrease, and they will appear apathetic toward therapy. However, when the student is encouraged to self-evaluate the task in terms of his own perspective of mastery, a sense of control and intrinsic motivation grows. We can view developing a sense of control as a cycle: (1) First, the teen views a task as challenging, (2) works to master the task, (3) which leads to increased intrinsic satisfaction, and (4) leads to the development of skills that allows the teen to become independent, that is, in control of his behavior.

The desire to control one's environment effectively is critical during this period when adolescents are searching to find themselves. Self-determination is defined through the question "Why am I doing this?" You can reinforce the teen's desire for control by the degree of choice making you permit in therapy. You must allow the adolescent to make choices regarding therapy tasks. You can provide the necessary information to help the student make an informed choice, but ultimately the decision should be left up to the adolescent. This requires a degree of flexibility on your part and having a lesson plan that is client driven.

When students are not allowed choice and control, they are not likely to learn strategies for self-regulated learning, nor will they learn the value of self-initiated learning (Zimmerman, 2000). It is hyphothesized that clinicians who are oriented toward autonomy provide a setting that fosters such learning (Deci & Ryan, 1992). Self-determination, or control, can also be reinforced through activities that are optimally challenging to teens, interesting, relevant within the context of their current life's events, and available in their immediate environment (e.g., talking to a friend in class, ordering lunch at a fast-food restaurant, or talking to the attendance clerk). Only the teen can tell you what is challenging, interesting, or relevant to him. You must be open and accepting of what teens have to say about their speech and ways they want to work on it.

Another aspect of control concerns the teens' beliefs about their ability to control stuttering. Attribution theory asserts that individuals who believe their poor performance is caused by factors out of their control are unlikely to see any hope of improvement (Anderman & Hicks-Midgley, 1998). Emphasizing the "doing" aspect of stuttering, in that stuttering is something they *do* therefore they can *undo,* may provide hope for teens trying to cope with repeated failure in controlling their stuttering. The literature on motivation and achievement clearly indicates when provided with choices over the types of tasks asked to perform and how much time to allot to each task, teens develop feelings of self-determination. You can foster this feeling also through problem-solving, helping teens break up large tasks into manageable portions, and providing guidelines for students to use when self-monitoring their own progress (p. 3).

Connectedness. Adolescence is a time of wanting to fit in and belong to a crowd. Crowds emerge in adolescence to help individuals master the developmental stage of autonomy and identity. The degree to which the adolescent is able to make friends and have an accepting peer group is of major importance. Adolescents need to belong to a group or be associated with others in some way. Many teens who stutter have no difficulty developing peer groups that are supportive. However, some teens experience severe social penalties because of their stuttering and fail to develop this sense of relatedness. Involvement in fluency groups and self-help organizations can ease the sense of isolation often felt by the teen who stutters. Many students with the disorder report never knowing another person who stutters. You must make every effort to schedule fluency clients together, even if they are in different grades. The opportunity to express their feelings with others who truly understand is very therapeutic. If grouping together is not possible, at least see the fluency teen individually so issues related to stuttering can be addressed in a personally safe environment. Some teens will not open up to others if they perceive negative consequences from sharing. The challenges facing the teen who stutters are unique and not easily understood by peers.

Another means of establishing feelings of connectedness is to learn about other people who stutter (e.g., famous stars and athletes who have become role models). Teens are often surprised to find out that Bruce Willis stutters or the voice of Darth Vader is James Earl Jones, another adult who stutters. Researching and discussing others who have struggled with this disorder can encourage teens to take a more active role in therapy. Teens, under your guidance, can use Internet resources to gather biographical information on famous people who stutter. This information can be used for reports or class presentations as the teen becomes more open about stuttering.

Also, teens can become Internet pals with other teens across the country through the Web site from Mankato State University, operated by Judith Kuster (see chapter 11). With modern technology, teens can engage in chat sessions, e-mail correspondence, and even join Web groups specifically involving people who stutter. The discussions on these electronic mailing lists help the teen gain a newer, different perspective on stuttering and perhaps open the door for hope. Each year at the National Stuttering Association Convention, teens gather together to share stories, make new friends, and visit with old acquaintances. For some, this is the first opportunity to socialize in meaningful ways with other teens who stutter (e.g., eating, dancing, sightseeing). Many of the connections made at these conventions are lifelines of support for the teen who stutters. Teens working together to educate others about stuttering is a wonderful experience. The active participation of students, once they feel there is a purpose to therapy, further motivates them to "do something about their speech."

TREATMENT DIRECTIONS

Therapy for adolescents who stutter must be designed around the particular interests, learning styles, and fluency profile of each teen. Teens are more likely to engage in activities that are related to their own personal goals and social needs (Deci & Ryan, 1992; Zebrowski, 2002). Clinicians and teens should work together to establish a common understanding of such goals and needs, a task that will establish a positive client/clinician relationship. Following the framework of the House That Jack Built allows for such individualization as the teen sees each student's needs being considered by the therapist (when designing the house). Some teens may have more social needs to be addressed in therapy; others need more functional skill development.

Two principles for working with adolescents who stutter involve the concepts of having fun and creating a favorable learning community. Weinstein (1996) reported four principles of fun at work: (1) Think about the people involved in therapy, their interests, and so on, (2) lead by example: the clinician discusses her own behavior and how it relates to the therapy process; (3) make therapy personally relevant to the teen; and (4) understand change takes time and clinicians must have patience and take pride in the small events that demonstrate student progress.

You are the ultimate motivator. You express concern and sincerity to students through your actions and enthusiasm for your work. Creating an environment conducive to learning involves three components: (1) Make yourself and your therapy room attractive to students, (2) focus their attention on individual and collaborative learning goals and help them achieve these goals, and (3) teach things that are worth learning, in ways that help students appreciate their value (Brophy, 1998). A positive learning environment should have walls decorated with student work, bulletin board displays created by students, and a comfortable seating arrangement for sharing with one another. Chairs placed in a circle display an open posture compared to the traditional setup with the therapist on one side of the table and students on the opposite.

Several therapy activities are recommended for use with adolescents who stutter. Haiku, a Japanese form of poetry, provides an excellent opportunity for students to find their own voice and share it with others. Haiku consists of three short lines of 17 syllables (5-7-5) with no consideration of rhyme and punctuation. Teens can brainstorm different emotions, compare and contrast themes, or be free with their words. Sharing these poems with the group or others allows the teen the opportunity of uncensored self-expression. You can encourage incorporation of themes around stuttering into the student's poetry as warranted. Figure 10.3 contains an excellent example of a young man's expression of his experience with stuttering, presented at the general session of the 2004 National Stuttering Association Conference. At the 2003 NSA conference, a songwriter presented a rap he had written about growing up with stuttering. This was his way of expressing himself, which resulted in a standing ovation from the audience. Again, during the 2004 NSA conference, teens created their own raps. Children, standing on stage, sang their songs to an audience of over 500 conference participants. This experience will undoubtedly stay in their minds for years to come. Figure 10.4 provides an example of one 18-year old's personal song shared with the group.

Encouraging students to set goals and monitor their progress will foster their active involvement in therapy. You must first model how to write specific behavioral objectives to ensure the teen will be able to have success. Identifying the components of a goal as "who" will do "what," "when," "where," and "how" aids in creating tasks that students can actually accomplish.

For example, "I will call my girlfriend on Tuesday evening, around 8:30, and ask if she has finished her homework. I will purposely stutter once during this conversation. Afterward, I will write in my journal the feelings, behaviors, and thoughts I

Untitled

I have a thought I want to share
But, to speak I must prepare
I take a breath, I say a prayer

I open my mouth
It all goes south

What will you think?
My dignity's on the brink
All because my words don't link

I'm in a block
Vocal cords won't unlock
Let go—I'm on the clock

It's all gone wrong
It's taking too long
Use your techniques! I can't prolong

It makes me shutter
I start to sputter
Oh God, get me through this stutter

I look at your face
"Come on, pick up the pace"
It's true, I'm losing the race

My throat is shut
I'm in a rut
This word is kicking my butt!

Unexpected, it burst through
nonetheless overdue!

I look around, I see them stare
On the next word, despite the glare
I take a breath, I say a prayer.

—Kevin P. Murphy

Figure 10.3
The expression of stuttering by a young man. Presentation at the 2004 National Stuttering Association Conference, Baltimore, MD.
Reprinted with permission from K. Murphy.

had while on the phone." Each teen writes specific short-term goals on index cards. Under each goal, they list three to five specific behaviors they can do to move toward the goal. These cards are kept in the therapy room and periodically reviewed by the students. You can facilitate the problem-solving process when students fail to reach their goals and help them generate explicit behaviorally oriented tasks to ensure success. For example, a teen writes on an index card "I would like to be less anxious when using the phone." His three behaviors are "I will answer the phone; I will

---

Freedom

It doesn't matter how I say it
It's what I'm saying
Get pass the block
and hear the message.
We all have the right
to be heard
no matter how we sound
I might get frustrated
and I might get sad
But I'm going to say
what's on my mind
If you don't like
the way I sound,
that's your problem.
Because we all have the right
to say what we feel
Talking may come easy to you
but for me, it's a struggle
I'm sick of getting those blank eyes
when I block
I'm tired of people finishing
my sentences
I get annoyed
when I have to repeat myself
I'm sick of the stereotyping
Enough is Enough
It's time to be free
I'm tired of being afraid of the telephone
I want to be able
to share my voice
without the taunting
Let's all share our voice
and be proud of who we are.

—Nicole Pratt

Figure 10.4
A teenager's song about stuttering. Presentation at the 2004 National Stuttering Association Conference, Baltimore, MD.
Reprinted with permission from N. Pratt.

relax before talking on the phone; and I will call my girlfriend once a day." The clinician, realizing these behaviors are too vague for actual implementation, reviews with the student the components of goals and helps him create concrete tasks geared for success.

Therapy activities involving small-group projects promote teamwork and socialization. Teens can become involved in two types of group projects: (1) those related to group interests and (2) those related to stuttering. You can engage students initially in small projects common to group members (e.g., driver's training, steps involved in planning a graduation party, or promoting a concert at school). As group members become familiar with one another, guide the group into projects involving stuttering, for example, promoting International Stuttering Awareness Day (ISAD), October 22, teacher inservice training on how to help teens in your class, or starting a teen support group on campus. Teens can generate their own survey on stuttering and decide who they will approach and where. Working with the Journalism Department, students can write an article for the school paper or even for submission to *Letting Go*, the newsletter of the National Stuttering Association.

Information learned through contextual learning will be retained over time. Incorporate real-life, everyday tasks students typically perform. Ordering food in a restaurant, making phone calls, asking a girl out on a date, or preparing for a job interview are challenging experiences for some teens who stutter. Through interactions with teens, you will discover the major issues facing each individual. Creative planning and schedule rearrangement may be necessary to provide the opportunity to go to Burger King for lunch and practice speech assertiveness. Use of role play is critical for this age group because they need to "do it" to "get it." Just talking about what they might say during a job interview or on the phone is not sufficient. Engagements in pretend scenarios approximates the real situation and better prepares the student.

For example, one senior high student had to make a presentation in speech class. The instructions were to bring three items that best represent you as a person. He selected his CD player, a DVD tape, and his speech journal. He wanted to tell his peers about his stuttering and saw this as an opportunity to educate them. During therapy, the clinician asked him to close his eyes and visualize the classroom, where the other students would be seated, where the teacher was, and where he would stand. He practiced deep breathing for relaxation as he tensed just picturing the event. He scripted out his speech so he could plan where to put in easy onsets and voluntary stuttering. Next, he stood up in the therapy room and rehearsed his speech with the clinician guiding him on general public speaking techniques. The session concluded with a discussion of when he would volunteer to give the speech. He identified the pros and cons of being first and last, deciding he would prefer to be among the first three speeches.

This session provides an example of a contextually relevant task of high importance to the student, directed by the student under the guidance of the clinician. The student made his choices regarding what he was to say, how he wanted to talk, and when he would present. From this author's experience, sessions like these foster motivation and engagement in the therapy process. However, you have heard the expression "You can lead a horse to water, but you can't make him drink." Although we cannot make him drink, we can increase the likelihood he will find interest in drinking on his own. The ultimate goal to therapeutic success always starts with an individual plan. You must realize the importance of designing therapy plans that best suit the needs of the adolescent. The following sections review other approaches for working with the adolescent who stutters.

Fluency-Shaping Approaches

Howard Schwartz

Schwartz (1993) described a contingent time-out, behaviorally oriented program for use with adolescents during the transfer and maintenance phase of therapy. The transfer component of this program includes both parental and peer group support systems to help the younger adolescent remember to use his fluency controls in situations beyond the therapy room. The adolescent is cued to change his speech when stuttering is present. Upon the third reminder with no change in speech, the client is put in a time-out condition for a predetermined amount of time. According to Schwartz, the older adolescent must learn to take responsibility for his transfer, which will be influenced by previous therapy experiences. Upon referral to an adolescent client, Schwartz attempts to answer three important questions:

1. Is this an individual who continues to stutter because of therapy programs that were inadequate to meet his needs?
2. Has this individual received a regular comprehensive therapy program and failed to make the necessary changes required to improve his speech?
3. Is this an individual who has never received any speech therapy and now requires attention?

Answers to these questions will guide you in jointly planning intervention. The plan will be modified according to the number of years of experience with stuttering, the degree of awareness of stuttering accompanied with emotional reactions, and the extent the adolescent is concerned with listener reaction. Schwartz noted the adolescent population should be considered a unique group with its own characteristics and not be treated with a blended approach from child or adult therapy paradigms.

Lena Rustin, Francis Cook, and Rob Spence

Rustin, Cook, and Spence (1995) published a book totally devoted to working with this population, *The Management of Stuttering in Adolescence*. Their communication skills approach stressed the importance of understanding the period of adolescence. They identify four common themes: (1) physical transformations, (2) intellectual growth, (3) peer pressure, and (4) the desire for independence. For the adolescent who stutters, they have observed difficulties in the area of social adjustment when compared to nonstuttering peers. Stuttering may inhibit adolescents' peer interactions in the following ways: avoidance of social contact, withdrawal from social interaction, and low rates of initiating social contacts. They developed an intervention paradigm that addresses the special affective, behavioral, and cognitive components of stuttering in adolescence.

Rustin's et al. (1995) adolescent program focuses on communication skill development in six areas: (1) fluency control, (2) relaxation, (3) social skills, (4) problem solving, (5) negotiation, and (6) environmental factors. Their program can be either intensive or nonintensive, depending on the needs of the individual adolescent. Stage 1 is subdivided into four components: normal speech production, stuttering, personal stuttering characteristics, and fluency controls, such as rate control, easy onsets, flow of speech, and breath control. Relaxation is approached in the same way as described in chapter 8. Social skills training focuses on the development of the adolescent's observation, listening, turn taking, as well as praise and reinforcement.

These authors wrote that many adolescents do not maintain eye contact during conversations; therefore, they do not observe the listener, which leads to misjudgments regarding listener reactions. Adolescents require instruction on how to reduce anxiety during conversations so they can listen adequately and respond appropriately. Additionally, anxiety reduction helps the adolescent learn how to initiate, maintain, and end conversations using appropriate turn-taking skills. Lastly, Rustin et al. stated that teenagers often lack confidence in their communicative competence. Incorporation of exercises in which teenagers actively evaluate their performance in positive ways aids in the enhancement of self-worth. An example used by these authors is having the client identify something he does well each day (e.g., make the bed, dress well, being punctual) and practice making positive self-statements daily to reinforce the action, for example, "I really made an effort to look my best today" (p. 66).

Problem-solving exercises are incorporated into therapy, as well as teaching adolescents negotiation skills. Rustin et al. defined negotiation as "having empathy for the other person's point of view, the facility to generate the alternative choices available, and an ability to present a reasoned argument on the basis of this understanding" (p. 68). Adolescents learn to differentiate among passivity, assertion, and aggression, which helps them deal with various relationships. An important emphasis of this approach involves the environment, or social system of the adolescent. Parents as partners in therapy help the adolescent transfer and maintain the gains made in treatment.

Stuttering Modification Approaches

Dorvan Breitenfeldt and Delores Lorenz

The Successful Stuttering Management Program (SSMP) (Breitenfeldt & Lorenz, 1989) is an intensive stuttering management program for adults and adolescents. This intervention paradigm involves 4 hours of work per day, plus homework over the course of 3 weeks. Participants work in group and individual sessions; most include some form of community interaction. The goals of the program are to increase awareness of stuttering (through tallying), identify the individual's behaviors of stuttering, and learn how to modify them. Decreasing fear and avoidance are critical for success with this program. A unique aspect of SSMP is that both adults and adolescents interact together during the treatment course, providing an opportunity to socialize with others who stutter. However, SSMP is an adult-oriented direct approach to the management of stuttering. It is presumed teens participating in this program would need to be intrinsically motivated with a strong desire to change their speaking patterns (see chapter 11 for more details on SSMP).

Table 10.5
Guidelines for working with adolescents who stutter.

1. Establish roles, goals, and responsibilities.
2. Know your subject, that is, the culture of the adolescent.
3. Talk less, listen more, and avoid overstatements.
4. Advance, retreat, and advance when interacting with the reticent teen.
5. Use humor in therapy.
6. Use writing as a tool for adolescents to express their feelings and ideas.

Source: Based on Zebrowski (2002).

Patricia Zebrowski

Zebrowski (2002) described a week-long intensive program for teenagers who stutter. Three critical principles are outlined for establishing a client/clinician relationship with teens who stutter: (1) Understand the period of adolescence, (2) allow the teens to get to know you, and (3) utilize coaching and counseling strategies. Directive teaching strategies will most likely result in disaster with this population. You have to follow the student's leads and interests, not your own agenda. Take time to get to know your teens beyond their stuttering. Find out their likes, dislikes, and hobbies, and share with them your own likes, dislikes, and hobbies. Learn from them how stuttering has shaped their lives. Zebrowski emphasized that the teen is the "expert" on his stuttering and only the teen can decide what strategy works best. Again, gently guide the teen; don't direct him. This type of clinician behavior will lead to active choice making rather than passive compliance with clinician requests.

Various procedures are used in this program to develop self-responsibility, self-discovery, and self-improvement. Treatment is described as a "journey" involving a series of guidelines (Table 10.5). Zebrowski used writing projects as a way for the adolescent to express ideas and feelings. Outside of questionnaires and surveys, teens are asked to write a self-characterization in third-person narrative. You can use these characterizations to determine if any personal constructs are working against the teen's possibility for speech change. Next, teens are presented with a series of open-ended sentences or questions to probe client understanding of stuttering disorders in general. Teens are also asked to maintain a journal and are assigned topics for reflection. This therapy program incorporates cognitive restructuring activities, as well as motor and mental training (e.g., self-talk, imagery).

Integrated Approaches

Gordon Blood

Blood's (1995) work with adolescents who stutter is categorized as an integrated approach with a strong emphasis on cognitive elements of treatment. After 25 hours of intensive work learning a modified version of the Stutter-Free Speech Program, teens are then involved in 50 hours of relapse prevention sessions. Blood reported that the motoric aspects of speech production will be maintained if the client develops positive coping strategies. Among the strategies recommended by Blood are self-responsibility and relapse management. To instill self-responsibility, clinicians must train clients to "attribute the acquisition of these skills to themselves and not some 'magic pill'" (p. 170). Additionally, the adolescent who has realistic expectations regarding use of his skills in real-life situations may be better able to cope with the daily fluctuations common in stuttering.

An important component of Blood's model for cognitive-behavioral treatment is his improvement criteria. "The management of stuttering is only as successful as the client's ability and willingness to assume responsibility for the day-to-day changes in his or her speaking behavior and attitudes" (p. 170). The teenager who stutters must have knowledge of the behaviors and attitudes that either facilitate or interfere with speech. They must also demonstrate proficiency in the use of fluency behaviors and positive attitudes. More important, the teen must exhibit functional use of these skills outside the therapy environment. To help maintain skill usage in these situations, Blood described a relapse management program called POWER^2 (Figure 10.5).

Blood defined "relapse as the tendency to revert to a previous mode of behavior" (p. 170). His relapse model includes three features: (1) squares representing factors that influence maintenance, (2) circles representing the actual program components, and (3) rectangles representing specific skills trained in the program. POWER^2 stands for *P*ermission, *O*wnership, *W*ell-being, *E*steem of one's self, *R*esilience, and *R*esponsibility. Teens are taught how to approach, understand, and solve problems related to their stuttering. Development of effective coping strategies is critical for maintenance of newly learned behaviors (cognitive or behavioral). Four coping strategies taught by Blood (1995) are (1) expressing negative emotion, (2) engaging in appropriate assertive responses, (3) bouncing back after a stuttering episode, and (4) dealing with interpersonal and intrapersonal variables. Blood's POWER^2 program is an innovative and creative way to address the unique needs of the adolescent who stutters.

Deborah Kully and Marilyn Langevin

Kully and Langevin (1999) described an intensive treatment, the Comprehensive Stuttering Program, a design for adolescent stutterers based on the philosophy that "adolescents are a distinctive population and warrant their own approach to treatment" (p. 139). Their treatment procedures follow an integrated approach to the treatment of stuttering disorders with emphasis on affective, behavioral, and cognitive components of stuttering. Table 10.6 outlines the goals of this program in each of these areas.

Before determining the adolescent's readiness for treatment, the clinician must assess three factors, the first being the client's desire to change. Second is the client's understanding or expectations of treatment. The adolescent must understand the process of change and the gradual nature of change that requires certain responsibilities from the client. Third, the adolescent must have the ability to handle treatment requirements, such as good attention span with appropriate cognitive and social skills to interact in group settings.

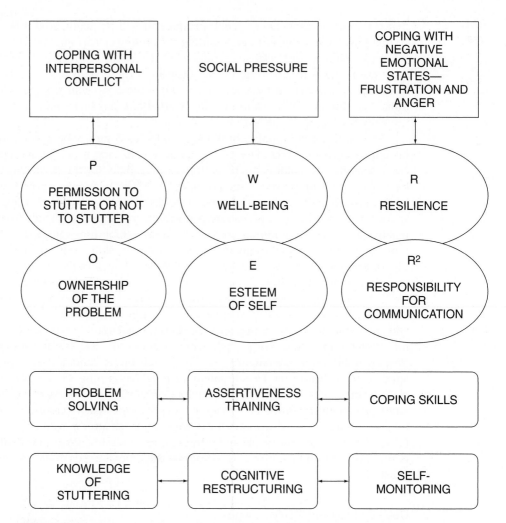

Figure 10.5
Relapse management program designed to help young adults deal with their feelings
and attitudes toward stuttering.
*Source: From "POWER² Relapse Management with Adolescents Who Stutter," by G. W.
Blood, 1995,* Language Speech and Hearing Services in Schools 26, *p. 171. Copyright
1995 by the American Speech-Language-Hearing Association. Reprinted with permission.*

Willie Botterill and Francis Cook

Botterill and Cook (1987) described the application of Kelly's personal construct theory to therapy for adolescents who stutter. They affirm that adolescents, who have had
previous therapy that has been relatively unsuccessful, may require a different approach to treatment. Repeated failures may have changed their personal construct

Table 10.6

Treatment goals for their intensive program for adolescents who stutter.

Speech-Related Goals	Emotional-Attitudinal Goals	Self-Management Goals	Environmental Goals
• Ability to sustain controlled fluency in all speaking environments • Ability to manage residual stuttering • Improved communication, social skills, and confidence	• Positive attitudes toward communication • Openness about stuttering and fluency-enhancing techniques • Reduced avoidance behavior • Ability to manage fear and anxiety • Ability to handle regression and recognize when relapse in occurring • Ability to deal with teasing and negative listener reactions	• Increased understanding of the etiology and development of stuttering and the long-term process of change • Problem-solving skills • Self-monitoring and self-evaluation skills • Ability to manipulate the environment to support needs • Ability to sequence practice activities	• Increased parental understanding of the etiology and development of stuttering and the long-term process of change • Parental ability to support the client during and after therapy

Source: Based on Kully and Langevin (1999).

belief system, which inhibits the ability to change speech. "Failure to maintain newly found fluency may have its roots in the psychological status of the individual rather than any 'deterioration' of treatment effects" (p. 148). The adolescent will require special assistance in making the transition from a person who stutters to a fluent speaker, necessitating a change in the person's constructs. (Refer to chapter 6 for more information on personal construct theory.)

Fry and Cook (2003) described this 2-week intensive program for young adults (15–18 years) in which participants meet daily from 10 a.m. to 3:30 p.m. Groups are relatively small, approximately 8 members, and facilitated by two therapists and students in training. The philosophy of the program is based on Aaron Beck's cognitive therapy principles of information processing: (1) Individuals make sense of the world by interpreting their experience; (2) underlying beliefs and assumptions shape this process; (3) the way an event is interpreted influences emotional, somatic, and behavioral responses; (4) interpretations may be biased, inaccurate, or unhelpful; and (5) behavioral responses may be counterproductive. This therapy program involves a process of seven steps designed to assist teens in combating negative automatic thoughts by learning how to confront and reframe thoughts (Table 10.7). A major advantage to this therapy paradigm is the power inherent in working with groups of teens. We know peer pressure and acceptance is critical at this time. Group cognitive therapy allows these young adults to express differing opinions, share experiences, and see alternative perspectives from their peers while gaining group acceptance.

Table 10.7
Guided therapy plan for young adults who stutter.

Participants will follow these steps:	
Step 1	"Buy into" the cognitive model of therapy.
Step 2	Learn to identify emotions and negative automatic thoughts (NATs).
Step 3	Critically evaluate their NATs.
Step 4	Use behavioral experiments to test reality.
Step 5	Apply problem-solving skills.
Step 6	Work on assumptions and beliefs if necessary.
Step 7	Develop an action plan.

Source: Based on Fry and Cook (2003).

Table 10.8
Advice for SLP (speech-language pathologists) from teens who stutter.

1. Learn about stuttering, the whole disorder. Keep up with the latest research and ideas about stuttering.
2. Concentrate on increasing comfort in communication.
3. Stress that it is OK to stutter.
4. Learn about the extreme difficulty involved in using the techniques on a daily basis, in real-life situations.
5. Be there for the individual who stutters.
6. Try to understand the motivation behind not talking and avoiding certain situations.
7. Be invested in the whole process.
8. Listen to your clients and incorporate their suggestions and thoughts into therapy.
9. Work on real-life situations.
10. Get involved in self-help groups for people who stutter.
11. Make an effort to build trust and mutual respect before expecting clients to work hard and take risks in therapy.
12. Be consistent.
13. Ask your client and their family what they need or want from therapy.
14. Assist your client in educating teachers, parents, family members, and peers about stuttering.

Source: Reaching Out, *by FRIENDS: The Association of Young People Who Stutter (2004).*

Caveat

Adolescents are a unique breed of people who stutter. Speech-language pathologists (SLPs) working with this age group must recognize this uniqueness and allow teens to express themselves in a free, unconditional setting. A key element of success with this age group is the ability to listen. At the 2003 Friends Convention, teens worked together to generate a list of suggestions for those professionals working with them (FRIENDS, 2004). Table 10.8 lists their recommendations. Any competent clinician would acknowledge the worthiness of their advice when guiding teens toward the path of better communication.

CHAPTER SUMMARY

The period of adolescence is characterized by turmoil and testing limits. Adolescents who stutter face challenges exacerbated by their difficulty communicating. Feelings of frustration, anger, and resentment toward therapy and clinicians negatively influence motivational levels. They continue to struggle with speech and develop avoidances as they try to fit in with their peers. Understanding the physiological, cognitive, and sociological changes occurring during this period is essential for meaningful interactions with teens.

The question of how to best service this population remains unanswered. Clinicians may have to resort to innovative therapy scheduling to engage adolescents in the therapy process. A particular concern of clinicians involves motivating teens who stutter. Motivation drives all humans to achieve through either intrinsic or extrinsic reinforcement. However, the transition from elementary school to middle and high school is characterized by a decrease in intrinsic motivation to learn with a shift toward extrinsic motivation. Accompanied by this shift is a lack of interest in the adult world (imposing the controls of extrinsic motivation), presenting a problem for the clinician trying to help teens modify their speech.

Clinicians who foster feelings of competence, control, and connectedness are more likely to engage these teens, motivate them to become involved in the learning process, and help them cope more effectively with stuttering. The literature provides little guidance with regard to treatment approaches designed specifically for adolescents who stutter. There are only a few fluency-shaping, stuttering modification, and integrated approaches appearing in the literature. It is speculated the reason why resources are limited is that few clinicians choose to focus on this group because of the discord often felt between adolescents and adults during this period. Adolescence can be a trying period for teens, parents, teachers, and clinicians. This chapter presented several strategies to make therapy more engaging, motivational, and successful for teens who stutter.

STUDY QUESTIONS

1. What makes working with the adolescent difficult for clinicians?
2. Describe the sociological changes taking place during this period.
3. Differentiate between intrinsic and extrinsic motivation.
4. How can the clinician foster intrinsic motivation?
5. Discuss the 3C's of motivation in relation to planning therapy for teens who stutter.
6. Describe how competency cues can either increase or decrease intrinsic motivation.
7. Compare and contrast two therapy approaches presented in this chapter.

11

Adults Who Stutter

CHAPTER OUTLINE

Advice from Adults Who Stutter
Fluency-Shaping Approaches
Stuttering Modification Approaches

Integrated Approaches
A Personal Account of Stuttering

LEARNER OBJECTIVES

- Identify the social, vocational, and therapeutic limitations of lifelong stuttering.

- Explain the interaction of affective, behavioral, and cognitive elements of stuttering to the adult.

- Identify the subgroups of adults who stutter who are classified as interiorized (covert) stutterers.

- Select appropriately the intensity and type of intervention based on client needs.

- Explain the advantages and disadvantages of group therapy to the adult client.

- Utilize skills during group therapy to enhance the participation of all members.

- Understand the phenomena of relapse and be able to explain it to the adult client.

- Inform the adult client of area and national support groups as an adjunct to therapy.

- Compare and contrast the various therapy methods described in the literature.

KEY TERMS

active listening
adjusting stage
clarification
covert stuttering
encouraging and supporting
informational exchange
interiorized stuttering
mini-lecturing
modeling

PFCT–R therapy
redirecting
regulating stage
reflection
relapse
repairing
rescuing
scanning

self-disclosure
self-help groups
silence
small talk
structuring stage
success
summarizing
targeting stage

A lifelong battle with stuttering leaves its mark on adults who stutter (Guitar, 1998). The challenges faced by adults vary, yet they can be grouped into three areas: social, vocational, and therapeutic. Socially, these adults have encountered numerous communication exchanges that have shaped their belief system regarding effective communication. Socialization experiences, such as dating, cocktail parties, and holiday gatherings, often leave memory traces filled with negativity and pessimism.

Vocationally, the adult who stutters may have chosen the path of least resistence, choosing jobs requiring little or no verbal demands. This author recalls a young adult who wanted to become a pilot but did not fulfill his lifetime dream because he believed it was impossible due to his stuttering. Instead, he chose a vocation that was neither verbally nor intellectually challenging. The shaping of the future because of stuttering does not always go in this negative direction. A medical student once shared with me his determination to become a doctor despite a severe stutter. He had the inner confidence, knowing he could tackle the textbook knowledge, but at times he doubted if he would succeed because of his speech. But this client won the battle, not letting stuttering shape his future—he became a doctor. Sadly, this is not the story for other adults who stutter. Gabel, Tellis, and Althouse (2003) presented results of a study confirming vocational stereotyping for adults who stutter in which participants reported certain careers were "more or less advisable" for people who stutter.

Therapeutically, adults who stutter have typically undergone numerous interventions throughout their life: different therapies, different therapists, intensive versus individual—producing little long-term change. They continue to stutter despite these efforts. Previous therapy, whether perceived as successful or not, shapes how adults view the prospect of future therapy. Questions remain unanswered: "Why didn't it work?" "What's new out there?" "Maybe if I try again, it will work." What brings the adult back into therapy is highly individual. For whatever reason, social, vocational, and therapeutic experiences create special treatment needs particular to each adult who stutters.

THE ABCs OF STUTTERING

Affective Components

The affective component of stuttering depends on prior experiences (successes and failures) of the adult who stutters. Feelings of frustration, fear, guilt, helplessness, and, more important, shame may influence everyday interactions and self-perceptions regarding one's ability to change the stuttering (Van Riper, 1971). When fluency has been established only to be lost later, clients begin to doubt the therapy process and the likelihood of ever getting better. With failure after failure (in their own eyes), shame festers and grows. Adults internalize this feeling of inadequacy and frustration, furthering the struggle to gain control over stuttering (Conture, 2001). For some adults, these emotions exacerbate the behavioral components of stuttering.

Behavioral Components

The behavioral component of stuttering is also highly variable depending on the adult's prior experiences with stuttering and his natural coping abilities. For the adult who continues to react emotionally to stuttering, the behaviors exhibited are more likely to be tense sound prolongations and blocks accompanied by secondary behaviors of escape and avoidance (Conture, 2001; Guitar, 1998; Manning, 1996; Van Riper, 1971). Trying hard not to stutter, the adult resorts to reactionary behaviors, such as tensing, pushing, avoiding, and other behaviors used to produce speech. If adults have given up on their struggle against stuttering, the behavior may be mild, consisting of short-sound syllable repetitions that are void of excessive tension. The behaviors of stuttering in adults depends on their current affective and cognitive states related to coping with this disorder.

Cognitive Components

The belief system of adults who stutter certainly varies because cognitive orientation is influenced by life's experiences (Conture, 2001; Cooper & Cooper, 1985; Daly, 1988; Guitar, 1998; Shapiro, 1999; Van Riper, 1971). Klein and Amster (2003) prescribed that adults reconsider their beliefs surrounding stuttering, communication, and the impact of one on the other. If the adult believes stuttering has negatively impacted his life's decisions, negative thinking and self-doubt regarding the ability to gain any degree of control over stuttering will be evident. These individuals may harbor anger and regret, believing they could be more than they are at the present time. Thoughts such as "If I didn't stutter, I would have a better job, a better marriage, or a better social life" ruminate in their minds, reinforcing a sense of helplessness over their current situation. Gabel, Blood, Tellis, and Althouse (2004) confirmed this tendency in a study investigating role entrapment and occupational stereotyping in adults who stutter.

For some adults, life's experiences are not overshadowed by stuttering. Stuttering becomes a part of them and does not encompass their entire self. They may not like the stuttering, but they have tired of fighting it and have gained a certain level of acceptance of the disorder. Other adults continue to avoid situations or difficult words when stuttering is anticipated, dreading its emergence. One subgroup of adults who stutter do anything in order to appear fluent: the covert stutterers.

Covert Stuttering: A By-Product of Affective and Cognitive Reactions

Covert stuttering, or **interiorized stuttering,** has interested clinicians for years (Cheasman & Everard, 2003; Douglas & Quarrington, 1952; Ham, 1999; Hood, 2003). A phenomenon on the rise (Cheasman & Everard, 2003), therapists are challenged by this subgroup of stutterers who maintain a facade of fluency at all costs. Covert stuttering arises when an interaction between the affective and cognitive domains of stuttering produces excessive fear and extreme avoidance behaviors in response to the mere thought of stuttering or being associated with stuttering. This subgroup of adults who stutter do anything not to stutter. Because covert stutterers are able to assume the role of fluent people, the rewards of fluency far outweigh the cost of their covert behaviors. The consequences of stuttering, albeit predominantly self-imposed, are viewed as punitive and reflective of a personal flaw.

Hood (2003) identified four factors that perpetuate the need for covert behaviors for these adults who stutter: fear, guilt, shame, and denial. *Fear* encompasses the fear of stuttering or the fear the person might stutter and look or sound different. Most important, the covert stutterer fears the secret of stuttering will be discovered by the listener. Covert stutterers feel *guilt* for what they do or might do, guilt for stuttering, and guilt for making the listener feel uncomfortable. *Shame*, the devaluation of oneself as a person of worth and a person who stutters, festers the need to hide stuttering. *Denial* of stuttering is easily accomplished because of high levels of fluency. This further complicates the profile, allowing the adult to further deny the need to work on resolving the stuttering.

Treatment for covert, or interiorized, stuttering requires explicit clinical skills. As the clinician working with a covert stutterer, you must realize that change in cognitive and affective domains is a gradual, lengthy process. Proficiency in the use of cognitive behavior therapy is vital. Remember that asking covert stutterers to confront stuttering is an attack on their self. It is as if stuttering makes them feel different and they do not want to be different. Group therapy is recommended for all clients covert in their behaviors in order to establish a group affiliation, reduce feelings of isolation, and develop a support system (Cheasman & Everard, 2003; Hood, 2003). Cheasman and Everard (2003) believed therapy should be nonintensive because change in identity does not occur rapidly. Their treatment course involves 24 2-hour sessions with only interiorized stutterers. Therapy focuses on avoidance reduction, speech modification, and cognitive analysis. Desensitization activities make up the bulk of the initial work for these groups, followed by speech modification. Challenging negative thoughts and identifying "hot thoughts" that contribute to increased negative emotion around stuttering are the foundation of this therapy approach.

Working with covert stutterers involves several key elements. First, therapeutic emphasis must be on desensitization to stuttering. Second, fluency should not be the focus of group discussions. Third, clients must be encouraged to take small risks based on a hierarchy of feared situations. Hood (2003) stressed the need to establish a feeling of *acceptance* of stuttering, that is, work to be more open, honest, tolerant, and accepting of stuttering. Hood recommends the following activities to adults to foster acceptance of stuttering:

1. Talk more openly about stuttering.
2. Mention your stuttering to family, friends, and colleagues.
3. Advertise your stuttering by wearing a NSA T-shirt or pin.
4. Insert voluntary stuttering on nonfeared words.
5. Make phone calls to strangers and insert voluntary stuttering.
6. Have reading material about stuttering in your office or home.

Covert stuttering presents a special challenge to even the experienced clinician. Using problem-solving strategies, you can help adults see the payoffs (advantages) and costs (disadvantages) of their avoidance behaviors. Engaging them in discussions and challenging their rationalizations and overgeneralizations can help them see how stuttering has defined and confined them as communicators. During these confrontations, clients develop the skills to make better decisions regarding therapy goals. Cheasman and Everard (2003) described SMART goals, which are *S*pecific, *M*easurable, *A*chievable, *R*ealistic, and *T*ime constrained. The covert stutterer must learn how to use SMART goals as stepping-stones toward the larger ultimate goal: being free of the shame of stuttering and accepting oneself as a person who stutters.

Sheehan's Iceberg of Stuttering

A unique way to visualize the affective, behavioral, and cognitive components of stuttering in the adult population is through Sheehan's (1986) Iceberg of Stuttering analogy. Sheehan conceptualized stuttering as an iceberg "with its greatest portion lying beneath the surface. What is seen and heard is the smaller portion; what is hidden from view is far greater and more dangerous and destructive" (p. 207). The affective and cognitive aspects of stuttering lie beneath the surface. Although the behaviors of stuttering may remain stable, what lies beneath the waterline may continue to grow. The shame, anger, and guilt fester underwater and become maintaining elements in stuttering, what Hicks (2002) referred to as the "emotional garbage" accompanying stuttering. You must be cognizant of the extent to which these factors are present in the profiles of adults who stutter. Hicks (2002, 2003, 2004), expanding on Sheehan's iceberg analogy, created a unique visual aid to help adults understand the development and maintenance of stuttering (see Figure 11.1).

The iceberg analogy is particularly relevant to adults who stutter because this group differs greatly in their manifestation of the ABCs of stuttering. The lifelong struggle with stuttering surfaces through different configurations of icebergs, varying in density, size, and hardness (Hicks, 2002). Hicks hypothesized that the visible part of stuttering, which you hear, comprises only 10% of the problem of stuttering. The hidden part is what lies beneath the water. This 90% comprises the fear, shame, guilt, anxiety, hopelessness, isolation, and denial. Therapy that addresses the behavioral aspect of stuttering (e.g., fluency shaping) works to melt the tip of the iceberg. However, Hicks noted that ice is less dense than water and the iceberg slowly rises out of the water again, another way of viewing relapse. The under-the-surface emotions not only bring about the reemergence of the tip of the iceberg but also increase the strength of these emotions. However, the development of icebergs differs for each adult. People each develop their own individualized iceberg, varying in density, size, and hardness.

Hicks (2003) wrote that for some adults, their iceberg is characterized by low density with extremely overt stutters and little emotional garbage accompanying them. Then there is a subgroup of adults who have medium-dense icebergs, like a typical iceberg. For some covert stutterers, their iceberg is highly dense with the majority of stuttering lying beneath the surface. This analogy continues with the size of each person's iceberg. For severe stutterers their iceberg is large, yet for mild stutterers it is small, or what Hicks (2003) calls "an ice cube." The hardness aspect of icebergs describes the temperament of the client. "Soft" icebergs represent clients who are cooperative, willing to try new strategies. "Medium" icebergs are the typical stutterers,

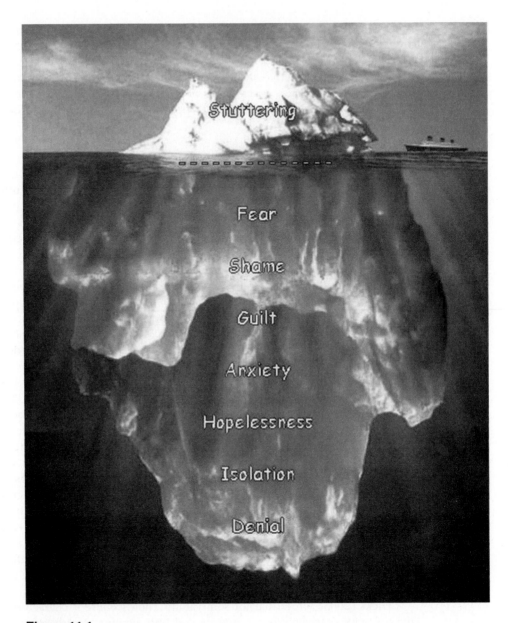

Figure 11.1
Hicks's (2004) representation of Sheehan's Iceberg of Stuttering analogy.
Source: www.russhicks.com/iceberg. Reprinted with permission.

wary but willing to learn. "Hard" icebergs refer to the reluctant clients, resistant to change and new ideas. Hicks summarized his analogy with the following comments:

> The captain of the *Titanic* looked out and saw this little iceberg and thought his ship was unsinkable. So he said "Full speed ahead!" What he did NOT see was the 90% of the iceberg under the water. And the ship sank . . . because he didn't really understand the awesome power of an iceberg. He would have made a lousy SLP! If he was a good SLP, he would have recognized that he wasn't seeing the whole iceberg. And that his ship—good though it really was—could NOT stand up to the huge berg. He MUST deal with the WHOLE iceberg, not just the tip of the surface.

Clinicians who work with adults who stutter must understand the dynamic interaction among the affective, behavioral, and cognitive components of stuttering. Being aware of how these factors impact one another (such as in the iceberg analogy) is critical to the effective management of stuttering and the prevention of relapse. When developing treatment plans, both clinicians and their adult clients need to consider the following special issues in this process.

SPECIAL ISSUES

Service Delivery Models

When determining the best model of therapy, you must consider the factors of intensity and type of intervention appropriate for each adult who stutters. Multiple factors influence the selection of a particular service delivery model with the decision ultimately the client's responsibility. Your role is to provide the adult client with all the necessary information, assist in the problem-solving process of advantages and disadvantages for each model, and be available to support the adult in whatever decision he makes.

Intensity

Intensity of treatment is one factor to consider when planning intervention for the adult who stutters. Intensity refers to the frequency and duration of treatment sessions. Intensity can range from 3-week all-day residential programs to once-a-year weekend workshops. Ingham (1999) described a residential intensive behaviorally oriented treatment program for adults. According to Ingham, the establishment phase of treatment consists of 8- to 12-hour days of practice over the course of approximately 9 days. Neilson (1999) described a cognitive-behavioral intensive treatment program used in Sydney, Australia. Intensive group treatment takes place over a 3-week consecutive period with weekends free. The first week focuses on establishing fluency, the second week transfers this fluency to everyday environments, and the last week involves the generalization of fluency skills to settings and situations relevant to each particular client. Clients return for follow-up sessions periodically over the course of the next year.

Webster (1980) conducts his intensive Precision Fluency Shaping Program in much the same way as Ingham and Neilson. Breitenfeldt and Lorenz's Successful Stuttering

Management Program (1989) is an intensive program whose emphasis takes the form of modified stuttering rather than fluency shaping. Bloom and Cooperman (1999) wrote about their synergistic approach to the treatment of stuttering, which includes a short-term intensive component along with a long-term nonintensive program. The intensive portion of the program is carried out via a "Weekend Workshop for Those Who Stutter." After this experience, the adult attends individual therapy sessions and participates in clinician-directed weekly support group meetings.

Type

Several types of service delivery models are used with adults who stutter: individual, group, or a combination of the two. An overview of the writings on treatment models for adults indicates frequent use of the combined individual and group session formats. Manning's (1996) treatment approach includes initial individual sessions followed by group support meetings. Onslow and Packman (1997) and Ingham (1999) utilize group and individual sessions for their intensive behavioral programs. In Bloom and Cooperman's (1999) synergistic approach to the treatment of stuttering, the adult attends individual therapy sessions and participates in weekly support group meetings. Neilson (1999) utilizes a pure group intervention design for her treatment program. Ham (1999) clearly stated that the type of service delivery model utilized is influenced by many factors outside the control of the clinician, such as work setting, time, resources, and money. Cassar and Neilson (1997) discussed extending the scope of service delivery into the workplace. Their unique approach for adults includes a collaborative effort of the clinician, adult client, and workplace members to facilitate therapy outcomes for the adult who stutters.

Group Therapy. Group therapy is often used as the sole treatment type for adults who stutter. Gregory (2003) noted three advantages of group treatment: (1) allows an opportunity for social skill practice, (2) creates a feeling of unity, and (3) provides a place to ventilate. He structures his group sessions into thirds, each portion designed to meet a specific goal. At the beginning of each group session, members participate in a structured relaxation exercise. Then the floor is open for discussion with topics ranging from shared stuttering experiences, previous therapies, or questions related to the disorder itself. The last third of the session incorporates direct practice on newly learned motor skills or role-play scenarios representing real-life situations difficult for group members. At the end of the session, the leader summarizes the session, demonstrating the relevance of the group work toward other activities the members may be engaged in between group therapy sessions. Table 11.1 outlines additional advantages and disadvantages to the group treatment model reported by other researchers (Bloom & Cooperman, 1999; Manning, 1996; Prins, 1984; Ramig & Bennett, 1997b; Webster & Poulos, 1989).

Specific issues arise when conducting group intervention. It requires establishing trust among the members of the group. When membership fluctuates, it may be difficult to establish or maintain genuine, trusting relationships. Group therapy works

Table 11.1
Advantages and disadvantages of group treatment.

Advantages	Disadvantages
Provides an environment for enhancing and maintaining change	Scheduling a time convenient to all likely participants
Helps with the client's feelings of isolation	Maintaining consistent attendance
Promotes an open discussion of stuttering	Securing a location for the meetings
Provides a safe environment where the person can stutter without penalty	Getting enough adults to participate in the group
Provides a structured setting for practicing strategies learned in individual treatment	Establishing a trusting environment when membership fluctuates
Enables the clinician to monitor client's progress in social contexts	Handling the situation when one adult controls the conversation
Provides an open forum for learning about stuttering disorders	Finding a group leader to facilitate group discussions
Serves as a good teaching tool for graduate students in speech pathology	Managing when levels of speech modification/management are drastically different among the participants
Builds a sense of community among participants	

best when there is a semiequivalent degree of skill development among the members. Having a new client who has not had the opportunity to learn techniques within a group of members who are more proficient in their strategies can produce an imbalance in the ability of all members to participate and benefit from the session. This may create too much downtime for some members because of the needs of one individual. When skill levels are somewhat similar, all group participants benefit from clinician instruction and the opportunity for structured practice on modification strategies.

Another issue surrounds group dynamics and the individual personality characteristics present within the group. Briefly, challenges arise when the exchange of ideas or opinions are not balanced among participants. All members must agree to accept each other's feelings and beliefs. Group work requires a proficient group leader who can direct and channel the discussions in positive ways. Let's look at specific skills a group leader needs to conduct group therapy.

Skills Required of Group Leaders

Ramig and Bennett (1997b) identified three skill clusters a group leader must develop to enhance the overall benefit of the group experience: cluster 1, process components; cluster 2, content components; and cluster 3, interpersonal components. Figure 11.2 visually presents these clusters and their individual elements, which facilitate group intervention.

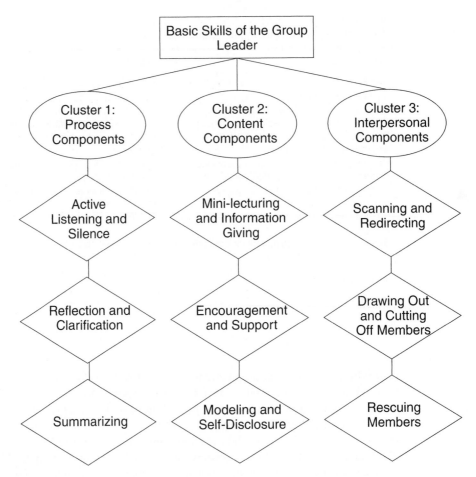

Figure 11.2
Outline of skills required of people functioning as the group leader.
Source: From P. R. Ramig & E. Bennett, "Considerations for Conducting Group Intervention with Adults Who Stutter." Seminars in Speech and Language *1997; 18(4): 346. Reprinted by permission.*

Cluster 1: Process Components

Briefly, process components describe *how* the group leader might respond to members through active listening and using silence, reflection and clarification, and summarizing. **Active listening** relates to the attention paid to the speaker's words, linguistic stress, and body language. The clinician looks for congruity among these elements of communication in order to understand the message relayed by the speaker. Rollin (1987) noted that "body language accounts for more than 50 percent of a message's impact" (p. 34). The group leader must attend to the client's facial expressions, gestures, body stance, and movement when engaged in active listening. To demonstrate this behavior, the group leader can use head nods, facial expressions, and minimal encouragers.

The use of **silence** by the group leader can be highly effective at facilitating on-going dialogue among group members. Luterman (1991) identified four types of silence relevant to group dynamics: (1) the embarrassed silence, (2) the changing-topic silence, (3) the reflective silence, and (4) the termination silence. The embarrassed silence occurs in the early stages of therapy, usually when members are expecting the group leader to direct the discussions. Ramig and Bennett (1997b) maintained that when the group leader does not fill in this silence, members are more likely to use this time as an opportunity to speak up and continue the discussion. The next type of silence involves changing the topic or when members are reflecting on whether they have something else to add to the discussion. During this silence, the leader may ask the members for any last comments and then introduce a new topic of interest to the group.

During group therapy, a variety of emotions may surface as topics are discussed. Members may express feelings of anger, hurt, frustration, and/or even hostility. The group leader may use reflective silence to provide an opportunity for members to experience these emotions in an accepting environment, communicating that all emotions are okay. Luterman noted that "the deepest feelings take place in silence, and . . . that all of the really important work is done in silence" (p. 105). Toward the end of the group session, the group leader may use the termination silence to bring closure to the session. This is followed by a summary of the group's work with a comment regarding the orientation of the next group session.

The use of reflection and clarification are two additional skills leaders may use to conduct group sessions. "**Reflection** involves the restatement of a comment, indicating that the listener has understood the content and feeling conveyed by the speaker" (Ramig & Bennett, 1997b, p. 347). The purpose of this strategy is to ensure that other group members understand the client's message and accompanying emotion. The group leader may make statements, such as "It seems that talking to your boss is a difficult task and you become embarrassed at times," to draw the group's attention to the speaker's communicative intent. This reflective statement could be followed up with an inquiry, such as "I wonder who else has had this experience?" **Clarification** statements are used when the speaker's message is not clear and it is evident other group members are not comprehending. Doyle (1992) identified three types of clarification responses: (1) perception checking, (2) clarifying alternatives, and (3) requesting further information or elaboration. Table 11.2 provides examples of each of these response types.

The last process-oriented strategy is called **summarizing,** a restating of the comments and concerns expressed by group members throughout the session. By consolidating the key elements of the session, group members are able to organize the session's discussion in a structured way. The group leader demonstrates the relevance of each theme to all members and how they might reflect on these themes during the time in between sessions. Ramig and Bennett (1997b) provided this example of summarizing:

> Each of you in today's session expressed a desire to change some aspect of your speech. Two of you plan on making more phone calls during the upcoming week. Tom committed to using voluntary stuttering at least once at the office. And John will pick one conversation with his wife where he will not change any words. As we close today, let's hear from the rest of you about the goals you've set for yourself. (p. 348)

Table 11.2
Examples of clarification responses used by group leaders.

Clarification Response	Examples
Perception checking	"It seems your major concern is . . . " "Are you feeling angry over the situation?"
Clarifying alternatives	"You are saying you're ready to confront your stuttering at work but you are unsure of how to do it. Let's talk about the choices you have . . . " "You seem to be confused about what exactly it is you want from therapy—to be more fluent or to have better control of your stuttering?"
Requesting further information or elaboration	"I am not sure if I understand what happened yesterday at work. Tell me again how the topic of your speech came up." "You say you don't mind how you talk. Could you tell the group more about this?"

Cluster 2: Content Components

The orientation of this cluster relates to *what* events may take part during group therapy sessions. **Mini-lecturing** and **informational exchange** provide a mode for dissemination of information about communication and the disorder of stuttering. Ramig and Bennett (1997b) believed mini-lecturing and information exchanges "serve to educate group members and deal with misinformation that may reduce benefits from intervention" (p. 348). Alm (1995) identified three positive outcomes of study groups conducted in Sweden: (1) increased understanding of oneself and stuttering, (2) created healthy identity and increased self-esteem, and (3) assisted persons who stutter to deal with problems and guided members in the selection of appropriate individual therapy.

Encouraging and supporting group members is an essential behavior for group leaders. To demonstrate encouragement and support, group leaders may use a variety of responses: (1) a person-of-value response, (2) an approval response, (3) a consolation response, and (4) a relaxation response (see Table 11.3). Some members may be hesitant to share their opinion for fear of disappointing the group leader and other members. It is important the leader communicate acceptance of all ideas and positively reinforce those who contribute to group discussions, whether in agreement or not. Remember that group members look to their leader for direction, feedback, and validation. Using a variety of encouraging and supporting responses will help achieve the feeling of acceptance.

Modeling and self-disclosure concludes this section on content components leaders utilize when conducting group therapy. As noted earlier in this text, **modeling** of behaviors, as well as attitudes and feeling, is essential to effective treatment. The leader who models enthusiasm for the therapy process and proficient use of strategies provides an incentive for members to approach treatment positively and hopefully. A leader who is unsure of herself, or is unhappy with the outcome of group treatment,

Table 11.3
Encouraging and supporting responses group leaders may use to communicate effectively with group members.

Type of Encouraging and Supporting Response	Examples
A person-of-value response (showing respect for the client beyond speech-related features)	"You handled that situation nicely." "It sounds like you had fun."
An approval response (showing support and helping client feel more positive)	"That was good of you to help." "You certainly have the ability to do it."
A consolation response (showing genuine caring and concern for the client)	"You are really facing a tough decision." "It must be so difficult knowing you are not going to get the support you want."
A relaxation response (showing interest for the client by asking him to relax during periods of his emotionality)	"Let's take a few minutes to close our eyes." "You are breathing quite fast. Take a full breath and exhale through your mouth."

subtly communicates these attitudes to group members, a condition not conducive to positive treatment gains. At times, it may be relevant for the group leader to use **self-disclosure** (relaying of personal information or experience to assist members with their progress). Self-disclosure helps others see that the leader understands their struggles and helps in the problem-solving process. "The guiding principle is that the helper's (*group leader*) self-disclosure should be for the helpee's (*group member*) benefit" (Okun, 1997, p. 274). Just as the group members share themselves with the leader, so might the leader share personal aspects of his or her experiences with the group.

Cluster 3: Interpersonal Components

Group leaders need certain interpersonal skills to conduct effective group sessions. Use of eye contact and awareness of rescuing behaviors among members can influence group development. To engage group members and facilitate equal involvement in the therapy process, group leaders need to be able to scan using eye contact, redirect members, draw out members, and cut off members.

Scanning is a highly effective tool for group leaders. It is important to make eye contact with every group member throughout the session. Eye contact creates a sense of identification with the member, encouraging him to participate in discussions. **Redirecting** is used to develop a sense of unity among group members. Often members look at the leader when making comments. To redirect group members effectively, Jacobs, Harvill, and Masson (1988) suggested the leader engage in four different activities: (1) Ask members to look at one another when sharing; (2) explain that the leader will not always be looking at them when talking; (3) scan the group while another member is talking, allowing the speaker to make contact with others; and (4) signal the member to talk to everyone by making a sweeping motion around the group with his or her hand (p. 89).

Not all group members participate easily in group therapy. The group leader can use eye contact to draw out a member who may be hesitant to share in front of the group. As a member is sharing his story, the group leader can establish eye contact with the reticent individual, smile, and nod her head as an encouragement to contribute. Nonverbal cues (such as a slight raise of the hand, fidgety hand movements, head nods indicating agreement or disagreement, or subtle subvocalizations) may indicate a readiness to share by the reticent member, and the group leader should attend to these signs, asking the member to provide his insight.

In contrast, there are members who may dominate the discussions, seemingly never stopping to pause. The group leader needs to develop cutting-off skills in order to allow all members to participate in the session. To cut off a member, the leader may remind everyone to allow all group members to participate. The leader may make eye contact with the "talker" of the group, initiate dialogue, and gradually shift eye gaze to another member. This subtle approach to cutting off a rambling member does not always work as planned. The leader may have to resort to a more direct approach, directly interrupting the speaker to gain control of the speaking floor. Ramig and Bennett (1997b) provided this example of cutting-off behaviors: "Ron, let me stop you. The reason why I am doing so is because . . . " or "Let me stop you all here, because I don't want us to lose sight of the point that Jack is trying to make" (p. 350).

The last interpersonal component group leaders must be aware of is **rescuing.** Jacobs et al. (1988) defined rescuing as efforts of group members to console one another when experiencing high emotionality. Comments such as "It'll be okay" or "Don't worry—it'll get better" demonstrate that the listeners are uncomfortable with the emotions being expressed and want the speaker to feel better. However, this could possibly provide false hope for the member. The group leader can talk about rescuing behaviors, when appropriate, with the group through confrontational comments such as, "John, how do you know Alma will be okay?"

Another form of rescuing occurs when members tell the speaker what to do in a particular situation. Although these members are trying to be helpful, they may be communicating to the speaker the belief that he is not able to solve his own problems. Luterman (1991) believed this type of behavior removes the responsibility for change from the individual, encouraging others to "fix it" for them. "Overt assistance, although often appreciated, is also a statement that the recipient is inadequate and needs aid" (p. 55). Both forms of rescuing can have negative effects on group dynamics and must be monitored by the group leader.

The Problem of Relapse

Another issue for discussion is the relative effectiveness of short-term intensive or long-term programs at maintaining treatment gains. Manning (1996) reported that, among the three stages of treatment, "maintenance is burdensome for the client, for he is working against many forces that are pulling in the direction of pretreatment performance and cognition" (p. 239). All of the intensive treatment approaches mentioned establish certain levels of fluency in a brief period of time, regardless of the path chosen. However, do these clients maintain their achieved fluency over time? Is the client able to take this newly learned fluency and hold on to it for any length of time? Bloom and Cooperman (1999) wrote that anywhere from 50% to 90% of adults who have attended intensive treatment programs experience some degree of relapse.

Relapse is defined as the recurrence of symptoms after a period of improvement (Webster & Poulos, 1989). Starkweather (1998) provided an excellent description of a client's belief system after obtaining certain levels of fluency. "Typically, the client, delighting in his newfound fluency, and perhaps assuming that the awful problem is completely behind him, simply stops thinking about it. He feels as though he has been cured of the malady. Why should he bother doing this or that exercise? Stuttering is behind him" (p. 3). However, the small "microstutters begin to occur," just like the weeds in the garden. The client soon finds himself in the throes of the stuttering cycle, struggling with and reacting to the building behaviors. Is this relapse or is it a reflection of a therapeutic failure that did not address the underlying fear of stuttering? Starkweather argued that failure to resolve "unfinished business" may be the underlying source for some relapse episodes. Failure to maintain treatment gains is a phenomenon regardless of the type, intensity, or orientation of treatment.

Explanations for relapse may be the lack of continued practice once treatment is terminated, treatment that stopped too soon, underdeveloped fluency skills, unnatural speaking patterns, continued avoidance behavior, and/or a lack of change in the client's self-perceptions. Peters and Guitar (1991) believed the client must assume responsibility for his ongoing progress. Starkweather (1998) affirmed that what is considered relapse may easily be attributed to either the client voluntarily discontinuing using the effortful, unnatural speaking techniques or the fear of stuttering was not completely eliminated in therapy.

As Manning (1996) pointed out, a high threshold or tolerance of fluency breaks on behalf of the clinician or client may lead to regression. Even the belief they are cured can contribute to relapse. If cured, the individual does not have to put forth the energy or effort to monitor speech. Webster and Poulos (1989) believed there are three major sources of interference interacting when a client fails to maintain newly learned skills: (1) ineffectual self-talk, (2) tension, and (3) avoidances. Another plausible explanation for relapse was described by Boberg in 1986, when he wrote,

> One possibility is that there exists a physiological basis for stuttering. An implication of this position is that maintenance might be a lifelong process. Stutterers who maintain treatment gains do so because they continue to exercise those skills that successfully compensate for the underlying physiological or neurological condition. (p. 508)

Regardless of why relapse happens, you must be proactive in preparing the adult for relapse. However, research is sparse in the area of maintenance of treatment gains. In fact, concentrated attention on this issue began to emerge in the late 1970s (Ham, 1999). Over a 32-year period, Henning and Tellis (2003) found only 25 treatment studies that addressed this issue. There was considerable variability in research design, maintenance approaches implemented, age of experimental group, and length of time posttreatment. Overall, they concluded the research literature is unable to guide clinicians in determining effective ways of achieving long-term maintenance of speech gains. Much of the knowledge about maintenance and relapse comes from clinical reports and the adults themselves who have suffered such disappointments.

Based on a review of the literature, the following is a list of principles or guidelines that facilitate maintenance of therapy gains (Boberg, 1986; Boberg, Howie, & Woods, 1979; Boberg & Kully, 1994; Conture, 2001; Culatta & Goldberg, 1995; Guitar, 1998; Ham, 1999; Ingham, 1984; Manning, 1996; Sheehan, 1984; Starkweather, 1998; Webster & Poulos, 1989).

1. Extend transfer activities into the real world early in the therapy process.
2. Adults must learn, in the beginning stages of therapy, to identify moments of stuttering quickly and accurately.
3. Discuss the nature and likelihood of relapse with clients.
4. Guide clients in determining their maintenance needs.
5. Let clients know they should not expect success every time they speak, and teach them to be tolerant of mistakes.
6. Gradually reduce the frequency of therapy sessions; just don't cut the client off "cold turkey."
7. Schedule planned follow-up sessions or regular contacts with the client.
8. Encourage the client to engage in scheduled daily practice and self-monitoring activities.
9. Teach the client to use visual reminders to apply skills learned in therapy.
10. Allow adult clients to continue in therapy for as long as they feel the need.
11. Encourage adults to attend weekly or monthly support group meetings.
12. Discuss and help the adults set realistic long-term fluency goals.

The maintenance phase of therapy is critical and should not be taken lightly by either the clinician or client. Getting clients fluent is a relatively easy task for the clinician knowledgeable in this disorder. Keeping them fluent is the challenge. Conducting maintenance programs has several roadblocks. First, it is often difficult to maintain contact with the client. Today's society is a highly mobile one and people change residences and phone numbers often. Keeping track of such changes, alone, can be a daunting task for any clinician. Second, it is a cumbersome and time-consuming process to obtain accurate out-of-clinic data concerning speech performance. Third, clients differ in many ways, so comparing group performances in varying environments can present its own flaws. Last, many different interpretations exist for the phrase *successful maintenance*. Prior to entering the maintenance phase of therapy, the clinician should help adults determine their own definition of success. Webster and Poulos (1989) defined **success** in terms of performance standards: (1) use of fluency skills in situations, (2) entering situations previously avoided, (3) reduced time and severity in blocking, (4) greater ease in communication, and (5) increased feeling of control. Measuring maintenance of therapy gains should be an individualized process because of the heterogeneity of the stuttering population. You must be cognizant of this variability when engaging adults during the maintenance phase of therapy.

Self-Help Groups

From the early days of 1977 to the present time, the role of **self-help groups,** also referred to as *support groups,* has greatly influenced the lives of many adults who stutter.
Members gathering with a common goal help build bonds that last a lifetime. Discussing
their stuttering stories, members are able to vent, share, cope, and, eventually, let go of the
shame of stuttering. Bradberry (1997) succinctly wrote that "meeting other people who
stutter provides emotional support while we share information about common concerns,
fears, and experiences" (p. 391). Most important, association with a support group helps
members cope with the feelings of isolation often held by people who stutter, a feeling
that they exist in a no-man's-land. Writers in the area of fluency disorders, as well as ASHA's
Guidelines for Practice in Stuttering Treatment, endorse this self-help movement as a
way to provide support, understanding, and sharing to people who stutter and the professional community inherently connected to them (Conture, 2001; Gregory, 1997; Ham,
1999; Krauss-Lehram & Reeves, 1989; Manning, 1996; Ramig, 1993c; Starkweather &
Givens-Ackerman, 1997). "Such a powerful therapeutic force cannot and should not be
overlooked by clinicians interested in doing everything they can to help clients talk more
easily and feel heard" (Starkweather & Givens-Ackerman, 1997, p. 139).

The Group

Specifically, self-help groups are defined as "self-governing groups whose members
share a common specific concern or situation and give each other emotional support
and material aid, charge either no fee or only a small fee for membership, and place a
high value on experiential knowledge in the belief that it provides a special understanding of a situation" (Pill, 2003, p. 1). Hunt (1987) described several features of effective self-help groups: (1) those whose members are somewhat older and more
self-aware, (2) members who have succeeded in establishing some degree of control
over their speech, (3) members who exhibit effective communication skills, and (4)
members who are willing to share their stories about coping strategies. Getting a support group started takes commitment, energy, and organizational skills. The challenges
of finding a meeting place, members to attend, and maintaining membership face the
group's organizers (Hunt, 1987). Fortunately, the NSA provides a manual for starting a
support group that includes many useful suggestions and resources. The benefits of
getting a support group started in the community are far greater than the inherent
challenges.

The Members

For the person who stutters, involvement in a self-help group can be a life-altering experience. Just take a look at any issue of *Letting Go,* the newsletter distributed by the
National Stuttering Association, to read about changes and eye-opening experiences
that adults report. As with any coming together of new people, it takes time to establish a sense of group membership. In his keynote address to the Fourth World Congress on Fluency Disorders, Pill (2003) described three stages members go through

when joining a support group. First, the member has feelings of victimization and helplessness in his approach to the disorder. Next, the member becomes a survivor, understanding the role stuttering has played in his life's decisions. Last, the member develops a mature outlook on stuttering and thrives on the continued growth provided by the group.

According to Diggs (1990), "Through such experiences, many self-helpers decide for the first time that they don't have to hide their problem. A sense of normalization grows from being with people who share a problem, and often a social support system emerges" (p. 33). Ramig (1993c), in a summary of surveys on the efficacy of self-help groups, concluded, "Involvement in self-help groups for many persons who stutter is a positive and beneficial experience" (p. 355). More specifically, a study conducted by Yaruss et al. (2002) found individuals involved in self-help groups reported the most beneficial aspect of support group participation was (1) meeting others who stutter, (2) talking about talking, and (3) learning to cope with stuttering more directly.

The Professional

The professional interested in stuttering disorders can gain a unique insight into both the disorder and people who have it by participating in self-help groups. Gregory (1997) summarized specific ways in which the professional speech pathologist can interact with self-help groups (see Table 11.4).

However, the clinician's attitude toward self-help groups certainly impacts the extent of their involvement. Several writers (Gregory, 1997; Manning, 1996; Pill, 2003; Ramig 1993c; Silverman, 1996) acknowledged the hesitant behaviors of speech pathologists to endorse self-help groups and attribute this hesitancy to a lack of understanding of the role of self-help groups; feelings of disappointment when a prior client seeks group support; failing to accept the fact that some adults will continue to stutter with or without therapy; and failure to recognize the impact stuttering can have on the life of a person who stutters.

Table 11.4
Ways the professional can interact with self-help groups.

1. Provide information at self-help meetings.
2. Help organize a group on a local level.
3. Conduct a therapy session at a self-help group meeting.
4. Give members of a group evaluations of how they are doing relative to speech and attitude change.
5. Attend meetings, acting as a consultant on issues that relate to professional interests and practices.
6. Act as a consultant to a governing board of a local or self-help organization.
7. Inform group members about available services.
8. Work on joint projects of such as public information, passing useful legislation, and so on.

Source: Based on Gregory (1997).

As a longtime member of the NSA, this author can attest to the multiple learning experiences and knowledge obtained through interactions at conventions. The young novice speech clinician attending her first NSA convention will learn more over the course of several days than ever garnered in the classroom setting. Textbook knowledge certainly provides a foundation. But talking with adults who stutter, interacting with many different PWS, and listening to their stories provides an introspection you cannot gain from reading a book. However, Gregory (1997) urged speech pathologists involved in self-help groups to evaluate continuously the rationale for their involvement. "They should be thinking always of self-help objectives such as increased understanding, sharing experiences, and non-judgmental acceptance. Just as it is not a self-help group's mission to embrace a treatment model including evaluation and therapy strategies, it is not a professional's place to change a self-help group into a therapy group" (p. 409).

Communication Skills

At a gathering of the National Stuttering Association in 2003, Kelso presented an excellent workshop on the development of communication skills for adults who stutter. It is not infrequent for adults to allow stuttering to inhibit social interactions. Living with the fear of ridicule and embarrassment for years may have kept adults who stutter from learning basic communication strategies to use in social situations. There is more to communication than speaking. Kelso described three types of communicators: poor communicators, average communicators, and skilled communicators. Poor communicators are those who say what they think with little regard for the listener. Related to stuttering, Kelso maintained that the individual who has a blatant disregard for how stuttering impacts communication would be classified as a poor communicator. Average communicators say what they think and monitor the listener's response to it. The adult who reacts to the listener's response would fall into this second group. Skilled communicators rely on their perception of how the audience thinks and feels and responds according to those thoughts and feelings. The person who stutters, acknowledging the role stuttering has in conversations, being proactive in advertising their stuttering, and engaging in active listening would be considered a skilled communicator. A person's underlying temperament, such as being shy, may even impact communication.

One might predict there is a subgroup of adults who stutter who describe themselves as "shy" and reticent to make small talk in social situations. Gabor (1997) defined **small talk** as "light and casual conversation that avoids obscure subjects, arguments, or emotionally charged issues" (p. 21) and has as its purpose getting to know someone or creating a positive first impression. For people who stutter, much energy is expelled worrying about and planning for these first impressions. Gabor (1997) suggested that shy people learn how to make small talk so others will see they are approachable and friendly. He presented 10 steps to mastering small talk and building one's confidence in making conversation (see Table 11.5). For whatever reason, these adults might benefit from group social skills training to improve conversational skills and build confidence.

Table 11.5
Ten steps for shy people to learn the skill of making small talk.

Strategy		Example/Hint
Step 1.	Before the event, identify several interests and experiences you are willing to discuss.	"What have I read lately that I enjoyed or found thought provoking?" "What restaurants could I recommend to someone who shares my taste in food?"
Step 2:	Search for individuals who seem receptive.	Look for people already talking or appearing as though they want to talk.
Step 3.	Establish eye contact and smile to send receptive signals.	Make eye contact for 5 to 10 seconds to indicate interest and curiosity. When the other person returns eye contact, smile back.
Step 4.	Be the first to introduce yourself and ask an easy, open-ended question.	"How do you know our host?" "What do you think of this spectacular view?" The earlier you introduce yourself, the better.
Step 5.	Listen carefully for the other person's name and use it in the conversation.	Focus only on the first name. Immediately repeat the name to make sure you got it right. Think of someone you know with the same name.
Step 6.	Listen carefully for facts, feelings, key words, free information, and implied statements	Pay attention to trigger statements, such as "I can't wait until . . . " or "excited about a new job." Follow up with a question, such as "You mentioned being in Chicago. That's where I grew up."
Step 7.	Disclose some of your background, interests, and experiences.	"One of my favorite things to do is . . . " "I've been working as a . . . for many years." "When I was growing up, . . . "
Step 8.	Explore the other person's interests by encouraging him or her to talk.	"I heard you mention earlier . . . " "Do you mind if I ask you about something you mentioned a few minutes ago?"
Step 9.	Highlight mutual interests.	"It's always good to meet someone who is interested in . . . "
Step 10.	Restate something you found interesting in the conversation and end with an invitation to meet again.	Keep farewells short. Mention the topics discussed, add that you enjoyed the chat, and if you desire, suggest the two of you meet again.

Source: Based on Gabor (1997).

TREATMENT DIRECTIONS

The third item for discussion involves the direction of treatment for the adult who stutters. Considering the unique combination of affective, behavioral, and cognitive aspects of each adult's profile, therapy should be designed specifically to meet these unique needs. Just as the clinician creates a profile-dependent treatment plan for a child and adolescent who stutters, the adult comes into the therapy process with many more experiences that have shaped his belief system around communication and will require an individualized treatment plan to meet his needs.

The philosophy behind the House That Jack Built applies similarly to the adult, with a few modifications. The adult may require more time at the initial stage of therapy. It is surprising how many adults enter therapy knowing very little about the disorder they have lived with for years. More time will be necessary to provide and discuss the research about stuttering so the adult can better cope and understand the journey ahead of him. The identification process is more tedious with adults who have had years of running past moments of stuttering, hiding stuttering, or avoiding situations requiring speaking. It takes a strong commitment on behalf of the adult to tally stutters, eliminate avoidances, and confront the fear of stuttering. Only time will dissolve the fears and conspiracy of silence upheld in the past. Time spent in avoidance reduction therapy is essential to long-term maintenance of gains made in speech therapy (Sheehan, 1986; Sisskin & Weadon, 2004).

As adults increase their knowledge of both normal speech production and their stuttering behaviors, ideally they have already begun to modify attitudes, behaviors, and cognitions, that is, to build the rooms of therapy. Again, change is not as rapid as seen with children, especially the younger preschool child. Change is a gradual process encumbered with trials and tribulations. Clients may become discouraged with the realization that a rapid cure is not on the horizon and therapy requires much effort and time. The fluency gained early in the therapy process provides the carrot dangling in front of the adult, but as we all know, this fluency is not long lasting. Understanding the cyclic nature of stuttering and the relapse phenomena already discussed are essential topics for adults who stutter. Confronting the moment of stuttering and acceptance of oneself as an adult who stutters must emerge within the client's self-concept in order to sustain the management skills learned in therapy and the subsequent fluency, that is, roof of fluency. Because of the unique needs of this group of stutterers, clinicians need to be cognizant of certain treatment topics, discussed next.

Treatment Topics: The Three A's of Adult Intervention

Working with adults who stutter provides an opportunity for you to delve into the components of stuttering with greater detail than with the school-age or adolescent who stutters. Just as with these other groups, using analogies or having a unique way of presenting information to adults helps them understand the therapy process. For adults, you might present the three A's of stuttering treatment: *A*wareness, *A*cceptance, and *A*voidance reduction (Figure 11.3). Awareness involves

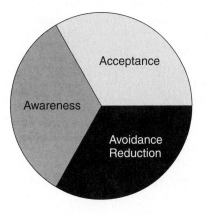

Figure 11.3
The three A's of adult treatment.

becoming more familiar with patterns of behaviors, feelings, and thoughts. Creating awareness is essential to growth for the adult. As objective awareness increases, you can lead the adult into discussions about acceptance. Acceptance, too, is necessary for long-term maintenance of gains made in therapy. Acceptance comes in many different forms, often referred to as advertising. While increasing awareness and acceptance, you can encourage the adult to eliminate, or at least reduce, avoidance behaviors. Avoidance, as discussed throughout this text, works to maintain stuttering and negative thought processes. Avoidances, one at a time, must be directly targeted.

Awareness: The Essentials of Identification

The identification phase of therapy should begin with the more observable moments of stuttering first, gradually drawing attention to the shorter, less tense moments. Stay away from the adult's stuttering patterns by having him identify episodes of stuttering in the speech of other group members or in the speech of the clinician. Insert pseudostuttering into your speech, varying the type and duration. As the adult becomes more proficient at catching your stutters, have him listen to a conversational speech sample on an audiotape, preferably of another person who stutters. You may choose to transcribe a speech sample prior to having the client perform this offline analysis. Having a transcription ahead of time allows you to focus solely on the client's identification skills.

When the adult demonstrates a high degree of proficiency at identifying stuttering (both the frequency and type), ask him if he is ready to listen to himself on the tape recorder. Let him know that in the current session, you will record him, and in the next session, you will listen to the tape and tally stuttering moments together. This time delay will help prepare him because the process of tallying one's own stuttering involves a greater degree of emotionality for the adult. Some adults have no difficulty listening to their speech on a tape recorder; others respond negatively to it. Keeping the identification tasks brief in the beginning helps desensitize the adult to listening to his own stuttering. As the adult becomes more comfortable with this process, you may choose to have him watch a videotape of his conversational speech. Again, seeing one's stuttering may produce negative reactions. You must become fine-tuned at reading the client's nonverbal signals of discomfort and address these feelings as they arise.

You will need to gauge when the adult is ready to perform online identification tasks, that is, tally/counting stuttering moments during ongoing speech production. This task is more difficult than offline analysis. It requires the adult to attend to what he is saying as well as how he is talking. The communication message is often interrupted by the tallying and subsequent reinforcing comments you make. Some adults may become frustrated because they are not able to complete their speech efforts. Introduce this task with comments that you will be interrupting the client while he is talking, the goal of the activity is to identify stuttering, and he should not worry about completing what he is saying. Let him know ahead of time that this therapy activity will be disjointed. After each successful identification, praise the adult for paying attention to his stuttering instead of running away from it. Focus on the identification goals and not the message.

Eventually, you must focus the adult's attention on any episode of stuttering, no matter how small. If brief moments go unidentified, they may grow into larger episodes if the adult has any remnants of negative reactions toward stuttering. As presented in the story "Speech Weeds" in chapter 9, brief moments of stuttering, if left unattended, fester and grow into larger moments. It is not uncommon for clinicians and adults to get comfortable once the noticeable stuttering has been removed. The adult may not physically feel these brief stutters and so ignores them. This places him at risk for relapse. Conture (2001) set an 80% criterion rate for the identification phase of therapy. Anything less than this allows for possibility that stuttering will reemerge, often more severe than the original.

If strong emotional reactions are attached to stuttering, the identification process may exacerbate this emotionality and increase stuttering. Some adults may not realize just how much they stutter (frequency) or how much time they spend in a moment of stuttering (duration). As adults become more aware, they report an increase in stuttering, believing they are getting worse. However, this observation is indicative of a positive therapeutic direction because, most likely, the adults are not avoiding stuttering, therefore allowing stuttering to emerge (Guitar, 1998; Van Riper, 1973). Conture (2001) identified five reasons why the client may exhibit increased stuttering during the identification phase of treatment: (1) The original estimates of stuttering were inaccurate; (2) the type of stuttering has changed from one that is minimally audible and visible (silent prolongations) to one much more audible and visible (sound, syllable repetitions); (3) the client is avoiding less, talking more, and in longer units; (4) the situations in which speech is now elicited differ from those using during the original evaluation; and (5) any of the reasons and more in combination (p. 304). You must help clients understand this progression. In the beginning of identification, discuss this phenomenon with the client. The client must understand the reasoning behind it and be prepared in case it happens.

One last comment about identification. Adults must learn to attend to the feelings involved during moments of stuttering. I often use the words *focus on the feeling* when the adult is in a moment of stuttering, helping him to become more aware of what he is doing with his articulators, breath stream, or vocal cords (Nelson, personal communication, 1990; Ramig, 1998). Identifying the loci of stuttering within the speech production system is critical to mastery of stuttering modification and long-term change.

Conture (2001) identified two elements necessary for change to occur: (1) correct, quick, and objective identification of when and what the adult does when stuttering, and (2) "most of this ability to identify must relate to the physical feelings (not emotions) of speech movements and muscular tension" (p. 295). Have the adult close his eyes, allowing him to focus his attention on the proprioceptive feeling in his speech mechanism (Ramig, 1998). The tuning out of visual information helps the senses tune into the tactile and kinesthetic input during speech. Having the adult practice triad drills and negative practice exercises are facilitating activities for developing a keener sense for feeling the moment of stuttering. As previously discussed, triads involve having the client say a word in a hard way, pause, repeat the word with an easy repetition, pause, and repeat it again using an easy prolongation. Negative practice involves having the adult say a word in a hard, stuttered way and then repeating it with a 50% reduction in tension. Again, focusing on the feeling provides a more immediate feedback loop than attending to the auditory signal.

Acceptance Through Advertising

A major obstacle to overcome for adults who stutter is acceptance of their stuttering. A small number of adults achieve total recovery, or remission, from stuttering and become fluent speakers (Finn, 1997). However, the majority of adults retain some degree or remnants of stuttering in their speech. A goal of therapy for adults is to accept stuttering as a part of them and stop fighting against it. To achieve this goal, clinicians have recommended advertising as a daily part of the adult's therapy plan (Breitenfeldt, 2003b; Breitenfeldt & Lorenz, 1989; Hood, 2003; Montgomery, 2003; Murphy, 1999; Quesal, 2002; Rentschler, 2003; Saitta & Madsen, 2004; Van Riper, 1973). Advertising can take several different forms, from wearing a pin with the saying "You Are Not Alone" from the National Stuttering Association to stuttering purposefully on non-feared words.

Advertising has as its main goal the demonstration of acceptance by the person who stutters. The rationale for engaging in advertising is to become and remain desensitized to the moment of stuttering as well as listener reactions. Adults often anticipate negative reactions to their stuttering and react accordingly. Concern over listener perceptions may consume their energies. Adults must come to understand that they cannot control how people will respond to their stuttering. Engaging in advertising puts them on the road to acceptance of their stuttering. Advertising can involve simple nonverbal demonstrations of an association with stuttering to the overt insertion of stuttering into one's speech and should be carried out in a hierarchical order (least to most stressful). Take every opportunity possible to provide positively reinforcing comments to the adults who engage in advertising, encouraging them to continue with the process.

The following is a sample of tasks that adults might choose to perform while on the journey toward acceptance:

- Wearing a T-shirt or a pin with a saying related to stuttering.
- Displaying a book about stuttering in the work or home environment.
- Framing a poster with famous people who stutter and taking the opportunity to discuss it when others show interest in it.
- Drinking your morning coffee from a mug with a saying related to stuttering.
- Distributing a pamphlet on "How to talk with a person who stutters" to work colleagues and discuss with them how you would like them to respond when you stutter.

- Initiating a conversation with an open comment about stuttering (e.g., "I'm a person who stutters so you might notice that my speech is different" or using a bit of humor say, "Have a seat—this may take a while because I stutter").
- Telling friends and coworkers that you are in therapy working to improve your speech.
- Selecting a person or situation each day to insert voluntary stuttering on non-stuttered words (e.g., you will use voluntary stuttering to the last person you talk to before lunch or the first phone call of the day you will initiate it with voluntary stuttering).
- Purposefully going up to people you do not know and introducing yourself as a person who stutters (e.g., walking into the shopping mall and introducing yourself to every salesperson you encounter).

Although some of these tasks seem simple and straightforward, there is nothing simple about advertising. These activities may be difficult for some adults to perform and require a thorough understanding of the rationale behind them. Guitar (1998) introduced discussing stuttering openly with the following excerpt:

> One way to become more comfortable with your stuttering is to discuss it openly with your family, friends, and acquaintances. When you get to the point of being open about your stuttering, you will lose much of the fear of it and be more relaxed. In most cases, your listeners know you stutter, you know you stutter, but nobody ever says anything about it. It's like the ostrich sticking his head in the sand in the face of danger, pretending it's not there. You would feel much more comfortable about your stuttering if you were open and at ease with your stuttering. (p. 243)

Advertising as a means of demonstrating acceptance of stuttering remains a tool for adults to use throughout their therapy plan as well as after therapy. This technique should become a major part of the maintenance plan, periodically using it whether they need to or not. It functions as a vaccination against any increase in negative reactions to stuttering—a defense mechanism necessary for long-term acceptance of being a person who stutters.

Avoidances Reduction

Elimination of avoidance behaviors is essential to long-term recovery from stuttering (Bloodstein, 1995, 1997; Fraser, 1978; Prins, 1997; J. G. Sheehan, 1953; V. M. Sheehan, 1986; Webster & Poulos, 1989; Williams, 1972; Van Riper, 1973). The adults who enter therapy most likely have a long inventory of sounds, words, people, or situations in which they avoid talking. As Sheehan (1953) wrote, the desire to speak works in opposition to the desire to avoid speaking. Ham cleverly stated, "Where there is stuttering, there will be avoidances (Ham's law)" (1999, p. 94). The payoffs of avoidance (i.e., the absence of embarrassment and shame) feed its continuation. The adult may experience relief when he changes a feared word or is able to get his needs met without talking. However, prolonged avoidance behavior diminishes any feeling of empowerment, making the person a victim of stuttering.

Table 11.6
Avoidance behaviors and their definitions.

Avoidance Behavior	Definition
Postponement	Any behavior designed to delay a speech attempt.
Starter	Any behavior whose production coincides with and helps initiate a feared word.
Retrial	When the fluent portion of the utterance is repeated several times before a feared word is produced.
Release	Any movement, gesture, or audible behavior inserted during the moment of stuttering to try to break the cycle, such as a sudden pitch rise.
Circumlocutions	Use of a phrase or multiple words to replace one feared word.
Substitution	Use of a synonym or other replacement word instead of the word originally targeted.
Withdrawal	Choosing not to talk, produce certain words/sound, or enter a specific situation because of the fear of stuttering.

Source: Based on Ham (1999).

Elimination of avoidance behavior is typically a goal of most adult treatment programs (Bloodstein, 1995; Bloom & Cooperman, 1999; Breitenfeldt & Lorenz, 1989; Conture, 2001; Guitar, 1998; Ham, 1999; Manning, 1996; Montgomery, 2003; Shapiro, 1999; Sheehan, 1953; Sisskin & Weadon, 2004; Starkweather & Givens-Ackerman, 1997; Van Riper, 1973). Table 11.6 contains a list of common avoidance devices along with their definitions.

Ham (1999) acknowledged that avoidance behaviors are hard to change; therefore, clinicians must thoughtfully prepare the adult before engaging in avoidance reduction tasks. When selecting which avoidance behavior to target initially, Ham defended starting with the one that will most boost the client's confidence level. However, this may also be one of the most difficult for the client to achieve. Therefore, consider the factors presented in Table 11.7 when selecting which avoidance behavior to target in therapy.

Sisskin and Weadon (2004) discussed their approach to avoidance reduction based on Sheehan's approach-avoidance theory. They identified four outcomes of avoidance reduction therapy: (1) reduce struggle, avoidance, and fear of speaking; (2) develop a comfortable, forward-moving speech pattern that may include some disfluency; (3) develop positive attitudes about oneself as a speaker; and (4) communicate effectively in a wide variety of speaking situations. Their ultimate goal is recovery from stuttering, which is defined as "to say what you want, when you want without interfering with communication, and without preoccupation with the negative impact of stuttering or listener reaction" (p. 5). Table 11.8 provides several useful tips for adults to follow when implementing self-directed avoidance reduction therapy.

Table 11.7
Criteria for selection of avoidance behaviors to target in the early stages of therapy.

Client Awareness	The more aware the client is of a particular behavior, the easier it should be to control or eliminate it.
Obviousness of Behavior	The more overt or obvious the behavior, the easier it is to bring into awareness. Subtle interjections, such as 'mmm,' may be hard to control, whereas multiple repetitions produced in a loud voice should be easy to eliminate.
Client Preference	The behaviors that bother the client, or significant others, are good candidates for elimination.
Frequency of Occurrence	Common behaviors offer more opportunities for elimination. Some avoidances occur only under special circumstances, at very high levels of anxiety, or on particular words.
Longevity	The life history of a particular behavior is important. The "older" an avoidance is, the harder it is to eradicate.
Proximity	The distance, in terms of space and time, between the behavior and the actual moment of stuttering is important to consider. • Space: the nearer, physically, an avoidance movement is to the speech mechanism, the more difficult it will be to gain control (e.g., a lip-licking postponement is harder to get hold of than a head-scratching behavior). • Time: the nearer in time to a moment of stuttering, the more difficult control will be. Postponements are more difficult than substitutions, but easier than starters. In turn, starters are easier than release efforts.
Singularity	The more unusual or nontypical a behavior is, the easier control will be.
Isolation	Avoidance behaviors that occur in isolation will be easier to gain control of than those embedded in a cluster of behaviors.
Effectiveness	Nothing succeeds like success, and avoidances are no exception. If a client feels the avoidance is really effective (i.e., really helps reduce stuttering), then enthusiasm for elimination may be minimal. The feeling will be increased if, during early control efforts, the stuttering increases in frequency and intensity.

Source: Based on Ham (1999, pp. 95–96).

Two Special Points

From the clinical experience of this author, working on the three A's often produces an increase in fluent speech. Some adults really like the fluency they have established and begin to believe they are finished with therapy. They take their suitcase of fluency, as it were, and go on vacation. However, they do not have a complete vacation plan. Engagement in routine outside assignments is a necessity that adults begin to overlook because they have become more fluent.

Be Aware of Lucky Fluency

The term *lucky fluency* refers to the spontaneous fluency that emerges as adults begin to change their speaking patterns. As clients replace the inappropriate patterns of speech production with appropriate strategies, their speech becomes more fluent. Do

Table 11.8
Self-therapy tips for adults who stutter engaged in avoidance reduction therapy.

Self-Therapy Tip 1: Become an Expert on Your Own Stuttering Pattern
- Identify behaviors that are maladaptive to forward moving speech.
- Identify attitudes and thoughts that promote avoidance and hiding.
- Increase awareness of these behaviors and thoughts as they occur.

Self-Therapy Tip 2: Have the Courage to Stutter Openly
- Develop a "no-tolerance" policy for word substitutions.
- Say all that you would like to say with the words you mean to use.
- Talk! Talk! Talk! . . . even when you don't need to.

Self-Therapy Tip 3: Approach Feared Speaking Situations
- Develop a hierarchy of speaking fears, lowest to highest.
- Starting with the least feared situation, enter feared speaking situations permitting yourself to stutter.

Self-Therapy Tip 4: Exercise Choice in the Way You Stutter
- In low feared situations, experiment with your stuttering pattern.
- Stay in the block long enough to make adjustments to reduce tension and release the block comfortably.

Self-Therapy Tip 5: Reveal Yourself as a Person Who Stutters
- Reduce fears related to disclosure by advertising yourself as a person who stutters.
- Stutter (in a comfortable, easy way) when you would normally be fluent just for the purpose of showing your stuttering.

Self-Therapy Tip 6: Become Your Own Speech Clinician
- Develop assignments based on your current state of comfort in communicating, situation fears, or degree of risk.
- Set specific assignments and criteria for success before you speak.
- Evaluate performance using the most realistic outcomes based on previous assignments.

Source: Based on Sisskin and Weadon (2004).

not confuse this fluency with that created through purposeful implementation of speech modification techniques. Conture (2001) cautioned against misinterpretation of such fluency as an indication of a readiness to be dismissed from therapy. This spontaneous fluency often does not last, especially if adults have not significantly reduced avoidance behaviors and worked on acceptance. Adults need to understand where this fluency is coming from and be praised for their efforts. However, they must continue to work on modifying moments of stuttering, despite the newly found level of fluency, in order to prevent a relapse from occurring.

Outside Assignments

The creation of outside assignments for adults who stutter is a systematic process involving both the clinician and adult. The three main reasons for doing homework are to (1) provide the client practice with habituating newly learned behaviors, (2) foster awareness of one's speech behavior and the need to change, and (3) demonstrate to clients that change is possible and "that they can really do something on

SWOT
Worksheet

Over the next few days, take the time to identify your particular speech strengths and weaknesses. During this time frame, what opportunities did you have to take charge of your speech? What threats (e.g., avoidances, mind reading) still exist that keep you from making change?

Figure 11.4
A worksheet to help the adult develop awareness and acceptance of stuttering.

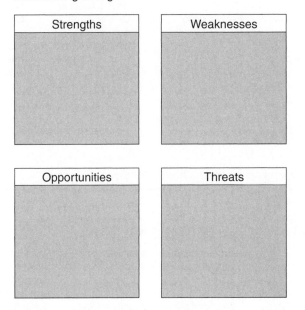

their own to help themselves" (Conture, 2001, p. 317). Assignments should begin with awareness activities and gradually incorporate modification tasks. Figure 11.4 provides an example of an awareness assignment in which the adult is required to focus on his strengths (*S*), weaknesses (*W*), opportunities for change (*O*), and threats (*T*) that keep him from changing (i.e., fears and avoidances). *SWOT* assignments, when designed by adults and completed on a routine basis, prepare them to become their own clinician.

However, it has been this author's experience that when the clinician designs a homework plan without input from the client, she is conveying the message of being in charge of this process, encouraging the client to assume the role of a passive therapy participant. After a period of time, the adult becomes dependent on the clinician for guidance about what to do about stuttering. Thus you should function, from the beginning of therapy, as a guide, allowing the adult to make decisions and design outside assignments. Model a problem-solving approach to designing assignments that begins in less stressful situations and gradually increases in level of difficulty. You may use a simple worksheet that identifies the major aspects of outside assignments,

Table 11.9
An example of an outside assignment log completed by an adult who stutters.

Who	When	Where	Strategy	What Will Be Said	Performance
Boss	First thing in morning	By coffee machine	Voluntary stuttering-bounce	G- g- good morning	Completed— felt great!
Secretary	Before lunch	At her desk	Easy prolongation	I————m leaving for lunch	Turned real but stayed with it.
Vendor	At lunch	Hotdog stand	Easy bounce	C- c- can I have a hotdog with relish?	No problem
Wife	Before leaving office	On the phone	Easy prolongation	I—m leaving the office now.	Had total control of it.

Table 11.10
A guide for implementing outside assignments for the adult who stutters.

Who will be present?	When will you do this assignment?	Where will this interaction occur?	What will you say exactly?	What type of speech strategy will you use?	Comments:
Sister	Morning before work	Kitchen	Ask her about college	Bounce on first word	Went too fast through bounce. Was disappointed with speed.
Friend	At lunch	Work cafeteria	Weekend plans	Bounce on first word	Better bounce, not as tight or fast as this morning.
Dad	Night	Garage	Car repairs	Acknowledge my stutters	Made a comment about having a good dad with my speech— no reaction from Dad. Felt nervous yet good about bringing up topic of stuttering.

that is, who, where, when, what will be said and how it will be conveyed (see Table 11.9). This teaches the adult how to plan for success and ensures compliance with assignments because the adult has a degree of ownership in the assignment. These assignments should be brief and practical, involving everyday events. Table 11.10 provides an example of adult assignments during the early stage of awareness and identification.

Advice from Adults Who Stutter

The strategies just described resonate with the practical advice provided by many adults who stutter. In an excellent publication by the Stuttering Foundation of America, *Advice for Those Who Stutter*, adults who stutter, many of whom are speech-language pathologists themselves, offer insights from their journeys with stuttering. Several common themes prevail through these stories: learning how to identify the stuttering, focusing on the feeling of stuttering, eliminating avoidances, accepting stuttering through advertising, and persisting with daily assignments. The following are samples of the advice provided.

David Daly

Daly (1998) detailed a history of struggle with stuttering that eventually led him to discover how his thoughts influenced his actual stuttering. His story provides hope for other adults wanting to achieve increased fluency. He provided the following insights into his own journey toward fluency:

- Trust in the clinician is essential to client progress.
- Set realistic, achievable goals.
- View stuttering as a challenge, not a curse.
- Practice 5 minutes each day and become aware of the small gains you have made.
- Start with tasks that are short and simple.
- Do your assignments, just don't talk about them.
- Keep a written account of your speech activities to demonstrate progress.

Daly emphasized consistent everyday practice along with visualization exercises. He argued that practice must be an ongoing event in order to sustain the adult's improved fluency. Relapse is a common factor in the adult's journey toward fluency. Daly wrote, "What had become easy to do, then becomes easy *not* to do" (p. 85). He suggested using the following quote as a daily mantra: "Practicing a little every day helps the smoother, more fluent speech stay" (p. 85). In an example of his practice routine, Daly described a concrete and simple activity he engaged in:

> I began by putting 10 paperclips in my left front pocket each morning. Each time that I attempted and completed a specifically planned sentence, e.g., asking for directions to a certain store, I would move a paperclip to my right front pocket. At the end of the day I would count and write down how many clips I had moved. On days when I found only one or two clips in my right pocket, I mentally gave myself a kick in the seat of the pants. I was realizing that unless I made the effort to improve, progress would not be possible. (p. 84)

Daly also used visualization exercises in his practice routine. He wrote that the adult must visualize himself clearly and vividly engaging in a communication exchange. "Visualize what you want, not what you don't want" (p. 86). These exercises incorporate relaxation principles that the adult should take a few minutes every day to practice. Daly stressed it is important to try something different to make change happen. To this end, Daly suggested "concentrated, focused speech practice and visualization exercises" should be a major part of the adult's daily schedule.

Gerald Johnson

Johnson (1998) outlined 10 rules for talking for adults who stutter. He suggested that adherence to these rules gives adults the opportunity to become effective communicators by not defining themselves with the dimension of stuttering. Risk taking, tolerating stuttering, modifying tension that produces stuttering episodes, and practice are just a few of his therapy tenets. He wrote that adults should enjoy talking in an easy, light manner and use visualization strategies to focus on their ability to talk smoothly. Johnson (2003) recommended that adults become aware of several "danger signs" that might interfere with their recovery process (see Table 11.11).

Larry Molt

Molt (1998) described a process of attacking the "iceberg of stuttering" through the tools of forgiveness, understanding, courage, and patience. To Molt, forgiveness entails forgiving yourself for your stuttering; forgiving yourself for the inability to make change; and forgiving yourself for the occasional setbacks that will happen and should be viewed, not as failures, but as opportunities to learn. Understanding is outlined into two components. First, the adult must understand that his beliefs about stuttering are different from those who do not stutter. To PWS, stuttering is a noticeable defect that makes the person different. However, to others who do not stutter, it is "often little

Table 11.11
Danger signs for speech management in adults who stutter.

- When you ignore speech tension
- When you are not spontaneous with speech
- When you don't use the mechanical rules
- When you do not approach speaking vigorously
- When your urge to communicate is stronger than your need to use your rules for modifying your stuttering
- When you ignore little stutterings
- When you concentrate on negatives rather than positives
- When you don't reward yourself with spontaneous talking
- When you don't increase your talking time
- When you feel tight and bound up
- When you do not feel spontaneous with speech
- When stuttering becomes a focal point in your life
- When you don't tolerate the good stuttering
- When you don't handle the right-locked type of stuttering
- When you substitute words
- When you don't tolerate some stuttering

Source: Based on Johnson (2003).

more than noticing that we're having a terrible time talking" (p. 112). Molt (1998) further noted that understanding others' reactions to stuttering is essential to progress. He stated that stuttering often catches the listener "off guard" and that people genuinely want to help out but just do not know what to do.

The next tool is courage. It takes courage to be open with stuttering and to stop running from it. Molt presented three strategies that are helpful when facing stuttering: (1) self-identification (i.e., letting the listener know you stutter); (2) voluntary stuttering (i.e., deliberately stuttering on nonstuttered words); and (3) playing around with stuttering voluntarily (i.e., inserting different types of stuttering into your speech, even tense hard blocks, to build up your tolerance).

The last tool is patience. It takes time to change old habits. Molt (1998) summarized the concept of patience with the following thoughts: "It's easy and very human to be overwhelmed by the immensity of attacking our stuttering, but remember, the longest and most important journeys begin with a single step, and that's all we need to worry about taking right now. Make up your mind to make just one small change today" (pp. 115–116).

William Murphy

Stuttering elicits feelings of anxiety, shame, and guilt. To overcome such feelings, Murphy (1998) recommended that adults engage in openness tasks, such as telling people they stutter and inserting voluntary stuttering on nonstuttered words. "Get the secret out," wrote Murphy, who defined success, not in terms of the degree of fluency, but in relation to being the best "stutterer" possible. Letting go of the need to control or stop the stutter is essential to the adult's recovery. Murphy noted that if emotional reactions continue, the adult should incorporate pseudostutters, which involve the purposeful imitation of real stuttering.

To deal with his ghosts of stuttering from the past, Murphy began to write shame stories. These described the avoidance, tricks, and other behaviors he had engaged in for years. As his shame dissolved, Murphy was able to heal his wounds from stuttering and gain better self-acceptance. A sign of this change is his practice of handing out pencils with "B-B-Bill" stamped on them. Murphy emphasized that the more the adult tries to control, prevent, or eliminate stuttering, the less likely he will achieve progress toward recovery.

Robert Quesal

Quesal (1998) outlined three concepts important to adults trying to cope with stuttering. Knowledge, understanding, and acceptance interrelate with one another in a nonlinear fashion. *Knowledge* encompasses the adult's journey to learn about stuttering both formally and informally. Formal study might include reading textbooks on the disorder or researching the leading journals for relevant articles. Informal study involves active participation in self-help organizations or interaction with Internet resources. *Understanding* what you do when you speak and how you stutter is critical to the coping process. Taking the time to pay attention to your fluency and stuttering helps you understand it better. *Acceptance* of stuttering as a part of the individual is critical. It might involve advertising through voluntary stuttering and openness comments or helping others understand the disorder. Quesal urged adults wanting to cope better with their stuttering to gain knowledge, understanding, and acceptance of the disorder.

Peter Ramig

Ramig (1998) described an eight-step process of self-initiated recovery from stuttering. This process begins with the realization that stuttering is not going to disappear magically overnight. Ramig discussed his early journey to overcome stuttering implementing the following eight points. First, the adult commits to the change process. Second, he must understand the physical speaking process: how the lips, tongue, and voice box interact when producing fluent and stuttered speech. Third, the adult must try not to recoil from stuttering but instead move forward. "Many people who stutter have learned to block silently at the tongue, lips, or vocal cords and/or recoil repetitively from their blocks and other dysfluent moments" (p. 47). Ramig wants the adult to stutter with forward movement, not retrace or repeat what he said fluently in hopes of pushing through or avoiding the upcoming stuttering. The fourth step is to pay attention to feeling how and where the lips, tongue, and voice box make specific sounds. He suggests the adult close his eyes as he says words and sentences repeatedly, visualizing the movement of the articulators. Then, Ramig suggested the adult begin to push hard during speaking and consciously contrast the difference in the feeling of easy versus hard speech efforts.

The fifth suggestion involves eliminating jaw clenching during speaking. Opening the mouth when talking helps counteract the habits learned from years of anticipating and holding back stuttering. Ramig's sixth suggestion is that the adult acknowledge, in a matter-of-fact manner, that he stutters. "Disclosure is a proactive strategy" to help diminish the effects of a conspiracy of silence around stuttering. Seven, the adult should confront stuttering by occasionally inserting pseudostuttering in his fluent speech. Ramig asserted that putting mild, easy stuttering into one's speech can lessen fear and apprehension of stuttering. Step 8 is "Never give up!" Ramig wrote, "Release yourself from the handicapping grip of stuttering" (p. 50), implying that with a committed effort, adults who stutter do not have to be held back by their stuttering. In summary, Ramig's steps to self-initiated recovery provide a solid foundation that can guide the adult client in the direction of a life not controlled by stuttering.

Kenneth St. Louis

St. Louis (1998) grew up with stuttering and shared his insights. His advice included the following five points: (1) Locate resources, (2) take stock regarding your stuttering, (3) reduce your burden, (4) change the way you stutter, and (5) work on your speech every day. The first point involves finding a competent SLP or a local self-help chapter. Taking stock means sharing your story of stuttering and asking yourself a series of questions. St. Louis suggested that the adult write or record (audio or video) himself talking about his journey with stuttering. This exercise can be very cathartic.

Table 11.12
Questions that adults must ask themselves as they venture into the therapy process.

1. How much has stuttering affected my life?
2. How much time or money are you willing to give up to improve your speech?
3. Who would support your efforts?
4. Who would not?
5. What other important challenges besides stuttering are you facing right now?
6. What positive things are going on?
7. What advice or therapy have you had that helped or didn't help? If it didn't help, how much was the fault of the advice or therapy and how much was your fault?
8. What are your future prospects for getting therapy?
9. Are you willing to tackle the very difficult problem of stuttering, even though you can't be guaranteed total fluency?

Source: Based on St. Louis (1998).

St. Louis also outlined a long list of insightful questions the adult must be prepared to answer if he is to make progress. Table 11.12 lists these questions.

To reduce the burden, St. Louis recommended three tasks. First, the client writes down all he tends to avoid because of stuttering. During this task, the adult should focus on the behavior of stuttering, that is, the *doing* part. For example, "I repeat the first sound three times before I can get the word out." Next, he suggested the adult stutter on purpose to gain the feeling of internal control. Last, the adult must do things he would typically avoid (e.g., leaving a message on an answering machine). St. Louis noted that the adult should not try to not stutter as he begins to change the way he stutters by eliminating any avoidance or tricks he uses. He should try to reduce the tension and duration of his stutters, resisting the urge to "push the sounds out." St. Louis suggested using gentle prolongations that are smooth and effortless. In summary, St. Louis stressed working on speech every day. Practice must become a routine event in the adult's journey toward more effective coping with stuttering.

There is no one way to conduct therapy, especially for the adult who stutters. There are many paths to one's destination and practicing clinicians must be aware of these different routes. As discussed in chapter 5, models of treatment can be divided into three major classifications: fluency-shaping, stuttering modification, and integrative approaches. Each approach has its own goals, objectives, and procedures as delineated by the following author(s) (provided in alphabetical order).

Fluency-Shaping Approaches

Einer Boberg and Deborah Kully

Boberg (1980) and Boberg and Kully (1994) described a 3-week intensive program for adults who stutter. Their program, originated by Boberg and now run by Kully and Langevin, is divided into seven phases: (1) baseline establishment; (2) identification of stuttering patterns; (3) early modification using fluency skills such as easy onset of phrases, soft contact on consonants, short phrases, and continuous airflow; (4) mastery of prolonged speech; (5) normalizing rate and correcting errors via cancellations; (6) self-monitored normal-sounding speech; and (7) transfer of normal-sounding speech into nonclinical environments. Criteria for advancing into phase 7 is production of speech at a normal syllable rate of approximately 190 spm with less than 1% disfluency and an emphasis on maintaining appropriate eye contact with the listener.

During transfer, the adult engages in a 5-minute talk time, which is recorded for later analysis. The client must obtain a 300-second speech sample and analyze it according to the following criteria: (1) 5 minutes of speech spoken at a normal rate, (2) less than 2% disfluency, and (3) acceptable prosody. Transfer assignments are ranked according to perceived level of difficulty and range from conversations with secretaries, conducting opinion surveys, shopping and phone assignments, and actual job interviews. These transfer activities are personalized to meet the specific needs of each adult. Adults are advised to develop some type of self-reinforcement schedule with simple rewards and consequences. However, Boberg and Kully acknowledged that some adults do not choose to use such schedules, noting that the fluency produced by their efforts is reinforcing enough. All transfer assignments are completed during the third week of treatment.

Barbara Dahm

Dahm (1997) described a "speech processing therapy" approach with the goal of changing "what people do when they produce speech so that the result will be fluent speech" (p. 2). Dahm's program can take the form of intensive (plan A) or nonintensive (plan B) based on client need. Intensive treatment begins with 3 weeks of group therapy, ranging from 6 to 7 hours per day of directed speech practice. Six months of self-help therapy follows the intensive portion of treatment. Self-help therapy incorporates telephone communications between clinician and client, hourly sessions once a month (or more, if indicated), and regular written reports from the client to the clinician.

Plan B treatment involves individual sessions with the frequency of sessions dependent on client needs. As the client is able to produce speech correctly, he attends 30-minute to 1-hour group and/or individual sessions in conjunction with self-help therapy between sessions involving telephone communications between clinician and client, as well as written client reports to the clinician. Both treatment plans are divided into two stages with differing goals. Stage 1 has as its goals (1) the understanding of speech production and stuttering, (2) the correct production of speech, and (3) the establishment of positive attitudes. Stage 2 involves a period of self-therapy: (1) the development of habits for producing correct speech in real-life situations, and (2) learning how to cope with attitudes and emotions that surface in these novel settings.

The initial stages of Dahm's approach are highly structured. Dahm outlined three phases of stage 1. The first is designed to help the client gain an understanding of what his speech goals should be if he is to achieve fluent speech. In phase 2, the client must develop the ability to produce consecutive vocal syllables, a major emphasis of Dahm's processing approach. Last, the client engages in intensive practice of correct production both inside and outside the clinic setting.

Stage 2 is less structured and also divided into three phases. The first requires the client to identify his own strengths and weaknesses. In phase 2, the client develops a flexible, yet individualized program to follow from week to week. Phase 3 incorporates monthly practice sessions held to ensure the client received guidance and support from the clinician.

Practice sessions teach the client to attend to vocal fold vibration during the production of multisyllabic words and sentences leading into spontaneous speech. Practice sessions are conducted at individual work stations with prescribed routines to follow. Exercises are arranged in a set order with a predetermined number of trials required to achieve stable fluency. These exercises are designed according to the following principles: (1) from simple processing to complex processing, (2) from short speech utterances to long speech utterances, (3) from slow production of speech to a normal rate of speech production, (4) from intentional behaviors to habitual behaviors, (5) from low-anxiety situations to high-anxiety situations, and (6) from clinician evaluation to self-evaluation.

From inspection of both the clinician and client manuals that accompany this program, it clearly focuses on fluency. However, Dahm addresses the cognitive processes that may interfere with fluent speech production. This program teaches clients to learn to identify negative thoughts and reframe them with more positive-oriented thoughts. Another major component is the early incorporation of client self-evaluation. Clients are assisted in developing the ability to evaluate their speech production efforts, which, according to Dahm, is necessary for the transfer and maintenance of gains acquired during participation in the program.

Roger Ingham

Ingham (1999), a longtime proponent of fluency-shaping programmed approaches for stuttering, described a performance-contingent management program for adults. His model involves a residential intensive treatment design utilizing prolonged speech production in which adults are taught to manipulate phonation intervals. The core program includes performance-contingent schedules, a token reinforcement economy, and stepwise hierarchy of tasks. Ingham, like Webster, uses technology to provide clients with feedback regarding their phonation intervals. Both task and time completion are criteria for advancement in the program. The organization of the program follows a traditional treatment paradigm of establishment, transfer, and maintenance phases. However, Ingham did find that when the client reaches the maintenance phase of treatment, greater variation in client plans is needed.

Mark Onslow and Ann Packman

Onslow and Packman (1997) conducted an intensive treatment program for adults who stutter in Sydney, Australia. Their behaviorally oriented paradigm establishes prolonged speech through operant conditioning, and the ultimate goal of treatment is controlled stuttered speech. The origins of this program can be traced back to the work of Goldiamond with delayed auditory feedback. Onslow and Packman have added two additional components to their implementation procedures: ongoing naturalness ratings and individual treatment strategies based on client need. They developed a protocol for designing a client's management procedures that is completed during the initial stage of therapy. For some clients, the intensive program may be more appropriate, whereas individual therapy works better for others. Five pretreatment issues often arise during this initial interviewing period: (1) whether the client's quality of life will improve as a result of controlling stuttering, (2) whether the client has the drive and determination to succeed with the task of controlling stuttering, (3) whether anxiety rather than stuttering is the predominant problem, (4) whether the client is sufficiently organized in a lifestyle for a commitment to treatment, and (5) whether it is the client or others who are the motivating force for seeking treatment (p. 371). Answers to these issues guide client and clinician decisions throughout treatment. Onslow (2003) reported positive long-term follow-up data for his clients up to 9 years posttreatment.

William Perkins

Perkins (1984) outlined his techniques for establishing fluency in adults who stutter. His program is based on the premise that adults eventually revert to their stuttered speech if their newfound fluency sounds unnatural. Perkins utilized seven fluency skills "to provide a voluntary method of obtaining normal fluency as an attractive alternative to stuttering" (p. 174). Table 11.13 lists these seven fluency skills with a brief description by Perkins.

These skills are learned in sequential order, meaning mastery of preceding skills is required before practice begins on the next. Perkins relies on the DAF device to teach the adult how to adjust his speaking rate, gradually decreasing the delay by 50 msec increments until he reaches a target rate of 150 to 200 syllables per minute. Mastery of all seven skills is required, although not all skills are implemented during conversation. To prepare or be proactive with regard to relapse, Perkins has adults analyze their stuttering episodes in relation to which of the seven skills failed during stutter-

Table 11.13
Sequence of fluency-shaping strategies utilized to replace stuttered speech.

Skill	Brief Description
Rate	Prolong all syllables to 2 seconds duration until all skills are established.
Phrasing	Limit phrase length to 2 to 5 syllables.
Phrase Initiation	Slow voice onset by breathy initiation of phrase with /h/.
Soft Contact	Reduce excessive articulatory pressures by using soft articulatory contacts.
Breathy Voice	Maintain air flow through the phrase by using breathy tone.
Blending	Remove within-phrase breaks in the air stream by blending words and syllables together.
Rhythm	Establish normal syllable duration values by prolonging stressed syllables for full 2 seconds, but unstressed syllables are touched briefly.

Source: Based on Perkins (1984).

ing. The adults practice recovering from stuttering by approximating their stuttering patterns and then implementing a particular skill selected to counteract the stuttering. In summary, Perkins (1984) stated,

> Fluency is viewed as a by-product of use of fluency skills; my focus is not on fluency but rather on solid mastery of the skills of which it is a function. Occurrence of stuttering is seen as evidence of a major lapse in use of these skills. The objective is to establish them firmly enough that when clients choose to use them, achievement is virtually assured. (p. 178)

George Shames and Cheri Florance

Shames and Florance (1980, 1986) view therapy from a multidimensional, interacting framework involving various aspects of the client and his family and social environments, interacting with a strong client/clinician relationship. The goal of their approach is to help clients "learn to produce elements of normal speech" (p. 447) through four treatment phases. First, the client replaces stuttered speech with volitional control over speech in the form of close monitoring of continuous phonation, rate, and prosody. Again, the DAF device is used to facilitate this learning process. Next, the client is trained to monitor and reinforce this stutter-free speech. Phase 3 involves the transfer and maintenance to environments outside the clinic with phase 4 concluding with the replacement of monitored speech with unmonitored, automatic speech. The Stutter-Free Speech program can be implemented in individual or brief, intensive residential settings.

Ronald Webster

Webster (1986) developed an intensive program format in early 1966 and has revised it several times since then. Currently, this 3-week intensive program is a behaviorally based speech reconstruction program called Precision Fluency Shaping Program. It incorporates behavioral and electronic technologies to achieve fluent speech production. Behavioral targets are practiced sequentially with specific emphasis on controlled gentle onset of voicing. Sounds are classified into four groups: group 1, vowels; group 2, voiced continuants; group 3, voiceless fricatives; and group 4, plosives. Delayed auditory feedback technology was initially used to promote prolonged speech. Now, the Voice Monitor, a special-purpose computer designed to measure criteria in single utterances or connected speech, provides feedback regarding the client's gentle onset productions.

Stuttering Modification Approaches

Dorvan Breitenfeldt

The Successful Stuttering Management Program (SSMP) (Breitenfeldt & Lorenz, 1989) is an intensive stuttering management program for adults and adolescents. Implemented for over 35 years, this intervention paradigm involves 4 hours of work per day, plus homework over the course of 3 weeks. Participants work in group and individual sessions in a variety of settings, most to include some form of community interaction. The program design is based on six premises: (1) stuttering is an incurable disease at the present time; (2) the goal is not fluent speech, but controlled/managed stuttering; (3) most therapy must be out of the therapy room; (4) the cause of stuttering is not emphasized nor dwelled on; (5) the adult who stutters must accept responsibility for stuttering and for change; and (6) group therapy is most advantageous.

Therapy is divided into two phases. Phase I goals include (1) the elimination of avoidances and purposeful movement into all blocks, (2) reduction of word and situation fears, and (3) learning about stuttering. Clients begin by videotaping a brief monologue used to catalog overt and covert stuttering symptoms. Emphasis is placed on maintaining eye contact during spoken interactions. Clients use the mirror to practice this skill designed to reduce negative reactions to stuttering. Advertising is considered the "most important" therapeutic technique and carried out in all situations. Phase I also includes in-depth analysis of stuttering episodes through mirror work, tallying, and freezing. Breitenfeldt (1998) stated that adults must engage in tallying of speech behaviors in order to achieve change. His tally technique involves the following steps:

- Go directly into the block without the use of starters, postponements, and other tricks.
- Stutter all the way through without retrials.
- Stop immediately after the stuttered word.
- Tally the block in a 3 × 5 memo book as 1 2 3 4 5 6, etc.
- Regain eye contact and continue until your next block, then mark in your tally book again, etc. (p. 10)

Elimination of word and situational fears is directly targeted through mass practice on making phone calls, introducing oneself, conducting surveys, and obtaining information from the community. Every interaction is initiated with an openness comment in which the adult advertises the fact that he stutters. SSMP participants learn much about the nature of stuttering, particularly in the area of genetics, gender bias, theories, development of stuttering, and unique aspects of stuttering (such as the adaptation effect, fluency-inducing conditions, and drug effects).

Phase II treatment goals are the following: (1) teach the stuttering handling techniques to control/manage stuttering; (2) transfer handling techniques into real life, outside speaking situations; (3) develop lifestyle changes; and (4) establish a maintenance program for posttherapy. The primary handling techniques used in SSMP are prolongation, pullouts, cancellation, and controlled normal speech. Transferring use of these strategies into real life involves entering feared situations prepared to use techniques, in shopping malls, restaurants, college classes, and even Toastmasters events. The adults go into the community in small groups with their clinician and ask for directions or information, all the while managing their stuttering. The group then discusses the experiences in relation to the ability to manage stuttering even when experiencing fear.

According to Brietenfeldt (2003b), the philosophy of the program is "taking risks and trusting others." To become their own clinician, the adults must be willing to take these risks in order to gain control over their stuttering. Last, a new component of SSMP involves a 5-day follow-up maintenance program incorporating 10 hours per day

Table 11.14
Ground rules used in his self-therapy book for adults who stutter.

1. Make it a habit of always talking slowly and deliberately whether you stutter or not.
2. When you stutter, stutter easily, gently, and smoothly without forcing, and prolong some sound of words you fear.
3. Stutter openly and do not try to hide the fact that you are a stutterer.
4. Identify and eliminate any unusual gestures, facial contortions, or body movements that possibly you may exhibit when stuttering or trying to avoid difficulty.
5. Do your best to stop all avoidances, postponement, or substitution habits.
6. Maintain eye contact with the person to whom you talk.
7. Analyze and identify what your speech muscles are doing improperly when you stutter.
8. Take advantage of block correction procedures to modify or eliminate your abnormal speech muscle stuttering behavior.
9. Always keep moving forward as you speak.
10. Try to talk with inflection and melody in a firm voice.
11. Pay attention to the fluent speech you have.
12. Talk as much as you can.

Source: Based on Fraser (1978).

of individual and group sessions based on the individual needs of the participants. This is called the "annual tune-up program" and coincides with the middle week of the intensive program.

Malcolm Fraser

Fraser (1978), the founder of the Stuttering Foundation of America, published the first book devoted to self-therapy for adults who stutter. *Self-Therapy* was designed for clients who, for whatever reason, choose to become their own therapists. Fraser strongly believed adequate therapy was not available for the majority of people who stutter, leaving the responsibility for change solely up to the adult. To initiate the program, the client must engage in an intensive period of self-study, paying attention and writing down both emotions and behaviors present when stuttering. He sets forth 12 basic ground rules to follow based on an integrated approach to the treatment of stuttering (see Table 11.14). Fraser recommends working on one rule at a time with the understanding that self-therapy is a long process, requiring much determination and time.

Evelyn Klein and Barbara Amster

Klein and Amster (2003) developed an intensive cognitive-behavioral therapy (CBT) plus a stuttering modification treatment design for adults who stutter. Their treatment program lasts 6 weeks with the first 3 weeks incorporating both individual and group therapy focused on cognitive behavior therapy. Weeks 4 through 6 introduce stutter modification techniques with a review of CBT concepts. Results of their study utilizing this program indicated significant changes in both stuttering frequency and attitudes toward communication.

The content of the CBT individual therapy included work on identifying and re-framing cognitive distortions, keeping a written journal of automatic thoughts, systematic desensitization utilizing guided imagery and relaxation, and discussing stuttering with others. Klein and Amster's individual modification program included exploration of the speech production process, contrasting forward versus stopping versus backward moving speech, negative practice, avoidance reduction, pseudostut-tering, and other speech modification strategies (cancellations, pullouts, preparatory sets, easy onsets, light contacts, etc.).

Group sessions for CBT explored values and rules that govern the way the clients live. They explored the automatic thoughts written in their journals and looked for evidence for rational thinking. Discussions included topics regarding listener reactions, anxiety, mind-sets, and ways of increasing feelings of self-esteem. Group modification sessions included mirror work, production of fluency targets, role-playing dialogues with peers, and exploring future plans. This combined CBT and modification approach helped adults understand the interaction among the affective, behavioral, and cognitive components of stuttering.

Walter Manning

Manning's (1996) major contributions to working with adults who stutter involved his insight into how the clinician directs the therapy process and the use of humor in therapy. Manning urged clinicians to "lead from behind" when engaging adults who stutter. The clinician must have a clear direction of where therapy might lead but should not engage in controlling behaviors. Clinicians are guides, providing advice, information, and opinions to clients in an open, unconditional manner. The following is an excerpt from Manning's writing exemplifying this therapeutic principle:

> Unquestionably, the clinician must have an overall plan and a direction for treatment and must be familiar with many associated treatments. However, we cannot control all aspects of the other person and make him into our own image of him. Our goal is to help him to self-manage his handicap, and we can direct that process. However, sometimes it is clear that we have to lead from behind, following the client where he needs to go and helping him to get there. We can assist him in developing new views of himself and new options concerning his fluency. With the right timing in response to changes by the client, we can help him to make better choices and to become less handicapped. We can also acknowledge that while we provide direction, insight, and information, the person who must ultimately take the lead in repairing the problem is the client. (p. 145)

His second contribution involves the strong belief in the healing nature of humor, an insightful topic particularly relevant to working with adults who stutter. In his review of the literature on humor, Manning (1996) identified three components essential to the implementation of humor in therapy: the conceptual shift, distancing with humor, and mastery of humor.

A conceptual shift occurs as the client gains new insight into his condition for the first time. The client begins to view stuttering from various perspectives. To achieve this paradigm change, Manning contended that adults must begin to distance themselves from the stuttering episode. The client steps back from a feared situation long enough to "gain objectivity by viewing the problem with the third eye of humor. Rather than endlessly reliving earlier experiences with the old view, new interpretations become possible. Humor promotes the possibility that the client will begin to play with the possibilities and have fun considering a variety of new interpretations of the experience" (p. 20).

As the client develops a feeling of mastery of a given task, the clinician may observe an increased use of humor in therapy. Manning noted that humor reduces stress and emerges when the client develops an internal locus of control (the ability to view events as a consequence of one's own behavior). In that humor is related to hopefulness, enthusiasm, and vigorousness, its use in therapy for stuttering can have many positive effects for both the clinician and adult who stutters.

In a paper presented online for the Second International Stuttering Awareness Conference, Manning (1999) addressed the issue of creating one's own map for change. An important first step is for the adult to accept the reality of stuttering and no longer hide from it. He outlined three prime directives necessary for change: Eliminate avoidances, learn to speak and stutter easily, and push the envelope and accept speaking challenges that are just beyond your reach. He adds several other suggestions for therapy regardless if the therapy is clinician directed or self driven. To better understand the surface features of stuttering, the adult must learn about the anatomy and physiology of speaking, as well as learn about the categories of speech sounds. Fluency-enhancing techniques, combined with stuttering modification strategies, must be mastered through hours of practice.

Manning maintained that it is liberating when, after years of trying not to stutter, the adult gives himself permission to stutter. Using voluntary stuttering takes courage and determination. Lastly, the adult must be willing to practice. The under-the-surface features of stuttering take longer to change. Changing the cognitive aspects of stuttering can be facilitated through support group involvement, learning about stuttering on the Internet, and by watching the many educational videotapes produced by the Stuttering Foundation of America and National Stuttering Association.

Gary Rentschler

Rentschler (2003) charged adults to take responsibility and ownership of their stuttering in a modification approach to treatment. A part of this treatment design is the focus on overall communication effectiveness. He strongly advocated that "effectively managing stuttering moments represents only one facet of communicating well" (p. 39). The adult who stutters must develop new perspectives regarding stuttering and communication through the implementation of basic principles he calls "Ten Tips for Better Stuttering." He dictated that "If you're going to stutter, be as good at it as you can be!"

Tip 1: *Become an expert on your stuttering*. Get to know your stuttering through mirror work and speech analysis. Focus on all three dimensions of your stuttering problem (affective, behavioral, and cognitive). It can form the basis for you to educate others about stuttering, too.

Tip 2: *Learn from the past*. Why do the same thing over and over again when it always results in a disfluency? Break up your stuttering habits so you know what you have to change. "If you always keep doing what you're doing, you get what you got."

Tip 3:   *Make observations without labeling*. Focus on describing behaviors, not labeling them emotionally with labels such as "that was awful" or "bad job." Don't focus on the fear. Stutter smarter by becoming a more objective observer of your behaviors.

Tip 4:   *Set realistic expectations*. Your goal should not be one of "speech perfection" because this is unattainable. Always remember, you don't start off at the top of the game. You work your way up.

Tip 5:   *Don't just speak, give a performance*. Use speaking opportunities to enjoy yourself purposefully talking. You have to work hard to succeed; it doesn't just happen.

Tip 6:   *Get out in front of your stuttering*. Be open about your stuttering. Tell people you stutter before you stutter. Tell people what they can do to help. Be proactive about your stuttering rather than reactive.

Tip 7:   *Script the story of the cause of your stuttering*. Write down in your journal what you think caused your stuttering. Putting words into print helps release emotionality. Comments in your "cause script" might include "My brain is wired differently than other people when I talk." Being the provider of information makes you the authority and helps to open up a dialogue about your speech.

Tip 8:   *Build your own support team*. Talk to your family, coworkers, and friends about stuttering. Tell them how it feels to stutter and how you are coping with the disorder. Learn to be your own best friend—don't beat yourself up because you stutter.

Tip 9:   *Own your stuttering*. Take responsibility for your stuttering behaviors; after all, it is yours. Figure out what *you* are doing that results in *your* stuttering.

Tip 10: *Develop a positive attitude about your stuttering and communication*. Become friends with your stuttering. Learn to coexist with it. You don't have to like it, but you must peacefully coexist with it. Focus on communication effectiveness rather than the absence or presence of stuttering. In spite of fluency, it's your ability to get the message across that's key.

Joseph and Vivian Sheehan

Sheehan and Sheehan (1984) adhere to the principles of avoidance reduction therapy subsequent to the suppression of stuttering, as seen in the covert stutterer. This therapy orientation does not look at levels of fluency because they view fluency as the byproduct of the adult's successful avoidance of stuttering. The key component of therapy is eliminating all avoidance behavior. To achieve this goal, the Sheehans use openness as the main vehicle. "Openness is a key to success, and suppression is a toboggan ride to failure" (p. 148). An action-oriented therapy similar to Van Riper, avoidance reduction therapy is divided into five stages of treatment: (1) self-acceptance, (2) monitoring and exploring, (3) initiative, (4) modification of patterns, and (5) developing a safety margin. Stage 1 emphasizes the use of purposeful eye contact in which the adult first looks at the listener and then begins to talk. Participants discuss stuttering openly with family, friends, and strangers to aid in exploring their feelings of shame and guilt. Adults engage in intellectual discussions about the nature of stuttering, a task that the Sheehans maintain facilitates motivation. Stage 2 involves monitoring one's own stuttering behaviors. This stage is purely one of awareness, and no modification of speech is accepted.

Stage 3, initiative, is proactive: The adult is encouraged to seek out difficult feared situations as challenges. "Don't wait for fear to descend upon you" (p. 149) is the motto during this phase of therapy. A major concept the Sheehans convey to the adult is that neither stuttering nor fear should be interpreted as failure. They are just opportunities to analyze and learn from to obtain feelings of self-acceptance. Stage 4 focuses on the modification of speech through the use of the slide, a slow, tension-free prolongation. Voluntary stuttering is implemented on nonfeared words, even when the adult can be fluent. This confrontation strategy reinforces tolerance of stuttering, which for so long was avoided. Stage 5 combines the four stages to create a margin of safety in which the adult balances the pressures for fluency and the capacity to deliver fluency honestly, void of tricks. Speech, at this point in therapy, is smooth flowing, yet the adult inserts a slide to conceal some of the fluency obtained through being open.

Charles Van Riper

Van Riper was a pioneer in the field of speech pathology. During the early years of the profession, his dogmatic approach to stuttering influenced many clinicians. His writings are among the most frequently cited in the field. He set the standards for treatment for adults who stutter. His textbooks, *The Nature of Stuttering* (1971) and *The Treatment of Stuttering* (1973), provided a keen perspective into the puzzle of stuttering.

As noted in chapter 5, Van Riper's therapeutic sequence is the framework for many of the clinical citations in this book. Figure 11.5 presents a visualization of his modification strategies. He proposed that therapy begin with the identification of the moment of stuttering. His premise was that unless clients knew what, when, where, and how they stuttered, they would be unable to change their speaking patterns. With this knowledge, clients then engage in various activities geared to desensitize them to stuttering. Emotionality attached to the stuttering moment must be reduced or eliminated in order to succeed at modifying stuttering. The stabilization phase of therapy involves daily

Steps taken during the learning phase of therapy

Figure 11.5
Van Riper's modification road.

Identification	Desensitization	Modification	Stabilization
Knowledge and Confrontation	Cancellations	Pullouts	Preparatory Sets

Steps taken during the maintenance phase of therapy

activities designed to maintain therapy gains and keep from allowing stuttering to control behavior. Therapeutic strategies were designed to be used during each phase of therapy.

Cancellations, pullouts, and preparatory sets are Van Riper's main modification techniques. Once clients master the cancellation (postblock correction), they may proceed to implement pullouts (within-block correction) when caught in a moment of stuttering. Preparatory sets are used before the moment of stuttering as a preblock correction strategy. Clients are taught to first use preparatory sets when they anticipate difficulty. If this fails, they may utilize the pullout, in which they stop in the midst of stuttering and slowly pull out of the moment. If this fails, they must implement the cancellation, where they stop after the moment of stuttering, exercise a time-out period to calm and relax the speech mechanism or themselves, and proceed with a modified version of the moment of stuttering through easy prolongations or syllable repetitions.

The sequence is reversed during the establishment phase of therapy. First clients must identify, classify, and understand stuttering moments before they venture into desensitization activities. Conquering feared situations, the stuttering bath, and voluntary stuttering are sample tasks during this phase of treatment. Next clients practice pullouts to handle any residual stuttering. As clients fear less and approach communication in positive ways, they are able to use preparatory sets whenever needed. In conclusion, the establishment stage of therapy proceeds from identification, cancellations, pullouts, and preparatory sets, whereas, during the stabilization phase of maintenance, clients first use preparatory sets, then pullouts, followed by cancellations, and when not successful, clients proceed with identifying the circumstances surrounding the episode that contributed to the feeling of loss of control.

As mentioned earlier, the Stuttering Foundation of America distributes a series of tapes featuring Van Riper demonstrating his modification of stuttering approach. These tapes are vital for anyone wishing to develop clinical proficiency in the area of stuttering disorders.

Dean Williams

Williams, often referred to as the master clinician, was another exemplar often emulated by others. His action-oriented, problem-solving approach reshaped how clinicians implemented therapy. Instead of just talking about the problem of stuttering, Williams emphasized the *doing* aspect of stuttering, helping clients identify what exactly they do to interfere with the normal speaking process. One key principle to his approach to therapy for adults was reframing how they talk about their stuttering. Williams (1972) described his treatment approach in *To the Stutterer*, a publication of the Stuttering Foundation of America series. He suggested, first, that the adult "ponder" how he thinks about his problem and identify what he does that he calls stuttering. It is the client's job to discover why he "does" what he "does." From this list, the adult marks the most helpful behaviors he does when he stutters and attempts to relate these behaviors back to his belief system of rights and wrongs. He now is able to mark those items that do not help him when he stutters. The next challenge is to determine why the adult behaves in such a manner. Williams emphasized the client's ability to self-reflect on the problem, not the clinician directing and telling him about his problem. He summarized his thoughts to the adult who stutters in the following way:

> You cannot solve a problem by acting like an innocent bystander waiting for someone else to answer questions that you never thought to ask. It is your problem and you must face it." (p. 99)

Integrated Approaches

Charleen Bloom and Donna Cooperman

Bloom and Cooperman (1999) presented a synergistic model of intervention that includes aspects of both fluency-shaping and stuttering modification programs. It was their belief "each person who stutters has developed individual and learned attitudinal and behavioral responses to the underlying neurological disorder. It is therefore important to us to integrate both of these approaches" (p. 9). They define this synergistic approach as the viewing of stuttering from multiple perspectives that vary with each individual and do not act independently. Within each system, the interactions among and between the physiological, psychological, linguistic, and social components comprise the whole picture of stuttering. Bloom and Cooperman thoroughly incorporated information from the field of psychology and counseling to assist clients with their attitudes toward communication.

Their discussion of Coopersmith's fundamental experiences that lead to increased self-esteem have particular relevance to the adult who stutters. Adults in therapy should be provided the opportunity to experience feelings of significance, competence, power, and virtue. Feelings of significance lie in the acceptance, attention, and affection of others. Clinicians who allow the adult to speak without the fear of punishment feel listened to and become encouraged. Feelings of competence are defined as "successful performance in meeting the demands for achievement." Therapy carefully structured through hierarchy analysis ensures client success, which leads to more success.

Especially with adults, the clinician must evaluate the client's readiness to perform all tasks before assigning them. Ask yourself, "Does the client have the skills necessary to be successful at this speech task?" If not, break down the task into smaller components until you reach the level where success is optimal. Clinicians want adults, who have experienced so much prior failure, to feel "able to do" or competent in their skills. Adults who stutter need to experience feelings of power, the ability to influence and control others. Letting the client make clinical decisions, being an active participant in the problem-solving process, and giving them choices fosters feelings of power. The development of self-responsibility and motivation needed for true change depends on these feelings of power. Lastly, feelings of virtue, adherence to moral and ethical standards, is achieved through experiences in which the client is actively engaged in helping others. Involvement in support groups, public service announcements, and speaking at PTA meetings and other organizations helps not only the adult but also his community to better understand the disorder of stuttering.

Eugene and Crystal Cooper

Cooper and Cooper (1985) outlined a comprehensive assessment and treatment program for children and adults who stutter: the Personalized Fluency Control Therapy—Revised (PFCT—R). This section addresses their specific therapy framework for the adult based on the following assumptions regarding the nature and treatment of stuttering:

1. Most chronic stuttering behavior is the result of multiple and coexisting physiological and psychological factors.
2. Central neurological deficits are among the major physiological factors involved.
3. Learning and anxiety are among the major psychological factors involved.
4. Stuttering may be viewed, for intervention purposes, as involving the discoordination of the processes of phonation, articulation, and respiration.
5. Most forms of stuttering observed in early childhood are amenable to early intervention.
6. Certain forms of chronic stuttering are resistant to voluntary control and, while alterable, are essentially incurable.
7. Comprehensive stuttering therapy programs must include activities for the modification of stuttering, as well as fluency facilitation and change in negative feelings and attitudes. (p. 125)

PFCT-R therapy involves a four-stage process that addresses the affective, behavioral, and cognitive components of stuttering. STAR stands for *S*tructuring, *T*argeting, *A*djusting, and *R*egulating attitudinal and behavioral aspects of stuttering. During the **structuring stage,** the clinician aids the adult in identifying and describing his stuttering behaviors, avoidances, and attitudes that impact his communication. The **targeting stage** begins by eliminating secondary behaviors that exacerbate the client's stuttering. Emphasis is placed on the client/clinician relationship at this stage in order to establish a trusting environment in which to modify feelings and attitudes toward stuttering that negatively impact the change process. The **adjusting stage** assists the client in developing fluency-enhancing attitudes, feelings, and behaviors in which self-reinforcing skills are learned. Here the adults experiment with different *FIGs* (*F*luency *I*nitiating *G*estures) to determine which strategies are the most comfortable and effective in implementing to change their stuttering. Finally, the **regulating stage** assists the client with the feeling of being in control of his fluency. Fluency control is contingent on the adult's (1) accurate perception (as judged by the clinician) of the stuttering behavior and the interpersonal ramifications of the behavior, (2) realistic emotional and intellectual appreciation of self, (3) capacity of self-reinforcement, and (4) knowledge, feeling, and belief in the capability to gain the feeling of fluency control (Cooper & Cooper, 1985, pp. 137–138). PFCT is a highly structured therapy program that includes many worksheets and examples. It is an excellent training tool to assist clinicians in learning how to conduct integrated behavioral and cognitively oriented therapy.

David Daly

Daly (1988) outlined his integrated approach for use with adults who stutter containing two major components: motor training and mental shift. Motor training, a fluency-shaping emphasis, involves the establishment of fluency targets at a 90% criterion level. The three major targets in this program are deliberate phonation, normal breath, and easy stretch. Daly's fluency therapy begins with mass practice on deliberate phonation on spondee compound word lists, single-word syllables, picture pairs, and word pairs. Daly called this practice "droning" and stressed the importance of not allowing clients to talk in their "easier, faster way of talking" (p. 11) during this practice regime. The second target incorporates practice on modifying the adult's breathing patterns and gradually phases into the third target, the easy stretch. This is defined as the even flow of talking and smooth transition between words. Incorporated into this target are light articulatory contacts, reduced volume, and phoneme prolongation.

The mental-shift component includes work in the cognitive domain through self-instructional strategies. Daly (1988) wrote that "too many of our clients get fluent in their mouths but not in their heads" (p. 103). This aspect of Daly's treatment involves four elements of instruction: guided relaxation, mental imagery, affirmation training, and self-talk strategies. What is different in Daly's program compared to others is his emphasis on mental imagery and affirmation training. Daly wants clients to see themselves in a new role by generating "pictures in the mind." Clients are to spend time engaging in mental rehearsal each day visualizing themselves performing in different ways. The affirmation training component has clients write goals, in positive first-person language on index cards, of what they want to be true in the future. This helps them "replace the faulty, old programming with something better" (p. 113).

Hugo Gregory

Gregory (2003) described his integrated approach to the treatment of adults as a process utilizing four areas of activity: (1) gaining insight into attitudes (thoughts and feelings about stuttering), (2) increasing awareness of muscular tension through the use of relaxation exercises, (3) analyzing and modifying speech, and (4) building new speech skills. The degree of emphasis in one area over another depends on the unique profile of each individual client. Gregory dictated a set of underlying principles that govern the therapy process for stuttering therapy:

1. Differential evaluation, differential treatment: A comprehensive evaluation to determine the client's relative strengths and weaknesses must be completed prior

to generating a treatment plan. Therapy goals should be formulated based on the diagnostic findings, thus individualizing treatment for each client.

2. Relationship between client and clinician: A bond must be established between the client and clinician that is reinforced through demonstrating an understanding of the client as a unique person with different experiences, thoughts, and feelings. The client comes to value the clinician's insight and accordingly "comes to identify with the clinician" (p. 72).

3. Counterconditioning, deconditioning, and desensitization: Speech change that replaces a maladaptive response to stuttering with a more adaptive response must occur in the early stages of therapy. Whether it is using an easier initiation of phonation or a modified version of stuttering, the clinician helps the client work through hierarchies to respond to anticipated stuttering in a positive manner.

4. Modeling: Gregory considers modeling "one of the most efficient and powerful teaching techniques the clinician possesses" (p. 73). Clinicians must be able to model speech modification techniques in all interactions with clients to promote vicarious learning and emphasize the importance of "practicing what you preach."

5. Guided practice: Clients must have the opportunity to rehearse behavior changes under the guidance of the clinician. It should not be assumed the client can perform a particular task if, during therapy, the clinician and client have not role-played the activity to ensure appropriate use and skills for a positive experience.

6. Positive reinforcement: Therapy should emphasize the use of positive reinforcement following the occurrence of a desired behavior. The clinician should recruit the adult's spouse or significant other to reinforce the use of newly learned skills in other environments besides the therapy room.

7. Self-monitoring, self-reinforcement: Therapy should emphasize the ability of the client to monitor and evaluate their own behavior. Table 11.15 provides a sample sequence of this principle.

Barry Guitar

Guitar (1998) described a program of modification and fluency-shaping techniques to establish fluency in the adult or advanced stutterer. He maintained that the slow movements and light articulatory contacts used during pullouts are similar to those speech movements used during slow, prolonged speech production. It is beneficial to the adult to have a repertoire of strategies to achieve three main fluency goals: (1) successfully apply skills when it is important to sound fluent (i.e., spontaneous fluency); (2) achieve a modified level of stuttering close to fluency when unable to achieve spontaneous fluency (i.e., controlled fluency); and (3) accept stuttered speech when it is not important to sound fluent and the client does not want to put the effort into modifying speech (i.e., acceptable stuttering). In addition to these behavioral goals, therapy must address the adult's feelings and attitudes toward stuttering. Elimination of avoidances and reduction in feared words or situations is essential to long-term speech improvement.

Table 11.15
Illustrated sequence designed to teach clients to self-monitor and evaluate their speech productions.

---

1. Clinician gives instruction and models the behavior.
   Client hears instructions and observes the clinician's model.
2. Clinician gives instructions and models the behavior.
   Client hears instructions and observes the clinician's model.
   Client emits the behavior.
   Clinician says, "Good" or "Try again. Watch my model."
3. Clinician instructs and models.
   Client listens, observes, and emits the behavior.
   Client evaluates, writing "+" or "−" on a concealed sheet.
   Clinician evaluates, writing "+" or "−" on a concealed sheet.
4. When the clinician and client are agreeing 90% of the time, proceed to:
   Clinician models; instructions may be very brief.
   Client emits the behavior.
   Client evaluates, "+" or "−".

Source: Based on Gregory (2003).

Guitar's (1998) clinical procedures encompassed various components from both modification and fluency-shaping approaches. The first phase of treatment has as its goal the understanding and confrontation of stuttering. The clinician structures tasks to decrease the mystery around stuttering by teaching the client about the speech mechanism and exploring stuttering. Phase 2 involves the reduction of negative feelings and attitudes and the elimination of avoidance behaviors. To achieve this goal, stuttering is openly discussed in clinical and nonclinical settings. The adult is instructed to talk about stuttering with family, friends, and even coworkers. Using feared words and entering feared situations is encouraged to help reduce negative emotionality. Another strategy Guitar used during this phase was to ask the adult to freeze or hold on to the moment of stuttering while remaining calm. Use of voluntary stuttering aids in desensitizing the adult to stuttering, reducing their shame, fear, and embarrassment. All of the strategies implemented during phase 2 of therapy are structured in a hierarchal manner from easy, less fear to complex, increased fear.

Phase 4 helps the adult integrate both fluency-shaping and stuttering modification strategies to achieve speech goals. Guitar describes two procedures used throughout this phase of treatment: *Fluency-Enhancing Behaviors (FEBs)* and modifying moments of stuttering. FEBs include slower rate, gentle onsets, soft contacts, and proprioception. To modify moments of stuttering, adults are asked to stutter easily without the use of secondary behaviors, saying the word in a slow and relaxed way. Guitar adds that the adult must be able to implement FEBs when approaching production of a problematic word. The last phase of treatment entails the maintenance of speech improvements through two procedures: (1) becoming your own clinician, and (2) establishing long-term fluency goals. Given the fluency-shaping and stuttering modification tools just discussed, Guitar stated that adults must assume responsibility for their treatment regime by tackling fear words and situations when they arise and identifying avoidance behaviors that reemerge with time. The adult must continue to organize assignments, preferably daily, that combat the development of fear and avoidance. Discussion regarding relapse is essential to reinforcing self-responsibility. Then adults must establish long-term fluency goals compatible with their unique set of needs.

Catherine Montgomery

Montgomery (2003) described an intensive integrated treatment design for adults who stutter attending the American Institute for Stuttering. Prior to starting the program, clients undergo a pretreatment evaluation that includes the following components: (1) case history questionnaire, (2) WASSP Scale, (3) the Perceptions of Stuttering Inventory (PSI), (4) the OASES, and (5) videotaped samples of the client's speech during conversation and reading. Participants attend the clinic for treatment all day, Monday through Friday, for a 3-week period. The overall goal is to provide a variety of comprehensive tools for effective speech and attitude management. To achieve this goal, participants engage in a series of activities involving identification, desensitization, speech and voice management, attitude modification, and transfer of skills into real life.

Montgomery outlined the following identification tasks conducted during the first few days of the program and gradually phased out: (1) tallying moments of stuttering and avoidances, (2) mirror work and freezing moments of blocks, and (3) classifying overt and covert speech behaviors. Desensitization to the moment of stuttering, as well as listener reaction, is an ongoing program component and includes tasks such as (1) making phone calls and telling the listener you stutter, (2) stuttering openly, and (3) conducting surveys about stuttering with family, friends, and strangers. Speech and voice management begins on the third or fourth day: Participants learn a combination of stuttering modification and fluency-shaping strategies to transform the muscular miscoordination that constitutes disfluent speech into a coordinated muscular coordination of the breath, vocal folds, and articulators. Easy initiation of phonation with coordinated breathing is practiced throughout the program. Attitude management incorporates discussions and readings on expectancy behaviors, fears and avoidances, and identifying the learned patterns that interfere with the implementation of speech management techniques.

By the end of the second and beginning of the third week of the program, skills are transferred to the real world through outside assignments. Participants enter the community to reinforce use of speech management and cognitive tools in everyday realistic and challenging conditions. Ultimately, depending on individual goals, each client takes over the self-as-clinician role and customizes his own approach to speech management. Next, a written, 2-month maintenance plan is developed during the final phase of treatment. A series of follow-up meetings are scheduled to include once-a-week support practice sessions, weekly, bimonthly, and monthly phone contacts, and 1-hour, 1-day, or 1-week refresher courses as needed.

Megan Neilson

Neilson (1999) outlined a *Cognitive-Behavioral Treatment* (CBT) program for adults who stutter. This intensive 3-week program follows the original therapy design of Ingham and Andrews with one major modification: increased emphasis on the cognitive aspects of therapy. The first week of therapy establishes smooth speech, a derivative of prolonged speech. During week 2, the client transfers learned fluency to everyday environments outside the clinic setting. The last week focuses on the transfer of skills to client-specific circumstances based on individual needs and lifestyle. Participants attend once-a-month follow-up sessions 1, 2, 3, 6, and 12 months after treatment. Neilson's CBT program included four elements: education (learning about the disorder, demands/capacity framework, rationale for speech modification strategy, the role of anxiety, and self-management); skill acquisition (learning smooth-speech technique); graded exposure exercises (using new skills in settings of increased difficulty); and cognitive restructuring (understanding the interaction between behavioral and cognitive change factors). Upon review of the information provided by Neilson, what is classified as an integrated approach appears to have greater emphasis on the behavioral component with "explicit cognitive restructuring proceeding largely on an ad hoc basis" (p. 194).

David Shapiro

Shapiro (1999) claimed there are two major treatment goals for the adult who stutters: (1) spontaneous-controlled fluency with acceptable stuttering if necessary and (2) the establishment and maintenance of positive attitudes toward communication. To achieve these goals, the adult must first establish fluent speech production, increase its use, and transfer the skills to various settings. Then the adult must develop resistance to fluency disruptions that threaten the maintenance of controlled fluency. For the second goal, the adult establishes and maintains positive feelings around communication. The client must maintain the fluency-inducing effects of treatment, particularly in the area of communication-related behaviors, thoughts, and feelings.

Shapiro's integrated approach incorporates components of both fluency-shaping and stuttering modification treatment designs, perhaps with a stronger emphasis on fluency development. Shapiro (1999) maintained that three events must transpire in order for the transfer of speech fluency to occur: (1) The client must assume an active role in treatment, (2) activities must be individualized, and (3) the client must gain the feeling and experience of fluency control. He recommended that clinicians create a "safe environment" for the PWS. Six components combine to make such a setting: (1) allow the client to express himself, his dreams, and what he hopes to accomplish; (2) accept the client's input on treatment objectives; (3) encourage active participation in therapy; (4) design communication hierarchies varying communication partners, audience size, location, and content; (5) provide opportunities for the client to experience fluency success; and (6) heighten his awareness of the speech fluency already present in his speech. He described a journal assignment that provides a means for creating this awareness. Adults are instructed to write one word per day that they were able to produce fluently in their "success journals." Gradually, words are added to this list.

Shapiro prescribed that clinicians follow a 3D therapy structure: *D*iscuss, *D*emonstrate, and *D*irect/coach. This organization provides the adult with the knowledge, model, and skills necessary to attend to his fluency regularly. Additional feature of Shapiro's approach to the disorder is an emphasis on the client/clinician relationship, the client's personal construct organization, and family dynamics that influence therapeutic outcomes.

C. Woodruff Starkweather and Janet Givens-Ackerman

Starkweather and Givens-Ackerman (1997) discussed a process of recovery from stuttering implemented at Temple University Stuttering Center. Their integrated approach to the treatment of stuttering involves a three-step therapy plan: (1) increasing awareness, (2) becoming more accepting of oneself at the moment of stuttering, and (3) change: getting out of the way. Step 1 is the most comprehensive stage: It emphasizes increased awareness in affective, behavioral, and cognitive dimensions of the disorder. With the use of two therapy tools, the tape recorder and journal, the client begins to reflect on the moment of stuttering, providing specific details. According to these authors, the rationale for increasing awareness in the adult who stutters is to provide a foundation of common knowledge and understanding used to discuss stuttering. It also facilitates increased acceptance and decreased denial. "Denial is the only defense immediately available against the psychological pain of the disorder" (p. 151). To counteract this defense mechanism, the client begins to identify, locate, and characterize stuttering behaviors. Table 11.16 contains a list of questions designed by Starkweather and Given-Ackerman to initiate conversations and thus increase awareness and understanding of stuttering behaviors.

Another part of the recovery process is to become more accepting of oneself at the moment of stuttering. Starkweather and Givens-Ackerman defined this as accepting the behavior for what it is at a particular point in time. They stress the importance of just letting the behavior happen, without struggle, avoidance, or fear. "Acceptance means simply surrendering to the current reality. For the moment, the person realizes that he or she is powerless to control the events that are occurring" (p. 163). The adult does not try to change this moment; nor does he judge it as in a "Oops, I did it again" statement. It just happens and that is all there is to it.

Last, step 3 involves change or, as these authors put it, "Change: Getting Out of the Way." They outline several techniques that may be helpful during this stage of change. **Repairing** simply means implementing a different speech behavior, which allows the individual to move forward in his speech (e.g., pullouts, slides, bounces). "Letting It Out" focuses on the feelings of anticipation and fear that accompany moments of stuttering. "Letting them out means an abandonment of all the struggling, forcing, and pushing that so often characterizes the speech of people who stutter" (p. 164). "Giving Oneself the Necessary Time" helps the person handle time pressure,

Table 11.16
Questions used to facilitate conversations that increase awareness of the behaviors of stuttering.

1. Am I stuttering now or not?
2. Where in my body is this happening?
3. What sound or word am I trying to say?
4. What is the purpose of my sentence?
5. Where in the sentence is the stuttering located?
6. With whom an I talking?
7. In what situation am I talking?
8. Is my voice pitched higher or lower than usual or is the quality different (strained, hoarse, tense)?
9. Is my articulation soft or hard? Am I saying a sound that has been a problem in the past (an articulation disorder or mispronunciation)?
10. Is this behavior a repetition, prolongation, blockage, broken word, tremor, or a combination of these?
11. Am I trying to force the word out; backing up; trying to get rhythmic support; postponing, avoiding, or hiding sounds, situations, subject, or silences; substituting; or doing some other trick?
12. Is this behavior struggled or easy? Is it rapid or slow in tempo?

Source: Based on Starkweather and Givens-Ackerman (1997).

either self-imposed or environmental, that often exacerbates one's ability to move forward in speech. "Say What One Wants," another principle of this recovery process, stresses the abandonment of word substitutions that reinforce denial. It is important that the adult learn to say the word he planned on saying and extinguish all substitutions. "Telling Listeners What One Needs Them to Do" is a proactive strategy designed to educate listeners on ways they can help the person who stutters. Starkweather and Givens-Ackerman contend that one way to handle a listener is to talk more to them. The last technique to change is "Being Open About Stuttering." As previously discussed, being open about one's stuttering directly confronts feelings of shame and denial.

A Personal Account of Stuttering

This chapter ends with a personal story from Michael Sugarman, past director and creator of the National Stuttering Project (now the National Stuttering Association). Reading the stories of adults whose educational, social, and career choices were greatly influenced by their speech helps us understand this disorder. St. Louis (2001), in the preface of his book *Living With Stuttering: Stories, Basic Resources, and Hope*, helps those of us who do not stutter to "put a human face on a problem that has afflicted untold millions of people through the ages" (p. 9) by sharing stories from adults who stutter. Each story has been colored by stuttering in one way or another. The uniqueness of each personal account helps establish an appreciation of these adults "as individuals, folks not to be regarded as victims but as people meeting the challenges of life just like everyone else" (p. 9). The following story by Michael Sugarman (St. Louis, 2001, pp. 78–81) personifies the struggles of the adult coming to grips with his stuttering.

> Acknowledging that I stuttered took incredible courage. And it took years. At twenty-one I was finally able to admit to myself and others that I stuttered. I was a college student and seeing a school psychologist. In the fourth session I told the psychologist that I was a "person who stuttered." It was then that I began to own my stuttering. My "admission" is what I needed to do in order to take the first step toward forging a new and more fulfilled Michael.
>
> Until then, my stuttering represented my entire self-image. I was dominated by my stuttering. It was difficult for me to express my wants and feelings. I stuttered and worried about what the listener would think of me as a person who stuttered. I struggled to push words out and felt helpless, anxious, afraid, shame, and guilty. When words emerged, I questioned myself: was I saying what I really meant, or was I just using words I could be fluent on, regardless of whether or not they truly expressed my intentions? I learned how to disguise my stuttering, hiding it in various ways. Often this meant substituting words that were easier to say.
>
> I became an expert at avoiding verbal communication. I dealt with many everyday situations in silence. I would point to what I wanted on the menu in restaurants. I asked family members or friends to buy the ticket for a movie or concert; if I had to do it, I'd use gestures as much as possible, my fingers, for example, indicating how many tickets I wanted. I answered questions by nodding or shaking my head. I didn't speak unless it was absolutely necessary. I'd try to let a short simple "yes" or "no" suffice. I even avoided people because they reminded me that I was unable to communicate verbally.
>
> In the first and second grades, I remember being placed in the "slow class." I played with blocks a lot. When I read out loud, I stuttered. Fortunately, a reading teacher eventually asked me to read silently and answer questions about what I had read. I did fine and mainstreamed back into my peer group class.
>
> When I was in the third grade, a yellow "speech card" was placed on the blackboard chalk ledge every Wednesday to remind me to go to speech therapy. The card also served as a silent reminder that I was different. I often walked out sheepishly from class and tried to hide in the bathroom. The school speech therapist worked on my "s" and "th" sounds, but never talked about my stuttering or how I felt.
>
> Throughout my school years, I recall using tricks to enable me to get through class presentations despite my blocks, blinking eyes, and head-jerking tension. These strategies were many and varied: talking in a low voice, talking very fast, nodding my head, and using filler words. I remember doing a talk on Copernicus in eighth grade. That day the word "okay" was my prop; I inserted it after almost every word. Without doubt, my grades suffered because of my stuttering.
>
> Other childhood memories involve my mother's constant advice to, "Stop. Think before you speak," and the ulcer I developed in the third and again in the seventh grade. Eating out at restaurants was torture. Waiters would mimic my stuttering when I tried to

order. I resorted to ordering cheeseburgers instead of a hamburger—what I really wanted—for sixteen years of life because it was easier for me to say.

After high school, I did a lot of study and research about stuttering. I read numerous articles, in search of answers and, hopefully, my cure. It was towards the end of this quest that I met with the university psychologist and started to really talk about my life and my stuttering. The psychologist recommended speech therapy. I followed through and began speech therapy for the third time in my life. This time, however, it was different. With therapeutic guidance, I began a year-and-a-half process of self-disclosure, discovery, practice, and ultimately, liberation.

I began to see how I used my stuttering as an excuse. It let me legitimize my lack of effort, interest, and aspirations. I felt that I couldn't participate fully in life because I stuttered, and so embraced an attitude of "Why assert myself?" The pursuit and development of interests, goals, and relationships had no place in my life, I figured. I felt ambivalence toward my parents and thought no one would marry me because I stuttered. Regarding academics, I was afraid to ask a question despite my thirst for knowledge and answers. And when I considered employment and a career, I couldn't imagine a profession that would not demand verbal faculty.

The speech therapist helped me look at past events that led me to assume the identity of "stutterer." I realized I needed to re-create myself, and with guidance, I was successful. Breaking away from the past was key. For me, this meant giving up the idea that I was a person who was unable to express feelings and desires without stuttering, and it meant trying to understand the behavior controlling me. For example, I noted how my stuttering seemed to worsen when I spoke of my family or myself. Gradually, I became less and less afraid of verbal communication, and more willing to take risks, speaking and otherwise.

I know that stuttering—its cause, patterns, and effects—is not the same for everybody. In my case, looking back, I know it was important that I objectified my stuttering behavior. This involved separating myself from a destructive self-concept and assuming a liberating self-concept.

As for the more technical side of my speech therapy, I spent hours working with a tape recorder. With the recorder on, I practiced reading from books, monologue, and conversation. At first I hated listening to myself and being reminded of how I spoke. However, in time, the tape recorder became less of an enemy and more of an ally in my journey.

Greatly inspired by my experience, I became involved in something incredibly important. One evening in 1976, a group of clinicians and clients from the University of California Santa Barbara Speech Clinic went out for dinner to celebrate the end of the term. I was sitting with five other people who stuttered and had also been in speech therapy.

While we were trying to have a relaxing conversation, the clinicians sat there counting our disfluencies. I decided to get up and move to another table. The rest of the people who stuttered joined me. That night in Santa Barbara, California, we formed the nation's first stuttering self-help group. Later that year, I met Bob Goldman and together we started the National Stuttering Project. Now known as the National Stuttering Association, it has over 2,700 members and self-help groups meeting in more than seventy-five cities around the country. Dealing with my stuttering and building bonds with other people who stutter has enriched my life tremendously.

CHAPTER SUMMARY

Adults who stutter manifest a highly variable, multidynamic mix of the affective, behavioral, and cognitive components of stuttering. The often lifelong experience of stuttering leaves its mark on the adult in the form of social, vocational, and therapeutic limitations. Clinicians must consider the heterogeneity inherent in this population when determining treatment options. Some adults will have buried their stuttering under a mountain of shame, as seen in the covert stutterer; others will have coped more positively with the disorder. The extent to which stuttering has impacted the self-concept of the adult who stutters will determine the degree of cognitive intervention required.

This chapter reviewed several approaches designed to assist the adult in developing effective communication. The intensity and type of therapy are variables to consider when planning treatment. Intensive short-term group programs versus individual long-term designs are both viable options for adults. Selecting the appropriate approach and design will be based on the adult's prior therapy experiences and the circumstances that bring him back into therapy. As part of therapy, certain issues will need to be addressed with this population. Issues of relapse, understanding and coping with this phenomena, must be discussed early in the therapy process. Clinicians must prepare the adult for the ups and downs of stuttering by providing useful coping tools. The treatment approaches discussed in this chapter can assist the clinician in determining which tools are most appropriate for each client. For most adults, involvement in self-help meetings greatly supplements and sometimes replaces the need for clinician-directed therapy. Self-help involvement provides an unconditional environment for adults to learn to accept themselves as people who stutter. Reduction of avoidance behaviors accompained with openness about their stuttering allows adults to move toward acceptance of stuttering and feelings of internal control. Finally, developing effective communication skills may be required for some adults who have permitted stuttering to impact their ability to interact socially.

STUDY QUESTIONS

1. What is the lifelong impact of stuttering for some adults?
2. Describe ways that some adults suffers vocationally due to this disorder.
3. In what phase of treatment would you spend a significant amount of time in therapy for the severe adult? Explain your answer.
4. Identify topics for discussion for an adult support group meeting. Justify the need to address your topics.

5. Generate five tasks you might ask the adult who exhibits covert stuttering to perform. State your rationale along with your response.

6. Why is the identification phase of treatment important?

7. Compare and contrast two of the fluency-shaping programs covered in the text.

8. Summarize your thoughts and feelings experienced when you read the advice from other adults who stutter.

9. How can you help the adult client handle the relapse phenomenon?

12

Cluttering
Another Fluency Disorder

Treatment Approaches
    David Daly
    Kenneth St. Louis and Florence Myers
    Charles Van Riper
Therapy Activities for Children Who Clutter
    Turn-Taking Activities
    Rate Control Activities

Speech Intelligibility Activities
Topic Maintenance Activities
Nonverbal Activities

LEARNER OBJECTIVES

- Define and identify the ABC characteristics of cluttering.
- List the challenges facing the clinician working with people who clutter.
- Differentiate between stuttering and cluttering features.
- Discuss current research trends in the area of cluttering disorders.

- Identify issues related to treatment effectiveness.
- Compare and contrast treatment approaches for cluttering.
- Understand the personal impact cluttering can have on the adult.

KEY TERMS

CAP (central auditory processing)
central language imbalance
pragmatics
tachylalia

Cluttering has been referred to as the "orphan" in the family of speech pathology (Daly, 1993b). Little has been written about this rare, intriguing, and complex disorder. Perhaps the reason for the lack of information and research on cluttering is that it is "not a clearly identifiable entity" (St. Louis, 1992). It is considered a low-incidence disorder, occurring in only 5% of all fluency disorders (Daly, 1996). Although onset occurs during early childhood, it is not typically identified until age 7 or 8 and even as late as 10 years (Diedrich, 1984; Luchsinger & Arnold, 1965). Unfortunately, cluttering is an understudied disorder.

A DEFINITION OF CLUTTERING

Weiss's 1964 text, *Cluttering*, is considered the classic source on this topic. He identified three signs of cluttering: (1) excessive repetitions of speech, (2) short attention span and concentration, and (3) lack of complete awareness of the problem. St. Louis (1992) defined cluttering as a speech-language disorder characterized by an abnormal fluency that is not stuttering and a rapid and/or irregular speech rate. Preus (1992) argued that cluttering should not be considered solely a fluency disorder because language and articulation difficulties contribute significantly to the disorder. "Cluttering interferes with the ongoing fluent expression of thoughts and ideas" (Daly & Burnett, 1999, p. 226). Weiss (1964) proposed that clinicians view cluttering as a **central language imbalance** that affects all communication modes. Daly and Burnett (1999) captured Weiss's viewpoint through their linguistic disfluency model of cluttering (Figure 12.1). They conceptualize cluttering as a multidimensional disorder with possible impairments in five broad communicative dimensions: cognition, language, pragmatics, speech, and motor. These features are clearly overlapping, interactive components of communication, and a deficit in one area has an impact on other areas.

The term *cognition* refers to the clutterer's apparent lack of awareness of his communication problems, further confounded by a short attention span and poor memory. Language organization is weak, often making discourse very difficult to follow for the listener.

Receptive and expressive *language* deficits are often reported in people who clutter. Narrative discourse is unorganized, with thoughts fleeting back and forth from one topic to another. Difficulty following directions, comprehension of both verbal and written language, and poor auditory memory are just a few weaknesses that may be present in the profile of the clutterer.

Pragmatics, the appropriate use of language in social situations, may also be impaired in cluttering. Knowing when to take turns in a conversation may be problematic for the clutterers who do not self-monitor their speech. They may talk too long and not allow others to contribute to the conversation or they may interrupt others to add their opinions. Maintaining, initiating, and terminating conversations may also be underdeveloped skills with clutterers, who appear to be oblivious to the nonverbal behaviors of their communication partners.

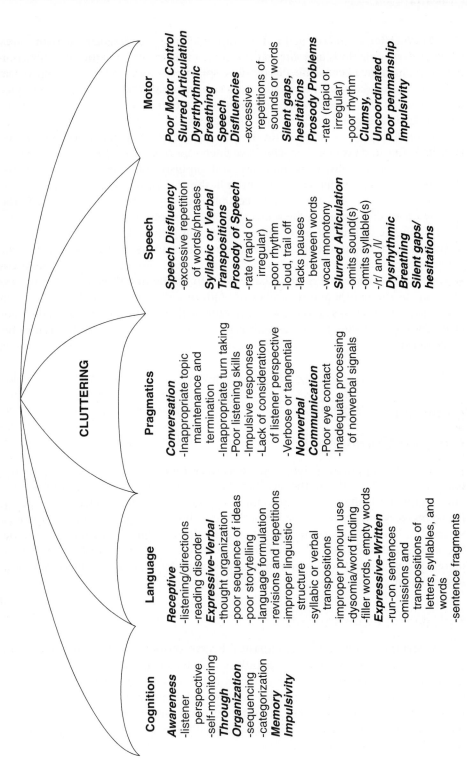

Figure 12.1

Linguistic Model of Cluttering illustrating possible impairment(s) with five broad communicative dimensions.
Source: From D. A. Daly & M. Burnett, Cluttering, Cluttering: Traditional Views and New Perspectives, in R. F. Curlee (Ed.), Stuttering and Related Disorders of Fluency, (2nd ed.). New York: Thieme Medical Publishers, 1999, pp. 242–243. Adapted by permission.

Speech deficits stand out in this disorder. Rapid, sporadic, irregular rate with sound transpositions, omissions, and slips of the tongue may be present in the clutterer's running speech. In the client's effort to produce speech at excessive rates, a compromise occurs in the accuracy of speech, that is, a speed-accuracy trade-off. Sounds and syllables, usually at the end of words, are omitted in order to maintain the fast rate of speech, severely impacting the client's intelligibility.

Motor difficulties comprise the last dimension in Daly and Burnett's model. Deficits in fine and gross motor skills have been reported in the literature, describing clutterers as clumsy, physically immature, and impulsive in their motor movements. The fine motor skill of penmanship is poor in the cluttering population. This linguistic model captures the central language imbalance described by Weiss and is the framework for discussions in the remainder of this chapter.

This chapter represents a compilation of details gathered after a review of the literature on cluttering disorders. However, there is a relatively small number of *current* readings on this topic, most written by the same set of authors: David Daly, Kenneth St. Louis and Florence Myers, and Charles Van Riper. The first three have written extensively on the nature and treatment of cluttering disorders in both children and adults. They used Weiss's (1964) text, *Cluttering*, as their guide into this intriguing disorder. They are considered, by this author, to be the most current, leading authorities on cluttering.

THE ABCs OF CLUTTERING

Affective Components

The affective component of cluttering is not as developed as with the person who stutters. We can attribute this to the fact that clutterers are often not aware of their communication difficulties; therefore, they do not react emotionally to speech breakdowns. Some clutterers may experience feelings of apprehension in situations where they have had prior communication difficulties. Feelings of frustration at not being understood have been observed in this population and often attributed to failure on the listener's part. The clutterer frequently denies the presence of any communication problem.

Behavioral Components

The behaviors of cluttering encompass a diverse set of features. First, the fluency characteristics typically seen in people who clutter are excessive speech rate (called **tachylalia),** frequent use of verbal revisions and interjections, jerky respiration and short respiratory span, and an excessive number of repetitions involving words or phrases. Iterations are effortless and long, sometimes up to 6 to 10 repetitions when formulating language. Typically, there is an absence of physical concomitants, lack of anticipatory behaviors, and sound or word fears, perhaps attributed to the clutterer's limited awareness. Speech is hurried and sometimes unintelligible due to sound/syllable omissions, consonant cluster reduction, irregular rate, sporadic bursts of speech, variable vocal intensity, and monotonous speech intonation. Slips of the tongue occur in conversation with the absence of repair behaviors.

The clutterer's language behaviors may include trouble formulating language and the presence of word-finding difficulties, which interact to create a lack of cohesion in their narratives. Cluttering often co-occurs with reading and written language difficulties. Physically, clutterers have been described as hyperactive or restless and respond impulsively to stimuli. There is a possible family history of stuttering or language disorders with the family reporting consistency in cluttering behaviors with no periods of fluency as seen in stuttering, being difficult to understand, and history of delayed speech and language development. Daly and Burnett (1999) provided a concise checklist of the behaviors typically associated with cluttering (see Figure 12.2).

Cognitive Components

The cognitive components of cluttering cluster around the individual's lack of awareness of the communication problem. If clients are unaware of their difficulties, negative thought processes will not likely emerge. Clutterers may think listeners have the problem and not attribute communication difficulties to any specific behavior they exhibit. As Dalton and Hardcastle (1989) noted, "many just do not realize the speed at which they are speaking and are genuinely puzzled by their listeners' failure to understand them" (p. 124). Clutterers do not attend to their speech production, exhibiting poor self-monitoring skills and ability to interpret nonverbal signals. Poor cooperation with therapy regimes confirms their cognitive denial of the problem, even when faced with real career-related consequences (e.g., the loss of a job because co-workers cannot understand them). However, as Daly (1992) noted, a subgroup of clutterers may develop negative thoughts around talking, seemingly "rooted in a negative frame of mind" (p. 115). He proposed that most clutterers come into therapy having tired of their cluttering and listener reactions, truly wanting to improve their speech.

SPECIAL ISSUES

Cluttering Differentiated from Stuttering

There is consensus in the literature that cluttering exists as a distinct disorder from stuttering (Dalton & Hardcastle, 1989; Daly, 1986, 1992, 1993a, 1993b, 1996; Daly & Burnett, 1999; Preus, 1992; St. Louis, 1992; St. Louis & Myers, 1995, 1997; Van Riper,

Checklist for Identification of Cluttering—Revised				

Client's Name: _____ Date: _____

Instructions: Please respond to each descriptive statement below. Your answer should reflect how accurately you believe the statement is true for the client.

Statement True for Client	not at all	just a little	pretty much	very much
1. Repeats words or phrases				
2. Started talking late; onset of words and sentences delayed				
3. Never very fluent; fluency disruptions started early				
4. Language is disorganized; confused wording				
5. Silent gaps or hesitations common				
6. Interjections; many filler words				
7. Little or no tension observed during disfluencies				
8. Rapid rate (tachylalia) or irregular rate; speaks in spurts				
9. Compulsive talker; verbose or tangential				
10. Respiratory dysrhythmia; jerky breathing pattern				
11. Slurred articulation (deletes, adds, or distorts speech sounds)				
12. Speech better under pressure (during periods of heightened attention)				
13. Difficulty following directions; impatient/disinterested listener				
14. Distractible, attention span problems; poor concentration				
15. Poor language formulation; storytelling difficulty; trouble sequencing ideas				
16. Demonstrates word-finding difficulties resembling anomia				
17. Inappropriate pronoun referents; overuse of pronouns				
18. Improper linguistic structure; poor grammar and syntax				
19. Clumsy and uncoordinated, motor activities accelerated or hasty, impulsive				
20. Reading disorder or difficulty reported or noted				

Figure 12.2
Cluttering checklist.
Source: From D. A. Daly & M. Burnett, "Cluttering: Traditional Views and New Perspectives." In R. F. Curlee (Ed.), Stuttering and Related Disorders of Fluency *(2nd ed.). New York: Thieme Medical Publishers, 1999, p. 251. Reprinted by permission.*

Statement True for Client (Page Two)	not at all	just a little	pretty much	very much
21. Disintegrated and fractionated writing; poor motor control				
22. Writing show omission or transposition of letters, syllables, or words				
23. Initial loud voice, trails off to a murmur, mumbles				
24. Seems to verbalize prior to adequate thought formulation				
25. Above average in mathematical and abstract reasoning abilities				
26. Poor rhythm, timing, or musical ability (may dislike singing)				
27. Variable prosody; improper/irregular melody or stress patterns in speaking				
28. Appears, acts, or sounds younger than age; immature				
29. Other family member(s) with similar speech problem(s)				
30. Untidy, careless, or forgetful; impatient, superficial, short-tempered				
31. Lack of awareness of self and/or communication disorder(s)				
32. Inappropriate turn taking				
33. Inappropriate topic introduction/maintenance/termination				
34. Poor recognition or acknowledgment of nonverbal signals				
35. Telescopes or condenses words (omits or transposes syllables)				
36. Lack of effective/sufficient self monitoring				
Diagnosis: _____ Clinician: _____ Total Score: _____				

Figure 12.2
Continued

1973; Weiss, 1964). Clinicians feel confident in their ability to differentially diagnose cluttering from stuttering (St. Louis & Rustin, 1992). Table 12.1 contains a list of features identified which typically differentiate one disorder from the other (Daly & Burnett, 1999).

However, there does exist a subgroup of clutterers who exhibit stuttering behaviors and stutterers who exhibit cluttering behaviors. Researchers have reported the emergence of stuttering once cluttering symptoms have been resolved. Bloodstein (1995) concurred with Weiss's contention that stuttering often begins as the child

Table 12.1
Inventory of characteristics that differentiate cluttering and stuttering disorders.

Feature	Cluttering	Stuttering
Started talking late; language delay	Typical	Atypical
Slurred articulation; telescope/condense/omit sounds or syllables	Typical	Atypical
Baby talking/lallying	Typical	Atypical
No remission of fluency disruptions; never very fluent	Typical	Atypical
Clumsy, uncoordinated; hasty motor activities	Typical	Atypical
Poor rhythm/musical ability	Typical	Atypical
Poor penmanship; disintegrated writing	Typical	Atypical
Repeats longer words and/or phrases	Typical	Atypical
Clonic-type disfluencies	Typical	Atypical
Speaks better under pressure or on demand	Typical	Atypical
Prosodic deviances; irregular rate, rhythm	Typical	Atypical
Initial loud voice trailing off to a murmur; mumbles	Typical	Atypical
Language formulation difficulties	Typical	Atypical
Disorganized discourse; poor sequencing/storytelling	Typical	Atypical
Word-finding difficulties	Typical	Atypical
Improper linguistic structure/syntax; grammatical errors	Typical	Atypical
Improper pronoun referents	Typical	Atypical
Reading disability	Typical	Atypical
Poor written expression; parallels verbal errors	Typical	Atypical
Inappropriate topic introduction/maintenance/termination	Typical	Atypical
Tangentiality and verbosity	Typical	Atypical
Poor listening skills; impatient listener	Typical	Atypical
Insufficient processing of nonverbal signals	Typical	Atypical
Impulsivity; carelessness	Typical	Atypical
Lacks awareness of communication difficulty	Typical	Atypical
Attention deficits	More frequent	Less frequent
Excels in math and science	More frequent	Less frequent
Fluent episodes	Atypical	Typical
Secondary characteristics	Atypical	Typical
Repeats sounds and short words	Atypical	Typical
Starter sounds and words used	Atypical	Typical
Tonic-type disfluencies	Atypical	Typical
Sound prolongations	Atypical	Typical
Tension/struggle behaviors	Atypical	Typical
Pitch changes	Atypical	Typical
Word substitutions and circumlocutions	Atypical	Typical
Fearful about speech; shy and anxious	Atypical	Typical
Heightened awareness of disfluencies	Atypical	Typical

Source: From D. A. Daly & M. Burnett, *"Cluttering: Traditional Views and New Perspectives." In R. F. Curlee (Ed.),* Stuttering and Related Disorders of Fluency *(2nd ed.). New York: Thieme Medical Publishers, 1999, p. 227. Reprinted by permission.*

tries to avoid cluttering. And Daly (1992) reported an increase in word-finding problems subsequent to cluttering therapy. Bloodstein (1995) summarized the research comparing stuttering and cluttering subjects on various tasks. The following features were found true for clutterers:

1. Brain wave differences exist for clutterers.
2. Greater differential effects of drugs on the speech of clutterers have been observed.
3. Use of the DAF device and procedures has decreased rate control affect for clutterers.
4. Mean pause time when reading is less for clutterers.
5. Reading rates are faster for clutterers.
6. Masking noise results in decreased benefit for clutterers.
7. Clutterers use fewer complex or complete sentences.

These individuals present a unique profile of challenges with regard to treatment. As with other concomitant disorders, working from a concurrent versus sequential framework may help reduce these challenges. As Myers (1992) advocated, treatment of cluttering symptoms should follow a synergistic framework, meaning a change in one dimension can result in changes in another. Therapy is always guided by the particular profile of strengths and weaknesses present in each case. It should incorporate significant others and be highly structured to help the client focus on his speech. The ultimate goal of therapy for cluttering is to get the client to self-monitor his own speech production and take appropriate actions when a breakdown occurs.

Treatment Effectiveness

Another major issue in working with clients who clutter is whether they can benefit from therapy. In the introduction to their discussion of the treatment of cluttering, Myers and Bradley (1992) provided an immediate disclaimer regarding treatment effects. "Before discussing intervention strategies for cluttering, it is important to note that results of therapy with clutterers have thus far not been uniformly favorable" (p. 98). St. Louis (1992) stated several reasons why cluttering is difficult to treat. First, cluttering is considered a multidimensional disorder with anomalies of rate, rhythm, language, articulation, and fluency. Therapy having to address so many parameters has inherent limitations. Second, there may be an organic basis for cluttering that negatively influences its prognosis. And third, clutterers are often not aware of their communication problems; nor are they focused on the impact the disorder has on communicative effectiveness. The scenario facing the clinician working with clutterers can become one of frustration and impatience. Lack of follow-through, difficulty remembering how to perform skills, and intersession regression in performance abilities are just a few of the problems. Add to this the inability to sustain attention and the impulsive bursts of speech, and one can understand why therapy is sometimes ineffective.

However, Daly (1992) reported good treatment effects when therapy addressed all aspects of the problem. He emphasized the role of repetition in discussing therapy rationales and procedures, stressing activities that strengthen the client's awareness of therapy goals. Incorporating cognitive tasks, such as visualization, imagery, relaxation, and positive self-talk, promotes therapy progress. He concluded his chapter with the following advice: "First, tell them what you are going to tell them, tell them, then tell them what you just told them. Finally, the importance of repetition and persistence when working with cluttering clients cannot be overstated" (p. 121).

Research Trends and Needs

There is a dearth of research in the area of cluttering. Because of its rarity, clinicians' limited experience with clutterers, and the profession's previous ignorance regarding this disorder, researchers have not embraced cluttering as they have stuttering, but this trend is changing. At the American Speech-Language-Hearing Association Convention in 2002, researchers interested in cluttering presented a double seminar on the most recent investigations and beliefs regarding cluttering. The following research trends were discussed and/or recommended for further investigation: (1) intelligence, (2) incidence rate, (3) brain organization and activity, (4) acoustic characteristics, (5) development trends, (6) genetic/organic basis, (7) impulsivity and temperament, (8) speech motor control abilities, (9) treatment efficacy, (10) social penalties, and (11) educational impact of cluttering. Recent speculations regarding cluttering include an association among central auditory processing (**CAP**) disorders, learning disabilities, and cluttering because of the similarity in symptomology (Myers et al., 2002). It was suggested that clutterers may even benefit from similar therapy activities used with children who have CAP.

TREATMENT APPROACHES

David Daly

Daly (1986, 1992, 1993a, 1993b, 1996) has published several assessment tools and articles focusing on cluttering disorders. Daly and Burnett (1999) presented three principles of therapy for the client exhibiting cluttering. The first principle states the client must understand the goals and rationale for therapy. The second principle states the clinician should provide immediate, direct feedback regarding speech skills. Use of video and audio equipment is highly effective in promoting client self-awareness and counteracting the presence of denial. The third principle specifically requires the involvement of parents and significant others throughout the entire therapy process. Involvement of others is essential for the transfer of skills into the home environment, as well as to assure accurate and consistent practice of skills.

Daly and Burnett (1999) proposed a linguistic model of cluttering comprised of five broad communication dimensions: cognition, language, pragmatics, speech, and motor. Following this model, they presented therapy activities and suggestions classified according to each communication dimension (see Table 12.2). The objective of cluttering therapy is to teach the client to produce a slower, more deliberate speech rate. To achieve

Table 12.2

Therapy strategies categorized according to their linguistic model of cluttering.

Targeted Deficit Area	Treatment Principles and Activities
Awareness: It is important to address awareness as a whole as it pertains to each deficit area.	• Provide rationale for each task and goal in each session • Utilize video and audio recordings • Provide immediate, direct feedback with positive reinforcement for appropriate performance/behavior • Multisensory feedback, i.e., vibro-tactile feedback, pacing board • Negative practice
Self-Monitoring Tasks for awareness also assist in improving self-monitoring and vice versa. Impulsivity also improves.	• Monitor the number of times the client self-corrects (e.g., an articulation error, self-cues to reduce rate, etc.) • Use of Delayed Auditory Feedback • Self-rating for specific task performance (i.e., demonstrating ability to judge accurately correct or desirable performance) • Train awareness and accurate response to listener feedback
Attention Span	• Measure time on task (sustained attention) • Tally number of times redirection to task is required • Use time or alarm to indicate task beginnings, endings • Listening for comprehension and details, following directions; selections of increasing duration • Auditory memory for increasingly longer series of numbers (forward or backward), words (related or unrelated)
Thought Organization/ Formulation Note that each activity may actually address multiple target areas simultaneously	• Naming attributes within given category for specific objects • Categorization of items or objects • Detailed description of objects, increased use of descriptors/adjectives • Describe similarities and differences of two objects • Sequencing activities, such as naming steps to complete a task or giving directions • Storytelling; structured with use of picture sequencing cards or unstructured narrative • Writing; same task as above with written responses
Semantics, Syntax, and Lexical Selection The activities in the sections above as well as these can be targeted in verbal or written exercises	• Unscramble words, sentences, paragraphs • Vocabulary-building exercises • Naming activities, including confrontation naming and naming of description or category • Cloze activities at sentence or paragraph level • Sentence framing • Combining simple sentences into one complex sentence
Pragmatics/Social Skills	• Listening activities requiring careful follow-through; blind board activities • Training appropriate means of requesting, clarification, questioning • Building awareness of specific behaviors through direct feedback (verbal, audio or video replay, role playing) • Overt practice of social skills (greetings, introductions, salutations) • Topic-specific discussion; attempt to make all remarks pertain to one topic • Overt or exaggerated practice of acknowledging nonverbals (reading expressions, body language) • Practice turn taking in activities and conversation; move from highly structured to less structured tasks • Appropriately tell jokes (proper sequencing, timing)

(continued)

495

Table 12.2
Continued

Targeted Deficit Area	Treatment Principles and Activities
Speech Production and Prosody Many suggestions in this section address speech and motor abilities	• Rate reduction programs; DAF; deliberate, exaggerated practice • Reduce repetitions via use of DAF, deliberate phonation, decreasing rate and increasing linguistic skills • Emphasize appropriate changes in inflection/intonation; stressing different words to change meaning, statements, versus questions • Breathing modifications for better coordination with speaking and increased use of pauses; appropriate use of "verbal punctuation" • Overarticulation and exaggeration of mouth movements; articulation drills, if necessary • Imitation or oral reading of nursery rhymes, poetry
Motor Skills	• Oral-motor skills training (e.g., Riley & Riley) • Recite tongue twisters • Address penmanship in written assignments • Practice various rhythmic patterns (tapped or verbalized)

Source: From D. A. Daly & M. Burnett, "Cluttering: Traditional Views and New Perspectives." In R. F. Curlee (Ed.), Stuttering and Related Disorders of Fluency *(2nd ed.). New York: Thieme Medical Publishers, 1999, pp. 242–243. Reprinted by permission.*

this goal, clinicians can use sequence pictures to elicit storytelling in a highly structured way, gradually increasing the length and complexity of the stories. Reading in unison helps control rate. Recording reading samples for client reference is recommended. Volitional accentuation of each syllable while reading is another effective therapy technique. Having clients underline the final consonants in written passage may facilitate their awareness when reading. Training on silent sentence formulation before verbalization may help reduce the number of interjections and retrials in the clutterer's speech.

Clients need to understand that silence is as much a part of communication as speech. Teaching them to monitor both silent periods and talking periods may aid in reducing tangential verbosity. Even with cluttering, clients need to learn the language of fluency. Clients must be able to verbalize what they are doing and why. Daly incorporated several cognitive strategies (relaxation, visual imagery, and breathing exercises) to enhance concentration and reinforce the possibility of success. Daly (1986) maintained that the major emphasis in therapy is to draw the client's awareness toward the details of speech production. When necessary, Daly (1993) used a series of oral-motor drills designed to develop speech motor coordination. Because of the presence of many deficit areas, Daly recommended working on more than one dimension in each session. Concurrent therapy is the only way to address the needs of the whole client. For this and other reasons related to self-monitoring and awareness, Daly believed therapy for cluttering usually takes longer than for stuttering. Maintaining a highly structured therapy routine is critical for the cluttering client. Daly (1992) wrote, "more than any other clients we have worked with, cluttering individuals benefit from highly specific, short-term goals" (p. 108). He urged clinicians to be prepared, positive, and persistent.

Kenneth St. Louis and Florence Myers

St. Louis (1992) and St. Louis and Myers (1995, 1997) described a synergistic approach to the treatment of cluttering disorders. They defined *synergistic* as "parts of the communication system working together in a highly coordinated and well timed or synchronous manner" (p. 324). A breakdown in one domain (e.g., rate of speech) may produce concomitant difficulties in another (e.g., language formulation). All dimensions of communication are inherently linked to one another; therefore, treatment requires work on all dimensions in a interrelated manner. Therapy is planned around the domains of speech production to include rate and rhythm, fluency, articulation-phonology, and language functions. St. Louis and Myers provided a list of six therapy principles with accompanying techniques to guide the clinician when planning intervention for the person who clutters.

Principles and Techniques for Improvement in Rate and Rhythm

1. Utilize a step-by-step outline of therapy tasks manipulating the amount of information the client is to produce. First, encourage the client to use short, simple utterances. Read lists of words and phrases to practice rate control. Gradually increase the number of phrases produced. When using written text, mark the phrases at the clause boundaries to provide a visual clue for the client. Move into answering questions requiring short single-word responses.
2. Provide instruction in the area of speech cadence to help the client with rhythmic speech production. Teach the client to increase loudness and pitch on stressed syllables and stretch the length of these syllables to decrease speech rate. The client can recite poetry, sing songs, and read simple scripts that contain built-in cadences to follow.
3. Use the DAF to reduce speech rate and provide the clutterer with the sensory feedback associated with slower speech production. The clutterer may not like the way slow speech "feels" and will need much practice to adapt to the difference in proprioception. When using the DAF, the client should not ignore the delay and should keep pace with the preset delay to produce the desired decrease in speech rate.

Principles and Techniques for Improvement of Articulation

1. The clutterer is often speaking at a speech rate that exceeds their natural abilities, resulting in poor articulation. Using phrasing and pausing are two techniques that address this discrepancy between the individual's capacity and the demands placed on the system.
2. Teach the client to prolong the end of the words. Have the client highlight the end of words in a written passage making sure to exaggerate his productions. This counteracts the clutterer's tendency to rush through the endings of words and utterances.
3. Discuss the features of speech production with the older clutterer, stressing how important information (such as plurals) is lost when the ending sounds are

omitted. The clinician can transcribe a speech sample with various omissions of sounds and syllables and have the client interpret the passage. Using metalinguistic skills may increase awareness of speech behaviors.

4. Target phoneme-specific misarticulations or phonological processes in conventional ways.

Principles and Techniques for Improvement of Language

1. Word-finding difficulties may compound the clutterer's ability to produce fluent speech and need to be addressed in therapy. Sometimes just reducing speech rate down will facilitate selection of the appropriate word and eliminate the appearance of this problem.
2. Work on semantics and syntax, especially relational words, helps the clutterer organize his language. Relational words include *because*, *unless*, *therefore*, *however*, *nevertheless*, and *but*. By emphasizing these words, the client learns to connect clauses and thoughts.
3. Mental mapping of narrative details can facilitate the organizational skills of the clutterer. By identifying the essential information in the passage and organizing events sequentially, the clutterer learns to use outlines to improve his narratives.
4. Help the client identify "maze" behaviors (fillers, empty words, revisions, incomplete phrases, etc.) by transcribing a discourse sample. Show the client how these speech behaviors impact listener comprehension. Highlighting each maze behavior can provide a visual display of how often the flow of communication is disrupted. The client then reads the sample, first with the mazes and then without, to experience the difference between the two narratives.
5. Social skills training may be necessary for some clutterers. Some clients appear to have a lack of "social awareness" and do not perceive subtle nonverbal cues the listener may be relaying. Learning how to repair conversations and engage in appropriate turn taking during conversations will be an added component to some clutterers' treatment plans.

Principles and Techniques to Improve Fluency

1. In that rate and language are the primary determinants of fluency, teach the client to implement rate control strategies to allow time to formulate and produce fluent speech.
2. Have the client underline the stressed syllable and focus on his productions when reading aloud. Then have the client underline the unstressed syllables or words within the utterance (such as *a* and *the*) to make sure they are fully produced.
3. Broadening the client's semantic network by working on antonyms and synonyms will help build linguistic fluency.
4. Teach the clutterer appropriate therapy techniques, such as light articulatory contacts and easy onsets, to help develop coping strategies for any "stuttering-like" behaviors that may be present in his speech profile.

Principles and Techniques to Improve Self-Monitoring

1. Engage the older child or adult in a discussion of the nature of cluttering and the interactions of speech and language that produce this disorder. Use analogies to help him understand what happens to communication when he speaks fast.
2. Use negative practice purposely to contrast slow versus fast speech production.
3. Have the clutterer identify "danger signs" for when speech is "getting into trouble." Danger signs might include repeating words multiple times, emergence of irregular rate, production of run-on sentences, listener nonverbal communication signals, dropping off sounds, and slurring speech.
4. Have the client close his eyes when practicing rate control strategies in order to heighten awareness of other senses, such as tactile, kinesthetic, or proprioceptive feedback.
5. Have clients manipulate other parts of their body (arms, legs, fingers) in contrastive slow and fast movements, focusing on feeling the difference between them.
6. Listen to audiotapes of too fast, too slow, and desired speech rates to enhance auditory awareness of rate differences.

Principles and Techniques to Improve Cognitive/Attitudinal/Emotional Components Associated with Speech

1. Cultivate a positive attitude toward speech.
2. Generate therapy goals in a collaborative way with client and clinician.
3. Be prepared to handle client resistance to therapy when it arises.
4. To foster a feeling of success, give homework assignments in small, manageable segments without undue difficulty.
5. Help the client focus on the relevant information in the session to decrease impulsivity to outside stimuli.

Myers et al. (2002) added several other suggestions to this synergistic therapy approach. To improve speech rate, clinicians can use the analogy of a speedometer to help the client gauge how fast he is talking (e.g., 55, 60, 70 mph). Explain how rate of speech needs to be modified according to "road conditions" and whether you are in the "city or country." Facilitate rate control by teaching the clutterer to say only one sentence at a time, called self-imposed phrasing, with a pause after the utterance to check for listener comprehension. Again, talking about talking and talking about cluttering fosters metacluttering awareness and may strengthen the client/clinician relationship. Myers sets her therapy goal for cluttering as the encoding of thought, language, and speech units in a well-timed and cohesive manner, at a rate suitable to the individual's capacity.

More recently, St. Louis, Raphael, Myers, and Bakker (2003) provided a clinical update on treatment strategies for use with people who clutter. They reinforce the concept of individual treatment planning to meet unique client needs. Several therapy strategies have been discussed over the years and were summarized by these authors. They prioritized these common goals and principles as follows: slowing rate; heightening monitoring; using clear articulation; using acceptable, organized language;

interacting with listeners; speaking naturally; and reducing excessive disfluencies (p. 20).The following is a summary of their therapy suggestions:

1. Slowing rate: Find an effective strategy that works for the client and remember that rate increases when topic emotionality increases; use delay auditory feedback; cue client when rate spurts occur; provide a slow speech model for the client to imitate; transcribe a sample of his speech (with no spaces between words) and have the client mark when to pause; and have the client match his speech productions with a prerecorded sample, as played on a language master device.

2. Heightening nonitoring: Requiring imagination and close observation on behalf of the clinician, teach clients to listen to their speech productions via audiotaped and videotaped conversations; use visualization and positive self-talk prior to speaking tasks; and tape-record clients' "worst, questionable, and best examples of speech and then help them adopt a discipline of listening to that tape several times a day to enhance monitoring" (p. 21).

3. Using clear articulation: Implement a systematic articulation regime; develop automaticity of correct speech productions; practice short sentences to elicit clear speech; and read word lists that include multisyllabic words stressing the inclusion of all sound.

4. Using acceptable, organized language: Implement language treatment to include simple, short sentences, and progress to complex sentences; transcribe samples of the client's cluttered utterances and identify the mazes and filler words; have the clients underline the content of their discourse (for example, who, what, when, how); and stress organizational and sequential aspects of their stories.

5. Interacting with listeners: Teach pragmatic aspects of language necessary when "anticipating, perceiving, and responding to standard cues provided by listeners during conversations" (p. 21); discuss rules for turn taking; demonstrate how to respond to signals indicating listener confusion; and have the client routinely ask the listener if he or she is understanding his speech.

6. Speaking naturally: Practice varying syllable durations and intonation contours; provide immediate feedback when speech becomes irregular; and use software programs, such as Visi-Pitch, to model intensity and frequency required of natural-sounding speech.

7. Reducing excessive disfluencies: Target this aspect of speech through fluency-shaping strategies.

Charles Van Riper

Van Riper's (1971) Track II classification clearly identified those people with cluttering disorders, although he did not refer to these clients as clutterers. He described this subgroup as exhibiting very disorganized speech with hurried and irregular repetitions with rare prolongations and fixations. Revisions, false starts, interjections, and more retrials occur in their conversations. Articulation is disrupted and accompanied by poor self-monitoring. Track II children do not typically develop fears, avoidances, or struggle behaviors because their awareness is limited. These children are described as children who do not listen to themselves. Van Riper clearly linked his Track II stutterers to

Weiss's "early cluttering-like speech" (p. 109); however, he argued that these "cluttering" children eventually merge into stuttering as they become aware of their disordered communication and the affective and cognitive components of stuttering develop.

Van Riper (1992), based on his experience with cluttering, offered these suggestions for working with the clutterer: (1) do not ask the clutterer to slow down, but find ways of slowing him down; (2) build the client's tolerance for a slower speech rate; (3) read in unison, beginning with a faster rate and gradually decreasing rate to normal; (4) use the shadow technique with the clinician's speech and that of others; (5) practice repeating phrases and sentences with varying tempos; (6) write down words before he starts to say them; (7) tap out the words before speaking; (8) record samples of the client's speech, then listen to them and transcribe them; (9) jointly analyze samples for omissions, repetitions, and slurring; (10) practice voluntary cluttering using written material; (11) pause and learn to tolerate the silence; (12) memorize short quotations and daily greetings; (13) paraphrase a reading passage implementing rate control strategies; and (14) role-play situations demanding coherent speech production.

THERAPY ACTIVITIES FOR CHILDREN WHO CLUTTER

Four major principles of therapy for working with children who clutter are recommended by this author: (1) Keep activities concrete using conceptually based tasks; (2) incorporate repetitive practice of stimuli through different therapy games (same set of words used for Concentration, Memory, Bingo, Guess What, word search, etc.); (3) develop a strict routine and structure to therapy; and (4) make therapy fun. Children who clutter benefit from therapy activities that incorporate language they are familiar with (e.g., trains). The clinician can use a known topic to teach a new concept to the child. Several of the following activities incorporate this philosophy. Additionally, children who clutter need multiple experiences producing the same words in order to develop automaticity of speech production. If each activity changes stimuli, the child has little opportunity to transfer skills within each session. This is particularly true during the beginning stages of therapy. Therapy for cluttering should be highly structured, instructing clients to limit their extraneous comments during drill work. Above all, therapy must be child centered, creative, and fun. The following are activities designed for children who clutter.

Turn-Taking Activities

LIPS AND EARS

Objective: Students will take communication turns.

Procedure: Gather materials needed for this activity: clip art picture of the ear and lips (have only one picture of lips and four or five pictures of an ear, depending on the size of your group), popsicle sticks, glue or tape. Introduce the lesson with a definition of communication: the exchange of ideas among people. There are two roles during communication, one of listener and one of speaker. Direct the student's attention to the ear and ask what we use the ear for. Do the same for the mouth. Instruct the students that during a conversation, only one person talks (the one with the mouth) and the others listen (the ones with the ears). After the mouth makes a comment, he passes the mouth to the next person and picks up the ear to become the listener. This continues until everyone has had the opportunity to contribute to the conversation.

TURN-TAKING TREE

Objective: Students will practice obtaining information from one another.

Procedure: Gather materials needed for this activity: tree trunk, top of tree, squares (four of each color), and branches cut out of craft foam board (see Figure 12.3 for shapes and visual representation). Introduce this activity with a discussion about the importance of involving others during a conversation. Tell the students the group will make a tree by adding squares to the top of the tree trunk each time they ask a question of another student. The first person puts down a square and begins to talk. They ask another person a question to follow up on the topic they introduced. This person then puts down his square and answers the question, elaborating if needed. He then asks another student a question, who then puts down his colored square. This continues until everyone has used their four squares to ask questions of the other students. Once you are out of squares, you can no longer contribute to the conversation. If someone interrupts, you lay a branch down to indicate a break in the tree (Winner, 2002). You can play this game numerous times, seeing how many squares the group can put down before getting a branch. Start over each time someone interrupts. Then put squares, a branch, a trunk, and tree top in a plastic sealable bag for students to take home and play the game with their family.

Rate Control Activities

PACING BOARD

Objective: Students will utilize phrasing when generating sentences.

Procedure: Gather materials needed for this activity: sentence strips cut into four pieces, markers, glue, and buttons. There are different types of pacing boards: one for a sound, one for syllables, and one for words. Depending

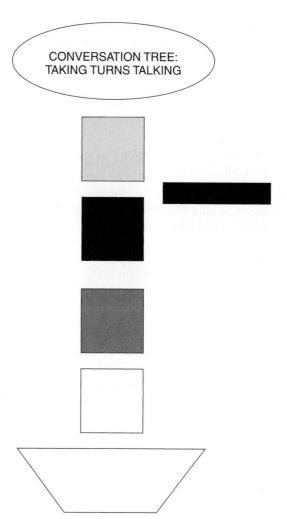

Figure 12.3
Conversation tree designed
to teach clients to take turns
talking without interrupting.
Source: M. Winner (2002).
Reprinted with permission.

on the extent of the client's rate mismanagement, draw two red lines on
the card, dividing the sentence strip into three sections. The color red
provides a visual cue for the student to stop. The student glues a button
in the middle of each section to represent either a syllable or a word (initially). It is recommended each section contain a different type or color
button. The student puts his finger on the button when he says the word.
The time it takes for the student to move his finger usually produces a
significant decrease in rate of speech. The student practices saying numerous phrases containing three words before moving to a more advanced stage where each section represents a phrase. Now the student
can make several new pacing boards, gluing three or four buttons in
each section to represent the clause unit. Explain that the number of

buttons represents the maximum number of words the student is to use in a phrase. He may select fewer words depending on what he is saying.

RED LIGHT—GREEN LIGHT

Objective: Students will phrase appropriately when provided with visual cues in written text.

Procedure: Gather the materials together for this activity: written passage and red and green pencils. This activity is intended for older children who are proficient in reading. Introduce the lesson by talking about street signals and the meaning of red, yellow, and green lights. Problem-solve the consequences when a person driving a car does not respond appropriately to these signals. Read aloud the first sentence in a fast manner and ask the group where you should have stopped to be "in charge" of your speech. Students mark this spot on the paper with a red vertical line. Right after the red line, the students draw an arrow ($\rightarrow$) under the first syllable of the next phrase. This green arrow is to cue them to start in an easy, gradual manner. You can create a set of brief two- to three-sentence paragraphs for students to practice deciding where to mark stops and easy starts. Have the students practice adhering to red lights or get caught by the other members if they run a red light. Gradually increase the length of the paragraphs as students demonstrate the ability to phrase. Eventually, phase out the visual cues on some sentences to see if the students use this skill on their own.

Speech Intelligibility Activities

WHERE'S THE CABOOSE?

Objective: Students will understand the importance of producing final consonants.

Procedure: Gather materials needed for this activity: a train set with an engine, one car, and a caboose, train cutouts, a set of pictures whose meaning is lost if the final consonant is deleted, and markers. To create an awareness of the presence of final consonants, tap the student's hand as you make the final sound of a consonant-vowel-consonant (CVC) word. This provides a tactile cue marking the presence of the sound at the end of the word. Gradually transfer this tapping to touching each part of the train as you say the word. Select a picture from the stack and say the word, tapping the engine for the onset consonant, the train car for the vowel, and the caboose for the final consonant. Practice this until the students understand the task. You can also use the language master machine and have the students listen to the word and identify the beginning, middle, and ending sounds. When a word does not have a final consonant, you comment, "Where's the caboose? Oh no, we lost the caboose. Help me find it." You can even mark the sounds on the train cutouts and hide the caboose and have the child find it.

SPEECH PUZZLES

Objective: Students will produce words including final consonants.

Procedure: Gather materials needed for this activity: index cards, markers, a list of CVC words at the age-appropriate level, scissors, and a plastic sealable bag. Introduce this activity by talking about puzzles and how each piece has a special place within the whole puzzle. Take an index card and cut it into three puzzlelike sections. Then write a letter on each puzzle piece. With the pieces apart, say each sound. Put the onset and vowel pieces together to show the students how you created a syllable. Then add the final puzzle piece to complete the word. The students then practice saying the word with and without the final consonant as you manipulate the final puzzle piece, trying to trip the students into leaving off the final consonant. Each student then makes his own puzzles, practices them in therapy, and then takes them home in the bag as his home assignment.

Topic Maintenance Activities

MAKING BRIDGES

Objective: Students will learn how to make a change in the topic of a conversation.

Procedure: Gather materials needed for this activity: paper bridges or die-cut bridges, pens, blue construction paper cut into shapes resembling water drops, and a list of familiar topics. To begin this activity, show the list of topics to the group. Have them select five topics they would be interested in discussing. Write each topic on an index card and put them aside. Divide the water drops among the group members. Select a bridge and put it in the middle of the table. Select a topic card and place it on the bridge. Students take turns placing water drops under the bridge as they make a topic-related comment. This continues until the group runs out of things to say or a student says, "I would like to bridge to _____ (new topic)." Place another bridge next to the first and begin to place water drops under the bridge. If another student wants to change the topic, he must ask to bridge. In the beginning, a student may change the topic immediately upon his speaking turn. Don't stop him from doing so. When the five topics have been discussed, draw the students' attention to the number of drops under each bridge. Probe for their understanding of rapid topic change resulting in only a few drops of water. The next time you play this game, set a lower limit of the number of water drops required before bridging topics. (This activity is a modification of an activity originally presented by Winner, 2002.)

BRANCHES ON MY TREE

Objective: Students will learn to maintain the topic of discussion.

Procedure: Gather materials needed for this activity: same as for the turn-taking tree activity. Instead of focusing on turn taking, the emphasis is now on topic maintenance. The procedures are the same as the preceding; however, when a student makes a nonrelated comment, a branch is placed next to his circle. You continue to play the game and see how many times (and by whom) comments are not related to the chosen topic.

Nonverbal Activities

MY FACE TELLS ABOUT ME

Objective: Students will interpret facial expressions.

Procedure: Gather materials needed for this activity: emotion cards, facial parts representing different expressions, blank faces cut out of construction paper, and scenarios to read aloud for which students will determine how the person feels. Open the discussion with the question "How do you know when someone is feeling sad?" Go through the emotion cards talking about the different shape of the eyes, nose, eyebrows, lips, and so on. Talk about situations in which a person feels happy, nervous, tired, and so on. Have the children draw an expression on their blank face. You can also use colorforms of facial expressions for the students to select from. Gradually merge into how people look when they do not understand what the other person is saying. Point out other nonverbal cues that signal the listener is not following your train of thought (e.g., sudden stop in head nods, breaks in eye contact, or fidgety behavior). Role-play conversations in which the listener begins to show signs of a lack of comprehension and have the speaker identify the signals. Make a list of what the speaker can do in these situations. Role-play situations in which the speaker changes some aspect of communication in response to listener nonverbal cues.

EMOTIONS BINGO

Objective: Students will learn about different facial expressions used to convey emotion.

Procedure: Gather materials needed for this activity: emotion bingo boards, chips, and calling cards. Use this game to reinforce the topic introduced with the preceding activity. Casually play bingo with one student being the caller for each game. As the caller, the student selects a calling card and imitates the facial expression. You discuss what you are *doing with your face and body* to show this emotion. Everyone puts a chip on the appropriate space that matches the emotion displayed by the student. Change the caller after each bingo game.

CHAPTER SUMMARY

Cluttering is a rare fluency disorder that presents several challenges. First, clinicians must understand the different affective, behavioral, and cognitive components and be able to differentiate them from stuttering. Because of the client's lack of self-awareness and monitoring skills, treatment has less than optimal impact. Many times clients terminate therapy because they do not believe they have a problem. Motivating the clutterer to put forth the effort necessary for significant speech change presents its own challenges. Cluttering disorders have not received the same research efforts or clinical attention as stuttering. Much remains unknown about cluttering, the person suffering from the disorder, and effective means of remediating it. The majority of current writings are attributed to David Daly, Kenneth St. Louis, and Florence Myers. All three authors have made major contributions to enlightening clinicians about this unique and isolated disorder. Whether with adults or children who clutter, the clinician will encounter these challenges and ideally be better equipped to manage them.

STUDY QUESTIONS

1. What are the differentiating features of cluttering disorders?
2. Discuss Daly and Burnett's linguistic model of cluttering.
3. Discuss strategies for increasing awareness in people who clutter.
4. What is the prognosis for clutterers in treatment? Support your answer with information from the chapter.

Final Thoughts

The original intent of the book was to provide information with an applied emphasis so clinicians could learn and become more comfortable working with people who stutter. Stuttering is comprised of factors related to affective, behavioral, and cognitive domains interacting together differently in each individual. From a theoretical standpoint, the clinician should be prepared to explain what is known and not known about stuttering and the people who suffer from it. Assessing the disorder, from a theoretical perspective, can be accomplished through the procedures explained in chapter 4. Determining whether a disorder exists is a time-consuming process; however, the time allocated to determine the independent profile of strengths and weaknesses of the client guides the clinician when planning treatment. The clinician may choose among various approaches of therapy (i.e., fluency shaping, stuttering modification, or an integration of these philosophies) when planning treatment. The clinician has the information to guide her in the problem-solving process when determining which approach produces the best fit for the client. When necessary, clinicians utilize various counseling techniques to assist clients, parents, and significant others in developing coping skills for handling the ups and downs of stuttering.

Treatment for stuttering is as variable as the people who exhibit it. For the preschool child who stutters, emphasis on parental involvement and direct fluency-shaping strategies produces significant speech change. Many preschool children spontaneously recover from stuttering; however, as children enter the elementary years with continued stuttering, it is less likely stuttering will recede. The demands of the school environment coupled with increased peer attention toward speech often exacerbate the underlying stuttering. Children begin to react more to their speech breakdowns, requiring intervention that addresses the affective and cognitive aspects of the disorder. A continuum of treatment options is available to the clinician working with this age group depending on the extent of the student's reactive behavior.

Multiple activities with concrete dialogue samples are included in this text to help the clinician address all components of the disorder.

Entering the middle school and high school years presents additional challenges for both the clinician and teenager who stutters. The literature has little to offer in the way of guidance and specific strategies for use with teens. Understanding motivation and the concepts of competence, control, and connectedness may help the clinician reach these students in positive, engaging ways. Living the life of a person who stutters leaves its mark on the adult. Adults may develop handicapping behaviors that impact their educational, social, as well as vocational advancement. Therapy models, whether intensive short-term or extensive long-term designs, should address the handicap and help adults cope effectively with lifelong stuttering. For some adults, spontaneous remission from stuttering is possible. The hope is out there, yet few achieve it. Adults frequently become fluent through therapy only to lose their skills with time, sometimes only months later, sometimes years later. Understanding relapse is essential for working with adults who stutter. Long-term maintenance of speech gains presents a challenge for both the clinician and client.

Ideally *Working with People Who Stutter* has provided a practical, hands-on learning experience. The many how-to ideas and guidelines have their origin in actual practice. As you reflect on the contents of this book, one question may arise in your mind: "How do I know these activities are effective?" The answer to this question is complex because leading authorities disagree on what to measure and how to measure it. What are the treatment outcomes clients, parents, teachers, and clinicians wish to achieve? Is the treatment being provided responsible for producing the desired outcomes? This book, therefore, concludes with a discussion on identifying treatment outcomes and the process of measuring them.

TREATMENT OUTCOMES

Manning (2004) provided an excellent discussion on the issues related to measuring change in people who stutter. Following the medical model often recommended in professional publications may not reflect accurately the efficacy of the treatment we provide. Using Wampold's findings from the literature on psychology, Manning stressed that "the medical model and associated criteria for empirically validated treatments does a poor job of explaining treatment outcomes" (p. 63). Measuring change beyond the surface features of stuttering, clinicians can document treatment through the way clients describe changes in their cognitive orientation toward speech. The following are two examples provided by Manning (2004, p. 64):

- "You know I stuttered as much as I always have talking to her, but as I walked away, I wasn't embarrassed as I have always been in the past."
- "Ninety-five percent of the time or more, stuttering is not an issue. It's there, I know it's there, and it's part of who I am, but it's not an issue in terms of decisions I make or in terms of what I've achieved. It just doesn't play a major role in my life."

Measuring treatment outcomes presents several challenges to the clinician. Yaruss (2004) outlined factors that may overtly or covertly impact outcome measures:

- Variability of speech behaviors.
- Variations in the characteristics of stuttering exhibited in PWS.
- Broad range of treatment approaches available to PWS.
- Different reactions of PWS.
- Client/clinician relationship.
- Client's overall feelings of satisfaction with treatment.
- Diversity of life experiences by PWS.
- Client's perceptions of changes in quality of life associated with treatment.

Yaruss contended that any combination of these factors can complicate the measurement of treatment effects. To document individual treatment outcomes effectively, he provided several suggestions to help clinicians evaluate the success of their therapy with PWS:

- Work with your client to determine the specific goals of treatment.
- Do not assume or require that all clients achieve the same outcomes in treatment.
- Collect meaningful baseline data and continue to collect data throughout treatment.
- Collect data in multiple situations, both in and out of the clinic.
- Collect data about more than just speech fluency.
- Do not be fooled by the variability of stuttering.
- Do not let your client be fooled by the variability of stuttering.
- Remember that the published empirical literature on stuttering is not yet complete.

Professional leaders addressed the topic of treatment outcomes at the ASHA 1997 Special Interest Division #4 Leadership Conference. Together, clinicians and researchers worked to determine the desired outcomes of fluency therapy. Outcomes were categorized as client outcomes, clinical outcomes, societal outcomes, financial outcomes, and funding source outcomes (Quesal, 1997b). The following are the specifics of these treatment outcomes:

The identified *client outcomes* for adults were these:

- I am satisfied with my therapy program and its outcome.
- My client/clinician jointly determined goals were met.
- I have an increased ability to communicate effectively.
- I feel more comfortable as a speaker.
- I like the way I sound.
- I have an increased sense of control over speech, including stuttering.
- My speech has become more fluent.
- I am independently able to employ a variety of techniques and strategies as appropriate.
- My understanding of stuttering and fluency has increased.
- My speaking skills have become more automatic.
- I have an increased ability to cope with variability of stuttering and relapse.
- I am better able to reach social/educational/vocational potential and goals.

- My knowledge of self-help/support options has been increased.
- Given my demonstrated ability to progress, I could benefit from continued therapy.

Preferred *clinical outcomes* were defined as the client demonstrating feelings, behaviors, and thinking that lead to improved communicative performance and satisfaction with the therapy process. Preferred clinical outcomes may be measured according to the following:

- Frequency and/or severity (duration, tension, evident struggle) of stuttering is reduced in a variety of settings.
- Speech sounds natural (intonation, loudness, rate) in a variety of settings.
- Speech fluency has increased.
- Volitional communication has increased.
- Speaking interactions are pragmatically appropriate (e.g., eye gaze, turn taking) in a variety of settings.
- Techniques are used independently in a variety of settings.
- Avoidance behavior have been reduced.
- Scores on standardized self-appraisal instruments reflect improvement.
- Knowledge and understanding of speech and stuttering has increased.
- Problem-solving skills are increased.
- Attitudes, feelings, and cognitions relative to speech and stuttering are improved.
- Coping skills used in response to negative environmental reactions are improved.
- Involvement of family and significant others has been an ongoing process.
- Knowledge of self-help/support options has increased.

The preferred *financial outcomes* of therapy should include the following:

- A reduction in need/expense of treatment if effective intervention is provided early in childhood.
- A close match between projected and actual costs of treatment is realized.
- Increased cost effectiveness for the client when fluency services are provided by a certified speech-language pathologist who is a specialist in fluency disorders rather than when services are provided by a noncertified speech-language pathologist or a speech-language pathologist who is not a specialist in fluency disorders.
- Reduction in duration and cost of therapy when attendance is consistent.
- More cost-effective therapy outcome if significant others are involved in therapy.
- Diminished cost effectiveness and increased duration of therapy may occur when concomitant conditions exist.
- Diminished cost effectiveness and increased duration of therapy may occur if extraordinary disrupting circumstances exist.

The preferred *funding source outcomes* relative to the payer include the following:

- Treatment is cost effective (in terms of therapy outcomes, frequency of treatment, duration of treatment, fees for treatment, structure of treatment, and utilization of resources).
- Fees for treatment are reasonable and justified.

- Long-term expenses are reduced.
- Services and results are reported using uniform terminology and standard codes.
- Continued treatment is justified based on functional progress.
- Client reports satisfaction with services provided and observed functional changes.

OUTCOME MEASURES

Determining what to measure can create as much debate as how it will be measured. Yaruss (1998) discussed a unifying framework for documenting treatment outcomes based on the World Health Organization's *International Classification of Impairments, Disabilities, and Handicaps.* To review, this system looks at the consequences of a disorder based on three levels: impairment, disability, and handicap. *Impairment* is defined as "any loss or abnormality of psychological, physiological, or anatomical structure or function" (p. 217). *Disability* is "any restriction or lack (resulting from an impairment) of ability to perform an activity in the manner or within the range considered normal for a human being" (p. 217). *Handicap* is "a disadvantage for a given individual, resulting from an impairment or disability, that limits or prevents the fulfillment of a role that is normal (depending on age, sex, and social and cultural factors) for that individual" (p. 217).

Yaruss viewed the ICIDH classification system as a more appropriate framework for evaluating stuttering treatment. If we conceptualize stuttering disorders as involving more than the behavioral component (what people *do* when they stutter, i.e., the impairment), outcomes must address the handicapping consequences of the stuttering behavior. Assessment of handicapping effects must be obtained before, during, and after treatment. However, gathering the data for progress reports, term-end summaries, or client reports is not enough. The data must be reported by clinicians to demonstrate treatment effectiveness, and our professional journals must be willing to publish clinical summaries that are not controlled efficacy studies. Ingham and Cordes (1999) criticized the profession for publishing articles, book chapters, and books that have not been "reliably and empirically documented" (p. 213). This view assumes the data does not exist. Conducting systematically controlled efficacy studies is very important but often not within the realm of possibility for the working speech-language pathologist. Clinicians continuously document the effectiveness of their treatment procedures in terms of progress toward the prescribed goals selected by the client, parents, teachers, and/or clinician. Yaruss (1998) made a good point when he described the difference between treatment efficacy and treatment effectiveness:

> According to the Agency for Health Care Policy and Research (1994), studies of treatment efficacy examine the extent to which a treatment can be shown to be beneficial under optimal (or ideal) conditions. Such studies typically involve careful selection of subjects and precise control of treatment parameters to establish that the treatment is actually responsible for the changes that are observed. Studies of treatment effectiveness, on the other hand, evaluate the extent to which treatment is shown to be beneficial under

typical conditions. These studies demonstrate the results of the treatment as it is actually administered by practicing clinicians in the real world; as such, they are often affected by a variety of factors that may not be related to the treatment itself. (p. 223)

The need to document the effectiveness of treatment is one reason ASHA established a Task Force on Treatment Outcomes and Cost Effectiveness for speech-language pathologists and audiologists in 1993 (Cooper & Cooper, 1998). A product of this task force was the National Outcomes Measurement System (NOMS), which established a 7-point Functional Communication Measure (FCM) scored by clinicians when clients enter and are discharged from therapy. Many clinicians have chosen to become involved in the NOMS project with hopes of practical FCMs in the area of stuttering disorders. Cooper and Cooper (1998) provided an example of a FCM related to stuttering therapy, *Prototype Scales for Assessing Preferred Functional Outcomes of Stuttering Therapy* (see figure). This tool encompasses the same philosophy of stuttering presented in this text, that is, stuttering is a complex syndrome of affective, behavioral, and cognitive components. Scales such as this one are in the process of being evaluated for their reliability and validity. But it is a starting point for all clinicians to reflect on the outcomes of their therapy. Clinicians document therapy progress on an ongoing basis. Whether it is information from the "Hands-Down" (Chmela & Reardon, 2001) worksheet placed in the client's folder or an updated Children Attitude Test (Brutten, 1984) administered prior to the Christmas break, clinicians are continually assessing client progress toward goals. The information is there; it just is not getting reported. Practicing clinicians must team with researchers who have had success publishing treatment effectiveness reports to learn the process and gain feelings of competence at writing for professional journals in the field.

Prototype Scales for Assessing Preferred Functional Outcomes of Stuttering Therapy

Affective Components

1. I enjoy communicating.

1	2	3	4	5	6	7
Strongly Disagree	Mildly Disagree	Disagree	Neutral	Agree	Mildly Agree	Strongly Agree

2. I feel comfortable as a speaker.

1	2	3	4	5	6	7
Strongly Disagree	Mildly Disagree	Disagree	Neutral	Agree	Mildly Agree	Strongly Agree

---

(continued)

3. I like the way I sound.

1	2	3	4	5	6	7
Strongly Disagree	Mildly Disagree	Disagree	Neutral	Agree	Mildly Agree	Strongly Agree

4. I feel I can modify my speech in even the toughest situations.

1	2	3	4	5	6	7
Strongly Disagree	Mildly Disagree	Disagree	Neutral	Agree	Mildly Agree	Strongly Agree

5. I am satisfied with my overall speech fluency.

1	2	3	4	5	6	7
Strongly Disagree	Mildly Disagree	Disagree	Neutral	Agree	Mildly Agree	Strongly Agree

Behavioral Components

1. I avoid speaking situations.

1	2	3	4	5	6	7
Never	Rarely	Sometimes	Half the time	More than half the time	Almost always	Always

2. I avoid words.

1	2	3	4	5	6	7
Never	Rarely	Sometimes	Half the time	More than half the time	Almost always	Always

3. My speech is becoming more fluent.

1	2	3	4	5	6	7
Never	Rarely	Sometimes	Half the time	More than half the time	Almost always	Always

4. I use fluency-enhancing techniques or strategies.

1	2	3	4	5	6	7
Never	Rarely	Sometimes	Half the time	More than half the time	Almost always	Always

(continued)

(continued)

5. When I stutter I do things such as blink my eyes or look away.

1	2	3	4	5	6	7
Never	Rarely	Sometimes	Half the time	More than half the time	Almost always	Always

Cognitive Components

1. I need speech therapy.

1	2	3	4	5	6	7
Strongly Disagree	Mildly Disagree	Disagree	Neutral	Agree	Mildly Agree	Strongly Agree

2. My speech negatively affects my vocational success.

1	2	3	4	5	6	7
Strongly Disagree	Mildly Disagree	Disagree	Neutral	Agree	Mildly Agree	Strongly Agree

3. My speech negatively affects my social success.

1	2	3	4	5	6	7
Strongly Disagree	Mildly Disagree	Disagree	Neutral	Agree	Mildly Agree	Strongly Agree

4. I understand my stuttering problem.

1	2	3	4	5	6	7
Strongly Disagree	Mildly Disagree	Disagree	Neutral	Agree	Mildly Agree	Strongly Agree

5. I am doubtful stuttering therapy can help me.

1	2	3	4	5	6	7
Strongly Disagree	Mildly Disagree	Disagree	Neutral	Agree	Mildly Agree	Strongly Agree

Appendix A Outside Assignment Log

Event 3	Event 2	Event 1		
			Before	Affective
			During	
			After	
			Before	Behavioral
			During	
			After	
			Before	Cognitive
			During	
			After	

Appendix B Child Case History Form

Date: _____

Personal Information

Name: _____   Date of birth: _____

Parents: _____   Date of evaluation: _____

Address: _____   Phone: _____

_____   Referral: _____

Child lives with: _____

Family Background

Father: _____   SS#: _____ Age: _____

Occupation: _____   Work phone: _____

Mother: _____   SS#: _____ Age: _____

Occupation: _____   Work phone: _____

Family members living in the home: _____

Language spoken in the home: _____ English _____ Spanish _____ Both _____ Other: _____

Language spoken by child: _____ English _____ Spanish _____ Both _____ Other: _____

Please describe the reason for your visit today:

_____

_____

_____

How have your child's difficulties changed since you first noticed them? _____

_____

_____

Check the items you feel apply to your child:

_____ Talks very little   _____ Has limited vocabulary   _____ Stutters

_____ Talks excessively   _____ Speech cannot be understood   _____ Has hearing problems

_____ Talks too fast   _____ Has nasal-sounding speech   _____ Has poor memory

_____ Uses poor grammar   _____ Has difficulty sleeping   _____ Eating peculiarities

Do any other members of your family have speech or hearing problems? Please explain.

_____

Have you ever questioned your child's ability to hear normally? _____ No _____ Yes   Why?

_____

Has your child had recurrent ear infections? _____ No _____ Yes   Please describe.

_____

Is your child currently under the care of a physician? _____ No _____ Yes

    Name of physician: _____

Is your child taking any medication? _____ No _____ Yes   If yes, please list medications:

_____

Has your child received speech therapy in the past? _____ No _____ Yes   If yes, please provide
information regarding such treatment. _____

_____

_____

Medical History

Prenatal
Did mother have any of the following during pregnancy? When?

Condition	*0–3 months*	*3–9 months*
German measles _____		
Hepatitis _____		
Toxemia _____		
Bleeding _____		
Anemia _____		
Extreme nausea _____		
Rh incompatibility _____		
High blood pressure _____		
Unusual fatigue _____		
Emotional upset _____		
Drugs administered _____		

Postnatal

Was delivery in a hospital? _____ No _____ Yes   Birth weight: _____

Length of pregnancy (weeks): _____   Length of labor: _____

Was labor induced? _____ No _____ Yes   Caesarian delivery: _____ No _____ Yes

Was baby premature? _____ No _____ Yes   Postmature: _____ No _____Yes

Did baby require oxygen? _____ No _____ Yes   Incubator: _____ No _____ Yes

Did baby leave hospital with mother? _____ No _____ Yes   If not, why?

_____

Were there any other complications at birth? _____

_____

_____

Health

Child has had (check the appropriate items):

Allergies	_____	Asthma	_____	Chickenpox	_____
Croup	_____	Colds	_____	German measles	_____
Draining ear	_____	Ear infections	_____	Sinusitis	_____
Headaches	_____	Dizziness	_____	High fevers	_____
Seizures	_____	Influenza	_____	Pneumonia	_____
Encephalitis	_____	Tonsillitis	_____	Myringotomy	_____

Has your child had any surgeries? _____ No _____ Yes   If yes, what type and when:

_____

_____

Describe any major accidents. _____

_____

_____

Developmental History

Check the appropriate items:

_____ Development appears to be usual in every way.

_____ Development unusual compared to other children in family.

_____ Sleeps excessively	_____ Considerate of others' feelings
_____ Sleeps little	_____ Dresses self
_____ Gets along with peers	_____ Child is aggressive
_____ Behavior is difficult	_____ Child is explosive
_____ Fearful in new situations	_____ Perfectionistic
_____ Coordination is poor	_____ Sensitive
_____ Child is impulsive	_____ Difficulty swallowing

Provide the approximate age at which your child began to do the following activities:

Crawl _____	Sit up _____	Stand _____	Walk _____
Feed self _____	Dress self _____	Tie shoes _____	Toilet trained _____

Provide the approximate age at which your child began to do the following activities:

Cooing _____	Babbling _____	Name objects _____	Single words _____
Combine two words _____	Make simple sentences _____		Ask questions _____
Engage in conversation _____			

Does your child have difficulty saying any sounds in particular? _____

_____

Do strangers have difficulty understanding your child's speech ? _____ No _____ Yes

Did your child develop skills and then lose them? _____ No _____ Yes   What skills?

_____

Does your child exhibit any unusual behaviors? _____ No _____ Yes _____

_____

Fluency History

Describe your concerns regarding your child's fluency difficulties:

_____

_____

_____

What do you think caused this difficulty? _____

_____

When was it first noticed? _____ By whom? _____

Describe the speaking situation present when you first noticed the difficulties.

_____

_____

Has the problem changed since it was first noticed? _____ No _____ Yes   If yes, describe:

_____

_____

Are any of the following behaviors present in your child's speech?

	Onset	Present
1. Repetitions of sounds (b b b boy)	_____	_____
2. Repetitions of syllables (bo bo boy)	_____	_____
3. Repetitions of whole words (boy boy boy)	_____	_____
4. Prolongation of sounds (ssssssssss star)	_____	_____
5. Inability to produce sounds at all	_____	_____
6. Facial distortions when trying to talk	_____	_____
7. Visible attempt to speak with no sound	_____	_____
8. Tension in speech efforts	_____	_____
9. Rise in pitch when having difficulty	_____	_____
10. Loss of eye contact with listener	_____	_____
11. Giving up on talking	_____	_____
12. Comments about speech difficulty	_____	_____

Describe situations in which your child's speech fluency is good:

_____

_____

Describe situations in which your child's speech difficulties are worse:

_____

_____

Do you feel your child is aware of his or her speech difficulties? _____ No _____ Yes   If yes, explain:

_____

_____

Is there a history of speech and language problems in your family? _____ No _____ Yes   If yes, explain: _____

Educational History

School: _____ Grade: _____ Teacher: _____

Educational performance: _____ Good _____ Average _____ Poor

Grades failed (if any)? _____

History of school problems? _____ No _____ Yes   Describe: _____

_____

Has difficulty with: _____ Reading _____ Math _____ Writing _____ Spelling _____ Behavior

Is your child receiving any special education services at school? _____ No _____ Yes

_____ Speech therapy   _____ Occupational therapy   _____ Resource assistance

_____ Physical therapy   _____ Content mastery   _____ ESL

Favorite playmates include: _____

Favorite hobbies include: _____

If your child is enrolled in speech therapy, what would your goals be for him or her?

_____

_____

_____

What specific questions do you have about your child you would like us to try to answer?

_____

_____

Appendix C Adult Case History Form

Personal Information

Date: _____

Name: _____
Date of birth: _____

Address: _____
Date of evaluation: _____

_____
Phone: _____

Educational Level: _____
Marital status: _____

Occupation: _____
Employer: _____

Name of spouse or nearest relative: _____

What is the purpose of your visit today?

_____

_____

_____

_____

Background Information

How long have you had this problem? _____

Have you received treatment for this problem? _____ Yes _____ No   If yes, where and when?

_____

Are you currently in speech therapy? If so, please describe.

_____

_____

Does any member of your family have a similar problem?

_____

What do you think caused the problem?

_____

_____

How severe is the problem today? _____ Mild _____ Moderate _____ Severe

How do others in your family view your speech difficulties?

_____

_____

Are you right or left handed? _____ Has anyone ever tried to change the hand you write with? (If so, please explain.)

_____

To the best of your recollection, describe your speech as a young child. _____

_____

_____

How did you feel about your speech growing up?

_____

_____

_____

Current Speech Behaviors

Do you avoid any speaking situations? If so, please explain.

_____

_____

Does the problem affect your job/school/social performance? _____

_____

_____

List any situations where you find it easy to speak.

_____

Do you usually know the words you will have difficulty saying? If so, please explain.

_____

Do you substitute other words for those you expect to have difficulty saying?

_____

Do you ever use facial grimaces or body movements to help you get through a difficult speaking situation?

_____

Do you ever pause, pretend to think, or recollect your thoughts in order to avoid speech difficulties?

_____

Are you ever unable to get any sound started without resorting to a starter or another device, such as _ah, uhm,_ or _you know?_

_____

Are there times when your speech is better or worse?

_____

_____

Would you say your speech today is typical or more or less nonfluent than usual? _____

_____

If enrolled in therapy, what do you hope to accomplish?

_____

_____

_____

_____

Please provide any additional information that may contribute to a better understanding of your speech difficulties.

_____

_____

_____

_____

_____

This form was completed by:

_____

Appendix D Sample Diagnostic Report: Child

NAME:	John Jackson
ADDRESS:	444 Genisus St.
	Sametown, America
D.O.B.:	May 4, 1989
CHRONOLOGICAL AGE:	13 years, 7 months
REFERRAL:	Cheryl Lynds, M.S., CCC-SLP
DATE OF EVALUATION:	February 18, 2003
DATE OF REPORT:	February 28, 2003
EXAMINER:	Ellen M. Bennett, Ph.D., CCC-SLP

SPEECH AND LANGUAGE EVALUATION

John Jackson, a 13-year 8-month-old male, was brought to the Speech Center on February 18, 2003. His mother, father, and infant sister accompanied John to the present evaluation. John was referred by his school speech language pathologist Cheryl Lynds. The goal of the evaluation was to determine the severity and nature of John's speech difficulties and to make the appropriate recommendations for therapy.

Background Information

John is the oldest of five children. He lives with parents, a younger sister, age 9, twin brothers, age 7, and an infant brother. Mr. Jackson is a nurse for the army and, due to frequent reassignment, John has attended many schools throughout his academic career. English is the primary language spoken in the home; therefore the present evaluation was conducted in English. Mrs. Jackson reported unremarkable prenatal, postnatal, and perinatal medical history. Overall health has been good with the exception of typical childhood illness, including allergies, colds, and chickenpox. Mrs. Jackson reported a negative history of otitis media. John's motor developmental milestones were reported as unremarkable.

Mrs. Jackson reported that John did not begin to speak until he began preschool at 4 years of age. Prior to age 4, John communicated through gestures and production of vowel /ʌ/. Mr. Jackson speculated that the delay in speech production may have been due to the fact that John did not have a need to speak because "he was raised by his grandmother who anticipated his every need." Age of first word, age at which two words were combined, and other speech milestones were reported as occurring at approximately the time John entered school, but no specific ages was reported.

Mrs. Jackson reported that John stuttered from the time he began speaking at age 4 and that the severity of the stuttering had increased with age. John has received speech and language services in the schools, however, was told at one point in time that he no longer qualified for services. Mrs. Jackson reported she has had to "fight" the school districts to get speech therapy services for John. There is a history of severe stuttering by John's maternal uncle.

Mr. Jackson reported that John's progress in school is good with honor roll status more recently. John reported a negative history of teasing at school; however, Mrs. Jackson stated that she has observed teasing behaviors. Mr. Jackson commented that John "holds back" academically due to his stuttering. Mrs. Jackson reported that he reacts negatively to being told by his parent's to "slow down." Parents' goals for John are for him to achieve his full potential academically and to increase his opportunities for success in the future.

Speech and Language Evaluation

John was cooperative and friendly during the testing session; however he stated that he was tired and yawned periodically during the session.

Hearing

Mrs. Jackson reported that John had received a hearing evaluation in the past and hearing was found to be normal. Observation during the testing situation suggested normal hearing acuity; therefore, a formal hearing screening was not conducted.

Intellectual Performance

The Test of Nonverbal Intelligence-3 (TONI) was administered to John to obtain information regarding his nonverbal intelligence. John obtained a total raw score of 20, which is equivalent to an intellectual quotient (IQ) of 91 and a percentile rank of 27. John's performance on this test is indicative of average intellectual functioning.

Oral Peripheral Examination

Informal examination of the oral mechanism revealed normal structure and function for speech.

Language

John's expressive language skills were assessed through the use of a language sample. John's semantics, syntax, morphology, and phonology were characteristic of average language performance. However, his narration was at times disconnected due to a large number of interjections. In addition, the majority of the sentences produced were linguistically simple. Communicative intent was not judged to be within normal limits during this activity due to the limited number of details provided when explaining the story line of the movie. However, during other interactions, John's communicative intent was age appropriate to observers and to the clinician. It is believed that John's language use during interactive situations appears delayed because of his desire to hide his stuttering. It is obvious that he is changing his words and engaging in circumlocutions to avoid episodes of stuttering.

Voice

Vocal quality appeared to be appropriate for John's age and gender. Pitch, loudness, and intonation were unremarkable.

Articulation

A standardized articulation test was not administered during this session due to the client's age and lack of concern reported by parents. Articulation ability was assessed informally throughout the session. The majority of John's speech was clear and intelligible with and without known context. John's speech was noted to be unintelligible during some portions of the session due to mumbling and covering his face with his hands.

Fluency

John's fluency was assessed through reading a passage, a mother/child interaction, and a monologue describing a movie. The Systematic Disfluency Analysis (Campbell & Hill, 1987) was used to analyze his patterns of disfluency. The disfluencies were categorized into two different groups: More Typical Disfluencies and Less Typical Disfluencies.

John's fluency breakdowns, patterns, and behaviors were characterized by consistent primarily of blocks, prolongations, and sound repetitions. Clusters, or combinations of any two nonfluent components of speech, were also observed. The clusters consisted of a block followed by a prolongation, a hesitation, or a sound repetition. Short, tense blocks were the most prevalent stuttering behavior throughout all interactions. It was apparent that John was avoiding certain words because he would frequently begin an utterance with "and," "and then," "so," or "well," as if to initiate phonation on a word that is not difficult for him to produce. Despite this coping strategy, John still had difficulty initiating speech and demonstrated secondary behaviors in reaction to these disfluencies. John's secondary characteristics included tension in the face and neck, facial grimace, protruding of jaw, moving head to the right, and puckering lips. The severity of the secondary characteristics was more pronounced during the mother-child interaction as compared to both the reading and monologue situations. It was interpreted that John was more relaxed when communicating with his mother and therefore let his guard down and allowed his true stuttering to emerge. The majority of John's speech patterns were consistent throughout the session, except for the significant increase in interjections during the monologue and the increase in blocks during the mother-child interaction.

	Reading	Movie Monologue	Mother/Child Interaction
More Typical Disfluencies			
Hesitations	0	0	0
Interjections	0	1	0
Revisions	2	4	4
Unfinished Utterances/Words	0	0	0
Phrase Repetitions	0	0	1
Word Repetitions	1	1	4
Clustered Components (2–3)	0	3	0
Clustered Components (4+)	0	0	0
Less Typical Disfluencies			
Word Repetitions	0	0	0
Syllable Repetitions	0	0	2
Sound Repetitions	0	3	3
Prolongations	3	4	8
Blocks	12	10	18
Clustered Components (2–3)	2	4	5
Clustered Components (4+)	0	1	1
Number of Syllables	210	213	322
No./Percentage More Typical Disfluencies	3/1%	9/4%	9/3%
No./Percentage Less Typical Disfluencies	17/8%	22/10%	37/11%
Total No./ Percentage Disfluencies	20/10%	31/15%	46/14%
Rate of Speech	normal	normal	normal

Linguistic Complexity

Shine's Systematic Fluency Assessment for Young Children (Shine, 1980) was administered to John to determine if an increase in linguistic complexity would adversely affect the amount of stuttering observed. At the start of the session, automatic responses were elicited, such as counting and naming the days of the week. John exhibited fluent speech during these automatic speaking situations where minimal language generation was required. As the linguistic demands increased, John began to stutter and exhibited an increase in secondary behaviors. John displayed no difficulty counting, saying the alphabet, or naming the days of the week. Limited disfluency was observed when he was asked to name pictures. As the language level increased, John exhibited an increase in stuttering behaviors including prolongations, repetitions, and blocks. Therefore, an increase in linguistic complexity and the generation of higher-level language adversely affects John's fluency.

Stuttering Severity

The Stuttering Severity Instrument-3 (Riley, 1994) was used to determine the severity of John's stuttering. Using speaking and reading tasks, John received an overall score of 31, which represents the 78–88 percentile range. Therefore, severity was judged to be in the severe range.

Speech Rate

A standardized procedure to assess speech rate was not administered. Perceptual judgment of articulatory rate indicates speech rate to be within normal limits.

Loci of Tension

Loci of tension appeared to be in the laryngeal area because respiration would not pass the vocal folds during a block. Tension was also noted during blocks in the face, particularly in the jaw and lips.

Communication Attitudes

John completed the Communication Attitude Test-R (DeNil & Brutten, 1991), which explores a child's attitude toward speech. John received a raw score of 21, which is indicative of attitudinal concerns. The following is a summary of John's responses to the questions on the CAT-R:

- Dislike of the way he talks
- Differences between his speech and that of his peers
- Reduced ease of communication, primarily when speaking in front of the class
- Increased difficulty in speaking with people
- Difficulty in producing words

In addition, The Perceptions of Stuttering Inventory was administered. John reported the following characteristics of his speech:

- Avoidance of talking, especially in front of a crowd or unfamiliar listeners
- Speech characteristics, including changing pitch to avoid stuttering, adding unnecessary sounds, repeating sounds, and making unusual sounds when speaking

- Body tension
- Avoidance of speaking to people
- Rearranging what he had planned to say

Mr. and Mrs. Jackson completed Cooper's Parent Attitudes Toward Stuttering Checklist (Cooper, 1985), which assesses parents' perception and beliefs regarding the disorder of stuttering. Mrs. Jackson reported that the following items concerned her in regard to her son's speech:

- Lack of knowledge regarding how to respond to John's speech
- Limited communication with John regarding his speech
- High degree of "worry" regarding John's speech
- The progression of the stuttering
- John's emotions due to the stuttering

Mr. Jackson reported the following concerns:

- Lack of knowledge regarding how to respond to John's speech
- Causation of stuttering
- Progression of stuttering
- Discussing stuttering with John

Diagnostic Impressions

John is a pleasant young man who exhibits a moderate to severe stuttering disorder including sound/syllable repetitions, prolongations, blocks accompanied by secondary behaviors including lip pursing, head jerking, and jaw protrusion. Voice, language, articulation, and hearing appear to be age appropriate. Prognosis for improvement with treatment is good due to parental involvement, John's intellectual capacity, and his desire to work on his speech. Prognosis for improvement without treatment is poor due to the progressive nature of stuttering, John's denial of negative incidents due to stuttering such as being teased, and the frequent moves and risks associated with his father's employment. Confounding variables include the family's frequent relocation and family history of stuttering.

Recommendations

The following recommendations were discussed with Mr. and Mrs. Jackson:

1. John should receive individual speech therapy twice a week.
2. John should be encouraged to learn more about stuttering through research on the Internet. He was provided with the Stuttering Foundation of America's *Guide to Teens* book as a resource for learning about this disorder and how to cope with it.
3. Therapy should include desensitization to stuttering episodes, increased awareness of stuttering behaviors and his reactions to them, and strategies for modifying his stuttering.

4. Parents should refrain from telling John to "slow down" when speaking because this elicits a negative response. Parents were given a book from the Stuttering Foundation that includes helpful suggestions for interacting with their son.

_____

Ellen Bennett, Ph.D., CCC-SLP
Speech Language Pathologist
Fluency Specialist
Texas License #44880

Appendix E Sample Diagnostic Report: Adult

NAME:	Matthew Holmes
ADDRESS:	1422 Pecos Road
	El Paso, Texas 79924
PHONE:	986–9142
D.O.B.:	October 1, 1965
DATE OF EVAL.:	March 27, 1997
EXAMINER:	Ellen M. Bennett, Ph.D., CCC-SLP

FLUENCY EVALUATION

Mr. Holmes, a 31-year-old male, contacted the Speech Therapy Group on March 27, 1997, regarding his communication difficulties. Mr. Holmes expressed concern regarding his stuttering problem and its impact on his ability to communicate and succeed in the career he is pursuing (teaching). Mr. Holmes was referred to this office by Dr. Jessie James, a professor in the education department.

Background Information

Mr. Holmes is single, lives alone, and works part time at Comet Cleaners. Although he considers himself bilingual in Spanish and English, this assessment was conducted in English. Mr. Holmes reported that he has stuttered all his life, receiving speech therapy off and on in both university and public school settings. Mr. Holmes believes he received little benefit from these services, "as best as he recollects." Parental reaction and openness to discussing stuttering were reported as positive. There is a history of familiar stuttering, grandfather and great uncle, on the maternal side of the family. A paternal uncle stuttered at some point in his life but now has recovered.

Mr. Holmes could not recall specific information about his speech therapy as a youngster. Previous therapy as an adult was described as following a stuttering modification orientation. Interactions with Mrs. Roberta Juarez, M. S., CCC-SLP, appeared to have influenced the development of positive beliefs around stuttering. Mr. Holmes reported that he is in "total acceptance" of his stuttering and has "learned to accept the situation." He noted that his stuttering is at the moderate level, although he is seeking help because he feels he needs a higher degree of fluency to succeed in teaching.

On the case history information, Mr. Holmes completed a checklist of daily behaviors. He reported a feeling of general body tension, flushing, difficulty breathing, and frustration when having difficulty with speech. He noted that during social situations, he experiences the following behaviors or feelings: timid, quiet, frank, uneasy, withdrawn, and shy. He does not report situational avoidances, although he does have difficulty with words that start with the /s/ sound.

Evaluation

Mr. Holmes's fluency was assessed in three different speaking situations: reading, monologue, and dialogue with the clinician. Systematic Disfluency Analysis (Campbell & Hill, 1987) was used to analyze his patterns of disfluency. This assessment classifies disfluencies into two groups: More Typical Disfluencies (that which are typical of normal disfluencies) and Less Typical Disfluencies (that which is characterized by stuttered speech). The following table shows the frequency counts obtained for these three samples:

	Monologue	Reading	Dialogue
More Typical Disfluencies			
Interjections	19	1	11
Revisions	7	0	3
Word Repetitions	5	0	4
Clustered Components 2–3	6	0	3
Clustered Components 4+	3	0	3
Less Typical Disfluencies			
Sound Repetitions	2	1	5
Prolongations	1	0	3
Blocks	21	14	26
Clustered Components 2–3	13	6	11
Clustered Components 4+	4	0	4
Number of Syllables	535	196	263
No./Percentage More Typical Disfluencies	40/7.5%	1/.5%	24/9%
No./Percentage Less Typical Disfluencies	42/7.8%	20/10.2%	49/19%
Total No./Percentage Disfluencies	82/15.3%	23/11.7%	73/28%
Rate of Speech	normal	normal	normal

Mr. Holmes's speech patterns consisted primarily of brief, tense blocks often surrounded by an interjection and accompanied with secondary features. During blocks, Mr. Holmes would either close his eyelids, shift eye contact by looking away, roll his eyes upward, or exhibit a quick head jerk in the upward direction. Sudden jaw dropping appeared to be an escape mechanism, although not always successful at releasing Mr. Holmes from a moment of stuttering. During the monologue and dialogue samples, Mr. Holmes exhibited a high number of interjections. These appeared to function as fillers, a means of buying time before speaking. However, they lost their effectiveness as Mr. Holmes continued to block on the interjections and exhibit secondary characteristics on this behavior.

Clusters (when the individual exhibits more than one type of disfluency during a moment of stuttering) were present in samples requiring a high degree of language formulation, such as when relating events about oneself (monologue) or engaging in communication exchanges with the clinician. Most clusters included an interjection followed by either a block or a sound repetition. It appeared that the interjections were used as starter devices, although not always effective. Mr. Holmes's speech is characterized by both more typical and less typical disfluencies in all except the reading sample. Disfluencies during the reading sample were predominantly less typical in nature. When reading, the client is unable to change or circumlocute around difficult words and, therefore, use of more typical disfluencies as postponement or stalling devices was not as predominant. During the monologue and dialogue samples, Mr. Holmes had the opportunity to use avoidance strategies. It is conjectured that the behaviors of interjections, revisions, and whole-word repetitions function as either postponement devices or false starters.

Linguistic Complexity

To determine the effect of linguistic complexity on Mr. Holmes stuttering behaviors, he was asked to perform a series of speaking tasks. He had extreme difficulty reciting his numbers, saying the ABCs, days of the week, and months of the year fluently. These are tasks in which the client is unable to avoid. Imitating responses appeared to be fluency shaping for Mr. Holmes. However, naming pictures resulted in interjections, sound repetitions, and blocks. As the language level increased, Mr. Holmes exhibited stuttering behaviors and interjections but had longer streams of fluency and it appeared to be less frustrating for him. Linguistic complexity inversely impacts Mr. Holmes's ability to be fluent.

Stuttering Severity

The Stuttering Severity Instrument-3 (Riley, 1994) was used to determine the severity of Mr. Holmes's stuttering. Using a job task and reading task, Matthew received a total overall score of 28, which represents the 61 to 77 percentile range. Severity was judged to be in the upper end of moderate.

Speech Rate

Perceptual judgment of articulatory rate indicates speech rate to be within normal limits for his age.

Loci of Tension

Loci of tension appeared to be in the laryngeal area with the initiation of voicing. Tension around the lips and jaw was apparent during blocks. Speech was characterized by tense articulatory contacts, particularly on the first sound of the utterance. Mr. Holmes did produce several intrasyllabic moments of stuttering on multiple-syllable words, although less frequently than the onset position of words.

Communication Attitudes

The Perceptions of Stuttering Inventory (PSI) and the Overall Assessment of the Speaker's Experience of Stuttering (OASES) were administered to assess Mr. Holmes's attitudes toward communication and stuttering. The PSI is a 60-item checklist in which the individual check items that are characteristic of his stuttering. It is divided into three equal subtests: Struggle, Avoidance, and Expectancy. On the PSI, Mr. Holmes received a total score of 40 comprised of the following components: Struggle: 8/20 (40%); Avoidance: 18/20 (90%); and Expectancy: 14/20 (70%). Avoidance and expectancy behaviors are what Mr. Holmes does to avoid stuttering, such as having other people talk for him, avoiding making a purchase, postponing speaking until he can be fluent, and terminating speaking when stuttering occurs. Mr. Holmes reported severe cognitive and affective reactions to his stuttering.

The OASES is a four-part criterion-referenced questionnaire assessing the impact of stuttering on the individual's life. Mr. Holmes received the following scores on this instrument:

Part I:	General Information	60
Part II:	Your Reactions to Stuttering	102
Part III:	Communication in Daily Situations	84
Part IV:	Quality of Life	49

Part I addresses general information about the client's speech, knowledge of stuttering and treatment options, and how the client feels about stuttering. The following concepts were indicated by Mr. Holmes as being relevant to his particular stuttering profile:

- Rarely says exactly what he wants to say
- Never uses strategies
- Rarely does his speech sound natural
- Negative feelings toward his speaking ability, communication skills, the way he sounds, variations in his stuttering, and being a person who stutters

Part II investigates what the individual feels about stuttering, how often one engages in particular behaviors, and the client's belief system regarding stuttering. Mr. Holmes indicated the following:

- Feelings of helplessness, anxiety, anger, shame, and loneliness
- Often feeling depressed, embarrassed, and frustrated
- Sometimes feeling guilty and defensive

- Always leaving a situation because he thinks he might stutter
- Frequently breaking eye contact with the listener, avoiding speaking situations, and letting somebody else speak for him
- Sometimes he will experience tension when stuttering, yet rarely exhibits secondary features
- Sometimes he will not say what he wants to say, use a filler word or starters, and experience a period of increased stuttering just after having stuttered on a word
- Agrees with the statement that he would be better able to achieve his goals if he did not stutter and he does not want people to know he stutters
- Strongly agrees with the statement that when stuttering, there is nothing he can do about it and he does not speak as well as other people
- Somewhat agrees he does not have confidence in his speaking abilities and he should do everything possible not to stutter

Part III evaluates the client's ability to speak in different situations as well as communication effectiveness in the work, social, and home environments. Mr. Holmes marked the following items:

- Somewhat difficult to talk to another person one on one, even people he knows
- Somewhat difficult talking on the phone, initiating conversations, continuing speaking regardless of listener reactions, and standing up for himself verbally
- Somewhat difficult to talk with clients, customers, or supervisors
- Somewhat difficult to tell stories or jokes or ask for information
- Somewhat difficult to talk to family and extended family members
- Very difficult to talk while under time pressure, talking with people he does not know well, giving oral presentations or speaking in front of people at work, and talking with coworkers
- Very difficult to participate in social events, ordering food in a restaurant, or ordering food at a drive-thru
- Extreme difficulty talking in front of a small or large group of people
- Extreme difficulty using the phone at work

Part IV assesses the extent to which stuttering interferes with the client's quality of life. The following items were rated by Mr. Holmes:

- Some negative impact on quality of life due to his reactions to his stuttering and other's reactions to his stuttering
- Some impact on his communication satisfaction in general, with a lot of interference at work and in social situations
- Some interference with his relationships with friends and his ability to function in society with a lot of interference with relationships with other people and intimate relationships
- Some interference with his ability to do his job and overall satisfaction with his job with a lot of interference with his ability to advance in his career

- Some inference with his personal life related to his sense of self-worth, outlook on life, confidence in himself, overall stamina or energy level, and spiritual well-being
- Little interference in his enthusiasm for life, overall health and physical well-being, and sense of control over his life

Diagnostic Impressions

Mr. Holmes is a pleasant gentleman who exhibits a moderate to severe stuttering disorder that dramatically influences his ability to communicate. His stuttering patterns are consistent across interactive exchanges and he does appear to be aware of his speech difficulty. Although case history information indicated Mr. Holmes has accepted his stuttering, the use of secondary behaviors reflect his reaction to stuttering. Currently, Mr. Holmes does not appear to have any effective way of coping with the moment of stuttering. Prognosis for improvement with treatment is good due to Mr. Holmes's desire to improve his speech so he can teach. Prognosis for the attainment of complete fluency is guarded due to the progressive nature of stuttering and the extent to which he is reacting. Confounding variables to progress might be Mr. Holmes's misperception regarding the degree of "acceptance of stuttering" he actually has and familial history of persistent stuttering.

Recommendations

The following recommendations were given to Mr. Holmes:

1. He should enroll in speech therapy twice a week for 1-hour sessions. Therapy should focus on increasing Mr. Holmes's fluency through stuttering modification principles with emphasis on building self-monitoring skills, developing positive attitudes toward stuttering, and developing automaticity with in-block correction strategies.
2. Therapy should use reading tasks as a means of facilitating fluency and providing encouragement for Mr. Holmes as he tackles the more difficult aspects of therapy.
3. Mr. Holmes is encouraged to contact the National Stuttering Association for peer group support and education. This would give him an opportunity to correspond with many other people who stutter and become desensitized to stuttering.

_____

Ellen Bennett, Ph.D., CCC-SLP
Speech-Language Pathologist
Fluency Specialist
Texas License #446611

Appendix F Exercises in Expressing Empathy

The following scenarios are presented as opportunities for you to practice using Egan's empathy formula with people who stutter. After reading the client's story, the clinician identifies the components of the client's core message and summarizes this using an empathetic statement. These samples are from Egan's workbook but have been modified to reflect the experiences common to people with stuttering.

EXERCISE 1

A 27-year-old man is talking with his therapist about a visit he had with his mother the previous day:

> I just don't know what got into me! She kept interrupting me the way she always does, filling in words she thinks I want to say. As she went on, I got more and more angry. (He looks away from the therapist toward the floor.) I finally began screaming at her. I told her to stop doing that. (He puts his hands over his face.) I can't believe what I did! I told her to shut up and then I left and slammed the door in her face.

A. **Key experiences:** mother interrupting him and filling in his words
B. **Key behaviors:** losing his temper, yelling at her, saying shut up, slamming the door
C. **Feelings/Emotions generated:** embarrassed, guilty, ashamed, disappointed in himself
   Note carefully: This man is talking about his anger, the way he let his temper get away from him, but while talking to the therapist, he is feeling and expressing the emotions listed.
D. **Empathetic Response:** "You feel disappointed in yourself because you yelled at your mother."

EXERCISE 2

A woman in a self-help group is talking about a relationship with a man:

> About a couple of months ago, he began making fun of my stuttering, calling me Porky Pig. To tell you the truth, that's why I joined this group, but I haven't had the courage to talk about it until now. The couple times I've tried to stand up for myself, he started to laugh and say it wasn't a big deal. That I was making more of it than it was. So I've been taking it, just sitting there taking it . . .

A. **Key experiences:** _____
B. **Key behaviors:** _____
C. **Feelings/Emotions generated:** _____
D. **Empathetic Response:** _____

EXERCISE 3

A teenager is talking to his therapist about asking this girl out on a date:

> It's no big thing. But this is the third time this month I've called her and left a message to call me back. I don't understand why she won't call me back. I see her in class but I can't get up the courage to confront her. You know, with my stuttering and all . . .

A. **Key experiences:** _____
B. **Key behaviors:** _____
C. **Feelings/Emotions generated:** _____
D. **Empathetic Response:** _____

EXERCISE 4

A high school senior is talking with his school counselor about college prospects:

> I want to go to college but I haven't got the courage to complete the applications. How am I going to complete the public speaking requirement? Even now when everyone knows I stutter, I can barely say a word in front of the class. I knew that one day my stuttering would keep me from doing what I want.

A. **Key experiences:** _____
B. **Key behaviors:** _____
C. **Feelings/Emotions generated:** _____
D. **Empathetic Response:** _____

EXERCISE 5

A parent of a preschool child who stutters is discussing evaluation results with the clinician:

> I had hoped that his speech would get better. The doctor said to just wait and see. Why did I have to listen to him? He should have known better. After all, he is the doctor. I should have gone with my instincts and called you sooner. If I had come in sooner, maybe he wouldn't be stuttering now. I just can't believe my stupidity.

A. **Key experiences:** _____
B. **Key behaviors:** _____
C. **Feelings/Emotions generated:** _____
D. **Empathetic Response:** _____

Appendix G Teasing and Bullying Questionnaire for Children who Stutter– Revised (TBQ-CS) *

Notes regarding administration:

1. This questionnaire is ideally completed with children individually but may also be completed in small groups (Langevin, Bortnick, Hammer, & Wiebe, 1998).
2. It is intended to facilitate discussion to gain a deeper understanding of any teasing and bullying that is occurring at school since children often report that teasing occurs primarily at school. It is also intended to facilitate a general discussion about teasing and bullying that is occurring in other places, (e.g., at extra-curricular sports such as hockey or soccer).
3. The questionnaire may be completed by the child individually and then discussed, or it may be completed with the child and administrator discussing items as the child progresses through them. Some children are reticent to discuss bullying but will be open to completing a questionnaire without discussion. For other children, this questionnaire provides a comfortable way to open a discussion.
4. For children known to have reading difficulties and those 8 years and under, items are read by the administrator.
5. For all children, the administrator reviews with the children the purpose, definition of bullying, and directions for completing the questionnaire.

*Contributed by Marilyn Langevin, M.Sc. SLP(C), CCC-SLP of the Institute for Stuttering Treatment & Research, Affiliated with the University of Alberta.

TEASING AND BULLYING QUESTIONNAIRE FOR CHILDREN WHO STUTTER–REVISED (TBQ-CS)

Name: _____   Date: _____

Male ___ Female ___

Purpose: This questionnaire will help us understand what happens when you are at school.

Definition of bullying: Students sometimes bully kids at school by deliberately and repeatedly hurting or upsetting them in some way. For example they may hit or push kids around, tease kids, say mean things, or leave kids out of things on purpose. Bullying occurs when someone tries to have power over you or tries to dominate you, but it is not bullying when two young people of the same strength have the odd fight or quarrel. Bullying includes teasing that is hurtful or upsetting. If you are being teased and you think it is funny, then that kind of teasing is not bullying.

Directions: There are two sections to this questionnaire. The first section is about teasing and bullying about your stuttering and the second section is about teasing and bullying about other things (other than your stuttering). Read each sentence and then circle the answer that is best for you. There are no right or wrong answers. Sometimes you will be asked to answer a question by writing the answer.

SECTION I

Teasing and bullying about STUTTERING that occurs at school.

1. Have you been teased/bullied about your stuttering at school?

    Never   Sometimes   Often   Very often

    If you circled "Never," please go to Section II. If you circled "Sometimes," "Often," or "Very Often," complete the following questions.

2. How often in the last 6 months have you been teased/bullied about your stuttering at school?

    Less than   About once or
    once a week   twice a week   Most days   Every day

3. How much did the teasing/bullying about your stuttering bother or upset you?

    Didn't upset   Upset me some   Upset me most   Upset me all
    me at all   of the time   of the time   of the time

4. In what places were you teased/bullied about your stuttering and how often were you teased in those places?

(a) Were you teased/bullied about your stuttering in the classroom?

    Never   Sometimes   Often   Very often

(b) Were you teased/bullied about your stuttering in the hallways at school?

    Never   Sometimes   Often   Very often

(c) Were you teased/bullied about your stuttering on the school playground?

    Never   Sometimes   Often   Very often

(d) Were you teased/bullied about your stuttering on the way to or from school?

    Never   Sometimes   Often   Very often

(e) Were you teased/bullied about your stuttering in other places? If so, what are the other places? Write those places here.

5. What happened when you were teased/bullied about your stuttering at school and how often did these things happen?

(a) Were you pushed or shoved when kids teased/bullied you about your stuttering?

    Never   Sometimes   Often   Very often

(b) Were you called names about your stuttering?

    Never   Sometimes   Often   Very often

(c) Were you kicked or hit when kids teased/bullied you about your stuttering?

    Never   Sometimes   Often   Very often

(d) Did kids spread rumors about you that related to your stuttering? That means they talked about you or said bad things about you to other kids about your stuttering.

    Never   Sometimes   Often   Very often

(e) Did kids imitate your stutter or repeat what you said and pretend to stutter?

    Never   Sometimes   Often   Very often

(f) Did kids threaten to hurt you when they teased/bullied you about your stuttering?

    Never   Sometimes   Often   Very often

(g) Did kids leave you out of things because of your stuttering?

    Never   Sometimes   Often   Very often

(h) Did kids make fun of your stuttering?

    Never   Sometimes   Often   Very often

(i) Did kids do other things to tease/bully you about your stuttering? If so, describe what they did here.

SECTION II

Teasing and bullying about OTHER THINGS that occurs at school.

The following questions are about teasing/bullying that is related to OTHER THINGS, NOT your stuttering. For example, some kids get teased about their hair, their name, the way they walk, or about being smart or not smart.

6. Have you been teased/bullied about other things at school?

    Never   Sometimes   Often   Very often

If you circled "Never" you are finished and may stop here. If you circled "Sometimes," "Often," or "Very Often," please complete the following questions.

7. How often in the last 6 months have you been teased/bullied about other things at school?

| Less than once a week | About once or twice a week | Most days | Every day |

8. How much did the teasing/bullying about other things bother or upset you?

| Didn't upset me at all | Upset me some of the time | Upset me most of the time | Upset me all of the time |

9. What are the OTHER THINGS that you have been teased/bullied about at school? Write them here.

10. In what places were you teased/bullied about other things and how often were you teased in those places?

(a) Were you teased/bullied about other things in the classroom?

    Never   Sometimes   Often   Very often

(b) Were you teased/bullied about other things in the hallways at school?

    Never   Sometimes   Often   Very often

(c) Were you teased/bullied about other things on the school playground?

   Never   Sometimes   Often   Very often

(d) Were you teased/bullied about other things on the way to or from school?

   Never   Sometimes   Often   Very often

(e) Were you teased/bullied about other things in other places? If so, what are the other places? Write those places here.

11. What happened when you were teased/bullied about other things at school and how often did these things happen?

(a) Were you pushed or shoved?

   Never   Sometimes   Often   Very often

(b) Were you called names about things other than your stuttering?

   Never   Sometimes   Often   Very often

(c) Were you kicked or hit?

   Never   Sometimes   Often   Very often

(d) Did kids spread rumors about you? That means they talked about you or said bad things about you to other kids.

   Never   Sometimes   Often   Very often

(e) Did kids threaten to hurt you?

   Never   Sometimes   Often   Very often

(f) Did kids leave you out of things?

   Never   Sometimes   Often   Very often

(g) Did kids make fun of you about other things?

   Never   Sometimes   Often   Very often

(h) Did kids do other things to tease/bully you? If so, describe what they did here.

Appendix H Zany Words

Write down your partner's answers on each line. Encourage your partner to think of funny and zany words—the crazier the better (Karsten, 1995, p. 28).

Item	Zany Response
1. Famous person's name	
2. Adjective	
3. Adjective	
4. Zoo animal	
5. School subject	
6. Verb	
7. Verb	
8. Funny action	
9. Animal home	
10. Carnival ride	
11. Verb	
12. Name of sports star	
13. Sound	
14. Color	
15. Verb	
16. Emotion	
17. Animal action	
18. Verb	
19. Something that makes noise	
20. Time of day or night	
21. Food	
22. Occupation	
23. Verb	
24. Adjective	
25. Emotion	

Appendix I How Absurd!

Transfer your list of zany words to the corresponding blanks in the story below to create a zany, absurd tale.

My name is _____ (1) but my friends call me _____ (2). Today I feel _____ (3). One of the things I think is special about me is my _____ (4). The thing that bothers me most about school is _____ (5). I'd rather _____ (6) than _____ (7). I like teachers who _____ (8). My favorite place to be is in a _____ (9). One of the things that bothers me the most is my _____ (10). When I am alone I like to _____ (11). The most important person in the world is _____ (12). Sometimes I like to listen to somebody _____ (13). I think the world should be _____ (14). I think that families should _____ (15) together. I think that school should be a place where you feel _____ (16). I feel nervous when I'm asked to _____ (17). More than anything else, I like to _____ (18). Sometimes I like to listen to a _____ (19). I get really angry when it's _____ (20). I feel proud when I have _____ (21). I wish that people would all be _____ (22) and I wish they wouldn't _____ (23). This year I hope I can become more _____ (24). One thing that I'd like you to know about me is that I'm _____ (25).

Appendix J A Story of Truth

Fill in the blanks with truthful answers about who you are and the things you like. When you are finished, compare this story with the absurd one.

My name is _____ but my friends call me _____. Today I feel _____. One of the things I think is special about me is my _____. The thing that bothers me most about school is _____. I'd rather _____ than _____. I like teachers who _____. My favorite place to be is in a _____. One of the things that bothers me the most is my _____. When I am alone I like to _____. The most important person in the world is _____. Sometimes I like to listen to somebody _____. I think the world should be _____. I think that families should _____ together. I think that school should be a place where you feel _____. I feel nervous when I'm asked to _____. More than anything else, I like to _____. Sometimes I like to listen to a _____. I get really angry when it's _____. I feel proud when I have _____. I wish that people would all be _____ and I wish they wouldn't _____. This year I hope I can become more _____. One thing that I'd like you to know about me is that I'm _____.

References

Adams, M. R. (1978). Further analysis of stuttering as a phonetic transition defect. *Journal of Fluency Disorders, 3,* 265-271.

Adams, M. R. (1981). The speech production abilities of stutterers: Recent, ongoing and future research. *Journal of Fluency Disorders, 6,* 311-326.

Adams, M. R. (1993). The home environment of children who stutter. *Seminars in Speech and Language, 14,* 185-191.

Adams, M. R., & Ramig, P. (1980). Vocal characteristics of normal speakers and stutterers during choral reading. *Journal of Speech and Hearing Research, 23,* 457-469.

Adams, M. R., & Runyan, C. M. (1981). Stuttering and fluency: Exclusive events or points on a continuum? *Journal of Fluency Disorders, 6,* 197-218.

Ainsworth, S., & Fraser, J. (1988). *If your child stutters: A guide for parents.* Memphis, TN: Stuttering Foundation of America.

Ajzen, I. (1988). *Attitudes, personality, and behavior.* Chicago: Dorsey Press.

Alm, P. (1995). Study groups for stutterers—a valuable part of stuttering therapy. In C. W. Starkweather & H. F. M. Peters (Eds.), *Stuttering: Proceedings of the first world congress on fluency disorders.* Nijmegen, The Netherlands: University Press Nijmegen.

Amabile, T. M., & Hennessey, B. A. (1992). The motivation for creativity in children. In A. K. Boggiano & T. S. Pittman (Eds.), *Achievements and motivation: A social-developmental perspective* (pp. 54-76). New York: Cambridge University Press.

Ambrose, N. G., Cox, N. J., & Yairi, E. (1997). The genetic basis of persistence and recovery in stuttering. *Journal of Speech, Language, and Hearing Research, 40,* 567-580.

Ambrose, N. G., & Yairi, E. (1994). The development of awareness of stuttering in preschool children. *Journal of Fluency Disorders, 19,* 229-246.

Ambrose, N. G., & Yairi, E. (1995). The role of repetition units in the differential diagnosis of early childhood incipient stuttering. *American Journal of Speech-Language Pathology, 4,* 82-87.

Ambrose, N. G., & Yairi, E. (1999). Normative disfluency data for early childhood stuttering. *Journal of Speech, Language, and Hearing Research, 42,* 895-909.

Ambrose, N., Yairi, E., & Cox, N. (1993). Genetic aspects of early childhood stuttering. *Journal of Speech and Hearing Research, 36,* 701-706.

American Speech-Language-Hearing Association. (1996). *A practical guide to applying treatment outcomes and efficacy resources.* Rockville, MD: Author.

Amster, B. (1995). Perfectionism and stuttering. *Proceedings from the 1st World Congress on Fluency Disorders* (pp. 540-542). Nijmegen, The Netherlands: Nijmegen University Press.

Anderman, L. H., & Hicks-Midgley, C. (1998). *Motivation and middle school students* [ERIC digest]. Champaign, IL: ERIC Clearinghouse on Elementary and Early Childhood Education. (ERIC Document Reproduction Service No. ED 421 281).

Anderson, J. D., & Conture, E. G. (2000). Language abilities of children who stutter: A preliminary study. *Journal of Fluency Disorders, 25,* 283-304.

Anderson, J. D., & Conture, E. G. (2004). Sentence-structure priming in young children who do and do not stutter. *Journal of Speech, Language, and Hearing Research, 47,* 552-571.

Andrews, G. (1984). The epidemiology of stuttering. In R. F. Curlee and W. H. Perkins (Eds.), *The nature and treatment of stuttering: New directions.* San Diego, CA: College-Hill.

Andrews, G., & Craig, A. (1988). Prediction of outcome after treatment for stuttering. *British Journal of Psychiatry, 153,* 236-240.

Andrews, G., Craig, A., Feyer, A., Hoddinott, S., Howie, P., & Neilson, M. (1983). Stuttering: A review of research findings and theories circa 1982. *Journal of Speech and Hearing Disorders, 48,* 226–246.

Andrews, G., & Cutler, J. (1974). Stuttering therapy: The relationship between changes in symptom level and attitudes. *Journal of Speech and Hearing Disorders, 34,* 312–319.

Andrews, G., & Harris, M. (1964). *The syndrome of stuttering. Clinics in developmental medicine,* no. 17. London: Spastic Society in association with Wm. Heinemann Medical Books.

Andrews, G., Howie, P., Dozsa, M., & Guitar, B. (1982). Stuttering: Speech pattern characteristics under fluency-inducing conditions. *Journal of Speech and Hearing Research, 25,* 208–216.

Andrews, G., & Ingham, R. (1971). Stuttering: Considerations in the evaluation of treatment. *British Journal of Communication Disorders, 6,* 129–138.

Archibald, L., & DeNil, L. F. (1999). The relationship between stuttering severity and kinesthetic acuity for jaw movements in adults who stutter. *Journal of Fluency Disorders, 24,* 25–42.

Armson, J., Jensen, S., Gallant, D., Kalinowski, J., & Fee, E. J. (1997). The relationship between degree of audible struggle and judgements of childhood disfluencies as stuttered or not stuttered. *American Journal of Speech-Language Pathology, 6*(1), 42–50.

Armson, J., & Stuart, A. (1998). Effect of extended exposure to frequency on stuttering during reading and monologue. *Journal of Speech, Language, and Hearing Research, 41*(3), 479–490.

Arndt, J., & Healey, E. C. (2001). Concomitant disorders in school-age children who stutter. *Language, Speech, and Hearing Services in Schools, 32,* 68–78.

Au-Yeung, J., Howell, P., & Pilgrim, L. (1998). Phonological words and stuttering on function words. *Journal of Speech, Language, and Hearing Research, 41*(5), 1019–1030.

Ayre, A., Wright, L., & Grogan, S. (1998). Therapy's long term impact on attitudes to stuttering at work. In E. C. Healey and H. F. M. Peters (Eds.), *2nd World Congress on Fluency Disorders: Proceedings* (pp. 403–406). Nijmegen, The Netherlands: University Press Nijmegen.

Baars, B. J. (1980). On eliciting predictable speech errors in the laboratory. In V. A. Fromkin (Ed.), *Errors in linguistic performance: Slips of the tongue ear, pen, and hand* (pp. 307–318). New York: Academic Press.

Baars, B. J., Motley, M. T., & MacKay, D. G. (1975). Output editing for lexical status in artificially elicited slips of the tongue. *Journal of Verbal Learning and Verbal Behavior, 14,* 382–391.

Baken, R. J., McManus, D. A., & Cavallo, S. A. (1983). Prephonatory chest wall posturing in stutterers. *Journal of Speech and Hearing Research, 26,* 444–450.

Bakker, K., & Brutten, G. J. (1989). A comparative investigation of the laryngeal premotor, adjustment, and reaction times of stutterers and nonstutterers. *Journal of Speech and Hearing Research, 32,* 239–244.

Bandura, A. (1977). *Social learning theory.* Upper Saddle River, NJ: Prentice Hall.

Bandura, A. (1986). *Social foundations of thought and action.* Englewood Cliffs, NJ: Prentice Hall.

Barasch, C. T., Guitar, B., McCauley, R. J., & Absher, R. G. (2000). Disfluency and time perception. *Journal of Speech and Hearing Research, 43,* 1429–1439.

Batik, J., & Bennett, E. M. (2001, November). *Recent findings regarding the intelligence of children who stutter.* Paper presented at the American Speech-Language-Hearing Association convention, San Francisco, CA.

Batik, J., Bennett, E. M., & Yaruss, J. S. (2003, August). *A preliminary investigation of the co-occurrence of word finding disorders in children who stutter.* Paper presented at the 4th World Congress on Fluency Disorders, Montreal, Canada.

Bennett, E. (1995). Shame in children who stutter. *Proceedings from the 1st World Congress on Fluency Disorders* (pp. 245–248). Nijmegen, The Netherlands: Nijmegen University Press.

Bennett, E. M. (2002, May). *Beyond the speech therapy room: Thinking outside the box.* Paper presented at the American Speech-Language-Hearing Association, Special Interest Division #4 Leadership Conference, Albuquerque, NM.

Bennett, E. M. (2003). Planning a teacher inservice for stuttering disorders. *Seminars in Speech and Language, 24,* 53–58.

Bennett, E. M., & Chmela, K. A. (1998). The mask of shame: Treatment strategies for adults who stutter. *Proceedings from the 2nd World Congress on Fluency Disorders* (pp. 340–342). Nijmegen, The Netherlands: Nijmegen University Press.

Bennett, E. M., & Louko, L. J. (1994, November). *Co-occurring fluency and phonological disorders: Treatment strategies and activities.* Paper presented at the American Speech-Language-Hearing Association convention, San Francisco, CA.

Bennett, E. M., & Orr, J. M. (2001, April). *Parental attitudes toward stuttering.* Paper presented at the Texas Speech-Language-Hearing Assocation convention, Austin, TX.

Bennett, E., Ramig, P., & Reveles, V. (1993, November). *Speaking attitudes in children who stutter: Summer fluency camps.* Poster session at the American Speech-Language-Hearing Association convention, Anaheim, CA.

Bennett-Mancha, E. (1990, April). *Parent support groups: For parents of children who stutter.* Paper presented at the Texas Speech-Language-Hearing Association convention, Houston, TX.

Bennett-Mancha, E. (1992). The House That Jack Built. *Staff* (Aaron's Associates, 6114 Waterway, Garland, TX 75043).

Berg, B. (1990). *The self-concept workbook: Exercises to improve and maintain self-esteem.* Los Angeles: Western Psychological Services.

Berkowitz, M., Cook, H., and Haughey, M. J. (1994). A nontraditional fluency program developed for the public school setting. *Language Speech and Hearing Services in the Schools, 25,* 94–99.

Bernstein Ratner, N. (1992). Measurable outcomes of instructions to modify normal parent-child verbal interactions: Implications for indirect stuttering therapy. *Journal of Speech and Hearing Research, 35,* 14–20.

Bernstein Ratner, N. (1993). Parents, children, and stuttering. *Seminars in Speech and Language, 14,* 238–250.

Bernstein Ratner, N. (1995). Language complexity and stuttering in children. *Topics in Language Disorders, 15,* 32–47.

Bernstein Ratner, N. (1997a). Leaving Las Vegas: Clinical odds and individual outcomes. *American Journal of Speech-Language Pathology, 6,* 29–33.

Bernstein Ratner, N. (1997b). Stuttering: A psycholinguistic perspective. In R. F. Curlee & G. M. Siegel (Eds.), *Nature and treatment of stuttering: New directions* (2nd ed., pp. 99–127). Needham Heights, MA: Allyn & Bacon.

Bernstein Ratner, N. (2000). Performance or capacity: The model still requires definitions and boundaries it dosen't have. *Journal of Fluency Disorders, 25,* 337–346.

Bernstein Ratner, N. (2001, June). *Treatment of early stuttering: Concepts, choices, and controversies.* Paper presented at the National Stuttering Association conference, Boston, MA.

Bernstein Ratner, N., & Sih, C. C. (1987). Effects of gradual increases in sentence length and complexity in children's dysfluency. *Journal of Speech and Hearing Disorders, 52,* 278–287.

Bernstein Ratner, N., & Silverman, S. (2000). Parental perceptions of children's communicative development at stuttering onset. *Journal of Speech, Language, and Hearing Research, 43,* 1252–1263.

Bilodeau, L. (1992). *The anger workbook: Working through your anger for positive results.* New York: MJF Books.

Bishop, J. H., Williams, H. G., & Cooper, W. A. (1991a). Age and task complexity variables in motor performance of stuttering and nonstuttering children. *Journal of Fluency Disorders, 16*(4), 207–218.

Bishop, J. H., Williams, H. G., & Cooper, W. A. (1991b). Age and task complexity variables in motor performance of children with articulation-disordered, stuttering, and normal speech. *Journal of Fluency Disorders, 16,* 219–228.

Black, J. W. (1951). The effect of delayed sidetone upon vocal rate and intensity. *Journal of Speech and Hearing Disorders, 16,* 56–60.

Blackmer, E. R., & Mitton, J. L. (1991). Theories of monitoring and the timing of repairs in spontaneous speech. *Cognition, 39,* 173–194.

Blomgren, M., Nagarajan, S. S., Lee, J. N., Li, T., & Alvord, L. (2003). Preliminary results of a functional MRI study of brain activation patterns in stuttering and nonstuttering speakers during a lexical access task. *Journal of Fluency Disorders, 28,* 337–356.

Blood, G. W. (1995). Power-2: Relapse management with adolescents who stutter. *Language, Speech, and Hearing Services in Schools, 26,* 169–179.

Blood, G.W., & Blood, I. M. (2004). Bullying in adolescents who stutter: Communicative competence and self-esteem. *Contemporary Issues in Communication Science and Disorders, 31,* 58–68.

Blood, G.W., Blood, I. M., Tellis, G., & Gabel, R. (2001). Communication apprehension and self-perceived communication competence in adolescents who stutter. *Journal of Fluency Disorders, 26,* 161–178.

Blood, G.W., Blood, I. M., Tellis, G., & Gabel, R. (2003). A preliminary study of self-esteem, stigma, and disclosure in adolescents who stutter. *Journal of Fluency Disorders, 28,* 143–159.

Blood, G., Blood, I., Tellis, G., Gabel, R., Mapp, C., Wertz, H., & Wade, J. (1998). Coping with stuttering during adolescence. In C. Healey & H. Peters (Eds.), *Proceedings of the Second World Congress on Fluency Disorders* (pp. 319–324). Nijmegen, The Netherlands: Nijmegen University Press.

Bloodstein, O. (1950). A rating scale study of conditions under which stuttering is reduced or absent. *Journal of Speech and Hearing Disorders, 15,* 29–36.

Bloodstein, O. (1958). Stuttering as an anticipatory struggle reaction. In J. Eisenson (Ed.), *Stuttering: A Symposium* (pp. 1–70). New York: Harper & Brothers.

Bloodstein, O. (1984). Stuttering as an anticipatory struggle disorder. In R. F. Curlee & W. H. Perkins (Eds.), *Nature and treatment of stuttering: New directions* (pp. 171–186). Needham Heights, MA: Allyn & Bacon.

Bloodstein, O. (1993). *Stuttering: The search for a cause and cure.* Boston: Allyn & Bacon.

Bloodstein, O. (1995). *A handbook on stuttering* (5th ed.). Chicago: National Easter Seal Society.

Bloodstein, O. (1997). Stuttering as an anticipatory struggle reaction. In R. F. Curlee & G. M. Siegel (Eds.), *Nature and treatment of stuttering: New directions* (2nd ed.), (pp. 169–181). Boston: Allyn & Bacon.

Bloom, C., & Cooperman, D. K. (1999). *Synergistic stuttering therapy: A holistic approach.* Boston: Butterworth-Heinemann.

Bluemel, C. S. (1932). Primary and secondary stuttering. *Quarterly Journal of Speech, 18,* 187–200.

Boberg, E. (1980). Intensive adult therapy program. *Seminars in Speech, Language and Hearing, 1,* 365–374.

Boberg, E. (1982). Behavioral transfer and maintenance programs for adolescent and adult stutterers. In J. Fraser (Ed.), *Stuttering therapy: Transfer and maintenance* (pp. 41–62). Memphis, TN: Stuttering Foundation of America.

Boberg, E. (1986). Postscript: Relapse and outcome. In G. H. Shames & H. Rubin (Eds.), *Stuttering: Then and now* (pp. 501–516). Columbus: Charles E. Merrill.

Boberg, E., Howie, P., & Woods, L. (1979). Maintenance of fluency: A review. *Journal of Fluency Disorders, 4,* 93–116.

Boberg, E., & Kully, D. (1994). Long-term results of an intensive treatment program for adults and adolescents who stutter. *Journal of Speech and Hearing Research, 37,* 1050–1059.

Boberg, J. M., & Boberg, E. (1990). The other side of the block: The stutterer's spouse. *Journal of Fluency Disorders, 15,* 61–75.

Bohart, A. C., & Todd, J. (1988). *Foundations of clinical and counseling psychology.* New York: Harper & Row.

Bosshardt, H. (1993). Differences between stutterers' and nonstutterers' short-term recall and recognition performance. *Journal of Speech and Hearing Research, 36,* 286–293.

Botterill, W., & Cook, F. (1987). Personal construct theory and the treatment of adolescent dysfluency. In L. Rustin, H. Purser, & D. Rowley (Eds.), *Progress in the treatment of fluency disorders* (pp. 147–165). London: Whurr.

Botterill, W., Kelman, E., & Rustin, L. (1991). Parents and their pre-school stuttering child. In L. Rustin (Ed.), *Parents, families, and the stuttering child.* San Diego, CA: Singular.

Bradberry, A. (1997). The role of support groups and stuttering therapy. *Seminars in Speech and Language, 18,* 391–399.

Bradshaw, J. (1988). *Healing the shame that binds you.* Deerfield Beach, FL: Health Communications.

Braun, A. R., Varga, M., Stager, S., Schulz, G., Selbie, S., Maisog, J. M., Carson, R. E., & Ludlow, C. L. (1997). Altered patterns of cerebral activity during speech and language production in developmental stuttering: An $H_2{}^{15}O$ positron emission tomography study. *Brain, 120,* 761–784.

Breitenfeldt, D. H. (1998). Managing your stuttering versus your stuttering managing you. In S. B. Hood

(Ed.), *Advice to those who stutter* (2nd ed.), pp. 7–12). Memphis, TN: Stuttering Foundation of America.

Breitenfeldt, D. H. (2003a). *Tale of the three little stutters and the big bad block.* Cheney, WA: Eastern Washington University.

Breitenfeldt, D. H. (2003b, August). *The successful stuttering management program with therapy "tune ups" for adolescents and adults.* Paper presented at the 4th World Congress on Fluency Disorders, Montreal, Canada.

Breitenfeldt, D. H., & Lorenz, D. R. (1989). *Successful stuttering management program.* Cheney, WA: Eastern Washington University.

Brisk, D. J., Healey, E. C., & Hux, K. A. (1997). Clinicians' training and confidence associated with treating school-age children who stutter: A national survey. *Language, Speech, and Hearing Services in Schools, 28*(2), 164–176.

Brophy, J. E. (1998). *Motivating students to learn.* Boston: McGraw-Hill.

Brown, S. F. (1938a). Stuttering with relation to word accent and word position. *Journal of Abnormal and Social Psychology, 33,* 112–120.

Brown, S. F. (1938b). A further study of stuttering in relation to various speech sounds. *Quarterly Journal of Speech, 24,* 390–397.

Brown, S. F. (1945). The loci of stuttering in the speech sequence. *The Journal of Speech Disorders, 10,* 181–192.

Brutten, G. (1984). *The attitude of children who stutter.* Unpublished manuscript.

Brutten, G. J., & Dunham, S. L. (1989). The Communication Attitude Test: A normative study of grade school children. *Journal of Fluency Disorders, 14,* 371–377.

Brutten, G. J., & Shoemaker, D. J. (1967). *The modification of stuttering.* Englewood Cliffs, NJ: Prentice Hall.

Brutten, G., & Shoemaker, D. (1969). Stuttering: The disintegration of speech due to conditioned negative emotion. In B. B. Gray & G. England (Eds.), *Stuttering and the conditioning therapy* (pp. 57–68). Monterey, CA: The Monterey Institute for Speech and Hearing.

Büchell, C., & Sommer, M. (2004). What causes stuttering? *PloS Biology, 2,* 0159–1163. Retrieved July 25, 2004, from www.plosbiology.org.

Buck, S. M., Lees, R., & Cook, F. (2002). The influence of family history of stuttering on the onset of stuttering in young children. *Folia Phoniatrica et Logopaedica, 54,* 117–124. Abstract retrieved July 25, 2004, from www.ncbi.nlm.nih.gov/PubMed.

Burnell, I. (1990). *The power of positive doing: Twelve strategies for taking control of your life.* Center Ossipee, NY: International Personal Development.

Burns, D. D. (1980). *Feeling good: The new mood therapy.* New York: Penguin.

Burns, D. D. (1989). *The feeling good handbook.* New York: Penguin.

Butterworth, B. (1992). Disorders of phonological encoding. *Cognition, 42,* 261–286.

Byrd, K., & Cooper, E. B. (1989). Apraxic speech characteristics in stuttering, developmentally apraxic, and normal speaking children. *Journal of Fluency Disorders, 14,* 215–229.

Campbell, J. H. (2003). Therapy for elementary school-age children who stutter. In H. H. Gregory (Ed.), *Stuttering therapy: Rationale and procedures* (pp. 217–262). Boston: Allyn & Bacon.

Campbell, J. H., & Hill, D. G. (1987). Systematic disfluency analysis. In *The Stuttering Foundation of America continuing education course for fluency specialists workbook,* Dallas, TX, 1990.

Campbell, J. H., & Hill, D. G. (1989). Handouts from *The Stuttering Foundation of America continuing education course for fluency specialists workbook,* Northwestern University, Evanston, IL.

Caruso, A. J. (1991). Neuromotor processes underlying stuttering. In H. F. Peters, W. Hulstijn, & C. W. Starkweather (Eds.), *Speech motor control and stuttering* (pp. 101–116). New York: Elsevier Science.

Caruso, A. J., Abbs, J. H., & Gracco, V. L. (1988). Kinematic analysis of multiple movement coordination during speech in stutterers. *Brain, 111,* 439–455.

Caruso, A. J., Max, L., McClowry, M. T., & Chodzko-Zajko, W. (1998). Cognitive stress and stuttering: An experimental paradigm for connected speech. *Contemporary Issues in Communication Science and Disorders, 25,* 65–75.

Caruso, A. J., Ritt, C. A., & Sommers, R. K. (2002). Interactions between fluency and phonological disorders. *Contemporary Issues in Communication Science and Disorders, 29,* 146-153.

Cassar, M. A., & Neilson, M. D. (1997). Workplace fluency management: Factoring the workplace into fluency management. *Seminars in Speech and Language, 18,* 371-389.

Chang, S., Ohde, R. N., & Conture, E. G. (2002). Coarticulation and formant transition rate in young children who stutter. *Journal of Speech, Language, and Hearing Disorders, 45,* 676-688.

Cheasman, C., & Everard, R. (2003, August). *Interiorised stammering—a group therapy program—clients' and therapists' perspectives.* Paper presented at the the 4th World Congress on Fluency Disorders, Montreal, Canada.

Cherry, C., & Sayers, B. (1956). Experiments upon the total inhibition of stammering by external control and some clinical results. *Journal of Psychosomatic Research, 1,* 233-246.

Chmela, K., Bennett, E., Campbell, J., Oyler, L., Scott-Trautman, L., & Tardelli, M. (2002). *Fluency specialists as consultants in the school setting.* Paper presented at the American Speech-Language-Hearing Association Convention, Washington, DC.

Chmela, K., & Reardon, N. (2001). *The school-age child who stutters: Working effectively with attitudes and emotions.* Memphis, TN: Stuttering Foundation of America.

Christmann, H. (1998a). Stuttering and communication. In E. C. Healey and H. F. M. Peters (Eds.), *2nd World Congress on Fluency Disorders: Proceedings* (pp. 397-398). Nijmegen, The Netherlands: University Press Nijmegen.

Christmann, H. (1998b). Stuttering and the labor market. In E. C. Healey and H. F. M. Peters (Eds.), *2nd World Congress on Fluency Disorders: Proceedings* (pp. 399-402). Nijmegen, The Netherlands: University Press Nijmegen.

Colcord, R. D., & Adams, M. R. (1979). Voicing duration and vocal SPL changes associated with stuttering reduction during singing. *Journal of Speech and Hearing Research, 22,* 468-479.

Commodore, R. W., & Cooper, E. B. (1978). Communication stress and stuttering frequency during normal, whispered, and articulation without phonation speech modes. *Journal of Fluency Disorders, 3,* 1-12.

Conture, E. G. (1991). Young stutterers' speech production: A critical review. In H. F. M. Peters, W. Hulstijn, & C. W. Starkweather (Eds.), *Speech motor control and stuttering* (pp. 365-384). New York: Excerptamedica.

Conture, E. G. (1997). Evaluating childhood stuttering. In R. F. Curlee & G. M. Siegel (Eds.), *Nature and treatment of stuttering: New directions* (pp. 239-256). Boston: Allyn & Bacon.

Conture, E. G. (2001). *Stuttering: Its nature, diagnosis, and treatment.* Boston: Allyn & Bacon.

Conture, E., & Caruso, A. (1987). Assessment and diagnosis of childhood dysfluency. In L. Rustin, H. Purser, & D. Rowly (Eds.), *Progress in the treatment of fluency disorders* (pp. 84-104). New York: Taylor & Francis.

Conture, E. G., Colton, R. H., & Gleason, J. R. (1988). Selected temporal aspects of coordination during fluent speech of young stutterers. *Journal of Speech and Hearing Research, 31,* 640-653.

Conture, E. G., & Guitar, B. (1993). Evaluating efficacy of treatment of stuttering: School-age children. *Journal of Fluency Disorders, 18,* 253-287.

Conture, E. G., & Kelly, E. M. (1991). Young stutterers' nonspeech behaviors during stuttering. *Journal of Speech and Hearing Research, 34,* 1041-1056.

Conture, E. G., & Melnick, K. S. (1999). The parent-child group approach to stuttering in preschool children. In M. Onslow & A. Packman (Eds.), *The handbook of early stuttering intervention* (pp. 17-52). San Diego, CA: Singular.

Cooper, E. B. (1984). Personalized fluency control therapy: A status report. In M. Peins (Ed.), *Contemporary approaches in stuttering therapy* (pp. 1-38). Boston: Little, Brown.

Cooper, E. B. (1993). Chronic perseverative stuttering syndrome: A harmful or helpful construct? *American Journal of Speech-Language Pathology, 2,* 11-15.

Cooper, E. B. (1997). Understanding the process. In J. Fraser (Ed.), *Counseling stutterers* (pp. 19-28). Memphis, TN: Stuttering Foundation of America.

Cooper, E. B., & Cooper, C. S. (1985). *Cooper personalized fluency control therapy—revised.* Allen, TX: DLM.

Cooper, E. B., & Cooper, C. S. (1991). A fluency disorders prevention program for preschoolers and children in the primary grades. *American Journal of Speech-Language Pathology, 1*(1) 28-31.

Cooper, E. B., & Cooper, C. S. (1996). Clinician attitudes towards stuttering: Two decades of change. *Journal of Fluency Disorders, 21*(2) 119-136.

Cooper, E. B., & Cooper, C. S. (1998). *The impact of identifying preferred treatment outcomes on conceptualizing, assessing, and treating chronic stuttering.* ISAD Internet Conference, October. Retrieved on October 13, 1998, from www.mankato.msus.edu/dept/comdis/isad/papers/cooper.html.

Cooper, E. B., & Rustin, L. (1985). Clinician attitudes toward stuttering in the United States and Great Britain: A cross-cultural study. *Journal of Fluency Disorders, 10,* 1-17.

Coriat, I. H. (1928). Stammering A psychoanalytic interpretation. *Nervous and Mental Disease Monogram, 47,* 1-68.

Coriat, I. H. (1943). The psychoanalytic conception of stammering. *Nervous Child, 2,* 167-179.

Coriat, I. (1972). The psychoanalytic conception of stammering. In L. L. Emerick & C. E. Hamre (Eds.), *An analysis of stuttering: Selected readings* (pp. 259-263). Danville, IL: Interstate.

Costello, Ingham, J. (1993). Behavioral treatment of young children who stutter. In R. F. Curlee (Ed.), *Stuttering and related disorders of fluency* (pp. 68-100). New York: Thieme Medical Publishers.

Costello, Ingham, J. (1999). Behavioral treatment of young children who stutter: An extended length of utterance method. In R. F. Curlee (Ed.), *Stuttering and related disorders of fluency* (2nd ed., pp. 80-109). New York: Thieme Medical Publishers.

Costello, J. M. (1980). Operant conditioning and the treatment of stuttering. *Seminars in Speech, Language and Hearing, 1*(4), 311-326.

Costello, J. M. (1983). Current behavioral treatments for children. In D. Prins & R. J. Ingham (Eds.), *Treatment of stuttering in early childhood methods and issues* (pp. 69-112). San Diego: College-Hill Press.

Costello, J. M., & Ingham, R. J. (1984). Assessment strategies for stuttering. In R. F. Curlee and W. H. Perkins (Eds.), *Nature and treatment of stuttering: New directions* (pp. 303-334). Needham Heights, MA: Allyn & Bacon.

Craig, A. (1990). An investigation into the relationship between anxiety and stuttering. *Journal of Speech and Hearing Disorders, 55,* 290-294.

Craig, A. (1998). Relapse following treatment for stuttering: A critical review and correlative data. *Journal of Fluency Disorders, 23*(1), 1-30.

Craig, A., & Hancock, K. (1998). Anxiety, communication attitudes and locus of control in children who stutter. *Proceedings from the 1st World Congress on Fluency Disorders* (pp. 129-132). Nijmegen, The Netherlands: Nijmegen University Press.

Crary, M. A. (1993). *Developmental motor speech disorders.* San Diego, CA: Singular.

Cross, D. E., & Luper, H. L. (1979). Voice reaction time of stuttering and nonstuttering children and adults. *Journal of Fluency Disorders, 4,* 59-77.

Cross, D. E., & Luper, H. L. (1983). Relation between finger reaction time and voice reaction time in stuttering and nonstuttering children and adults. *Journal of Speech and Hearing Research, 26,* 356-361.

Crowe, T. (1997). *Applications of counseling in speech-language pathology and audiology.* Baltimore: Williams and Wilkins.

Crowe, T. A., & Cooper, E. B. (1977). Parents' attitudes toward and knowledge of stuttering. *Journal of Communications Disorders, 10,* 343-357.

Crowe, T. A., & Walton, J. H. (1981). Teacher attitudes toward stuttering. *Journal of Fluency Disorders, 6,* 163-174.

Crystal, D. (1991). *A dictionary of linguistics and phonetics.* Cambridge, MA: Blackwell.

Culatta, R., Bader, J., McCaslin, A., & Thomason, N. (1985). Primary school stutterers: Have attitudes changed? *Journal of Fluency Disorders, 10,* 87-91.

Culatta, R., & Goldberg, S. (1995). *Stuttering therapy: An integrated approach to theory and practice.* Boston: Allyn & Bacon.

Cullinan, W. L., & Springer, M. T. (1980). Voice initiation times in stuttering and nonstuttering children. *Journal of Speech and Hearing Research, 23,* 344-360.

Curlee, R. F. (1999). Identification and case selection guidelines for early childhood stuttering. In R. F. Curlee (Ed.), *Stuttering and related disorders of flu-*

ency (2nd ed., pp. 1-21). New York:Thieme Medical Publishers.

Curlee, R. F. (2000). Demands and capacities versus demands and performance. *Journal of Fluency Disorders, 25,* 329-336.

Curlee, R. F., & Perkins, W. H. (1969). Conversational rate control therapy for stuttering. *Journal of Speech and Hearing Disorders, 34,* 245-250.

Curlee, R. F., & Yairi, E. (1997). Early intervention with early childhood stuttering: A critical examination of the data. *American Journal of Speech-Language Pathology, 6*(2) 8-18.

Curry, F. K. W., & Gregory, H. H. (1969). The performance of stutterers on dichotic listening tasks thought to reflect cerebral dominance. *Journal of Speech and Hearing Research, 12,* 73-82.

Dahm, B. (1997). *Generating fluent speech: A comprehensive speech processing approach.* Eau Claire, WI:Thinking Publications.

Dalton, P., & Hardcastle, W. J. (1989). *Disorders of fluency* (2nd ed.). London:Whurr.

Daly, D. A. (1986). The clutterer. In O. St. Louis (Ed.), *The atypical stutterer* (pp. 155-192). New York:Academic Press.

Daly, D. A. (1988). *Freedom of fluency.* Tucson, AZ: LinguiSystems.

Daly, D. A. (1992). Helping the clutterer: Therapy considerations. In F. L. Meyers & K. O. St. Louis (Eds.), *Cluttering: A clinical perspective* (pp. 107-124). Kibworth, Great Britain: Far Communications.

Daly, D. A. (1993a). Cluttering: Another fluency syndrome. In R. Curlee (Ed.), *Stuttering and related disorders of fluency* (pp. 151-175). New York:Thieme Medical Publishers.

Daly, D. A. (1993b). Cluttering: The orphan of speech-language pathology. *American Journal of Speech-Language Pathology, 2,* 6-8.

Daly, D. A. (1996). *The source for stuttering and cluttering.* East Moline, IL: LinguiSystems.

Daly, D. A. (1998). Some suggestions for gaining and sustaining improved fluency. In S. B. Hood (Ed.), *Advice to those who stutter* (2nd ed., pp. 83-87). Memphis,TN: Stuttering Foundation of America.

Daly, D. A., & Burnett, M. L. (1999). Cluttering: Traditional views and new perspectives. In R. F. Curlee (Ed.), *Stuttering and related disorders of fluency* (2nd ed., pp. 222-254). New York:Thieme Medical Publishers.

Darley, F., & Spriestersbach, D. (1978). *Diagnostic methods in speech pathology* (2nd ed.). New York: Harper & Row.

Dayalu, V. N., Kalinowski, J., Stuart, A., Holbert, D., & Rastatter, M. P. (2002). Stuttering frequency on content and function words in adults who stutter: A concept revisited. *Journal of Speech and Hearing Research, 45,* 871-878.

Deci, E. L., & Ryan, R. M. (1992). The initiation and regulation of intrinsically motivated learning and achievement. In A. K. Boggiano & T. S. Pittman (Eds.), *Achievement and motivation: A social-developmental perspective* (pp. 9-36). New York: Cambridge University Press.

Dell, C. W., Jr. (1979). *Treating the school age stutterer: A guide for clinicians.* Memphis,TN: Stuttering Foundation of America.

Dell, C. W., Jr. (1993). Treating school-age stutterers. In R. F. Curlee (Ed.), *Stuttering and related disorders of fluency* (pp. 45-67). New York:Thieme Medical Publishers.

Dell, C. W., Jr. (2000). Fluency disorders. In E. P. Dodge (Ed.), *Survival guide for school-based speech-language pathologists.* Belmont, CA: Delmar.

Dell, G. S. (1986). A spreading-activation theory of retrieval in sentence production. *Psychological Review, 93,* 283-321.

Dell, G. S., & Juliano, C. (1991). Connectionist approaches to the production of words. In H. F. M. Peters, W. Hulstijn, & C. W. Starkweather (Eds.), *Speech motor control and stuttering* (pp. 11-36). New York: Elsevier Science.

Dell, G. S., Juliano, C., & Govindjee, A. (1993). Structure and content in language production: A theory of frame constraints in phonological speech errors. *Cognitive Science, 17,* 149-195.

Dell, G. S., & Reich, P. A. (1980). Toward a unified model of slips of the tongue. In V. A. Fromkin (Ed.), *Errors in linguistic performance* (pp. 273-286). New York:Academic Press.

Dembowski, J., & Watson, B. C. (1991). Preparation time and response complexity effects on stutterers' and nonstutterers' acoustic LRT. *Journal of Speech and Hearing Research, 34,* 49-59.

DeNil, L. (1995, November). *Linguistic and motor approaches to stuttering: Exploring unification.* A panel presentation at the annual convention of the American Speech-Language-Hearing Association, Orlando, FL.

DeNil, L. F. (1999). Stuttering: A neurophysiological perspective. In N. B. Ratner & E. C. Healey (Eds.), *Stuttering research and practice: Bridging the gap* (pp. 85-103). Mahwah, NJ: Lawrence Erlbaum Associates.

DeNil, L. F., & Abbs, J. H. (1991). Oral and finger kinesthetic thresholds in stutterers. In H. F. M. Peters, W. Hulstijn, & C. W. Starkweather (Eds.), *Speech motor control and stuttering* (pp. 123-130). New York: Excerptamedica.

DeNil, L. F., & Brutten, G. J. (1991). Speech-associated attitudes of stuttering and nonstuttering children. *Journal of Speech, Language, and Hearing Research, 34*(1), 60-66.

DeNil, L. F., Kroll, R. M., & Houle, S. (2001). Functional neuroimaging of cerebellar activation during single word reading and verb generation in stuttering and nonstuttering adults. *Neuroscience Letters, 302,* 77-80.

DeNil, L. F., Kroll, R. M., Kapur, S., & Houle, S. (2000). A positron emission tomography study of silent and oral single word reading in stuttering and nonstuttering adults. *Journal of Speech, Language, and Hearing Research, 43*(4), 1038-1053.

DeNil, L. F., Kroll, R. M., Lafaille, S. J., & Houle, S. (2003). A positron emission tomography study of short- and long-term treatment effects on functional brain activation in adults who stutter. *Journal of Fluency Disorders, 28,* 357-380.

Denny, M., & Smith, A. (1997). Respiratory and laryngeal control in stuttering. In R. F. Curlee & G. M. Siegel (Eds.), *Nature and treatment of stuttering: New directions* (2nd ed., pp. 128-142). Boston: Allyn & Bacon.

Devour, J., Nandur, M., & Manning, W. (1984). Projective drawings and children who stutter. *Journal of Fluency Disorders, 9,* 217-226.

Diedrich, W. M. (1984). Cluttering: Its diagnosis. In H. Winitz (Ed.), *Treating articulation disorders: For clinicians by clinicians.* Baltimore: University Park Press.

Diedrich, S., Jensen, K. H., & Williams, D. E. (2001). Effects of the label "stutterer" on student perceptions. *Journal of Fluency Disorders, 26,* 55-66.

Diggs, C. C. (1990). Self-help for communication disorders. *ASHA, 32,* 32-34.

Doody, I., Kalinowski, J., Armson, J., & Stuart, A. (1993). Stereotypes of stutterers and nonstutterers in three rural communities in Newfoundland. *Journal of Fluency Disorders, 18*(4), 363-374.

Dorsey, M., & Guenther, R. K. (2000). Attitudes of professors and students toward college students who stutter. *Journal of Fluency Disorders, 25*(1), 77-83.

Dougherty, A. M. (1990). *Consultation: Practices and perspectives.* Pacific Grove, CA: Brooks/Cole.

Douglas, E., & Quarrington, B. (1952). The differentiation of interiorized and exteriorized secondary stuttering. *Journal of Speech and Hearing Disorders, 17,* 377-385.

Doyle, R. E. (1992). *Essential skills and strategies in the helping process.* Pacific Grove, CA: Brooks/Cole.

Dworkin, J. P., Culatta, R. A., Abkarian, G. G., & Meleca, R. J. (2002). Laryngeal anesthetization for the treatment of acquired disfluency: A case study. *Journal of Fluency Disorders, 27,* 215-226.

Egan, G. (1998). *The skilled helper: A problem-management approach to helping* (6th ed.). Pacific Grove, CA: Brooks/Cole.

Eger, D. L. (1999, April). *School-based service delivery options, caseload management, and customer feedback.* Paper presented at the New York State Speech-Language-Hearing Association convention, Syracuse, NY.

Ellis, A. (2001). *Overcoming destructive beliefs, feelings, and behaviors: New directions for rational emotive behavior therapy.* Amherst, NY: Prometheus.

Ellis, A., & Harper, R. A. (1975). *A new guide to rational living.* Englewood Cliffs, NJ: Prentice Hall.

Emerick, L. (1988). Counseling adults who stutter: A cognitive approach. *Seminars in Speech and Language, 9,* 257-267.

Erickson, R. L. (1969). Assessing communication attitudes among stutterers. *Journal of Speech and Hearing Research, 12,* 711-724.

Ezrati-Vinacour, R., Platzky, R., & Yairi, E. (2001). The young child's awareness of stuttering-like disfluency. *Journal of Speech, Language, and Hearing Research, 44,* 368-380.

Faber, A., & Mazlish, E. (1980). *How to talk so kids will listen and listen so kids will talk.* New York: Avon.

Feinberg, A. Y., Griffin, B. P., & Levey, M. (2000). Psychological aspects of chronic tonic and clonic stuttering: Suggested therapeutic approaches. *American Journal of Orthopsychiatry, 70,* 465–473. Abstract retrieved July 24, 2004, from www.ncbi.nlm.nih.gov/PubMed.

Felsenfeld, S. (1996). Progress and needs in the genetics of stuttering. *Journal of Fluency Disorders, 21,* 77–104.

Felsenfeld, S. (1997). Epidemiology and genetics of stuttering. In R. F. Curlee & G. M. Siegel (Eds.), *Nature and treatment of stuttering: New directions* (2nd ed., pp. 3–23). Boston: Allyn & Bacon.

Felsenfeld, S. (1998). What can genetics research tell us about stuttering treatment issues? In A. K. Cordes & R. J. Ingham (Eds.), *Treatment efficacy for stuttering: A search for empirical bases* (pp. 51–67). San Diego: Singular.

Felsenfeld, S. (2002). Finding susceptibility genes for developmental disorders of speech: The long and winding road. *Journal of Communication Disorders, 35,* 329–345. Abstract retrieved July 24, 2004, from www.ncbi.nlm.nih.gov/PubMed.

Felsenfeld, S., Kirk, K. M., Zhu, G., Statham, D. J., Neale, M. C., & Martin, N. G. (2000). A study of the genetic and environmental etiology of stuttering in a selected twin sample. *Behavioral Genetics, 30,* 359–366. Abstract retrieved July 24, 2004, from www.ncbi.nlm.nih.gov/PubMed.

Ferguson, T. J., Stegge, H., and Damhuis, I. (1991). Children's understanding of guilt and shame. *Child Development, 62,* 827–839.

Field, L. (1995). *The self-esteem workbook: An interactive approach to changing your life.* Rockport, MA: Element.

Finn, P. (1997). Adults recovered from stuttering without formal treatment: Perceptual assessment of speech normalcy. *Journal of Speech, Language, and Hearing Research, 40*(4), 821–831.

Finn, P., Ingham, R. J., Ambrose, N., & Yairi, E. (1997). Children recovered from stuttering without formal treatment: Perceptual assessment. *Journal of Speech, Language, and Hearing Research, 40*(4), 867–876.

Flanagan, B., Goldiamond, I., & Azrin, N. (1972). Operant stuttering: The control of stuttering behavior through response-contingent consequences. In L. L. Emerick & C. E. Hamre (Eds.), *An analysis of stuttering: Selected readings* (pp. 745–750). Danville IL: Interstate.

Foundas, A. L., Bollich, A. M., Corey, D. M., Hurley, M., & Heilman, K. M. (2001). Anomalous anatomy of speech-language areas in adults with persistent developmental stuttering. *Neurology, 57,* 207–215. Abstract retrieved July 24, 2004, from www.ncbi.nlm.nih.gov/PubMed.

Fox, P. T., Ingham, R., & Ingham, J. (1996). A PET study of the neural systems of stuttering. *Nature, 382,* 158–162.

Franck, A. L., Jackson, R. A., Pimentel, J. T., & Greenwood, G. S. (2003). School-age children's perceptions of a person who stutters. *Journal of Fluency Disorders, 28,* 1–15.

Fraser, M. (1978). *Self-therapy.* Memphis, TN: Stuttering Foundation of America.

Frattali, C. M. (1996). How outcomes information can lay the groundwork for efficacy research and outcomes research. In *A practical guide to applying treatment outcomes and efficacy resources* (pp. 9–16). Rockville, MD: American Speech-Language-Hearing Association.

Freeman, F. J. (1979). Phonation in stuttering: A review of current research. *Journal of Fluency Disorders, 4,* 79–89.

Freeman, F. J., & Ushijima, T. (1978). Laryngeal muscle activity during stuttering. *Journal of Speech and Hearing Research, 21,* 538–562.

FRIENDS: The Association of Young People Who Stutter. (2004, January-February). Advice for SLPs from teens who stutter. *Reaching Out,* p. 1.

Froeschels, E. (1943). Pathology and therapy of stuttering. *Nervous Child, 2,* 148–161.

Fromkin, V. A. (1973). *Speech errors as linguistic evidence.* The Hague: Mouton.

Fromkin, V. A. (1993). Speech production. In J. B. Gleason and N. B. Ratner (Eds.), *Psycholinguistics.* Orlando, FL: Holt, Rinehart & Winston.

Fry, J., & Cook, F. (2003, August). *Using cognitive therapy in group work with young adults.* Paper presented at the 4th World Congress on Fluency Disorders, Montreal, Canada.

Gabel, R., Blood, G. W., Tellis, G. M., & Althouse, M. T. (2004). Measuring role entrapment of people who stutter. *Journal of Fluency Disorders, 29,* 27-49.

Gabel, R., Tellis, G., & Althouse, M. T. (2003, August). *Perception of people who stutter: Effects of familiarity.* Paper presented at the 4th World Congress on Fluency Disorders, Montreal, Canada.

Gabor, D. (1997). *Talking with confidence for the painfully shy: How to overcome nervousness, speak-up, and speak-out in any social or business situation.* New York: Random House.

Gaines, N. D., Runyan, C. M., & Meyers, S. C. (1991). A comparison of young stutterers' fluent versus stuttered utterances on measures of length and complexity. *Journal of Speech and Hearing Research, 34,* 37-42.

German, D. J. (1989). *National College of Education Test of Word Finding (TWF).* Austin, TX: Pro-Ed.

Ginsberg, A. P. (2000). Shame, self-consciousness, and locus of control in people who stutter. *Journal of Genetic Psychology, 161,* 389-399. Abstract retrieved July 24, 2004, from www.ncbi.nlm.nih.gov/ PubMed.

Glasner, P., & Rosenthal, D. (1972). Parental diagnosis of stuttering in young children. In L. L. Emerick & C. E. Hamre (Eds.), *An analysis of stuttering: Selected readings* (pp. 382-390). Danville, IL: Interstate.

Goldberg, S. A. (1997). *Clinical skills for speech-language pathologists.* San Diego, CA: Singular.

Gonzalez, M. P., Barrull, E., Pons, C., & Marteles, P. (1998). *What is emotion?* Retrieved March 19, 2002 from www.biopsychology.org.

Gracco, V. L. (1991). Sensorimotor mechanisms in speech motor control. In H. F. M. Peters, W. Hulstijn, & C. W. Starkweather (Eds.), *Speech motor control and stuttering* (pp. 53-78). New York: Excerptamedica.

Gregory, H. H. (1979). The controversies: Analysis and current status. In H. H. Gregory (Ed.), *Controversies about stuttering therapy.* Baltimore, MD: University Park Press.

Gregory, H. H. (1982). Definitions. In *Stuttering therapy: Transfer and maintenance* (Publication No. 19) (p. 11). Memphis, TN: Stuttering Foundation of America.

Gregory, H. H. (1986). Environmental manipulation and family counseling. In G. H. Shames & H. Rubin (Eds.), *Stuttering: Then and now* (pp. 273-294). Columbus: Charles E. Merrill.

Gregory, H. H. (1991). Therapy for elementary school-age children. *Seminars in Speech and Language, 12,* 323-335.

Gregory, H. H. (1997). The speech-language pathologist's role in stuttering self-help groups. *Seminars in Speech and Language, 18,* 401-410.

Gregory, H. H. (2003). *Stuttering therapy: Rationale and procedures.* Boston: Allyn & Bacon.

Gregory, H., & Hill, D. (1980). Stuttering therapy for children. *Seminars in Speech and Language, 1,* 351-363.

Gregory, H. H., & Hill, D. (1993). Differential evaluation—differential treatment for stuttering children. In R. F. Curlee (Ed.), *Stuttering and related disorders of fluency* (pp. 23-44). New York: Thieme Medical Publishers.

Gregory, H. H., & Hill, D. (1999). Differential evaluation—differential treatment for stuttering children. In R. F. Curlee (Ed.), *Stuttering and related disorders of fluency* (2nd ed., pp. 22-42). New York: Thieme Medical Publishers.

Guitar, B. (1976). Pretreatment factors associated with the outcome of stuttering therapy. *Journal of Speech and Hearing Research, 19,* 590-600.

Guitar, B. (1997). Therapy for children's stuttering and emotions. In R. F. Curlee & G. M. Siegel (Eds.), *Nature and treatment of stuttering: New directions* (2nd ed., pp. 280-291). Boston: Allyn & Bacon.

Guitar, B. (1998). *Stuttering: An integrated approach to its nature and treatment* (2nd ed.). Baltimore: Williams and Wilkins.

Guitar, B. (2003). Acoustic startle responses and temperament in individuals who stutter. *Journal of Speech and Hearing Research, 46,* 233-240.

Guitar, B., & Bass, C. (1978). Stuttering therapy: The relation between attitude change and long-term outcome. *Journal of Speech and Hearing Disorders, 15,* 393-400.

Guitar, B., Guitar, C., Neilson, P. D., O'Dwyer, N., & Andrews, G. (1988). Onset sequencing of selected lip muscles in stutterers and nonstutterers. *Journal of Speech and Hearing Research, 31,* 28-35.

Guitar, B., & Marchinkoski, L. (2001). Influence of mothers' slower speech on their children's speech rate. *Journal of Speech, Language, and Hearing Research, 44*(4), 853–861.

Guitar, B., Schaefer, H. K., Donahue-Kilburg, G., & Bond, L. (1992). Parent verbal interactions and speech rate: A case study in stuttering. *Journal of Speech and Hearing Research, 35,* 742–754.

Hall, K. D., & Yairi, E. (1992). Fundamental frequency, jitter, and shimmer in preschoolers who stutter. *Journal of Speech and Hearing Research, 35,* 1002–1008.

Ham, R. E. (1990). *Therapy of stuttering: Preschool through adolescence.* Upper Saddle River, NJ: Prentice Hall.

Ham, R. E. (1999). *Clinical management of stuttering in older children and adults.* Gaithersburg, MD: Aspen.

Hancock, K., & Craig, A. (1998). Predictors of stuttering relapse one year following treatment for children aged 9 to 14 years. *Journal of Fluency Disorders, 23*(1), 31–48.

Hanson, B. R. (1978). The effects of a contingent light-flash on stuttering and attention to stuttering. *Journal of Communication Disorders, 11,* 451–458.

Harackiewicz, J. M., Manderlink, G., & Sansone, C. (1992). Competence processes and achievement motication: Implications for intrinsic motivation. In A. K. Boggiano & T. S. Pittman (Eds.), *Achievement and motivation: A social-developmental perspective* (pp. 115–137). New York: Cambridge University Press.

Hargrave, S., Kalinowski, J., Stuart, A., Armson, J., & Jones, K. (1994). Stuttering reduction under frequency-altered feedback at two speech rates. *Journal of Speech, Language, and Hearing Research, 37,* 1313–1319.

Harrison, E., & Onslow, M. (1999). Early intervention for stuttering: the Lidcombe Program. In R. F. Curlee (Ed.), *Stuttering and related disorders of fluency* (2nd ed., pp. 65–79). New York: Thieme Medical Publishers.

Harter, S. (1992). The relationship between perceived competence, affect, and motivational orientation within the classroom. In A. K. Boggiano & T. S. Pittman (Eds.), *Achievement and motivation: A*

social-developmental perspective (pp. 77–114). New York: Cambridge University Press.

Hayden, P. A., Adams, M. R., & Jordahl, N. (1982). The effects of pacing and masking on stutterers' and non-stutterers' speech initiation times. *Journal of Fluency Disorders, 7,* 9–19.

Healey, E. C., Mallard, A. R., & Adams, M. R. (1976). Factors contributing to the reduction of stuttering during singing. *Journal of Speech and Hearing Research, 19,* 475–480.

Healey, E. C., & Scott, L. A. (1995). Strategies for treating elementary school-age children who stutter: An integrative approach. *Language, Speech, and Hearing Services in Schools, 26,* 151–161.

Healey, E. C., Susca, M., & Trautman, L. S. (2002, May). *What challenges does the child present: Aspects of stuttering that should be addressed.* Paper presented at the American Speech Language Hearing Association, Special Interest Division #4 Leadership Conference, Albuquerque, NM.

Healey, E. C., Trautman, L. S., & Susca, M. (2004). Clinical applications of a multidimentional approach for the assessment and treatment of stuttering. *Contemporary Issues in Communication Science and Disorders, 31,* 40–48.

Hegde, M. N., & Brutten, G. J. (1977). Reinforcing fluency in stutterers: An experimental study. *Journal of Fluency Disorders, 2,* 315–328.

Heinze, B. A., & Johnson, K. L. (1985). *Easy does it—1: Fluency activities for young children.* East Moline, IL: LinguiSystems.

Heinze, B. A., & Johnson, K. L. (1987). *Easy does it—2: Fluency activities for school-aged stutterers.* East Moline, IL: LinguiSystems.

Henning, M., & Tellis, G. (2003, August). *A maintenance study using stuttering modification techniques in extra-clinical settings.* Paper presented at the 4th World Congress on Fluency Disorders, Montreal, Canada.

Hicks, R. (2002). Stuttering is like an iceberg. Retrieved on July 25, 2004, from www.russhicks.com/ iceberg.

Hicks, R. (2003). *Iceberg analogy of stuttering.* Paper presented at the International Stuttering Awareness Day (ISAD) Online Conference. Retrieved on July 25, 2004, from www.russhicks.com/ iceberg.

Hicks, R. (2004, June). *The iceberg matrix of stuttering.* Paper presented at the National Stuttering Association Conference, Baltimore, MD.

Hillman, R. E., & Gilbert, H. R. (1977). Voice onset time for voiceless stop consonants in the fluent reading of stutterers and nonstutterers. *Journal of the Acoustical Society of America, 61,* 610-611.

Hood, S. (2003, June). *Successful communication: Realistic outcomes for adults who stutter.* Paper presented at the National Stuttering Association Conference, Nashville, TN.

Howell, P., & Au-Yeung, J. (1995). The association between stuttering, Brown's factors, and phonological categories in child stutterers ranging in age between 2 and 12 years. *Journal of Fluency Disorders, 20,* 331-344.

Howell, P., Au-Yeung, J., & Sackin, S. (1999). Exchange of stuttering from function words to content words with age. *Journal of Speech, Language, and Hearing Research, 42,* 345-354.

Howell, P., Au-Yeung, J., & Sackin, S. (2000). Internal structure of content words leading to lifespan differences in phonological difficulty in stuttering. *Journal of Fluency Disorders, 25,* 1-20.

Howell, P., Sackin, S., & Rustin, L. (1995). Comparison of speech motor development in stutterers and fluent speakers between 7 and 12 years old. *Journal of Fluency Disorders, 20,* 243-256.

Howie, P. (1981). Concordance for stuttering in monozygotic and dizygotic twin pairs. *Journal of Speech and Hearing Disorders, 24,* 317-321.

Hubbard, C. P., & Prins, D. (1994). Word familiarity, syllabic stress pattern, and stuttering. *Journal of Speech and Hearing Research, 37,* 564-571.

Hubbard, C. P., & Yairi, E. (1988). Clustering of disfluencies in the speech of stuttering and nonstuttering preschool children. *Journal of Speech and Hearing Research, 31,* 228-233.

Hugh-Jones, S., & Smith, P. K. (1999). Self-reports of short- and long-term effects of bullying on children who stammer. *British Journal of Educational Psychology, 69,* 141-158. Abstract retrieved July 25, 2004, from www.ncbi.nlm.nih.gov/PubMed.

Hulit, L. M., & Wirtz, L. (1994). The association of attitudes toward stuttering with selected variables. *Journal of Fluency Disorders, 19,* 247-268.

Hultberg, P. (1988). Shame—a hidden emotion. *Journal of Analytical Psychology, 33,* 109-126.

Hunt, B. (1987). Self-help for stutterers: Experience in Britain. In L. Rustin, H. Purser, & D. Rowley (Eds.), *Progress in the treatment of fluency disorders* (pp. 198-212). London: Whurr.

Hutchinson, J. M., & Navarre, B. M. (1977). The effect of metronome pacing on selected aerodynamic patterns of stuttered speech: Some preliminary observations and interpretations. *Journal of Fluency Disorders, 2,* 189-204.

Hutchinson, J. M., & Norris, G. M. (1977). The differential effect of three auditory stimuli on the frequency of stuttering behaviors. *Journal of Fluency Disorders, 2,* 283-293.

Ingham, R. J. (1984). *Stuttering and behavior therapy: Current status and experimental foundations.* San Diego, CA: College Hill Press.

Ingham, R. J. (1999). Performance-contingent management of stuttering in adolescents and adults. In R. F. Curlee (Ed.), *Stuttering and related disorders of fluency* (2nd ed., pp. 200-221). New York: Thieme Medical Publishers.

Ingham, R. J. (2001). Brain imaging studies of developmental stuttering. *Journal of Communication Disorders, 34,* 493-516. Abstract retrieved July 25, 2004, from www.ncbi.nlm.nih.gov/PubMed.

Ingham, R. J., & Cordes, A. K. (1998). Treatment decisions for young children who stutter: Further concerns and complexities. *American Journal of Speech-Language Pathology: A Journal of Clinical Practice, 7,* 10-19.

Ingham, R. J., & Cordes, A. K. (1999). On watching a discipline shoot itself in the foot: Some observations on current trends in stuttering treatment research. In N. Bernstein Ratner & E. C. Healey (Eds.), *Stuttering research and practice: Bridging the gap.* Mahwah, NJ: Lawrence Erlbaum Associates.

Ingham, R. J., Fox, P. T., Ingham, J. C., & Zamarripa, F. (2000). Is overt speech a prerequisite for the neural activations associated with chronic developmental stuttering? *Brain and Language, 75,* 163-194.

Ingham, R. J., Fox, P. T., Ingham, J. C., Zamarripa, F., Martin, C., Jerabek, P., & Cotton, J. (1996). Functional-lesion investigation of developmental stuttering with positron emission tomography. *Journal of Speech and Hearing Research, 39,* 1208-1227.

Ingham, R. J., Ingham, J. C., Finn, P., & Fox, P.T. (2003). Towards a function neural systems model of developmental stuttering. *Journal of Fluency Disorders, 28,* 297-318.

Ingham, R. J., Kilgo, M., Ingham, J. C., Moglia, R., Belknap, H., & Sanchez, T. (2001). Evaluation of a stuttering treatment based on reduction of short phonation intervals. *Journal of Speech, Language, and Hearing Research, 44,* 1229-1244.

Ingham, R. J., Moglia, R.A., Frank, P., Costello-Ingham, J., & Cordes, A. (1997). Experimental investigation of the effects of frequency-altered feedback on the speech of adults who stutter. *Journal of Speech, Language, and Hearing Research, 40,* 361-372.

Ingham, R. J., & Packman, A. (1979). A further evaluation of the speech of stutterers during chorus and nonchorus reading conditions. *Journal of Speech and Hearing Research, 22,* 784-793.

Jackson, S. M., & Robbins, A. K. (1990). *Learning about our speech helpers.* Greenville, SC: SuperDuper School Company.

Jacobs, E. E., Harvill, R. L., & Masson, R. L. (1988). *Group counseling: Strategies and skills.* Belmont, CA: Wadsworth.

James, J. E. (1981). Punishment of stuttering: Contingency and stimulus parameters. *Journal of Communication Disorders, 14,* 375-386.

James, J. E. (1983). Parameters of the influence of self-initiated time-out from speaking on stuttering. *Journal of Communication Disorders, 16,* 123-132.

Jancke, L. (1994). Variability and duration of voice onset time and phonation in stuttering and nonstuttering adults. *Journal of Fluency Disorders, 19,* 21-37.

Janssen, P., Wieneke, G., & Vaane, E. (1983). Variability in the initiation of articulatory movements in the speech of stutterers and normal speakers. *Journal of Fluency Disorders, 8,* 341-358.

Jayaram, M. (1984). Distribution of stuttering in sentences: Relationship to sentence length and clause position. *Journal of Speech and Hearing Research, 27,* 338-341.

Jeffers, S. (1988). *Fell the fear and beyond.* New York: Ballantine.

Jezer, M. (1997). *Stuttering: A life bound up in words.* New York: Basic.

Johnson, A. (1996). Outcomes and efficacy: Some considerations for practitioners in audiology and speech-language pathology. In *A practical guide to applying treatment outcomes and efficacy resources* (pp. 1-8). Rockville, MD: American Speech-Language-Hearing Association.

Johnson, G. F. (1998). Rules for talking. Retrieved on March 16, 2003, from www.mankato.msus.edu/dept/comdis/kuster/gjohnson/rulesfortalking.html.

Johnson, G. F. (2003). Danger signs. Retrieved on March 16, 2003, from www.mankato.msus.edu/dept/comdis/kuster/gjohnson/dangersigns2.html.

Johnson, W., & Knott, J. (1937). Studies in the psychology of stuttering: Vol. 1. The distribution of moments of stuttering in successive readings of the same material. In L. L. Emerick & C. E. Hamre (Eds.), *An analysis of stuttering: Selected readings* (pp. 537-539). New Jersey, IL: Interstate.

Johnson, W., & Rosen, L. (1937). Studies in the psychology of stuttering: Vol. 7. Effect of certain changes in speech pattern upon frequency of stuttering. *Journal of Speech Disorders, 2,* 105-109.

Johnson, W., et al. (1942). A study of the onset and early development of stuttering. *Journal of Speech Disorders, 7,* 251-257.

Johnson, W., and associates. (1959). *The onset of stuttering.* Minneapolis: University of Minnesota Press.

Jones, M., Onslow, M., Harrison, E., & Packman, A. (2000). Treating stuttering in young children: Predicting treatment time in the Lidcombe program. *Journal of Speech, Language, and Hearing Research, 43*(6), 1440-1450.

Jones, R. K. (1966). Observations on stammering after localized cerebral injury. *Journal of Neurology, Neurosurgery and Psychiatry, 29,* 192-195.

Juan's Secret. (1990). *Staff* (Aaron's Associates, 6114 Waterway, Garland, TX 75043).

Kalinowski, J., & Saltuklaroglu, T. (2003). Choral speech: The amelioration of stuttering via imitation and the mirror neuronal system. *Neuroscience and Biobavioral Reviews, 27,* 339-347. Abstract retrieved July 24, 2004, from www.ncbi.nlm.nih.gov/PubMed.

Kalinowski, J., & Stuart, A. (1996). Stuttering amelioration at various auditory feedback delays and speech rates. *European Journal of Disorder of Communication, 31,* 259-269. Abstract retrieved July 24, 2004, from www.ncbi.nlm.nih.gov/PubMed.

Kalinowski, J., Stuart, A., & Armson, J. (1996). Perceptions of stutterers and nonstutterers during speaking and nonspeaking situations. *American Journal of Speech-Language Pathology, 5,* 61-67.

Kalinowski, J., Stuart, A., Wamsley, L., & Rastatter, M. P. (1999). Effect of monitoring condition and altered auditory feedback on stuttering frequency. *Journal of Speech, Language, and Hearing Research, 42,* 1347-1354.

Karen, R. (1992, February). Shame. *Atlantic Monthly,* pp. 40-43, 46-50, 53-55, 58, 60-62, 64-65, 68-70.

Karnoil, R. (1995). Stuttering, language, and cognition: A review and a model of stuttering as supresegmental sentence plan alignment (SPA). *Psychological Bulletin, 117,* 104-124.

Karsten, M. (1995). *Developing health self-esteem in adolescents.* Grand Junction, CO: Good Apple.

Kaufman, G. (1980). *Shame: The power of caring.* Rochester, VT: Schenkman.

Kaufman, G., & Rafael, L. (1990). *Stick up for yourself: Every kid's guide to personal power and positive self-esteem.* Minneapolis: Free Spirit.

Kay, D. W. K. (1964). The genetics of stuttering. In G. Andrews & M. M. Harris (Eds.), *The syndrome of stuttering.* London: Heinemann.

Kelly, E. M. (1993). Speech rates and turn-taking behaviors of children who stutter and their parents. *Seminars in Speech and Language, 14,* 203-213.

Kelly, E. M. (1994). Speech rates and turn-taking behaviors of children who stutter and their fathers. *Journal of Speech and Hearing Research, 37,* 1284-1294.

Kelly, E. M. (1995). Parents as partners: Including mothers and fathers in the treatment of children who stutter. *Journal of Communication Disorders, 28,* 93-105. Abstract retrieved July 24, 2004, from www.ncbi.nlm.nih.gov/PubMed.

Kelly, E. M. (2000). Modeling stuttering etiology: Clarifying levels of description and measurement. *Journal of Fluency Disorders, 25,* 359-368.

Kelly, E. M., & Conture, E. G. (1991). Intervention with school-age stutterers: A parent-child fluency group approach. *Seminars in Speech and Language, 12,* 310-322.

Kelly, E. M., & Conture, E. G. (1992). Speaking rates, response time latencies, and interrupting behaviors of young stutterers, nonstutterers, and their mothers. *Journal of Speech and Hearing Research, 35,* 1256-1267.

Kelly, E. M., Martin, J. S., Baker, K. E., Rivera, N. I., Bishop, J. E., Krizizke, C. B., Stettler, D. S., & Stealy, J. M. (1997). Academic and clinical preparation and practices of school speech-language pathologists with people who stutter. *Language, Speech, and Hearing Services in Schools, 28,* 195-212.

Kelso, K. (2003, June). *"What to ask when you don't know what to say": Improving communication and conversation for the person who stutters.* Paper presented at the National Stuttering Association Conference, Nashville, TN.

Kendall, D. L. (2000). Counseling in communication disorders. *Contemporary Issues in Communication Science and Disorders, 27,* 96-103.

Kent, R. D. (1983). Facts about stuttering: Neuropsychologic perspectives. *Journal of Speech and Hearing Disorders, 48,* 249-255.

Kent, R. D. (1984). Stuttering as a temporal programming disorder. In R. F. Curlee & W. H. Perkins (Eds.), *Nature and treatment of stuttering: New directions* (pp. 283-302). Needham Heights, MA: Allyn & Bacon.

Kidd, K. D. (1984). Stuttering as a genetic disorder. In R. F. Curlee and W. H. Perkins (Eds.), *Nature and treatment of stuttering: New directions* (pp. 149-170). Needham Heights, MA: Allyn & Bacon.

Kidd, K. K. (1980). Genetic models of stuttering. *Journal of Fluency Disorders, 5,* 187-201.

Klein, E. R., & Amster, B. J. (2003, August). *The effects of cognitive behavioral therapy with people who stutter.* Paper presented at the 4th World Congress on Fluency Disorders, Montreal, Canada.

Klevans, D. R. (1988). Counseling strategies for communication disorders. *Seminars in Speech and Language, 9,* 185-207.

Kloth, S. A. M., Janssen, P., Kraaimaat, F. W., & Brutten, G. J. (1995). Communicative behavior of mothers of stuttering and nonstuttering high-risk children prior to the onset of stuttering. *Journal of Fluency Disorders, 20,* 365-378.

Kolk, H. (1991). Is stuttering a symptom of adaptation or of impairment? In H. F. M. Peters, W. Hulstijn, & C. W. Starkweather (Eds.), *Speech motor control and stuttering* (pp. 131-140). New York: Elsevier Science.

Kolk, H., & Postma, A. (1997). Stuttering as a covert repair phenomenon. In R. F. Curlee & G. M. Siegel (Eds.), *Nature and treatment of stuttering: New directions* (2nd ed., pp. 182–203). Boston: Allyn & Bacon.

Kraaimaat, F., Janssen, P., and Brutten, G. J. (1988). The relationship between stutterers' cognitive and autonomic anxiety and therapy outcome. *Journal of Fluency Disorders, 13,* 107–113.

Krauss-Lehrman, T., & Reeves, L. (1989). Attitudes toward speech-language pathology and support groups: Results of a survey of members of the National Stuttering Association. *Texas Journal of Audiology and Speech Pathology, 15,* 22–25.

Kubler-Ross, E. (1969). *On death and dying.* New York: Macmillan.

Kully, D., & Langevin, M. J. (1999). Intensive treatment for stuttering adolescents. In R. F. Curlee (Ed.), *Stuttering and related disorders of fluency* (2nd ed., pp. 139–159). New York: Thieme Medical Publishers.

Langevin, M. (2000). *Teasing and bullying: Unacceptable behavior.* Edmonton, Alberta: Institute for Stuttering Treatment and Research, University of Alberta.

Langevin, M. (2002). *Teasing and bullying questionnaire for children who stutter—revised (TBQ-CS).* Edmonton, Alberta: Institute for Stuttering Treatment and Research, University of Alberta.

Langevin, M., Bortnick, K., Hammer, T., & Wiebe, E. (1998). Teasing/Bullying experienced by children who stutter: Toward development of a questionnaire. *Contemporary Issues in Communication Science and Disorders, 25,* 12–24.

Langlois, A., Hanrahan, L., & Inouye, L. (1986). A comparison of interactions between stuttering children, nonstuttering children, and their mothers. *Journal of Fluency Disorders, 11,* 263–273.

Larson, V. L. & McKinley, N. (2003). *Communication solutions for older students.* Ean Claire, WI: Thinking Publications.

LaSalle, L. R., & Conture, E. G. (1991). Eye contact between young stutterers and their mothers. *Journal of Fluency Disorders, 16,* 173–200.

LaSalle, L. R., & Conture, E. G. (1993, November). *Relation of self-repairs to stuttering in children's disfluency clusters.* Paper presented at the American Speech-Language-Hearing Association convention, Anaheim, CA.

LaSalle, L. R., & Conture, E. G. (1995). Disfluency clusters of children who stutter: Relation of stutters to self-repairs. *Journal of Speech and Hearing Research, 38,* 965–977.

Lass, N. J., Ruscello, D. M., Pannbacker, M., Schmitt, J. F., Kiser, A. M., Mussa, A. M., & Lockhart, P. (1994). School administrators' perceptions of people who stutter. *Language, Speech, and Hearing Services in Schools, 25,* 90–93.

Lass, N. J., Ruscello, D. M., Schmitt, J. F., Pannbacker, M. D., Orlando, M. B., Dean, K. A., Ruziska, J. C., & Bradshaw, K. H. (1992). Teacher's perceptions of stutterers. *Language, Speech, and Hearing Services in Schools, 23,*(1) 78–81.

Laver, J. (1980). Monitoring systems in the neurolinguistic control of speech production. In V. A. Fromkin (Ed.), *Errors in linguistic performance: Slips of the tongue, ear, pen, and hand* (pp. 287–305). New York: Academic Press.

Lechner, B. K. (1979). The effects of delayed auditory feedback and masking on the fundamental frequency of stutterers and nonstutterers. *Journal of Speech and Hearing Research, 22,* 343–353.

Lee, B. S. (1951). Artificial stutter. *Journal of Speech and Hearing Disorders, 16,* 53–55.

Leith, W. R. (1984). *Handbook of stuttering therapy for the school clinician.* San Diego, CA: College-Hill Press.

Leith, W., Mahr, G., & Miller, L. (1993). *The assessment of speech related attitudes and beliefs of people who stutter.* Baltimore: ASHA.

Lerner, H. G. (1985). *The dance of anger: A woman's guide to changing the patterns of intimate relationships.* New York: Harper & Row.

Levelt, W. J. M. (1983). Monitoring and self-repair in speech. *Cognition, 14,* 41–104.

Levelt, W. J. M. (1989). *Speaking: From intention to articulation.* Cambridge, MA: MIT Press.

Levelt, W. J. M. (1992). Accessing words in speech production: Stages, processes and representations. *Cognition, 42,* 1–22.

Levelt, W. J. M., & Wheeldon, L. (1994). Do speakers have access to a mental syllabary? *Cognition, 50,* 239–269.

Levitt, A., Healy, A. F., & Fendrich, D. W. (1991). Syllable-internal structure and the sonority hierarchy: Differential evidence from lexical decision, naming, and reading. *Journal of Psycholinguistic Research, 20,* 337–363.

Lewis, K. E., & Golberg, L. L. (1997). Measurements of temperament in the identification of children who stutter. *European Journal of Disorders of Communication, 32,* 441–448. Abstract retrieved July 25, 2004, from www.ncbi.nlm.nih.gov/PubMed.

Lewis, M. (1992). *Shame: The exposed self.* New York: Free Press.

Lincoln, M., Onslow, M., & Reed, V. (1997). Social validity of the treatment outcomes of an early intervention program for stuttering. *American Journal of Speech-Language Pathology, 6,* 77–84.

Logan, K. J., & Caruso, A. J. (1997). Parents as partners in the treatment of childhood stuttering. *Seminars in Speech and Language, 18,* 309–327.

Logan, K. J., & Conture, E. G. (1995). Length, grammatical complexity, and rate differences in stuttered and fluent conversational utterances of children who stutter. *Journal of Fluency Disorders, 20,* 35–62.

Logan, K. J., & Conture, E. G. (1997). Selected temporal, grammatical, and phonological characteristics of conversational utterances produced by children who stutter. *Journal of Speech, Language, and Hearing Research, 40,* 107–120.

Logan, K. J., & LaSalle, L. R. (1999). Grammatical characteristics of children's conversational utterances that contain disfluency clusters. *Journal of Speech, Language, and Hearing Research, 42,* 80–91.

Logan, K. J., Roberts, R. R., Prieto, A. P., & Morey, M. J. (2002). Speaking slowly: Effects of four self-guided training approaches on adult's speech rate and naturalness. *American Journal of Speech-Language Pathology, 11,* 163–174.

Lougeay, J., & Anderson, N. (2002, May). *Tricks for talking: An innovative collaboration for children who stutter.* Paper presented at the American Speech Language Hearing Association, Special Interest Division #4 Leadership Conference, Albuquerque, NM.

Louko, L. J. (1995). Phonological characteristics of young children who stutter. *Topics in Language Disorders, 15,* 48–59.

Louko, L. J., Conture, E. G., & Edwards, M. L. (1993). Simultaneously treating stuttering and disordered phonology in children: Experimental treatment, pre-

liminary findings. *American Journal of Speech-Language Pathology, 2*(3), 72–81.

Louko, L. J., Conture, E. G., & Edwards, M. L. (1999). Treating children who exhibit co-occurring stuttering and disordered phonology. In R. F. Curlee (Ed.), *Stuttering and related disorders of fluency* (2nd ed., pp. 124–138). New York: Thieme Medical Publishers.

Louko, L. J., Edwards, M. L., & Conture, E. G. (1990). Phonological characteristics of young stutterers and their normally fluent peers: Preliminary observations. *Journal of Fluency Disorders, 15,* 191–210.

Luchsinger, R., & Arnold, G. (1965). *Voice-speech-language, clinical communicology: Its physiology and pathology.* Belmont, CA: Wadsworth.

Ludlow, C. L. (2000). Stuttering: Dysfunction in a complex and dynamic system. *Brain, 123,* 1983–1984.

Ludlow, C. L., & Loucks, T. (2003). Stuttering: A dynamic motor control disorder. *Journal of Fluency Disorders, 28,* 273–296.

Luper, H. L., & Mulder, R. L. (1964). *Stuttering: Therapy for children.* Englewood Cliffs, NJ: Prentice Hall.

Luterman, D. M. (1991). *Counseling the communicatively disordered and their families* (2nd ed.). Austin, TX: Pro-Ed.

MacKay, D. G. (1969). Effects of ambiguity on stuttering: Towards a theory of speech production at the semantic level. *Kybernetik, 5,* 195–208.

MacKay, D. G. (1982). The problems of flexibility, fluency, and speed-accuracy trade-off in skilled behavior. *Psychological Review, 89,* 483–506.

MacKay, D. G., & MacDonald, M. C. (1984). Stuttering as a sequencing and timing disorder. In R. F. Curlee and W. H. Perkins (Eds.), *Nature and treatment of stuttering: New directions* (pp. 261–282). Needham Heights, MA: Allyn & Bacon.

Mallard, A. R. (1991). Using families to help the school-age stutterer—a case study. In L. Rustin (Ed.), *Parents, families, and the stuttering child* (pp. 72–101). San Diego, CA: Singular.

Manning, W. H. (1996). *Clinical decision making in the diagnosis and treatment of fluency disorders.* Albany, NY: Delmar.

Manning, W. H. (1999). *Creating your own map for change.* Paper presented at the 2nd International Stuttering Awareness Day Online Conference. Retrieved

October 13, 1999, from www.mankato.msus.edu/dept/comdis/isad2/papers/manning2.html.

Manning, W. H. (2003). Counseling adolescents who stutter. *Perspectives on Fluency and Fluency Disorders, 13,* 11-14.

Manning, W. (2004). "How can you understand? You don't stutter!" *Contemporary Issues in Communication Science and Disorders, 31,* 58-68.

Manning, W. H., Burlison, A. E., & Thaxton, D. (1999). Listener response to stuttering modification techniques. *Journal of Fluency Disorders, 24*(4), 267-280.

Martin, N., Weisberg, R. W., & Saffran, E. M. (1989). Variables influencing the occurrence of naming errors: Implications for models of lexical retrieval. *Journal of Memory and Language, 28,* 462-485.

Martin, R. R., & Haroldson, S. K. (1967). The relationship between anticipation and consistency of stuttered words. *Journal of Speech and Hearing Research, 10,* 323-327.

Martin R., & Haroldson, S. K. (1979). Effects of five experimental treatments on stuttering. *Journal of Speech and Hearing Research, 22,* 132-146.

Martin R. R., & Haroldson, S. K. (1982). Contingent self-stimulation for stuttering. *Journal of Speech and Hearing Disorders, 47,* 407-413.

Mayer, J. (1999). *Success is a journey.* New York: McGraw-Hull.

McClean, M. D., Kroll, R. M., & Loftus, N. S. (1991). Correlation of sutttering severity and kinematics of lip closure. In H. F. M. Peters, W. Hulstijn, & C. W. Starkweather (Eds.), *Speech motor control and stuttering* (pp. 117-122). New York: Excerptamedica.

McClean, M. D., Tasko, S. M., & Runyan, C. M. (2004). Orofacial movements associated with fluent speech in persons who stutter. *Journal of Speech and Hearing Research, 47,* 294-303.

McCombs, B. L. (1991). Overview: Where have we been and where are we going in understanding human motivation? *Journal of Experimental Education, 60*(1), 5-14.

McKay, M., Rogers, P. D., & McKay, J. (1989). *When anger hurts: Quieting the storm within.* Oakland, CA: New Harbinger.

McKnight, R. C., & Cullinan, W. L. (1987). Subgroups of stuttering children: Speech and voice reaction times, segmental durations, and naming latencies. *Journal of Fluency Disorders, 12,* 217-233.

Meece, J. L (1991). The classroom context and students' motivational goals. In M. Maehr and P. Pintrich (Eds.), *Advances in motivation and achievement* (pp. 261-286). Greenwich, CT: JAI Press.

Meier, S. T., & Davis, S. R. (2001). *The elements of counseling* (4th ed.). Belmont, CA: Brooks/Cole Thomas Learning.

Melnick, K. S., & Conture, E. G. (2000). Relationship of length and grammatical complexity to the systematic and nonsystematic speech errors and stuttering of children who stutter. *Journal of Fluency Disorders, 25,* 21-46.

Melnick, K. S., Conture, E. G., & Ohde, R. N. (2003). Phonological priming in picture naming of young children who stutter. *Journal of Speech, Language, and Hearing Research, 46,* 1428-1443.

Menzies, R. G., Onslow, M., & Packman, A. (1999). Anxiety and stuttering: Exploring a complex relationship. *American Journal of Speech-Language Pathology, 8,* 3-10.

Meyers, S. (1991). Interactions with pre-operational preschool stutterers: How will this influence therapy? In L. Rustin (Ed.), *Parents, families, and the stuttering child.* San Diego, CA: Singular.

Meyers, S., & Freeman, F. (1985a). Interruptions as a variable in stuttering and disfluency. *Journal of Speech and Hearing Research, 28,* 428-435.

Meyers, S., & Freeman, F. (1985b). Mother and child speech rate as a variable in stuttering and disfluency. *Journal of Speech and Hearing Research, 28,* 436-444.

Meyers, S., & Woodford, L. (1992). *The fluency development system for young children.* Buffalo, NY: United Educational Services.

Middleton-Moz, J. (1990). *Shame and guilt: The masters of disguise.* Deerfield Beach, FL: Health Communications.

Miles, S., & Bernstein Ratner, N. B. (2001). Parental language input to children at stuttering onset. *Journal of Speech, Language, and Hearing Research, 44,* 1116-1130.

Molt, L. (1998). Attacking the iceberg of stuttering: Icepicks, axes, and sunshine. In S. B. Hood (Ed.), *Advice to those who stutter* (2nd ed., pp. 111–116). Memphis, TN: Stuttering Foundation of America.

Montgomery, C. O. (2003). Personal e-mail communication (September 13, 2003).

Montgomery, J. K. (1994). Service delivery issues for schools. In C. Fratalli & R. Lubinski (Eds.), *Professional Issues in Speech Language Pathology & Audiology.* San Diego, CA: Singular.

Mordechai, D. (1979). An investigation of the communicative styles of mothers and fathers of stuttering versus nonstuttering preschool children. *Dissertation Abstracts International, 40,* 4759-B.

Mower, O. H. (1967). Stuttering as simultaneous admission and denial: Or, What is the stutterer "saying"? *Journal of Communication Disorders 1,* 67-71.

Murphy, W. (1998). Recovery journal. In S. B. Hood (Ed.), *Advice to those who stutter* (2nd ed., pp. 101-106). Memphis, TN: Stuttering Foundation of America.

Murphy, W. (1999). A preliminary look at shame, guilt, and stuttering. In N. Bernstein Ratner & E. C. Healey (Eds.), *Stuttering research and practice: Bridging the gap.* Mahwah, NJ: Lawrence Earlbaum Associates.

Murphy, W. (2002, June). *Working with school-age children who stutter: Modifying negative feelings and attitudes and increasing self-esteem.* Paper presented at the National Stuttering Association Conference, Anaheim, CA.

Murphy, W. P., & Quesal, R. W. (2002). Strategies for addressing bullying with the school-age child who stutters. *Seminars in Speech and Language, 23,* 205-211.

Murphy, W. P., & Yaruss, J. S. (1999). Adolescents and stuttering therapy. In A. Bradberry and N. Reardon (Eds.), *Our voices: Inspirational insights from young people who stutter.* Anaheim Hills, CA: National Stuttering Association.

Myers, D. G. (1992). *Psychology* (3rd ed.). New York: Worth.

Myers, F. L. (1992). Cluttering: A synergistic framework. In F. L. Meyers & K. O. St. Louis (Eds.), *Cluttering: A clinical perspective* (pp. 71-84). Kibworth, Great Britain: Far Communications.

Myers, F. L., & Bradley, C. L. (1992). Clinical management of cluttering from a syngeristic framework. In F. L. Meyers & K. O. St. Louis (Eds.), *Cluttering: A clinical perspective* (pp. 85-105). Kibworth, Great Britain: Far Communications.

Myers, F. L., St. Louis, K. O., Bakker, K., Raphael, L. J., Wiig, E. H., Katz, J., Daly, D. A., & Kent, R. D. (2002, November). *Putting cluttering on the map.* Paper presented at the American Speech-Language-Hearing Association Convention, Atlanta, GA.

Nathanson, D. L. (1992). *Shame and pride: Affect, sex, and the birth of the self.* New York: W. W. Norton.

National Stuttering Association. (2001). *Transitional years: Top 10 "to do" list for teens.* Unpublished brochure.

Natke, U., Grosser, J., Sandrieser, P., & Kalveram, K. T. (2002). The duration component of the stress effect in stuttering. *Journal of Fluency Disorders, 27,* 305-318.

Neelley, J. N. (1961). A study of the speech behavior of stutterers and nonstutterers under normal and delayed auditory feedback. *Journal of Speech and Hearing Research, 10,* 63-82.

Neidecker, E. A., & Blosser, J. L. (1993). *School programs in speech-language: Organization and management.* Englewood Cliffs, NJ: Prentice Hall.

Neilson, M. D. (1999). Cognitive-behavioral treatment of adults who stutter: The process and the art. In R. F. Curlee (Ed.), *Stuttering and related disorders of fluency* (2nd ed., pp. 181-199). New York: Thieme Medical Publishers.

Neilson, M. D., & Neilson, P. D. (1991). Adaptive model theory of speech motor control and stuttering. In H. F. M. Peters, W. Hulstijn, & C. W. Starkweather (Eds.), *Speech motor control and stuttering* (pp. 149-156). New York: Excerptamedica.

Neumann, K., Eulelr, H. A., Von Gudenberg, A. W., Giraud, A., Lanfermann, H., Gall, V., & Preibisch, C. (2003). The nature and treatment of stuttering as revealed by fMRI: A within- and between-group comparison. *Journal of Fluency Disorders, 28,* 381-410.

Newman, L., & Smit, A. (1989). Some effects of variations in response time latency on speech rate, interruptions, and fluency in child's speech. *Journal of Speech and Hearing Research, 32,* 635-644.

Nippold, M. A. (1990). Concomitant speech and language disorders in stuttering children: A critique of the literature. *Journal of Speech and Hearing Disorders, 55,* 51-60.

Nippold, M. A. (2002). Stuttering and phonology: Is there an interaction? *American Journal of Speech-Language Pathology, 11,* 99-110.

Nooteboom, S. G. (1980). Speaking and unspeaking: Detection and correction of phonological and lexical errors in spontaneous speech. In V. A. Fromkin (Ed.), *Errors in linguistic performance: Slips of the tongue, ear, pen, and hand* (pp. 87-96). New York: Academic Press.

Okasha, A., Bishry, Z., Kamel, M., & Hassen, A. H. (1974). Psychosocial study of stammering in Egyptian children. *British Journal of Psychiatry, 124,* 531-533.

Okun, B. F. (1997). *Effective helping: Interviewing and counseling techniques* (5th ed.). Pacific Grove, CA: Brooks/Cole.

Olson, E. D., & Bohlman, P. (2002). IDEA '97 and children who stutter: Evaluation and intervention that lead to successful, productive lives. *Seminars in Speech and Language, 23,* 159-164.

Onslow, M. (1992). Identification of early stuttering: Issues and suggested strategies. *American Journal of Speech-Language Pathology: A Journal of Clinical Practice, 1*(4), 21-27.

Onslow, M. (1996). *Behavioral management of stuttering.* San Diego, CA: Singular.

Onslow, M. (2003, August). *The bittersweet tale of empiricism in stuttering treatment research.* Paper presented at the 4th World Congress on Fluency Disorders, Montreal, Canada.

Onslow, M., & Packman, A. (1997). Designing and implementing a strategy to control stuttered speech in adults. In R. F. Curlee & G. M. Siegel (Eds.), *Nature and treatment of stuttering: New directions* (2nd. ed., pp. 356-376). Boston: Allyn & Bacon.

Onslow, M., & Packman, A. (1999). The Lidcombe program of early stuttering intervention. In N. B. Ratner & E. C. Healey (Eds.), *Stuttering research and practice: Bridging the gap* (pp. 193-210). Mahwah, NJ: Lawrence Erlbaum Associates.

Onslow, M., Packman, A., & Harrison, E. (2003). *The Lidcombe program of early stuttering intervention: A clinician's guide.* Austin, TX: Pro-Ed.

Oyler, M. E., & Chmela, K. A. (2003). The role of the stuttering specialists in the school setting. *Seminars in Speech and Language, 24,* 47-52.

Oyler, M. E., & Ramig, P. R. (1995, December). *Vulnerability in stuttering children.* Paper presented at the Annual Convention of the American Speech-Language-Hearing Association, Orlando, FL.

Packman, A., & Onslow, M. (1998). What is the take-home message from Curlee and Yairi? *American Journal of Speech-Language Pathology, 7,* 5-9.

Packman, A., Onslow, M., & Menzies, R. (2000). Novel speech patterns and the treatment of stuttering. *Disability Rehabilitation, 22,* 65-79. Abstract retrieved July 24, 2004, from www.ncbi .nlm.nih.gov/ PubMed.

Paden, E. P., Ambrose, N. G., & Yairi, E. (2002). Phonological progress during the first 2 years of stuttering. *Journal of Speech, Language, and Hearing Research, 45,* 256-267.

Paden, E. P., & Yairi, E. (1996). Phonological characteristics of children whose stuttering persisted or recovered. *Journal of Speech, Language, and Hearing Research, 39,* 981-990.

Paden, E. P., Yairi, E., & Ambrose, N. G. (1999). Early childhood stuttering: II. Initial status of phonological abilities. *Journal of Speech, Language, and Hearing Research, 42,* 1113-1124.

Patterson, J., & Pring, T. (1991). Listeners' attitudes to stuttering speakers: No evidence for a gender difference. *Journal of Fluency Disorders, 16,* 201-206.

Peins, M. (1961). Consistency effect in stuttering expectancy. *Journal of Speech and Hearing Research, 4,* 397-398.

Pellowski, M. W., & Conture, E. G. (2002). Characteristics of speech disfluency and stuttering behaviors in 3- and 4-year-old children. *Journal of Speech, Language, and Hearing Research, 45,* 20-34.

Perkins, W. H. (1984). Techniques for establishing fluency. In W. H. Perkins (Ed.), *Stuttering disorders* (pp. 173-181). New York: Thieme-Stratton.

Perkins, W. H. (1986). Postscript discoordination of phonation with articulation and respiration. In G. H. Shames & H. Rubin (Eds.), *Stuttering: Then and now* (pp. 82-92). Columbus: Charles E. Merrill.

Perkins, W. H., & Curlee, R. F. (1969). Clinical impressions of portable masking unit effects in stuttering. *Journal of Speech and Hearing Disorders, 34,* 360-362.

Perkins, W. H., Kent, R. D., & Curlee, R. F. (1991). A theory of neuropsycholinguistic function in stuttering. *Journal of Speech and Hearing Research, 34,* 734-752.

Perkins, W. H., Rudas, J., Johnson, L., & Bell, J. (1976). Stuttering: Discoordination of phonation with articulation and respiration. *Journal of Speech and Hearing Research, 19,* 509–522.

Peters, H. F., & Hulstijn, W. (1984). Stuttering and anxiety: The difference between stutterers and nonstutterers in verbal apprehension and physiologic arousal during the anticipation of speech and non-speech tasks. *Journal of Fluency Disorders, 9,* 67–84.

Peters, H. F., & Hulstijn, W. (1987). Programming and initiation of speech utterances in stuttering. In H. F. M. Peters and W. Hulstijn (Eds.), *Speech motor dynamics in stuttering.* Vienna: Springer-Verlag.

Peters, H. F. M., Hulstijn, W., & Starkweather, C. W. (1989). Acoustic and physiological reaction times of stutterers and nonstutterers. *Journal of Speech and Hearing Research, 32,* 668–680.

Peters, H. F. M., & Starkweather, C. W. (1989). Development of stuttering throughout life. *Journal of Fluency Disorders, 14,* 303–321.

Peters, T. J., & Guitar, B. (1991). *Stuttering: An integrated approach to its nature and treatment.* Baltimore: Williams and Wilkins.

Pill, J. (2003, August). *Self-help and the international scene.* Paper presented at the 4th World Congress on Fluency Disorders, Montreal, Canada.

Pindzola, R. (1987). *Stuttering intervention program.* Austin, TX: Pro-Ed.

Platt, J. M., & Olson, J. L. (1997). *Teaching adolescents with mild disabilities.* Pacific Grove, CA: Brooks/Cole.

Pool, K. D., Devous, M. D., Sr., Freeman, F. J., Watson, B. C., & Finitzo, T. (1991). Regional cerebral blood flow in developmental stutterers. *Archives of Neurology, 48,* 509–512.

Poplin, M., & Weeres, J. (1993). Listening at the learner's level. *The Executive Educator, 15,* 14–19.

Postma, A. (1991). *Stuttering and self-correction: On the role of linguistic repair processes in disfluencies of normal speakers and stutterers.* Unpublished doctoral dissertation. Nijmegen Institute for Cognition and Information, Nijmegen, The Netherlands.

Postma, A., & Kolk, H. (1990). Speech errors, disfluencies, and self-repairs of stutterers in two accuracy conditions. *Journal of Fluency Disorders, 15,* 291–303.

Postma, A., & Kolk, H. (1992a). The effects of noise masking and required accuracy on speech errors, disfluencies, and self-repairs. *Journal of Speech and Hearing Research, 35,* 537–544.

Postma, A., & Kolk, H. (1992b). Error monitoring in people who stutter: Evidence against auditory feedback defect theories. *Journal of Speech and Hearing Research, 35,* 1024–1032.

Postma, A., & Kolk, H. (1993). The covert repair hypothesis: Prearticulatory repair processes in normal and stuttered disfluencies. *Journal of Speech and Hearing Research, 36,* 472–487.

Postma, A., Kolk, H., & Povel D. (1991). Disfluencies as resulting from covert self-repairs applied to internal speech errors. In H. F. M. Peters, W. Hulstijn, & C. W. Starkweather (Eds.), *Speech motor control and stuttering* (pp. 141–148). New York: Elsevier Science.

Potter-Efron, R., & Potter-Efron, P. (1989). *Letting go of shame: Understanding how shame affects your life.* San Francisco: Harper & Row.

Poulos, M. G., & Webster, W. G. (1991). Family history as a basis for subgrouping people who stutter. *Journal of Speech, Language, and Hearing Research, 34,* 5–10.

Power-deFur, L. A., & Orelove, F. P. (1997). *Inclusive education: Practical implementation of the least restrictive environment.* Gaithersburg, MD: Aspen.

Preus, A. (1992). Cluttering and stuttering: Related, different or antagonistic disorders. In F. L. Meyers & K. O. St. Louis (Eds.), *Cluttering: A clinical perspective* (pp. 55–70). Kibworth, Great Britain: Far Communications.

Prins, D. (1984). Treatment of adults: Managing stuttering. In R. F. Curlee & W. H. Perkins (Eds.), *Nature and treatment of stuttering: New directions* (pp. 397–424). Needham Heights, MA: Allyn & Bacon.

Prins, D. (1991). Theories of stuttering as event and disorder: Implications for speech production processes. In H. F. M. Peters, W. Hulstijn, & C. W. Starkweather (Eds.), *Speech motor control and stuttering* (pp. 571–580). New York: Excerptamedica.

Prins, D. (1997). Modifying stuttering—the stutterer's reactive behavior: Perspectives on past, present, and future. In R. F. Curlee & G. M. Siegel (Eds.), *Nature and treatment of stuttering: New directions* (2nd ed., pp. 335–355). Boston: Allyn & Bacon.

Prins, D., Hubbard, C. P., & Krause, M. (1991). Syllabic stress and the occurrence of stuttering. *Journal of Speech and Hearing Research, 34,* 1011–1016.

Prosek, R. A., Walden, B. E., Montgomery, A. A., & Schwartz, D. M. (1979). Some correlates of stuttering severity judgments. *Journal of Fluency Disorders, 4,* 212-222.

Quesal, R. W. (1997a). A perspective on attitudes in stuttering. Retrieved May 26, 2002, from Bob Quesal Talks About Stuttering Web site: www.wiu.edu/users/mfrwg.atts.html.

Quesal, R. W. (1997b). Preliminary preview/review of outcome statements from the 1997 SID#4 Leadership Conference. Retrieved on December 1, 1997, from SID4@vm.temple.edu.

Quesal, R. W. (1998). Knowledge, understanding, and acceptance. In S. B. Hood (Ed.), *Advice to those who stutter* (2nd ed., pp. 129-134). Memphis, TN: Stuttering Foundation of America.

Quesal, R. (2002). Dean Williams' approach to stuttering therapy: "Forward Moving Speech." Retrieved on March 18, 2002, from www.mnsu.edu/comdis/kuster/TherapyWWW/Williams.html.

Quesal, R. W., & Shank, K. H. (1978). Stutterers and others: A comparison of communication attitudes. *Journal of Fluency Disorders, 3,* 247-252.

Quesal, R. W., & Yaruss, J. S. (2000). Historical perspectives on stuttering treatment: Dean Williams. *Contemporary Issues in Communication Science and Disorders, 27,* 178-187.

Ramig, P. R. (1993a). High reported spontaneous stuttering recovery rates: Fact or fiction? *Language, Speech, and Hearing Services in Schools, 24,* 156-160.

Ramig, P. R. (1993b). Parent-clinician-child partnership in the therapeutic process of the preschool- and elementary-aged child who stutters. *Seminars in Speech and Language, 14,* 226-237.

Ramig, P. R. (1993c). The impact of self-help groups on persons who stutter: A call for research. *Journal of Fluency Disorders, 18,* 351-361.

Ramig, P. R. (1998). Don't ever give up! In S. B. Hood (Ed.), *Advice to those who stutter* (2nd ed., pp. 45-50). Memphis, TN: Stuttering Foundation of America.

Ramig, P. R., & Adams, M. R. (1980). Rate reduction strategies used by stutterers and nonstutterers during high- and low-pitched speech. *Journal of Fluency Disorders, 5,* 27-41.

Ramig, P. R., & Adams, M. R. (1981). Vocal changes in stutterers and nonstutterers during high- and low-pitched speech. *Journal of Fluency Disorders, 6,* 15-33.

Ramig, P. R., & Bennett, E. M. (1995). Working with 7-12 year old children who stutter: Ideas for intervention in the public schools. *Language, Speech, and Hearing Services in Schools, 26,* 138-150.

Ramig, P. R., & Bennett, E. M. (1997a). Clinical management of children: Direct management strategies. In R. F. Curlee & G. M. Siegel (Eds.), *Nature and treatment of stuttering: New directions* (2nd ed., pp. 292-312). Needham Heights, MA: Allyn & Bacon.

Ramig, P. R., & Bennett, E. M. (1997b). Considerations for conducting group intervention with adults who stutter. *Seminars in Speech and Language, 18,* 343-356.

Ramig, P. R., & Wallace, M. L. (1987). Indirect and combined direct-indirect therapy in a dysfluent child. *Journal of Fluency Disorders, 12,* 41-49.

Ratner, N. B. (1993). Parents, children, and stuttering. *Seminars in Speech and Language, 14,* 238-250.

Rather, N. (2004). Research Update 2004: Translating the scientific literature. Presentation at the National Stuttering Association Annual Conference, Baltimore, MD, June.

Reardon, N. A., & Reeves, L. (2002). Stuttering therapy in partnership with support groups: The best of both worlds. *Seminars in Speech and Language, 23,* 213-218.

Regan, J. (1978). Involuntary automatic processing in color-naming tasks. *Perception and Psychophysics, 24,* 130-136.

Rentschler G. (2003 June). *Ten tips for better stuttering.* Paper presented at the National Stuttering Association Conference, Nashville, TN.

Rice, F. P. (1999). *The adolescent: Development, relationships, and culture.* Boston: Allyn & Bacon.

Ridge, H., & Ray, B. (1991). *Fluency at your fingertips: Pragmatic and thematic therapy materials.* Tucson, AZ: Communication Skill Builders.

Riley, G. D. (1981). *The stuttering prediction instrument.* Austin, TX: ProEd.

Riley, G. D. (1994). *Stuttering severity instrument for children and adults* (3rd ed.). Austin, TX: Pro-Ed.

Riley, G. D., & Riley, J. (1979). A component model for diagnosing and treating children who stutter. *Journal of Fluency Disorders, 4,* 279-293.

Riley, G., & Riley, J. (1983). Evaluation as a basis for intervention. In D. Prins & R. J. Ingham (Eds.), *Treatment of stuttering in early childhood: Methods and issues.* San Diego, CA: College Hill Press.

Riley, G. D., & Riley, J. (1984). A component model for treating stuttering in children. In M. Peins (Ed.), *Contemporary approaches in stuttering therapy* (pp. 123-172). Boston: Little, Brown.

Riley, G. D., & Riley, J. (1986). Oral motor discoordination among children who stutter. *Journal of Fluency Disorders, 11,* 334-335.

Riley, G., & Riley, J. (1991). Treatment implications of oral motor discoordination. In H. F. M. Peters, W. Hulstijn, & C. W. Starkweather (Eds.), *Speech motor control and stuttering* (pp. 471-478). New York: Excerptamedica.

Riley, G., & Riley, J. (2000). A revised component model for diagnosing and treating children who stutter. *Contemporary Issues in Communication Science and Disorders, 27,* 188-199.

Riley, J. (2002). Counseling: An approach for speech-language pathologists. *Contemporary Issues in Communication Science and Disorders, 29,* 6-16.

Rogers, C. R. (1961). *On becoming a person.* Boston: Houghton Mifflin.

Rogers, C. R. (1986). The attitude and orientation of the counselor. In G. H. Shames & H. Rubin (Eds.), *Stuttering: Then and now* (pp. 295-315). Columbus: Charles E. Merrill.

Rollin, W. J. (1987). *The psychology of communication disorders in individuals and their families.* Englewood Cliffs, NJ: Prentice Hall.

Roth, F. P., & Worthington, C. K. (2001). *Treatment resource manual for speech-language pathology* (2nd ed.). San Diego, CA: Singular.

Runyan, C. M., & Runyan, S. E. (1986). Fluency rules therapy program for young children in the public schools. *Language Speech and Hearing Services in Schools, 17,* 276-284.

Runyan, C. M., & Runyan, S. E. (1993). Therapy for school-age stutterers: An update on the fluency rules program. In R. F. Curlee (Ed.), *Stuttering and related*

disorders of fluency (pp. 101-114). New York: Thieme Medical Publishers.

Runyan, C. M., & Runyan, S. E. (1999). Therapy for school-age stutterers: An update on the fluency rules program. In R. F. Curlee (Ed.), *Stuttering and related disorders of fluency* (2nd ed., pp. 110-123). New York: Thieme Medical Publishers.

Ruscello, D. M., Lass, N. J., Schmitt, J. F., & Pannbacker, M. D. (1994). Special educators' perceptions of stutterers. *Journal of Fluency Disorders, 19,* 125-132.

Ruscello, D. M., St. Louis, K. O., & Mason, N. (1991). School-aged children with phonologic disorders: Coexistence with other speech/language disorders. *Journal of Speech and Hearing Research, 34,* 236-242.

Rustin, L., Botterill, W., & Kelman, E. (1996). *Family interaction: Assessment and therapy for young dysfluent children.* San Diego, CA: Singular.

Rustin, L., & Cook, F. (1995). Parental involvement in the treatment of stuttering. *Language, Speech, and Hearing Services in Schools, 26,* 127-137.

Rustin, L., Cook, F., & Spence, R. (1995). *The management of stuttering in adolescence: A communication skills approach.* London: Whurr.

Rustin, L., & Purser, H. (1991). Child development, families, and the problem of stuttering. In L. Rustin (Ed.), *Parents, families, and the stuttering child* (pp. 1-24). San Diego, CA: Singular.

Ryan, B. P. (1971). Operant procedures applied to stuttering therapy for children. *Journal of Speech and Hearing Disorders, 36,* 264-280.

Ryan, B. P. (1974). *Programmed therapy of stuttering in children and adults.* Springfield, IL: Charles C. Thomas.

Ryan, B. P. (1984). Treatment of stuttering in school children. In W. H. Perkins (Ed.), *Stuttering disorders* (pp. 95-106). New York: Thieme Medical Publishers.

Ryan, B. P. (1986). Operant therapy for children. In G. H. Shames & H. Rubin (Eds.), *Stuttering: Then and now.* Columbus: Charles E. Merrill.

Ryan, B. P. (1992). Articulation, language, rate and fluency characteristics of stuttering and nonstuttering preschool children. *Journal of Speech and Hearing Research, 35,* 333-342.

Ryan, B. P., & Van Kirk Ryan, B. (1995). Programmed stuttering treatment for children: Comparison of two establishment programs through transfer, maintenance, and follow-up. *Journal of Speech and Hearing Research, 38,* 61–75.

Ryan, B. P., & Van Kirk Ryan, B. (2002, May). *The public schools are still the best place to offer treatment for stuttering.* Paper presented at the American Speech Language Hearing Association, Special Interest Division #4 Leadership Conference, Albuquerque, NM.

Ryan, R. M., Connell, J. P., & Grolnick, W. S. (1992). When achievement is not instrinsically motivated: A theory of internalization and self-regulation in school. In A. K. Boggiano & T. S. Pittman (Eds.), *Achievement and motivation: A social-developmental perspective* (pp. 167–188). New York: Cambridge University Press.

Sabournie, E. J., & de Bettencourt, L. U. (1997). *Teaching students with mild disabilities at the secondary level.* Columbus: Prentice Hall.

Saitta, E., & Madsen, B. (2004, June). *Advertising your stuttering.* Paper presented at the National Stuttering Association Conference, Baltimore, MD.

Santrock, J. W. (1987). *Adolescence: An introduction* (3rd ed.). Dubuque, IA: Wm. C. Brown.

Satir, V. (1976). *Making contact.* Millbrae, CA: Celestial Arts.

Scheuerle, J. (1992). *Counseling in speech-language pathology and audiology.* New York: Macmillian.

Schneider, C. D. (1977). *Shame, exposure, and privacy.* New York: W. W. Norton.

Schum, R. L. (1986). *Counseling in speech and hearing practice* (Clinical Series No. 9). Rockville, MD: National Student Speech Language Hearing Association.

Schwartz, H. D. (1993). Adolescents who stutter. *Journal of Fluency Disorders, 18,* 289–302.

Schwartz, H. D., & Conture, E. G. (1988). Subgrouping young stutterers: Preliminary behavioral observations. *Journal of Speech and Hearing Research, 31,* 62–71.

Sermas, C. R., & Cox, M. D. (1982). The stutterer and stuttering: Personality correlates. *Journal of Fluency Disorders, 7,* 141–158.

Shames, G. H., & Florance, C L. (1980). Stuttering treatment: Issues in transfer and maintenance.

Seminars in Speech, Language and Hearing, 1, 375–388.

Shames, G. H. & Florance, C. L. (1980). *Stutter free speech: A goal for therapy.* Columbus, OH: Charles E. Merrill.

Shames, G. H., & Florance, C. L. (1986). Stutter-free speech: A goal for therapy. In G. H. Shames & H. Rubin (Eds.), *Stuttering: Then and now* (pp. 447–453). Columbus: Charles E. Merrill.

Shane, P. (1980). Shame and learning. *American Journal of the Orthopsychiatric Association, 50,* 348–355.

Shapiro, A. I. (1980). An electromyographic analysis of fluent and dysfluent utterances of several types of stutterers. *Journal of Fluency Disorders, 5,* 203–231.

Shapiro, D. A. (1999). *Stuttering intervention: A collaborative journey to fluency freedom.* Austin, TX: Pro-Ed.

Shattuck-Hufnagel, S. (1979). Speech errors as evidence for a serial order mechanism in sentence production. In W. E. Cooper & E. C. T. Walker (Eds.), *Sentence processing: Psycholinguistic studies presented to Merrill Garrett.* Hillsdale, NJ: Lawrence Erlbaum Associates.

Shattuck-Hufnagel, S. (1992). The role of word structure in segmental serial ordering. *Cognition, 42,* 213–259.

Sheehan, J. G. (1953). Theory and treatment of stuttering as an approach-avoidance conflict. *Journal of Psychology, 36,* 27–49.

Sheehan, J. G. (1958). Conflict theory of stuttering. In J. Eisenson (Ed.), *Stuttering: A symposium* (pp. 121–166). New York: Harper & Brothers.

Sheehan, J. G. (1968). Stuttering as a self-role conflict. In H. H. Gregory (Ed.), *Learning theory and stuttering therapy* (pp. 72–83). Evanston, IL: Northwestern University Press.

Sheehan, J. G. (1969). The role of role in stuttering. In B. B. Gray & G. England (Eds.), *Stuttering and the conditioning therapy* (pp. 199–210). Monterey, CA: The Monterey Institute for Speech and Hearing.

Sheehan, J. G. (1984). Problems in the evaluation of progress and outcome. In W. Perkins (Ed.), *Current therapy of communication disorders: Stuttering disorders* (pp. 223–239). New York: Thieme-Stratton.

Sheehan, J. G. (1997). Principles of therapy. In *Counseling stutterers* (pp. 69–79). Memphis, TN: Stuttering Foundation of America.

Sheehan, J. G., & Sheehan, V. M. (1984). Avoidance-reduction therapy: A response suppression hypothesis. In W. Perkins (Ed.), *Stuttering disorders* (pp. 147–151). New York: Thieme-Stratton.

Sheehan, V. M. (1986). Approach-avoidance and anxiety reduction. In G. H. Shames & H. Rubin (Eds.), *Stuttering: Then and now* (pp. 201–212). Columbus: Charles E. Merrill.

Sherman, D. (1952). Clinical and experimental use of the Iowa Scale of Severity of Stuttering. *Journal of Speech and Hearing Disorders, 17,* 316–320.

Shields, L. W., & Kuster, J. M. (2003). Finding good resources for treating school-age children. *Seminars in Speech and Language, 24,* 7–12.

Shine, R. E. (1980). Direct management of the beginning stutterer. *Seminars in Speech, Language and Hearing, 1,* 339–350.

Shine, R. E. (1984). Assessment and fluency training with the young stutterer. In M. Peins (Ed.), *Contemporary approaches in stuttering therapy* (pp. 173–216). Boston: Little, Brown.

Shine, R. E., Johnson, P. J., Demarco, S., Hough, M., & O'Brien, K. (1991, November). *Word-finding ability in preschool stuttering and nonstuttering children.* Paper presented at the Annual Convention of the American Speech-Language-Hearing Association, Atlanta, GA.

Shipley, K. G. (1997). *Interviewing and counseling in communicative disorders* (2nd ed.). New York: Macmillan.

Sidoli, M. (1988). Shame and the shadow. *Journal of Analytical Psychology, 33,* 127–142.

Siegel, G. M. (2000). Demands and capacities or demands and performance? *Journal of Fluency Disorders, 25,* 321–327.

Silverman, F. H. (1970). Concern of elementary-school stutterers about their stuttering. *Journal of Speech and Hearing Disorders, 35,* 361–363.

Silverman, F. H. (1996). *Stuttering and other fluency disorders* (2nd ed.). Needham Heights, MA: Allyn & Bacon.

Sisskin, V. (2002). Therapy planning for school-age children who stutter. *Seminars in Speech and Language, 23,* 173–179.

Sisskin, V., & Weadon, M. (2004, June). *Peer mentoring in avoidance reduction therapy for stuttering, Part I & II.* Paper presented at the National Stuttering Association Conference, Baltimore, MD.

Smith, A. (1990). Factors in the etiology of stuttering. American Speech-Language-Hearing Association Reports. *Research Needs in Stuttering: Roadblocks and Future Directions, 18,* 39–47.

Smith, A. (1999). Stuttering: A unified approach to a multifactorial, dynamic disorder. In N. B. Ratner & E. C. Healey (Eds.), *Stuttering research and practice: Bridging the gap* (pp. 27–44). Mahwah, NJ: Lawrence Erlbaum Associates.

Smith, A., & Kelly, E. (1997). Stuttering: A dynamic, multifactorial model. In R. F. Curlee & G. M. Siegel (Eds.), *Nature and treatment of stuttering: New directions* (2nd ed., pp. 204–217). Boston: Allyn & Bacon.

Smith, A., Denny, M., & Wood, J. (1991). Instability in speech muscle systems in stuttering. In H. F. M. Peters, W. Hulstijn, & C. W. Starkweather (Eds.), *Speech motor control and stuttering* (pp. 231–242). New York: Excerptamedica.

Sommers, R. K., & Caruso, A. J. (1995). Inservice training in speech-language pathology: Are we meeting the needs for fluency training? *American Journal of Speech-Language Pathology, 4,* 22–28.

Stager, S. V., & Ludlow, C. L. (1991). Do fluency-evoking conditions elicit continuous voicing in normal speakers? In H. F. M. Peters, W. Hulstijn, & C. W. Starkweather (Eds.), *Speech motor control and stuttering* (pp. 355–364). New York: Excerptamedica.

Stager, S. V., & Ludlow, C. L. (1993). Speech production changes under fluency-evoking conditions in nonstuttering speakers. *Journal of Speech and Hearing Research, 36,* 245–253.

Stager, S. V., & Ludlow, C. L. (1998). The effects of fluency-evoking conditions on voicing onset types in persons who do and do not stutter. *Journal of Communication Disorders, 31,* 33–51. Abstract retrieved July 24, 2004, from www.ncbi.nlm.nih.gov/PubMed.

Starkweather, C. W. (1987). *Fluency and stuttering.* Englewood Cliffs, NJ: Prentice Hall.

Starkweather, C. W. (1991). The language-motor interface in stuttering children. In H. F. M. Peters, W. Hulstijn, & C. W. Starkweather (Eds.), *Speech motor control and stuttering* (pp. 385–392). New York: Excerptamedica.

Starkweather, C. W. (1997a). Learning and its role in stuttering development. In R. F. Curlee & G. M. Siegel (Eds.), *Nature and treatment of stuttering: New directions* (2nd ed., pp. 79–96). Boston: Allyn & Bacon.

Starkweather, C.W. (1997b). Therapy for younger children. In R. F. Curlee & G. M. Siegel (Eds.), *Nature and treatment of stuttering: New directions* (2nd ed., pp. 257–279). Boston: Allyn & Bacon.

Starkweather, C.W. (1998). *Relapse: A misnomer?* Paper presented at the 1st International Stuttering Awareness Day Online Conference. Retrieved October 13, 1998, from www.mankato.msus.edu/dept/comdis/isad/papers/starkweather.html.

Starkweather, C. W., & Givens-Ackerman, J. (1997). *Stuttering.* Austin, TX: Pro-Ed.

Starkweather, C.W., & Gottwald, S. R. (1993). A pilot study of relations among specific measures obtained at intake and discharge in a program of prevention and early intervention for stuttering. *American Journal of Speech-Language Pathology, 2,* 51–58.

Starkweather, C.W., Gottwald, S. R., & Halfond, M. H. (1990). *Stuttering prevented: A clinical method.* Englewood Cliffs, NJ: Prentice Hall.

Steinberg, L. (1989). *Adolescence* (2nd ed.). New York: Knopf.

Stephenson-Opsal, D., & Bernstein Ratner, N. (1988). Maternal speech rate modification and childhood stuttering. *Journal of Fluency Disorders, 13,* 49–56.

St. Louis, K. O. (1991). The stuttering/articulation disorders connection. In H. F. M. Peters, W. Hulstijn, & C.W. Starkweather (Eds.), *Speech motor control and stuttering* (pp. 393–400). New York: Excerptamedica.

St. Louis, K. O. (1992). On defining cluttering. In F. L. Meyers & K. O. St. Louis (Eds.), *Cluttering: A clinical perspective* (pp. 37–53). Kibworth, Great Britain: Far Communications.

St. Louis, K. O. (1998). Your life is too important to spend it worrying about stuttering. In S. B. Hood (Ed.), *Advice to those who stutter* (2nd ed., pp. 141–146). Memphis, TN: Stuttering Foundation of America.

St. Louis, K. O. (2001). *Living with stuttering: Stories, basic resources, and hope.* Morgantown, WV: Populore.

St. Louis, K. O., & Durrenberger, C. H. (1992). *Clinician preferences for managing various communication disorders.* Paper presented at the American Speech-Language-Hearing Association Convention, San Antonio, TX.

St. Louis, K. O., & Hinzman, A. R. (1988). A descriptive study of speech, language, and hearing characteristics of school-aged stutterers. *Journal of Fluency Disorders, 13,* 331–355.

St. Louis, K. O., & Lass, N. J. (1980). A survey of university training in stuttering. *Journal of the National Student Speech Language Hearing Association, 10,* 88–97.

St. Louis, K. O., & Lass, N. J. (1981). A survey of communicative disorders students' attitudes toward stuttering. *Journal of Fluency Disorders, 6,* 49–79.

St. Louis, K. O., Murray, C. D., & Ashworth, M. S. (1991). Coexisting communication disorders in a random sample of school-aged stutterers. *Journal of Fluency Disorders, 16,* 13–23.

St. Louis, K. O., & Myers, F. L. (1995). Clinical management of cluttering. *Language, Speech, and Hearing Services in School, 26,* 187–195.

St. Louis, K. O., & Myers, F. L. (1997). Management of cluttering and related fluency disorders. In R. F. Curlee & G. M. Siegel (Eds.), *Nature and treatment of stuttering: New directions* (2nd ed., pp. 313–332). Boston: Allyn & Bacon.

St. Louis, K. O., Raphael, L. J., Myers, F. L., & Bakker, K. (2003). Cluttering updated. *ASHA Leader, 8,* 4–5, 20–22.

St. Louis, K. O., & Rustin, L. (1992). Professional awareness of cluttering. In F. L. Meyers & K. O. St. Louis (Eds.), *Cluttering: A clinical perspective* (pp. 23–35). Kibworth, Great Britain: Far Communications.

Stocker, B. (1980). *The Stocker probe technique for diagnosis and treatment of stuttering in young children.* Tulsa, OK: Modern Education Corporation.

Strein, W. (1995). *Assessment of self-concept.* ERIC Digest No. ED389962. Retrieved on March 18, 2002, from www.ed.gov/databases/ERIC_Digests/ed389962.html.

Stuart, A., Kalinowski, J., Armson, J., Stenstrom, R., & Jones, K. (1996). Fluency effect of frequency alterations of plus/minus one-half and one-quarter octave shift in auditory feedback of people who stutter. *Journal of Speech and Hearing Research, 39,* 396–401.

Subramanian, A., Yairi, E., & Amir, O. (2003). Second formant transitions in fluent speech of persistent and recovered preschool stutterers. *Journal of Communication Disorders, 36,* 59-75.

Susca, M. (2002). Diagnosing stuttering in the school environment. *Seminars in Speech and Language, 23,* 165-171.

Sussman, H. M. (1984). A neuronal model for syllable representation. *Brain and Language, 22,* 167-177.

Tavris, C. (1989). *Anger: The misunderstood emotion.* New York: Simon & Schuster.

Tavris, C., & Wade, C. (1987). *Psychology.* New York: Harper & Row.

Telser, E. B. (1971). *An assessment of word finding skills in stuttering and nonstuttering children.* Unpublished doctoral dissertation, Northwestern University, Evanston, Il.

Throneburg, R. N., & Yairi, E. (2001). Durational, proportionate, and absolute frequency characteristics of disfluencies: A longitudinal study regarding persistence and recovery. *Journal of Speech, Language, and Hearing Research, 44* (1), 38-51.

Throneburg, R. N., Yairi, E., & Paden, E. P. (1994). Relation between phonologic difficulty and the occurrence of disfluencies in the early stage of stuttering. *Journal of Speech and Hearing Research, 37,* 504-509.

Till, J. A., Reich, A., Dickey, S., & Sieber, J. (1983). Phonatory and manual reaction times of stuttering and nonstuttering children. *Journal of Speech and Hearing Research, 26,* 171-180.

Travis, L. E. (1931). *Speech pathology.* New York: Appleton-Century.

Travis, L. E. (1978). The cerebral dominance theory of stuttering: 1931-1978. *Journal of Speech and Hearing Disorders, 43,* 278-281.

Van Borsel, J., Achten, E., Santens, P., Lahorte, P., & Voet, T. (2003). fMRI of developmental stuttering: A pilot study. *Brain and Language, 85,* 369-376. Abstract retrieved July 25, 2004, from www.ncbi.nlm.nih.gov/PubMed.

Van Borsel, J., Reunes, G., & Van den Bergh, N. (2003). Delayed auditory feedback in the treatment of stuttering: Clients as consumers. *International Journal of Language and Communication Disorder, 38,* 119-129. Abstract retrieved July 25, 2004, from www.ncbi.nlm.nih.gov/PubMed.

van Lieshout, P. H. H. M., Hulstijn, W., & Peters, H. F. M. (1991). Word size and word complexity: Differences in speech reaction time between stutterers and nonstutterers in a picture and word naming task. In H. F. M. Peters, W. Hulstijn, & C. W. Starkweather (Eds.), *Speech motor control and stuttering* (pp. 311-324). New York: Elsevier Science.

Van Riper, C. (1971). *The nature of stuttering.* Englewood Cliffs, NJ: Prentice Hall.

Van Riper, C. (1973). *The treatment of stuttering.* Englewood Cliffs, NJ: Prentice Hall.

Van Riper, C. (1992). Foreword. In F. L. Myers & K. O. St. Louis (Eds.), *Cluttering: A clinical perspective* (pp. vii-ix). Kibworth, Great Britain: Far Communications.

Vanryckeghem, M. (1995). The Communication Attitude Test: A concordancy investigation of stuttering and nonstuttering children and their parents. *Journal of Fluency Disorders, 20* (2), 191-204.

Vanryckeghem, M., & Brutten, G. J. (1992). The Communication Attitude Test: A test-retest reliability investigation. *Journal of Fluency Disorders, 3,* 177-190.

Vanryckeghem, M., & Brutten, G. J. (1996). The relationship between communication attitude and fluency failure of stuttering and nonstuttering children. *Journal of Fluency Disorders, 21,* 109-118.

Vanryckeghem, M., & Brutten, G. J. (1997). The speech-associated attitude of children who do and do not stutter and the differential effect of age. *American Journal of Speech-Language Pathology, 6,* 67-73.

Vanrychkeghem, M., Glessing, J. J., Brutten, G. J., & McAlindon, P. (1999). The main and interactive effect of oral reading rate on the frequency of stuttering. *American Journal of Speech-Language Pathology, 6,* 164-170.

Vanryckeghem, M., Hylebos, C., Brutten, G. J., & Peleman, M. (2001). The relationship between communication attitude and emotion of children who stutter. *Journal of Fluency Disorders, 26,* 1-16.

Van Wijk, C., & Kempen, G. (1987). A dual system for producing self-repairs in spontaneous speech: Evidence from experimentally elicited corrections. *Cognitive Psychology, 19,* 403-440.

Wall, M. J., & Myers, F. L. (1995). *Clinical management of childhood stuttering* (2nd ed.). Austin, TX: Pro-Ed.

Wall, M., Starkweather, C. W., & Cairns, H. (1981). Syntactic influences on stuttering in young child stutterers. *Journal of Fluency Disorders, 6,* 283-298.

Wallace, W. A. (1993). *Theories of personality.* Needham Heights, MA: Allyn & Bacon.

Walton, P., & Wallace, M. (1998). *Fun with fluency: Direct therapy with the young child.* Bisbee, AZ: Imaginart International.

Watkins, R. V., & Yairi, E. (1997). Language production abilities of children whose stuttering persisted or recovered. *Journal of Speech, Language, and Hearing Research, 40,* 385-399.

Watkins, R. V., Yairi, E., & Ambrose, N. G. (1999). Early childhood stuttering. III: Initial status of expressive language abilities. *Journal of Speech, Language, and Hearing Research, 42,* 1125-1135.

Watson, B. C., & Alfonso, P. (1982). A comparison of LRT and VOT values between stutterers and nonstutterers. *Journal of Fluency Disorders, 7,* 219-241.

Watson, B. C., & Freeman, F. J. (1997). Brain imaging contributions. In R. F. Curlee & G. M. Siegel (Eds.), *Nature and treatment of stuttering: New directions* (2nd ed., pp. 143-166). Boston: Allyn & Bacon.

Watson, J. B. (1987). Profiles of stutterers' and nonstutterers' affective, cognitive, and behavioral communication attitudes. *Journal of Fluency Disorders, 12,* 389-405.

Watson, J. B. (1988). A comparison of stutterers' and nonstutterers' affective, cognitive, and behavioral self reports. *Journal of Speech and Hearing Research, 31,* 377-385.

Weber-Fox, C. (2001). Neural system for sentence processing in stuttering. *Journal of Speech and Hearing Research, 44,* 814-825.

Webster's Collegiate Dictionary: The new lexicon of the English language. (1990). New York: Lexicon.

Webster, L. M. (1977). A clinical note on psychotherapy for stuttering. *Journal of Fluency Disorders, 2,* 253-255.

Webster, R. L. (1980). Evolution of target-based behavioral therapy for stuttering. *Journal of Fluency Disorders, 3,* 303-320.

Webster, R. L. (1986). Stuttering therapy from a technological point of view. In G. H. Shames & H. Rubin (Eds.), *Stuttering: Then and now* (pp. 407-414). Columbus: Charles E. Merrill.

Webster, W. G. (1993). Hurried hands and tangled tongues. In E. Boberg (Ed.), *Neuropsychology of stuttering* (pp. 73-111). Edmonton, Alberta: University of Alberta Press.

Webster, W. G., & Poulos, M. G. (1989). *Facilitating fluency: Transfer strategies for adult stuttering treatment programs.* Tucson, AZ: Communication Skill Builders.

Weiner, A. E. (1984). Stuttering and syllable stress. *Journal of Fluency Disorders, 9,* 301-305.

Weinstein, M. (1996). *Managing to have fun.* New York: Simon & Schuster.

Weiss, A. L. (1993). The pragmatic context of children's disfluency. *Seminars in Speech and Language, 14,* 215-225.

Weiss, A. L. (1995). Conversation demands and their effects on fluency and stuttering. *Topics in Language Disorders, 15,* 18-31.

Weiss, A. L., & Zebrowski, P. M. (1991). Patterns of assertiveness and responsiveness in parental interactions with stuttering and fluent children. *Journal of Fluency Disorders, 16,* 125-142.

Weiss, A., & Zebrowski, P. M. (1992). Disfluencies in the conversations of young children who stutter: Some answers about questions. *Journal of Speech and Hearing Research, 35,* 1230-1238.

Weiss, D. (1964). *Cluttering.* Englewood Cliffs, NJ: Prentice Hall.

Wenker, R. B., Wegener, J. G., & Hart, K. J. (1996). The impact of presentation mode and disfluency on judgments about speakers. *Journal of Fluency Disorders, 21,* 147-159.

Westbrook, J. B. (1991). Specialization. *Texas Journal of Audiology and Speech Pathology, 17,* 37.

Westbrook, J. B., et al. (1992). *Let's go camping! Alternative therapy models for children who stutter.* Paper presented at the American Speech-Language-Hearing Association Convention, San Antonio, TX.

Wieneke, G., & Janssen, P. (1991). Effect of speaking rate on speech timing variability. In H. F. M. Peters, W. Hulstijn, & C. W. Starkweather (Eds.), *Speech motor control and stuttering* (pp. 325-332). New York: Excerptamedica.

Wijnen, F., & Boers, I. (1994). Phonological priming effects in stutterers. *Journal of Fluency Disorders, 19,* 1–20.

Wilkenfeld, J. R., & Curlee, R. F. (1997). The relative effects of questions and comments on children's stuttering. *American Journal of Speech-Language Pathology, 6*(3), 79–89.

Williams, D. E. (1971). Stuttering therapy for children. In L. E. Travis (Ed.), *Handbook of speech pathology.* New York: Appleton-Century-Crofts.

Williams, D. E. (1972). Some suggestions for adult stutterers who want to talk easily. In S. Hood (Ed.), *To the stutterer* (pp. 99–104). Memphis, TN: Stuttering Foundation of America.

Williams, D. E. (1979). A perspective on approaches to stuttering therapy. In H. H. Gregory (Ed.), *Controversies about stuttering therapy* (pp. 241–268). Baltimore: University Park Press.

Williams, D. E. (1984). Working with children in the school environment. In J. F. Gruss (Ed.), *Stuttering therapy: Transfer and maintenance* (pp. 29–40). Memphis, TN: Stuttering Foundation of America.

Williams, D. E. (1985). Talking with children who stutter. In J. Fraser (Ed.), *Counseling stutterers* (pp. 35–45). Memphis, TN: Stuttering Foundation of America.

Williams, D. F., & Brutten, G. J. (1994). Physiological and aerodynamic events prior to the speech of stutterers and nonstutterers. *Journal of Fluency Disorders, 19,* 83–111.

Williams, D. F., & Dugan, P. M. (2002). Administering stuttering modification therapy in school settings. *Seminars in Speech and Language, 23,* 187–194.

Wingate, M. E. (1969). Sound and pattern in "artificial" fluency. *Journal of Speech and Hearing Research, 12,* 677–686.

Wingate, M. E. (1976). *Stuttering: Theory and treatment.* New York: Irvington.

Wingate, M. E. (1981). Sound and pattern in artificial fluency: Spectrographic evidence. *Journal of Fluency Disorders, 6,* 95–118.

Wingate, M. E. (1984a). Stuttering and syllable stress. *Journal of Fluency Disorders, 9,* 301–305.

Wingate, M. E. (1984b). Stuttering as a prosodic disorder. In R. F. Curlee and W. H. Perkins (Eds.), *Nature and treatment of stuttering: New directions* (pp. 215–236). Needham Heights, MA: Allyn & Bacon.

Wingate, M. E. (1988). *The structure of stuttering: A psycholinguistic approach.* New York: Springer-Verlag.

Winner, M. (2002). *Inside out: What makes a person with social cognitive deficits tick?.* San Jose, CA: Center for Social Thinking.

Winslow, M., & Guitar, B. (1994). The effects of structured turn-taking on disfluencies: A case study. *Language, Speech, and Hearing Services in Schools, 25,* 251–257.

Wolk, L., Blomgren, M., & Smith, A. B. (2000). The frequency of simultaneous disfluency and phonological errors in children: A preliminary investigation. *Journal of Fluency Disorders, 25,* 269–282.

Wolk, L., Edwards, M. L., & Conture, E. G. (1993). Coexistence of stuttering and disordered phonology in young children. *Journal of Speech and Hearing Research, 36,* 906–917.

Wood, F., Stump, D., McKeehan, A., Sheldon, S., & Proctor, J. (1980). Patterns of regional cerebral blood flow during attempted reading aloud by stutterers both on and off haloperidol medication: Evidence for inadequate left frontal activation during stuttering. *Brain and Language, 9,* 141–144.

Woods, C. L. (1974). Social position and speaking competence of stuttering and normally fluent boys. *Journal of Speech and Hearing Research, 17,* 740–747.

Woolf, G. (1967). The assessment of stuttering as struggle, avoidance, and expectancy. *British Journal of Disorders of Communication, 2,* 158–171.

Wu, J. C., Maguire G., Riley, G., Fallon, J., LaCasse, L., Chin, S., Klein, E., Tang, C., Cadwell, S., & Lottenberg, S. (1995). A position emission tomography [18F] deoxyglucose study of developmental stuttering. *NeuroReport, 6,* 501–505.

Yairi, E. (1997a). Disfluency characteristics of childhood stuttering. In R. F. Curlee & G. M. Siegel (Eds.), *Nature and treatment of stuttering: New directions* (2nd ed., pp. 49–78). Boston: Allyn & Bacon.

Yairi, E. (1997b). Home environment and parent-child interaction in childhood stuttering. In R. F. Curlee & G. M. Siegel (Eds.), *Nature and treatment of stuttering: New directions* (2nd ed., pp. 24-48). Boston: Allyn & Bacon.

Yairi, E. (1999). Epidemiologic factors and stuttering research. In N. B. Ratner & E. C. Healey (Eds.), *Stuttering research and practice bridging the gap* (pp. 45-54). Mahwah, NJ: Lawrence Erlbaum Associates.

Yairi, E. (2004). The formative years of stuttering: A changing portrait. *Contemporary Issues in Communication Science and Disorders, 31,* 92-104.

Yairi, E., & Ambrose, N. G. (1999). Early childhood stuttering. I: Persistency and recovery rates. *Journal of Speech, Language, and Hearing Research, 42,* 1097-1112.

Yairi, E., Ambrose, N., & Cox, N. (1996). Genetics of stuttering: A critical review. *Journal of Speech and Hearing Research, 39,* 771-784.

Yairi, E., Ambrose, N., Paden, E. P., & Throneburg, R. N. (1996). Predictive factors of persistence and recovery: Pathways of childhood stuttering. *Journal of Communication Disorders, 29,* 51-77.

Yairi, E., & Carrico, D. M. (1992). Early childhood stuttering: Pediatricians' attitudes and practices. *American Journal of Speech-Language Pathology, 1,* 54-62.

Yairi, E., & Lewis, B. (1984). Disfluencies at the onset of stuttering. *Journal of Speech and Hearing Research, 27,* 154-159.

Yaruss, J. S. (1997). Clinical measurement of stuttering behaviors. *Contemporary Issues in Communication Science and Disorders, 24,* 33-44.

Yaruss, J. S. (1998). Describing the consequences of disorders: Stuttering and the international classification of impairments, disabilities, and handicaps. *Journal of Speech, Language, and Hearing Research, 41,* 249-257.

Yaruss, J. S. (1999a). Current status of academic and clinical education in fluency disorders at ASHA-accredited training programs. *Journal of Fluency Disorders, 24,* 169-184.

Yaruss, J. S. (1999b). Utterance length, syntactic complexity, and childhood stuttering. *Journal of Speech, Language, and Hearing Research, 42,* 329-344.

Yaruss, J. S. (2000). The role of performance in the demands and capacities model. *Journal of Fluency Disorders, 25,* 347-358.

Yaruss, J. S. (2002). Facing the challenge of treating stuttering in the schools. *Seminars in Speech and Language, 24,* 153-157.

Yaruss, J. S. (2004). Documenting individual treatment outcomes in stuttering therapy. *Contemporary Issues in Communication Science and Disorders, 31,* 49-57.

Yaruss, J. S., & Conture, E. G. (1993). F2 transitions during sound/syllable repetitions of children who stutter and predictions of stuttering chronicity. *Journal of Speech and Hearing Research, 36,* 883-896.

Yaruss, J. S., & Conture, E. G. (1995). Mother and child speaking rates and utterance lengths in adjacent fluent utterances: Preliminary observations. *Journal of Fluency Disorders, 20,* 257-278.

Yaruss, J. S., & Conture, E. G. (1996). Stuttering and phonological disorders in children: Examination of the covert repair hypothesis. *Journal of Speech and Hearing Research, 39,* 349-364.

Yaruss, J. S., LaSalle, L. R., & Conture, E. G. (1998). Evaluating stuttering in young children: Diagnostic data. *American Journal of Speech-Language Pathology, 7,* 62-76.

Yaruss, J. S., Quesal, R. W., Reeves, L., Molt, L., Kluetz, B., Caruso, A. J., Lewis, F., & McClure, J. A. (2002). Speech treatment and support group experiences of people who participate in the National Stuttering Association. *Journal of Fluency Disorders, 27,* 115-135.

Yaruss, J. S., & Quesal, R. W. (in press). Overall Assessment of the Speaker's Experience of Stuttering (OASES). *Proceedings of the Fourth World Congress on Fluency Disorders.*

Yaruss, J. S., & Reardon, N. A. (2002). Successful communication for children who stutter: Finding a balance. *Seminars in Speech and Language, 23,* 195-203.

Yaruss, J. S., & Reardon, N. A. (2003). *Preschool children who stutter: Information and support for parents* (2nd ed.). New York: National Stuttering Association.

Yeakle, M. K., & Cooper, E. B. (1986). Teacher perceptions of stuttering. *Journal of Fluency Disorders, 11,* 345-359.

Yovetich, W. S., Leschied, A. W., & Flicht, J. (2000). Self-esteem of school-age children who stutter. *Journal of Fluency Disorders, 25,* 143-154.

Zackheim, C. T., & Conture, E. G. (2003). Childhood stuttering and speech disfluencies in relation to children's mean length of utterance: A preliminary study. *Journal of Fluency Disorders, 28,* 115-142.

Zebrowski, P. M. (1993). Parents' judgments of children's fluency. *Seminars in Speech and Language, 14*(3), 192-202.

Zebrowski, P. M. (1997). Assisting young children who stutter and their families: Defining the role of the speech-language pathologist. *American Journal of Speech-Language Pathology, 6,* 19-28.

Zebrowski, P. M. (2002). Building clinical relationships with teenagers who stutter. *Contemporary Issues in Communication Science and Disorders, 29,* 91-100.

Zebrowski, P. M., & Conture, E. G. (1998). Influence of nontreatment variables on treatment effectiveness for school-age children who stutter. In A. K. Cordes & R. J. Ingham (Eds.), *Treatment efficacy for stuttering:* *A search for empirical bases* (pp. 293-310). San Diego, CA: Singular.

Zebrowski, P. M., Conture, E. G., & Cudahy, E. (1985). Acoustic analysis of young stutterers' fluency. *Journal of Fluency Disorders, 10,* 173-192.

Zebrowski, P. M., & Kelly, E. M. (2002). *Manual of stuttering intervention.* Clifton Park, NY: Delmar.

Zembrowski, P. M., & Schum, R. L. (1993). Counseling parents of children who stutter. *American Journal of Speech-Language Pathology, 2,* 65-73.

Zimmerman, B. J. (2000). Attaining self-regulation: A social cognitive perspective. In M. Boekaerts, P. R. Pintrich, & M. Zeidner (Eds.), *Handbook of self-regulation* (pp. 13-39). San Diego, CA: Academic Press.

Zimmerman, G. (1980a). Articulatory behaviors associated with stuttering: Cinefluorographic analysis. *Journal of Speech and Hearing Research, 23,* 108-121.

Zimmerman, G. (1980b). Articulatory dynamics of fluent utterances of stutterers and nonstutterers. *Journal of Speech and Hearing Research, 23,* 95-107.

Name Index

Subject Index